The Launching of Duke University

The Launching

of Duke University

1924–1949

ROBERT F. DURDEN

Duke University Press   *Durham & London 1993*

© 1993 Duke University Press

All rights reserved

Printed in the United States of America on acid-free paper ∞

Designed by Mary Mendell

Typeset in Berkeley Medium by Tseng Information Systems, Inc.

Library of Congress Cataloging-in-Publication Data appear on the last

printed page of this book.

This book is dedicated,
with abiding love and gratitude, to
M. O. D. R., M. F. D.,
and W. I. R.

Contents

Preface

〜⧉〜

THAT EACH AMERICAN university shares many features with all the
others while also being in various ways unique is a truism. While
the unique aspects derive from many things—such as location,
mission, and origins—all of these are bound up and reflected in the institution's history. The early, nineteenth-century portion of Duke's history
has been competently and fully covered in Nora C. Chaffin's *Trinity College, 1839–1892: The Beginnings of Duke University* (Durham, N.C.: Duke
University Press, 1950). From the modest school begun by Methodist
and Quaker farmers in Randolph county in Piedmont North Carolina to
the move of Trinity College to Durham, Chaffin recounts in a careful,
scholarly fashion how the institution evolved from Brown's Schoolhouse
to Union Institute Academy and finally, in 1859, to Methodist-sponsored
Trinity College. Chaffin shows how the remarkable dedication, sacrifice,
and leadership of one man, Braxton Craven, kept the small, struggling
institution alive. Indeed, the most remarkable thing about Trinity College
down to 1892 was that it survived.

Picking up the story where Chaffin stopped, Earl W. Porter, in *Trinity
and Duke, 1892–1924: Foundations of Duke University* (Durham, N.C.:
Duke University Press, 1964), splendidly reveals how Trinity College
gradually became a strong liberal arts college by the time of World War
I and how under the leadership of three outstanding presidents—John F.
Crowell, John C. Kilgo, and William P. Few—the institution finally began
to solve its hitherto unending financial problems and came to be supported by Washington Duke and his family. Although a significant portion

of Duke University's history was rooted in and foreshadowed by Trinity's history, especially after 1892, there seemed to be no point in going back over ground that Chaffin and Porter have well covered. Thus this history focuses on the organization of a research university around Trinity College after December, 1924.

The term "research university" was not commonly used in the 1920s, and President Few and his allies talked of building a "major university" or a "national university." James B. Duke, the principal underwriter of the new university, spoke of his hope that the institution would attain "a place of real leadership in the educational world" and explicitly endorsed the plan of organization that Few had provided. Because "university" is and always has been a loosely used, imprecise word in the United States, I have chosen to use throughout the term "research university," since that was precisely what Duke was meant to be and quickly became.

Duke's history as a research university has a certain larger interest and significance partly because of timing. With the Johns Hopkins University leading the way in 1876, a group of older, private institutions in the Northeast and state-supported ones in the Midwest soon partially emulated the Johns Hopkins model and also became research universities. By the turn of the century these various universities had clearly established themselves as the premier educational institutions of the nation. Complex and expensive, they formed an increasingly important, elite segment of the nation's educational system.

Primarily because of persistent and widespread poverty, the South long failed to share in the revolution that reshaped much of higher education in the other sections of the country. State-supported universities in Charlottesville, Virginia; Austin, Texas; and Chapel Hill, North Carolina, did, however, begin to arouse and gradually transform themselves in the early decades of the twentieth century. And Trinity's President Few had the audacity to hope that the college in Durham might become the nucleus or heart, as he preferred to say, of the first voluntarily supported research university in the South.

By the 1920s, when Few and J. B. Duke collaborated, the strengths as well as the hazards of the research-university model were quite clear. Duke, therefore, became such an institution in a more self-conscious, deliberate, and expeditious fashion than was true in most other cases. Few and his coworkers meant for Duke to be a different kind of research university in two particular ways. First, Few believed, quite correctly, that in the rush to emphasize research and the training of graduate and professional students, many universities had woefully shortchanged undergraduates and liberal education. He meant for Duke to be different and to keep its undergraduate colleges and their students as priority items right alongside the graduate and professional schools. The task would prove to be difficult but certainly not impossible, and the university's development during its first quarter-century would show the largely successful realization of Few's plan.

President Few wanted Duke to be different in another way also, and that was in the area of religion. He believed that many research universities had for various reasons either downplayed or actually ignored the religious dimension of life and the place of religion in higher education. Without religious tests for either students or faculty, Duke, according to the plans of Few and his collaborators, would try to maintain its friendly but not constricting relationship with the Methodist church; to treat religion, both as a subject for study and as an aspect of life, with great respect and to provide for it supportive policies; and to afford every opportunity for students voluntarily to participate in religious activities.

The new university encountered many problems, of course, some to be expected, some unforeseen and growing out of special circumstances. Perhaps the most predictable problem, and one certainly shared with at least a few other research universities that strove for balance, was the tension between research and teaching, a tension that was reflected not only in various university policies and appointments but in the lives of individual faculty members and in the operations of their departments. Although Few himself had a mistaken notion that those faculty members who primarily taught undergraduates could be differentiated from those who dealt with advanced students, the effects of that shortsighted view were overcome, at least in most departments, by chairmen and senior faculty members who from the first tried to recruit scholar-teachers, that is, men and women who were capable of doing significant research as well as interested in and willing to undertake the teaching of undergraduates. Moreover, there turned out to be less money available for the university than was originally anticipated, and practical exigencies soon dictated that senior faculty members, including the most distinguished ones, had to share in the teaching of both undergraduate and graduate students.

The largest unforeseen problem, aside from the shortage of funds, that Duke encountered arose from the fact that the university had its own governing board of trustees, while the perpetual philanthropic trust that J. B. Duke established late in 1924, the Duke Endowment, had a separate board of trustees. Since down to World War II the university derived approximately half of its annual income from the Endowment, the fact that the trustees of the Endowment were empowered, under certain circumstances, to withhold funds from the university turned out to be a troublesome and dangerous matter for President Few and the university and one that, from the late 1920s until the mid-1930s, caused Few his greatest worry. While he finally worked out a solution to the problem that proved to be satisfactory, at least during his lifetime and during President

Robert L. Flowers's administration in the 1940s, the matter of potential conflict between the two boards was a most serious one.

By the early 1990s, the relationship between the Duke Endowment and Duke University had been maintained successfully for nearly seventy years. While the support that the university received from the Endowment grew steadily larger in dollar amounts over the decades, the proportion of that valuable, even indispensable support to the whole amount of the university's annual income shrank as income increased from tuition, the university's own endowment, and governmental as well as private agencies. Looking back from the early 1990s, therefore, one might be tempted to conclude that a smooth and largely happy outcome was inevitable, but that would be reading history backwards and would distort the sometimes painful realities and uncertainties of the early years.

Another problem that was unique to Duke as a research university was that it inherited from Trinity a strong, deep-rooted commitment to be of as much service as possible to North Carolina and the southeastern region. At the same time, Duke aspired to be a national university (and, later in the century, an international one). This double mission brought problems, especially concerning admissions and with the university's trustees and older alumni. In the main, Few and Flowers, aided by numerous others, managed to keep a balance and remain in pursuit of both objectives. It took considerable effort, however, and added another, distinctive theme to Duke's history.

The first quarter-century of the university's history forms a unit, therefore, not merely because it happened to coincide with the administrations of Few and Flowers but primarily because those were the formative and most critical years for the expanded institution. No other president of Duke has faced or will ever face quite the challenges and opportunities that came to William P. Few. He necessarily looms large in the pages that follow, although a vast number of other people assisted significantly in the building of the university.

When a troubled time came to Duke in the years immediately after World War II, the institution both suffered in certain respects and took various steps that better prepared it for the last half of the century. As Few once said, Duke was successfully embarked on a long journey.

This is not, in any sense, an authorized or official history of Duke's first quarter-century. Acting completely on my own, I began the research for it almost a decade ago and undertook the project because it needed doing and because, in one sense, it continued a story that I had begun to tell in *The Dukes of Durham* (Durham, N.C.: Duke University Press, 1975). There the focus had been on Washington Duke and his family, especially the two youngest sons, Benjamin N. and James B. Duke. While such a family history naturally included considerable attention to the family's involvement in the tobacco, textile, and electrical power industries, a main theme throughout the book was the family's philanthropic activity and particularly the Dukes' creative entanglement with Trinity College from about 1890 onward. The philanthropic culmination came late in 1924, when James B. Duke established the Duke Endowment and made possible the organization of a new university around Trinity College. Those matters are dealt with in the last two chapters of *The Dukes of Durham*. In this study the focus shifts from the family to the university itself, and to President William Preston Few and his associates, who began to create the university that James B. Duke's gift had made possible.

Too many people have generously befriended me in this undertaking for me to risk the attempt to list them here. Nevertheless, I greatly appreciate all the help. A large number of active and retired members of the faculty kindly read portions of the manuscript that dealt with their own departments or schools. One group of friends and colleagues, however, critically read all or a large portion of the manuscript, so I particularly thank Frances Brown, Jeff Crow, Paul Escott, Charles Flynn, Bill Holley, Bill King, and Harold Parker.

My research was done largely in our first-rate University Archives, a treasure trove of data not only about Duke but also about American higher education—and myriad other matters—in this century. For graciously taking me on as practically a live-in researcher and constantly helping me in countless ways, I thank William E. King, the archivist, and his associates, Thomas Harkins and Doris Parrish.

In the history department, Vivian Jackson and Grace Guyer, as they have done for many years and other writings of mine, efficiently and graciously typed all the chapters. I am deeply indebted to them and value their friendship as well as their services.

Three chapters in this volume have appeared earlier, in somewhat different form, in the *North Carolina Historical Review*, and I am grateful to its publishers for permission to reprint them.

Anne Oller Durden, my wife, has patiently listened to more Duke history than she ever bargained for. Moreover, she has promised to help, as usual, with the onerous task of compiling what promises to be a whopping index. I can hardly thank her enough and, at the same time, I hope that she will share the mixed pleasures, Providence willing, of a future volume in Duke's history.

Robert F. Durden
Duke University
May, 1992

The Launching of Duke University

1

The Origins of the University Idea

at Trinity College

⤸

W HEN THE TRUSTEES OF Trinity College named John Franklin
Crowell as president of the small, struggling institution in
1887, they undoubtedly did not realize what the long-range
consequences of their action would be. Not only would the Pennsylvanian, who was only twenty-nine years old when he took the job, succeed
in moving the institution some fifty miles eastward, from its rural isolation in Randolph County to the booming factory town of Durham, but he
also had even more ambitious ideas about transforming the little college
into a university.[1]

After attending school in New Berlin, Pennsylvania, young Crowell
went to Dartmouth for a year, transferred to Yale in 1880, and, after receiving his undergraduate degree there in 1883, spent a year in Yale's
divinity school and another in its fledgling graduate school before serving
as a school principal for two years.[2]

Crowell's ambitious hopes for a "Greater Trinity," a university-type
institution, were way ahead of their time and doomed to failure. Since
Trinity was not yet, in fact, a strong liberal arts college, Crowell's talk of
professional schools and other features of a university suggest a certain
naiveté and lack of realism on his part. Yet the fact that he brought such
ideas with him to Trinity points up an important truth about American
higher education in the late nineteenth century.

Although the term "university" was, and is, used with notorious loose-
ness in the United States, there is widespread agreement among historians
that the nation's first authentic university—what would later on in the

twentieth century be known as a research university—opened its doors in 1876. The Johns Hopkins University in Baltimore, Maryland, deliberately modeled itself on the German universities that were then widely hailed as the best in the world. The training of graduate students, through relatively small seminars where research was the principal concern and the new doctor of philosophy degree the goal, was the prime mission of Johns Hopkins, and its example quickly influenced the whole pattern of American higher education.[3]

While other forces were also at work, the Johns Hopkins example inspired a select group of American institutions to transform themselves, gradually and in varying fashions, into research universities. In the Midwest and Far West, several state-supported universities—most prominently Illinois, Michigan, Minnesota, Wisconsin, and California—emulated Johns Hopkins and added to their historic mission of teaching that of the advancement of human knowledge through research as one of their primary purposes. In the Northeast, several of the nation's oldest educational institutions—especially Harvard, Yale, Princeton, Pennsylvania, and Columbia—bestirred themselves to meet the new competition and by around 1900 were widely recognized as belonging in the top group of research universities. Joining the five state-supported universities and the five Ivy League institutions, five important new, voluntarily supported universities were launched after the Civil War: Cornell in 1868, Massachusetts Institute of Technology in 1865, Johns Hopkins in 1876, Stanford in 1891, and Chicago in 1892. These fifteen institutions, according to a prominent historian of American research universities, "fully embody the emergence of research as a fundamental goal in American higher education."[4]

Twelve of the fifteen institutions named above were among the fourteen founding members of the Association of American Universities. Its creation in 1900 was an important milestone in the emergence of the American research universities, for the leading Ph.D.-granting institutions of the era not only thereby declared their equality with the much older European universities but also set about strengthening the standards for the doctorate and guaranteeing the value of the best American degrees against "cheaper" domestic and foreign competition.[5]

Although Johns Hopkins is in the border state of Maryland, the revolution that transformed the top echelon of American higher education in the late nineteenth century virtually bypassed the South. This happened primarily because deep, widespread poverty gripped the South for many decades after the Civil War. The large amounts of money that research universities required—from state governments, wealthy alumni, or philanthropists like John D. Rockefeller and Leland Stanford—simply did not exist in the vast area between the Potomac and the Rio Grande. Consequently, just as public schools in the South generally lagged pitifully behind those in most other parts of the country, the colleges and universities in the region remained distinctly weaker than the nation's best.

Yet individuals, such as John F. Crowell at Trinity, began the process of transmitting the ideas and aims of the educational revolution long before certain southern institutions themselves could be recognizably transformed. Individuals comparable to Crowell no doubt acted as key transmitters or conveyers at state-supported universities in Charlottesville, Virginia; Chapel Hill, North Carolina; and Austin, Texas, as well as at various other ambitious institutions in the South. Trinity College, when it moved to Durham in 1892, was a far cry indeed from a research university; nevertheless, it slowly began to reflect important changes wrought by Crowell and other transmitters like him and to move toward acquiring genuine strength as a liberal arts college.

Certainly one major academic advantage that Trinity College derived from the move to Durham was that, since most of the former faculty members proved unable or unwilling to leave Randolph County, Crowell had to recruit a largely new faculty. Since he did so at the new graduate-training universities in the East, Trinity quickly acquired a young, well-prepared faculty with advanced degrees from Johns Hopkins, Yale, Cornell, and one or two other institutions. Contact with these enthusiastic, relatively cosmopolitan professors soon inspired such recent and promising Trinity graduates as John Spencer Bassett and William Ivey Cranford, who were serving as instructors in the college, to go themselves for graduate study at one of the major universities.[6]

Armed with the new Ph.D. degree from Johns Hopkins, John Spencer Bassett returned to teach history at Trinity in 1894 and within less than a decade, according to one historian, "acquired a reputation as the South's foremost scholar in the field of history."[7] More important than his professional reputation, however, was the impact or influence that Bassett had on Trinity College.

Even more directly than Crowell, perhaps, Bassett may be seen as an example of the transmitter par excellence of many of the ideas and values of the research university. Unlike some university-trained scholars who became so enamored of research that they disdained teaching "mere" undergraduates, Bassett apparently did not lose his zest for the classroom, though with a teaching load of at least fifteen hours per week—and sometimes more—plus other duties, his schedule would be considered cruel and intolerable by later standards. That he managed to keep a personal touch and to relate with his students is suggested by a former student who recalled that Bassett was the only member of the small Trinity faculty who "believed that Jesus Christ had died for freshmen too."[8]

Neither the amount of his teaching nor its apparently caring quality was as significant as the fact that Bassett, bringing to Trinity the methods he had learned at Johns Hopkins, required his students to write research papers based in part on original source material in the library.[9] Rejecting the timeworn class routines that involved a near-sacred textbook and student memorization of data from it or from the professor's lectures, Bassett was among a small group of pioneers at Trinity who believed that undergraduates, no less than graduate students, needed to be trained in analytical, critical thinking and the writing of clear, correct English.

If such an approach was to be used, however, there were obvious implications for the college library, and Bassett was one of the first in a long line of Trinity faculty members who put library development at the top of the institution's list of priorities. Bassett's predecessor at Trinity, Stephen B. Weeks, who was also a Johns Hopkins Ph.D., led interested students and faculty to organize the Trinity College Historical Society in the spring of 1892. Its object, as stated in its constitution, was "to collect, arrange and preserve a library of books, pamphlets, maps, charts, manuscripts, papers, paintings, statuary and other materials illustrative of the history of North Carolina and of the South; . . . [and] to encourage original work in the field of Southern history and to promote the study of the same by means of lectures and publications." Weeks left Trinity before such an ambitious program could be effectively started, but Bassett, recognizing the potential in the organization, proceeded vigorously to utilize the historical society and pursue its aims. "There is reason to believe," one presumably impartial historian concludes, "that no local historical association ever succeeded better in effecting its program than the society at Trinity College."[10]

Using the historical museum with its miscellaneous artifacts and relics to catch the interest of the students and the public, Bassett had a more serious purpose in mind for the manuscripts and other historical documents that he and other members of the historical society went after: they were to form the nucleus of a research collection. In 1898, four years after Bassett's return to Trinity, he proudly informed his mentor at Johns Hopkins that whereas Trinity had previously owned no documentary collection, it now possessed over two thousand documents, and he had been promised a fireproof vault in which to keep them. In addition to Bassett's many other duties, the trustees named him "manager of the library," though in 1898 the college also acquired its first full-time librarian, Joseph P. Breedlove.[11]

John Carlisle Kilgo, who succeeded Crowell in 1894 as Trinity's president, declared in 1901 that the library was "the one department that measures the future development of the college."[12] This was hardly a commonplace view among college presidents in that era, especially in small, church-related institutions, and it was almost certainly an insight or policy that Kilgo himself acquired from Bassett and other young university-trained Ph.D.'s on the faculty. A native of South Carolina and a graduate of Wofford College, Kilgo was a spellbinding and controversial Methodist preacher who quickly earned the admiration and confidence of two groups that were vitally important to Trinity College: the faculty and the family of Washington Duke.

Benjamin N. Duke, Washington Duke's son, had given $1,000 to Trinity in 1887 and become a trustee of the school in 1889. He and especially his father played central roles in moving the college to Durham three years later. Once there, the chronically poor condition of the college's financial situation did not improve, as President Crowell had hoped, but drastically worsened. Washington Duke, having retired from the family's tobacco business in 1880 at the age of sixty, left most important business and philanthropic decisions and negotiations to his son Ben Duke. Moreover, all of the dissension and wrangling that both preceded and followed the college's move to Durham led Washington Duke, for a time, to regret his involvement with Trinity. Yet since the family had become entangled with it, Ben Duke, together with his sister, Mary Duke Lyon, and his younger brother, James B. Duke, agreed to extend emergency financial assistance that would at least keep the college in operation, even if on a spartan basis that was a far cry indeed from the ambitious program that Crowell had envisioned.[13]

Kilgo's arrival on the scene soon brought a dramatic change in the college's situation, for not only did Ben Duke consider him "a very strong man in every way" and one "admirably fitted for the position he holds," but Washington Duke was equally captivated by Kilgo and again became keenly interested in the welfare of Trinity College. In 1896 he offered to give it $100,000 for endowment, a princely sum in that era, if it would "open its doors to women, placing them in the future on an equal footing with men."[14] Since the college had earlier enrolled women as students, although on an irregular and nonresidential basis, and since Kilgo and others on the faculty were sympathetic with the idea, the college promptly accepted Washington Duke's offer. The residentially separate or coordinate college for women that Crowell had proposed and that Kilgo preferred would have to wait for another generation and larger resources; but beginning in September, 1897 a small number of women entered Trinity College and lived in the first dormitory for women, the Mary Duke Building.[15]

While Washington Duke gave yet another $100,000 to the college's endowment in 1898, with additional large gifts in subsequent years, Ben Duke began to make annual contributions to Trinity's operating budget and to meet specific needs as they arose. Serving on the executive committee of the college's trustees, Ben Duke, both before his father died in 1905 and afterward, served as the family's chief agent for a wide range of philanthropic activities in North Carolina, with Trinity College always at the top of the list.

There is no documentary evidence to prove the case, but there is a strong probability that Ben Duke, possibly aided by his father, persuaded his younger brother, James B. Duke, to make his first sizeable gift to the college in 1900. Having moved to New York City in 1884, James B. Duke, who was known only to family and a few intimate friends as "Buck," never again lived in Durham—though he maintained close ties with his family, especially his father and his brother Ben. What a later generation would know as a "workaholic," J. B. Duke was primarily involved in the giant American Tobacco Company, which he helped to create in 1890 and long led as president. That task left him little time or taste for the endless letter-writing and conferring with Methodist preachers, college administrators, and others that Ben Duke endured. At any rate, J. B. Duke agreed to give Trinity a handsome library with a capacity of 100,000 volumes and $10,000 for the purchase of books to go in it. Thus the concern of Bassett and others for Trinity's library resources reached, via Kilgo and Ben Duke, to the youngest, and eventually the richest member of the family.

Support from the Dukes provided the financial security that Trinity College had always desperately but vainly sought. The college, by national standards, was a long way from being affluent. But by comparison with most other educational institutions in the poverty-stricken South at that time, Trinity was fortunate, and it could gradually begin to build toward the academic strength that it coveted. Enrollment climbed from 150 students when Kilgo became president to 197 by 1903, when the new library was dedicated. Since income from the tuition of $50 per year amounted to little more than 10 percent of the college's total income, the significance of the support from the Dukes is readily apparent. The endowment income and the annual gifts from the Dukes were such, in fact, that Kilgo proposed and got in 1900 the establishment of fifty tuition scholarships to be awarded on the basis of ability and character and twelve graduate student awards for those seeking the master of arts degree.[16]

While a strong library was essential if Trinity was to become the academically vigorous college that Kilgo, his faculty, and their benefactors envisioned, Bassett may also be used to illustrate another development at Trinity that reflected the practice of the research universities more than it did that of the typical small college of that time. A prodigious researcher himself, Bassett published, among other works, pioneering studies of slavery in North Carolina and of antislavery leaders in the state. Both subjects were then rather novel, and Bassett's critical, scholarly stance even more so. Since historians, unlike major novelists or poets, write in sand, Bassett's scholarship has long since been washed away by the tides of revisionism. More enduring, however, was the example he set of scholarly investigation and of the careful search for truths about the South's past, a past which had to be painfully stripped of romanticism and evasion before it could even begin to be understood.

Since the validity of scholarship must be judged by other scholars as well as by educated laypersons who might be interested, Bassett also brought with him from Johns Hopkins the idea that academically serious institutions had an obligation to support and encourage scholarly publication. Accordingly, in 1895 he inaugurated the *Historical Papers of the Trinity College Historical Society*, a long-lasting series of scholarly monographs produced by both students and faculty. One of the few scholarly historical publications in the South at that time, it was the only one in North Carolina. Since the *Historical Papers* aimed at a limited, scholarly audience, however, Bassett sought another medium through which to reach a larger public. With the support of Kilgo and others on the faculty, in 1902 he launched the *South Atlantic Quarterly*.

Now approaching its centennial, the *South Atlantic Quarterly* is the second oldest such general and literary quarterly in the nation. A later editor of the magazine, William B. Hamilton, noted that Bassett and his allies intended it both as a medium of publication and as an incentive to continued scholarly effort. "The satisfactions of a teacher are the college professor's meat, but publication is his wine," Hamilton declared. "It stimulates him to new efforts, and it prevents his meat from going dry in his mouth."[17] The quarterly was meant to serve a larger purpose, however, than as a mere vehicle for scholarly publication. The South, as the young Ph.D.'s at Trinity College saw it, was a well-loved region that desperately needed to be shaken and awakened. In Hamilton's words, "there were poverty and sloth," and "a tendency to whine that the South's troubles were caused by Yankees." As in the antebellum South concerning slavery, dissent was not tolerated about the region's second peculiar institution, the increasingly rigid and legally mandated system of Jim Crow segregation. With the weakest school systems in the nation, Southerners wrote and read little, and social ills ranging from blatant racial injustice to child labor and notorious political demagoguery cried out for remedial action. "The young men of Trinity girded themselves," Hamilton noted, and "the *South Atlantic Quarterly* was their spear."[18]

Bassett hurled his most famous "spear" in the issue of October, 1903. Long privately critical of the racial tactics employed by Southern Democrats in general and Tar Heel Democrats in particular, Bassett fumed when the "White Man's Party" routed its Republican and Populist opponents in the rabid "white supremacy" campaigns of 1898 and 1900. Although African-American voters were effectively disfranchised as a result of the latter election and the Democratic party was more solidly entrenched in its one-party domination than ever before, many leading Democrats, including especially such powerful politico-journalists as Josephus Daniels of the Raleigh *News & Observer*, kept up a noisy drumfire of racist appeals and attacks. In a *Quarterly* article entitled "Stirring Up the Fires of Race Antipathy," Bassett issued a quiet, reasoned analysis and protest and, among other things, predicted that some day in the future Negroes would win equality. That there would be continuing conflict between the races, Bassett conceded, but he saw it as "the duty of brave and wise men" to "seek to infuse the spirit of conciliation into these white leaders of white men." The conflict could become less dire only if whites substituted a "spirit of conciliation" for their insistence on the inferiority of blacks.[19]

The angry outcry that soon followed upon the appearance of Bassett's article, an outcry orchestrated by but not confined to Daniels' *News & Observer*, led to the famed "Bassett affair" and an important crisis in the life of Trinity College. Since the affair has been extensively written about elsewhere, there is no need to repeat the story here.[20] From the vantage point of the late twentieth century, one has difficulty understanding the genuine fury of those who saw Bassett as a "traitor to the Southern way of life," a "heretic" who should be promptly dismissed from his position at Trinity. Also, since it was a time when colleges had to worry about recruiting qualified students rather than one when students worried about being admitted to college, Trinity faced a genuine dilemma about its "clientele." Bassett, in the face of the clamor and recognizing the danger to the college, offered to submit his resignation, and the crucial question became whether Trinity's trustees, in a specially called session on December 1, 1903, would bow to the storm and sacrifice the professor.

Although Bassett had certainly never intended for such to happen, he inadvertently gave Trinity College—and therefore Duke University—its finest hour. With Kilgo, the faculty, and the student body all solidly lined up in support of Bassett's right to express his views freely, the trustees voted eighteen to seven in favor of keeping Bassett and of academic freedom at Trinity. Though occasionally talked about, academic freedom scarcely existed anywhere in the United States, much less in the South, in the early years of the century. Trinity's decision in the Bassett affair and the eloquent statement issued by the trustees thus became historic landmarks: "A reasonable freedom of opinion is to a college the very breath of life; and any official throttling of the private judgment of its teachers would destroy their influence, and place upon the college an enduring stigma."[21]

Although John Spencer Bassett left Trinity in 1906 to go to Smith College, he left both tangible and intangible monuments. The *Historical Papers* and the *South Atlantic Quarterly* would long continue, the former in changed format into the 1960s, the latter still appearing regularly. On the intangible side, Bassett provided a model for the teacher-scholar that lasted long after a university had been organized around the college. Bassett's student at Trinity, William K. Boyd, went to Columbia for his doctorate in history and succeeded Bassett as chairman in history, a position he held until his death in 1938. A prodigious collector of manuscripts and other research materials, Boyd also served as director of libraries in Duke University for several years and gave the *Papers of the Trinity College Historical Society* even more substance and merit than they had earlier possessed. When Boyd's son-in-law, William B. Hamilton, who obtained his doctorate in history at Duke and remained there to teach, became editor of the *South Atlantic Quarterly* in 1958, it represented in one sense the third generation of the Bassett-style teacher-scholar.

Although none was quite the obvious, even dramatic transmitter of university values and practices that Bassett was, there were, of course, numerous other important transmitters in other fields of study at Trinity. When William H. Pegram in the chemistry department retired in 1919 after forty-six years of service, he was succeeded by the young Paul M. Gross, who received his doctorate at Columbia. In addition to being a vital transmitter himself, Gross was destined to play a major role in the development of Duke University. In economics, William H. Glasson came from Columbia in 1902 and would spend his entire career at Trinity-Duke. In romance languages, A. M. Webb came from Yale, and in German, William H. Wannamaker, an undergraduate at Wofford College, did graduate work at Trinity before continuing it at Harvard and various German universities. Wannamaker, who joined the Trinity faculty in 1902, would play a major role in the university until his retirement.

The English department was strong in Trinity College, and several members of it played significant roles in both strengthening the institution and transplanting the university idea. Edwin Mims, after graduating from Vanderbilt and remaining there for two years of graduate work, joined the Trinity faculty in 1894. A passionate lover of literature who thought philology and other technical matters were best left to graduate students, Mims was both an inspiring, well-loved teacher and a productive scholar; a biography of Sidney Lanier published in 1905 helped establish Mims as a leading literary critic in the South.[22] In that same year he took over the editorship of the *South Atlantic Quarterly* from Bassett.

Mims had gone in 1896 to Cornell to complete his doctorate, and his presumably temporary replacement for a year was a young South Carolinian named William Preston Few.

No transmitter of the university idea to Trinity College was as important as Few. That was true both for what he admired in such institutions as Harvard and Johns Hopkins and for what he rejected. After graduating from Wofford College in 1889, Few taught school for three years before going to Harvard in 1892 for his doctorate in English. His four years in

Cambridge were important ones in Few's life, not with reference to his character or personality, for they were already shaped, but in terms of his ideas about higher education. A highly intelligent, hardworking person, Few became an able professional scholar at Harvard and acquired both an understanding of and a respect for true scholarship. His own career was destined to be steered early toward administration, but it is significant that he was a scholar first. Moreover, as he often recalled later, he had been fascinated to observe at first hand what President Charles W. Eliot was in the process of doing at Harvard: changing "a provincial New England college into a true American university."[23]

Understandably impressed by the growing excellence of Harvard, both in the arts and sciences and in its professional schools, Few nevertheless developed profound reservations about certain aspects of the then new research university. One misgiving centered on what he believed to be the tendency of the universities and their highly specialized faculties to neglect or minimize undergraduate teaching and to forget that, in Few's words, "the speculative pursuit of new truth" should not be the main end of undergraduate education. Deeply religious, Few clung to an old-fashioned educational notion that the values, character, and even physical health of undergraduates should concern colleges as much as the intellectual development of their minds. "What profiteth a man though he speak with the tongues of men and of angels and leave college a dyspeptic," Few posited, "though he understand all knowledge and have the habit of spending money that does not belong to him . . . ?"[24]

Few was not, of course, the first person—and certainly not the last— to understand the profound tension that arose particularly in the universities between undergraduate teaching and research. A recent historian of research universities puts the matter succinctly: "The bane of American higher education from the perspective of would-be university builders has traditionally been its large teaching burdens." Compared with their European counterparts, American professors "have been condemned to provide extensive basic instruction to large numbers of relatively poorly prepared undergraduates." Yet, since "American society has chiefly rewarded its universities for the undergraduate education that they provided," the universities, in order to provide the costly resources for research, have accepted their fate.[25]

Johns Hopkins, from its establishment until well into the twentieth century, was different. With more graduate students than undergraduates and admittedly oriented largely toward graduate and professional training, particularly in medicine, it seized a vanguard position as a research university. William P. Few, however, saw Johns Hopkins as an attempt "to transplant to American soil a full-grown German university." The experiment had been useful, he concluded in 1909, but except in its medical school (and, he should have added, its graduate school of arts and sciences), it had "not been successful."[26]

All of these ideas, formed and gracefully articulated by Few long before there was any notion of organizing a university around Trinity College, were later to become vitally important in that development. At this early stage, however, Few was merely one of a group of faculty members and others led by President Kilgo who were attempting in the years around and after the turn of the century to make Trinity into a strong college. In Few's own case, English became the first two-person department when Mims returned with his doctorate and Kilgo and his colleagues decided that Few should be retained nevertheless. Ben Duke, as in other such cases, made the decision possible by agreeing to pay the extra salary involved. Edwin Mims, in thanking Duke, was more prophetic than he could realize when he suggested that Few's retention was "one of the most important steps that Trinity has made."[27]

In 1902 Kilgo persuaded the trustees to make Few the dean of the college, the first such official in the institution's history. Kilgo not only delegated most of the academic administration to his new dean, but, regarding the post as a kind of vice presidency, gave various other responsibilities to Few. One of six founding members of the Southern Association of Colleges and Preparatory Schools in 1895, Trinity, while strengthening itself, had moved to the forefront of those institutions that struggled to raise the entire region's educational standards. Mims and Few were especially active in the work of the Southern Association, an important relationship that Few maintained until the end of his life.

With an endowment that had grown from $22,500 in 1894 to $440,000 by 1903 (thanks largely to Washington Duke), Trinity had developed greatly during its decade or so in Durham. There had been only nine faculty members when Kilgo assumed the presidency in 1894, but by 1903 the number had grown to twenty-three. New buildings, and particularly the library given by J. B. Duke, met important needs and made the campus more attractive. With the college shaping up satisfactorily, Kilgo suggested in 1902 that the time had come for the trustees to consider the future development of Trinity.

The first two lines of expansion recommended by Kilgo were a separate, coordinate college for women and a law school. The number of women students enrolled at Trinity had risen from four in 1896 to thirty-five by 1902. Since the majority of them, however, came from Durham, Kilgo argued that more adequate facilities for women would be required to achieve a greater geographical distribution. While the trustees did approve Kilgo's plan for the coordinate college, and he pushed it forward again in 1904, its implementation required resources that were not yet available.[28]

Kilgo's proposal for a law school was more fortunate. Determined that

Trinity's venture into legal training would follow high standards, Kilgo gained a pledge of annual support from the Duke brothers, and at a time when many law schools all over the country required only a high school education (and, in fact, many persons still became lawyers without attending law school at all), Trinity required the completion of two years of college work for admission to the three-year program in law. Opened in 1904 with the colorful and able Samuel Fox Mordecai as dean and senior professor, the school would remain small—there were six students in 1904 and seventeen in 1910—but the year after its establishment, Trinity's law school became the second member from the South, after the University of Tennessee, in the newly organized Association of American Law Schools.[29]

There was talk of a medical school at Trinity, an idea that Crowell had encouraged. Such a school would meet an undoubted need. Although Shaw University in Raleigh had opened a medical school for African Americans in 1882, it was sadly underfinanced and finally ceased operations in 1918. The first decades of the twentieth century found North Carolina without a four-year medical school for white students and, like most of the Southern states, lagging far behind in the fields of health and medicine. Kilgo, however, wisely held to the view that Trinity should not tackle new ventures unless the resources to support them were in sight. He agreed that, in due time, Trinity might begin with a two-year course in medicine and pharmacy. Again in 1909 there was a flurry of interest in the possibility of a medical school at Trinity, but the old question of money soon arose. The medical school, like the coordinate college for women, would have to wait.

Upon Kilgo's election to the Methodist episcopacy in 1910, the trustees promptly named the forty-two-year-old Few as his successor. Although Few shared many of Kilgo's ideas about educational administration and leadership—in fact, Few clearly learned how to be president primarily from Kilgo—the two men were vastly different in style. Whereas Kilgo was a spellbinding orator, Few spoke diffidently in public and excelled only in writing. Where Kilgo thrived on controversy, and aroused a great deal of it throughout his presidency, Few was a quiet peacemaker. Both men had strong, deeply held convictions about education, religion, and other important matters, but they expressed and acted on them quite differently.

Since Kilgo had first won and then held the loyal support of Washington Duke and his sons, many observers speculated that when Trinity lost Kilgo to the episcopacy it would also lose the backing of the Dukes. The observers could hardly have been more wrong. Ben Duke, like Few, was a quiet, reticent person. Although a businessman with only one year at New Garden School (later Guilford College), Ben Duke from the early

1890s onward grew to know higher education, as represented by Trinity College, and to become a close friend as well as working ally of Kilgo, Bassett, Few, and others. A year after Few's inauguration, itself an elaborate occasion that had led Ben Duke to say he felt "prouder of Trinity than ever before," he informed a friend that Few was "making a rousing good college president." The college, Duke boasted, had so many students that it was "almost impossible to take care of them."[30] As he had done for two decades, Ben Duke, and through him his younger brother, stood staunchly behind the college as it grew.

Precisely when James B. Duke first began to think of large-scale philanthropy that involved Trinity College is not known. William R. Perkins, a native Virginian who became J. B. Duke's chief legal counselor in 1914, later declared that almost from that time he had in his desk an early, rough draft of what became, a decade later, the indenture establishing the Duke Endowment.[31] Clearly the entrepreneurial genius of a hard-working, business-minded family, J. B. Duke had a vast talent for thinking and planning on a large scale. Moreover, he had the persistence and drive to see his projects through. After the Supreme Court of the United States ordered the dissolution of the American Tobacco Company in 1911 on the grounds that it violated the nation's antitrust law, J. B. Duke removed himself completely from the domestic tobacco industry. He remained, however, as president of the globe-circling British-American Tobacco Company, with its headquarters in London, and was deeply involved with building a vast, pioneering hydroelectric power company in the two Carolinas that would ultimately become the Duke Power Company.[32]

Many members of the Trinity faculty had never even met J. B. Duke. Kilgo, Few, Robert L. Flowers, and a handful of others had but were certainly not as close to him as they were to Ben Duke. At any rate, beginning in 1914 Few began to have occasional direct contact with J. B. Duke, never as much as Few would have preferred but nonetheless important. After conferring in New York with the Duke brothers in March, 1914, Few wrote what may have been his first letter directed solely to J. B. Duke. "We want you to understand what we are doing and to approve of it," Few explained. "But I do want you to feel that we will live within our means; that we will incur no added financial responsibilities without the approval beforehand of your Brother and yourself, and that any further contributions are to be free will offerings made because you feel like making them and not because they are expected of you." Then, in closing, Few struck a thoroughly characteristic note and employed an idealistic concept to which he returned many times: "And speaking for myself I am particularly anxious that you shall get enduring personal satisfaction and happiness out of what you have done for Trinity College, because you are able to feel that through it you have done some permanent good upon the earth."[33]

Never one to speak about ultimate motives or aspirations, J. B. Duke may or may not have been attracted by Few's idea of doing "permanent good upon the earth." The fact remained, however, that the family had become thoroughly entangled with the life and welfare of Trinity College, and beginning in the fall of 1914, Ben Duke, long the chief agent for family philanthropy, became ill. Suffering from debilitating "nervousness" and a "dizziness in the head," he gradually slipped into semi-invalidism. While he would have interludes of improved health and partially restored vitality, Ben Duke at age fifty-nine entered into a prolonged physical decline that lasted for the remaining fifteen years of his life.

Perhaps it was partly because J. B. Duke had always been remarkably close to his older and now unwell brother that he began around 1915 to put more of his own time and a steadily increasing amount of his wealth into the family's philanthropic work. A great lover of gardens and horticulture, as his father and brother were also, J. B. Duke assigned his own landscape architects to work on Trinity's new campus and gave $10,000 to be used on the grounds. Starting in 1915 he began making an annual contribution of $10,000 to supplement the funds of the two Methodist conferences in North Carolina for their superannuated preachers and the widows and children of deceased preachers. J. B. Duke requested Trinity College, that is, Few, to disburse the fund, and later used the same procedure with the $25,000 he gave each year for the building and support of rural Methodist churches.[34]

With the growing involvement of J. B. Duke in both Trinity College and other Methodist affairs, Few later said that around 1916 he, like Crowell and Kilgo before him, began "definitely" to think about plans for a university.[35] Few also said, repeatedly and eloquently, that the greater service that Trinity could render to humanity—in North Carolina, the South, and the nation—if it were expanded and organized as a major university was the essential reason for wanting the change. While that was no doubt true in Few's own thinking as well as in the minds of many others who supported him in the endeavor, there was more to the matter than such high-minded idealism.

Few, born in 1867, belonged to a generation of Southerners who knew poverty and defeat at first hand. After being reared in a deeply religious family and receiving a morally and academically sound education in South Carolina, he ventured into another and much more sophisticated world at Harvard in the 1890s. Although he never harped on the matter, Few undoubtedly became even more sensitized about the South's backwardness through his four years in the highly prosperous, rapidly developing, cosmopolitan university world at Cambridge. A quintessential Southerner in his love of his native region and his abiding sense of history, Few, like Woodrow Wilson, was very much "reconstructed" insofar as acceptance, even approval, of the outcome of the Civil War was concerned. But he remained deeply mortified by the conditions that continued to prevail in the postwar South, economically, politically, racially, and educationally. "Why is it," he asked in 1905, "that a civilization which has produced such men as Washington, Jefferson, Madison, Marshall, and Lee is now without commanding leaders of national reputation, . . . without ancient and famous institutions of learning, . . . without artists and writers, without so many of the good things of life that make civilization strong and great and beautiful?" Few confessed that he did not have a satisfactory, single answer to the questions he posed, but he believed that there were "two fundamental causes that had made all kinds of high intellectual attainment impossible" even in the antebellum South: "a belated survival at the South of the spirit of English feudalism" and the institution of slavery. The first, he argued, was essentially aristocratic, and while a sense of personal honor at its best was a fine thing, it could and did all too "easily degenerate into a regard for reputation and little concern for character." Just as English chivalry had centered on knights and ladies, the Old South's civilization had been "almost exclusively for the benefit of the well-to-do classes, and there was no chance to build up a great middle class, the mainstay of all modern civilizations." Too well satisfied with things as they were, the privileged groups of the South before the war fixed their gaze upon the past, and "when thought must run in certain, fixed conventional grooves," there could be no competition in the marketplace of ideas.

Slavery, Few suggested, strongly reinforced those tendencies in southern life, while it also was against the civilization of the nineteenth century. At war with the thinking of the rest of the Western world, southerners, he asserted, felt bound to defend themselves and concentrated their thought and energies on that defense rather than on a search for the truth which liberates. With cries of "white supremacy" and "Negro inferiority" even more raucous around 1900 than before the war, Few argued that southerners had to escape from the "miasmatic intellectual regions where we have lived for three quarters of a century," give truth and freedom their old ascendant place in life, and "hold aloft in our democratic Southern society high, national, universal standards of excellence in all human concerns."[36]

In short, Few passionately wanted his beloved South to have a major university, a research university, both because the region did not yet have one and because he believed such an institution could play a significant role in the work of intellectual and spiritual liberation that he deemed necessary. Few's long, patient, and ultimately successful wooing of James B. Duke involved a great deal more than mere ambitions for Trinity College.

Few claimed to have begun contemplating the idea of a university just before the United States entered World War I, but involvement in that war naturally affected Trinity as it did so much else in the nation.

The college faced a series of new problems, including the loss of male students and some faculty to military service, the increased enrollment of female students without adequate facilities for them, and particularly the war-induced inflation that eroded the college's real income from its endowment and pitifully shrank the buying power of faculty salaries.

Although J. B. Duke agreed in 1918 to Ben Duke's suggestion that he become a trustee of Trinity, he did not attend meetings of the board, for he strongly disliked all the talk involved in what he called "town meetings." If Few could not manage to confer in person with J. B. Duke, he could at least write to him, and in a particularly forceful letter late in 1918 Few advised the elusive industrialist that ever-improving conditions in the Methodist church in North Carolina were largely attributable to Trinity College. It not only furnished a large part of the Methodist preachers in the state but was "the inspiration of North Carolina Methodism." The strength of the church, therefore, was inevitably tied to Trinity's ability "to keep pace with the growing needs of a growing section of the country in a time of rapid change." Few ended his letter with a frank appeal: "I shall be grateful if you will allow me, as opportunity affords, to talk freely to you upon these questions and then leave action to your judgment and to your own good time. I am giving my life to these things that seem to me to be most worth while. That is all I can do, except to bring the needs and possibilities of these great causes to the attention of a man like you."[37]

The letter must have worked, for early in 1919 J. B. Duke met with Few and apparently for the first time began to get more specific about his philanthropic plans, which at that stage apparently involved giving a significant portion of his equity in the electric power industry for the support of Trinity College and of certain Methodist causes in the Carolinas. "As I have thought of your plan," Few wrote J. B. Duke soon after their talk, "it grows in my mind." Few believed that it was a sounder idea than that around which any other large benevolence in the county had been built. In another letter shortly afterwards, Few advised J. B. Duke that if he and his lawyer found that the property could not be administered under the charter of Trinity College, then Duke could "create a separate corporation, perhaps to be called the James B. Duke Foundation or Fund, as you might prefer." The self-perpetuating trustees of the fund could be the seven members of the executive committee of Trinity's board of trustees. "To carry out your ideas as I understand them," Few continued, "I think the charter of the Foundation ought to provide that the income is to go to Trinity College, Durham, N.C., and to the building of rural Methodist churches and the supplementing of rural Methodist preachers in the states of North Carolina and South Carolina."[38]

Few's hopes seem to have soared, but he was not yet aware that there was to be an inevitable delay. James B. Duke simply was not ready to act. For one thing, he believed that the stock of the power companies was not paying what he considered to be adequate dividends and could not do so until the rates could be adjusted upwards. Too, Duke, already heavily involved in strengthening and expanding his utility holdings in the Carolinas, was about to become the prime mover in the construction of what would be the world's largest hydrostation up to that time, in a remote region of the Canadian province of Quebec.

While J. B. Duke's delay was perfectly understandable from his point of view, President Few could not allow the vision of future good fortune to distract him from grim realities close at hand, such as woefully inadequate faculty salaries and the college's rusting heating plant, which had somehow to be replaced. Ben Duke, as always, remained Few's strongest ally despite his illness. Another important friend of Trinity, who was also one of Few's closest personal friends, was Clinton W. Toms. A former superintendent of the Durham schools, as were several other able young men whom the Dukes recruited for top positions in the tobacco industry, Toms long served as a trustee of Trinity and as a member of the executive committee. Quiet and always offstage, he ultimately became president of the Liggett & Myers tobacco company and a vital link between Trinity and Few on the one hand and the Duke brothers on the other. Individuals like Toms, who were as sympathetic with and informed about higher education as they were about big business, were rare, and for many years Few relied on Toms in a variety of routine as well as critical matters. In an uncharacteristic moment of gloom in 1919, when worries about salaries, the heating plant, and other such immediate problems kept mounting, Few confessed wearily to Toms: "If we can within the next two or three years make adequate provision for six hundred men and for a relatively small number of women who will come here I shall be content to leave further developments to a windfall or to future generations." [39]

The normally indefatigable Few soon recovered from his passing moment of fatigue and shriveled hope. Concerning the most urgent problem, that of inflation-hit faculty salaries, Ben Duke offered $12,000 and informed Few that he had talked over the situation at Trinity with his brother and persuaded him to give another $12,000. "I am very sorry he did not make it at least double this amount," Ben Duke added. [40]

Immensely relieved by the assistance, Few also took heart from a campaign among the townspeople of Durham to raise money for a women's dormitory at Trinity. It would be a memorial to the recently deceased James H. Southgate, longtime chairman of Trinity's board of trustees and a widely respected citizen. Clinton Toms in New York sent encouraging word in September, 1919, that as best he could learn progress was "being made on the formation of the Trust to be administered by the College and that within a year it would yield a very substantial income to the College."[41]

Toms's information turned out to be incorrect, for J. B. Duke was still not ready to act. He did, however, yield to the nudgings of Ben Duke, Toms, and other champions of Trinity and promise to give $100,000— $20,000 a year over a five-year period. Few promptly thanked him for the "generous gift" that would "help relieve the strain put upon us by the rapid growth of the College at the very time the value of money has fallen to the lowest level this generation has known."[42]

From one perspective, the Duke brothers might well have protested the demands that Trinity College made on them, for in the final analysis each additional student admitted to the burgeoning college cost them money. This was because Trinity, long proud of its accessibility to "poor boys"—and, to a more limited degree, "poor girls"—clung to a tuition rate of $50 per year. Even that was remitted for all pre-ministerial students, sons and daughters of preachers, and often for others who pled hardship or emergency. From 1910 to 1916, for example, enrollment increased by 60 percent, but income from tuition increased only 30 percent. By 1924 Trinity had 980 undergraduates (245 of whom were women), and since that was almost double the number in 1916 (551), one explanation for the soaring costs became obvious.[43]

Since neither of the Duke brothers was in any sense blind or dumb, they well knew that postwar inflation was not the only cause of Trinity's problem. Yet they, like Few and so many others connected with Trinity, accepted the burden of service that was the mission of the college and acknowledged the reality of the poverty and hard times that again struck home in North Carolina after 1921. Few, like Kilgo before him, had always insisted, however, that Trinity was more interested in quality than in numbers or size. From about 1920 on Few began to ponder the matter of selective admissions for the college.

As the student body grew, so did the faculty, which numbered 103 by 1924. More important than the size, however, was the quality of at least a significant portion of the group. John Spencer Bassett had early on counseled his protégé and successor, W. K. Boyd, that he should make his "stand for scholarship; it is what Trinity needs most and what the South needs most." Bassett went even further by adding that they needed scholarship "more than influence or numbers or even religion."[44] Precisely to help faculty members along that line, Few appointed a faculty committee on research in 1919 and made available a small fund to award research grants to faculty members and to help pay travel expenses to professional meetings. The first volume bearing the imprint "Trinity College Press" appeared in 1922, and the beginning of the sabbatical-year policy—a year's leave every seventh year at half-pay or a half-year at full pay—meant that more faculty members would have the time to write books for Trinity's or some other press.

Trinity established a committee on graduate instruction as early as 1916, and gradually the requirements for the degree of master of arts were clarified and formalized. Boyd and his Johns Hopkins–trained colleague who had come to Trinity in 1909, William T. Laprade, had long urged both a required thesis and greater concentration in a major field. Those features, as well as residence and foreign-language requirements, were spelled out by 1923, and in the following year the college had forty-one graduate students. A significant number of them were in the Department of Education, which Holland Holton, an alumnus and former superintendent of Durham county schools, led with marked vigor and flair.

With Trinity clearly maturing as a liberal arts college, symbolized by its finally winning a much-coveted chapter of Phi Beta Kappa in 1920, soon after the war Few turned again to the matter of Trinity's attempting to do something about the increasingly obvious need in North Carolina for a full-fledged, four-year medical school. As early as 1916 Few established contact with Dr. Abraham Flexner, the author of a famous report for the Carnegie Foundation in 1910 that helped to revolutionize medical education in the United States. Among other things that Few learned from Flexner was that medical education, if done properly and well, was enormously expensive.

Knowing that the General Education Board was interested in encouraging soundly conceived and adequately financed medical schools in the South, Few approached George W. Watts of Durham, longtime business partner of the Dukes first in tobacco and then in other ventures, about a plan to link a medical school with Watts Hospital, which Watts had given to the city in 1895. The school and hospital could also seek the cooperation of the two-year medical school at the University of North Carolina in nearby Chapel Hill. The death of Watts in March, 1921, interrupted but did not halt the plan, for Watts's widow and his son-in-law, John Sprunt Hill, were also interested in it.

Before Few could pursue the matter further, the situation became complicated by a discussion about a four-year medical school that began in Chapel Hill and in the state legislature. Controversy soon arose as to whether the school should be located in Chapel Hill, then still a small town, or in the much larger city of Charlotte. Few, assured privately of J. B. Duke's support, thanks in part to Clinton Toms, then made a somewhat audacious effort for an unusual compromise.[45]

The president of the University of North Carolina at the time was Harry W. Chase, a major figure in the transformation of the venerable school into a modern research university. Having gained the support of

Chase for his plan, as well as that of Governor Cameron Morrison, Few proposed late in 1922 that Trinity College and the University of North Carolina cooperate to build a medical school in Durham that would be operated in conjunction with Watts Hospital. The Baptists' Wake Forest College and the Presbyterians' Davidson College would also be invited to cooperate in the venture, which would be a highly unconventional but obviously economical merging of effort by state-supported and voluntarily supported institutions. Given North Carolina's great need of a full-fledged medical school, the high cost involved, and the prevailing economic realities, there was obviously much to be said for the plan.

Opposition to Few's scheme, however, arose quickly in various quarters. Josephus Daniels and the Raleigh *News & Observer*, favoring a school controlled solely by the University of North Carolina, opposed the plan, and some Baptists were reported to be disturbed by any proposed mingling of church and state. Once again, too, disputes arose about which city would be the best site for such a school. When even Chase, who had to worry about other needed appropriations from an economy-minded legislature, decided that the matter should be postponed and his trustees rejected the scheme, Few was disappointed but not particularly unhappy. He had privately explained part of his motivation for the plan by saying, "We are planning for large expansion here, but I am anxious to get rid of Trinity College [alone] tackling a medical school."[46] A little later, when the plan had clearly collapsed, Few advised the president of the state medical society that he could "safely assume that Trinity will build a medical school without too much delay." Looking back much later, Few observed that the abortive plan had served two purposes: "It kept the road open for a first-rate School of Medicine later on, and it put Mr. James B. Duke on his mettle."[47]

If Few had come to recognize the expensiveness of medical education, J. B. Duke was also beginning to appreciate that fact. Just how much else he learned from the episode may only be conjectured, but one of Few's strongest supporters in the effort for a cooperative medical school was Dr. Watson S. Rankin, then the secretary of the state board of health. Rankin warned, however, that a full-fledged medical school, as much as it was needed, would not alone alleviate the shortage of doctors in North Carolina, which remained one of the most predominantly rural states in the nation. Rankin believed, on the basis of his study of the experience in the Canadian province of Saskatchewan and elsewhere, that the principal remedy for the shortage of medical care in much of the state would be the establishment of local hospitals jointly financed by the state and counties. Both B. N. Duke and J. B. Duke had a long-standing interest in Watts Hospital as well as in Lincoln Hospital, which they had given to Durham's African Americans in 1901. But Few's early efforts in seeking a medical school and Dr. Rankin's emphasis on local hospitals clearly exerted a great influence on J. B. Duke's thinking about his projected philanthropy.

In the midst of his unsuccessful efforts to secure a medical school, Few made his most elaborate and ultimately influential move to prod J. B. Duke into action. Hospitalized throughout much of the summer of 1920, probably as much from sheer fatigue as anything else, Few continued to be intermittently unwell through the following winter. During his convalescence from pneumonia in the spring of 1921 he had time for reflection, and a number of ideas, many of them foreshadowed by earlier efforts or proposals, finally fell into place in his mind. He produced the initial blueprint for a "Duke University" that could be organized around Trinity College. The plan was not a hastily conceived scheme to lure a large gift. Rather, it was the carefully considered synthesis of a number of Few's ideas that had long been evolving and of developments in Trinity College that had long been underway.

As his starting point, Few held passionately to the notion, as he expressed it in 1919 and repeated many times, that the best American universities "have at their heart a great college of arts and sciences."[48] A simple fact, perhaps, but it was one that some educators as well as much of the public either minimized or failed to understand. Few not only saw the undergraduate college as the heart of any true university, but he placed effective teaching, especially of freshmen, near the top of his list of educational priorities. Much of the strength that Trinity College had obviously achieved by the early 1920s derived from the fact that a significant proportion of the faculty shared Few's faith in the college and in teaching. Yet beginning with Bassett and others like him, many of the faculty also liked to do research and, despite the inevitable tensions, wanted an opportunity to engage meaningfully in both teaching and investigation.

While the law school that was established in 1904 had been a respectable one in that era, it appeared increasingly inadequate in light of developments in legal education after World War I. The hope for a coordinate college for women had resurfaced at various times since Washington Duke's gift in 1896, but Trinity's commitment to the education of women was simply not yet matched by adequate facilities for them. In addition to the possible medical school, Trinity's interest in theological education was manifested in the early 1920s by a significant expansion in that area, and Few pushed for a school of religion. A department of engineering had long existed in the college, but it too needed strengthening and development. If Trinity were to be enlarged, why not keep it as the "heart" and use another name for a university that might be built around it?

The idea for naming the enlarged institution "Duke University" came from Few. The principal reason that he gave for favoring it was that there was already a Trinity University in San Antonio, Texas, and several other

Trinity Colleges in the United States. In Great Britain and elsewhere in the English-speaking world numerous other institutions were named Trinity. Not wishing to share a name with so many, Few turned to the idea that various people had begun to suggest as early as the 1890s. There is no evidence, however, that any member of the Duke family had ever shown any interest in changing the institution's name.

Thus it was that Few, pulling together all his ideas in the spring of 1921, submitted the following statement, which he apparently hoped J. B. Duke would sign.

I wish to see Trinity College, the law school & other schools expanded into a fully developed university organization. It has been suggested to me that this expanded institution be named Duke University as a memorial to my father whose gifts made possible the building of Trinity College in Durham, and I approve this suggestion. I desire this university to include Trinity College, a coordinate College for Women, a Law School, a School of Business Administration, a School of Engineering (emphasizing chemical & electrical engineering), a Graduate School of Arts & Sciences, and, when adequate funds are available, a Medical School. I desire this enlarged institution to be operated under the present charter with only such changes, if any changes at all, as the enlargement may require. To this university that is to be thus organized I will give ———— millions of dollars. I agree to pay in within ———— years ———— millions in cash or good securities.[49]

Few, as soon as he was able to get out, took the plan to Ben Duke, who was in residence at his home in Durham at the time. He promptly approved the whole idea, but when Few soon thereafter went to New York, J. B. Duke was still not prepared to commit himself so definitely and refrained both from filling in the all-important blanks in Few's memorandum and from signing the document. J. B. Duke apparently gave some sort of general approval to the scheme, however, for when Trinity's trustees met in June, 1921, Few alluded briefly to a possible reorganization looking toward the status of a university. To one or two of the closest friends of the college he mentioned "great plans which I think in due course will be completely realized" and hinted about "our reorganization for the future." Conferences between Few and J. B. Duke followed, one later in 1921, but the record reveals nothing about them except that they occurred.[50]

Movement toward the creation of J. B. Duke's foundation accelerated in 1923. Duke had once told a friend that the electric power industry would never be as profitable for the owners as the tobacco industry had been.[51] Yet Duke and his allies had succeeded finally in getting the rates adjusted upward, and with what Duke regarded as a more adequate return on the investment, he was ready to proceed with his philanthropic plans.

Early in 1923 Duke arranged for Few to meet George Garland Allen, who in the final years of Duke's life became his close associate in business and who was destined to play a highly important role in the early history of Duke University. A native of Warrenton, North Carolina, Allen had attended business school after completing high school and had become a bookkeeper for the American Tobacco Company in 1895. Working his way up through that and J. B. Duke's other organizations, he finally became Duke's chief lieutenant in the early 1920s. Although Allen had no previous connection with Trinity College, his relationship with J. B. Duke and the large plans concerning the institution led to Allen's election to the board of trustees late in 1923.

Amidst all the various confidential preparations, J. B. Duke found, as he told one friend, that it had been easier to accumulate his wealth than it was to give away a large portion of it wisely.[52] Nevertheless, he proceeded as carefully and systematically in his approach to philanthropy as he always had in his business affairs. One who took much pleasure in the physical construction involved with certain large enterprises, J. B. Duke probably looked forward to the extensive building that would go on at Trinity as much as anything else. He picked his architectural firm in 1923, and Horace Trumbauer of Philadelphia, whose staff had designed Duke's mansion on New York's Fifth Avenue as well as some elaborate greenhouses at Duke's estate near Somerville, New Jersey, began to correspond with Few about the overall plan of the campus.

In the spring of 1924, Few and Frank C. Brown, the chairman of the English department, who was a good friend of Ben Duke and a key aide to Few in matters pertaining to the grounds and buildings, went on an extensive tour of a large number of colleges and universities in the North. After conferring first with Trumbauer, Few and Brown carefully studied the stone buildings at Bryn Mawr College that were constructed in what was usually referred to as the collegiate Gothic or Tudor Gothic style of architecture.

At Princeton University, where handsome dormitories in the Tudor Gothic style had been built before World War I, Few and Brown collected pictures, some blueprints, and much information about the buildings as well as about such prosaic matters as arrangements for the kitchens and mail delivery. J. B. Duke's country estate was not far from Princeton, and he had seen and liked the newer stone buildings there. His half-brother, Brodie Duke, had much admired the buildings at Oxford University on a visit to Britain in 1891. The Duke brothers probably could not have explained all of their reasons for being attracted to this architectural style, but they seemed to share, even if half unconsciously, the thinking of Woodrow Wilson, who offered this explanation early in the century while he was still president of Princeton: "By the very simple device of constructing our new buildings in the Tudor Gothic style we seem to have added to Princeton the age of Oxford and of Cambridge; we have added a thousand years to the history of Princeton by merely putting those lines in our architecture which point every man's imagination to historic traditions of learning in the English-speaking race."[53]

Few and Frank Brown certainly shared Woodrow Wilson's notion about the Tudor Gothic style, and they studied it further at Yale, Cornell, the City College of New York, Chicago, and on other campuses. At Harvard they took special notice of the Widener Memorial Library, which Trumbauer's firm had designed, and at Johns Hopkins and particularly at the University of Virginia, as well as at some other schools in Virginia, they were impressed by the felicitous use of red brick and white columns in buildings of neoclassical or Georgian design.[54]

By September, 1924, still three months or so before the public knew anything about the projected university, J. B. Duke, after conferences with Few, Brown, and Trumbauer, had decided that the new buildings to be erected on the Trinity campus would be constructed of stone in the Tudor Gothic style. Few reported happily to Ben Duke that it was "distinctly my first choice." Clearly elated by the prospect of what lay ahead, Few declared, "It is but the sober truth to say that when these buildings as now planned are put on the grounds we will have here the most harmonious, imposing, and altogether beautiful educational plant in America."[55]

George G. Allen predicted to Few in September, 1924, that when once J. B. Duke had made up his mind definitely to go ahead, he would "see that a most creditable job is done."[56] Duke had indeed concluded to move ahead on his large project, and in October, 1924, Robert L. Flowers, now vice president of Trinity and Few's close associate in administration, began sending to Few from New York some most interesting, handwritten letters marked "personal & confidential." Flowers got much of his information from Alex. H. Sands, Jr., the executive secretary of the Duke brothers, and from Allen, as well as from William R. Perkins. A native Virginian, Perkins graduated in law from Washington and Lee University and worked for the American Tobacco Company before becoming chief legal counselor to B. N. and J. B. Duke around 1914. The principal author of the indenture creating the Duke Endowment, Perkins, like Allen, would play a key role in Duke University's early history.

Flowers found that explaining various aspects of Trinity College and of higher education in general to New York businessmen was not always easy. Still, he remained optimistic. "I think everything is going all right," he assured Few. "From what they all tell me, Mr. J. B. is right behind the thing now. Mr. B. N. is greatly interested." Later that same day, Flowers dispatched more substantial and important news: "Mr. J. B. is undecided how to have the trust fund administered." During the five or more years of preliminary discussion and planning, the idea apparently had been to have the executive committee of Trinity's board of trustees administer the foundation. Now, however, Flowers reported a significant development: "They have been to confer with the Rockefeller Foundation and at present they are very much inclined to have fifteen trustees of the fund." Flowers confessed that he thought it might be unfortunate for Trinity to have the trustees of the foundation too widely separated from those of the college. Yet he believed that the people on the foundation's board would be the crucial element, and he found both Allen and Perkins eager to "get in touch with the College."[57]

Ben Duke, who probably shared Andrew Carnegie's belief that rich philanthropists should carry out their plans during their lifetimes rather than trust to posthumous arrangements, had long urged J. B. Duke to act. Now, Flowers found Ben Duke in "better shape than for a long time" and in "fine spirits." Flowers credited Allen with "spurring up Mr. J. B. not to wait longer to establish his trust," and at long last "Mr. J. B. is pushing things just as fast as he can."[58]

Flowers proved to be quite correct about J. B. Duke's "pushing things" rapidly, for early in December, 1924, Duke arrived in Charlotte with his wife, his twelve-year-old daughter Doris, Allen, Perkins, and several other associates. They were soon joined at Duke's home in Charlotte by the top officers of the power company, and for part of the time by Few, Flowers, and one or two others. Duke announced that, after working on his philanthropic project for a number of years, he now wanted the group to remain assembled until the job of polishing and completing the indenture that would establish the perpetual trust was finished. Unfortunately for history's sake, no record of the meeting was kept, but the group worked steadily for about four days and discussed, section by section, the draft of the indenture that W. R. Perkins had prepared. Many years later, one participant recalled no substantial alterations or additions that the group made. "Of course, Mr. Duke . . . was a positive man," this participant added, "and when he made a positive assertion very few people controverted it."[59] J. B. Duke might have been better served by candid, critical suggestions from the group, for the indenture was not without flaws, and at least one of them, to be discussed later, would cause much unnecessary embarrassment to Duke himself.

Even before Duke could formally sign the indenture at his legal residence in New Jersey on December 11, 1924, news of the large philanthropy leaked out in the newspapers. While the nation at large paid ample heed to the story, the news had its largest impact in the Carolinas, where all of the beneficiaries were located. Securities worth approximately $40,000,000—mostly, but not exclusively, in the electric power company—were turned over to the trustees of the Duke Endowment, and the annual income from the principal was to be distributed among educational institutions, hospitals, orphanages, and the Methodist church in a manner specified in the indenture.[60]

While three other educational institutions were named as beneficiaries—Davidson College (Presbyterian, near Charlotte), Furman University (Baptist, in Greenville, South Carolina), and Johnson C. Smith University (an institution for African Americans in Charlotte)—the lion's share, 32 percent of the annual income, was designated to go to "an institution of learning to be known as Duke University." To establish it the trustees were authorized to spend $6,000,000 from the corpus of the trust. "However, should the name of Trinity College . . . be changed to Duke University" within a three-month period, then the $6,000,000 and the annual income should go to that institution.

Starting back in the 1890s, Ben Duke had acted for the family in disbursing modest sums for a variety of charitable purposes, with Trinity College heading the list. In 1924, J. B. Duke apportioned the income from a $40,000,000 perpetual trust that was destined to grow much larger, for it would be more than doubled by the terms of J. B. Duke's will. Moreover, he made Duke University the prime beneficiary. The striking point, however, is not really the difference in the sums of money in the 1890s and 1920s but the continuity in the purpose of the giving. The creation of the Duke Endowment, with its large commitment to Duke University, was certainly not inevitable, for many rich individuals have found countless other ways to dispose of their wealth. Yet the Duke Endowment was the culmination of a deeply rooted tradition and pattern of giving that Washington Duke had initiated, that Ben Duke had supervised for many years, and that J. B. Duke, the youngest and by far the richest of the clan, freely chose to institutionalize for posterity on a princely scale.

As Christmas approached in 1924, no North Carolinian could have been happier than William P. Few. "Then after all, my dream and your dream is to be realized in full," he exulted to Ben Duke. "Isn't it glorious?"[61] In truth, it was to be glorious in many ways, but unforeseen trouble also lay ahead for Few and Duke University.

2

Building on Two Campuses:

"The Most . . . Beautiful

Educational Plant in America"

⌁

ALTHOUGH PRESIDENT FEW privately expressed his fear that some of the Trinity College alumni might object to the organization of a new university around the old college, he quickly secured overwhelming support from the great majority of the institution's alumni and friends. "Personally, when it comes to that point where Trinity can take the lead in educational circles of the entire South," one alumnus wrote, "I am inclined to shout with Shakespeare: 'WHAT'S IN A NAME?'" Another prominent alumnus declared: "As you are aware, changing the name to Duke University has been my wish for some years, and it is with genuine satisfaction that I now see a realization of this about to take place."[1]

While alumni and the public focused on the matter of the new name, Few concentrated on more important matters and prepared for the crucial called meeting of Trinity's trustees on December 29, 1924. Apparently untroubled as yet about any problems that might arise from the indenture creating the Duke Endowment, Few first submitted his carefully drawn statement of Trinity's response to J. B. Duke's offer to Joseph G. Brown, the chairman of the trustees. Brown commended Few's draft and thought it made "perfectly clear that the college is not in the hands of that [Endowment] board and yet we know that a great many do not get the idea that the Trustees of the fund are simply to handle the business at that end of the line."[2] Voting unanimously to accept J. B. Duke's offer and issuing the statement drafted by Few, the trustees declared, among other things: "We have found that the university is to be developed according to plans that are perfectly in line with our hopes for the expansion of this historic college. . . ." Furthermore, they added: "The control of Duke University and all its relations to its constituency will remain identical with the control and relations to constituency that Trinity College has had."[3]

Few and the trustees also responded to ideas that J. B. Duke had advanced in his indenture. He had included Duke University as a principal beneficiary, he explained, because he believed that "education, when conducted along sane and practical, as opposed to dogmatic and theoretical lines, is next to religion, the greatest civilizing influence." J. B. Duke requested that the institution "secure for its officers, trustees and faculty men of such outstanding character, ability and vision as will insure its attaining and maintaining a place of real leadership in the educational world. . . ." For its students he urged that "great care and discrimination be exercised" to admit "only those whose previous record shows a character, determination and application evincing a wholesome and real ambition for life." Finally, he advised that the courses at Duke University should be arranged "first, with special reference to the training of preachers, teachers, lawyers and physicians, because these are most in the public eye, and by precept and example can do most to uplift mankind, and, second, to instruction in chemistry, economics and history, especially the lives of the great of [the] earth, because I believe that such subjects will most help to develop our resources, increase our wisdom and promote human happiness."

The trustees in their statement responded that Duke University would "be concerned about excellence rather than size" and would "aim at quality rather than numbers—quality of those who teach and quality of those who learn." Moreover, the university would be developed "with a view to serving conditions as they actually exist" and would be "for the use of all the people of the State and Section without regard to creed, class or party, and for those elsewhere who may seek to avail themselves of the opportunities it has to offer."[4]

Enthusiastically supported by the students then enrolled at Trinity-Duke, Few also received an encouraging word from an important neighbor. President Harry W. Chase of the University of North Carolina, a generous and broad-visioned man like Few, declared prophetically: "Two universities, located as ours are, growing up side by side, the one in response to private benefaction and the other under State control, should supplement each other, and each, I believe, will be a stimulus to the other's development." Chase suggested that J. B. Duke's gift to Duke University would "advance at the same time the whole level of thinking about higher education in the State and in the South."[5]

While happy harmony seemed to reign among J. B. Duke, Few, the trustees, and most of the alumni, there were a few scattered dissents. A small number of alumni objected to the new name for the institution.

One opposed not so much the name as the location in Durham and J. B. Duke's failure to consider Asheville, in the mountainous region of North Carolina, as the site for the university. "The Divinity which engineered the building of the Pyramids in the desert sands of Egypt probably understands why Duke University is going ahead in Durham County," the irate alumnus declared, "but His great plan does not comprehend that people outside of Durham should understand it." Few, ever patient, explained that he had once discussed with J. B. Duke the possibility of "going to Asheville" but found him opposed to the idea. "When you go out to get $40,000,000 from a man," Few noted, "you will find that he has some ideas of his own." When the stubborn champion of Asheville retorted by arguing that "nothing short of a *miracle* can ever establish a truly great university in a place like Durham," Few closed the correspondence magisterially: "We have never thought of ourselves as miracle workers but we have not a shadow of doubt that we can work the miracle that may seem to be necessary to build a great university here."[6]

More serious perhaps than the complaints of a small handful of unhappy alumni was the widespread and long-lasting misunderstanding about the role of J. B. Duke in the naming of Duke University. This arose from a clumsily worded section of the indenture that could easily have been avoided. The document had provided that $6,000,000 should be used to establish "an institution of learning to be known as Duke University," but "should the name of Trinity College . . . be changed to Duke University" then it would receive the $6,000,000.

Journalists and others across the entire nation promptly seized on this section of the indenture and interpreted it, understandably enough, as a blatant case of "Buck Duke's buying himself a university" or "bribing" a college in order to memorialize himself and the family name. That seemingly obvious interpretation was simply not correct. In the first place, since the idea of building a university around Trinity and naming it Duke had originated with Few, the popular interpretation was hardly fair to J. B. Duke. Secondly, the widespread emphasis on the "name change" helped obscure the important facts that a new university was to be organized around an old college, and that, furthermore, Trinity College would actually continue to exist as the undergraduate college of arts and sciences. Yet J. B. Duke and W. R. Perkins were themselves primarily responsible for the unnecessarily awkward language that inspired the whole furore. Few issued explanatory statements to the public and privately confessed that he was "only sorry that the legal phrasing in the Indenture of Trust seemed to put Mr. Duke in a bad light."[7]

Unfortunately, history is replete with examples that illustrate how truth often never catches up with error, particularly when the falsehood may be turned to witty, amusing ends. H. L. Mencken's *American Mercury* specialized in sophomoric attacks on J. B. Duke and his alleged presumption in thinking he could buy himself a university to be built from scratch.[8] Numerous other journalists for many years ignored Few's repeated efforts to set the record straight. An additional twist was soon added with the allegation that J. B. Duke had first tried to "buy" Princeton (because of its proximity to his estate in Somerville, New Jersey?) but, having failed there, turned to a small college in the South that was unknown to many in the Northeast. Oddly enough, students and even some faculty members at Duke University itself have for decades passed along the tale about J. B. Duke and Princeton. A 1973 version in the student newspaper at Duke put it this way: "Many years ago, before the expansion of Trinity College, James Duke tried to 'buy' Princeton so that he would have a little school to which to give his name." A variation appeared in another publication: J. B. Duke is "reputed to have first urged his money (and his name) on Yale. Rebuffed by Yale, he decided to rival it in prestige and physical beauty. Thus was Duke University grandly formed from Duke's millions."[9]

The examples could be multiplied endlessly, but most of the utterly groundless tales arose out of ignorance not only about President Few's role in the naming of the university but more especially about Trinity College and the Duke family's long and close relationship with it. At any rate, if J. B. Duke ever became aware of the brouhaha about the name change, one must doubt that he lost any sleep over the matter. He had long before developed a tough hide, possibly too tough for his own good, when it came to what journalists had to say about him and his activities. On the one hand, such indifference to public image stands in refreshing contrast to a tendency in the later twentieth century for image often to seem more important than substance or reality. On the other hand, indifference to the public's opinion could easily leave one's actions open to serious misinterpretation. As a long career in business had demonstrated, however, J. B. Duke believed that he had more important things to do than worry about misunderstandings on the part of the public.

Starting early in 1924, many months before the Duke Endowment was officially established, J. B. Duke and Horace Trumbauer, or some of the latter's associates, visited the Trinity Campus from time to time in connection with the contemplated expansion. In January, 1924, Few informed Duke that he had given much thought to the "re-laying out of our campus along the general lines you suggested to me in Charlotte the other day." Sending preliminary sketches, Few expressed his eagerness to cooperate in the planning.[10]

Essential for the projected expansion was the acquisition of additional land. Despite the fact that Trinity's campus was already spacious—approximately 108 acres—it was not big enough for all the new buildings that J. B. Duke planned to give to the university. Land to the north of the campus, particularly between it and Watts Hospital, would be needed for the possible medical school. By the spring of 1924 Few's agents had been quietly securing options for land around the campus for more than a year. When informed in May, 1924, that the price of the various parcels of land under option totalled $161,000, J. B. Duke sent word to Few that "it would be all right to go that far but not to pay any more than that, and to be sure that you get all of it."[11]

Getting "all of it" at reasonable prices, however, proved to be increasingly difficult as rumors spread through Durham about Trinity's expansion, and land prices rose accordingly. By October, 1924, Few was still optimistic about acquiring the desired land but confessed that "it will require some time."[12] Impatient with the delays and angered by what he regarded as the price-gouging of landowners in the vicinity of Trinity's campus, J. B. Duke made threatening noises about giving up in Durham and trying to build a university in Charlotte. One kinswoman to whom he allegedly said something along those lines reported that she made this reply: "Uncle Buck, that would be awful. This is the place you all were born; your father started that college and he lived here and had great faith in Trinity College and all, and [going to Charlotte] would look awfully silly and foolish." When J. B. Duke responded that the university was going to be a large one and that Charlotte might be better able to handle it, the staunch partisan of Durham and Trinity recalled saying, "Well, you do it, but I don't think it is a true memorial to the Duke family or to your father if you move it to Charlotte."[13]

If J. B. Duke was merely trying to light a fire under Few and his associates with the talk of Charlotte—and he probably was attempting just that—he succeeded admirably. Few, walking with his sons through a lovely wooded area a mile or so to the west of the Trinity campus, hit upon the idea of expanding in that direction rather than north towards Watts Hospital. The ground rolled gently, there were pine and hardwood forests, and no one, including the landowners, had even dreamed of Trinity's going that far afield. "It was for me a thrilling moment," Few later wrote, "when I stood on a hill . . . and realized that here at last is the land we have been looking for."[14]

J. B. Duke agreed to an effort to acquire land in the new direction, and while some limited buying continued north of the old Trinity campus, Robert L. Flowers, operating with great discretion and quietness, put an agent to work. Securing the first option on November 7, 1924, Flowers had, by the spring of 1925, succeeded in acquiring at reasonable prices much more land than was immediately needed. In fact, purchases to round out the holdings continued for many years, and Duke University, in addition to two spacious campuses, eventually wound up owning approximately 8,000 acres, most of it in a forest preserve. The university would never face the problem of land scarcity that has plagued so many educational institutions.[15]

"The acquisition of the land," Flowers informed his old friend Ben Duke, "has been to me one of the most absorbing things I have ever been connected with." All who saw the new land, Flowers declared, were "carried away with the prospect," and there had never been "any greater mystery in Durham than the land transaction."[16] For several months while the new land was being acquired, however, no one knew for sure whether or just how it might be used. J. B. Duke had the final word on that, and not until late March, 1925, was his decision made.

The North Carolina Piedmont, with its abundant dogwood and redbud trees along with other native flowering shrubs scattered among pines and hardwood trees, can be a glorious place during the long, slow spring season. Such it was when J. B. Duke finally inspected the new land and, in consultation with Few and others, quickly made a series of decisions that had a far-reaching impact on Duke University. The Tudor Gothic buildings, J. B. Duke decided, would have a soaring chapel at their center and would be built on the new land on a crest overlooking a deep ravine. There J. B. Duke, who had a penchant for lakes and fountains, envisioned a lake, and a large fountain in the central quadrangle would send water cascading down a series of terraces into the lake. The long-desired coordinate college for women, instead of being crowded into the northwest corner of the old Trinity campus, would occupy the entire campus. Several of the existing buildings would be retained but some would have to go in order to make room for eleven new buildings to be constructed of red brick and white marble in the Georgian or neoclassical style.

One of the few documentary sources for the important decisions concerning Duke University's physical plant that J. B. Duke, Few, and their associates made late in March, 1925, is a prosaic work diary or notebook kept by Horace Trumbauer's construction superintendent, B. M. Hall. He merely noted: "Met Mr. Duke today and went over the ground for the new university." On the following day Hall recorded that he had met with Trumbauer and another of the architects and "explained the new location of the layout on top of the hill moving the chapel forward so it will come on the high ground." The superintendent added that the library was "to be moved over to a high spot to the right of where shown on plans, this being Mr. Duke's idea of how the layout should be." Further on, after mentioning various other matters, Hall wrote: "Went over to the new location and Mr. Duke approved of the general layout but ordered another fountain on the opposite hill [where the traffic circle would be built] to flow down into the lake. . . ."[17]

Amidst all this activity, the trustees of the Duke Endowment were meeting in Durham, in Ben Duke's home. Many years later two things about the meeting remained vivid in the memory of one of the trustees who was present. The first was that during one of the trustees' sessions twelve-year-old Doris Duke entered the room, climbed onto the knee of her father, J. B. Duke, and remained quietly there for the remainder of the meeting. The other memory was that J. B. Duke invited the trustees to inspect the new land with him. "We walked all over those grounds," Dr. Watson Rankin stated, "jumping ditches and crossing wagon roads and going through shrubbery and all that kind of thing, with Mr. Duke always in the lead. Again I was impressed with the man's vigor."[18]

On the third day of all the intense activity and planning, Few, Flowers, and Frank Brown attended a "full meeting" where a reduction of over 900,000 cubic feet was made in the plans, but at a subsequent session, B. M. Hall noted, "a goodly portion of our saving was put back by Mr. Duke and Mr. Allen."[19] Trumbauer and his associates headed back to Philadelphia with instructions to proceed with working drawings, first for the new Georgian buildings on the Trinity campus, which was soon to be known as the East campus, and then for the Gothic structures eventually to be erected on the new land, or the West campus. Much of the preliminary planning for the two campuses of Duke University had been accomplished in three busy spring days of 1925.

Apparently unbeknownst to most people at the time, the self-effacing but brilliant architect who worked quietly along with others in Trumbauer's office in Philadelphia and who actually designed the new buildings for Duke University was Julian Abele. The first African-American graduate of the University of Pennsylvania's architectural school, Abele had also studied at the Ecole des Beaux Arts in Paris. Now known as the designer of Harvard's Widener Library and the Philadelphia Museum of Art, among other important public buildings, Abele, following the practice in Trumbauer's large firm, did not put his signature on any of the blueprints for Duke University until after 1938. While Few no doubt met Abele early on and corresponded on occasion with him in later years, J. B. Duke may neither have met nor known of Abele. In light of Washington Duke's and his family's generous attitude toward African Americans, however, one may safely conjecture that J. B. Duke would have been pleased by Abele's important role in Duke University's architectural history.[20]

Concurrently with the matter of the new land and the siting of the buildings on it, J. B. Duke helped to decide another matter that much interested him, and this concerned the kind of stone to be used in the Tudor Gothic buildings. He originally thought that the stone should come from one of the well-known quarries in the North, in Pennsylvania, New Jersey, Indiana, or Massachusetts. He therefore arranged for carloads of various samples of stone to be shipped to Durham and for test walls to be built on the Trinity campus. In the meantime, Frank Brown investigated the possibility of North Carolina stone and found in the possession of the state geologist some specimens of volcanic stone from an abandoned quarry near Hillsborough, only a few miles from Durham. On the eve of J. B. Duke's inspection of the new land in March, 1925, Brown informed Trumbauer that a sample wall of the local stone revealed that it was "much more attractive than the Princeton wall" and "much warmer and softer in coloring." Brown estimated that it could be quarried and delivered on the ground at not more than $3.50 per ton, whereas he thought that the Princeton stone would cost approximately $21.00 per ton. When Flowers informed George Allen about the exciting possibilities of the local stone and how cheaply the "entire ridge" with "an almost unlimited supply" of stone could be purchased, J. B. Duke ordered the acquisition of the quarry and further testing of the stone.[21]

J. B. Duke, pleased by the wide range of colors in the local stone as well as reassured of its durability by tests conducted both in the state geologist's office and in the Bureau of Standards in Washington, proudly led the trustees of the Duke Endowment to the sample walls in late March, 1925. Balloting there indicated an overwhelming preference for the native stone, but J. B. Duke wanted additional test walls built with "less of the yellow and gold colors." Accordingly, Frank Brown suggested a wall showing "as predominating colors the dark blue, the light blue, the light green, the light gray and the dark blue with face mottled with dark brown." All these colors, Brown believed, could be obtained from the Hillsborough quarry in "unlimited quantities."[22] Thus it turned out that while the original buildings of the university's West campus were inspired by a venerable style of English architecture, the warmly colored stone came from a neighboring hillside in Piedmont North Carolina.

Like Washington and Ben Duke, J. B. Duke loved horticulture and landscaping, and to lay out the grounds of the new campus as well as to redesign those of the old Trinity campus, he selected one of the leading firms in the nation, Olmsted Brothers of Boston. The firm had been founded by Frederick Law Olmsted, the creator of Central Park in New York and of many other famous gardens and parks. Even before J. B. Duke had seen the new land, he requested that contour maps of its central portion show all the large trees, for he clearly hoped to build the new campus in such a fashion as to save as many of the significant trees as possible. In emphasizing the physical setting or environment in which educational activities were to occur, J. B. Duke unknowingly concurred with John Spencer Bassett. Although he had left Trinity some years earlier, Bassett remained keenly interested in the institution, and in 1920 he had admonished Few that educated persons in the South needed "to turn to this aesthetic problem." Bassett thought that Trinity College (thanks to the Dukes) could "afford to spend money liberally for beautiful grounds and artistically designed buildings well placed." They were "educational in just the way we need education just now."[23] J. B. Duke probably would never have articulated the matter in the way that Bassett had, but the industrialist-turned-philanthropist instinctively understood and acted accordingly.

One of the most important attributes of Washington, Ben, and J. B. Duke as the enablers or backers of Trinity-Duke was that they gave, generously and repeatedly, but they never interfered in the academic side of the institution. In the particular case of J. B. Duke, he strongly agreed with Few on the intention to have Duke University maintain an emphasis on religion and the tie with Methodism, to pursue excellence rather than mere bigness or numbers, to be of as much service as possible, and to have a national as well as regional orientation. J. B. Duke apparently intended to provide the buildings, the grounds, and as much of the monetary means as he could and leave the rest to Few, Flowers, Wannamaker, and their associates in the university. All of this was somewhat ironic in light of what would happen after J. B. Duke's death, but in early 1925 he concerned himself with large planning problems, such as the location and even the style of the projected chapel, and with small details, such as the width of the hallways in the women's dormitories (he wanted, and got, wider ones). Even the arrangements of the rooms within the projected new buildings on the East campus, where construction was to begin later in the year, interested him.[24]

As greatly interested as J. B. Duke was in the physical construction of Duke University, he still had other large projects of vital concern to him. In July, 1925, he, George Allen, and various officials of the Aluminum Company of America visited the Saguenay River in Canada to inspect the vast hydroelectric plant there that Duke had swapped for a one-ninth interest in the aluminum company. At the same time a serious drought in the Carolinas posed massive problems for the Duke Power system, and J. B. Duke had visited Charlotte to wrestle with the urgent need for more coal-burning steam plants.

Joining his wife and daughter at the mansion in Newport, Rhode Island, that he had purchased for them in 1922, J. B. Duke continued to confer there with associates who came up to deliver important papers or to gain a final decision on some question. Robert L. Flowers visited him about university matters, and in September Allen sent word from Newport that J. B. Duke, who believed in going first class, had decided to use the "pinkish granite" rather than the less expensive gray granite in certain parts of the new Georgian buildings and that marble rather than limestone would be used, even though the former cost $350,000 more.[25]

Despite J. B. Duke's continuing interest in university and other affairs, he became ill at Newport in late July, 1925. A month later his wife continued to be optimistic, for she wrote Few that "though Mr. Duke's improvement has been slow, it still continues from day to day." She thought it would be "at least two or three months, however, before he is back to his normal health again."[26] When Duke's illness only seemed to grow worse, he was carried in his private railway car to New York, and there his doctors discovered in September that he suffered from what they diagnosed as pernicious anemia. On October 10, 1925, J. B. Duke died in his mansion on Fifth Avenue. He would have been sixty-nine years old on December 23.[27]

Death seems to have caught J. B. Duke by surprise, for he had been vigorous for a man of his age and had suffered few serious health problems during the two decades or so before his death. Happily involved in building Duke University and in the problems of the power company, he had mentioned to several close associates that he hoped to live long enough to see his favorite projects completed. Even on his deathbed he continued to make important decisions concerning them. Earlier in the year he had added $2,000,000 to the original building fund of $6,000,000. Few had hammered away at J. B. Duke about the great expensiveness of medical education, and in the indenture creating the Duke Endowment Duke had incorporated Few's own guarded phrasing about the university's including a medical school "as and when funds are available." Carefully refraining from committing the university until funds were clearly in sight, Few persisted in reminding J. B. Duke about the need to make special provision for a medical school if he truly wanted to see one built at Duke University. In his will that had been signed in December, 1924, when the Endowment was established, Duke specified that an additional $10,000,000 be given to the Endowment and that $4,000,000 of that sum should be used for the construction of a medical school, hospital, and nurses' dormitory at Duke University, with the annual income from the remainder to go to the university. Another provision of the will left the remainder of his estate after all other bequests—which turned out eventually to be more than the equivalent of the original $40,000,000—to the Endowment.[28]

Not content with those provisions that were not made public until after his death, J. B. Duke continued to worry about the adequacy of the funds for building the university. Consequently, on October 1, 1925, nine days before his death, he signed a codicil to his will leaving an additional $7,000,000 for "building and equipping" Duke University. Altogether, then, and apart from the annual income that the university would derive from its share of the Endowment, J. B. Duke provided $19,000,000 for the building of Duke University on its two campuses.[29]

Ben Duke, a semi-invalid who was already saddened by the accidental death of his only son, Angier Buchanan Duke, in 1923, was particularly crushed by the death of his younger brother. Shortly before that happened,

Ben Duke made one of his most significant gifts to Duke University. To commemorate his dead son, he established the Angier B. Duke Memorial, Incorporated, which immediately became and remained a principal source of scholarships and loan funds in the university. Institutionalizing on a large scale something that he, his father, and others in the family had been doing constantly since the early 1890s—helping able but needy students attend college—Ben Duke could hardly have selected a more useful way to erect a special kind of monument to his son.[30] Having earlier divided much of his fortune among his wife, son, and daughter, Ben Duke, despite increasingly frail health, spent much of his time during the last four years of his life dividing nearly $3,000,000 among a large number of churches, orphanages, and especially colleges, both for whites and for African Americans, in the South.[31]

One who kept Ben Duke much in mind was William P. Few. As he had done for many years, Few regularly wrote long, personal letters to Ben Duke in New York reporting on the progress of construction at Duke University and on various other matters that he knew would be of interest. "You would get extreme pleasure out of it, I am sure," Few declared to Ben Duke in 1926, "if you could see here with your own eyes the wonderful developments that have come from the small beginnings that you nourished in the big formative years of the past quarter-century." Earlier, on Ben Duke's seventy-first birthday, Few had written that he spoke to the students in a chapel assembly about "what you have meant to this institution in all its strivings" for thirty-five years or more. Few added: "I told them if they or their successors in the long future ever allowed themselves to forget all this then they would be unworthy of their great heritage. But they will never forget in this or in any other generation."[32]

One matter that Few did not discuss with Ben Duke, or with anyone else for that matter except Clinton Toms and a few other intimates, was an embarrassing situation that had to do with Duke University and its needs. On the one hand, the new university being organized around an old college was spectacularly blessed and richly endowed. The South, certainly, had never known its like, and the whole nation was taking much notice of the good fortune of Duke University. But on the other hand, Few had first suggested in his memorandum of 1921, and J. B. Duke had included in his indenture creating the Duke Endowment, a large number of tasks for Duke University. By comparison, Princeton University, another relatively small institution in size and only one generation older than Duke as a university, had a much larger and richer body of alumni. Moreover, despite its wealth, Princeton had no coordinate college for women nor a medical school, law school, divinity school, or one or two other professional schools that Duke University included. In other words, J. B. Duke, at Few's suggestion, had called for a most ambitious undertaking at Duke

University. If J. B. Duke had lived, matters might have been different, and Few would not have felt the embarrassing financial constraints that he knew to be a painful fact but could hardly explain to a public dazzled by Duke University's good fortune.

A leading historian of American research universities has suggested that the leaders of many if not most of them tended to be "gambler[s], dealing in university 'futures.'" The common tendency was to expand the institution in advance of guaranteed resources, then hope, pray, and struggle that "benefactors could be goaded into alleviating the consequent plight by responding to the 'emergency.'" William R. Harper and John D. Rockefeller had such a relationship with the University of Chicago, and so did G. Stanley Hall and the benefactor of Clark University.[33]

When the dust began to settle and various realities became clear after J. B. Duke's death, no one knew better than Few that his "gamble," if such it had been, had resulted in a large, embarrassing difficulty. More likely, neither Few nor anyone else knew just how much money would be needed to build as large and complex an institution as Duke University was intended to be. The Duke Endowment would eventually, of course, grow much larger, for J. B. Duke had more than doubled it by the terms of his will—though tax problems would force his estate to remain unsettled for several years. Moreover, he had specified in the indenture creating the Endowment that the trustees should, after dividing among themselves 3 percent of the annual income as compensation for their services, set aside 20 percent of the annual income to be added to the principal until the original corpus of the trust had been doubled in size. While the future, therefore, held great promise for Duke University's support from the Duke Endowment, the immediate situation in the late 1920s was much more problematical.

Few, painfully aware of and embarrassed about his own share of responsibility for the situation, could only confess privately his own—and Duke University's—dilemma, as he did for example to Dr. W. S. Rankin.

> I am frankly worried. It was just as clear to me the day Mr. Duke died as it is now that we do not have either in hand or in sight sufficient resources to develop the other departments of the University as Mr. Duke expected us to develop them and also support the sort of medical school and hospital that the public expects of us and that all of us want to see here.

Few went on to admit that he did not yet see a solution but, eternal optimist that he was, insisted that his faith had "always been that what ought to be done can be done." To another good friend of both Duke University and the Duke family, James A. Thomas, Few explained that J. B. Duke had "done one of the greatest things in the whole history of America; still he died before he had finished his work." Few continued with an appeal: "To do promptly all the things he expected us to do involves an overwhelming financial burden unless the burden can be rather widely distributed. The good friends who help now help twice because they help quickly."[34]

The widespread, persistent public misunderstanding about the resources actually available to Duke University added enormously to Few's problem. Despite careful efforts on the part of Few, Allen, Perkins, and others to issue exact statements for the public, many journalists garbled the facts and informed readers that the entire income of the Duke Endowment went to Duke University. The New York *Evening Post*, for example, declared that Duke University was "thinking over the best ways to use its $80,000,000 endowment." Even more erroneous was the widely repeated assertion that Duke had become the "richest endowed university in the world."[35]

Few gave liberally of his time to visiting journalists, and the university's own news bureau attempted to set the record straight. But it was uphill work. "It will be wise I am sure," Few advised one concerned alumnus, "for all our graduates and entire constituency during the next few years to exercise a good deal of patience." Many people were going to write about Duke University, Few continued, and he had spent numerous hours with reporters from the Baltimore *Sun*, *New York Times*, New York *World*, and other newspapers. Nevertheless, Few insisted that it would be "quite unfair to hold any of us responsible for what is written about us in the way of interpreting either the past, present and future." He concluded on a characteristic note: "I am trying my best to keep it all straight, and I am trying my best to see that nothing goes into the building of this new institution that will not be true and abiding in its power for good."[36] A few years later, a wearier but still indefatigable Few confessed to the same alumnus, "While I am something of a reformer, I have given up all hope of keeping straight the facts in newspapers even as they affect Duke University." Few declared to another friend of the school, "Nobody in America should become excited by anything in a newspaper until he first makes sure that he has the bottom facts."[37]

Despite the general public's exaggeration of the university's wealth, Few, Flowers, Allen, and Perkins grappled with a painfully tight budget even for the massive building program and had to cut down on various plans in order to stay within the limits of available income. The lake that J. B. Duke had envisioned on West campus and that preliminary plans had shown had to be eliminated, as were the two great fountains that he had wanted on West. On the East campus a fountain that J. B. Duke planned for the large circle between the handsome Georgian library and the matching Union building had to be omitted. More serious perhaps were the cuts that had to be made in the plans of the Gothic dormitories on West, for various amenities, such as commons or assembly rooms, had to be eliminated, and the cubic space of various buildings reduced.[38]

Few saw to it that news of these stringencies and curtailments did not reach the increasingly frail Ben Duke, for toward him Few felt two primary obligations. On the immediate and personal level, Few tried through his letters to cheer and support his old friend and longtime ally as best he could. As for the larger obligation and the future, Few desperately wished to have within Duke University some fitting memorial to Ben Duke, whose long years of service and generosity to Trinity-Duke had been overshadowed by his younger brother's spectacular philanthropy. "Speaking for myself," Few wrote to one friend of Ben Duke's, "may I say to you that there is not one thing about this whole big development here which concerns me more than the building up here of an appropriate and adequate memorial to Mr. B. N. Duke? And I so much wish that we could get this done in his life time."[39]

As had been the case for many years, Clinton Toms stood by in New York to assist Few, for Toms also was keenly interested in honoring Ben Duke. Toms and Few first hit on the idea of a specially designated Benjamin Newton Duke Endowment Fund, with the securities that had been given by Duke himself as the nucleus. Since he had, however, contributed annually for so many years to the operating budget of the institution and given various buildings and other improvements on the Trinity campus, the amount of endowment attributable directly to B. N. Duke was not extensive, being only about $400,000.[40]

Persisting in the search for a sizable and significant memorial to B. N. Duke, Few in 1928 advanced the idea of a "Benjamin Newton Duke Institute for the Advancement of Knowledge" to be established within Duke University. Essentially Few had in mind a graduate school of arts and sciences, a research council to assist in scholarly enterprises, and a few other features designed to enhance the advanced research and teaching in the university. An ambitious plan that clearly focused on a vital center of any true research university, Few's proposal attracted much faculty support. Flowers spoke further about the plan when he unveiled a marble bust of B. N. Duke in the library on the occasion of Ben Duke's seventy-third birthday. If B. N. Duke had not been born, Flowers declared, probably without exaggeration, "Trinity College would never have been in Durham . . . and Duke University would never have existed."[41]

Ben Duke died in his home in New York on January 8, 1929, and Few never succeeded in obtaining a special memorial to him alone. Immediately after the death, Few renewed the call for the institute that he thought would be a significant, living memorial as well as a vital contribution to the scholarly mission of the university. Friends of the Duke family, however, and particularly James A. Thomas, who was joined by George Allen and W. R. Perkins, proposed the creation and incorporation of "The Duke Memorial." It would attempt to raise money for a suitable memorial to all three of the major philanthropists of the family—Washington, B. N., and J. B. Duke. Thomas appealed widely to the students and staffs of the various educational institutions that had been assisted by the Dukes and also to the employees of the power and tobacco companies, the well-to-do business associates of the Dukes in New York and elsewhere, and even the schoolchildren and other groups in the Carolinas.[42]

Before it became clear that Few's plan had lost out, however, W. K. Boyd, chairman of Duke's history department and an outspoken fighter for worthy academic causes, wrote an interesting letter to his friend James A. Thomas. "It seems to me that the Dukes represent as no other group of persons," Boyd declared, "the latent productive power of men which was unloosed by the Civil War." He saw the family as typifying "the creative forces of Southern society of the modern period." The most appropriate memorial to them would therefore be, Boyd argued, one which "stimulates and serves creative power," especially "the creative power of mind." Boyd continued: "And this is just what the South needs, particularly it is what Duke University needs more than anything else." As chairman of the Library Council as well as of the university's Committee on Research, Boyd claimed intimate knowledge of the university's resources for advanced scholarly work. He had concluded that "those resources must be multiplied by three before Duke University can take rank with the *real* universities of this country—and then it will rank only with small real universities, such as Stanford, Princeton and some of the western state universities." Boyd insisted that his comparison was also true with respect to the other universities in the South, for he asserted that "not one of them is on a par in equipment with such institutions as I have just named." He strongly advocated, in conclusion, the establishment of a "Duke Foundation for the Advancement of Knowledge," with the income to be used to increase the intellectual resources of the university. Art should be included within the scope of "knowledge," Boyd added, especially since he believed that no southern institution then had a "high-grade curriculum and equipment" in the area of the fine arts.[43]

Other influential persons on the faculty agreed with Boyd in supporting Few's proposal. Paul M. Gross, the able young chemist who had come to Trinity in 1919, studied J. B. Duke's indenture creating the Duke Endowment and concluded that, above all, J. B. Duke had been interested in the service which Duke University could render its section of the country. "The proper rendering of this service by the university will call for ever increasing expenditures for research and investigation in the social and natural sciences," Gross maintained, "both for the acquirement of new knowledge and for the application of knowledge already in existence."[44]

All of the arguments of Few and his academic allies were in vain, for Thomas, Allen, and others in New York had early decided that the chapel, or some part of the chapel, to be erected on the West campus would be the most appropriate form for the memorial to take. Construction of the chapel, the centerpiece of the Gothic campus as originally envisioned by J. B. Duke, had not begun when B. N. Duke died and was not scheduled to begin until 1930. It was to be, in fact, the last of the original Gothic structures to be erected.

Few accepted with good grace the defeat of his own plan. "It is a big matter you are engaged in," he assured Thomas, "and it is being laid down along lines that not only assure immediate success but even larger ultimate good to Duke University." Few conceded that the "B. N. Duke Foundation for the Advancement of Knowledge . . . will have to wait perhaps," but he hoped that in the long run the efforts of Thomas and his associates might also help that cause.[45]

With Few's blessings, therefore, Thomas and his associates set out to raise money for the memorial to Washington Duke and two of his sons. Thomas had once hoped to raise more than a million dollars, but the crash of the stock market in the fall of 1929 ended that dream. With the approximately $135,000 that actually was raised, the Duke Memorial, Inc., contributed primarily to three things: the creation of the small Memorial Chapel to the left of the chancel in the chapel of Duke University; the three marble sarcophagi with recumbent statues in the Memorial Chapel where rest the remains of Washington, B. N., and J. B. Duke; and the bronze statue of J. B. Duke which stands on the quadrangle in front of the chapel.[46]

Few could accept with equanimity the frustration of his hopes for some significant memorial to B. N. Duke because, to a greater degree than most persons, William P. Few lived in the realm of the mind and the spirit. As much as he loved the rich architecture and the handsome grounds of Duke University, no one needed to tell him that those were hardly of central importance. A great college or university, Few once suggested, was essentially an "assembling of great personalities." Deeply conscious always of the long future as well as of the past, Few believed that "an institution like this [Trinity-Duke] lives on and will live as long as American civilization endures, and it cherishes the memory of those who have served it."[47]

Few's failure to sell the idea of significant support for the graduate school and the research council as a memorial to B. N. Duke is important for several reasons. First, the proposal itself shows that Few well understood, despite his deep commitment to the undergraduate colleges and the teaching that went on therein, that the graduate school of arts and sciences was the sine qua non of a research university, what Boyd had called a "real" university. Few's failure, however, is also instructive, for not only do many donors or potential donors to educational institutions prefer to give tangible things such as buildings—or statues—but the graduate school of arts and sciences and its central role in research universities are matters that are not always understood even by many groups that are vitally important to such institutions. Professional schools, especially those for law and medicine, are another matter. But the myriad ways in which the graduate school of arts and sciences is inextricably tied to and interwoven with the undergraduate college (or colleges in Duke's case) of arts and sciences—through faculty, libraries, and laboratories, to name only three—was a matter that Few, just like the leaders of most other research universities, had difficulty in getting across. The connection was hard to explain not only to the public but even to many trustees—and certainly to most undergraduates, their parents, and all those who saw Duke and other research universities mostly through their eyes.[48]

Even as Few tried and ultimately failed to raise money for Duke's graduate school, he was simultaneously coping with an even more urgent problem about financing for the projected medical school. Convinced that Duke could not open a proper four-year medical school, no matter how much it might be desired and needed, unless additional support for it could be obtained, Few set out to obtain funds for the medical school from other philanthropic foundations. It was that process that led Few to his first agonizing awareness about Duke University's problem concerning governance and ultimate control. Coping with the problem over a period of seven or eight years, Few later said that nothing else connected with the launching of the university caused him so much worry and trouble.[49]

Sympathetic with and supportive of Few in his search for outside funding, George G. Allen as the chairman of the Duke Endowment and William R. Perkins as its vice chairman were destined to play leading roles in the formative period of Duke University's history. As new to the world of higher education as J. B. Duke had been, both men exerted an enormous influence on both the Endowment and the university. Since J. B. Duke's widow had limited interest in his business affairs and philanthropy and his daughter, Doris, was only thirteen when he died, Allen and Perkins became, for all practical purposes, the primary inheritors of much of the late multimillionaire's power and the chief interpreters of his plans and intentions.

Just as Few, patiently and diplomatically, had earlier undertaken to inform and educate J. B. Duke about the needs and aspirations of Trinity College, he also tackled a similar task involving Duke University with Allen and Perkins. Both men, of course, were unlike Few in that they had to deal with many large business affairs, especially those of the Duke Power Company. Yet as Few tackled the job of gaining essential support and approval for Duke University from the powerful Rockefeller-funded General Education Board (GEB), he had to have the help and cooperation of Allen and Perkins.

Having invited Wallace Buttrick, the distinguished chairman of the GEB's board, to visit Duke early in 1926, Few sought his help in trying to find "big outstanding men" to head the new or reorganized professional schools and to fill certain posts in the arts and sciences. Buttrick replied that he and his associates would be happy to help and that he had been quite favorably impressed by what he had seen at Duke and what Few had told him. "I believe you are on the right track," Buttrick concluded, "and in the way of doing great service for the well-being of mankind."[50]

Buttrick then helped Few to arrange a meeting at the Johns Hopkins Medical School in early March, 1926, and that eventually led to Few's brilliant and lucky choice of Dr. Wilburt C. Davison to become the first dean and organizer of the projected medical school. Unfortunately, however, Buttrick's death forced Few, in a sense, to start anew. In late June, 1926, after conferences with GEB officials in New York, Few wrote a long, detailed letter to Dr. Abraham Flexner, also with the GEB and a leading authority on medical schools and their costs, explaining that since J. B. Duke's residuary estate had not yet been settled, the exact amount of his gifts to Duke University could not yet be ascertained. Aside from the medical school and hospital buildings, for which the philanthropist had made special provisions, Few noted that the hospital was assured of as much as $75,000 a year from the Duke Endowment's hospital fund, and he asked for the GEB's help toward establishing an initial endowment of $6,000,000 for the medical school and hospital. Few added that despite the uncertainty caused by the unsettled estate, enough was already known for him "to say definitely that if the medical school is otherwise endowed we shall then have for the support of the other departments an endowment of not less than $25,000,000." J. B. Duke had believed, according to Few, that in accordance with the provisions of the indenture the endowment would eventually increase so as to raise the $25,000,000 to an endowment for the university of $40,000,000 within a period of a dozen or so years. Flexner and his associates already knew, Few concluded, that "we are committed to the policy of trying to do well what we undertake to do—of trying to build up a university which while adapting itself to the conditions and needs here in the South will at the same time . . . keep in line with the best educational standards and ideals of our time."[51]

After additional conferences and letters back and forth, the GEB in early March, 1927, refused Few's request. Not only was Few disappointed, but he also now grew profoundly worried as he gradually learned that the officials of the GEB had made their negative decision because they did not believe that Duke University had adequate monetary resources, and, even more importantly, they were skeptical of its system of governance because of the division between the two boards of trustees.[52]

Down but by no means out, Few set to work to convince the GEB that its judgment was mistaken. As for the monetary resources, Few could not argue too much, for he was obviously knocking as hard as he knew how on the GEB's door. As far as governance was concerned, and that seemed to be the most crucial problem in the eyes of the GEB, Few felt confident that the complicated relationship between the university and the Duke Endowment could be satisfactorily explained. He proceeded to draft two documents, both of which he ultimately had printed for private distribution, one on the history and the various charters of Trinity-Duke and one on the relationship between the university and the Endowment.

The latter pamphlet proved to be the crucial one. In it Few, after quoting the scattered provisions in the indenture concerning the university, argued that the trustees of the endowment were "in a very real sense . . . also trustees of Duke University, providing as they do, a large part of the income and responsible as they are, for seeing that the University keeps true to the purpose for which it was founded." After elaborating on his confidence in the trustees of the Duke Endowment and in their whole-hearted devotion to Duke University, Few expressed his belief that they would "never under any circumstances be a menace to the educational integrity of the University. . . ."

Perhaps the most important part of Few's pamphlet was his explanation that as president of the university, he had adopted a policy of presenting to the trustees of the Duke Endowment, or to a committee of the same, for their consideration "all proposals, before the proposals are fully adopted and made effective, if they call for expenditure of money by the University or involve changes of importance in the operations of the University and come under the terms of the Trust Indenture establishing The Duke Endowment." Few, in effect, meant that he already was giving and expected to continue giving a veto power over most matters of large policy and planning concerning the university to Allen and Perkins.

Few concluded by noting that the above procedure had been approved by all concerned, was working well, and would most likely be recognized by all as "a safe procedure that is apt to become permanent." Since both boards were self-perpetuating and not apt to be "subject to violent changes," there would be every likelihood that they would pass on from one generation to the next whatever procedure that "has been proved to be good."[53]

Working with Allen and Perkins on the pamphlet and the application to the GEB as closely as circumstances allowed, Few also suggested to them his belief that within a year or two there probably should be worked out in the university's charter from the legislature an addition which provided for the arrangement he had described. Perkins replied that he and Allen sympathized with Few's effort to get the Endowment's trustees "hitched in advance" of any university action or policy. "At the same time," Perkins continued, "we do not see how the trustees in advance can tie their hands so that if the outcome is not what they thought they are powerless later on to object. . . ." Pledging cooperation towards the best possible results, Perkins concluded in semi-legal language that may have puzzled Few: "We think the best practical course is not to try to adopt any hard and fast program which by seeking to bind will warrant to void [*sic*]; but to let the harmonious cooperation that has existed continue until it becomes a course of procedure by experience and lapse of time."[54]

Not having quite gotten the urgency of the matter across, Few resorted to Clinton Toms. Just as Few had constantly sought Tom's help in making discreet overtures to both B. N. and J. B. Duke, he now asked him to work his magic with George Allen. Toms soon reported that he had conferred with Allen and Perkins about the importance of using the university's executive committee to obtain closer relations between the university and the Duke Endowment. They pledged agreement and cooperation, Toms added, but "reminded me that they were very busy men, with many things to look after." Concerning the application to the GEB, Toms noted that he had urged Allen to see Flexner and explain fully about the Endowment. "When I left, however, I did not feel sure that he [Allen] would present the thing to Dr. Flexner in just the right way," Toms confessed, "but I went over and over the matter with him and emphasized the importance of securing this money from the Rockefeller Foundation."[55]

Despite all these efforts, the GEB again declined to assist the medical school so that it could open on schedule as a full four-year medical school rather than a two-year school. Equipped with multiple copies of his two printed pamphlets, Few sent them off to the GEB with a letter that emphasized his main theme, namely, that the trustees of the university and those of the endowment were "completely at one in the common purpose to realize in and through Duke University its full possibilities." Then, laying his passionately felt convictions on the line, Few added: "I consider it of the first importance that the officers of Duke University and of the General Education Board go through to the end of this matter. For, under all the circumstances, a failure of the General Education Board to give recognition to Duke University would be, in the judgment of time, a reflection on the administration here or there. I feel this deeply and I know you will not mind my saying it to you." Few concluded with the suggestion that if the GEB should prefer to cooperate in some way other than about the medical school, then Duke University was prepared to submit suggestions.[56]

Few's strong letter, coupled with his pamphlet on the Duke Endowment and Duke University (the GEB requested twenty-five additional copies), and a conference which he and Davison had with GEB officers in New York in early November, 1929—all these finally won the day. Later that month the GEB made a grant to Duke University of $300,000 to be distributed on a diminishing basis over a period of five years. In other words, the university could now move ahead with the plans for opening its four-year medical school in 1930 and, if developments went as hoped, plan to increase the income to the medical school and hospital from student and hospital fees each year by an amount equal to the annual reduction in the grant from the GEB.[57]

As pleased as Few was about the money, he considered that the stamp of approval which the GEB had finally given to the university and to its system of governance was infinitely more important for the long run. "We need the money," Few admitted to Clinton Toms, "but the implications are even more valuable to us now than the money." Feeling that things were "clearing up gradually all along the line" for Duke University, Few exulted that "more and more the road seems opening up for us."[58]

Few was never one to coast along, however. Believing the governance problem to be more or less solved—save perhaps for some slight tinkering with the university's charter—he tried to focus the attention of Allen and Perkins, as well as of others connected with the university, on the critical need for additional endowment. Though the Wall Street stock market had collapsed in October, 1929, Few, like most Americans, seemed unaware that an unprecedentedly severe economic depression was getting underway. No reference to "unfavorable" business conditions appeared in his correspondence until June, 1930. Not realizing, therefore, that raising large sums for additional endowment was soon going to be indeed problematical, he launched his campaign with Allen and Perkins in January, 1930.

Few believed that as matters then stood, Duke's medical school was "better set up than any other one department of the university." But on the overall picture for Duke, he candidly spelled out some gloomy forebodings.

But the simple fact is, without increased endowment we cannot possibly build a great university. Indeed, unless we get a great deal more endowment Duke will drag indefinitely, just as Cornell dragged for twenty or thirty years until a new generation came with reinforcements and put that university at least within the running of the greater universities of the country. Johns Hopkins, except in its School of Medicine, still drags. What we all, of course, want to do is to put Duke across in our generation, as was done at Chicago and so insure Duke's "attaining and maintaining a place of real leadership in the educational world."[59]

Events in the near future were about to prove Few wrong. Money, as it turned out, had not become the university's most urgent need, though it was a real one. The governance problem, far from being resolved, was about to reappear in a more serious and potentially dangerous form than ever. Few and Duke University would ultimately ride out the crises, but at a price, and resolving them required all the skill, diplomacy, and effort that William Preston Few could muster.

3

Crisis in University Governance

✧

GOVERNANCE became the most critical problem facing Duke University late in 1930. A small difference of opinion about tuition increases preceded but did not cause the real trouble. As the nation's economy began its unrelentingly downward spiral after the stock market crash—and the South's agricultural economy had remained sick throughout most of the 1920s anyhow—a private debate occurred between Few and his associates in the university, on the one hand, and George G. Allen, William R. Perkins, and their allies among the trustees of the Duke Endowment on the other. The university's trustees had voted to raise Duke's tuition (including a matriculation fee) from $90 to $150 for the academic year 1928–29. Furthermore, the trustees agreed that as the university's equipment and facilities improved and as financial necessities of the university required, there would be further hikes from time to time.[1]

Though the Endowment's trustees were the strongest advocates of tuition hikes, Few supported the policy and publicly and privately argued that the American people who were able to do so, including those in the South, were going to have to become accustomed to paying more for higher education; and as tuition fees increased, scholarships for able students who could not pay would have to be increased also. This, he felt, was particularly true in the endowed universities that were attempting to provide the highest quality of instruction and facilities. He understood, too, that Duke University had inherited from Trinity College an increasingly anachronistic policy of low tuition, a policy made possible through support of the college from the Duke family. With Duke at $150 in 1928, Vanderbilt was at $227 and the older, endowed universities of the Northeast mostly in the $300 to $400 range.[2] With the increasingly hard times, however, Few, hoping for more endowment funds rather than tuition increases, urged careful thought about any hike beyond the figure of $250 that had been set for the year 1930–31.

In the midst of this ongoing debate between those in Durham and those in New York, what might be called the Norman Thomas affair exploded—privately and only through the United States mail, but critical and dangerous for the university nonetheless. Before Few was finally able to defuse the situation, at its most volatile point Allen and Perkins unlimbered their biggest gun: their power under J. B. Duke's indenture creating the endowment to withhold funds from Duke University.

Frequently speaking on college campuses during as well as between presidential-election years, Norman Thomas, the Princeton-educated socialist and Presbyterian minister, spoke at Duke in December, 1930; he had spoken in Chapel Hill and on many other campuses in 1928, and after his talk at Duke he proceeded to North Carolina State College. Though Allen and Perkins received newspapers from Durham, they learned of Thomas's visit to Duke from the *Southern Textile Bulletin*, whose rabidly ultraconservative editor in Charlotte, North Carolina, put socialists, communists, and labor union leaders into one anathematized lump. Enclosing a photostatic copy from the *Textile Bulletin*, Perkins wrote that he and Allen would like to have Few's views "as, frankly, I am wondering how Duke University came to select such a man for its program."[3]

Few wobbled slightly at first. He pointed out that Duke University had not invited Thomas and that he (Few) had been in Atlanta at an educational meeting when a discussion group on campus, composed of a small number of faculty members and a larger number of students, had invited the well-known socialist to speak. But, Few continued, "if I had been there I think I should have been obliged to let the matter go as it did go; namely, just to ignore it and let him have his say." After attacking some of the *Textile Bulletin*'s wild charges about Thomas's alleged atheism, interracial mixing, advocacy of free love, and so on, Few suggested that "however misguided we may think him, he is in all probability sincerely interested in the well being of mankind." Then, warming to his subject, Few offered his "frank opinion." Many thoughtful people had originally feared that "organized religion might seriously handicap the development of a University like Duke here in the South." He had not, however, seen from any church source "unfairness and little-mindedness" such as that displayed by the *Textile Bulletin*. "There has always been danger in the old South of the prostitution of higher education by politics," Few continued, but in North Carolina, at least, he thought that fight had been won. "It develops now to my surprise," Few boldly ventured, "that our chief danger may come from the groups that are primarily interested in industry and economics," for many of the "leaders in these fields seem to be afraid of their shadows."

For the peace of mind of all and for the good of Duke as well as of the nation, and especially its southern portion, Few eloquently argued,

> I think we must take the firm stand that it is the business of Duke University to hear both sides of all questions that are fairly debatable; that we have been careful in the selection of our men, particularly in subjects that in our time are highly inflammable, like Government, Economics and Sociology; Psychology and Philosophy; and that having selected such men we give them a free hand to find and proclaim the truth as they see it. Unless all of us with influence at Duke University come to this sort of "university-mindedness" we can never hope to build a university, in our day or in any other day.

Expressing his profound desire to see the South develop a "highly industrialized civilization in which not stark materialism but things of the mind and spirit shall prevail," Few declared that he thought the region might have the "best chance in the English speaking world" to develop "a civilization of really great and enduring qualities." Duke University was destined to have a large role in all of that, Few asserted, and "we shall especially need the open mind and a willingness to give a fair hearing to every well-meaning man." Then, forgetting that a sense of humor might not, under the circumstances, be prominent among the attributes of his correspondents, Few concluded with an appeal that he obviously meant to be lighthearted: "Meanwhile, let's not allow the 'saints' about Charlotte or elsewhere to vex our spirits unduly."[4]

The New York duo was neither amused nor mollified. "We have given the most earnest consideration to your statements," Perkins noted, "because they worry us exceedingly." Surely Few had not been his "normal self" in making the statement that the best thing to do was to ignore Thomas and let him have his say. "The nature and extent of your responsibility forbid such an attitude," Perkins admonished, since "you are in charge of boys and girls whose parents have committed them to your care at a most impressionable age." If protecting the young from impure food, drink, and communicable diseases was necessary, Perkins reasoned, then how "infinitely more important is it that our attitude towards the mental and moral health of the student body should be one of throwing around them every possible safeguard against pernicious influences." Agreeing with Few's contention that the university should hear both sides of all questions that were fairly debatable, Perkins nonetheless insisted that the doctrines of socialists such as Thomas were not in that debatable category of ideas. "Would not a proper pasteurization and filtration eliminate Norman Thomas and his ilk and their doctrines?" Perkins queried.

After quoting lengthy excerpts of speeches by Thomas in which he had attacked President Herbert Hoover and his policies as well as expressed strong sympathies for the textile strikers at Gastonia, North Carolina, Perkins rebuked Few for his "uncharitable" references to the "saints" around Charlotte. Few's comment about materialism drew an especially strong reprimand: "What is the 'stark materialism' which you fear? Not so many years ago, even in North Carolina, Mr. J. B. Duke was denounced as the arch-industrialist of them all. This attack was led by Mr. Josephus Daniels who, like Mr. Thomas, has a wonderful ambition for his own political preferment." Noting that the list of businessmen who had also been conspicuous philanthropists was a long one, Perkins argued that "the one example of Mr. Duke" was enough "to show the folly of classifying so-called 'Capitalism' as 'stark materialism'" and that "the capitalist as well as the laborer" was "God-created and performing a God-given part in the great economy of things." After pondering these matters, would Few please respond? [5]

At that point, if Few had been clairvoyant, he would have caught the next train to New York. Since he was not, he labored carefully over his reply to the New Yorkers and began with the confession that he was "sorely discouraged by the fact that words of mine could have been so misunderstood by two men whom I have known for a good many years." Declaring that he feared he would "be gun-shy the rest of my life when confronted with the duty" of expressing himself in writing on difficult questions, Few suggested that it might be best to "defer the effort to clear up these misunderstandings" until the three of them could talk together.

"And when that time comes," Few continued, as he proposed an agenda for the conference,

> I shall desire also to discuss with you three practical questions suggested to me by our correspondence: (1) Since the University had nothing to do with the invitation to Thomas and its officers knew nothing about it until his coming was announced, do you think that I, or in my absence some other officer representing me, should have refused to allow Thomas to speak in our buildings? (2) Is it the business of the University to protect its students from any except the orthodox views of economics and government, and particularly should students be forbidden to discuss those economic and governmental doctrines involved in what is known as Socialism? (3) Should I as President of the University be expected to know the ultimate truth in all the great fields of human knowledge and so at all times be ready to rule out questions that are not "fairly debatable," in eco-

nomics and government, in psychology and philosophy, in zoology, in Biblical criticism and theology, and in all other subjects of university instruction?

The whole theory of university education is, I think, involved in those three questions, and on these questions educational administrators are apt to take one view and business men another. I should like to have opportunity to go to the bottom of these great questions with both you and Mr. Allen whenever occasion may offer.

Suggesting that he could come to New York later in the month, Few attempted to strike a conciliatory note by pointing out that he and Perkins had "been on the same side of all public and political questions" since they had known each other and that they were "probably not far apart" in their personal views, "our recent letters to the contrary notwithstanding."[6]

"We are rejoiced to know that you think we have misunderstood you," Perkins (and Allen) shot back, with perhaps a touch of sarcasm, "but do not see that your numbered statements get us very far." Few's first question, Perkins declared, "simply puts a premium on official ignorance." Would it not prevent Few from objecting "to young men bringing immoral women into the dormitories," since university officials could truthfully say that they had not invited the women and knew nothing of their presence unless and until they were discovered? As for the second and third questions, they simply ran to "theoretical extremes," according to Perkins. "Far be it from me to ascribe omniscience or perfection to any mortal, be he a college president, who generally speaking, are scholars and not mere businessmen," Perkins asserted in some syntactical disarray. "But that is quite different from saying that we have to throw up our hands and open the floodgates to all the debris that may be coming down the current of life." Surely James B. Duke had not thought so, Perkins continued, for he had explained in the indenture that he had selected the university as one of the principal objects of his trust " 'because I recognize that education, when conducted along sane and practical, as opposed to dogmatic and theoretical, lines, is, next to religion, the greatest civilizing influence.' " And furthermore—and here came the big gun—his indenture gave the trustees of the Duke Endowment authority to withhold funds from the university if it was not " 'operated in a manner calculated to achieve the results intended hereby.' "[7]

Few went to New York. Neither what was said in the conference there nor what concessions Few had to make is known. While he had a long record as a patient peacemaker, he was dealing with two obviously adamant and powerful men. Few loved Duke University a great deal indeed, and for it he would go far rather than see its future be jeopardized by dangerous quarreling between its president and the men who controlled the purse strings. In all probability Few promised that in circumstances where university officials might properly have a say concerning speakers who were to be invited to the university, great care and discretion would be exercised. Few knew quite well, and he may have persuaded Allen and Perkins to accept the fact, that university officials could not possibly influence or control all invitations issued by some groups on campus, be they student, faculty, or a mix of both. But many lectures require a hall, and through the power to grant or deny use of university facilities some control could be and was exercised.

Certainly the papers of William H. Wannamaker—vice president in the university's academic division, dean of the university, and Few's chief officer in charge of both student and faculty matters—suggest that throughout the 1930s he, and later certain of his subordinate deans, kept an ever-watchful eye on the lists of proposed speakers for groups at Duke.[8] In carrying out such a policy, Few was actually doing what was common on most college and university campuses in that era. Yet in the wake of Few's problems about Norman Thomas, Duke may well have had a more restrictive policy than some of its peers in the world of research universities.

The specter of Norman Thomas, however, would not disappear. In the presidential election of 1932, a number of academic persons, together with many other North Carolinians, signed a petition to have Thomas's name placed on the ballot. In doing so, various faculty members at both Duke and the University of North Carolina explained publicly that while they themselves were not necessarily supporting the Thomas candidacy, they believed that the voters of the state should have the opportunity to express their sentiments. Reading the report of this development in the newspapers, George G. Allen this time undertook the investigation. Since Thomas would socialize all public utilities if he were in a position to do so, Allen argued, how could faculty members at Duke possibly lend even indirect support to a man who would rob the Duke Endowment, and therefore the university, of the major portion of its income? "No doubt you will be good enough to look into this," Allen wrote to Few, "and let me know the facts."[9]

Few replied that while he had not signed the petition, fearing that such an action might be misunderstood, he agreed with those who did sign it that "it is on the whole best for the country to give 'all voters a chance to express their sentiments.'" He went on to explain that most of those at Duke who had signed the petition—and he probably knew personally most of the approximately 350 persons then on the faculty—were not socialists. "So far as I know there are only four people here that are interested in that cause," Few stated, and "two of them are wives of our professors." He added that some of the students might have a theoretical interest in socialism, but he personally knew of only one, "a junior who comes from Boston, Massachusetts."

Then, still trying to explain the ethos of the university world to two men who seemed slow to understand or accept it, Few again tried reasoning.

> It would be more comfortable for you and for me if we could always have a concurrency of opinion concerning great moral, religious, economic, social and political questions, but it seems that in our world today this is impossible. Duke University is now in the stream of the world and we must allow a certain amount of give and take. The public has a right to expect that our teachers be men of "outstanding character, ability, and vision" but we must not allow the public to hold us responsible for the opinions of our teachers. Unless we succeed in this we shall always be in hot water. This institution in all its ramifications now touches people in many ways and there will always be somebody to complain about the scientific, theological, economic, or political views of our men. Our only hope is to get the best men we can, particularly in the headships of our schools and departments, and then allow a reasonable freedom of opinion in all mooted questions.

Every effort was needed, Few argued further, to help the public understand that the business of education was not "to indoctrinate students" but, first, to "try by all possible means to teach them to think" and, second, to use "this intellectual medium," together with all of the university's physical and social and moral agencies, to try to make of students "wise and good" persons. While the conduct of students had to be controlled, the "hand of authority" should be lifted from their minds and souls, all of which required "immense moral energy and vitality on the part of our officers and influential teachers." Few concluded by noting that he had been trying for "a quarter of a century to make all this plain to everybody interested in this institution and in the future of our civilization," and he hoped Allen would pardon him for going into it so lengthily.[10]

Sweet reason again batted zero. Allen, opening with the comment that Few's letter pained him very much, quoted at length from one of Thomas's speeches wherein he had outlined his policies and goals concerning government ownership of banks, public utilities, and other means of production. Agreeing ostensibly that it was "the discussion of divergent views on important matters which finally leads to the truth," Allen nonetheless insisted that there were "certain matters concerning which the truth has already been established." Allen included in that category of determined or established truths questions about slavery, about "rebellion against our government," and, finally, "what will just as surely bring about destruction of our government as rebellion, and that is democratization of property through the Norman Thomas conception of socialism." Allen went on to say that he realized that in dealing with a large faculty Few could not "always pick winners and mistakes are bound to occur." Nevertheless, the public had a right to hold those in charge of Duke University responsible "for the *kind* of teachers we suffer to remain and the *kind* of teaching they give to the youth." Few should ascertain which faculty members were "following false gods so that they may be weeded out and their influences removed from the young students." As for Few's argument that it was not the purpose of education to indoctrinate students, Allen countered that Thomas and his followers were the ones who were attempting to indoctrinate students with "false doctrine." After making additional attacks on both Thomas and those at Duke who had signed the petition, Allen concluded: "We are looking forward with pleasure to having you with us at the end of this month." [11]

One may well doubt that Few looked forward to that meeting. Once again he clearly felt forced to make certain concessions. While the records show that academic freedom for tenured members of the faculty at Duke was never impaired, the spirit of academic freedom—insofar as certain of the younger, untenured instructors were concerned and as academic freedom would later come to be understood—may well have been violated. After Norman Thomas spoke again at Duke, at the invitation of "older students in the School of Religion" and despite Few's repeated efforts to prevent the visit, a battered Duke president confessed to Allen that he had learned of the speech only when "it was too late to intervene unless I had broken up the meeting by force of authority; and that I decided not to undertake."

Having dealt with that seemingly perennial problem, Few went on to describe some "changes" which he said he had promised Allen and Perkins when in New York. "I have already arranged to let out three more of the younger men who seem to [those of] us most concerned to be more apt to make trouble for us than to render large service," Few reported. "I am inclined to think it would be unwise," he continued, "but if you and Mr. Perkins think I ought to do so, I would undertake, before another election comes round, to request our people to keep themselves free from compromising political entanglement." Few expressed the belief that the New Yorkers might hear more about the political and economic aspects of university life than he did. Disgruntled Methodists in North Carolina, according to Few, were bemoaning both Duke's alleged lack of denominational emphasis and the "worldly amusements" that seemed to preoccupy the students. "We are in a topsy-turvy world," Few declared. "All but the steadiest and wisest people are liable now to do foolish things. If those of us on the inside can stick together through thick and thin, I feel confident that in the end cooperation can bring us to our goal." [12]

Few's obvious eagerness to avoid a rupture with the two men who in effect ran the Duke Endowment sprang from more than just his concern about Duke University, though that was certainly the overriding factor. The unfortunate truth was that Few, like so many millions of other Americans at the Great Depression's worst point, was ensnared in debt. Through no fault of his own, actually, members of his family, both in South Carolina and in Durham, had incurred obligations which fell ultimately on one who described himself privately as "just a missionary" for education and certain other good causes. The situation became so extreme that Few and his wife had to rent out to young instructors all but three of the upstairs rooms in the spacious new house that the Endowment's building committee had erected for the university's president in 1931. That rent, Few explained to a close friend, about took care of the household expenses.[13] Finally, Few had to obtain sizeable personal loans from Allen, Perkins, and probably one other wealthy trustee of the university.[14]

As Few grappled privately with both his personal debts and the volatile relationship between the university and the Duke Endowment, he also turned again to the matter of a basic change in the legal basis for the governance of the university. He had decided back during his negotiations with the General Education Board in the late 1920s that it might be wise to have a formal, statutory arrangement that utilized the executive committee of the university's trustees to link the Endowment more closely to the university. The tensions and dangerous confrontations that occurred concerning Norman Thomas renewed Few's zeal to try to protect the university with a change in its charter from the state legislature that would require that at least three of the trustees who sat on the executive committee be also trustees of the Duke Endowment. Such an arrangement, Few argued, "would still leave the actual work of governing the University where I think it ought to remain, in the hands of the Executive Committee," but it "would let the Endowment trustees in on any fundamental changes in the University; and just that opportunity for them is what I am personally anxious to protect for the long future." Few's plan was to have Allen become a member of the executive committee as soon as possible. Since William N. Reynolds, of Winston-Salem's tobacco family, was already a member of that committee as well as a trustee of the Duke Endowment, Few's plan would be close to realization in fact. Moreover, while Flowers, an Endowment trustee, was not a voting member of the executive committee, he served as its recording secretary and was always active in the committee's business. (Perkins was already a trustee of the university but not yet on the executive committee.) "Let us try the plan out thoroughly for a year or two," Few urged, "with all of us straining a point to make a success of it, and then I will undertake to get it constitutionalized." Few believed he could "get this done without a jar."[15]

Few's sense of urgency about the charter change was such that, abandoning the idea of a trial period of a "year or two," he pressed the New Yorkers to approve the idea so that he might begin discussion about it with the university's trustees at their meeting scheduled for late February, 1934. While the matter was too important to rush, Few insisted that he regarded it "as the most important single thing for those of us most intimately concerned with the University to get done before our opportunity has passed."[16]

Few proved mistaken in his idea that the change in the charter could be hastily approached and that it could be sold to the university's trustees "without a jar." There were serious obstacles, as the chairman of the university's trustees, John F. Bruton of Wilson, North Carolina, made amply plain to Few. But before the matter could be resolved, a chain of events that had begun in the fall of 1933 ended in the last great crisis in governance at Duke University that Few encountered. It was also the only one that, at least as far as a portion of it was concerned, received considerable local and even national publicity. This was the somewhat mislabeled "student revolt" of February, 1934, which was actually a protest movement by male undergraduates. Its background was far more complex and its ramifications more far-reaching than most of those who took part in or observed it could have realized.

Conditions at Duke, as at other colleges and universities in the nation, were, in some respects, grim in 1933–34. Franklin D. Roosevelt and his New Deal program brought at least hope to millions; and even Few, a staunch Prohibitionist who had publicly supported Herbert Hoover in 1928 and 1932, conceded early that the "Roosevelt program seems to have brought about something of a change in the feelings of the American people," who seemed "more hopeful as to the future. . . ."[17] Still, economic recovery for a nearly prostrate nation was only a hope, and students and faculty even at a relatively privileged institution such as Duke felt the pinch in many ways.

As stock prices and then dividends plummeted in the years after October, 1929, the university's support from the Duke Endowment fell accordingly. In the fiscal years from 1927 through 1930 money from the Endowment approximated a half million dollars each year, making up roughly half of the university's total receipts. In 1930–32 the Endowment's contribution was approximately double the earlier level, but since the number of students had risen and the tuition had been raised, the Endowment still supplied close to half of the university's total receipts. In 1933–34 the Endowment's contribution shrank back to the 1927 level—and Duke University faced a difficult time.[18]

Since some colleges were even forced to cease operation during the depression and most educational institutions faced more severe and earlier retrenchment measures than occurred at Duke, the university was actually quite fortunate. Expansion at Duke had been halted in 1932 and various economy measures were taken; but there were no cutbacks in the number or salaries of faculty members and staff until the fall of 1933. By then the dreaded step had to be taken, and a 10 percent cut in salaries took effect in the fall of 1933, with a graduated surtax beginning at $1,000. For example, Few's cut came to 20 percent ($4,200) of his annual salary of $21,000.[19]

While Few, looking out from the president's office, thought morale at Duke remained high in the straitened times, he probably indulged in some optimism, for, regardless of the comparative situation, there were grumblings among some of the faculty and staff. One recently employed professor of law, whose salary of $10,000 a year was more than twice what most senior professors were paid in arts and sciences, even threatened legal action against the university because of breach of contract. While some of the faculty groused about the pay cuts and "the administration" that had implemented it, some of the students, many facing dire personal economies, made their usual complaints about the food in the dining halls, restrictions and regulations forced on them by an allegedly hard-hearted administration, and other such grievances that students often feel—and express—in almost any era. Coach Wallace Wade's Blue Devils went undefeated in nine straight football games only to have Rose Bowl hopes smashed by a defeat at the hands of Georgia Tech. "Johnny Long's Collegians," along with occasional orchestras imported from outside, played for many dances. Still, despite the happy diversions, there were problems and tensions caused by the new policy of deferred fraternity rushing, which had been mandated, in fact if not theory, by Wannamaker; that is, only academically eligible freshmen could join a fraternity at the beginning of the spring semester. The new "cut system" allowing a total of five excused and unexcused cuts from a class also brought howls of protest from some students.[20]

This was the atmosphere in which there mysteriously appeared on the Duke campus in the fall of 1933 "The Vision of King Paucus." Consisting of a single legal-size page, printed on both sides, it contained neither any four-letter words nor any sexual allusions. By late-twentieth-century standards, it was indeed tame stuff. But in 1933 a satirical attack on President Few and his top associates in the administration titillated many and, no doubt, scandalized quite a few also. While "King Paucus" (Few), wearing an academic gown and a crown of gold thorns, scratches his head and "goatish beard," "Prince Struttabout Blossoms" (Flowers), "a sonorous say-nothing dressed in a curious suit of armor fashioned from coins," stands by faithfully, as does "Lord Willie Wanna-B-King" (Wannamaker), a "pasty sort of ham-and-egg man wearing an academic robe." They kneel on a costly Oriental prayer rug and chant before a portrait of "the Duke," and a procession of professors and students in chains enters; Paucus explains that they are "those terrible radicals who wouldn't conform to our rules and regulations." And so forth. It was a sophomoric satire, which attempted to highlight the irony of Duke's Gothic splendor amidst the depression's poverty and the New Deal's brave liberalism. Yet the relatively young dean of Duke's law school, Justin Miller, sent a copy of "King Paucus" to William R. Perkins in New York and noted solemnly that "it has a very serious significance as indicating a disorderly condition and an unruly situation generally."[21]

Ernest Seeman, the director of the Duke University Press, was not, as many persons suspected at the time, the author of "King Paucus." He was merely the inspirer of the piece, which was written by a student friend of his.[22] Forty-six years old in 1933 and largely self-educated, Seeman became the first full-time director of Duke's press in 1926 primarily because he was himself a writer who knew well the world of printing and because his father had founded Seeman's Printery in Durham, a firm with which first Trinity College and then Duke University had had a long, close connection. A clarinetist, composer, cartoonist, handwriting analyst, and self-styled political liberal, among other things, Seeman had some trouble at the press from the start. This was primarily because he had little patience with a certain professor of English whom he alleged to be "pedantic," and he collided head-on finally with the senior professor of history, William K. Boyd, who was closely involved with press matters.[23] After continuing trouble about Seeman's frequently getting "things mixed up," Flowers, in September, 1933, took advantage of the university's financial straits to give a year's notice of contract termination to Seeman.[24]

In addition to working at the press, Seeman played an interesting extra-curricular role, for in 1931 he was the guiding spirit behind the launching of a popular organization at Duke known as the Explorers' Club. A rare mixture of faculty, staff, and students, this large, loosely organized group enjoyed frequent "explores" in the Duke Forest and the lovely hills around the Eno, Little, and Flat rivers in the northern part of Durham county. Hikes followed by food, coffee, songs or instrumental music, and conversation around a campfire—all these attracted a sizeable, frequently changing group in the early 1930s. One of the stalwarts from the first outing in October, 1931, was Justin Miller.[25]

Determined to launch Duke's reorganized and expanded law school in the strongest possible way, Few, in consultation with Perkins and others and after an elaborate search lasting several years, picked the forty-two-year-old Miller as its first dean in 1930. A native Californian with both undergraduate and law degrees from Stanford, Miller moved rapidly upward through a large number of jobs, academic and nonacademic, to become dean of the law school at the University of Southern California in 1927.[26] Few, initially delighted by his choice of Miller, declared to Perkins: "I am confident he is the right man, and that we can build up a great law school."[27]

Few virtually gave Miller a blank check in the matter of recruiting additional professors for the law school and rapidly building up its library. The widespread opinion was and still is that Miller did a superb job. Flowers, reporting Miller's enthusiasm after a visit in New York with Perkins, admitted that it was taking quite a bit of money, but he thought Duke now had "one of the ablest faculties to be found in any Law School in the country."[28]

Just how quickly the bloom faded from the rose is not clear. From a fairly early stage, however, Miller revealed a certain condescension toward Duke and its heritage from Trinity College. That perhaps did not matter too much, but he literally bombarded Few and Flowers with long memoranda in which he demanded various and sizeable expenditures for the law school. Then, at a time when most Duke professors had to share offices, sometimes even up to three and four persons in the same office, Miller announced that the prevailing "practice in the better law schools" in the country was to have exclusive use of the building; therefore, the twelve members of the department of economics and political science who had offices in the law school building, which was then adjacent to the library on Duke's West campus, would have to get out, as would the approximately fifty-four undergraduate classes that were held in the building.[29] Few boggled at the salary of $12,000, or possibly $14,000, that Miller wanted to pay one promising recruit for his faculty, but Perkins supported Miller's argument, and the new law professor came to Duke. Yet as the depression began to affect the university's income and restrictions loomed on expenses for travel, book purchases, and equipment, Miller began to chafe. After Few pointed out that enrollment in the law school had actually dropped from eighty-four students in 1930 to seventy-five in 1931— despite a huge outlay of money—Miller lashed out against the administration's thinking about the law school and charged that it was based upon the experience "with the sub-standard law school maintained" in the days of Trinity College.[30] In short, by the fall of 1933, for very different reasons, Justin Miller and Ernest Seeman, good friends from their Explorers' Club experience, had ample grievances against Few and his associates in the administration and clearly would have been happy to see them, at the least, thoroughly embarrassed.

The embarrassment came all right, but in a manner that no one could have planned or foretold. Dean Wannamaker inadvertently sparked the action. The Pan-Hellenic Council, which was then the men's version of an interfraternity council, decided in early February, 1934, that one of the fraternities had violated rushing rules and should be penalized by having its rushing period delayed for a month. Wannamaker, seizing on the technical constitutional point that he had not been present at the council's meeting, declared the ruling void and called for a new meeting. Incensed at what they perceived as high-handed, even autocratic and insulting treatment, a large group of men students, including most of the leaders, met informally in a fraternity section of one of the dormitories and issued a call for a mass protest meeting at the gymnasium the following evening. They also fired off telegrams to Perkins and another official of the Duke Endowment declaring that "the conditions on Duke campus at the present time are such that you should come at once to see for yourself that student opinion means nothing to the present administration." The students went on to assert that they were being "treated like children not men" and that "real universities do not treat student opinion with contempt."[31]

The morning after the initial student meeting the *Durham Morning Herald*, under the grossly erroneous headline "Duke Students Stage Riot Against University Heads," began a series of detailed and ingeniously but anonymously written accounts of events at Duke. Using unidentified sources and freely mixing facts and rumors, the *Herald*'s writer asserted that the students claimed that unrest had been growing at Duke for several years, had focused increasingly on Wannamaker, and that with his assumption of "autocratic powers over all student activities" student self-government "has been rendered impotent."[32]

The *Herald*'s exaggerated headlines and stories were picked up by other newspapers in the state, and even *Time*, in its issue of February 19, 1934, carried its usual *Time*-style account of the "Revolt at Duke." By the time the meeting in the gymnasium was held, however, Few, acting through staff and faculty members, was able to steer the protest into a more orderly channel by arranging for an assembly of students, faculty, and administrators in Page Auditorium. There, with various administrators and student leaders on the platform, the president of the men's student government association presided as well as outlined student grievances concerning the administration's treatment of student organizations, the food and prices in the dining halls, and other matters. Not specifically addressed was what the *Herald*'s reporter called a "startling resolution" that the students had strongly endorsed at the earlier meeting in the gymnasium, namely that "criticism of the administration by faculty members publicly is not only an indication of lack of loyalty on the part of such men, but is also a demoralizing influence on our student body." Subsequently the *Herald*'s writer alleged that the campus was "rife with claims" that the student making the surprise resolution had "received orders from or was unduly influenced by the administration."[33]

With the appointment at the assembly of a committee of nine students and three faculty members charged with the responsibility of investigating student grievances and recommending what if any remedial steps should be taken, the "student revolt" was over. Before the semester ended, the committee made its report, and the majority opinion, not shared by a few dissenters, seemed to be that it had done a thorough and fair job.[34]

A strange twist was given to the student protest at Duke by stories that appeared in the Durham *Sun* and in other newspapers in the state as well as, to a certain extent, in *Time* magazine's piece. This was to the effect that underlying the affair was a struggle between those who had long been identified with Trinity College, on the one hand, and newer men whose lot was cast wholly with the new Duke University—as well as with Franklin D. Roosevelt's New Deal. The prominence and popularity of Dean Justin Miller, this story continued, "coupled with his well known modernism" and youth, made "the Duke youngsters feel that their desires in this widening democracy within academic walls would have a far better chance of expression under a new deal. . . ."[35]

William Preston Few was never given to paranoia, so when he wrote to Perkins that there were "some people here not students who are seeking for their own purposes to get control of the University," the harassed president obviously meant what he said.[36] He need not have worried too much. Not only did he and his associates deftly handle the problems that had concerned the students, but the overwhelming majority of the faculty, the trustees, and, crucially, Allen and Perkins stood solidly behind him. Before many months had passed, Justin Miller, possibly embarrassed by recent events and certainly chagrined by Few's tough new approach to various matters affecting the law school, requested and was granted a year's leave of absence to serve in a federal post in Washington. Later during that year Miller resigned as dean to begin a long, distinguished career in the capital in both the public and private sectors.[37] By mid-1934 Few declared that "the University as an operating proposition is better off right now than it has been," and a bit later he asserted, "On the whole I consider Duke University in better condition than it has ever been."[38]

Despite such confidence and optimism, Few believed he still had vital and unfinished business concerning certain formal, legal provisions for the governance of the university. He had once thought he could obtain the desired change in the university's charter "without a jar." But as he kept pushing the matter late in 1934, John F. Bruton, the chairman of Duke's board of trustees, finally spelled out his opposition in strong terms. "I am distressed to learn that you still count it your duty," Bruton informed Few, "to insist upon a revision of the charter of Duke University. . . ." Bruton insisted that he had tried to see the matter as Few did and had "earnestly prayed over it," but all he could see in it were "results embodying an almost unpardonable mistake and irreparable injury to Duke University."[39]

Faced with such strongly felt opposition, Few dropped the idea of tampering with Duke's charter. He settled instead for the much less complicated procedure of changing the university's by-laws in order to guarantee that the Duke Endowment would have three of its trustees on the university's executive committee. But even that, Bruton feared, would be "full of mischief" and might lead to injury to both Duke and Few. Bruton argued that already there was a feeling on the part of some of the university's trustees that they were "regarded as mere figureheads." Despite Bruton's fears and worries, Few ultimately won him over, for when Few proposed the change in the by-laws to the full board on March 27, 1935, it was adopted unanimously.[40]

Few, remembering the painful questions about Duke's two different boards that the General Education Board had first raised in the late 1920s as well as the scares he had suffered during the controversies about Norman Thomas, felt great satisfaction about the outcome. When Perkins soon joined Allen and Reynolds on the executive committee, the change was complete. Few believed that Duke had come to a wise solution of its governance problem and that, unless there was a weak spot that he had not detected, the university's leaders now had "a sound foundation upon which to build a very great university, if we can keep the country from falling in on us."[41] During his lifetime and for some years beyond, Few was proved to be correct. The fundamental problem of the two separate boards would reemerge at a later time and in a different set of circumstances, however, and would cause profound difficulties for Duke University.

Moreover, Few had been forced to pay a price in order to maintain a close working relationship with Allen and Perkins, a relationship that he rightly considered essential for the well-being of Duke University. There were limitations, partly hidden and subtle, on academic freedom at Duke in the stormy early 1930s. Yet those limitations should not be exaggerated. In response to a public attack on Duke by Ernest Seeman, Dr. William A. Perlzweig, a professor in Duke's medical school and former president of the local chapter of the American Association of University Professors, offered a trenchant reply. Perlzweig explained that he had grown up in the liberal tradition and had taught at other universities and research institutes for fifteen years before coming to Duke in 1930. Admitting that Duke had an atmosphere of "newness, of growth and emergence," Perlzweig insisted that it nevertheless had "as much academic freedom as any other university within my ken and a great deal more of such freedom and of spirit of tolerance than in many others that I know of." Perlzweig conceded that Duke University, like many others, had been established by a "great captain of industry" and that "his purpose was to perpetuate rather than destroy the system which bore and nurtured him. . . ." Moreover, it was equally clear that J. B. Duke's friends and business associates who controlled the Duke Endowment shared his ideas. "That under the circumstances a large measure of tolerance and of free flow and exchange of ideas is flourishing at our university," he concluded, "is to me one of these unmitigated blessings of our democracy which compensates at least in part for its many shortcomings."[42]

Just as a large measure of academic freedom continued at Duke even in one of its most inwardly troubled periods, so did the university make giant strides toward its goal of becoming a major research university. This was true despite the dual problems of an inadequate endowment and a dangerously divided system of governance. Building on a strong foundation that had been laid in Trinity College before 1925, Few and his colleagues at Duke set about strengthening the arts and sciences in such a manner that in the relatively short span of thirteen years, the Association of American Universities acknowledged the worthiness of the result by admitting Duke to membership.

4

Strengthening the Arts and Sciences:

The Natural Sciences, Mathematics,

and Engineering

‹Ͽ

PRESIDENT FEW'S REPEATED insistence that Trinity College, the undergraduate college of arts and sciences, was to remain the heart of Duke University was as much a moral imperative as it was a practical strategy.[1] The experience of the older research universities that were voluntarily supported—such as Harvard, Yale, and Princeton—made abundantly clear that the financial support of alumni, most of whom came from the undergraduate college, was essential for the well-being of these complex and expensive institutions. Aside from that practical consideration, however, there was a more fundamental matter of sheer honesty and integrity: if Duke University, like Trinity College before it, existed first of all to be of service and to try to make a difference in the lives of its students, then the best possible teaching of them became morally requisite.

Unfortunately for historians, there is no one grand academic blueprint that Few and his faculty drew up in the months after December, 1924, no precise chart for expansion. Certain strategies, however, Few clearly rejected. A professor at Harvard writing to a prominent new member of the Duke faculty, who passed the letter on to Few, obviously regarded quick prestige in academia, or certain portions thereof, as the prime desideratum. He thought the best way to achieve it was to concentrate resources on maybe a half dozen cognate departments, such as mathematics, physics, chemistry, and possibly physiology, or, as another possible grouping, history, government, economics, and psychology. By paying quite large salaries to attract distinguished heads for whichever group of cognate departments might be selected and then giving them substantial budgets to build up their departments, Duke could immediately attain recognized leadership, at least in certain disciplines.[2]

Such a specialized or one-sided faculty as the Harvard professor's approach would mean was clearly not what Few and his colleagues had in mind. Even if Duke had then possessed the money required for such an approach, which it did not if the professional schools were also to be developed, the pursuit of prestige at the price of lopsided development of the college of arts and sciences was not an attractive option. A slower approach aiming at a more comprehensive development of a large number of disciplines or departments was dictated both by the history of the institution and its multifaceted mission of service.

While there was no blueprint for expansion, there is an enlightening but undated memorandum in Few's papers, which internal evidence suggests was written by Few around 1927. He may have prepared it for a meeting of the trustees or with top administrators and possibly certain departmental chairmen. At any rate, the document begins with the statement that yearly income from all endowment sources was figured to be $967,000, to which should be added the (small) income from tuition and fees. Moreover, $360,000 of the total sum would be the income from the $6,000,000 that J. B. Duke had designated for the particular endowment of the medical school.

"The primary effort at present," the memorandum continues, "should be gradually but surely to strengthen and develop the University's undergraduate work. . . ." This was to be done by employing a "superior teaching force"; strengthening the teaching personnel in departments already established; developing "science work"; better equipping laboratories and further developing the library, "etc." The first step in this procedure would be the employment during the next year of "six outstanding teachers at a cost of approximately $36,000."

There should be gradual effort to raise the standards of admission, though in doing this, consideration had to be given to "conditions in the states adjacent to the University and the competitive state institutions, and it should be handled in such a way as not to decrease the patronage." Beginning in September, 1928, combined tuition and fees (for the college) should go up from $90 to $150 per year, and further increases should be made "from time to time as the necessity of the University may require." Loan funds to the extent of $100,000 per year were to be made available, thanks to the Angier B. Duke Memorial fund ($470,000 par value at the time) and the much smaller ($69,000) loan fund of the university itself. Great care was to be taken in making loans, with each note being endorsed by two persons and with "the interest of the University" being "carefully safeguarded."

Then, in a portion of the memorandum that clearly reflected the vital relationship between the university and the Duke Endowment, which was run by businessmen, the role of Robert L. Flowers as secretary-treasurer (and vice president for finance) was emphasized. Not only was he to concentrate on the "business end of the institution," but he was to have under him a "capable auditor" in charge of accounting. "The system of accounting [is] to be thoroughly organized, the records to be kept in the best possible way, and everything in connection with the business end of the institution to be handled the same as in big business corporations." No expenditures were to be made except upon the approval of the executive committee of the trustees or the administrative committee of the university, consisting of the president (Few), the secretary-treasurer (Flowers), and the dean of the university (Wannamaker).

Turning to the graduate and professional dimension of the new university, the memorandum merely stated that the graduate school was to be gradually developed as funds became available. The contemplated expansion of the law school should not be emphasized until the new buildings on the West campus were completed and "until it is certain that sufficient funds are available." Meantime, steps should be taken to "put the right foundation under the present Law School, so that at some later date we would be able to develop a fully organized Law School."[3]

The medical school and hospital "should be established," but there was not at hand sufficient endowment; in fact, there was only about two-thirds of what was required. "In establishing the Medical School," the memorandum continued, "we must know just how we now stand—just what funds from every source are available—and we should not employ a faculty or incur expenses unless the funds are available."

Turning to more general matters, the memorandum noted that since there was "not at present sufficient income from endowment and students to carry out at this time all the plans which Mr. J. B. Duke had in mind," everyone "must realize the necessity for securing increased endowment." The alumni, friends, and patrons of the university should be kept fully informed of plans and purposes, and "all matters affecting the constituency of the University must be handled carefully and with a clear knowledge of all conditions."

Touching only briefly on the matter that would increasingly loom larger in Few's mind, the memorandum noted that it was "highly desirable that there be at all times the closest cooperation between the Trustees of Duke University and the Trustees of the Duke Endowment." Everyone connected with or interested in the university, in the academic world or the general public, should understand that the two groups of trustees intended "to develop and carry out cautiously, carefully, and yet surely, the plans which were in Mr. Duke's mind." It could not be done hastily or even in a few years, but "ultimately—ten years, twenty years from now—there will be the great Duke University."

In the meantime, it was most important that expenditures of all kinds, large and small, be watched closely and that "no extravagant notions be encouraged." (Tales of President Few's turning off lights in unoccupied rooms long survived on campus.) "There is danger of getting on a wrong basis," the memorandum declared. "There is danger of those connected with the institution, as well as the general public, getting the idea that the institution has unlimited resources."

The document closes on a note that is completely characteristic of Few, whose own actions closely paralleled his admonitions: "There should be at all times the most friendly, considerate attitude toward North Carolina institutions and institutions in adjoining states." Every one should understand—"without assuming any attitude of superiority, without any spirit of boastfulness—that we are going ahead to build an institution which is to help the South, and, for that matter, this county—in other words, let every one understand the genuine, sincere spirit which we have in mind—a spirit which would help everybody and pull down nobody." It would be only by "having in our minds just the right feeling towards this institution, by the exercise of great patience, by proper consideration, by putting our heads and hearts together, that we shall be able to accomplish the great task."[4]

As the memorandum indicated, the first concrete step toward dealing with "the great task" was to strengthen the university's undergraduate work. In addition to expanding various existing departments, this meant adding several disciplines that Trinity College had not included. While Few and Wannamaker were involved in all appointments to the faculty to a larger extent than became true of the top administrators in a later era, in the case of the more well-established departments, the president and the dean were not usually the primary agents; the departmental chairmen and their senior colleagues were.

Given the limited resources available to Duke in the late 1920s, that there were relatively few prestigious professors, or academic "stars," added to the Duke faculty should occasion no surprise. There were a few such appointments, and the perception of some faculty members already on the scene may have been that there were more high-powered additions than there actually were. Harvie Branscomb, an able young professor in Duke's School of Religion after 1926, many years later noted that Duke, in trying to upgrade its faculty in the late 1920s and 1930s, brought in each year one outstanding person by paying whatever was necessary to do so. The person, according to Branscomb, turned out to be quite ordinary in some instances, academically eccentric in others, and in most cases difficult to integrate into a preexisting department. He claimed that he then concluded that if he ever had an opportunity similar to President Few's—which Branscomb did have, in fact, after 1946 as a revitalizing chancellor of Vanderbilt University—he would eschew the "star" approach to appointments and put his money on promising younger scholars.[5]

Branscomb, looking back from considerable distance to his younger days, may have been a bit harsh and unfair about the relatively few "star" appointments that Duke made. But he had a point. Certainly, in largely pursuing able, younger scholars out of financial necessity, the university had either a significant amount of luck or remarkably good judgment, or, more likely, some combination of the two. A significant number of the beginners who were recruited in the late 1920s and 1930s went on to establish themselves as nationally recognized scholars in their fields. Moreover, that approach had an additional benefit to the university, one that was either unforeseen at the time or unmentioned: a large number of the young scholars who "grew up" at and, in one sense, with Duke developed a high degree of institutional loyalty. Many of them, serving in various leadership roles both within their disciplines and within the university, would eventually turn down college presidencies or more lucrative employment elsewhere to spend their entire professional careers at Duke. The risk of being invidious is large, but examples only from the arts and sciences such as Calvin B. Hoover in economics, Taylor Cole in political science, Marcus Hobbs in chemistry, and Paul Kramer in botany would at least start a list that could be considerably longer.

In contrast to the complex and exacting standards of appointment-making in the late twentieth century, Duke's procedures in its early period as a university were relatively simple. What various critics would much later assail as the "old-boy network" operated, and departmental chairmen, once authorized by Few and/or Wannamaker, requested suggestions from their own mentors at the well-established research universities and from chairmen or members in other leading departments. Duke, because of its Woman's College, was more receptive to a limited number of appointments for women scholars than was the case with the majority of research universities.[6] The appointment process on the whole, however, was one that involved mostly white males.

Although Few clearly recognized the importance of the research dimension in appointing faculty members for what was meant to be a research university, he and especially Wannamaker put more emphasis upon a prospective faculty member's teaching potential than would be the case in the late twentieth century. Writing to a job applicant in 1931, Wannamaker, echoing Few's values and emphasis, explained that Duke was "deeply interested in the vital problem of proper instruction in undergraduate courses, especially for freshmen and sophomores" and was, therefore, "more than willing to get here properly trained men of sound character, of inspirational powers, with interest in undergraduate work."[7] Even more explicitly, Wannamaker a year or so later advised a chairman who wished to make an appointment that the new instructor "ought to be given to understand that if we bring him here, we are doing so with the distinct understanding that he is to give a good account of himself in his teaching, first of all." If the instructor made good in that and showed promise for research, he could "devote a reasonable part of his time to that [latter] sort of undertaking." But if he wanted to go largely into research, "we ought not to bring him here."[8] Pursuant to instructions, the chairman promptly informed the job candidate that, while the department was largely composed of young people who had the future ahead of them and an opportunity to make their professional reputations, both administrators and members of the department desired "to give first class instruction, especially to elementary students." The success of the instructor (who came and remained at Duke) would "depend to a great extent on your teaching ability," but there would be ample opportunity for research—in the summer.[9]

Wannamaker, as dean of the university and vice president for educational affairs, remained consistent in his priorities until his retirement in 1949. Explaining Duke's policy concerning promotion and tenure to a fellow administrator at another university in 1945, Wannamaker noted that while Duke put "great stress upon effective teaching, we also expect our teachers to keep alive and alert through study, and we emphasize the importance of research and productive scholarship though that is only one of our requirements for promotion and it is not the one that counts most in the lower brackets of the Faculty."[10]

Some chairmen learned the hard way that Few was deadly serious about the matter of teaching. On one occasion, Wannamaker authorized W. T. Laprade, at Trinity-Duke in history since 1909, to name a novice as a part-time instructor in that department, though the dean conceded that Few, who was out of town, had final authority in such matters. Furthermore, Wannamaker noted, the policy had been to secure experienced teachers, especially for freshmen. When Few returned and refused to approve the appointment, Wannamaker had the task of so notifying both Laprade and the job candidate.[11]

The policy of emphasizing teaching, both as an ability and a responsibility, had an interesting ripple effect. Once underway, Duke's graduate school, or rather certain departments in it, would pioneer in requiring candidates for the Ph.D. to take noncredit courses in college teaching, as will be discussed in a later chapter. "In the administration of the teaching of our graduate fellows and assistants," one leading scientist at Duke explained, "we are making an earnest effort to discover and develop teaching ability—to establish ideals and give some insight into methods by practice."[12]

While job candidates normally visited the campus to be appraised by both top administrators and members of the department concerned, once a person was appointed the matter of gaining tenure was not the complicated, tension-packed process that it became in the latter part of the century. In fact, the matter was hardly discussed at all, though a quite active chapter of the American Association of University Professors, the leading watchdog organization of the academic profession, was established at Duke in 1926. While there is very little concerning tenure in Wannamaker's extensive files, there are various indications of a generally relaxed policy. That is, when an instructor—and that rank even for new Ph.D.'s remained very much alive at Duke until the 1960s—was rehired for the second year, unless the appointment was explicitly made temporary, the general expectation was that the person would remain at Duke. "Generally the teaching staff are engaged with the expectation that they will become permanent members," Wannamaker explained. It followed, therefore, that the "most reliable protection to the institution is the observance of great care and wisdom in bringing new persons into the teaching staff."[13]

Despite a general and somewhat vague expectation that went along with the unconditional rehiring of an instructor for the second year, more secure tenure came with the promotion to the rank of assistant professor. "Except for extreme reasons," Wannamaker explained, "our teaching personnel holding assistant professorships, associate professorships, or professorships are never discharged."[14]

Given these policies in the powerful dean's office, much depended on the judgment of the departmental chairmen. As was then the prevailing practice in most universities, Duke's chairmen tended to serve indefinite, more or less permanent terms; and while the wiser ones invariably consulted with at least their senior colleagues, no university or departmental by-laws existed to mandate such procedure. An emphasis on teaching ability, or to be more exact, an emphasis on a job candidate's willingness to teach and interest in teaching, was undoubtedly salutary for Duke's students. When such an emphasis was coupled with attention to the candidate's ability and inclination to conduct investigation in the appropriate field of inquiry—to grow professionally and intellectually—then the process had the best chance of being successful in the context of a research university.

Since a large portion of Duke's faculty had Ph.D.'s from older leading research universities, Few and Wannamaker were no doubt correct in believing that the training of the chairmen had tilted them, or certainly most of them, towards research and that a special effort was needed in order to restore teaching to its proper role in the equation. Yet lively, able teachers at age thirty, whose relative youth and enthusiasm often made them especially attractive to students, could be in trouble, albeit tenured trouble, when they reached age forty or fifty without having continued to investigate and keep up in their own fields of expertise. As noted in an earlier chapter, a Duke professor put the matter wittily and well when he declared: "The satisfactions of a teacher are the college professor's meat, but publication is his wine. It stimulates him to new efforts, and it prevents his meat from going dry in his mouth."[15]

Teachers in Duke's arts and sciences, more so than in the professional schools, had ample opportunity for their "meat" to go dry in their mouths, for they taught roughly twice as much as would their successors later in the century. Officially, as Few occasionally liked to promulgate, the teaching load for the majority of the faculty was supposed to be five courses or fifteen hours per week. In fact, four courses or twelve hours per week became standard practice fairly soon after the university was organized, with those performing important administrative duties (such as chairing a department) or teaching a significant number of graduate students gaining nine-hour loads. A survey of liberal arts colleges accredited by the Southern Association of Secondary Schools and Colleges in 1945 revealed that Duke was one of six institutions in the region having a standard twelve-hour teaching load, while 90 percent of the responding institutions still had fifteen hours as standard.[16]

At Duke the whole matter could be quite tricky, for in those science courses involving laboratory work and in certain other teaching situations, the counting of teacher-student contact hours became complicated. It was a problem that Wannamaker sought to leave largely in the hands of departmental chairmen. During World War II, when an accelerated, complex academic calendar combined with a shrunken faculty caused many departments at Duke to have staffing problems, one harassed chairman sought enlightenment from Wannamaker about the "standard" teaching load. The dean, knowing full well that practice had long ago become different from theory, responded that Few had several years earlier named a committee to investigate the problem, but no specific decision had been reached; Few, however, then wrote a memorandum stating that the teaching load was fifteen hours in the undergraduate colleges and twelve hours in the graduate school and that the fifteen-hour load could be reduced to twelve and the twelve to nine only by special permission. The inquiring chairman found this murky (and unrealistic) answer not altogether helpful and made a second request for an authoritative ruling. Wannamaker thereupon replied that he had no further information on the subject and concluded, somewhat loftily, "I wonder, after all, if the question is of such a pressing nature. All of us have a plenty of other things to do."[17]

What most of the Duke faculty had to do, of course, was teach, and one must recognize that reality in attempting to assess the quality of the faculty in arts and sciences during the university's first quarter-century. There was probably more concern about and interest in teaching, especially of undergraduates, than in most other research universities, with the exception of Princeton. While a significant number of Duke faculty members also turned out to be productive scholars, and some achieved national distinction, there was inevitably a certain amount of "dead wood" among the faculty, or what Harvie Branscomb termed "bulbs of low wattage."[18]

In reading Wannamaker's files, one can discern, in at least a few cases, mediocrity being built into a department. Since a tenured appointment could last for forty or so years, the resulting loss to the university, not to mention the students, was great. In one case, which is perhaps unusually stark, Wannamaker played a key role in the appointment in 1927 of an instructor whom he had doubts about even as to teaching ability. Another member of the Duke faculty had met the man and was not impressed. "While I am not absolutely sure of his perfect adaptability for this place," Wannamaker conceded, "I do believe he is a good man."[19] In another letter on the same day, Wannamaker explained that he had hesitated about the appointment but finally decided that the new instructor was "probably the best man available."

Five years later Wannamaker conceded that the person in question was "by no means a strong teacher but I do not know that we could at this time make any change." The man had "quite a load to carry with his family on his hands." Yet Wannamaker recognized that the small department in question needed to develop greater interest in scholarship in its members, for it "cannot expect to get many graduate students unless more is done in the way of independent research."[20]

Meantime, in the same department another instructor had been appointed in 1930. In 1936 the chairman, Wannamaker's chief collaborator in what could be taken as a model of how not to build a department, reported that the second man (the one hired in 1930) was not especially interested in research or in teaching advanced courses but was valuable in introductory work, which ought to entitle him to a permanent spot. "My records show," the collaborator wrote, "that I reported to you on his good work in 1931 and after that I probably considered that we had accepted him as a regular member of the department." As for the man hired in 1927, the report was quite mixed: he was a steady, reliable teacher who met his classes regularly (as if that were noteworthy) and used unique methods to gain and hold the attention of the students. He had begun to grade more strictly and make more demanding assignments (meaning that the courses were probably well known as "crips" or easy rides), and he had published more articles than most young instructors. His chief weakness was his "lack of vigorous personality and a consequent lack of compelling influence on the weaker ones among his students." He was, in short, probably "the weakest member of our staff." If he was not to be retained, the decision should be made soon. (In fact, it was several years too late by the seven-year standard of the American Association of University Professors for a negative decision, and the man had already gained tenure more or less by default.)

The collaborator, obviously a highly optimistic person, concluded that the work of the six-person department was "of a very high order indeed" and that it ranked "about as high as any in teaching ability and general efficiency." Ending on a resigned, wistful note, he observed that it was difficult "to change the mild or rather passive character of some college instructors."[21]

The whole episode was, admittedly, atypical of Duke's normal hiring practices in the period. Moreover, Wannamaker, an intelligent and hardworking dean, did not generally collude in standard-lowering. Yet the story does dramatically illustrate how mistakes with long-lived consequences could and did occur. Fortunately for Duke University, if Wannamaker did slip and let his guard down, most departments had chairmen and senior members who took a careful and conscientious approach to recruiting.

Those faculty members who were recruited to come to Duke in the arts and sciences in the late 1920s and 1930, a few "stars" excepted, did not come because the salaries proffered were large. By prevailing standards in the South, Duke's salaries were quite good, but by comparison with other research universities, particularly the older and better ones, the Duke pay scale was not dazzling. In the heady days of 1925, maybe even into 1926, before financial realities at Duke had become clear, Few had certainly envisioned a more ambitious recruiting program and higher salaries. He, no doubt in consultation with various advisors, even had at one time a list of national leaders in various fields whom he hoped to approach about coming to Duke, and he showed the list to one of J. B. Duke's well-to-do business associates in New York, who was a trustee of the Duke Endowment. When that trustee inquired in late 1927 how Few was succeeding with his list, the chastened president explained that it had seemed wise, even necessary, to see through the financial situation a bit more clearly before going on with the recruitment of well-established faculty members.[22]

The whole subject of salaries paid at Duke was handled in a highly secretive manner. Moreover, the American Association of University Professors would not get into the business of collecting and publishing salary data until after World War II. At Duke, the matter was both complicated and made more sensitive by the organization of a research university around an older liberal arts college and the consequent necessity of adding new faculty members to the existing faculty of Trinity College. Even to officials in the Southern Association of Secondary Schools and Colleges, who gathered general data on salary ranges, all Few would say is that salaries at Duke were higher than salaries elsewhere in the South (which was not saying much), but that inevitable complications arising from the reorganization led to great unevenness in salaries. "We prefer not to go on record concerning salaries," Few confessed, "until we are further along in our development."[23]

Data in the Few and Wannamaker papers, however, make it possible to generalize about salary ranges in the arts and sciences in the late 1920s. Since most salaries would actually shrink in the Great Depression (only belatedly and temporarily at Duke, in 1933–34), the ranges for the 1930s were close to those established in the late 1920s. There were, of course, numerous exceptions, but pay for instructors generally ranged from $2,000 per year to $2,900; for assistant professors from $3,000 to $3,900; for associate professors from $3,750 to around $4,500; and for professors from $4,500 to $7,500, with rather few at the top figure.[24]

The starting salary was not necessarily the determining factor in the decision of some new Ph.D.'s who came to Duke. Offering $2,000 in 1931 to one young scientist (Paul J. Kramer) whom the botanical wing of the biology department wanted, Wannamaker stressed that Duke was "trying to bring here a goodly number of young, ambitious scientists, with the hope that in teaching ability as well as in interest in their field of work they will justify our promoting them as rapidly as possible." Accepting the offer, Kramer confessed that the salary was somewhat lower than he had expected to be offered a Ph.D., but if there was "an opportunity for advancement, when deserved," the starting salary was not such a serious matter. "I am more interested in building for the future," he explained, "than in securing immediate remuneration and judging from what I have heard concerning your policies [at Duke] I should have a good opportunity to do so at Duke."[25]

Although salaries and salary ranges by rank were closely kept secrets, rumors and suspicions flourished, as they normally do in such situations. Salaries in all of Duke's professional schools, and particularly law and medicine, were significantly higher than in arts and sciences, and that discrepancy acutely displeased some veteran faculty members. Refusing to recognize that market forces necessarily operated to a certain extent even within academe, W. K. Boyd, who had been on the faculty at Trinity-Duke since 1906, fired off protests to Few and Wannamaker. Boyd argued that as a matter of justice, there should be a general raise in the salary scale for those in arts and sciences. A majority of the faculty members "who really think about the University as a whole, who are willing to give their surplus time from teaching to the promotion of the University['s] affairs in general," he maintained, "are in the non-professional schools." He thought the "future of academic teaching" was at stake, for if too great a proportion of salary funds went to the professional schools, "the disparity will react upon the caliber of the personnel" in arts and sciences. "Time and again this very thing has happened in American institutions," Boyd concluded, "namely that the college has suffered at the expense of the professional schools."[26] Needless to say, protests neither from Boyd nor from any others in arts and sciences had the least effect on the situation, and faculty salaries in the professional schools remained larger than those in arts and sciences.

Another aspect of Duke's faculty salaries in the years before World War II that differed from the situation later in the century was that there were no annual raises and no across-the-board raises at all. Given the painful deflationary realities of the 1930s, that should not be surprising. Still, for academics in the late twentieth century, who often have difficulty realizing that inflation and a rising price-and-salary scale have not always characterized American life, it might come as a shock to know that in 1939, for example, only forty-two of the nearly two hundred faculty members in arts and sciences received raises for the next academic year, and most of those raises were in the $100 to $250 range.[27]

In light of the salaries and opportunities offered in arts and sciences at Duke after December, 1924, one might well ask what actually happened in the staffing of the various departments. Few's undated memorandum of around 1927 had emphasized that work in science especially needed development, and the various departments in that area grew considerably, both in terms of size and quality.

Chemistry had a certain advantage among the sciences because Paul M. Gross chaired the department. A graduate of the City College of New York, he received his Ph.D. from Columbia and had come to Trinity in 1919. As able as he was energetic and forceful, he carefully balanced the research and teaching dimensions both in adding staff and in leading what became a strong department. Although a productive scholar himself, Gross excelled at planning, organizing, and administering, and he would eventually move into prominent positions of leadership within both Duke University and the national scientific community. He periodically lectured and studied abroad, in England or France or Germany, and kept in touch with developments and leaders in the field of chemistry both nationally and internationally.

An undated and unsigned memorandum, which may have been written by Gross around 1925 or 1926, reveals some sharp thinking about how a chemistry department should be built. "The great need and opportunity in the South," the memorandum asserts, "is for a university department of chemistry which will carry on active investigative work and teaching in the pure science aspects of the subject." Since it was generally conceded that advances in applied chemistry could most easily be made when there was a firm theoretical basis, the development of that base was necessary before work in applied chemistry or chemical engineering could be begun. The type of department envisioned should develop strong subdivisions covering the fields of physical or theoretical chemistry, analytical chemistry, organic chemistry, colloid chemistry, physiological chemistry, and biological chemistry. All of these were, the memorandum added, especially important to the study of medicine and to medical research, and the first three subdivisions were important in the development of electrochemistry.

Then the memorandum turned to the matter of staffing and revealed an approach or insight that was both somewhat different from that of President Few and, in the long run, much sounder and more realistic. In covering a given scientific field, the document continued, the members of the department concerned could be divided on the basis either of graduate-versus-undergraduate teaching or according to fields of specialization. There was no question as to the superiority of the second method as applied to chemistry and other scientific departments in general, for it led to a well-balanced department and made possible the offering of a logical sequence of courses. The first method of staffing (graduate versus undergraduate teaching) led, in a small department, to one-sided development in a relatively narrow specialty, or else resulted in a superficial survey; in either case, normal growth was difficult. (The memorandum did not include the point, but might well have, that, with rare exceptions, few professors of any ability or ambition would long be content to remain on the lower level of a two-tiered system of staffing that confined some exclusively to undergraduate teaching and gave others the rewards and challenges of graduate teaching. In the type of research university that Duke wished to be, the crucial need was for persons able and willing to do both kinds of teaching, at least eventually.) [28]

Not only, then, did the chemistry department have a sound rationale for its expansion, but there was a plan or timetable for it, obviously based on the correct assumption that enrollment would grow. One new instructor should be named for 1927–28 and provision made for sixty-five hours of instructional help in laboratory work from three graduate teaching assistants and two fellows. After increasing only the latter kind of help in 1928–29, another new instructor should be added in 1929–30 and another in 1930, with the help from the teaching assistants and fellows going up to 105 hours a week in 1931–32. The cost of the five-year plan, exclusive of the cost for the four-person staff in 1926, was estimated to be $5,000 for 1927–28; $5,600 the next year; and so on, up to $10,800 in 1931–32.[29]

The chemistry department at Duke clearly did not grow willy-nilly.

Neither did the handsome new Tudor Gothic building for the department that was being planned in 1926–27 and was then built in 1929–30 go up without substantial input from Gross and his colleagues, particularly Robert N. Wilson, who like Gross was a carryover from the Trinity College era.[30] Wilson found a useful place in the expanded department as the person who supervised and helped teach the important introductory course. A skillful and dedicated teacher, he helped to "break in" most of the young instructors who joined the department.[31]

In the palmy first year or so after the university was established, before budgetary realities began to hit home around 1927, Gross and Few may have considered the possibility of a "star" appointment in chemistry. Few, at any rate, inquired of a professor whom he had met in Cambridge, Massachusetts, whether a certain chemist then at the University of Pennsylvania, whom Duke was considering, could be ranked already among "the foremost chemists of America," or did he give clear promise of attaining such a rank?[32] Regardless of the unknown answer to the query, nothing ever came of the matter, and the chemistry department had to settle for a slower route toward winning recognition from chemists elsewhere. Remembering Warren C. Vosburgh as a classmate at Columbia, Gross, who was in Germany at the time, suggested him in an emergency in 1928 as a possible addition to the department. When George B. Pegram—Trinity alumnus, son of Trinity's William H. Pegram, and prominent dean at Columbia University—informed Wannamaker that Vosburgh's teachers had a high opinion of his ability and productivity and found him thoroughly scientific, industrious, reliable, and easy to get along with, Vosburgh, who had been teaching at the University of Iowa, became an assistant professor at Duke.[33]

Gross, seeking a topic of regional importance for investigation, began research related to the tobacco industry and added Frederick R. Darkis to the department in a research capacity in 1928. A pioneer in tobacco research whose training had been at the University of Maryland, Darkis joined Gross in working closely with the research headquarters in Durham of the Liggett & Myers tobacco company and later served as a vice president of the company.

Small colleges and even some university departments that grow smug and complacent about themselves or fearful of "foreign" influences sometimes slip into what the academic world calls "inbreeding," that is, a pattern of preferential hiring of their own alumni. On the other hand, self-confident colleges or departments, given a certain mix of non-alumni already on the staff, do not hesitate to add one of their own products if there is an opening and if the person's past record is strong and the promise of future achievement is real. Such was the case in 1928 when the chemistry department added one of its first Ph.D. alumni, John H. Saylor, as an instructor.

Lucius A. Bigelow, a Yale Ph.D. teaching organic chemistry at Brown University, informed Gross late in 1928 that he found himself blocked from advancement in his position there and would be interested in coming to Duke if there should be an opening. After further investigation and with proper authorization, Gross invited him as an assistant professor in 1929, and so another longtime member of the department was added. In the same year, Charles R. Hauser, with his doctorate from the University of Iowa, came as an instructor.[34] A slow but steady, patient investigator, he would later become the first member of the Duke faculty elected to the National Academy of Sciences.

In the cases of both Vosburgh and Bigelow, Gross managed to advance their professional and personal growth through exchange professorships. He capitalized on the fact that his former adviser at Columbia had moved to the University of Edinburgh, Scotland, and arranged to send Vosburgh there in 1932–33 and Bigelow in 1933–34. The Duke department no doubt benefitted from the presence of the Scottish professors who visited in exchange, but Gross knew the value of such an experience for his own staff. In Vosburgh's case, Gross urged him to take advantage of the summer following his year at Edinburgh to travel on the continent and specifically to see something of the scientific work being done in Germany and Denmark.[35]

While the expansion in the chemistry department down to around 1930 had not been exactly as forecast in 1926, it had been close, and in 1931 two other instructors who would spend their full, productive careers at Duke were added. As is discussed in the chapter on the Woman's College, its needs made Duke more receptive to a limited number of women scholars than was the case in many research universities in that era. Accordingly, in 1931 Gross found a promising young woman chemist, Frances Brown, who had gone on from Agnes Scott College to obtain her doctorate at Johns Hopkins. Joining her as a new instructor in the same year, Douglas Hill had received his doctoral training at Princeton. A year after Brown and Hill came to Duke, Gross reported in Wilson's absence on the work of the instructors in freshman chemistry. (That the dean annually requested such reports reflects the importance that President Few attached to the teaching of freshmen.) Saylor was in charge of the course during Wilson's absence, Gross noted, and had done a fine job. Hill had proved to be a "hard worker and is generally well liked by both students and faculty." The instruction of first-year women, all done on the East campus, had been under the direction of Brown and had been "better organized" and shown "definite improvement" over previous years. Two advanced sections of the introductory course, organized on the basis of a placement test given at Duke, had also been introduced and had gone well. In short, Gross concluded, in words that undoubtedly comforted Few and his deans, there had been definite improvement in the instruction of freshman chemistry.[36]

Spotting another Duke product that seemed well worth hanging on to, Gross and his senior colleagues added Marcus Hobbs as an instructor in 1935. Fresh from his doctoral work, done under the supervision of Gross, Hobbs was destined to become, like his mentor, an academic statesman as well as a well-known, productive chemist.

In 1937 Gross managed to land one of his and Duke University's prize catches, Fritz London. Although still a relatively young man at thirty-seven, London had already achieved an international reputation in theoretical chemistry and physics by the time Gross arranged to hear him read a paper and to meet him at a conference in Paris in the fall of 1937. Gross immediately wrote Wannamaker that London, who had formerly been in the Kaiser Wilhelm Institute in Berlin, was one of the many Jewish scholars who had lost their positions in Germany because of Nazi laws excluding persons of Jewish origins from state appointments. London had worked earlier with Enrico Fermi in Rome and after losing his post in Berlin had worked in the Clarendon Laboratory of Oxford University for several years. In January, 1937, he had gone to the Institut Henri Poincaré of the University of Paris and worked with Irène Curie and her husband, F. Joliot-Curie.

"In some ways," Gross reported, "he [London] is the same type intellectually as [Edward] Teller though he is if anything quite a bit better known." London had good prospects of eventually attaining a professorship at the Poincaré Institute, Gross explained, but since he and his wife were "essentially German," they did not "feel they would be content to stay in France." Reminding Wannamaker that President Few had earlier expressed a willingness to add one of the displaced German scientists to the chemistry department if the right person could be found, Gross noted that he thought London could be brought to Duke as an associate professor of chemistry at the standard salary. Gross favored a one-year appointment, subject to renewal if mutually satisfactory to both parties, since that was then the prevailing practice at Duke except for those appointed at the professorial level.[37]

Wannamaker, after conferring with Few and Flowers, soon informed Gross that they were all keenly interested in trying to hire London and were, in this case, quite willing to rely on Gross's judgment. Furthermore, a prominent scientist had written urging all university departments of chemistry to add as quickly as possible thoroughly competent mathematical chemists, and London gave promise of fitting exactly into that category.[38]

London, understandably enough, suggested that he and his wife could decide more freely and knowledgeably about moving permanently to the United States if he first visited Duke for a semester, without resigning from his position in Paris. After that was arranged, London came as a visiting lecturer in 1938 and then permanently, as a professor of chemistry, in the fall of 1939. Vosburgh, when the matter was being arranged, urged that the appointment be given ample publicity, for someone had remarked upon seeing the report on Duke to the rating committee of the American Chemical Society that the "one thing we [at Duke] lacked was a man with a big name." [39]

Along with the "big name" added just as World War II began in Europe, the chemistry department elected to bring back Charles K. Bradsher as an instructor in 1939. A Duke undergraduate who had gone to Harvard for his doctorate, Bradsher, like Saylor and Hobbs, was destined to become a successor to Gross in chairing the department. From four full-time members in 1926, it had grown to twelve on the eve of the war and had become a conspicuously strong department in the new research university.

Biology, containing both botany and zoology, was another of the science departments that grew quickly and impressively at Duke. The fact that it also, like the chemistry and physics departments, was given its own handsome new Tudor Gothic building on the West campus was more evidence of the university's determination to strengthen the natural sciences. The biology building stood on the east side of the northern arm of the quadrangle directly opposite the chemistry building, and since both were less than a stone's throw from the south or quadrangle entrance to the medical school and hospital buildings, there were obvious advantages in proximity for the natural and health sciences at Duke. The physics building stood next to the biology building and faced the law school across the quadrangle. Although not many years would pass before Duke's science departments began to complain of inadequate space and facilities, in the early days of the university the sciences clearly had certain physical or spatial advantages over both the humanities and the social sciences.

Two carryovers from the Trinity College faculty, Bert Cunningham in zoology and Hugo L. Blomquist in botany, formed the original nucleus of the department. Cunningham was a native of Illinois who, after receiving both a bachelor's and a master's degree from Wesleyan University, had taught school in Durham for several years before serving as an instructor at Trinity College and obtaining a master's degree in zoology there in 1916. Receiving his Ph.D. from Wisconsin in 1920, he was named professor of zoology and chairman of the biology department at Trinity in that same year. Perhaps because of his experience as a schoolteacher as well as President Few's eagerness to have Trinity be of maximum service to North Carolina's public schools, Cunningham devoted much time and energy to working with science teachers in the secondary schools.

Hugo L. Blomquist (known familiarly as "Bloomy") was born in Sweden and brought to the United States as a young child in 1892. After later becoming a naturalized citizen, he farmed in North Dakota for a number of years, obtained sufficient education to become a high school principal, and eventually went to the University of Chicago for both an undergraduate and a doctoral degree in botany, the latter being awarded in 1921. Coming to Trinity College in 1920, he soon began investigating the ferns, grasses, and peat mosses of North Carolina and other southern states and gradually achieved scholarly prominence through his published papers and books. Many years later an especially intriguing and beautiful portion of the Sarah P. Duke Gardens would be devoted solely to native plants and flowers and quite appropriately named the Blomquist Garden.

Both Cunningham and Blomquist were only in the beginning stages of their careers when the university was organized. Furthermore, since the two men apparently eyed each other somewhat warily, foreshadowing tension between the two wings of the conjoined department, Few and Wannamaker probably decided that one of the relatively few "star" appointments to be made should be in the biology department. The fact that the prominent zoologist who was finally selected for that appointment had been one of Cunningham's teachers at Wisconsin no doubt helped to lessen the political or interpersonal trickiness of the move.

If, as Few once noted, a university is essentially a collection of great personalities, then Arthur S. Pearse should rank fairly high among the colorful and significant scholars in Duke's early history. A complex, idiosyncratic man, he spent the last two decades of his teaching career at Duke and remained both active and influential there for a number of years after his retirement in 1948. With his doctorate from Harvard, Pearse had taught at the University of Michigan and elsewhere before joining the faculty at the University of Wisconsin. Many biologists travel frequently for research in exotic places around the globe, and Pearse was no exception. On his way via London to Nigeria and other parts of Africa when Few talked with him at Duke in 1926, Pearse continued his far-flung travels for many years. With books and papers in the fields of ecology and parasitology, he served as president of the Ecological Society of America in 1926 and would hold prominent positions in other important professional organizations later in his career.

Reporting for duty at Duke early in 1927, Pearse informed a friend that he found "things at Duke rather unorganized, and from a scientific point of view, undeveloped, but the prospects for the future have promise."[40] In a more positive vein, he informed another person that his son, Richard Pearse, had been "perfectly delighted" with his senior year at Duke after the first three years of college at Wisconsin. Having been initiated into Phi Beta Kappa at Wisconsin and made the highest average in Duke's senior class, the son declared that "he had made more friends here [at Duke] in one semester than he did in 14 years at Wisconsin."[41]

An impetuous, outspoken man, Arthur Pearse gradually developed grievances about what he regarded as the excessive amount of teaching required at Duke, and he focused much of the blame on Few. Looking back as he wrote a short memoir in the early 1950s, Pearse was more understated and mellow than some of his letters to Few in the 1930s had been. In 1926 Few had said, Pearse recalled, that Pearse would be one of about eight graduate professors who would teach only advanced-level courses and be free of administrative and other types of restraints. But upon arriving at Duke, Pearse wrote, he found the reality quite different and eventually concluded that Few, "though a fine gentleman and in some respects a great man, was a dreamer."[42]

That Pearse could be much more direct in making his point is suggested by a letter he wrote to a graduate student in zoology whom Duke had dropped and who wrote Pearse requesting a recommendation. After consulting his colleagues and finding that all agreed that they would not recommend the student, Pearse wrote to him: "Personally, I feel that your trouble is that you are incompetent, unreliable, lazy, and rather proud of being an abnormal non-conformist in the present social scheme."[43] Loyal and helpful to colleagues and conscientious students, Pearse obviously suffered those he regarded as fools less gladly than more timid souls might.

Soon after the arrival of Pearse, Blomquist informed Wannamaker that he and Pearse had discussed the matter carefully and had agreed that the biology department should be divided into two separate departments. Failing that, and as a temporary arrangement, Blomquist urged that Pearse be named chairman, since Blomquist perceived that the administration only nominally regarded Cunningham, whose interests were confined to his own field, as chairman. Wannamaker replied nervously that he did not think it wise even to discuss the matter at that time, though he promised to talk later with Blomquist.[44] Nevertheless, in 1928 Pearse was named to chair the department, though he claimed not to want the job. Since Blomquist led in the matter of recruiting the botanists, he was in effect a sub- or associate chairman, without, however, such a title. Both wings of the department grew quickly and developed considerable strength by the time of World War II.

Even before Pearse arrived at Duke, Frank G. Hall, a physiologist who had received his doctorate at Wisconsin under the supervision of Pearse, had come in 1926 to join the zoologists. Described by Pearse as "a genius" when it came to understanding the operation of all sorts of intricate equipment, Hall was put in charge of aeromedical physiology at Wright Field during World War II, and he transferred to the physiology department of Duke Medical School after the war.[45]

Other zoologists who joined the department in its formative stage were Irving E. Gray and George T. Hargitt, both of whom were appointed in 1930. Gray, another Wisconsin Ph.D. (1926) and a student of Pearse's, took cuts in both pay and rank to come to Duke from Tulane. An especially conscientious and effective teacher, Gray researched the blood and respiration of fish and the development of insects and succeeded Pearse as chairman of the zoology department in 1940. Hargitt, a Harvard Ph.D. who had taught at Northwestern and Syracuse prior to coming to Duke, published numerous papers in cytology and protozoology, excelled at graduate-level teaching, and shared with Pearse the distinction among early zoologists at Duke of having his name starred in *American Men of Science*.[46]

Another boost for biology at Duke came around 1930, when Pearse took the lead in launching and then long serving as editor of *Ecological Monographs*, a journal which Duke University Press published. Inspired by a tip from the editor of the Duke Press that, since it was already publishing two journals in other fields and a third was about to appear, a journal in the scientific area might be in order, Pearse went to work.[47] He consulted with various leaders in the field of ecology and found that a journal which could carry longer studies than were suitable for the existing journal, *Ecology*, would be valuable for the field. Since the administrative leaders at Duke were eager to have the university and its young press do their share in the way of scholarly publication, Pearse in 1928 easily gained approval for the venture from Flowers (who first consulted Few and officials of the Duke Endowment). The appearance of the journal was delayed until early 1931 because Pearse took a leave of absence from early 1929 to the fall of 1930 to do research in Japan and elsewhere in Asia, with support from the Rockefeller Foundation. Receiving a copy of the first issue of *Ecological Monographs* shortly before Christmas, 1930, a prominent biologist at the University of Chicago congratulated Pearse on the journal's general appearance and noted that "American ecology is now in a position to move forward in a dignified manner so far as research publication facilities are concerned."[48]

Three additional appointments rounded out the ranks of the zoologists in the prewar period. Cazlyn G. Bookhout, in cytology and embryology, received his Ph.D. from Duke in 1934 and joined the faculty as an instructor in 1935. He had earlier received a master's degree from Syracuse and taught for a couple of years at the Woman's College of the University of North Carolina before beginning his career at Duke. In 1937 Mychyle W. Johnson, with his doctorate from Indiana University, came from the Carnegie Institution's department of genetics at Cold Spring Harbor; his research centered on cytology of the nucleolus. Also in 1937, Katherine R. Jeffers, not the first woman in zoology but the first to stay for a significant period, came to Duke. A graduate of the University of Missouri who had obtained her doctorate at Bryn Mawr College, she had taught at her undergraduate alma mater before coming to Duke to be in charge of the zoology courses in the Woman's College. Jeffers may or may not have even noticed Wannamaker's choice of pronouns, but in answering her request for more information about the position at Duke, the dean assured her: "If a person convinces us that he has in him the quality necessary for a first-rate teacher or for research, we are glad to recognize him and to promote him as rapidly as we can."[49] (Wannamaker was not, of course, alone among males in that era's academic world, or elsewhere, in so using the language.)

Growth in the botany department paralleled that in zoology. Blomquist, like Gross and Pearse, actively sought teacher-scholars and succeeded in assembling a small but strong staff of seven full-time members before the war. The first of these to come, in 1927, was Frederick A. Wolf. A Nebraskan who had received his Ph.D. at Cornell in 1911, he had worked at state experiment stations in Alabama and then North Carolina and for two years at the United States Department of Agriculture before coming to Duke. Praised by a biologist at the University of Wisconsin as "one of the best men in Plant Pathology of his age in the United States," Wolf did work on fungi and tobacco diseases that would earn him also, like Pearse and Hargitt, a star in *American Men of Science*.[50]

Ruth M. Addoms, with a Wellesley arts baccalaureate and a Ph.D. from Wisconsin, was one of several women who came to Duke in 1930 when the separate Woman's College opened. She proved to be one of the most outstanding in the group, both in her scholarly activity in the field of plant physiology and in her teaching and various types of services to Duke. Taking a cut in pay from her position at Wisconsin and turning down better-paying jobs at women's colleges in the East to come to Duke, Addoms quickly gained strong approval and support from Blomquist, Pearse, and other colleagues. The second semester after she arrived, Pearse described her as "a very unusual woman, a most excellent teacher, and a good scientist who is doing research." Some years later, Wannamaker, in responding to an inquiry about Addoms as a possible college president, declared that he had a "very high opinion" of her and that she was a "woman of strong personality and absolutely dependable character," one who was highly thought of not only by members of her department but by the university as a whole.[51]

The arrival of Paul Kramer in 1931 has already been mentioned. His work in plant physiology and related areas would later lead to his election as president of the American Society of Plant Physiologists and membership on the editorial boards of several professional journals as well as in the National Academy of Sciences. By assuming the directorship of the Sarah P. Duke Gardens in 1945, Kramer performed one of his most valuable and long-lasting services not only for Duke but for the tens of thousands of visitors who come annually to the gardens. They were begun primarily to serve an aesthetic purpose, but Kramer, while enhancing the original purpose, helped to give the gardens an educational dimension that would grow steadily over the years.

Two new appointments in 1932 both proved significant and long-lasting for the botany department at Duke. Henry J. Oosting had recently received his doctorate at the University of Minnesota when Blomquist found him; since Oosting was an ecologist, Blomquist described the extensive Duke Forest as a feature that would appeal to him. Moreover, Blomquist pointed out that there were many ecological problems in North Carolina on which very little work had been done. Those features plus the promise of fair treatment concerning a pay increase and promotion brought Oosting to Duke as an instructor.[52]

Joining Oosting as a newcomer that same fall of 1932, H. S. Perry came as a geneticist and cytologist with a new Ph.D. from Cornell. As mentioned earlier, Blomquist, at Wannamaker's insistence, had made clear to Perry that Duke insisted on ample attention to teaching and was not interested in faculty members who only wanted to do research and work exclusively with graduate students. Perry accepted the offer, pointing out that a continuation of the work in genetics he had begun on corn would, after all, provide excellent material for course work. Making some important discoveries in years that lay ahead, Perry would also endear himself to many neighbors and colleagues by sharing the surplus sweet corn that was a by-product of his research interests.[53]

The fact that Lewis E. Anderson, another cytologist, became a lifelong member of Duke's botany department was partly a fortunate accident. With Blomquist going on leave in 1936–37, the department needed a temporary replacement for him. A Duke alumnus, Anderson was finishing up his doctoral work at the University of Pennsylvania and seemed a likely choice for the one-year instructorship. As happened in several other Duke departments and professional schools, however, the presumably temporary appointment became permanent. In Anderson's case Blomquist argued that he needed help in plant cytology because his workload was too heavy and, furthermore, Anderson had proven to be an "excellent scientist, a hard worker, and easy to get along with."[54] Since the budgetary crunch of 1933–34 had passed, Wannamaker, Few, and Flowers agreed to Anderson's remaining, and the pre–World War II staff in botany was assembled.

As Blomquist had earlier, Pearse too pushed for separate departments for zoology and botany. Writing to Few in 1933, Pearse complained that certain problems in the two-winged department caused him worry and trouble that hampered his scholarly endeavors. He argued, without giving any evidence, that the "administrative and pedagogical problems" were quite different in the two fields and that there was no particular community of interests between the two groups (which were contained in one department in many universities aside from Duke). Pointing out that botany had its own budget and that the botanists pretty much managed their own affairs until problems arose with the administration, Pearse asserted that he was then supposed to jump in and pull their chestnuts from the fire. "Sometimes my feeling is that the nuts are wormy or rotten," Pearse added, "but I have no choice but to jump in and burn my fingers." Since the botanists did not like having a zoologist as chairman, he continued, and he felt uncomfortable in the job, "Why not turn them loose?"[55]

Pearse got what he had suggested, for in 1935 zoology and botany became separate departments, headed respectively by Pearse and Blomquist. Despite the alleged friction, many members of the two departments actually did share overlapping or related professional interests. For one thing, Pearse himself described the Duke Forest as the "best asset for biological field work at Duke University."[56] Many of the botanists certainly agreed, and several of them taught courses in forestry and then served on the faculty of the School of Forestry when it was formally opened in 1938.[57]

Just as the rich presence of the Duke Forest facilitated and even encouraged interdisciplinary work, so did another important venture that Pearse took the lead in launching, the Duke University Marine Laboratory at Beaufort, North Carolina. The United States Fish and Wildlife Service maintained a laboratory at Beaufort, and Pearse had worked there, when not globe-trotting, during several summers. Pearse noted Beaufort's location near Cape Hatteras, which he described as the northern limit of many typically southern marine animals and the southern limit of many northern types. When the opportunity arose for Duke to buy eight and a half acres on a protected harbor at the southern end of Pivers Island, Pearse, envisioning a future marine station such as those at Woods Hole in Massachusetts and in the Tortugas, persuaded the administration to buy the land.[58]

Beginning modestly with a few frame buildings, the Marine Laboratory was opened officially for summer classes and research in 1938, and while World War II would delay its development, important beginnings were made before and even during the war. Late in 1941, but before Pearl Harbor, Pearse secured a grant from the General Education Board to cover the salary of a resident investigator at the Marine Laboratory for a three-year period and to help cover the cost of supplies and equipment. In June, 1942, Harold J. Humm, who would soon receive his Duke doctorate under the supervision of Wolf in botany, became the resident investigator. Humm's research on Atlantic Coast seaweeds and on agar-digesting bacteria was not only important scientifically, but since agars (used as culture media for bacteriologists, in adhesives, etc.) had been largely imported from Japan before the war, the work had significance for the American war effort. Upon Pearse's retirement, Humm was named director of the Marine Laboratory.[59]

Not only, then, were many zoologists and botanists more related to each other in their scientific investigations than Pearse and Blomquist wanted to admit, but Pearse also happens to afford an interesting example of how Duke's relative smallness as a research university and the physical proximity of its various science buildings facilitated communication and contact across departmental lines. Remembering a dinner club he had enjoyed in Madison, Wisconsin, Pearse took the lead in organizing the eight-member "Octopus Club" at Duke. Consisting originally of Pearse in zoology, Wolf in botany, Gross in chemistry, Nielsen in physics, Bayard Carter in obstetrics-gynecology, David Smith in bacteriology, Joseph Markee in anatomy, and William Perlzweig in biochemistry, the group obviously could never bog down in narrow specializations during its gatherings. Another club to which Pearse belonged, this one for weekly luncheons on campus, had an even broader composition, for in addition to Pearse, Gross and Markee from the dinner group, John Tate Lanning in history, Calvin D. Hoover in economics, Taylor Cole in political science, Clarence Gohdes in English, Glenn Negley in philosophy, and Benjamin Powell, the librarian of Duke University, constituted its membership for a number of years.[60]

Clearly a lively person, both professionally and socially, Pearse also required special handling, for like many, possibly most, academics he was all too human in his need for ego sustainment. President Few, upon receipt of a copy of a new book by Pearse, thanked and congratulated him and added an extra stroke or pat by saying that he (Few) took the opportunity again "to express to you my particular satisfaction in having you as one of us."[61] Although Few was certainly no manipulator or glad-hander, he probably did more of that type of morale-building in informal conversations. Yet Pearse, for reasons that are only partly clear, gradually began to criticize Few's administrative leadership. When the depression hit Duke in the spring of 1933, Few and Flowers, trying their best to avoid reduction in the work force, asked all heads of departments and schools for suggestions about economy measures. Pearse responded with a long letter that must have been hard for Few to evaluate, for it combined serious suggestions with extreme ones that may or may not have been seriously intended. Pearse began by pointing out a painful but probably correct fact: Duke, even in normal times, was "trying to develop more types of activities than can be taken care of with the available income." From that premise, Pearse argued that rather than maintain "a mediocre, widely-advertised, and inadequately financed graduate school," it might be better to abandon the graduate school altogether (and cease to be a research university). If not that, why not seize the opportunity offered by the global economic crisis and drop certain whole fields of endeavor? The engineering department, Pearse argued, was undeveloped, and he suggested it as a likely target for elimination.

Coming down to more limited suggestions, Pearse pointed to the separate classes for freshman and some sophomore women as a costly, inefficient arrangement, particularly in the natural sciences. He proposed eliminating the free tuition for the children of Methodist ministers and abolition of the "News Service, Comptroller [Frank Brown], Chief Engineer, Dean of Freshman, and the Y.M.C.A." Pearse opposed any reduction in stipends for graduate students, wages for service employees, or support for the library and closed with a few practical suggestions for cost-cutting in the biology department.[62] Altogether the letter was something of a grab bag, and Few probably knew, or thought he knew, which parts to take seriously and which to dismiss as the musings of one who frequently "spouted off."

More serious, perhaps, was Pearse's chronic complaint that members of the zoology department were overburdened with teaching—and zoology was a popular major for pre-medical students. Having earlier argued the point, he wrote Few in 1938 that he had read the president's annual report in which Few emphasized the strengthening of the graduate school. "Please accept my resignation as chairman of the Department of Zoology," Pearse continued, for he claimed that he could no longer "look the department in the face." The department's request for an additional instructor had been denied; the undergraduate teaching load was so great that there was no "time to build up graduate work"; the biology building was crowded by the presence of the School of Forestry, and so on. Claiming that zoology had 61 students per faculty member while botany had 34 and forestry 4.6, Pearse noted that a new instructor had been authorized in botany. "My feeling is that I have been a complete failure as Chairman of the Zoology department," Pearse concluded, and he wished to resign. "Apparently hard work and honest service are of no value. Perhaps I am incompetent. I am certainly a troublemaker."[63]

Few did not reply in writing to Pearse's letter and did not accept the resignation. Pearse may well have talked even earlier of resigning from the chairmanship, for on at least two occasions, in a different context, he had threatened to resign as editor of *Ecological Monographs* but then been mollified and gone on with the task. At any rate, the following year Pearse took his grievances to Wannamaker and, after arguing for four additional instructors in zoology, again offered his resignation and blamed his "personal deficiencies" for the department's problems.[64]

Pearse may or may not have been surprised, but Few and Wannamaker in 1940 finally did accept Pearse's resignation and named a reluctant Irving E. Gray as chairman of zoology. As Gray generously noted a year or so later, Pearse continued to be "the guiding force and inspiration for the department." Pearse, Gray reported, worked untiringly for both graduate and undergraduate students and used his own resources to help some of the first group; an internationally recognized zoologist, he remained "the most popular man on our staff."[65]

Henry Oosting, an ecologist in the botany department, was a different type of man from Pearse, but in an interesting, reflective letter prompted by the ending of his tenth year at Duke, Oosting furnished another perspective on Duke in the 1930s and early 1940s before the impact of World War II was fully felt on campus. Teaching both graduate and undergraduate (including freshman) students each year, Oosting noted that he had supervised ten master's theses and four doctoral dissertations, engaged in various activities both on campus and in professional organizations, and published eleven papers, with two more in press and two manuscripts in preparation. "I have done some good research," he declared. "None of it has been spectacular but all has been sound." Ecological work in the Southeast was relatively new, and he thought his could not be disregarded for some years to come.

Oosting noted that he had the major responsibility of student advising for all of the male undergraduates in botany and for some of the women. Moreover, he and his wife had entertained students in their home regularly, sixty-seven of them in the semester just ending and some of them more than once; they had served as faculty sponsors for a sorority and attended their meetings and parties; and they had supported a program to foster student-faculty relations, which was sponsored by the Young Men's Christian Association and the Young Women's Christian Association, by entertaining the Sunday evening groups once or twice each semester and attending student-faculty luncheons.

In replying graciously to Oosting's letter, Wannamaker pointed out that in exerting themselves to have personal and friendly contact with students, the Oostings were doing something important. Wannamaker might well have added that all of those who had known Trinity College before 1925, both alumni and faculty, hoped fervently that in the process of becoming a research university Duke would not lose the friendliness and human warmth that had characterized the smaller, less complex institution. Clearly, as long as there were people like the Oostings around, the old tradition survived.[66]

The physics department at Duke, at least initially, was not as lucky as either chemistry or biology in making the transition from small college to research university. Short of numerous miracles, the whole transformation was bound to pose multiple problems, and one of the more discernible of them came in physics. Interpersonal difficulties within the department hampered its development, so much so that at one point in the mid-1930s Wannamaker declared privately to Few that he hesitated to suggest bringing any young person into the department, for he considered it "really a no-man's land, totally lacking direction and guidance and [it] is becoming worse."[67]

Charles W. Edwards, who had become professor of physics in Trinity College in 1898, chaired the department. Having grown up in Randolph County near Trinity before its relocation in Durham, Edwards had long, close associations with the college and graduated from it in 1894. He then took a master's degree at Tulane, studied a year at Columbia, and then received another master's from New York University in 1898. The lack of a Ph.D. did not prevent Edwards from becoming an energetic, effective teacher at Trinity and a popular lecturer in the schools and colleges of the region. Having been at Trinity-Duke about as long as Flowers and Few had, he obviously represented an important link with the past. He also wrote a few scientific papers and collaborated with a prominent physicist, Robert A. Millikan, on a standard college textbook in physics. But the lack of the doctorate clearly posed problems when the training of candidates for that degree became a prime purpose of Duke's graduate school, and that lack, and various problems growing from it, may have lain at the root of the department's problems.

Charles C. Hatley, another graduate of Trinity in the class of 1913, taught physics at Southern College in Florida for several years before returning to teach at Trinity in 1917. Hatley, however, took off long enough to obtain his doctorate at Columbia in 1924.

When the expansion began in 1925, the first to join Edwards and Hatley was Walter M. Nielsen. With a new Ph.D. from the University of Minnesota, Nielsen came as an instructor in the fall of 1925. Winning a National Research fellowship a few years later, he showed real promise as an investigator in the field of cosmic ray research, but obviously was only at the start of what would be a long, productive career, including significant service to Duke.

Trouble began early. Neither the full scope nor the exact nature of it can be discovered and understood at this late date, but that hardly matters. The fact that Edwards fell out with and had deep misgivings about both Hatley and Nielsen is clear from the record. Writing about just that matter to Few in 1926, Edwards sought to win the president's support and included a somewhat strange warning: "With the hearty support of the administration I can be a real asset to the University. Under present conditions I will be quite the opposite."[68]

Given this problem, which had to be lived with rather than solved, Few involved himself much more in the building of the physics department than was the case with either chemistry or biology. He sought, in fact, to make a "star" appointment that would at one stroke, he hoped,

solve the problem of departmental governance and raise the national profile of physics at Duke. Writing to one leader in the field, Few explained
that Duke needed an outstanding man "who would be widely recognized
as being among the foremost physicists in the country." He added that
there were no other needs in physics, or in other departments, except for
very promising young men who might in time become "teachers or [sic]
scholars" of the first rank.[69]

Edwards too apparently joined in the search, for a distinguished physicist at Minnesota, who had taught Nielsen and who was the managing
editor of *Physical Review*, wrote Edwards that under certain conditions he
might be interested in coming to Duke. The first consideration would be
the quality and number of graduate students, which would largely depend
on fellowship support, and the second important concern would be the
adequacy of the laboratories and equipment. He would leave Minnesota
reluctantly, the physicist explained, and in view of his position and prospects there, he would not consider a salary of less than $10,000 a year.[70]
Since that salary was out of the ballpark in arts and sciences at Duke, as
well as at most other universities at that time, the Minnesotan obviously
had no serious interest in the possible move.

Persisting in the search for a distinguished physicist, Few, even as he
coped with numerous larger problems such as obtaining the additional
money needed to open a four-year medical school, may have at least come
close to landing a prize catch. In the course of his search for a top-flight
physicist he had quickly encountered the name of Arthur H. Compton, a
recent Nobel Prize winner at the University of Chicago. The record is not
clear, but Compton may have visited Duke, and he and Few seem to have
hit it off rather well. At any rate, in July, 1929, Compton wrote Few that
the invitation to come to Duke was "the only one of a dozen recent offers"
to which he had given "serious attention." Despite the attractions of the
position at Duke, however, Compton explained that he could not help but
feel that "the place for me to do my best work is at Chicago." He doubted
that his position there would ever be as attractive financially as the offer
Few had made (and the record does not reveal what it was), but Compton
believed that he could simply carry on his scientific investigations better
at Chicago than at any other place he knew.[71]

In explaining Compton's decision to George Allen in New York, Few
noted that Compton was "a wise and good man as well as a great scientist, and no doubt reached his conclusion out of considerations as to
how he may make his life count for most in the service of science and
humanity." Few added that, as far as he could tell, the "thing that counted
most" with Compton was "whether in any near future we could build up
strong and well-balanced departments in the allied sciences which would
be necessary for the satisfactory pursuit of his researches in physics." The

whole episode, Few concluded, showed clearly "how very difficult it is today to get men of the highest order." Nevertheless, Few avowed that "I am trying my best to learn the lesson and to do my best to remove every obstacle I can remove from the way of such men who may from time to time consider the question of coming to us."[72]

In the final analysis, perhaps the major obstacle in the way of attracting outstanding figures such as Compton was one that Few struggled valiantly but futilely to overcome: the lack of adequate endowment for Duke University. Officials at the Rockefeller Foundation held that view, which they privately conveyed to Few, and he believed that somehow Compton too had been made aware of the foundation's appraisal. Few, at any rate, seized the occasion to advise William R. Perkins that he wished soon to discuss the whole matter with Perkins, Allen, and, if possible, Mrs. James B. Duke.[73] Few had no way of knowing, of course, that events soon to take place on Wall Street in October, 1929, would make further discussion of adding to Duke's endowment highly moot for quite a long period.

Although the physics department had not yet been set up on the "new university basis," as Few put it, physics had to be taught to a significant number of students. To help in that task, the department in 1929 added David W. Carpenter as an instructor. A native North Carolinian who received three degrees from Duke—bachelor of science, master of science, and Ph.D.—Carpenter soon became the department's supervisor for freshman studies and for many years would fill that post in a highly conscientious and effective fashion. The following year, 1930, Frank Woodbridge Constant joined the department. A Princeton undergraduate, he had received his doctorate at Yale and taught briefly at the California Institute of Technology before coming to Duke. And although Few found that even providing the sometimes expensive laboratory facilities for promising experimental physicists could be a problem, another was added in 1932. James Carlyle Mouzon came to Duke the same year he received his Ph.D. from the California Institute of Technology. Mouzon had been an undergraduate at Southern Methodist University and was the son of a prominent Methodist bishop who was a close friend of Few's. In advising the bishop about the situation in physics at Duke, Few noted that Duke had an excellent "college department, with a staff adequate in number, I think, and thoroughly first-rate for college physics." Some of the young experimental physicists on the staff had promise, if the university could provide the facilities they needed, but the attempt to lure Compton to Duke had failed. Consequently, Few continued, Duke was experimenting with "young men of the highest promise, in the hope of developing some of them into distinguished physicists." They were not paid much at first, and their only hope for advancement was "through work of the highest order."[74] No doubt fully apprised of the situation by his father, young Mouzon accepted the challenge that Few had described and began his distinguished career at Duke, although he would leave the university for other opportunities during and after World War II.

A lucky windfall brought Hertha Sponer, one of the top women physicists in the world, to Duke in 1936. Born in Germany in 1895, Sponer received her doctorate from the University of Göttingen in 1920, studied for a year at the Kaiser-Wilhelm-Institut, and returned to Göttingen to teach. The publication in 1925 of her study of molecular spectra and their application to certain chemical problems, along with other scholarly papers, helped place her in the front ranks of women physicists. When Hitler's Nazis came to power in Germany, however, Sponer found her academic and scientific future jeopardized. She was not Jewish, but the Nazis frowned on women in academic posts (rather than in the home, having babies), and Sponer fled Germany in 1934 to teach at the University of Oslo in Norway.[75]

An official of the Rockefeller Foundation, which sponsored a program to assist displaced German scholars, informed Edwards in late 1933 of Sponer's possible availability. Edwards strongly endorsed the idea of trying to secure Sponer, though how others in the department felt about the matter is not known. A woman historian at Duke who had known Sponer in California reported that, aside from speaking English fluently, Sponer, of all the German women she had known, "fitted most successfully into an American academic atmosphere." Along with "feminine charm," she was said to have "a distinctly academic outlook and attitude, and a thorough appreciation of the problem of 'fitting in.'" In short, Sponer was described as "everything that one could look for in an academic woman."[76]

Few and Wannamaker, possibly because of the continuing governance problem in the physics department, may at first have dragged their feet a bit about Sponer. Wannamaker, as noted earlier, described the department about this time as a "no-man's land" that lacked direction and a situation into which he hesitated to bring any young scholar. Nevertheless, in the spring of 1935, the administrators authorized Edwards to invite Sponer to come to Duke that fall. Because she had work that she wished to complete at Oslo, Sponer asked, and Duke agreed, that she be allowed to come in the spring of 1936. Not many weeks after her arrival, Few informed the Rockefeller Foundation that since Duke liked Sponer, and vice versa, the university would, with partial help from the foundation for three years, like to keep her. "We are glad to have a scholar of her standing and promise," Few declared. The foundation promptly agreed to help, and Hertha Sponer threw in her lot with Duke.[77]

One of the many persons from whom Few sought advice about Duke's problems in physics was Robert A. Millikan of the California Institute of

Technology. Not long after the people at Duke had made their positive assessment of Hertha Sponer, Millikan advised, among other things, that in "introducing young blood into a department of physics" he should expect to go farther in influence and get more for his money if he "picked one or two of the most outstanding younger men, rather than if I filled one of my openings with a woman."[78]

Unfortunately for Few's reputation among feminists, he remained, in replying to Millikan, very much a male of his era. Admitting that he mainly agreed with Millikan's position, Few explained that Duke had a coordinate college for women, and from the spokesperson of the relatively few women on the faculty (Alice Baldwin) came a "constant pressure to have brought in a small number of more distinguished women." Help from the Rockefeller Foundation had made Sponer's case easier, and she was, of course, Few concluded, "like the other women on the Woman's College foundation."[79] Just what that "foundation" was, Few did not explain, but it obviously gave him some sort of consolation to think there was such a thing.

While Few may well have later grown more fully to appreciate Sponer's presence at Duke, it did not, after all, solve the department's basic problem. And it was one with which Few and Wannamaker continued to wrestle. In 1935 Few returned to Duke's staunch friend and alumnus at Columbia, George Pegram, and asked if he could not find "a man in Physics of the caliber of Dr. Gross, whom you secured for us in Chemistry some years ago." Pegram replied that what Few requested was not an easy task, for he knew of only one person in physics of whom he was as certain as he had been about Gross—and that person was someone at Columbia whom Pegram wanted to keep there.[80]

Acting on advice from Gross, Few and Wannamaker next went after a rising young theoretical physicist named Edward Teller, who was also a refugee from Germany and was then at George Washington University in the nation's capital. When Teller declined Wannamaker's first offer, Few wrote him asking if he would be willing to come as a visiting professor for a year, with Duke paying his regular salary ($4,400) plus $1,000 for any additional expenses he might have. Few added that Teller's schedule could be arranged so that he could spend three days in the middle of the week at Duke and have long weekends in Washington to keep up with the experiments he had going there. "At the present stage of the development in Physics here," Few somewhat plaintively concluded, "you could be of service to us and to the cause." Despite the entreaty, Teller responded that he simply could not spend so much time away from his work in Washington, but he hoped to continue to pursue the common research interests he held with Sponer and Nielsen.[81]

The situation in the department had become such that Charles Hatley took it upon himself in 1936 to write Wannamaker urging that Nielsen and Mouzon be promoted. Hatley argued that both men were doing work of the highest type, with Nielsen for all practical purposes supervising the graduate work in the department and Mouzon teaching graduate (as well as undergraduate) courses and directing theses. Yet after eleven years at Duke Nielsen was still an assistant professor and Mouzon an instructor. They could do their work no better if promoted, Hatley admitted, but it would put the department in a better light.[82]

What Hatley did not explain, perhaps because he knew that Wannamaker well understood, was that students, especially graduate students, often became the indirect but quite real victims when departments developed problems such as physics had. The problems for students could take many forms, but academia is full of stories, by no means all apocryphal, of graduate students who fail their qualifying examinations or their dissertation defense, at least initially, upon getting caught in the crossfire of feuding professors.

At any rate, by 1936 Few and Wannamaker obviously decided that they had been patient, humane, and politic long enough. Few quietly named a committee consisting of Wannamaker, Nielsen, and Hatley to supervise the operations of the physics department and prepare the budget. Then, in 1937, Walter Nielsen was named chairman to replace Edwards, who continued teaching in the department until his retirement in 1944.[83]

As Nielsen assumed the chairmanship, another important newcomer joined the department in the fall of 1937. Lothar Wolfgang Nordheim was another displaced German scholar who, as in many other such cases, enriched the United States as he fled Nazi Germany. With his Ph.D. from Göttingen in 1923, Nordheim was a theoretical physicist who taught at several universities in Germany and elsewhere in Europe before coming to the United States. At Purdue when Few invited him to come to Duke, Nordheim promptly accepted the offer. In his case also, Duke received temporary help from the Rockefeller-funded Emergency Committee in Aid of Displaced German Scholars. Nordheim was destined to play a prominent role as a nuclear physicist at the Oak Ridge, Tennessee, laboratories during World War II and continued to add distinction to Duke's physics department long after the war.[84]

Development of physics at Duke had been partially handicapped for about a decade. But with Nielsen as chairman and Sponer, Nordheim, and some of the younger members on the staff, the department was finally ready to move. World War II would, of course, interfere with that process, but the war had barely ended before Duke began making large, auspicious plans for its physics department.

Closely related to physics was the mathematics department. In Trinity College, for many years after 1891 the name of Robert L. Flowers was synonymous with mathematics. A graduate of the United States Naval Academy whose later and universally used title of "Doctor" was strictly honorary, Flowers apparently made no pretense of being a research scholar. The record abundantly suggests, however, that he was a popular, even beloved teacher whose patience, skill, and charm captivated Trinity students over a long period. Towards the end of World War II, when Flowers was in his mid-seventies and president of Duke, a former student wrote to him:

> Twenty-six years have passed since I sat in your class room. The kindness [toward] and love for your students which you reflected in your class room is to me to-day as fresh and alive as then. I do not remember so much of the mathematics you taught . . . but I have carried in my heart and mind all these years those principles and truths of righteous living which you in your unconscious influence shed on those of us who had the honor and privilege to sit with you.[85]

Having been named secretary of the college in 1910 when Few became president, Flowers had important administrative responsibilities from that time onward, and the job of treasurer or business manager was also assigned to him soon after 1910. When the university was organized Flowers became the vice president for finance while also keeping his older title of secretary-treasurer. Although he continued to teach until 1926, he had, of course, curtailed the amount of teaching after 1910. A more convivial and accessible person than Few, Flowers enjoyed great popularity with alumni and friends of Trinity. Yet the fact that Flowers retained the nominal title of chairman of the mathematics department perhaps complicated its development in the early years of the university.

Two other mathematicians from the Trinity era carried over into the new university. Charles B. Markham was a Trinity alumnus (1906) who had continued in the college for a master's degree in mathematics and then joined the teaching staff in 1909. Named assistant treasurer in 1911, he continued to teach in the department until 1929, though, like Flowers, he was obviously not full time there. In 1941 he was named treasurer of the university and would play a key administrative role until his death in 1955. The other carryover, Karl B. Patterson, joined the Trinity faculty in 1920. A graduate of Roanoke College with a master's degree from Princeton in 1905, Patterson had taught for a number of years in Lenoir College and then Durham High School before coming to Trinity.

The first Ph.D. in the department came in 1925, William W. Elliott. A graduate of Hampden-Sydney College who received his doctorate at Cornell in 1923, Elliott would eventually write a widely used textbook in college mathematics. And at the end of his forty-three years of teaching at Duke, he calculated that he had taught over ten thousand students.[86]

Another newcomer, William W. Rankin, arrived in 1926. Also one who taught predominantly undergraduates, Rankin graduated from North Carolina State before obtaining a master's degree at the University of North Carolina in Chapel Hill. He taught at a number of colleges before coming to Duke and carried on the Trinity-Duke tradition of service by founding and for many years running the Duke University Mathematics Institute for Teachers.

The graduate aspect of work in mathematics had not been forgotten, for in 1927 Few corresponded with an established mathematician at the University of Illinois about the chances of his coming to Duke. Part of the package that Few offered was the possibility of launching a new, Duke-supported journal in mathematics. The Illinois professor ultimately decided against coming to Duke, but the idea of a journal to be edited and published at Duke remained alive.[87]

George B. Pegram at Columbia helped Few in determining the ideas of leading mathematicians about a new journal at Duke and reported that there was considerable sentiment in favor of the proposal. Likewise, the secretary of the American Mathematical Society advised Few that since the production of scholarly papers had increased steadily through the 1920s, some journals were already too large, and a "crisis" loomed in the field. He thought the society would welcome a new journal.[88] The onset of the depression after 1929 delayed the new journal at Duke for several years, but apparently it was in conjunction with that venture and the search for an editor of the projected journal that Duke made one of its most high-powered appointments in mathematics during the early years.

Joseph M. Thomas did his undergraduate and graduate work at the University of Pennsylvania, completing the latter in 1923. The fact that he won a National Research fellowship and worked at Princeton, Harvard, and in Paris during the years from 1924 to 1927 marked him as a mathematician of great promise. Coming to Duke in 1930 after teaching at Pennsylvania, Thomas proved unable to obtain any outside funding to help in the launching of the new journal, and the appearance of the *Duke Mathematical Journal*, edited by Thomas, was delayed until 1935. When it did appear, however, the secretary of the Mathematical Society conveyed congratulations to Thomas, Few, and Flowers. "It was not thought by anybody that a new journal could start off at such a high level in quality and quantity," the prominent mathematician declared, "and I have heard very many compliments about the first volume." He thought the journal had already assumed a distinguished place "among the significant mathematical periodicals of the world."[89] Thomas would win a star in *American Men of Science* and remain at Duke until his resignation in 1965. Yet in one sense, as will be explained, Thomas and Duke were mismatched, at least in that early era.

In 1929, a year before Thomas came to Duke, Arthur Hickson joined the department. A Canadian who graduated from Acadia University, Hickson received his doctorate at Chicago in 1928 and would remain at Duke until his retirement many years later.

In 1930 Julia Dale became the first woman mathematician at Duke. She had received her doctorate from Cornell in 1924 and apparently proved to be a highly regarded teacher in the Woman's College, for upon her untimely death from an illness in 1936, Dean Alice Baldwin and other faculty and students in the Woman's College established in her memory the annual Julia Dale Prize in mathematics.[90]

John H. Roberts and Leonard Carlitz were two important additions in 1931 and 1932 respectively. Roberts was a Texan who received his undergraduate degree as well as his doctorate from the University of Texas. Also a National Research fellow at Pennsylvania in 1929–30, Roberts would toward the end of his forty-year career at Duke serve as chairman of the department. Carlitz was another find at Pennsylvania, where he had done both his undergraduate and doctoral work. His supervising professor there reported that Carlitz "so far excelled the other students here as to be literally in a class by himself." Only the "serious financial situation" at Pennsylvania, the professor explained, kept them from offering Carlitz a position there, and he was being considered at several major universities. From Oxford University, where Carlitz was doing postdoctoral work, came word that a paper published by him in the *Oxford Quarterly Journal* had made an excellent impression and shown that he was "fully master of the technique of his trade." The Oxford don opined that Carlitz was no doubt "better equipped in the analytic theory of numbers than anyone else in America."[91] Coming to Duke in 1932, Carlitz fully lived up to the glowing recommendations, for he would have a highly creative and distinguished career entirely at Duke.

In 1933, the year following the arrival of Carlitz, one of Duke's first Ph.D.'s in mathematics became a member of the department. Francis G. Dressel obtained a B.S. at Michigan State before receiving a master's degree at the University of Michigan in 1929. He then came to Duke, where he completed his doctorate the same year that he became an instructor. A productive scholar as well as a conscientious and effective teacher, he too would spend his full career at Duke.

Within less than a decade the mathematics department had clearly been vastly strengthened insofar as its scholarly or research dimension was concerned. Joseph M. Thomas believed that dimension to be the only one that truly mattered and proceeded to fight vigorously for his viewpoint. For reasons that are discussed more fully in the chapter on the Woman's College, Dean Alice Baldwin strongly argued that at least some women should be named to Duke's faculty in arts and sciences. Moreover, Few generally supported that policy, within certain limits. When Julia Dale died in 1936, Few and Wannamaker agreed with Baldwin that a woman mathematician should be found to replace Dale.

Thomas vehemently disagreed. He began his argument with the proposition that Duke's administration wanted a mathematics department comparable with the best, and he thought that such an end was achievable— *if* every opportunity to make an appointment were used with that goal in view. Thomas then noted that the reputation of the department rested "solely upon its accomplishments in research," and that "the really good teachers in University work are almost invariably found among research men." Thomas maintained that "a person who does not do research in his chosen subject is as a rule not mentally alert enough to make a good teacher."

Turning to the mathematicians already at Duke, Thomas asserted that "an optimistic estimate of the dead weight [i.e., nonresearchers] would be over 60 percent, and there is no superiority in teaching as an offset." As for appointing a woman, Thomas maintained that "such a course would probably only increase the dead weight in the end because there is no suitable woman candidate in the United States." Thomas went even further and argued that there was "no woman mathematician who has been actively engaged in research for at least the last ten years and none who gives any promise of becoming such a mathematician."[92]

Several of Thomas's colleagues joined him in another letter soon after the first one, and they hammered away at the proposition that "the position should be given to the best qualified person available, irrespective of sex, and that the primary qualification, the sine qua non, is research: a record in the past, activity at present and promise for the future." An examination of the records of the women candidates who had been suggested revealed that "none of them satisfies the standard to which we wish future members of the Department to conform." Thomas and his allies suggested that the opportunity be seized to appoint a man who not only had the qualifications stressed above but who could also solve the department's problem with the chairmanship. They believed they had just such a man in John J. Gergen.[93] Since women scholars in mathematics were, in fact, then a scarce commodity, and since even Alice Baldwin, who was herself a genuine scholar, conceded that there were too few productive women scholars in mathematics, Thomas and his allies won their point. Gergen received the appointment.

A Minnesotan who had received his undergraduate training at the University of Minnesota, Gergen got his doctorate from Rice in 1928 and won a National Research fellowship that allowed him to work at several leading universities in this country and in Europe over a two-year period. He was teaching at the University of Rochester when he came to Duke as an associate professor in 1936. In the following year he became chairman of the department and tenaciously held that position until his death in 1967. Gergen's name had come up at Duke as far back as 1932, in fact, when a Harvard professor had written that Gergen aimed "very high indeed" and was "on the track of *important* things in the field of analytic number theory." The Harvard man thought Gergen was "sure to be a mathematician of importance and that he may go very far indeed."[94]

In gaining Gergen, Thomas and those in the department who agreed with him had made an important point: in a research university, scholarly productivity, either proven or clearly promised, had to be a prime consideration. Aside from the special situation of the Woman's College, few persons in a research university could seriously disagree with the principles that Thomas and his allies had enunciated. Thomas, however, actually carried the argument one step further, and there he came into serious conflict with one of Duke's main purposes.

As envisioned by Few and then supported by Wannamaker and various others, Duke was to be a different kind of research university in that undergraduates and the teaching of them were to be valued and emphasized alongside the graduate and purely scholarly aspects. It was certainly a difficult, tension-filled policy—both for the administrators of the policy and for the individual faculty members who lived with and exemplified it. That it was not impossible, however, was clearly shown in many cases at Duke. Thomas, probably like a few other more timid or less articulate faculty members at Duke, had no interest in teaching undergraduates or sympathy with the idea that it was an important matter that deserved consideration. This became clear when Gergen, Carlitz, and Roberts joined in recommending a younger member of the department for promotion to assistant professor. They argued that the person in question was a competent, demanding teacher; had proven to be dependable and cooperative in carrying on the work of the department; and had a publication record that, while "not impressive," was "not vacuous" either and promised to improve. Thomas, on the other hand, argued that the department was already top-heavy and that the instructor's alleged skill as a teacher was a judgment based on the untrustworthy basis of students' opinions. "As a general proposition," Thomas added, "I should like to protest against students' opinions being given any weight in determining promotions." Only "indisputable scientific achievement," Thomas declared, should carry weight in considering promotion.[95]

Thomas lost that particular battle, and the instructor gained the promotion and a raise. Many years later, when Thomas angrily resigned from Duke only a couple of years before the time he would have had to retire anyhow, he no doubt had an accumulation of grievances against both his department and the university. One that he made explicit, however, was the "continuing attempt to coerce me to teach courses some of which were at the undergraduate level and none of which were of my choosing."[96] For some thirty-six years, Thomas had managed to put up with his mismatch with Duke, but it obviously became ultimately intolerable to him.

Engineering at Duke in its early phase had no scholars at all comparable to Thomas, for the subject was taught not in a separate college or school but in an undergraduate department. In fact, for a decade or so after the university was organized, Few and his advisors seemed uncertain as to what to do about engineering, and only gradually and pragmatically did they move toward a solution to the problem.

Introduced into Trinity College as early as 1887 by President Crowell, engineering was taught by Robert Flowers when he arrived from the Naval Academy. The field of study more or less disappeared from 1893 until 1903, but from then on it became a regular offering.

William H. Hall in civil engineering joined the Trinity faculty in 1915. After attending the Naval Academy for two years, he had transferred to Trinity, graduated in 1909, and taught school for several years before returning to Trinity for a master's degree. The year before he joined the Trinity faculty, Hall went to the University of Michigan for another bachelor's degree in civil engineering. An important link between Trinity and Duke in the field of engineering, Hall received a master's degree from Wisconsin in 1927 and would later become the first dean of the College of Engineering when it was organized in 1939.

Few, in his important memorandum to J. B. Duke in 1921, had included "a School of Engineering (emphasizing chemical and electrical engineering)" along with the other professional schools that he hoped to see established in the new university. Following Few's original outline fairly closely, J. B. Duke in his indenture creating the Duke Endowment had listed the various components of the proposed Duke University, naming as the last two "a Medical School and an Engineering School, as and when funds are available."

The final phrase turned out to be more significant than J. B. Duke perhaps realized, for as matters turned out there certainly were not sufficient funds for a separate school of engineering. Even if there had been, a "school," as that name was originally used at Duke, would have made no sense, for the pattern of engineering education as involving only or primarily a four-year, undergraduate education had been well established in the nineteenth century. With Rensselaer Polytechnic Institute (1824) and then the Massachusetts Institute of Technology (1865) as standard-setters, engineering courses and departments had been added in numerous liberal arts colleges some years before Trinity made the innovation in 1887.[97] In other words, Few had used the term "school" somewhat carelessly in his 1921 memorandum, for the professional schools he envisioned, and that actually took shape at Duke, were essentially for the post-baccalaureate training of those students who had graduated from four-year colleges and not, certainly, for undergraduates. At any rate, undergraduate engineering was alive and well at Trinity as the university was organized, but it too needed strengthening along with the other departments.

The first addition was destined to be a most important one, for Walter J. Seeley, who came in 1925 to teach electrical engineering, played a large role in the steady development of engineering at Duke. Born in Pennsylvania in 1894, Seeley graduated from the Polytechnic Institute of Brooklyn in 1917. After serving as an ensign in the United States Navy in World War I, he became an instructor at the University of Pennsylvania and received a master's degree in physics just before taking the job at Duke. Many years later, as Seeley was retiring in fact, a newspaperman described him in words that would no doubt have been just as applicable to the young man of 1925. Terming Seeley, who was short in stature, a "human dynamo," the journalist wrote: "He arrived exactly at the appointed hour, this ramrod-straight little man whose youthful, dapper appearance, eye-twinkle and springy step belie his nearly 70 years."[98]

In 1926 Harold C. Bird in civil engineering joined Hall and Seeley. A Yale-trained engineer, Bird taught at Pennsylvania Military College for a number of years and briefly worked in industry before coming to Duke. He would later serve for many years as the head of the Department of Civil Engineering.

Guided and influenced in the case of engineering as in many other areas by the discipline's chief accrediting body, Few and Hall kept in close touch with the national Society for the Promotion of Engineering Education. Apparently in response to the society's suggestions, in 1927 engineering at Duke was reorganized into separate departments of civil and electrical engineering, and the following year the bachelor of science degree, requiring 138 semester hours (as compared to 126 hours for the arts degree), was reinstated for engineers. The curricula of both civil and electrical engineering were revised to correspond closely to standards set by the accrediting body.[99]

When the new buildings on the West campus were opened in the fall of 1930, the engineers became unique by being the only male students left behind on East campus. Southgate became the engineers' dormitory, and a group of old buildings in the northwest corner of the campus, buildings that had been used by Trinity Park Preparatory School until its demise in 1922, housed the classrooms and laboratories for the engineers. Bivins, which was used by the civil engineers, had been described when new by the *Durham Recorder* in 1900 as "truly a work of art . . . a three-storied structure, built of face brick, covered with slate and trimmed with granite."[100] Thirty years later, and in comparison with the sparkling new Georgian buildings on East campus, Bivins probably did not look as impressive as it had in 1900. Asbury building, which had served as the classroom building for Trinity Park School, housed the electrical engineers.

To launch mechanical engineering at Duke, young Ralph T. Mathews, fresh from his graduation at Tufts College, came in 1930. Mathews may have been the only teacher at Duke who had the distinction first of helping to choose his own boss and then later of designing his own building. The boss was Ralph S. Wilbur, who came in 1933 and beginning in 1937 chaired the new Department of Mechanical Engineering. A graduate of Tufts in 1908, Wilbur taught at several schools, including a long stint at the Naval Academy's postgraduate school, before coming to Duke.

With the first six mechanical engineers graduating in 1934, the department was not large, but it grew steadily, and housing the equipment needed in its laboratories was a problem. Mathews later recalled that in motoring down the East Coast in his new Model A Ford to assume the post at Duke, he had stopped at Yale, Princeton, Pennsylvania, Johns Hopkins, and a couple of other schools to see their mechanical engineering laboratories. He had been struck by the huge size and obsoleteness of the old steam engines, pumps, and boilers he saw in those laboratories and had vowed that "Duke would have small but modern equipment with good instruments for measurement, if I had any say in the matter."

Mathews did gain a say, and when workmen began in the fall of 1934 to tear down the old Branson building, which had been a four-story dormitory for the school, Wilbur and Mathews persuaded Flowers to have a new Branson built for mechanical engineering. Wilbur and Mathews successfully argued that some of the old building material could be reused, in combination with face brick, for the new Branson. "I worked day and night for a couple of weeks drawing up the plans," Mathews later explained. The administration promptly approved the plans, and in about three months' time the new Branson was completed. Small but efficiently designed for its purpose, Branson served as the mechanical engineering laboratory until after World War II and then, in a strange turnaround, became for many years the venue for theater-in-the-round productions by the Duke Players.

Mathews, in addition to his role as a mini-Trumbauer, also offered interesting insights into certain policies that were followed in engineering in the 1930s. In the courses in mechanical engineering, he noted, basic theory and principles were emphasized and applied courses in diesel engines, airplanes, and so on were ruled out. The faculty members were urged to concentrate on "becoming good teachers" rather than dividing their time and energy between teaching and research, "doing neither well." The laboratory facilities were not for research but to provide the students with practical demonstrations of theories and principles; and those facilities were modern with small or medium-size equipment and the best instruments and apparatus.[101]

A third person in mechanical engineering, Frederick J. Reed, came in 1935. A graduate of Stevens Institute of Technology, Reed worked in industry while studying part-time for his master's degree at the University of Pittsburgh. He obtained that degree in 1931 and taught at Vanderbilt for several years before coming to Duke.

Electrical engineering also expanded. Otto Meier, Jr., joined that department in 1934, replacing a faculty member who had resigned. With an undergraduate degree from the University of Pennsylvania, Meier also received a master's degree at the University of Michigan and after World War II would obtain a Ph.D. at Pennsylvania. He would spend his full career at Duke and serve his discipline as well as the larger university community in a variety of ways.

In civil engineering, James Wesley Williams joined Hall, Bird, and one or two others in 1937. A Duke A.B. in 1930, Williams went to the Georgia Institute of Technology for his degree in civil engineering. He taught at Weaver Junior College and Brevard for a few years before returning to Duke for graduate work the year before he was appointed as an instructor; he would later receive a master's degree at Harvard.

Growth in engineering at Duke during the 1930s closely paralleled that in the larger departments in arts and sciences. In 1930 there had been four faculty members, and in 1938 there were nine. The student body numbered 101 in 1930 and rose to 167 by 1937 and 201 in the following year. But there clearly were problems. Uncertainty about the permanence of the engineering department's location was a handicap and may have affected the morale of the faculty. Engineering had a larger number of young instructors who remained only briefly at Duke than was the case in other departments.

President Few was aware of the problem. Harold Bird informed him in 1936 that while alumni and visitors were pleased with the obvious progress engineering had made, they often failed to appreciate the small classes and personal attention enjoyed by engineering students. Rather, "they immediately contrast our buildings with those [Gothic buildings] on the New Campus." Bird thought a new, well-equipped dormitory for engineers built adjacent to Bivins, Branson, and Asbury would vastly improve the situation.[102]

Few and others obviously agreed, for the next month, as Few began planning for the building program and fund-raising effort that were to be features of Duke's centennial celebration in 1938–39, he asked Trumbauer to prepare preliminary plans for an engineers' dormitory on East. Few advised the architect, however, not to bother at that stage about the inside of the building, for he was explaining in the publicity statements about the proposed building program that the dormitory would be designed and built so that it could be converted into an apartment house. Some people at Duke, Few noted, objected to putting money into a building on the East campus that all hoped would only be a temporary home for engineers.[103]

Nothing would ever come of those plans for a new dormitory for engineers on East, but pressure for strengthening Duke's program in engineering came from a well-placed source. Duke, like Trinity before it, wanted no part of any academic program that was not fully accredited, and when the national Engineers' Council for Professional Development growled a bit, Duke responded quickly and with significant results. A committee of the council visited Duke in the spring of 1937, and the council's chairman subsequently informed Flowers that the committee had been impressed by the ability of the faculty in engineering and by the good cooperation between the science and mathematics departments and engineering. The visiting committee felt, however, that the engineering departments at Duke were inadequately housed on the old campus and were too far removed from the facilities on the new campus.

Moreover, the committee believed that Duke had inadequate administrative arrangements for engineering. There was no dean and therefore no one person to coordinate and represent engineering. Then, in words that undoubtedly caught the attention of Few, Flowers, and others, the chairman of the council concluded: "It would appear that those determining the educational policies of the University are by no means sure that engineering education has a place in the scheme of things at Duke."[104]

The lack of a dean or coordinator in engineering had bothered some of the engineering faculty long before the Council for Professional Development focused on the issue. Walter Seeley, in fact, pointed out to Wannamaker as early as 1934 that the group in engineering was virtually functioning as a school but lacked that name and a dean. "The problems of administration are getting to the point where we are badly in need of a dean," Seely declared, "and we could function so much more efficiently if we had one."[105]

Wannamaker and Few did not heed Seeley's recommendation, but when the council revealed its displeasure in 1937, Few immediately replied that if Duke had the funds and if engineering were taught on the graduate level, as was the case with the work in the other professional schools at Duke, then the university would gladly organize a school of engineering. But to change from that scheme for the professional schools, Few insisted, "would require a modification of the whole underlying plan upon which the University is built and organized." Noting that in the past year he had given all of his "extra" time to the development of the Graduate School of Arts and Sciences, Few added that he was also actively involved in efforts to strengthen the departments of classics, philosophy, and physics. But now the engineering area would receive prompt attention.

As a first step, Few advised that a Division of Engineering was being established with a director to head it. Then civil and mechanical engineering would be divided into separate departments and a chairman named for each of them and for electrical engineering.[106] With W. H. Hall as the division's director and Seeley, Bird, and Wilbur as the chairmen under him, the new arrangement went into effect in the fall of 1937. It was clearly only a stopgap measure, for careful plans were being made for further steps to advance engineering at Duke.

In replying to the criticism from the Engineers' Council for Professional Development, Flowers also spoke up for his former discipline. Since Few was covering the organizational changes envisioned, Seeley advised Flowers to point out that engineering at Duke had, by 1937, 30,000 square feet of space, or about six times what it had occupied a decade earlier. Both Asbury and Bivins were being completely renovated for the particular purposes which the engineering departments needed. With their own buildings and a special dormitory (Southgate), the engineers formed an independent group and, Seeley suggested, came as near being "a completely integrated college within a university as could be desired." While there were plans for an even more directly contiguous new dormitory, Seeley argued that there was no handicap whatever in being removed from West campus. After recapitulating the growth in the size of the faculty and the student body, Seeley urged Flowers to point out that Duke had made its first exception in granting a uniform degree to its undergraduates when the bachelor of science degree had been reinstated for engineers in 1928. In short, in light of all the growth and the above-mentioned changes, Seeley thought it farfetched for anyone to say that the Duke administration had not properly supported engineering. Flowers, in a diplomatic letter to the Council, closely followed Seeley's suggestions.[107] Subsequently, Flowers informed the chairman of the council that a committee of the Duke trustees had been named to study and report on engineering early in 1938. Few was also studying the matter in order to deal with it in the president's report in 1938. Both investigations, Flowers noted, were following three lines: engineering as taught in some of the better colleges, such as Swarthmore and Lafayette; an engineering college for undergraduates as at Princeton and Yale; and finally a graduate school in engineering, "the idea we have up to now had in mind and even now our first preference if we could find the money with which to carry the idea out." In conclusion, Flowers assured the council that Duke was fully exerting itself to find out what its obligations and opportunities were in engineering and how it could best live up to and realize them.[108]

While all of these negotiations and studies were taking place, it is doubtful that the engineering students themselves were in the least disturbed. There is evidence, in fact, that being the only males in residence on the same campus with hundreds of women students was not something the engineers regarded as a hardship. They slept, studied, and ate in "The Shack," as Southgate was popularly called; there was also a gymnasium there where pep rallies and dances were frequently held. Calling the students on West campus various rude names, the engineers fielded intramural teams that won a large number of trophies. Sometimes, clad in pajamas and robes, they carried kerosene lanterns and staged late-night serenades in front of the women's dormitories; for football games on West, the engineers marched together to the stadium, carrying banners inscribed "The Duke Engineers."[109] In short, the engineers in the 1930s and during the World War II era clearly did enjoy many aspects of their situation and probably possessed an *esprit* that would be hard to rival later, when engineers finally did move westward after World War II and became residentially integrated with the students of Trinity College.

The trustee committee's report early in 1938 was clearly based on the thinking of Few, Flowers, Hall, Seeley, and other senior members of the engineering faculty. After an historical overview and recapitulation of the advances made since 1925, the report argued that there was, particularly in the South, a place for a college of engineering kept on a small, intimate scale with limited enrollment (225 students being the suggested maximum) and selective admission. Conceding that uncertainty about location had been a handicap, the trustees, echoing some of the engineering faculty, pointed to the advantages in the existing arrangement, particularly the atmosphere of a small college combined with various facilities of a larger university. Better landscaping of the engineering complex was needed (especially since the main quadrangles on both West and East were then models of academic landscaping). But more importantly, all three curricula in engineering had been fully accredited; and since there was then neither the money nor the demand for the organization of a full-fledged professional school—which might be a goal for the future—the report recommended that a college of engineering should be established. It would dignify the work in engineering, increase its prestige in the eyes of the engineering profession generally, and probably improve the morale of both faculty and students.[110]

Since new appointments to the faculty in engineering had to be made and therefore adequate funding had to be assured, the trustees did not formally authorize the establishment of the College of Engineering until June, 1939. At that time they also named W. H. Hall as the first dean. With five new instructors appointed in 1939, the faculty numbered a dozen, and since the engineers took courses in English, history, and other humanistic and social science areas, as well as in the natural sciences and mathematics, some twenty faculty members in those areas were associated with key faculty members in the new College of Engineering in an active Council on Engineering Instruction.

Three of the new faculty members named in 1939 did not remain long at Duke, but two of them did and would continue to play large roles in the maturation of the College of Engineering. Edward K. Kraybill came straight to Duke after receiving his degree in electrical engineering at Pennsylvania State University. After World War II he would go for a master's degree at the University of Michigan and even later for a Ph.D. at the same institution. Filling various important roles in the administration of the College of Engineering, Kraybill would remain at Duke for over thirty years.

Charles R. Vail also came as a new instructor in electrical engineering in the fall of 1939. A Duke graduate in engineering in 1937, he too would go after World War II first for a master's degree at the University of Michigan and then later for a doctorate at the same institution. An effective and admired teacher as well as an active participant in the life of the university as a whole, Vail would spend a large part of his professional career at Duke before accepting another position in 1967.

With alumni in engineering organized and active from 1937 onward and with a student body that grew to 201 in 1938–39, the college was clearly on its way. The annual Engineers' Show staged by the students each spring had begun in 1933 and grown larger and more popular with the university and Durham communities each year. Students in each department in the college vied to show off various technological marvels and improvements, such as the electrical engineers' mind-boggling display of a telephone-television booth in the late 1930s. Unlike the schools of forestry and law, which were hard-hit by the wartime draft of young men, the College of Engineering would boom during World War II. At the end of it, however, the engineers would lose their special place on East and be the first to benefit from Duke's postwar building program on the West campus.

Geology, unfortunately, did not before World War II enjoy the growth and "happy ending" that characterized engineering. Never taught in Trinity College, geology was a subject that Few as well as various others at Duke much wanted to see introduced. A. C. Lee, the able engineer who headed the construction company that was formed to erect all the new buildings at Duke after 1925, obviously had direct, professional interest in the matter. When he questioned Few in 1931 about the possibility of introducing geology, the harassed president explained that he was eager to do it but that the university was not then financially able. Not exaggerating at all, Few added that Duke was already committed to do all that it actually could do.[111]

By 1935, however, the worst of the economic depression had passed for Duke, and Few and Wannamaker were ready to make a start, albeit a strictly limited one, in geology. Apparently in response to inquiries sent out by Wannamaker or someone authorized to act for him, a young geologist then at Ohio State University, Edward Willard Berry, applied for and got the Duke position. With both his undergraduate and Ph.D. degrees from Johns Hopkins (he received the latter in 1925), Berry had spent three years in Peru working for an industrial concern before going to Ohio State University. The depression had by no means lifted there by 1935, for Berry wrote that the state legislature had made no appropriations for the university, the governor was hostile to it, the faculty had no contracts, and even the heat and lights in the buildings had been cut off. His chairman at Ohio State, in strongly recommending Berry, added that salaries at Ohio State had been cut and there had been virtually no promotions or increases "during this long dark period."[112]

Berry, therefore, was obviously quite happy to come to Duke as an assistant professor in the fall of 1936. A shortage of space on West campus forced Wannamaker to house Berry, who for a number of years was the sole member of the geology department at Duke, in the Science building on the East campus, which would much later house the Duke Art Museum. While constituting a one-man department no doubt caused various problems for Berry, he took it in good stride, taught a variety of courses, became a founder of the Carolina Geological Society, and remained quite active in both national and international professional organizations.

While geology had not been taught in Trinity College, a relatively new discipline in the social sciences, psychology, had been taught only piecemeal and, as at many other institutions at the time, it had been taught by members of the philosophy department. In a research university, psychology deserved better, and accordingly, it became a separate, new department at Duke. In fact, to launch it, Few pulled off what he regarded as Duke's greatest coup in the area of the arts and sciences.

5

Strengthening the Arts and Sciences:

The Social Sciences and the Humanities

&

O F THE THREE TRADITIONAL divisions of learning in a liberal arts college—the humanities, the natural sciences and mathematics, and the social sciences—the last-named was, on a comparative basis, probably the least developed in Trinity College. William G. Glasson brought considerable strength in the area of economics when he came to Trinity in 1902 with his new doctorate from Columbia. Glasson, however, also had to teach sociology for many years, and government (or political science) was long subsumed under economics. As at many other institutions at the time, the relatively new discipline of psychology was taught in the philosophy department, generally by persons who had only incidental training in psychology, although in 1924 Trinity appointed a full-fledged psychologist, only to have him leave the following year.

From the outset of the reorganization into a research university, President Few signalled Duke's intention to have philosophy and psychology in separate departments and to try to "make them very strong." On a three-week tour of major universities in the East and in Chicago in the spring of 1926, Few met and interviewed various academic leaders. Upon returning to Duke, he particularly requested a contact he had at his graduate alma mater, Harvard, to ask one of the leading psychologists there, William McDougall, if he could suggest some first-rate persons in his field for Duke.[1]

A distinguished British pioneer in the field of psychology, McDougall had obtained a medical degree after graduating from Cambridge University in 1894. Finding medicine too narrowly focused to contain his

y, took part in an
d that psychology
is "direct attack on
perimental psychol-
t University College,
ding role in organiz-
became, according to
ologist by far" and in

wrote to make sugges-
een proposed to Few,
and good character but
rsion of psychology that
id."⁴ Although behavior-
ehavior and its dismissal
unmeasurable categories,
quarters of academic psy-
sons, wanted no part of it,
he had "dropped the man
iced the problem of finding
promising young man."⁵

, Few was no doubt as sur-
he end of one of McDougall's
letters concerning v... post at Duke he dropped the
remark that he himself might be "a possi...lity." Not only, he explained,
had he been charmed by the glimpse he had had of the South, but he was
not "entirely satisfied" with his salary at Harvard. But, he concluded, at
fifty-four he was "probably at an age too advanced" for Few to consider.
Few replied promptly that he was deeply interested in what McDougall
had written and was prepared to "follow it up to the limit." Perhaps they
could meet in Boston or New York.⁶

The two men apparently did meet and then continued their negotiation through the mail. Concerning his status in the psychological field,
McDougall noted that he "had many strong supporters among the more
philosophically minded, and many strong opponents among those numerous academic psychologists who teach a dogmatically materialistic doctrine." McDougall considered his preparation for teaching and research in
psychology quite thorough, "probably more so than that of any other man
now living." After recapitulating his academic and extensive field training,
he mentioned that he had specialized for five years during the Great War
in the study of neurotic and mental disorders. Even before that, he had
been elected a Fellow of the Royal Society of London in 1912.⁷

Few was, of course, too careful an administrator merely to take Mc-

Dougall at his own word. Among the various letters that he or those acting for him received concerning McDougall, one of the most balanced and judicious reported that a competent authority believed that McDougall clearly ranked among the top ten psychologists in the world. Yet he had not "taken the place of leadership in American psychology that he undoubtedly expected to take." This, the informant continued, was because McDougall was more of a "speculative psychologist" than an experimental one; perhaps he was, in the eyes of many American psychologists, "more of a philosopher than a psychologist." The conclusion was that if Duke wanted an experimental psychologist who would command a place of leadership in the American field, McDougall was not the man. "But if you want a big man in speculative psychology and social philosophy," the letter concluded, "who will bring you prestige in these fields, will represent the university well in public address on important occasions, and will be a reasonably good yoke-fellow if you give him his daily meed of praise—yes."[8]

For Few, eager to gain such an eminent ally in the eternal war on both materialism and any mechanistic view of the mind, the answer was a quick yes. Although Few may not have fully realized the actual precariousness of Duke's financial situation as early as mid-1926, he still may have boggled momentarily when McDougall explained that he attached "considerable importance" to salary and named a figure. He thought that since Harvard was "a little inclined to trade on her prestige and other attractions," it might be beneficial to her and to the academic profession in general if Harvard "were made to feel that she cannot safely do this any more." At any rate, McDougall noted that he was then being paid $7,500 per year; was expecting an advance to $8,000; and would not consider going to Duke for less than $9,000. Though no other professor in the arts and sciences received a salary anywhere even near that figure—and most received about half of that amount—Few promptly agreed, and after some delay, William McDougall became Duke's first "star" appointment. In Few's eyes, moreover, McDougall was not only the first such appointment but always by far the most distinguished and preeminent.[9]

One prominent aspect of McDougall's antimaterialism had long been his interest in psychical research, and it was that which attracted young Joseph B. Rhine and his wife Louisa to take up study at Harvard in 1926. With doctorates in botany from the University of Chicago, both of the Rhines were spiritually sensitive people who quested for a bridge between science and religion. Although the Rhines' year at Harvard proved disappointing in many ways, primarily because McDougall went off on a year-long leave just as they arrived, when McDougall moved to Duke, in 1927 the Rhines soon followed him there. With Few's approval, J. B. Rhine a bit later became McDougall's research assistant and also a part-time instructor. "I think your experiments are highly important," Few assured McDougall, "and Duke University is anxious to give you all possible cooperation." [10]

For other appointments in the burgeoning psychology department, Few relied heavily on McDougall's guidance, and the small but able group that was soon assembled reflected that fact. Responding to Few's request for names of some young psychologists who could best begin by offering courses primarily for undergraduates, McDougall suggested, among others, two of his former students, Karl Zener and Donald K. Adams. Zener, who came to Duke in 1928, was the first recruited. After obtaining his doctorate at Harvard in 1926, he had received a National Research fellowship for study in Berlin and then taught for one year at Princeton. A specialist in psychophysical experimentation, he would later chair the department and spend his full career at Duke. Adams worked with McDougall while getting a master's degree at Harvard. He went on to Yale for his doctorate in 1927, taught at Wesleyan University for a year, and also received a National Research fellowship for two years' study in Berlin before coming to Duke in 1931.

Along with the suggestions for new staff members that Few had requested, McDougall, in advance of his arrival at Duke, made it clear that the psychology department would require space for a laboratory. "I am not one of those who thinks that laboratory psychology is the sole or most valuable kind," McDougall explained, but he nevertheless saw the need for such a facility. His own research at the time, he noted, was in animal psychology, and he had an experiment underway on mental heredity in rats.[11] Psychology got the laboratory, though a few years after McDougall arrived at Duke he argued that the scattered space allotted to the department in several buildings on both campuses was inadequate. He had collected documents showing the facilities for psychology at a number of universities, such as Princeton and the University of North Carolina, and insisted that the Duke department would feel cramped until it had rooms equivalent in number and size to those at the other universities.[12] While psychology did gain additional space, many years would pass before suitable space entirely on the West campus became available to the department.

Helge Lundholm, somewhat older than Zener and Adams, joined the department in 1930. A native of Sweden who had received his doctorate from the University of Stockholm, Lundholm came to the United States in 1919 and worked in pathological psychology for ten years at McLean Hospital in Waverly, Massachusetts. Lundholm, while a research fellow at Harvard in the 1920s, had come into contact with McDougall and greatly admired his broad, humanistic approach to psychology. In describing one of his own books to a layman some years after his arrival at Duke, Lundholm noted that there was little reference to experiments in the work. Rather, there was "much non-technical reflection upon human life and human nature in the broadest sense of these words." There was also, he continued, "inescapable reflection upon universal nature and upon man's place in nature." He concluded by saying that the work was "metapsychological or philosophical, as all psychological writing, if one frankly admits its most distant postulates or implications, is—forever—compelled to be."[13]

A sixth member joined the psychology department in 1934 when the opportunity arose to bring another distinguished, displaced German scholar to Duke. William Stern was born in Germany in 1871 and had taught at several German universities before becoming director of the Psychological Institute of Hamburg. A pioneer in the field of child psychology, he had introduced the method of mental measurement known as the intelligence quotient (IQ), though he came to deplore some of the uses to which popularizers later put his concept. Stern confessed to Few that his command of spoken English was inadequate for teaching, but Duke, with assistance from the Rockefeller Foundation, nevertheless appointed him as a professor of psychology in the fall of 1934.[14] Another psychologist in the McDougall-Lundholm mode, Stern also insisted on the close relation of psychology with philosophy and in fact was given a joint appointment in the latter department a year before he died in 1938.

Along with the new appointments in psychology, McDougall wanted and got a new quarterly journal published by Duke University Press. With the first issue appearing in September, 1932, *Character and Personality: An International Quarterly of Psychodiagnostics and Allied Studies* also was published in a German edition. The editor of the journal, Robert Saudek, lived in London, but Ernest Seeman, the director of the Duke University Press, served as associate editor until Karl Zener took over that job in 1934.[15]

In sponsoring J. B. Rhine at Duke, McDougall no doubt never dreamed that the younger man's name and work would become world famous before the 1930s ended, but that is exactly what happened. Encouraged and assisted both by McDougall and by several of his other colleagues, Rhine began his own particular program of experimentation in psychic phenomena around 1930. Attempting to be as careful and scientific in his procedures as possible, Rhine began the work in telepathy and clairvoyance that he dealt with at length, along with other related matters, in his book *Extra-Sensory Perception*, which was published in 1934. As reputable historians of science have suggested, Rhine's early work at Duke and especially his book on ESP transformed the field of psychical research or parapsychology. The first person to institutionalize psychical research within a university, Rhine helped to give the field an academic respectability that it had hitherto lacked. He and his work also, thanks to lavish attention from the popular media of the day, became well known to a much larger public than most academics ever have. Both Rhine and parapsychology also became highly controversial.[16]

While Rhine's colleagues initially shared his interest in psychical research and agreed that it had a place in the university, they also feared the possibility that such research might overshadow the conventional research and training offered in a department of psychology. In 1934, Zener, Adams, and Lundholm complained to McDougall about several of Rhine's alleged promotional activities on behalf of his own research interests, and they warned that psychical research should not be allowed to "attain a dominance which would exclude the investigation of psychological problems in general."[17]

Rhine, upon learning of his colleagues' complaints and fears, was offended and began actively seeking a way to do something that he had earlier thought about anyhow: establishing a university-based research institute that would be independent of the psychology department. Again assisted by McDougall and encouraged by Few, Rhine, who happened to be a personally charming and impressive-looking man, also benefitted from the fact that his was a field in which a number of well-to-do people, for various reasons, had special interest. While Rhine would not get his separate institute until soon after World War II, beginning in 1935 he succeeded in securing substantial contributions from private donors. Duke accepted the funds to enable Rhine to establish the Parapsychology Laboratory. It continued to have nominal ties with the psychology department, and Rhine, a highly popular teacher, continued to offer one course per semester. But a portion of the outside money was used to pay part of Rhine's salary, another portion to pay for a research assistant in parapsychology, and another portion for various expenses involved in the work. Another gift provided for two graduate fellowships in parapsychology.[18]

Not content with the stronger position of parapsychology at Duke, Rhine decided that the new field needed a professional journal of its own. "A regular periodical would do a great deal, I believe, to standardize work in the field," Rhine argued. "It would considerably stabilize and command respect for parapsychology to have a scientific journal in the hands of academic people . . . and publishing only first quality experimental material."[19] Again with encouragement from McDougall and the help of a private donor, Rhine launched the *Journal of Parapsychology*, published by Duke University Press, in April 1937.

Few was quite aware that the work of Rhine, as well as some of McDougall's ideas, aroused considerable hostility in many academic circles. Without seizing the opportunity to link Duke's support for both men with the principle of academic freedom, Few nevertheless strongly backed them. Congratulating Rhine on one of his articles that had appeared in *Forum* magazine, Few added the comment that perhaps some day, after Rhine had "digested many experiments," he could "write a book with the excellence of [William] James' 'Varieties of Religious Experience,'—with a dash of ultimate wisdom into the bargain." Rhine replied graciously that while he could never hope to follow successfully in the footsteps of James, that great philosopher and McDougall did represent his "highest ideals." Then Rhine added: "I could not with safety venture into the fields I am engaged in, departing from the lines (although not from the methods) of orthodox mechanistic science, without the examples before me of those hardy pioneers of thought, and, may I add, without the confidence and backing of our [Duke] administration."[20]

While Few obviously hoped to nudge Rhine toward even greater achievement, he felt no such impulse concerning McDougall. Upon receiving a copy of McDougall's new book, *Religion and the Sciences of Life*, in 1934, Few thanked the author: "I speak the words of soberness when I say that I know nobody in the world today who is doing so much [as you] towards bringing about right thinking in great fundamental things. You can count on me to cooperate with you to the uttermost now and all the way."[21]

McDougall became ill early in 1938. (Four years earlier, Few had allowed him to reduce his teaching responsibilities by half, i.e., one semester per year, but to continue receiving full pay.) As McDougall lay in the hospital, Few wrote him: "It is a supreme satisfaction to me to be able to believe that Duke University may have been of some service to you in the great work that you have done for humanity. I believe that your thinking and writing will influence in the right direction the generations that are to come and therefore will be a part of the heritage of the ages."[22]

McDougall died in November, 1938. Although later decades would see a renewed interest in and respect for certain of his ideas, in the 1930s a growing number of psychologists were coming to regard McDougall's views as old-fashioned and even irrelevant.[23] At Duke, however, he had not only supported Rhine and the institutionalization of the work in parapsychology, but he had also brought in a small but able group of other psychologists—Zener, Lundholm, and Adams—who would form the nucleus of a considerably expanded and stronger department in subsequent years.

Just as the psychology department was something new for Duke, so too was the creation of a separate department for another relatively new discipline in the social sciences, sociology. The subject had been taught in Trinity, but usually not under that name, and by professors, such as Jerome Dowd and William Glasson, who included sociology along with economics or some other social science.[24] Although Glasson helped in the search for an established scholar in the field of sociology and the person named was an old classmate of his at Cornell, the initial appointment reflected Few's values and orientation, as had McDougall's appointment in psychology.

Charles A. Ellwood, born in upstate New York in 1873, was one of the nation's pioneer sociologists. Upon graduating from Cornell, he studied for a year in Berlin and then obtained his Ph.D. at the University of Chicago. After a brief stay at the University of Nebraska, he accepted a position at the University of Missouri in 1900 and remained there until he came to Duke in 1930. Author of about a dozen books, including a widely used textbook, Ellwood helped organize the American Sociological Society in 1905 and later served as its president. Some of his books were translated into various foreign languages, and he also served as president of the International Institute of Sociology.

In accepting the offer from Duke, Ellwood noted that there was a struggle being waged in his field "between the materialists and the idealists," and he professed his pleasure in coming to an institution such as Duke that would give him "full support" in his battle to obtain recognition for the "spiritual values" in American social life.[25] Ellwood was correct in expecting full support from Few, for the department developed along the lines desired by Ellwood, albeit not as rapidly as he would have preferred.

The first person Ellwood recruited to join him was Howard E. Jensen. A native Kansan, Jensen received a bachelor's and a master's degree from the University of Kansas before getting his divinity degree and doctorate at Chicago, the latter in 1920. He taught at Butler University and then briefly at the University of Missouri before coming to Duke in 1931. Ellwood assured him that the Duke administration was eager to develop sociology, and as for Few, Ellwood declared, "I have never worked under a more liberal and progressive man." It was probably true, Ellwood thought, that North Carolina was less liberal about labor and property questions than about "the negro problem." Since industrialization and unions were relatively new, the people were not adjusted to them. There was, however, a "hopeful element" in the picture: "The Southern people are religious and it is always possible to talk about labor problems from the religious point of view." Furthermore, Ellwood assured Jensen that Few wanted the faculty to "feel free and undertake pioneering work in the social studies."[26]

Jensen, who was an ordained minister in the Disciples of Christ denomination, apparently did "feel free" at Duke. Certainly he involved himself more closely in the life of the Durham community than did most of his faculty colleagues. A pioneer in the professional organization of social work, he helped organize Durham's Social Planning Council and served as its first president. He also drew up the first plan for the Durham Community Fund, which later evolved into the United Way Fund, and, working closely with the divinity students whom he and Ellwood taught in the School of Religion, he helped organize the Edgemont Community Center in an underprivileged section of Durham. He and his wife led in the establishment of the Durham Juvenile Court and detention center for youthful offenders, and for many years Jensen chaired the North Carolina Commission for the Blind after its establishment in 1935.

Edgar T. Thompson, the third member to join the sociology department, was not so involved in Durham affairs as Jensen, but since race relations and plantation societies were among his primary fields of scholarly interest, he too found useful ways to serve the larger society in addition to teaching and publishing his scholarly studies. A native South Carolinian, he took a master's degree at the University of Missouri after graduating from the University of South Carolina in 1922. A decade later, and after holding various teaching posts, he received his doctorate at Chicago. He came to Duke in 1935 and became a prime mover in efforts to foster interdepartmental study of the South and its problems.

Duke's early sociologists faced ample challenge from some students. Ellwood informed Few that on the final examination in the introductory sociology course one student had presented evidence about the value the course had possessed for him: it had taught him his "place in the society of humanity." The student explained further that his ideas about a number of things had been altered: "I firmly believed that the negro should *not* be educated, because 'an educated nigger is too uppity!' and negroes were meant to be the servants of the white man. Now I know that the negro should be educated—socially educated." Instead of still thinking that the family was a pleasant but essentially economic convenience, the student claimed to have learned that it was actually the basis for all harmonious living together. And economic depressions, rather than being inevitable, could be avoided "by intelligent precaution and insurance in times when economic conditions are good."[27] Both Ellwood and the student had their own reasons, of course, for wanting such positive outcomes to be known, but the isolated case at least reveals a portion of what went on in a sociology class in the early 1930s.

In response to Ellwood's pressure for additional appointments needed to strengthen the department, the administration authorized the hiring of Hornell Hart in 1938. He had been spotted by Ellwood earlier in the decade, but Duke's financial constraints around 1933–34 had forced a delay in the appointment. A graduate of Oberlin who had received a master's degree from Wisconsin, Hart earned his doctorate at the University of Iowa in 1921 and had taught at Iowa, Bryn Mawr, and Hartford Theological Seminary before coming to Duke. An energetic scholar who interested himself in a wide variety of subjects, Hart, like Jensen and Thompson, would remain at Duke until retirement.

With three full professors and only one assistant professor (Thompson), the sociology department was top-heavy. Ellwood pressed for additional staff at the junior level and admitted that during the department's first decade the emphasis had been on graduate instruction.[28] Beginning as early as 1934, Ellwood urged that an anthropologist be added to the department because he considered anthropology and ethnology the foundation sciences for sociology. Despite that argument, however, appointments in other areas apparently took precedence, and not until 1941 was an anthropologist brought to Duke and the department's name changed to the Department of Sociology and Anthropology.

John P. Gillin, an expert in Latin American anthropology, received a bachelor's and a master's degree from Wisconsin before obtaining his Ph.D. from Harvard in 1935. He taught at several universities before coming to Duke in 1941, and he would resign shortly after World War II. His appointment, however, signalled a victory for Ellwood's insistence that anthropology should be taught at Duke.

While both the psychology and the sociology-anthropology departments represented new components at Duke, the Department of Economics and Political Science inherited from Trinity a relatively strong basis on which to build. Split into two separate departments in 1934, both would recruit young members and become conspicuously strong even before World War II.

William G. Glasson played a key role in the strong start that the two departments got, for he had a large part in picking the able scholar-teachers who became the core faculty. After receiving his doctorate from Columbia in 1900, Glasson had come to Trinity in 1902 to become the professor of economics and social science. President Few named him chairman of the committee on graduate instruction in 1916, when the college had the grand total of six candidates for the master's degree, and in 1926 Glasson became the first dean of the Graduate School of Arts and Sciences while continuing to chair the Department of Economics and Political Science. A quiet, methodical scholar and administrator, Glasson had help in the political science wing of the department from one or two instructors who preceded the important appointment in 1925 of Robert R. Wilson.

A native Texan, Wilson graduated from Austin College before obtaining a master's degree at Princeton and then, in 1927, a doctorate from Harvard. Men of Wilson's type, his major professor at Harvard commented, "are none too common."[29] As impeccable in his scholarship in the field of international law as he was in his gentle southern manners, Wilson became a nationally recognized authority in his field, and when political science became a separate department in 1934 he served as its first chairman. Even before that time, Wilson undoubtedly worked closely with Glasson in recruiting the other political scientists for the department.

The first of those named, Robert S. Rankin, came in 1927. He was a graduate of Tusculum College in Tennessee who obtained his Ph.D. at Princeton. A specialist in American state and local government, Rankin was an energetic, even ebullient scholar who helped to organize the Southern Political Science Association and, like Wilson, played a large role in its activities as well as in those of the American Political Science Association. Rankin, whose lifelong loyalty to Duke quickly became evident, kept in close touch with his mentor at Princeton and reported after several years at Duke that he and Wilson aimed at having "one of the best Political Science Departments in the South."[30]

An appointment in 1935 clearly pushed the Duke department closer to its goal. When R. Taylor Cole, another Texan, joined the political science department at Duke, he was not a rank beginner, for, after receiving his bachelor of arts and master of arts degrees from the University of Texas, he had taught for several years at Louisiana State University. Cole interrupted that teaching, however, to pursue a doctorate at Harvard. A fellowship there allowed him to spend over a year studying developments in Germany in the early 1930s. Upon completion of his dissertation in 1935, Cole could have returned at a higher salary and rank to Louisiana State University, but the assistant professorship offered to him at Duke proved more attractive in light of the growing political problems and turmoil in Huey Long's Louisiana. While Wilson had known Cole earlier in Texas, the glowing letters about him from his professors at Harvard clearly carried weight. The departmental chairman noted, among other things, that Cole was "a Southerner, a gentleman and scholar in every sense of the word, and I recommend him to you without reservation." Another Harvard political scientist observed that the presence of two established experts in Cole's field of comparative government prevented Harvard from trying to hold on to him but that "no junior member of the department has been more unanimously liked and approved of here than Cole."[31] In light of Cole's later career both in his professional field and as a highly skillful top administrator in Duke University, one would have to give his Harvard teachers high marks for accuracy and prescience.[32]

Not content with the three fields being taught in political science at Duke by 1935—public or international law, American state and local government, and comparative government—Wilson pushed for additional appointments in Far Eastern institutions and colonial governments, political theory, and public administration. He gained the administration's approval for the first of those appointments in 1937 and found Paul M. A. Linebarger to fill the position. A Johns Hopkins Ph.D. (1936) who had traveled extensively in the Orient and Europe and had lived off and on in China for about eight years, Linebarger would leave Duke during World

War II, but his appointment marked the department's and the university's commitment to that important area of study.

In public administration, Wilson recruited George A. Shipman in 1938. A Cornell Ph.D. (1931) who taught for several years at West Virginia University, Shipman also worked in a local government survey conducted by Princeton before he came to Duke. He too would leave Duke for work in Washington during World War II.

Two other early members of the political science department were Duke-trained scholars. The first of these, William H. Simpson, was a graduate of Tusculum College in 1926. After obtaining a master's degree at Duke and while continuing to work on his doctorate, which he received in 1935, Simpson became an instructor in 1930. A well-known teacher to many generations of Duke students who took courses in American government, Simpson did research concerning small-loan problems and Southern textile workers and their communities. William M. Gibson also received his doctorate from Duke (1936) and had become an instructor in the department before that. Although his dissertation and his first book dealt with the United States government's treatment of aliens, Gibson began to develop a specialization in Latin American governments even before he entered military service during the war.

Wilson's hope for a specialist in political theory was realized in 1941 when Duke appointed John H. Hallowell, Jr., as a visiting assistant professor to substitute for Taylor Cole, who was on leave. A Harvard graduate who came to Duke for a master's degree, Hallowell went on to Princeton for his doctorate and taught briefly at the University of California, Los Angeles, before returning to Duke. As happened in other cases, Hallowell's "visiting" status soon changed, and he would spend his full career at Duke.

With a marked pattern of Texas, Harvard, and Princeton influence, Duke's relatively new Department of Political Science had achieved considerable strength by the time the nation entered World War II. A strong foundation had been built for the department's important role at Duke and its climb in national rankings during the postwar decades.

The Department of Economics and Business Administration began as and remained a larger one than political science. In addition to Glasson, William J. H. Cotton served as a professor of economics in Trinity College after 1920. A graduate of Temple University and the University of Pennsylvania, he taught industrial management and labor relations before his untimely death in 1932.

Perhaps the most important new appointment in economics, from the standpoint of both the department and the university, came in 1925 when Calvin Bryce Hoover came to Duke with his brand-new Ph.D. from Wisconsin. An undergraduate at Monmouth College in Illinois, Hoover taught briefly at the University of Minnesota before his Duke appointment. A quiet, thoughtful person and imaginative scholar, Hoover also had, as one of his distinguished students later noted, "the great journalist's instincts for being in the right place at the right time."[33]

Hoover displayed that instinct by winning a Social Science research fellowship for study in Russia during 1929–30, and the result was a trail-blazing scholarly study, *The Economic Life of Soviet Russia*, which appeared in 1931. Hoover soon after spent a year, 1932–33, in Germany and then published another widely read and influential volume, *Germany Enters the Third Reich*. Other important publications followed, but Hoover's first two books quickly established him as one of the nation's most promising and literate economists, one who could reach both intelligent laypersons and specialists. Keeping him at Duke was not easy, for not only did New Deal agencies in Washington seek to lure him away, but various colleges and universities sought him for a professorship or even an institutional presidency. In 1934, when Hoover was on leave with the Department of Agriculture in Washington, he felt attracted both by the prospect of helping in the New Deal's ambitious programs for economic reform to benefit the nation's desperate farmers and by the higher salary promised by the federal government. While Glasson made a strong appeal to Hoover to return to Duke, President Few's efforts may have proved decisive. "I and others of us have given your case more careful consideration than any other case in our whole history," Few explained to Hoover. Stressing the department's and the university's need for Hoover and strong desire to keep him, Few pointed to the financial stringencies caused by the depression as the great obstacle facing Duke. "We must all go in part by faith," Few noted, though he felt "great confidence in the future of Duke University." There was a great deal yet to do, and Hoover could undoubtedly "do a good deal towards the building up of Duke to the stature that we expect it to attain." Commending the adage that "it is better to travel pleasantly than to have arrived," Few also promised Hoover a substantial raise in salary and promotion to full professor. Hoover telegraphed his willingness to return to Duke.[34] Succeeding Glasson both as chairman of economics and in 1938 as dean of the graduate school, Hoover would long play a key role in university affairs and bring considerable distinction to Duke.

Earl J. Hamilton, who became an internationally recognized authority on the economic history of Spain and its empire, joined the department in 1927. A native Mississippian who did his undergraduate work at Mississippi Agricultural and Mechanical College (Mississippi State), Hamilton taught high school and coached for several years while working on his master's degree from the University of Texas. Then he obtained his doctorate from Harvard in 1929. Lured by the University of California, Berkeley, in 1936, Hamilton noted that while he was happy at Duke, it was the Berkeley policy "to promote on the basis of productive scholarship," and he confessed "the hope of being able to survive in this form of competition." He added that his Harvard mentors would regard his going to Berkeley as "a long forward step," and since he could not count indefinitely on support from foundations for his expensive but essential research travel, he might be better off at Berkeley in that respect also. Despite all these western attractions, Hamilton remained at Duke when Wannamaker, after conferring with Few, offered a substantial raise in salary. Yet by 1944, when Duke's salaries had begun to lag behind in national competition, Hamilton moved on, first to Northwestern and then to Chicago.

Among a large number of young instructors and assistant professors in economics and business administration, there were several who would spend their full careers at Duke. In 1926, both Charles E. Landon in economic geography and John H. Shields in accounting and finance joined the department. Landon did undergraduate work at the University of Kansas and his graduate work at Illinois, while Shields graduated from the University of Texas before doing graduate work at Columbia.

The first Duke-trained Ph.D. to join the department was Benjamin U. Ratchford, who began teaching at Duke in 1928. A North Carolinian and a Davidson graduate, Ratchford established a solid reputation with the publication in 1941 of his authoritative *American State Debts* and would remain at Duke until taking a position in the Federal Reserve banking system in 1960.

Another Duke-trained Ph.D. in economics, Robert S. Smith, joined the staff in 1932, the year he received his doctorate. A graduate also of Amherst, Smith specialized in Hispanic economic thought and Latin American economic history. His highly regarded books and articles, along with Earl Hamilton's work in the 1930s and related studies done by members of the history department, helped make Duke a nationally recognized center for Hispanic studies from the 1930s onward.

Martin Lee Black, Jr., who would teach accounting to countless Duke students over more than four decades, joined the department in 1930. A native of Charlotte, North Carolina, who had been a Duke undergraduate (1926), Black worked as an auditor in Chicago for several years and obtained a master's degree in business administration from Northwestern. Winner of a gold medal from the Illinois Society of Certified Public Accountants for the highest honors in the accounting examinations given in that state in 1930, Black would much later serve as president of the American Accounting Association.

Another addition to the department in 1930 was Benjamin F. Lemert. An economic geographer, he had an undergraduate and a master's degree from Ohio State and a doctorate from Columbia. He published books on, among other things, the cotton textile industry in the South and tobacco manufacturing in North Carolina.

Joseph J. Spengler, brought as a visiting associate professor in 1932 to replace Hoover temporarily, remained at Duke throughout the rest of his career and became one of the university's most distinguished as well as colorful scholars. Having received B.A., M.A., and Ph.D. degrees from Ohio State, Spengler taught for two years at the University of Arizona before coming to Duke. Initially interested in the growth and distribution of population and its relationship to other socioeconomic problems, Spengler published *France Faces Depopulation* in 1938. A prodigious researcher and publisher, Spengler moved into the history of economic and social theory and boldly crossed disciplinary lines in a large body of scholarly writing. As one noted commentator observed, Spengler pursued truth "with a daring, vigor, and all-consuming erudition rare in the history of economics."[35]

Noted for working late into the night at his home, Spengler once remarked puckishly, "I always tried to sleep on the job; I didn't want to waste my own time." Concerning his fellow economists, he noted that they "have a few techniques and a few solutions, mostly for non-existing problems, which they look for blind to the fact that economics is not a theoretical science, but one whose content is institutionally determined." He added: "One is reminded of the carpenter who, having only a hammer in his toolkit, pretends that everything is a nail."[36]

Regarding university administrators as a special affliction—or, and one could never be sure, pretending to so regard them—Spengler fired off to them long letters of criticism and protest on a wide variety of subjects. Calvin Hoover, a patient man and close friend of Spengler's, finally had enough at one point in the harassed early years of World War II and responded in kind to one of Spengler's epistolary outbursts. "My answer may seem intemperate," Hoover explained to Wannamaker, "but I have had to put up with Spengler's bluster and attempted terrorization of everyone in the Department until I am sick of it."[37] Hoover, like most who knew Spengler well, no doubt soon forgave and forgot all about the episode. As for Spengler, he, like Hoover, would later become president of the American Economic Association, the Southern Economic Association, and several other national scholarly organizations. For all of his occasional bluster, he also proved to be a conscientious and kindly teacher.

One who was much more of a team player than Spengler, Frank T. deVyver, joined the economics department in 1935. He was a graduate of Oberlin who received his doctorate at Princeton and taught there while doing graduate work. A convivial as well as able man, deVyver was quickly recognized at Duke as one whose presence strengthened his department and the university. Commending him for promotion and a raise, Hoover explained: "It is a difficult matter to find a Labor economist who is at once humanitarian in his point of view and also not in some degree unbalanced emotionally and intellectually." Hoover thought that deVyver met Duke's needs "exceptionally well."[38] A future chairman of the department as well as vice provost of the university, deVyver also served for many years as vice president for personnel and labor relations in the Erwin textile mill in Durham.

A distinguished refugee scholar from the University of Bonn in Germany, Herbert von Beckerath, added to the strength of the economics and political science department in the years before World War II. With partial support from the Rockefeller Foundation, Duke and the University of North Carolina cooperated in 1935 to obtain and share von Beckerath's services. While von Beckerath proved to be eminently satisfactory, Few and Wannamaker, still clinging to the notion that the Duke faculty should be proximate and readily available to the students and university community, objected to the fact that the German scholar maintained his residence exclusively in Chapel Hill. Accordingly, von Beckerath, while keeping his apartment ten miles away, arranged to stay at Durham's Washington Duke hotel on weeknights in the semester that he taught at Duke.[39]

While the education department at Duke produced no scholars quite comparable to Spengler, Hoover, or Hamilton, it was, nevertheless, a most important component in the new university. This was so in the first place because of the institution's history. In the 1850s, Braxton Craven, desperately seeking financial support for the school that would eventually become Trinity College and then Duke University, recognized North Carolina's dire need for properly trained teachers in the public schools, which were then in their infancy in the state and nonexistent in most of the South. Accordingly, Craven persuaded the state legislature in 1851 to charter Normal College, which had earlier been Union Institute, as a teacher-training institution. Craven was absolutely correct about the state's need, but the legislature, accurately reflecting the chronic and deep-seated aversion to taxes on the part of North Carolina's citizenry, refused to provide financial support for the school. Accordingly, in 1859, when the institution became affiliated with the North Carolina Methodist church, the name was again changed, this time to Trinity College. Yet the early interest in training teachers never disappeared, and one of Trinity's most valuable services to the larger public in the late nineteenth and early twentieth centuries lay in the institution's close, constantly cultivated relationship with the public schools.[40]

Aside from that long, proud history of public service, James B. Duke, in his indenture creating the Duke Endowment, had amply demonstrated his own awareness of the Trinity tradition and the importance which he attached to it. In one place in the indenture, where the different components of the proposed research university are named, a "School for Training Teachers" is listed among various other professional schools. Further on in the indenture, J. B. Duke advised that courses at Duke University should "be arranged, first, with special reference to the training of preachers, teachers, lawyers, and physicians."[41]

While the indenture had also included a "School of Business Administration" among the professional schools to be established, that would not become a reality until more than forty years after the organization of the university. Few did attempt in the late 1920s to find a donor who would underwrite a business school at Duke; after those early efforts failed, Few and his successors long maintained that since training in business was available in the Department of Economics and Business Administration, that arrangement met the spirit, if not the letter, of the indenture.

In the case of education or teacher training, the evidence is skimpy, but what there is suggests that Few never intended or desired to have a separate professional school in that area at Duke. One of the scant references to the matter in the records came in 1926, when Edmund D. Soper, the first dean of the School of Religion and vice president for student life, answered a query about the issue: "There is a situation here [at Duke] which makes it necessary in the view of President Few to delay for some time the plans for the School of Education. . . . President Few is a little in doubt as to the relationship the school ought to have to the other departments and other schools." He wished to study the question more before making any plans for such a school.[42] Too canny to be categorical about a potentially controversial subject, Few never spoke publicly about his lack of interest in the idea of a separate professional school of education. His and the university administration's belief in and support for the Department of Education, in both its graduate and undergraduate aspects, were, however, both genuine and extensive.

The pattern and high standard for leadership in the education department at Trinity had been set by Eugene Clyde Brooks. He was a Trinity alumnus who, after extensive experience in the state's public schools and in the State Department of Public Instruction, became professor of education at the college in 1907. An energetic and charming man, Brooks played a key role in North Carolina's early-twentieth-century educational awakening to the vital importance of the public schools. Not only did the Durham city school system rank for a while as the best in the state, thanks in part to Trinity's and Brooks's close involvement, but his years at the college, according to one historian, "gave the institution a pre-eminence throughout North Carolina in teacher training."[43]

When Brooks left Trinity in 1919 to become state superintendent of public instruction, he was succeeded, after a two-year interval, by one of his former students, Holland Holton. His career duplicated that of Brooks in many respects, for he too was a Trinity alumnus (1907) who served as a principal in various public schools and then as superintendent of Durham county schools. He attended Trinity's law school for two years and also went to the University of Chicago during two summers before the nation entered World War I. Named to the Trinity faculty in 1921, Holton, like several other faculty members, recognized the need for stronger credentials when the university was organized, took a leave of absence in 1926–27, and obtained the doctor of jurisprudence degree in law at the University of Chicago. As Holton explained, he expected, quite correctly as matters turned out, that graduate work in education would grow in the new university, and with the legal aspect of school administration as his specialty he hoped to have that field to himself in North Carolina and probably in the South.[44] Inheriting Brooks's zest for and talent at achieving close involvement with the state's public schools, Holton helped to put Duke's education department where Trinity's had been: in the forefront of those parts of the institution that rendered direct, vital service to the people of North Carolina, the South, and, increasingly, much of the nation.

Aside from Holton, two other members of the Trinity faculty in education carried over into the new university. Arthur M. Proctor, another Trinity alumnus (1910), joined the faculty in 1923 after serving as a school administrator in Georgia and North Carolina. With M.A. and Ph.D. degrees from Teachers College of Columbia University, the latter degree in 1930, he too had been a student under Brooks and joined enthusiastically in the movement to strengthen North Carolina's public school system.

Benjamin G. Childs, who joined the department in 1924, received his A.B. and master's degrees (1921) from the University of Virginia and taught in the public schools and at Randolph-Macon College before coming to Trinity. Professors of education at Duke were, like the professors of religion, in great demand throughout the state as speakers for commencements, various civic occasions, and such. Childs, who was quite active in Methodist as well as educational affairs, proved to be one of the most popular of Duke's faculty members in that respect.

In 1926 John W. Carr, Jr., joined the department of education. Another Trinity graduate (1917) and student of Brooks, Carr received a master's degree from the Teachers College of Columbia in 1921 and a doctorate in 1927. A specialist in childhood education, he too had held administrative positions in the public schools before becoming a college professor, and he would later serve as chairman of the department.

Two additional appointments strengthened the department in 1930, those of William A. Brownell and Howard Easley. Since both men received their training at places other than Trinity-Duke, they also helped diversify the department. A graduate of Allegheny College who received his doctorate at Chicago in 1926, Brownell taught at several universities before joining the Duke faculty as professor of educational psychology. He was the author of several textbooks and monographs as well as numerous articles and became the editor of the *Duke University Research Studies in Education*. Only after his appointment did the education department begin to offer a doctoral program, and for a number of years it was limited to educational psychology. Brownell would leave Duke in 1949.

Howard Easley, the other new appointment in 1930, was also in the field of educational psychology. A Tennessean whose doctoral degree was from George Peabody College in Nashville, Easley would later be forced by health problems to retire early (in 1957) and would become prominent as an outspoken, salty-tongued politician as well as a farmer on the banks of the Eno River who generously shared produce, particularly sweet corn, with a host of friends.

The last appointment in education prior to World War II was that of Douglas E. Scates in 1939. Another Chicago Ph.D., like Brownell, Scates was interested in the application of educational measurements and research to practical problems in the schools and had taught at Indiana University and worked as a research specialist in the Cincinnati school system before coming to Duke. Editor of the *Review of Educational Research* for several years after 1939, he would later serve as president of the American Educational Research Association and resign from the Duke faculty in 1948.

The members of the education department not only played a key role during the regular academic year, but because the patronage for Duke's booming summer sessions in the years before World War II came so largely from schoolteachers, the faculty members in education, and particularly Holland Holton, were conspicuously important in that area also. Trinity College, following a nationwide trend resisted only by relatively few private colleges and universities mostly in the East, began holding regular summer school in 1919, though various types of summer institutes and training programs had been held earlier. With Holton as director of the summer school and with the college insisting on the same standards as in the regular year, it quickly caught on, and by 1924 the enrollment was over 800; well over half of the students were schoolteachers. For a few years a Trinity-Duke seashore summer school was held at Oriental, North Carolina, and for a longer period another branch of the school operated in the mountains, at Lake Junaluska, North Carolina.[45]

So committed was Duke to the teacher-training tradition that it gave to teachers who were in full-time service in schools and colleges a remarkable deal: they could attend up to four six-week summer sessions in a six-year period without paying any tuition. After their fourth full session, they had to pay regular tuition charges, and there was also a registration fee ($17.00 per term in 1930; $18.50 in 1940). This arrangement proved to be a special lure in the depression-wracked 1930s, and the summer school attracted students from a growing number of states. At the close of the summer session in 1930, Holton reported to Few that the enrollment for both terms at Duke and the Junaluska branch had totalled 1,502, with over a third of the first-term students enrolled in the graduate school and many of them working on master's degrees. The out-of-state enrollment grew steadily after the organization of the university, with the accompanying national publicity about the mammoth building program on two campuses. Holton believed, in fact, that the ultimate limit to the expansion of the summer school would probably be set by the capacity of the educational plant.[46]

When Duke's annual tuition and matriculation fee went up to $250 in 1930, Holton proposed that the summer charge should go from $1.50 per semester hour of credit to $4.00. The student who took the regular load of two courses (six hours) would therefore pay $24 tuition plus a $17 registration fee—a total of $41, or approximately one-fifth of the cost of the regular year.[47] Even in the depression, Duke's summer school was a bargain, especially for teachers, and by 1936 Few informed a close friend that the summer school had overflowed from the West campus to the East (Woman's College) campus. The surprised president had come to believe that the summer school, the medical school, and the Woman's College were Duke's most direct "roads to a strong south-wide and even nation-wide constituency."[48]

Both of the largest and perhaps strongest departments in Trinity College, English and history, had long had close ties with the work of the education department, and their faculty members, or certainly most of them, shared in the zeal for service in the matter of the public schools. William Kenneth Boyd, a Trinity alumnus and Columbia Ph.D., and William T. Laprade, with a Ph.D. from Johns Hopkins, were the two veteran members of the history department who carried over into the new university a long-standing interest in training teachers at all levels. Their zeal in that respect was passed on to a number of the newer members of the department.[49]

With Boyd in United States and particularly Southern history and Laprade in European and British history—he was one of the first Ph.D.'s in the South to be trained in European history when he came to Trinity in 1909—the history department gained significant strength through new appointments even before the organization of the university. E. Malcolm Carroll joined the department in 1923. With both his undergraduate and doctoral degree from the University of Michigan, Carroll had written his dissertation in United States history, and his first book, *The Origins of the Whig Party* (1925), which was in that field, was one of the early books published by the fledgling Duke University Press. John Spencer Bassett, who remained in close touch with affairs at Trinity-Duke, congratulated Flowers and Few on their support for the publication of Carroll's book and insisted that there was "no better possible publicity than this kind of a thing." The educational world had great interest in how Duke University would use its "wonderful gifts," Bassett added, and support for scholarly endeavors such as Carroll's would furnish one most satisfactory answer.[50]

Carroll did not long remain in United States history, however, and he serves as an early example of how certain scholars tailored or changed their own interests and research partly to meet the needs of the department. With both Boyd and a younger man, Randolph G. Adams (who soon left Duke), in United States history, and Laprade primarily in British history, there was obviously a need for someone in continental European history. Accordingly, Carroll, a meticulous scholar who already had a strong background in European history, shifted into that area and soon established, through a series of important books and articles, a solid national reputation in the field of modern European diplomatic history.

Alice M. Baldwin proved to be a significant bonus for the history department. Brought to Trinity in the summer of 1923 as a temporary dean of women, Baldwin impressed President Few, Boyd, and others as an able, mature, and scholarly woman. She ended up accepting an offer to become not only the dean of women but an assistant professor of history, the first woman to hold a full-fledged appointment to the faculty. A graduate of coeducational Cornell just after the turn of the century, Baldwin had early plans to pursue a doctorate in history, but they had been thwarted by family circumstances. She instead taught the subject for a number of years before going to the University of Chicago in 1921 to pursue the Ph.D. in colonial American history, which degree she received in 1926. With the publication in 1928 of her excellent dissertation, *The New England Clergy and the American Revolution*, Baldwin established her credentials in the field and, though she was only part-time in history, became an even more significant asset for the department.[51]

Joining Baldwin and Carroll as newcomers in history on the eve of the university's organization, Paul Neff Garber came into the department in 1924. An undergraduate at Bridgewater College in Virginia, Garber attended Crozer Theological Seminary for two years but then changed his career plans and obtained a doctorate in United States diplomatic history at the University of Pennsylvania. He remained in Duke's history department only two years, however, before he moved over to join the faculty of Duke's new School of Religion when it opened in 1926. Quickly establishing himself as a prominent historian of Methodism, Garber would eventually serve as dean of the school and then as a bishop in the Methodist church.

With five lively teacher-scholars when the university was organized—
Boyd, Laprade, Carroll, Baldwin, and Garber—history had a relatively
strong base on which to build. More than in certain other Duke departments, there was also from the beginning, thanks largely to Boyd and
Laprade, a clear understanding of what the transition from liberal arts
college to research university actually meant and of certain principles
that should be followed in making the transition. During the first month
of the new university's existence, Boyd advised Flowers, the university's
chief financial officer, that there were, he thought, two preeminent factors that distinguished a university from a college: a larger collection of
books and primary source materials in the library, and the publication
by the faculty of scholarly contributions to knowledge. Boyd suggested
that Trinity had been making some progress along those lines even before
the organization of the university, and now he and his colleagues were
eager to move farther and faster. Much involved in the operation of the
Duke University Press, Boyd noted that he and his colleagues had three
manuscripts ready for publication in 1925 and the promise of three others
for 1926. As for the university library, Boyd coolly suggested for a starter
that $10,000 be spent in the following year to build up collections in the
history of the southern United States and of Great Britain and her dominions.[52] Although no one on the faculty was more aggressive and energetic
in library-building than Boyd was, not even he got everything he wanted,
though he obtained a surprising amount.

As for the direction of the department itself, Boyd explained to Few
that the historians did not aspire to expand to teach all periods and all
phases of their subject; that would not only be too costly but would also
work against "the one thing essential in any group organization," that is,
a similarity in point of view and unity of effort. Rather, Boyd suggested
that the department, both in library purchases and appointments, should
try first to build on its strength in American and southern history and in
British history, with the latter to include the dominions. For the former,
Boyd now suggested that there should be an allocation of $2,000 per year
thereafter. Boyd argued that no collection of material from the British
dominions then existed in the United States, and the Duke library could
become "the mecca of all American students interested in these subjects."
While Laprade did get leave for research and library-building in England
in 1926–27, he did not get as much money as Boyd had suggested.

The second aspect of European history that the department wished to
emphasize, Boyd explained, was the growth of nationalism and diplomatic history since 1870. Rather than seek a graduate professor in that
field, however, Boyd urged that Carroll should be fully supported in his
desire to redirect his interests, for he had reportedly made an auspicious
beginning in that direction already.[53]

Boyd suggested that John Spencer Bassett be brought back to Duke to teach American social and intellectual history, but whatever might ultimately have come of that idea, Bassett was killed in a vehicular accident in Washington, D.C., early in 1928. The department had hoped to develop Garber as an historian of United States diplomacy, the subject of his dissertation and first book, but when he moved to the School of Religion, Boyd and Laprade in 1926 brought in J. Fred Rippy to teach that subject as well as Latin American history. A Berkeley Ph.D. who taught at the University of Chicago before coming to Duke, Rippy would leave Duke to return to Chicago in 1936. Before that happened, however, he played a significant role in making Duke a nationally recognized center for Latin American studies. Also contributing to that end, Boyd had, even before Rippy's appointment, gone after and succeeded in bringing to the Duke Press the *Hispanic American Historical Review*. The advantage of having that "high class" periodical published at Duke, Boyd explained, was that it would "put us on the map, and it will bring us contacts in foreign countries, the journal being of an international as well as national character."[54]

Not content with the Hispanic-American journal, Boyd at one time explored the possibility of bringing the *American Historical Review* to Duke. Although he failed in that endeavor, the American Historical Association did meet in Durham late in 1930, and the members were given ample opportunity to see the two campuses that had been so highly publicized. Boyd explained, while on leave in Cambridge, Massachusetts, that he wanted the *Review* for Duke in order to "knock a *solar plexus* into Yankeedom & turn Southward the center of historical scholarship." He added: "Harvard would be O.K. if it could only be born again into a socialized view of scholarship as well as of life. The Library & museums are O.K. but all else should be made over."[55]

While Boyd's somewhat jaundiced view of Harvard should not be taken too seriously, the fact was that Harvard went unrepresented in history at Duke for quite a few years. Although Boyd himself was a Trinity alumnus, he had obviously avoided anything resembling inbreeding in all of the department's early appointments. Yet when history did begin to retain certain of its own early Ph.D.'s, by and large the results were remarkably good.

The first of these was Robert H. Woody, who began teaching at Duke in 1929 and received his doctorate there the following year. Woody, who had been an undergraduate at Emory, was a native of the North Carolina mountain country who all his life took pride in his heritage and reflected it in his speech and friendly, unassuming manner. Upon Boyd's death in 1938, Woody took over the graduate courses in Civil War and southern history. He remained for many years a key figure in the department's graduate as well as undergraduate program, for Boyd and Laprade emphasized from the beginning that all of the "graduate professors" were to teach some undergraduate courses too. Woody would also later play an important role as director for a number of years of the George W. Flowers Memorial Collection of Southern Americana in the Duke library.

Alan K. Manchester, another early Ph.D. in history at Duke, was a Vanderbilt undergraduate (1920) who for five years in the 1920s taught school in Brazil and then served as president of a college there. Given Manchester's strong command of the Portuguese language, Brazilian history was a natural choice of specialization for him, and from 1930 onward he added further strength to Duke's Latin American program. Becoming dean of freshmen in 1934, Manchester revealed marked ability in administration and would later serve as the academic dean of Trinity College.

John Tate Lanning, who eventually became Duke's most distinguished specialist in Hispanic-American studies, was a Duke undergraduate who went to the University of California, Berkeley, for his doctorate (1928). Brought back to teach at Duke in 1927, Lanning turned out to be a fortunate backstop for Rippy, for upon the latter's resignation in 1936, Lanning was ready to take over in the Hispanic-American field. He would serve for many years as editor of the *Hispanic American Historical Review*, win various prizes and awards for his finely crafted books and articles, and serve the university's scholarly interests through his work on the Research Council.

Ernest William Nelson, a specialist in the Renaissance-Reformation era, came to Duke in 1929. With the A.B. and master's degrees from Clark University, Nelson received his Ph.D. at Cornell in 1925. An empathetic teacher who long supervised the instruction in the history department's important introductory course, Nelson also contributed greatly to the cultural, especially musical, life of the Duke and Durham communities.

Although Duke's financial problems in the early 1930s temporarily halted further expansion in history, Boyd argued strongly for the addition of a specialist in Far Eastern history. Admitting that with Carroll and Rippy the department had made a strong start in the international area, Boyd insisted that Duke needed scholars "to handle problems of present international importance as well as those of remoter interest." He believed that the future of international relations lay in the Far East, for there were the "vast man-power and the vast resources of the civilized world which I think will become the great stakes of diplomacy and economics." In addition to the Far Eastern historian, Boyd urged that an economic geographer and a specialist in comparative government should also be appointed for that area.[56]

Not until 1937, however, did Duke acquire the Far Eastern historian. Paul H. Clyde, a Canadian who was a naturalized citizen of the United

States, had received both his undergraduate and doctoral degrees from Stanford, the latter in 1925. He taught at Ohio State, Stanford, and the University of Kentucky before coming to Duke and had already acquired, through his books and articles, a solid reputation. At Duke he would later play a key role in helping to launch a most successful program in British Commonwealth studies and would capably direct the summer session for a number of years.

Seeking to find someone who could teach United States diplomatic history, which Rippy had taught before his resignation, and perhaps also constitutional history, the history department wound up making a crucial appointment that turned out quite differently than originally envisioned. Charles S. Sydnor, then teaching at the University of Mississippi, taught in Duke's summer school in 1935 and favorably impressed all who came to know him. A graduate of Hampden-Sydney, he received his Ph.D. from Johns Hopkins. Although his main interests and publications were in the field of antebellum southern history, Sydnor had competence in United States constitutional history and came to Duke in 1936 ostensibly to teach that. In recommending him to the administration, Boyd and Laprade noted that Sydnor was "a gentleman and a scholar, apparently of the Virginia gentry type" and added that he appeared to fit admirably "in our scheme."[57] The prediction turned out to be eminently sound, for Sydnor ultimately became one of the leading scholars in the country in the field of southern history. Moreover, Laprade would later write that, "If any single man is indispensable for the [department's] future, it is Professor Sydnor." Laprade explained that Sydnor had good judgment and was able, while supporting his own view of a matter, to understand a different one. Tactful in all human relations, he was genuinely interested in his work and in Duke. "In case of a change in the chairmanship of the department," Laprade concluded, Sydnor was "the only man in his age group who would satisfactorily fill the place."[58] Laprade's recommendation turned out to be prophetic, but Sydnor's untimely death in 1954, less than two years after he had succeeded Laprade as chairman, would rob the department and the university of his remarkable skills and services.

The appointment of Sydnor turned out to be the last in which Boyd played a large role, for he became ill in 1937 and died early in 1938. Since he had for many years worked closely with Laprade, who had also served at various times as acting chairman, the transition in departmental leadership was a smooth one. Nevertheless, Laprade, in an early example of semiformalized consultation of his more senior colleagues, began to meet regularly with the professors and associate professors in the department. They reported the practice to Few early in 1938, explained their intention to continue it, and made recommendations concerning the various administrative posts in the department. In words that they well knew would please the president, the senior historians avowed that they were interested in and expected to continue to concern themselves "with both the undergraduate and the graduate phases of the work of the department." The satisfactions that arose from teaching undergraduates, they explained, were somewhat different from those with graduates, and all members desired "to share in both."[59]

Whether it was this collegial approach that helped or just sheer good luck, the appointment of five young men in the late 1930s was destined to have a profound as well as a salutary impact on the history department and the university. All would spend their entire careers at Duke (except for service during World War II in the case of several) and, in various ways, would make highly significant contributions.[60] The first of these was William B. Hamilton, who came as a relatively mature graduate student in 1934, began to teach two years later, and received his doctorate from Duke in 1938. With both B.A. and M.A. degrees from the University of Mississippi, Hamilton taught in the public schools of his hometown of Jackson, Mississippi, for five years before coming to Duke. Laprade and others quickly spotted Hamilton as a person of unusual ability and promise, one who, in Laprade's words, seemed "likely to develop into a distinct personality and leader among the younger men on campus as well as into a scholar and good teacher." Not only was Hamilton industrious, quick, and imaginative, Laprade explained, but he possessed "friendly, human qualities" that enabled him to meet young and old on easy, equal terms and to sympathize with students.[61]

Laprade turned out to be remarkably prescient, for Hamilton did indeed prove to be a memorable teacher as well as a mover and shaker in the university, much as had been his father-in-law, W. K. Boyd. Although his dissertation and initial publications focused on early Mississippi history, he was particularly interested in the transmission of English law to the American frontier. This led naturally to an interest in British constitutional and legal history and, later, to the history of portions of the British Commonwealth. Thus, as in the case of Carroll, in pursuit of his own interests and better to meet the needs of the department, Hamilton became an historian of Britain and the Commonwealth. A lifelong supporter of the Duke library, he would later serve as editor of the *South Atlantic Quarterly* and become one of the principal architects of plans whereby the Duke faculty gained an important, meaningful voice in the governance of the institution. He would rank high among the "colorful personalities" that Few had once described as the essence of a university.

Theodore Ropp, who came to Duke in 1938, was in his own way as distinctive as Hamilton. The first Harvard Ph.D. in history at Duke, Ropp did his undergraduate work at Oberlin and taught for a year at Harvard before coming to Duke. With a strong background in modern European history,

Ropp faced the challenge during World War II of teaching naval history to huge throngs of Duke students in the United States Navy's V-12 officer-training program. From that experience as well as from his own interests, he became a military historian, and with the publication later (1959) of his highly acclaimed *War in the Modern World*, he became a nationally and even internationally recognized authority on the subject and the key figure in an outstanding program in military history at Duke.

On the eve of World War II, three other young scholars, all of whom came to Duke in 1939, joined Hamilton and Ropp as newcomers to the department. Harold T. Parker, arguably the most outstanding teacher that a department noted for strong teaching has produced, received both his undergraduate and doctoral degrees from Chicago, the latter in 1934. A year at Cornell (1929–30), where he studied with, among others, the noted historian Carl Becker, also benefitted Parker. A first-rate scholar in the area of the French Revolution and Napoleon, Parker would spend the larger part of his time and energy in his long career at Duke in teaching both graduate and undergraduate students and in administrative work for the department as well as important committee work for the university. Upon receiving one of several awards for his superb teaching, Parker would later say, quite characteristically, that he accepted it on behalf of Duke University, for he thought that Duke had long offered him "an environment favorable to good teaching," had encouraged and rewarded it, and possessed a central core of fifty to sixty "very effective teachers" who learned from each other. Moreover, Parker noted that he had taught at Duke "superior students, complex and sophisticated, who educate each other and their teachers."[62]

Several years younger than Parker, Arthur B. Ferguson, another Canadian and naturalized citizen, also joined the history department in 1939. After receiving his undergraduate degree at the University of Western Ontario, Ferguson obtained his doctorate at Cornell the same year he came to Duke. A quiet, highly individualistic scholar, Ferguson would gradually establish, through several books and many articles, a strong national reputation as an intellectual and cultural historian of the English Renaissance.

Rounding out the trio of newcomers in 1939 was Richard L. Watson, Jr. With both undergraduate and doctoral degrees from Yale, Watson, like Parker and Ferguson, took extended leave for military service during World War II. Though his dissertation had focused on nineteenth-century United States political history, he would gradually move into the Progressive era of the early twentieth century and develop strong courses as well as publications in that area. An energetic person who liked to administer as well as teach, he would later serve as chairman of the department and as an influential leader of the faculty in the area of university governance.

From six members in 1925 (one member an administrator and therefore part-time) to eighteen in 1939 (two members were also administrators and therefore part-time), the history department had grown and diversified remarkably. Yet through Boyd first and then Laprade the department had strong ties with the traditions of Trinity College, traditions which were partly embodied in the then still-flourishing Trinity College Historical Society. It continued to serve as an institutional link with the past and as the principal meeting ground for faculty, graduate students, a few undergraduates occasionally, and others in the university with interest in history.

Just as history benefitted from a strong start in the Trinity era, so too did English, by far the largest department in the area of the humanities. While Few had finally given up his class in Shakespeare by 1921, he kept a special interest in the department and helped in various ways to strengthen it. Frank C. Brown, the chairman of the department for many years before and after the university was organized, had come to Trinity in 1909. A native Virginian with a doctorate from Chicago (1903), Brown was a handsome, energetic person whose main claim to scholarship was as an assiduous collector of folklore. Seven volumes of materials that he collected would be edited by certain of his colleagues after his death and published by the Duke Press. By 1924, and for many years afterward, Brown was so deeply involved in the planning and then the building of the plants on both of Duke's campuses that he obviously had little time to spend on departmental affairs. Trusted and liked by Few and B. N. and J. B. Duke, Brown came to serve as a liaison between the Trinity-Duke administration on the one hand and Trumbauer's architectural staff and A. C. Lee's construction company on the other. Actually the configuration was a bit more complicated than that, for Brown had also to deal with the Duke Endowment's building committee, which, in effect, meant George G. Allen and William R. Perkins. Few gave Brown the additional title of comptroller of the university to cover his nebulous but important and time-consuming duties.

While Frank Brown played a central role in the physical transition from college to university, more important in the scholarly aspect of the English department was the part played by a younger man, Newman I. White. A Trinity alumnus who went to Harvard for his doctorate (1918), he taught briefly at Washington University in St. Louis before returning to teach at Trinity in 1919. A courageous man of independent, liberal views, he gained the respect of his colleagues in English as well as of the faculty at large. He edited and published pioneering anthologies of

African-American poetry and folk songs in the 1920s and, in the words of an historian of the English department, "reached stardom" in 1940 with a splendid two-volume biography of the English poet Shelley.[63] White succeeded Brown as chairman of English when the latter died in 1943.

Allan G. Gilbert, another outstanding scholar, joined Trinity's English department in 1921. A Cornell undergraduate, he went to Yale for a master's degree and then back to Cornell for his doctorate in 1912. Teaching at Cornell, Rice, and the University of Tennessee before coming to Trinity, Gilbert in 1921 was already on his way to establishing a preeminent national, even international, reputation as a scholar of Renaissance literature in Italy and England. An energetic, colorful person, he was a zealot for physical fitness, and many decades before jogging became popular, Gilbert's neighbors marvelled at the sight of him in his track clothes as he dashed about the streets. He would continue the practice long after he retired from Duke, but not from teaching, in 1957.

The third scholar who strengthened Trinity's English department was Paull F. Baum, who came in 1923. A graduate of Hamilton College, Baum spent several years studying at various leading universities in Germany and France before obtaining his doctorate at Harvard in 1915. He remained there to teach until he came to Trinity. An unusually well equipped philologist and medievalist, Baum proved to be a valuable resource in the launching of Duke's graduate school, in the building of the library, and, in the late 1920s, in the operations of the Duke Press.

Since Baum, White, and Gilbert would long stand out as among Duke's most prominent scholars in English, their arrival considerably before the university's organization is another sign of Trinity's maturation as a college in the years after World War I. Since the best and most prominent work of the three English professors still lay in the future in 1925, Few and Frank Brown apparently believed initially that the department needed the appointment of a "star." Few, at any rate, wrote his longtime friend at Harvard, George L. Kittredge, for help in finding a "very promising young scholar" who would have as his chief responsibility the giving of advanced classes and helping to build up the graduate program and the library. Few, in the early period when he was still thinking big about salaries, wrote another old friend from Harvard days that in English at Duke "we shall want some of the best men available and for the very best men we shall expect to pay as much as anybody else pays and under some conditions probably something more."[64]

That kind of talk did not last long. When one of Few's correspondents suggested in 1927 the name of an established scholar at the University of Illinois who might be induced to go to Duke, Few replied that he thought it would be unwise to attempt to hire the man, for Duke already had built up "an admirable teaching machine" in English. "All the men are young,"

Few explained, "with their spurs yet to be won." They represented the strongest graduate schools in the nation as well as Oxford, and bringing in an established scholar at a salary higher than those prevailing in the department would only tend to hurt morale.[65]

English acquired no new, big name comparable to that of McDougal in psychology, but the department did make several important appointments. In thinking about the direction in which the department should go and the shape it should take, Few invited some of the younger members to express their views. Gilbert, grappling with the department's inescapable responsibility of staffing the numerous sections of English composition, two semesters of which all freshmen were required to take, pointed out that "first-class men content to teach composition only" could not be found. Yet he also argued that a person who was unwilling to teach any composition class to freshmen was not sufficiently in contact with or sympathetic with students to teach literature. Someone else added to Gilbert's long memorandum that the department, aside from the matter of English composition, should aim to stimulate an appreciation of literature, a desire to do creative writing, and a love of research.[66] The department never adopted an official statement of aims, but its staffing and course offerings reflected all three emphases. At the same time, all members of the department long taught at least one section of the large freshman and sophomore courses in English.

Among the teachers whom several generations of Duke students knew well were several who labored mainly, and intensely, in the basic composition courses. Archibald C. Jordan was a Trinity alumnus (1918) who taught in the Trinity Park preparatory school before it was phased out in 1922. After attending Trinity's law school, he got a master's degree from Columbia and began to teach freshman English at Duke in 1925. He was famous as a stickler for proper grammar, and "A. C. Jordan's English" became a well-known institution within the university. From the perspective of a more grammatically relaxed (and sloppier) later period, one is intrigued to find a memorandum in which A. C. Jordan and two of his colleagues bluntly spelled out a list of six errors, any one of which would result in a grade of F on an English theme: (1) one misspelled word (three in an impromptu, in-class theme); (2) one incomplete sentence (exceptions for "effect" might be starred); (3) one comma fault or fused sentence; (4) one disagreement of subject and predicate (except in one or two special cases); (5) one dangling modifier; and (6) one serious incorrect sequence of tenses.[67]

In light of such standards, which would probably sink many, many young sailors on academic seas in the late twentieth century, one is not surprised to discover that in the fall of 1941, when Duke was still very much a civilian and "normal" campus, 7.5 percent of the entire freshman class of 781 students flunked English I. While an additional 19 percent made a grade of D, only 3 percent received the top grade of A. The C students also vastly outnumbered those who got B—50 percent versus 19 percent.[68]

There were others who toiled mainly in the composition classes in the early years, and some of them became well-known figures in Duke's English department. William M. Blackburn was a graduate of Furman University (1921) who won a Rhodes scholarship for study at Oxford University, where he received the B.A. and M.A. degrees. Coming to Duke in 1926, Blackburn also received a Ph.D. from Yale in 1943. Not a run-of-the-mill scholar by any means, Blackburn gradually demonstrated that his particular strength lay in supervising honors students and in nurturing creative writers. His classes at Duke would later be crucial in the training of, or perhaps it would be more accurate to say the inspiring of, a significant number of the most outstanding novelists in the nation, including, among others, William Styron, Reynolds Price, and Anne Tyler.

Another who came in the early years of the university was Lewis Patton. Also, like Blackburn, a Furman graduate (1923), Patton received his doctorate from Yale in 1937. A Coleridge scholar, Patton would later serve as director of the freshman English course. Charles Ward, a graduate of Baker University, began teaching part-time at Duke in 1927, while he was still a graduate student. Receiving his Duke Ph.D. in 1934, Ward was a specialist in seventeenth-century Restoration literature and would later in the 1950s serve as chairman of the department as well as dean of undergraduate studies.

Marie Updike White, wife of Newman White, received the B.A. and master's degrees from Washington University in 1915 and 1916, respectively. A witty, outspoken woman, she taught freshman English from the mid-1920s on but became best known for her popular classes in the modern drama. She and Mary H. Vance, another instructor in English, were the first women to be members of the department.

The appointment of Jay B. Hubbell in 1927 was particularly important, for it meant a new significance for American literature not only at Duke but, ultimately, in the nation and world. While courses in the subject had been taught occasionally in Trinity College, there had been no specialist in the field since Edwin Mims had left Trinity in 1909. Having received his undergraduate degree at the University of Richmond (1902), Hubbell got a master's at Harvard and then in 1922 a Ph.D. at Columbia. He taught at a number of institutions, including Southern Methodist University, before coming to Duke. A sound scholar as well as an academic entrepreneur in the best sense of the word, Hubbell played a leading role in helping to organize the growing number of specialists in the rising field of American literature into their own section of the Modern Language Association and in getting Duke University and its press to cooperate with that section in launching a research journal in 1929. Known simply as *American Literature*, it was long edited by Hubbell and quickly became the leading journal in the field, a field which acquired increasing international dimensions as the century advanced.

As part of Hubbell's mission at Duke, he undertook to build up the library's collection in American and especially southern literature. "'Southern literature' is intrinsically less important than other fields," Hubbell conceded in a letter to Few, "but it is important enough, I think, for one Southern university to pay some attention to it." None of the northern graduate schools were paying much attention to the field, Hubbell noted, and since Duke held such rich collections in southern history, thanks primarily to Bassett and then Boyd, it would only seem logical to have literary materials as a complement. Hubbell got the special appropriation that he requested.[69]

To backstop and assist Hubbell, a younger man, Clarence L. F. Gohdes, came in 1930. An undergraduate at Capital University, Gohdes went to Harvard for a master's and then to Columbia for the Ph.D. he received in 1931. He soon became the co-managing editor of *American Literature* and would later serve for many years, after Hubbell's retirement, as editor.[70]

The appointment of Walter K. Greene as professor of English in 1928 was more important perhaps for the undergraduate colleges as a whole than for the department, for he played a highly creative and important administrative role as the first dean of undergraduate instruction. A native South Carolinian, he was, like Few and Wannamaker, also a graduate of Wofford College (1903). He got a master's degree from Vanderbilt and taught in secondary schools for a number of years before obtaining his Ph.D. at Harvard in 1923. An active, prominent Methodist layman, Green served as a professor and dean at Wesleyan College in Georgia before coming to Duke. Sharing a great many of Few's concerns about academic excellence and the ethical dimensions of education, Greene helped bring about significant curricular changes.[71] Announcing Greene's appointment early in 1928, Few noted that Duke was undertaking to make a fairly sharp distinction between undergraduate work in the first two years and that of the junior and senior years. With advanced sections for the abler freshmen and sophomores, Duke hoped to select their teachers for personal qualities and "teaching power" as well as for knowledge of the subject taught. The aim was not only the intellectual development of the students but the shaping of their personalities and characters.[72] Greene would resign in 1942 to become the president of Wofford, and his departure would contribute to the emergence of serious problems that developed in the 1940s and especially in the years immediately after World War II.

Another appointment in English that had a significant impact on the larger university community was that in 1930 of Alfred T. West in the field of drama. A graduate of Alabama Polytechnic Institute (Auburn) who received a master's at the University of Alabama, West also studied at the American Academy of Dramatic Arts in New York before coming to Duke. Reorganizing the Taurian Players at first, West eventually launched the Duke Players, which became and long remained the students' chief vehicle for dramatic productions.

In the mid-1930s several persons who would long remain joined the English department. William H. Irving was a Canadian who, after graduating from Mount Allison University, went as a Rhodes scholar to Oxford, where he received the B.A. and M.A. degrees. Then, after obtaining the Ph.D. at Harvard in 1926, he taught there and at Northwestern before coming to Duke in 1936. Sharing Blackburn's appetite and talent for the supervision of honors work, Irving specialized in eighteenth-century literature and would later serve as chairman of the department.

C. Richard Sanders came to Duke in 1937, at first to supervise the instruction in the large freshman course. With undergraduate and master's degrees from Emory, Sanders received his Ph.D. at Chicago and taught at Emory prior to accepting the Duke appointment. A specialist in nineteenth-century British literature, Sanders would later launch, in collaboration with professors at the University of Edinburgh, a monumental edition of the correspondence of Thomas Carlyle, a project that would continue long after Sanders's retirement.

Two of Duke's own Ph.D.'s in English, Mary Poteat and George C. Harwell, began teaching in 1935 and remained until they retired. Over the years both taught composition to countless numbers of students, mostly women students in the case of Poteat and engineers in the case of Harwell.

Even as the English department burgeoned and grew more diverse, Few kept a special interest in it and particularly in the creative-writing courses. When Newman White explained that his course in the writing of poetry could not be scheduled and treated like any ordinary course for undergraduates, Few quickly understood and lent support. White argued that it was "essentially absurd" to expect a person to be poetic for one hour on Monday, Wednesday, and Friday at 9:10 A.M. He preferred, therefore, to treat the verse-writing class more like honors-type independent study and to meet the class one evening a week at his home.[73] "I know a few students here who give great promise [at writing verse]," Few advised one correspondent, "and am anxious to see them stimulated and encouraged as fully as possible." On another occasion, when Few learned that a potentially promising poet had applied for a fellowship at Duke, the busy president wrote the dean at the young man's college, asked for his opinion, and explained that he (Few) was doing whatever he could "to encourage so-called creative writing."[74] By the time of Few's death in October, 1940,

1   William P. Few, president of Trinity College, 1910-1924; president of Duke University, 1924-1940.
2   Robert L. Flowers, president of Duke University, 1940-1948.

3

3 Alice M. Baldwin, dean of the Woman's College of Duke University, 1930-1947.

4 William H. Glasson, dean of the Graduate School of Arts and Sciences.

5 Edmund D. Soper, dean of the School of Religion and vice-president for student life, 1925-1928.

6 Wilburt C. Davison, dean of the Medical School, and students pose for artist Wayman Adams, ca. 1947.

7 Justin Miller, dean of the School of Law, 1930-1934.

8 Clarence F. Korstian, dean of the School of Forestry.

9 Bessie Baker, dean of the School of Nursing.

4

5

6

7

8

9

10 James B. Duke and a group of his business associates in the early 1920s.
Duke is fourth from left in front; on his left is George G. Allen and between them
in back is William R. Perkins. Alex H. Sands, Jr., who also played an important
role in Duke University's history, is wearing dark glasses in the second row on the
right.

11   Construction begins on the old Trinity (East) Campus,
summer 1925. Memorial Gymnasium is in the background.
12   Early stages of the Science Building (later the Art Museum) on
East Campus, April, 1926. Epworth, Aycock, and East Duke are in
the background.

11

12

13   By August, 1926, the Library, Alspaugh, and Pegram become recognizable.

14   Construction begins on the "new land" (West Campus) in the summer of 1927. This is a view of what would become Chapel Drive looking toward the traffic circle, with Wannamaker Drive on the right and Flowers Drive on the left.

13

14

15 Doris Duke, not yet 16, participates in the cornerstone-laying on West
Campus, June, 1928. George G. Allen, chairman of the Duke Endowment, is
on the right and A. C. Lee, chief engineer for construction, is on the left.

16

17

16   First occupied in September, 1930, West Campus gets its first trees planted in the quadrangles that autumn.

17   By May, 1930 the Union, Library, Law, and Medical School buildings are virtually complete. Note that construction on the Chemistry Building has not begun and will not until the railway track into the main quadrangles can be removed.

18   Begun last among the original Tudor Gothic buildings, the Chapel had reached this stage by late summer, 1931.

18

19

20

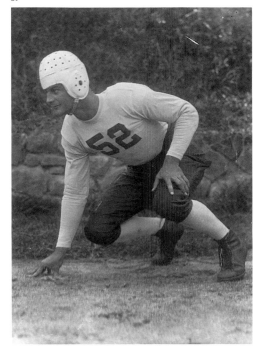

21

19   A graduating senior, Louise Bullington, represents "The University Woman" in the 1926 *Chanticleer* yearbook.

20   Voted the football team's most valuable player in 1930, Bill Murray also served as president of the Men's Student Government Association.

21   The "Big 3"— Flowers, Few, and Wannamaker—welcome Wallace Wade (second from the left) to Duke in January, 1931.

22   Johnny Long and his Duke Collegians in an early broadcast from the West Campus Union's lobby (Alumni Lounge) in May, 1934.

23

24

25

23   As the Wade-coached football teams win more and more victories, pre-game pep meetings grow livelier. Note the pajama-wearing fad of 1936.

24   "East is East and West is West, But *Ever* the Twain Shall Meet" in the 1939 *Chanticleer*.

25   Formally attired, Dukies swing into the Big Band era with Jimmy Lunceford's orchestra in January, 1938. (Photograph for 1938 *Chanticleer*.)

26 Dean Mary Grace Wilson gives last-minute instructions to Woman's College students who are about to help serve at a tea in 1940.

27 Candle-lit and civilized dining, rare for the men on West, occurred frequently in the East Campus Union.

28   Students rehearse for the first show to be staged by Hoof and Horn. (From the 1941 *Chanticleer*.)

29   Although World War II was well underway the United States was not yet in it, and Benny Goodman's band played for the men's Pan-Hellenic dances in 1941.(From the 1941 *Chanticleer*.)

30   The tag end of the Homecoming Parade at Five Points in Durham,
October, 1941.

31   The receipt of Duke's second invitation to the Rose Bowl late in
1941 inspires Duke students to celebrate in downtown Durham.

32   Coach Wade and the Duke bench watch Oregon State defeat the
Blue Devils in January, 1942, when the Rose Bowl game was played in
Durham.

31

32

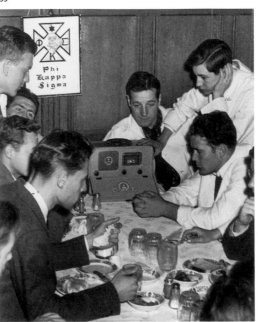

33   Students in a West Campus dining hall listen as President F. D. Roosevelt asks Congress for a declaration of war against Japan on December 8, 1941.
34   Even before the Navy's V-12 unit virtually took over West Campus, students in the Woman's College joined in the war effort.

34

35   A Marine unit, commanded by Major Walter G. Cooper, was a part of the
V-12 program at Duke.

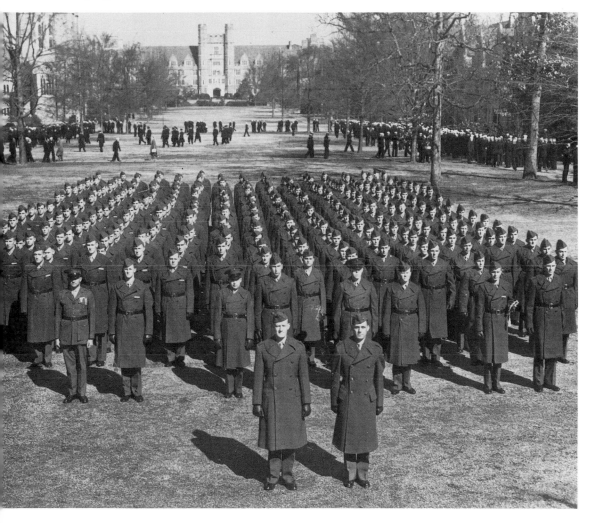

36

36   Uniformed Duke students ponder
the big news of June, 1944.
37   With Duke back on a peace-time
footing, cabin parties off campus
become popular with the students.
(From the 1946 *Chanticleer*)

37

38   President Flowers, Dean Baldwin, and Vice-President and Mrs. Charles Jordan
(right to left) greet new students at a reception on the grounds of "Four Acres," the
former home of the B. N. Duke family, in September, 1946.

39

40

39   Fraternity men serenade a Woman's
College student who has just received a
fraternity pin from a brother. (From the
1947 *Chanticleer*.)

40   After the dorm closes to visitors at
10:30 on weeknights, the women of
Bassett House on East enjoy a pajama
party. (From the 1947 *Chanticleer*.)

41   After World War II, beer becomes
more openly a part of student social life,
as is shown by these Duke students at a
local steak house in 1948. (From the
1948 *Chanticleer*.)

42   A class in the late 1940s with some
less-than-alert students in the rear ranks.

43   A. Hollis Edens is named as Duke's third president in late 1948.

44   Paul M. Gross, chemistry chairman and dean of the Graduate School, whom President Edens agreed to have named as vice president for education.

he had every reason to be proud of the English department. Not only was it an "admirable teaching machine," as Few had noted earlier, but various members of the department had already demonstrated outstanding scholarly ability and several of the younger professors showed clear signs of future outstanding achievement.

Unfortunately for the humanities at Duke in the early years of the university, no other department in that division was a match for English. Romance languages, a considerably smaller department, was still chaired in the last years of the Trinity era by Albert M. Webb, who had joined the faculty in 1903. With B.A. and M.A. degrees from Yale, Webb had also studied at the Sorbonne, in Madrid, and in Florence, and he continued to serve as chairman of the department until his retirement in 1947.

In addition to Webb, two other faculty members in romance languages carried over from Trinity into the university and were many years at Duke. Frederick A. G. Cowper received B.A. and M.A. degrees from Trinity College in Connecticut. Between the two degrees, however, he studied at the universities of Strasbourg and Geneva and, after coming to Trinity in North Carolina in 1918, received a Ph.D. from Chicago in 1920. He would later publish, among other things, a critical edition of a twelfth-century French writer, Gautier d'Arras. Edward H. Young joined the Trinity faculty in 1923. With an undergraduate degree from St. Stephens College, he had a master's from the University of Western Ontario, studied one year at the University of Pittsburgh, and spent several years at different times studying at the Sorbonne.

The first two long-term appointments in romance languages after the university was organized were those of Brady R. Jordan in 1927 and Loring B. Walton in 1929. An undergraduate at Princeton, Jordan later studied at the Sorbonne in 1921 and received his Ph.D. at Wisconsin in 1926. Having also taught at a number of schools and colleges before teaching at Wisconsin during his graduate study, Jordan was at the University of Tennessee for one year before coming to Duke. Loring Walton was another Princeton alumnus from the same class as Jordan (1916), and Walton also received a degree from the Sorbonne. Teaching at Princeton for several years before coming to Duke, Walton received his Ph.D. from Chicago in 1943 and published in the field of modern French literature, including a book on Anatole France.

Gifford Davis, a native of Maine who never lost his Down East accent but nevertheless made a graceful transition into being a Tar Heel, came to Duke in 1930. He was a graduate of Bowdoin who went to Harvard for the Ph.D. that he received in 1933. While Davis initially taught both French and Spanish, his advanced courses and publications were in the field of medieval and nineteenth-century Spanish literature.

Neal Dow and his French-born wife, Marie-Thérèse Dow, came to Duke in 1934 and for more than three decades were a prominent couple in matters related to French language and culture. With his doctorate from the University of Pennsylvania, Neal Dow also studied at universities in France and, in addition to writing textbooks for the study of French, translated a number of American books into that language. Madame Dow, as countless Duke students called her, not only taught the language but for many years directed and even costumed student productions of plays by Molière, Beaumarchais, and other notable French playwrights.

Two junior members of the romance language department were well known to many students in the 1930s and 1940s. Mary Lois Raymond, with a B.S. degree from Mount Holyoke (1912) and a master's from Radcliffe, came to Duke in 1931 and remained until her death in 1949. Lanier W. Pratt was a Davidson graduate (1934) who received a master's degree from Duke in 1938 and became an instructor in the department in 1940. Pratt's academic career was interrupted first by his service as an officer in the United States Navy during World War II and then later when he was called back into service during the Korean War. Before and after that latter service, however, he became a popular teacher as well as a much-admired assistant dean until his career was cut short by his death in 1956.

Just as Few apparently played no significant role in appointments made in romance languages, which was a different matter from English, so too did the president leave the department of German largely in the hands of Wannamaker. He, after all, had continued to serve as chairman in German even after becoming dean of the college in 1917 and then later dean of the university. A Wofford graduate who came to Trinity as a graduate student and part-time instructor, Wannamaker received a master's degree from Trinity in 1901 and another from Harvard in 1902. After extensive study at several German universities, he returned to Trinity as professor of German in 1905. One who enjoyed teaching and a highly efficient administrator, Wannamaker moved away from the classroom slowly and with reluctance only when his duties as Few's chief educational officer became too demanding. As late as the academic year 1924–25 Wannamaker taught, as he said "for the love of it," nine hours (three classes) per week, including "a wonderful class in Goethe's Faust." While he added that he realized that his duties as dean would no longer allow that much teaching, he avowed that he should "always cherish a great love for the work of teaching."[75]

In addition to Wannamaker, two other men in German carried over from the Trinity era. Charles A. Krummel came to Trinity in 1922, soon after receiving his doctorate at Wisconsin. Prior to that he had done undergraduate work at Central Wesleyan College (1905), received a master's degree at Syracuse, and studied at several other institutions including the University of Marburg in Germany. He taught at several schools but longest at Ohio Wesleyan before coming to Trinity. The year following Krummel's appointment, Frederick E. Wilson joined Trinity's German department. With a B.A. from Oberlin and a master's from Columbia, he had also studied at Harvard and Leipzig and taught at the American University of Beirut prior to coming to Trinity.

With the organization of the university, Wannamaker quite understandably sought to find what he termed "an outstanding man" to appoint in German. "I want this man in German to measure up well with some of the other bigger men we are bringing here," Wannamaker explained.[76] Presumably he felt that he had found what he was looking for when he brought Clement Vollmer to Duke in 1926. An undergraduate at Heidelburg College in Ohio, Vollmer went to Pennsylvania for graduate work and received his Ph.D. in 1915. He taught one year at Cornell and ten years at Pennsylvania prior to the Duke appointment and had published a book, *The American Novel in Germany*, in 1918. Vollmer eventually succeeded Wannamaker as chairman.

Two additional younger men were soon added in German. Lambert A. Shears received his B.A. degree from Columbia in 1912 and his Ph.D. from the same institution in 1922. He taught at several institutions before coming to Duke. Then in 1930, to round out the staff in the years before World War II, William Cary Maxwell began teaching German at Duke. A Duke undergraduate (1926) and probably one of Wannamaker's protégés, Maxwell went to the University of Heidelburg for the doctorate, which he received in 1932.

Wannamaker took pride in the fact that the study of German had not declined at Trinity during World War I, which was not the case in many other institutions. In the late 1920s he continued to take satisfaction from healthy enrollments in German and declared that Duke had more students in German than the combined number from all the other colleges in North Carolina, in fact "far more here than in any other southern institution of learning."[77] What he did not explain, however, was that the students studying German were very largely undergraduates and that the department, like Duke's other foreign language departments at that time, attracted too few graduate students for an ambitious research university.

The departments of Greek and Latin, which were not combined into a single Department of Classical Studies until much later, were both smaller than the German department. In Latin, Arthur M. Gates was the veteran link with Trinity. He had come there in 1909, the year before he received his doctorate from Johns Hopkins. Prior to that he had received the B.A. and M.A. degrees from Wesleyan University in the mid-1890s and then taught in several preparatory schools for a number of years.

Joining Gates in 1925, Ruskin Raymond Roseborough had two doctorates: one from Pennsylvania and one from the University of Louvain. An undergraduate at Stetson, Roseborough was a fellow at the American Academy in Rome from 1922 to 1924 and taught for a year at the University of North Carolina before being made chairman of Duke's Department of Latin and Roman Studies.

Jesse Lee Rose began teaching in the Latin department in 1936. With an A.B. from the College of Charleston, he received his master's and Ph.D. at Duke.

A final and important appointment in Latin before World War II came in 1937 when Robert S. Rogers joined the department. Having received an undergraduate degree at Pennsylvania in 1920, he went to Columbia for a master's degree and then received his doctorate from Princeton in 1923. He too was a fellow at the American Academy in Rome and taught at Western Reserve University before coming to Duke. Author of books and articles dealing with the early Roman Empire, Rogers succeeded Roseborough as chairman of the department in 1939.

In the small Greek department, Charles W. Peppler was the veteran from Trinity College. He had received both his A.B. and his Ph.D. degrees from Johns Hopkins (the latter in 1898) and had taught at Emory before coming to Trinity in 1912. Although the number of undergraduates studying Greek had declined markedly as the nineteenth century's classical curriculum gave way to the elective system and modern languages, Peppler found himself, as a one-man department, pushed hard. In 1930 he finally got some help when two younger men joined the Greek staff.

James N. Truesdale was a Duke graduate all the way: A.B. in 1928, master's in 1929, and Ph.D. in 1936. Beginning his teaching career in 1930, he gradually gained a long-lived reputation as a conscientious, kindly professor who introduced countless students to "the wonder and glory of Hellenism," as one former student declared. Describing Truesdale as a "marvellous blend of quiet dignity and genuine friendliness in and out of the classroom," this same Duke alumnus, who himself became a professor, paid Truesdale the ultimate academic tribute: "You were my finest teacher and the most significant influence upon my own academic development."[78] In the same year that Truesdale began teaching at Duke, 1930, Vernon E. Way joined the staff in Greek and remained for nearly three decades.

Philosophy, another small humanities department, was headed by a widely admired veteran of the Trinity era, William Ivey Cranford. Actually, when the university was organized Cranford was the sole member of the department, since another member who had taught both philosophy and psychology had resigned. A graduate of Trinity in 1891, Cranford had gone to Yale for his Ph.D. (1895) and then returned to become professor of philosophy at Trinity. When Few became president of Trinity in 1910,

Cranford had taken over as dean of the college; he served in that post for seven years. When he died at age sixty-eight in 1936, he was the oldest alumnus in service at Duke, and Few said about him, among other things: "He was loyal, competent, and unselfish—a rare combination—and the sort of man that is to an educational administrator as the shadow of a great rock in a weary land."[79]

Attempting earlier to build up the department, no doubt in consultation with Cranford, Few made overtures in 1927 to at least two philosophers at other institutions. Failing in those efforts, Few decided that Duke needed a "great personalistic philosopher" and that "we are more apt to get him from Great Britain than from America."[80] Few may have gotten his notion about more desirable hunting in Britain from his experience with McDougall, who came to Duke in 1926. At any rate, another transplanted Englishman proved to be one of the two important new appointments in philosophy.

Alban G. Widgery, who came to Duke in 1930, held both B.A. and M.A. degrees from Cambridge. After teaching for two years at Bristol University, he studied at Marburg, Jena, and the Sorbonne. He then spent a decade or so teaching at the University of Bombay and returned to Cambridge as a lecturer in the philosophy of religion in 1923. Crossing the Atlantic to teach at Bowdoin in 1928 and the following year at Cornell, Widgery decided to make his home in the United States and accepted the Duke post. A much-published scholar, he served as chairman of the department for ten years after Cranford's death and became president of the American Theological Society in 1940.

In some ways Widgery may never have comfortably adapted to the American university system, which differs greatly in many respects from the British model. At Duke, as at most other American colleges and universities before and for a considerable interlude after World War II, even full professors were expected to check class rolls for attendance. Furthermore, a student's absences from class at Duke beyond the allowed maximum could result in the loss of "quality points." Widgery, rebelling against the system approved by the Duke faculty and upheld by the administration, refused to report absences because he felt the penalty for excessive absences could result in the misrepresentation of the scholarly capacity of a student. "I feel myself in the position of a person who in former times in England," he advised the dean, "would not be an informer about stealing sheep because of the penalty of hanging." From such refusals and protests by individuals, he argued, the law was eventually changed.[81] Wannamaker, unmoved by the argument, stood by Duke's regulations, and Widgery presumably complied with them. A former student of Widgery's described him, in Dr. Johnson's phrase, as "a clubbable man," one who made his home in the Duke Forest area "almost a club for younger philosophers."

Yet this same Duke alumnus also noted: "We could not help sometimes feeling that were he to turn his formidable analytical skills upon his own views with the same ruthlessness that he applied them to ours, he would have come to different philosophical conclusions."[82]

While Widgery was obviously a distinctive addition to philosophy in 1930, he was not the only one, for Katherine Everett Gilbert also joined the department in that year and thus became also the first woman at Duke to hold the rank of full professor. A graduate of Brown whose doctorate was from Cornell, Gilbert published well-received books and articles in the field of aesthetics, and in 1942, while continuing to teach in the philosophy department, became the organizing chairwoman of a new Department of Aesthetics, Art, and Music at Duke.[83]

A younger man, Furman G. McClarty, began to teach in the philosophy department in 1933. A Duke undergraduate (1927), he went to Oxford as a Rhodes scholar and received the B.A. there in 1930. After obtaining a master's at Harvard, he returned to Duke to teach and work for the Ph.D., which he received in 1935. McClarty specialized in Hellenistic philosophy and the history of philosophy.

Around the mid-1930s President Few involved himself in an effort to strengthen philosophy even further, along with the departments of Latin and physics. The first appointment, in philosophy, to result from this endeavor was that of George A. Morgan, Jr., in 1936. He was an alumnus of Emory who went to Harvard for his Ph.D. (1930) and taught first at Harvard and then at Hamilton College before joining the Duke faculty as a specialist in ethics and social philosophy. Another Harvard man, Henry S. Leonard, came in 1937. With three degrees from Harvard (the Ph.D. in 1931), he taught there before coming to Duke in the field of logic and the philosophy of science.

By the eve of World War II, philosophy had grown from a one-person department in 1925 to one having six well-qualified specialists in a variety of areas. Furthermore, a distinguished visiting professor, Homer H. Dubs, taught Oriental philosophy and religion in the department from 1937 until 1943. Unfortunately, a kindred department in the humanities, religion, had a more problematical development.

Duke's undergraduate Department of Religion long had something of an identity problem, for it was included in and overshadowed after 1926 by the new School of Religion, which was renamed the Divinity School in 1941. Yet with all Duke undergraduates required to take two semesters of Bible, a curricular provision inherited from the Trinity era, there were obviously large staffing problems. Required courses involving quite large numbers of students are risky, difficult things. Sometimes departments and teachers rise to the challenge, and sometimes they do not. Perhaps an example of the latter situation in religion is furnished by a Duke student of the 1940s who remembers seeing little more of the instructor in the required Bible course than the green eyeshade worn by the teacher, who sat at a desk and scrupulously read notes or lectures to the class. Most members of the religion department did better, of course, but in its undergraduate dimension, religion would not come into its own as an important, vibrant department until quite a few years after 1925, in fact, until after World War II.

That lag in the development of the undergraduate Department of Religion was ironic, for President Few was probably more closely involved in the staffing and operations of it than was the case with any other department. This was true not only because of his keen personal interest in and commitment to religion, in both its intellectual and spiritual dimensions, but because of his oft-proclaimed assertion that one of the ways in which Duke was to be a different kind of research university was that religion and religious values were to be treated in the university with the utmost seriousness and respect.[84] In the case of the undergraduate Department of Religion, however, an unfortunate dichotomy in Few's mind between "good teachers" and "first-class scholars," or, to put the matter another way, between undergraduate and graduate-level teaching, led to an imbalance between Duke's undergraduate Department of Religion and the graduate-level professors in the School of Religion.

There were three professors of religion who carried over from the Trinity era, and all three were Trinity alumni: Hersey Spence, James Cannon III, and Jesse Ormond. Spence, the first of the three to be appointed, held two degrees from Trinity, a B.A. in 1907 and an M.A. the following year. Ordained as a Methodist preacher, he served in various pastorates, taught English at Trinity during one three-year interval, and then in 1918 was named professor of religious education. Receiving his Bachelor of Divinity degree from Duke in 1927, he was one of the first graduates of the School of Religion. A popular speaker and raconteur, Spence became conspicuous on the Duke campus for many years as the producer of religious pageants and dramas.[85]

James Cannon III, the son of a well-known Methodist bishop with the same name, graduated from Trinity in 1914. He too became a Methodist minister and, after obtaining a master's degree at Princeton University, joined the Trinity faculty in 1919 to teach courses in the Bible and world missions. The year the university was organized, 1924–25, he was on leave and at Princeton Theological Seminary obtaining a B.D. degree.

Jesse M. Ormond, the third of the Trinity College carryovers, graduated from Trinity in 1902 and received his divinity degree from Vanderbilt in 1910. After serving a number of Methodist churches in North Carolina, he taught pastoral and practical theology at Southern Methodist University for a year before joining the Trinity faculty in 1923. He soon became a specialist in rural church work and participated in the School of Religion's pioneering scholarship program which involved summer internships for divinity students and was financed by the Duke Endowment.

After the organization of the university, the first new appointment to have an important impact on the undergraduate Department of Religion was that of Hiram E. Myers. Another Trinity alumnus (1915), Myers became a highly successful Methodist preacher whom the bishop assigned in 1923 to Duke Memorial Methodist Church in Durham, where members of the Duke family as well as many of the Trinity faculty, including Few, were communicants. Myers had already obtained a bachelor's degree in theology from Boston University's School of Theology in 1920 and, at Few's suggestion, returned there for a master's degree in 1925. Returning to Durham to join Duke's faculty in that year, Myers became a mainstay in the undergraduate Department of Religion and may have become a de facto chairman of the department (in consultation with Few and the dean of the School of Religion) before he was officially given that title in the Duke bulletin for the academic year 1936–37.

The organizing dean of the School of Religion, Edmund D. Soper, was appointed in 1925 and insisted from the outset that there had to be a clear demarcation between the new School of Religion and the undergraduate work in religion.[86] For the faculty in the former, Soper wanted persons who held the Ph.D. Soper believed that James Cannon III had the potential to develop into an effective graduate-level teacher, and indeed, quite a few years later Cannon would become dean of the Divinity School. As for Spence, Ormond, and Myers, Soper recommended that they should, at least initially, be primarily utilized in undergraduate teaching.

The clear demarcation that Soper desired between undergraduate and graduate-level work took some time to be achieved, but by the mid-1930s, when the graduate Department of Religion was organized to offer the M.A. and Ph.D. degrees through the Graduate School of Arts and Sciences, the complicated arrangement of three distinct but interlocking entities in religion was complete: the undergraduate department, the School of Religion, and the graduate department. In the late 1920s and 1930s, the School of Religion grew steadily but was still small enough so that undergraduates had some access to certain strong scholars, such as Harvie Branscomb and Ray Petry, who were primarily in the professional school and teaching on the graduate level. But much of the undergraduate teaching was done in the early years by Spence, Ormond, Cannon, and Myers.

They were assisted after 1929 by two other new appointees. Bessie Whitted Spence taught sections or classes in the required Bible course for many years in the Woman's College. With B.A. and M.A. degrees from Trinity in 1906 and 1909, respectively, she married Hersey Spence, taught for a number of years in secondary schools, and was one of the first women to receive the bachelor of divinity degree from Duke's School of Religion (1929).

The other new appointment for undergraduate religion was that of Mason Crum in 1930. A graduate of Wofford in 1909, Crum, after studying at both Vanderbilt and Harvard, tried several jobs before being ordained as a Methodist preacher in 1919. While serving as a professor of religious education for ten years at Columbia College, he obtained a Ph.D. in education at the University of South Carolina in 1925. Much interested and involved in race relations work, Crum became a close student of the social history of the South Carolina Sea Islands, and in 1940 the Duke University Press published his book, *Gullah: Negro Life in the Carolina Sea Islands*.

In the years after World War II, the undergraduate Department of Religion would cease to be so preponderantly Methodist and inbred, that is, made up largely of Trinity-Duke alumni. The greater diversity and more scholarly attributes of the postwar appointments would vastly strengthen both the department and the humanities division at Duke.

Two departments in the humanities that later became important at Duke, music and art, were barely begun before World War II.[87] Trinity College prior to World War I was not alone in neglecting the fine arts, for American colleges and universities in general were slow to give up the practice of regarding music, art, and drama as essentially extracurricular matters.[88] By the 1920s, however, the situation was changing in many institutions, and after the university's organization, Duke needed to begin filling the void in fine arts inherited from Trinity.

President Few, keenly aware of the new university's weakness in the area, supported moves by Alice Baldwin, W. K. Boyd, and others to improve the situation. Yet the financial constraints that Few began to comprehend after about 1927, and especially in the early 1930s, limited Duke's initial efforts.

The first appointment in the fine arts was that of Louise Hall in 1931. A graduate of Wellesley, Hall received a degree in architecture from the Massachusetts Institute of Technology and also studied at the Sorbonne. She had to exert great initiative and ingenuity to obtain the slides, projectors, and library acquisitions that she needed for the first courses in art at Duke, but those courses were solidly established after Hall's arrival. Hall would much later, in 1954, receive her doctorate in architecture from Harvard. By 1934, when a second person in art was appointed (one who did not long remain at Duke), the catalog listed eleven courses in art.

Because numerous art exhibitions and other related activities took place in the handsome library of the Woman's College, President Few early in 1936 requested the university's architect to provide preliminary plans and cost estimates for an addition to that building that would meet the needs of the existing and projected art department.[89] Before anything along that line developed, however, Few's plans were totally altered late in 1936 when negotiations began with a wealthy art-lover and southerner, William Hayes Ackland, about his offer to Duke of an art museum and an endowment for it. In 1941, after Few's death, the executive committee of the university's trustees rejected the Ackland bequest, and Duke would not obtain an art museum until the 1960s.[90]

Despite the lack of adequate space and facilities, the art department slowly grew. When enrollment in art courses reached a point justifying another appointment, Alice Baldwin and Louise Hall persuaded Few and Wannamaker that the appointment of a male scholar to chair the department would be helpful in countering the notion that the study or teaching of art was for women only. Alexander D. McDonald, with an A.B. and a master's of fine arts degree from Princeton, was appointed in 1936; unfortunately, he not only lacked the doctoral degree but proved not to possess the administrative ability needed in a chairman, and he resigned in 1942. An appointment in art that turned out to be much longer in duration was that of Elizabeth Sunderland in 1939. With her undergraduate degree from the University of Michigan, Sunderland received her doctorate from Radcliffe in 1938 and specialized in the field of medieval architecture. Like Hall, Sunderland would spend her career at Duke.

Music as an academic discipline and department lagged only slightly behind art in its development at Duke. While J. Foster Barnes began his long tenure as director of the men's glee club in 1927 and his wife, Myrtle Preyer Barnes, led the women's choral group, those were extracurricular activities, as was the Duke band and orchestra that Robert Fearing, an alumnus with formal training in music, began to direct in 1935. The first course in the history of music came with the appointment of Edward H. Broadhead in 1933. A graduate of Denison, he was a skilled organist and, after obtaining a master's degree in history and education from Duke in 1933, also became the chapel organist. To teach courses in musical theory, Henry A. Bruinsma, with both his A.B. and master of music degree from Michigan, was appointed in 1938. Thanks to the insistence and help of Dean Baldwin, another appointment, one that proved to be long-lasting, was made in 1939 when Julia Wilkinson (later Mrs. Earl Mueller), a violinist trained at the Eastman School of Music, joined the department.

Since Broadhead, like McDonald in art, lacked a Ph.D. and the small group in music needed leadership, Few and Wannamaker, as a stopgap measure, named Alice Baldwin as acting chair in music in 1940. Then, as mentioned earlier, in 1942 the dual problems of the fledgling departments in art and music were solved by putting them into a new Department of Aesthetics, Art, and Music chaired by Katherine Gilbert.

With the large exception of English and perhaps philosophy, the humanities departments at Duke prior to World War II did not keep pace with the generally stronger departments in the natural sciences (including mathematics) and the social sciences. Yet the entire faculty in arts and sciences had grown remarkably, both in quantity and quality, after the organization of the university. Though Few always insisted that the undergraduate colleges were the heart of the university, he also realized that much of Duke's reputation in the educational world would rest on its Graduate School of Arts and Sciences and the advanced students who were trained there. Since the faculty members responsible for that training also taught undergraduates, Duke's graduate school shared virtually all of its faculty members with both Trinity College and the Woman's College. While not as physically distinct and visible as the professional schools, the Graduate School of Arts and Sciences was, in fact, the absolutely essential component, literally the sine qua non, of Duke as a research university.

6

The Graduate School of Arts and Sciences and Other Essentials for Mind and Spirit

⬦

Lᴛʜᴏᴜɢʜ ᴛʜᴇ ɢʀᴀᴅᴜᴀᴛᴇ sᴄʜᴏᴏʟ of Arts and Sciences was the sine qua non of Duke as a research university, it got no building of its own. As at most other major universities, the dean of the graduate school and the relatively small staff that operated under the dean's direction were housed in a few offices in the administration building. At Duke, since Allen building was not erected until the early 1950s, the administrative offices were located first in East Duke building and then, after September, 1930, in what later became Flowers building on the West campus. Just as clothes do not "make the man"—despite the hucksters' claims—buildings do not necessarily reflect the significance of what goes on within them. Yet the lack of sheer visibility for the Graduate School of Arts and Sciences, as compared to the law school or the medical school for example, may be one reason why so many people—including some groups who are important to universities—remain vague about both the function and the importance of the graduate school.

Princeton, without any of the professional schools that most research universities possess, gradually transformed itself into a major research university during the early decades of the twentieth century largely by building up its graduate school of arts and sciences as it simultaneously sought to keep its undergraduate college strong. Duke, on the other hand, opted for the more traditional pattern in research universities and sought to develop a number of professional schools along with its undergraduate colleges and a graduate school. This strategy meant, in light of the limited resources available, that Duke's Graduate School of Arts and Sciences would be developed slowly, more slowly than either its law or medical school.

Aside from the lack of physical visibility, the graduate school possessed other distinctive features, including a peculiar situation about alumni. On the one hand its alumni, especially its Ph.D. alumni, became important representatives of Duke in the world of higher education and, in certain scientific fields, in industrial research. Their achievements, or lack thereof, inevitably reflected on Duke. On the other hand, given the economic realities of the teaching profession, which most Ph.D.'s in the 1930s and 1940s entered, relatively few of the Ph.D. alumni could be expected to become wealthy. Even if they did so by some unusual turn of events, many of the Ph.D. alumni had earlier loyalties to their undergraduate colleges. Or, when they became college or university teachers themselves, many developed loyalties to the institutions where they spent the greater part of their professional lives. In short, the Graduate School of Arts and Sciences could not usually—and there were certainly important exceptions—look to a significant body of alumni who were financially able and willing to contribute the help that voluntarily supported institutions in the United States must inevitably seek. Princeton, as mentioned in an earlier chapter, did a much better job than most universities, including Duke, in educating the alumni of its undergraduate college and its trustees and friends about the vital role of its graduate school in attracting and keeping a strong faculty and in establishing Princeton's reputation in the educational world.[1]

President Few and many of his colleagues on the faculty were fully aware of the graduate school's importance. Few's abortive efforts to raise substantial sums of money for a memorial to B. N. Duke in the form of a graduate school and a related research council have already been noted. Even without those sought-for resources, however, the new graduate school quickly took shape and began promptly fulfilling its mission of offering in a number of departments the most advanced training available for scholars and researchers.

Duke, unlike some research universities, had a unitary faculty in arts and sciences and deliberately avoided naming faculty members who wished to teach only graduate students. Most full professors taught at least one undergraduate course, and from the beginning the policy was that undergraduates, particularly seniors and a limited number of juniors, had access to certain advanced-level or graduate courses (the 200-level courses at Duke) that were usually taught by members of the graduate faculty. This was the common practice, in fact, at a number of universities. A new faculty member's admission to the graduate faculty, however, did not come as early or as easily in the early decades as would be the case in the late twentieth century. A new Ph.D., once appointed at Duke, normally taught only undergraduates for several years; tangible evidence of prowess in research, as demonstrated through various types of publications, had to be in hand before the graduate school, acting through its executive committee or graduate council, approved a faculty member for admission to the graduate faculty. Once admitted, the faculty member could direct students who were writing doctoral dissertations or master's theses and serve on the examining committees of the candidates for those degrees. In summary, all members of Duke's graduate faculty in arts and sciences taught both graduate and undergraduate students, but the younger or less research-minded faculty members taught only undergraduates.

W. H. Glasson, chairman of the economics department, had become chairman of Trinity College's committee on graduate instruction before the organization of the university. Reporting to Few in June, 1925, Glasson noted that there had been ninety-two graduate students during the 1924 summer session and forty-one during the following school year. During the preceding eight years, Trinity had conferred fifty-three master's degrees, and twenty-seven were to be conferred in June, 1925. Glasson explained that the committee had spent many hours studying the requirements both for admission and for advanced degrees, and the faculty had adopted the recommended plans for the M.A. and the new master of education degree. New regulations increased the distinction between graduate and undergraduate work, spelled out the requirement of a master's thesis, and provided for an examination of the thesis and its author by a faculty committee. Ten teaching fellowships worth $600 each had been established, and the value of the twelve graduate scholarships had been increased.

Glasson suggested that Few should nominate to the board of trustees a dean of the graduate school and that a graduate council should be named to supervise graduate work and prepare plans for the final organization of the graduate school and for the requirements for the Ph.D. The council would be available for advice concerning the selection of the graduate faculty and policies about fellowships and scholarships.[2]

Since the master's degree and thesis would undergo various forms of dilution and weakening later in the century, perhaps one should note that in the 1920s and for several decades thereafter, the M.A. thesis at Duke was a substantial production that required considerable work from the degree candidate. Moreover, the examination of the thesis by the faculty committee was no mere pro forma exercise but a genuine intellectual probing and interchange between candidate and committee. Since the M.A. would long be required at Duke as a prerequisite for those wishing to work for the Ph.D., the solid standards for the first degree were obviously important.

When Few failed to act promptly in the matter of naming a dean, Glasson, writing for the committee on graduate instruction, again asserted that nothing could accomplish so much in giving Duke a recognized place among the nation's leading universities as the development of an outstanding graduate school. "Since there is no great Graduate School in the South," Glasson added, "we have an attractive chance to enter a field where competition is not so keen as it is in the North and West." The committee recognized that Duke could not initially provide a comprehensive program of graduate instruction in all departments but suggested that a logical first step would be to start it in those departments in which James B. Duke, in his indenture establishing the Duke Endowment, had expressed a special interest: chemistry, economics, history, and English. (Glasson might well have added that those departments also happened to be among the strongest ones anyhow.) The committee recommended that two graduate professorships be filled in each of those departments and, if sufficient funds were available, that an annual stipend for books and equipment should be attached to each professorship.

The committee now recommended that the word "teaching" be dropped from the title of the $600 fellowships and that four or five $1,000 university fellowships for second-year graduate students should be established. The committee had considered the requirements for the Ph.D. but was holding back on publicizing them until decisions had been made about the graduate courses that would be available in the 1926–27 academic year. Many inquiries were coming in; graduate enrollment had risen from forty-one students to sixty; a graduate bulletin should be published as early in the spring of 1926 as possible; and a dean should be named.[3]

Dean Wannamaker recognized the urgency of providing graduate courses leading to the Ph.D. in several departments, and early in 1926 presented a long list of staffing needs to Few.[4] Biology's need for a "big man" to offer graduate courses, for example, was soon met by the appointment of A. S. Pearse, as discussed in an earlier chapter. And while few other departments gained scholars with reputations to match those of Pearse or of William McDougall in psychology, many promising younger scholars began to join the Duke faculty.

Not until September, 1926, did Few formally name Glasson to serve as the first dean of the graduate school.[5] Since Few in 1926 was actively searching for new deans for the law and medical schools, beginning his protracted negotiations with the Rockefeller Foundation, and involved in countless other matters related to Duke, his delay in naming Glasson is perhaps understandable. But the mere naming of a dean by no means solved all the problems related to the expansion of Duke's graduate work. The whole university was still crowded onto the old Trinity campus in the late 1920s, and it was the scene of a massive construction project. Right before Christmas, 1926, the professors in the social science departments gave Few a "present" in the form of a lengthy list of problems and needs connected with graduate training. First of all, the faculty members noted that in view of the "emergency" caused by the increased number of graduate and undergraduate students, the library should be kept open continuously six days a week from 8:30 A.M. until 10:30 P.M. Then three seminar rooms should be provided—one each for history, economics, and political science—and a separate office assigned to each faculty member. Each department needed both a telephone and a secretary, and, perhaps nearest to the professors' hearts, the teaching load should be reduced "in conformity with the practice in the best universities." "The fixing of the schedule of [the professors in] the School of Religion at nine hours a week," the professors noted, "appears to be a step in the right direction." As for the future, one of the new Tudor Gothic buildings to be erected on West campus should be designated for the social sciences and history.[6]

While certain of the demands were soon met, such as longer library hours and seminar rooms, it would be many years before Duke would be able to provide uniformly the separate offices and other facilities that the faculty members requested. As for the separate building on West for the social sciences, that would not materialize until after World War II, and historians would not be housed in the building even then.

If Few and Duke were unable to provide many of the facilities that would be so vastly expanded and rather taken for granted later in the century, Few came through in other ways that had an indirect but nonetheless quite real effect on teaching at Duke. In the wake of Tennessee's famous Scopes trial, various groups in the South and elsewhere clamored for laws against the teaching of Darwinian theories about evolution. Few, at a meeting of the Educational Association of the Methodist Episcopal Church, South, early in 1927 wrote and introduced a resolution expressing opposition to all legislation that would interfere with the proper teaching of scientific subjects in American schools and colleges. Regardless of individual opinions about such matters, the resolution declared, restrictive legislation would be "futile and can serve no good purpose." Reading of Few's role in the nearly unanimous passage of the resolution, an attorney in Charlotte declared that the action would have "incalculable benefit in discouraging this foolish legislation all over the country" and was easily the most outstanding stand taken by any large church organization.[7] A young alumnus, Julian Boyd, who would later become a distinguished historian and Jeffersonian scholar, informed Few that "there are some alumni who got more of a thrill out of the courageous stand you took with such calm dignity at Memphis than they have out of even the most notable athletic achievements of the University."[8] The chairman of the commission on higher education of the Southern Association of Colleges and Secondary Schools thanked Few for the resolution and pointed out that while similar resolutions coming from groups outside the South might have proved counterproductive, to have "one of the strongest influences in the South lined up on the right side" was truly helpful. William Louis Poteat, president of Wake Forest College and himself a courageous champion of academic freedom, hailed the Methodist resolution as proof that "obscurantism does not possess the whole field."[9]

While Few no doubt appreciated the plaudits, he would undoubtedly have appreciated even more some tangible help for the graduate school. He submitted a memorandum concerning the school to the Rockefeller-backed General Education Board. Its president agreed with Few's proposition that in "any university the School of Arts [and Sciences] should be the heart of the institution" and considered it unfortunate but true that no well-developed graduate school of arts and sciences then existed in the South. The development of such an institution would stimulate education on all levels in the region, he thought, and he indeed hoped that Few could put his plans into operation.[10] Help from the GEB, when Few was finally able to obtain it after a long and difficult struggle, went, however, to the medical school. Duke's Graduate School of Arts and Sciences had to move ahead as best it could on inadequate resources.

A. S. Pearse, whose own zoological research was partly underwritten by the Rockefeller Foundation, advised an officer there that Duke's administrative leaders were looking to him for help in the scientific areas. "We do not have money enough to do much," Pearse confessed. "We have too few scholarships and those we have do not carry large enough stipends. Our faculty is weak in many places and we have too few high class men." Pearse expected further expansion of the faculty when the new West campus was opened and believed that Few had a "good slant" on Duke's opportunities in science, with a strong emphasis on pure rather than applied science.[11]

Despite the stringencies, Duke managed to come up with some important innovations in its graduate program. Just how many of the senior faculty members shared Few's long-standing worry about the fact that graduate training focused exclusively on research is not known. He as well as other critical observers of American higher education recognized, however, that teaching too was an honorable, vital part of most professorial lives. Yet most graduate schools seemed to operate on the assumption that their newly produced Ph.D.'s could easily and quickly, maybe even casually, acquire a knack and appetite for teaching.

Probably inspired by Few, Duke's plan called for each of the larger departments offering graduate work to appoint either a faculty member or a committee to have charge of teacher training for the advanced graduate students in the department. The faculty member or the committee was, first of all, to provide opportunities for the doctoral candidates who planned to become teachers to gain practical, supervised experience in teaching, and secondly, to arrange for seminar sessions devoted to the problems of teaching. "We shall expect those who receive degrees in our Graduate School to demonstrate the ability to carry on research and to advance knowledge," Few declared, "but we desire to discriminate in selecting our degree holders to be recommended for teaching positions."[12]

In history, for example, candidates for the Ph.D. who had passed their preliminary or qualifying examinations (usually after at least two years of course work) were long required to take a noncredit seminar in college teaching which functioned much as Few had originally envisioned. Other large departments, such as English and chemistry, which employed advanced graduate students as teaching or laboratory assistants made their own adaptations of the program. No one could prove that Duke's new Ph.D. graduates became better college teachers because of the teaching seminars, but at the least Duke Ph.D.'s in several important disciplines were made aware of the importance and challenging nature of the teaching dimension of the academic profession. Equally important, perhaps, was the fact that advanced graduate students at Duke worked with professors who, in most cases, took their teaching responsibilities at all levels with great seriousness. The fact that the president of the university cared deeply about the matter clearly made a distinct difference, not only during Few's lifetime but for two or three decades afterward.

Early in 1930, before the full significance and ramifications of the Wall Street crash in October had become clear, Few engaged in some inventorying and long-range thinking that involved the graduate school. Having just hired Justin Miller as the dean of Duke's law school, Few was acutely conscious of the fact that its reorganization and expansion would cost a lot of money. Yet, as he pointed out to George G. Allen, other schools, "especially the School of Medicine and even more the Graduate School of Arts and Sciences, will need all [the money] that we can get for them from every possible source, if we are to build a really great university." Few confided that he and his colleagues were working hard in arts and sciences to make Duke eligible for membership in the prestigious Association of American Universities. "Unless we succeed in this," Few insisted, "our degrees will be invalidated and we shall have to take a second-rate position as a university." He concluded, however, by noting, "I have been working a long time at all this and still have a vast store of patience."[13]

Writing in a similar vein to W. R. Perkins, Few reported that the recent national meetings in Durham of both the American Association of University Professors and the American Historical Association had seemed "uncommonly successful," with much praise from the visitors about Duke's new plant on two campuses. "Such contacts as these," Few added, "will help us to go forward." Yet in studying the list of faculty members added in the previous four years, Few recognized that "too large a proportion of them, even in the medical faculty, are young men who have not yet won their spurs." While most of them would be in the "high-price class" within five years or so, Few thought, he feared that Duke might soon lose one faculty member to Harvard and one to Cornell. "If it were a mere matter of salary we could hold them," he explained, "but it is also a matter of educational, especially library, facilities, and to build these up in short order requires a great outlay of money." No doubt hoping to inspire his coworkers in the Duke Endowment even as he deftly educated them about the university world, Few concluded that "these rapidly passing years remind me that we must all use our every opportunity to get our big day's work done before the day is over." [14]

Both the slowly developing economic depression and the bitter fight about the appearances of Norman Thomas at Duke would soon force Few to shift attention from his efforts on behalf of arts and sciences and the graduate school. Nevertheless, Duke made a fairly quick entry into advanced graduate training. The first Ph.D. degrees, two of them, were awarded in 1928 in the field of zoology. Dean Glasson reported in July, 1930, that there had been 193 graduate students enrolled in the academic year that had just ended. In the first summer term of 1929 there had been 223 and in the second term 94. While 268 of the total number of graduate students came from North Carolina, 150 were from other states and four foreign countries. At commencement in June, 1930, fifty-five M.A. degrees were awarded, six M.Ed. degrees, and eight Ph.D. degrees. Included in the last-named category was the first woman to receive a Duke Ph.D., Rose M. Davis in chemistry, who was a Trinity alumna (1916) and a professor at Randolph-Macon Women's College. While Robert Rankin served as the assistant dean of the graduate school, Dean Glasson continued to teach two courses each semester and to serve also as chairman of the rapidly growing Department of Economics and Business Administration. "The situation has been such," he confessed, "as to place a heavier burden of routine work upon me than I feel that I can continue to carry." [15] Although Glasson's obvious case of overload was not unique in Duke's early years, it serves as a good example of the price that some faculty members and administrators paid in service to the institution.

In one development that was important for Duke's graduate school, however, it was Few rather than Glasson who played the key role, and that concerned cooperative arrangements with the University of North Carolina. Despite athletic rivalry that grew more intense than ever in the 1930s, Duke and Carolina pioneered throughout the decade in finding ways for a voluntarily supported research university and a state-supported one to pursue cooperative and mutually advantageous policies. Few enjoyed cordial relations with Harry W. Chase, the president of the University of

North Carolina, who played a key role in its expansion and emergence as a modern research university in the 1920s. Chase left North Carolina, however, in 1930 and was succeeded by a younger man, Frank P. Graham, who was a liberal, reform-minded historian.

Few and Graham probably did not know each other well at the start of the latter's important tenure as president, but they soon developed what seems to have been a good working relationship based on mutual respect, despite marked differences in age and temperament. Early on in Graham's presidency, when a division of the university in Chapel Hill became interested in making an offer to a professor at Duke, Graham inquired about Few's reaction to the idea. "I have had a feeling for a good many years, and have acted on it," Few explained, "that two institutions located so near together as ours would do well to avoid drawing the one from the staff of the other." He thought that President Chase had come to share that view but conceded that they both might have been mistaken to hold it. "I shall, however, probably continue to act on that principle," Few concluded, "but I hope that you will be free to use your own judgment in the whole matter." Graham soon responded that he "would not want to do anything that would mar the spirit of our relations and the intercollegiate good will," so the University of North Carolina would not pursue the matter further.[16]

With the no-raiding policy thus reaffirmed, the two presidents began to express interest in finding ways to interact in a more direct, positive fashion. Speaking at the inaugural dinner for Graham, Few praised him as an alumnus of the University of North Carolina who already enjoyed an "uncommon influence" among the alumni, and as a former college teacher who would have the vital problems of the college of arts and sciences close to his heart. In the following month, Few explained to an influential correspondent that Duke's plans for its sociology department were partly influenced by the nature of the strong department in that discipline at Chapel Hill. "I think we all have a growing feeling," Few noted, "that these two universities ought to reinforce each other." Neither one of them could be strong at all points, for no university could still afford that aim.[17]

Graham might well have shared Few's ideas about the mutual reinforcement of the two institutions even if the economic depression had not happened. But by 1932, hard times had indeed fallen upon North Carolina along with the rest of the nation, and state support for higher education was necessarily curtailed sharply. The University of North Carolina, in fact, felt painful repercussions from the depression even before they affected Duke.

Addressing an assembly of his students late in 1932, Graham declared that through the cooperation of the University of North Carolina and Duke "one of the great spiritual and educational centers of the world might be established in North Carolina." The goal might be approached, he thought, through such measures as the sharing or exchange of courses, professors, and material from the two best libraries in the South.[18] Getting down to practical first steps, Graham subsequently suggested to Few that they should name a joint committee to plan for the cooperation of the two institutions. The two deans of the graduate schools and representatives from the two libraries would be, along with others, important members of such a committee, Graham thought, and there could be special subcommittees to deal with student affairs, public occasions, and various other matters.[19]

Few quickly agreed and named a high-powered group to represent Duke on the joint committee. It began its work in 1934 and soon had spotlighted a number of areas, some more important than others, where the two institutions hoped to work together. One of the most significant steps was in the area of library development, and a grant of $25,000 to each library from the General Education Board signified that foundation's warm support for the idea of cooperative library-building.[20]

Few informed W. R. Perkins about the program and explained some of his private thoughts about it. "Most of all I hope it will tend to break down certain prejudices that exist out among the alumni," Few noted, "and while existing are always liable to do harm, as for example in the State Legislature." Mindful that Perkins and Allen might be wary of Duke's linking itself too closely with the University of North Carolina, Few added that "we are going to watch our steps and be careful at every stage."[21]

Actually, Few himself was not as wary of the relationship as he thought his friends in New York might be. Both he and Graham encouraged their respective faculties to find their own ways to cooperate. Proposing a joint committee to plan for the staffing of the two classics departments, Few seized the occasion to point up what he regarded as the silliness surrounding the public image, at least in some quarters, of himself and Graham: "And an undertaking like this particular one [in classics] could give nobody occasion to urge that I am a Capitalist and you a Red; and how we do look the parts!"[22]

Summarizing some of the accomplishments by the spring of 1937, Graham thought the pattern of cooperation between the two libraries set an example for all other departments and divisions. In addition to the joint appointment of Herbert von Beckerath in economics and the sharing of one or two additional professors, the two classics departments had made an effort to build complementary strengths and cross-listed courses in the two catalogs; the staffs of the two law schools and of the two botany departments were meeting regularly; numerous departments had collaborated to hold national meetings of professional organizations in Durham and Chapel Hill; and there was a three-year experiment in allowing graduate students of each university to take courses at no extra cost on the other campus. Going on to mention other types of cooperation, Graham expressed his belief that the steps already taken were sound and provided a basis for even wider development under realistic guidance.[23]

Frederic M. Hanes, Duke's co-chairman of the joint committee, echoed Graham in reporting some two dozen types of cooperative endeavor. Hanes, sounding much like Few, suggested that the two universities were "competitors only in the laudable endeavors of building in North Carolina institutions of ever increasing usefulness to our people, mutually helpful in every way, and living proof that the petty acrimonies of the athletic field have no place in shaping the intellectual activities of our two universities."[24]

The program of graduate-level cooperation that Graham mentioned was particularly significant for Duke, for the University of North Carolina— that is, Graham and the dean of his graduate school—played important roles in helping Duke to attain the highly coveted membership in the Association of American Universities (AAU). That elite organization of American research universities invited the University of North Carolina to become a member in 1922. In private remarks to friends and coworkers, Few made no bones about the fact that the AAU was "the one organization in the country to which we need admission and have not secured it."[25] In a discreet but nonetheless careful and thorough fashion, Few and his associates set about doing what they could to attain the goal. Presidents and deans of the graduate schools normally attended the meetings of the AAU, and when the group arranged to meet at the University of North Carolina in the fall of 1931, Glasson, with the approval of the graduate dean in Chapel Hill, arranged for the visitors to have a meal at Duke and to meet various members of the faculty.

By the mid-1930s, Few, Glasson, Calvin Hoover, and others at Duke began to think seriously about the best strategy for gaining the desired membership. Since a university did not apply for inclusion but had to be nominated by an existing member, Duke's moves had to be discreet. Glasson pointed out to one correspondent that a committee on graduate instruction of the American Council on Education had recently conducted a study of graduate schools; one hundred scholars in each discipline were asked to indicate by a majority vote the institutions deemed to have an adequate staff and equipment to offer the Ph.D. in that field. Duke's graduate school, according to Glasson, was found to have satisfactory provision for Ph.D. work in more fields than was the case with several universities which had long been members of the AAU.[26]

Despite such measurement, Glasson well knew that, as in so many human institutions and organizations, there was a good bit of plain old politics involved in the AAU. That was a game that Few, from long experience in both higher education and the Methodist church, knew well how to play. A Duke faculty member, on leave at Princeton, reported that he was following Few's suggestion and doing nothing overtly about the matter of the AAU. The dean of Princeton's graduate school, however, was on his own initiative proceeding tactfully in Duke's behalf.[27] Meantime, Wannamaker made the suggestion, which was acted upon, that Duke should invite speakers for commencement, the annual Phi Beta Kappa address, and other such occasions with an eye to the AAU matter.[28]

When Few learned early in 1938 that Frank Graham had nominated Duke for membership, the Duke president went into high gear. He advised an old friend who had become associated with the Association of American Colleges that "if on the side you find it possible to help [Duke] along, I shall appreciate it."[29] George B. Pegram, a Trinity alumnus and graduate dean at Columbia, received a similar letter, as did certain other well-placed friends of Duke.

Few informed Frank Graham that, in accordance with the latter's advice, Duke had a whole series of influential graduate deans coming to the campus at intervals throughout 1938. When one of those deans spoke at a dinner meeting at Duke, Graham attended, spoke briefly of the cooperative program of the two universities, and emphasized that together they were doing more advanced graduate work than all the rest of the South.[30]

In the month before the AAU would meet to act on the nomination of Duke for membership, W. W. Pierson, the dean of Carolina's graduate school, visited Calvin B. Hoover, who had succeeded Glasson as Duke's graduate dean. After the conference, Hoover wrote a long, careful letter addressing the key matters that had been raised and arming Graham and Pierson for troublesome questions that were likely to be raised about Duke and particularly about its relationship with the Duke Endowment and the Duke Power Company. After quoting from Duke's catalog about the composition and function of the seven-person executive committee of the board of trustees, Hoover explained that the committee provided "the channel for the cooperation of the Trustees of the Duke Endowment with the trustees of Duke University in the supervision of the affairs of the university." The faculty, Hoover noted, was not conscious of any direct intervention in administration of the university by either of the two boards of trustees, since the executive committee functioned largely as a reviewing and advisory organ in its relation to the president. Then Hoover quoted Few directly:

The Trustees of the Duke Endowment do not consider that they have any obligations in the educational administration of Duke University; these Trustees have never intervened, not to say interfered, with

University affairs. The advice and cooperation of the three members of the Executive Committee from the Board of Trustees of the Duke Endowment have been most valuable. These three members have, without exception, approved every proposal and every nomination the President has ever made to the Executive Committee.

(Few, in saying that Allen and Perkins had never "intervened" in university affairs had apparently either conveniently forgotten about the episodes concerning Norman Thomas or else chose to regard them as passing and unimportant.)

After dealing with that tricky matter, Hoover turned to what had obviously been Pierson's concern about Duke University's relationship with the Duke Power Company and noted that Duke's law school offered a course dealing with public utilities. While the Department of Economics did not offer such a course, Hoover declared it certainly could if it so chose.

As for Duke's overall policy concerning graduate work, Hoover explained that there was no ambition to develop all fields. For example, there was no graduate work planned in astronomy or in a number of other fields; geology at Duke was offered only on an undergraduate basis. "The graduate departments in which we expect to concentrate a larger proportion of our resources," Hoover added, "are those of the physical sciences and the social sciences." The existence of Duke Medical School both required and facilitated the focus on the sciences, Hoover suggested, and the "urgency of national and sectional social and economic problems argues for the most comprehensive and effective research and graduate training in the social sciences."[31]

The arguments which Few and Hoover supplied Graham and Pierson must have been persuasive, for when the AAU met in November, 1938, of the four institutions nominated for membership, Duke was the only one to be approved. Immensely gratified, Few promptly thanked Graham and Pierson for their "indispensable services" in the matter. "I shall never cease to be grateful to you," Few declared, "and will try even harder if possible to make Duke University what it ought to be in the service of education and kindred causes."[32] Soon afterwards, Few reminded Graham that there were still matters, such as tuition exchange and transportation between the two campuses, that the joint committee could hardly deal with and that the two presidents needed to address. And Few, in one of his last letters on the matter, also wanted to know if Duke and Carolina could not find ways to cooperate in the area of Latin American studies and thereby be in a stronger position to obtain support from the Rockefeller Foundation.[33]

As for Duke's new membership in the AAU, Few realized that while it was certainly important and something of a seal of approval for the twelve-year-old graduate school from the leading universities in the country, it did not signify in any sense that Duke had achieved the level of excellence to which it aspired. There were too many large gaps in too many departments for complacency.

Few also used the new membership in the AAU to do a most characteristic thing: he wrote the head of Vanderbilt University, which was considerably older than Duke as a university but not yet a member of AAU, that he would be interested in nominating Vanderbilt "when you feel you are ready for it." Admission was primarily on the basis of the graduate school, Few explained, and the only advice he could offer was to "feel sure that you are reasonably ready before there is any nomination to membership." There was "no dog in the manger policy" at Duke, Few added, but rather a concern about "the welfare of other institutions particularly those in the Southern states," where more strong educational centers were badly needed.[34] The Vanderbilt chancellor thanked Few but confessed that he and his associates did not feel ready to seek the membership. (Vanderbilt would, in fact, become a member of the AAU in 1949.)

Essential for the growth of graduate work in the arts and sciences at Duke was the strengthening of the library. Beginning as early as the 1890s, there had been certain faculty members at Trinity who fully realized that a strong library was a prerequisite for the academic excellence to which the institution aspired. John Spencer Bassett, an energetic collector of historical material for the library, not only passed along his passion for library-building to his student, William K. Boyd, but together with Few, Mims, and others helped to educate President Kilgo about the library's role. Consequently, Kilgo declared in 1901 that the library was "the one department that measures the future development of the college."[35] Reflecting that viewpoint, which had apparently been adopted and passed along by Ben Duke, James B. Duke made his first significant, separate gift to Trinity in 1900 in the form of the money for a handsome new library building and $10,000 to purchase books for it. With an alumnus, Joseph P. Breedlove, earlier named as the first full-time librarian in 1898, Trinity's library remained small but with certain strengths in English literature and American history. A number of special gifts, such as the Anne Roney Shakespearean collection, supplemented books purchased by the college.[36]

In 1923, not long before the establishment of the university, Trinity's trustees established an important policy concerning the library: for each undergraduate enrolled a book fee of five dollars was to go to the library for the purchase and binding of books and periodicals. Moreover, this supplementary income was not to limit or affect the annual appropriation for the library from the general funds of the college. That policy together with the carryover of a strong tradition of individual benefactions to Trinity's library would be important factors in the steady, impressive growth of Duke University's several libraries.[37]

The most important individual in the early building of Duke's library proved to be William K. Boyd. Long a key member of Trinity's library committee, he became the first chairman of the larger and more powerful Library Council when President Few and the trustees established that body in 1928. As the completion of the Gothic buildings on the West campus approached, Few and others realized that cooperation and coordination would be necessary for the efficient, economical operation of Duke's five libraries (not counting the departmental libraries in the sciences and mathematics): the University or Main Library, the Woman's College Library, the Medical School Library, the Law Library, and the School of Religion Library. Consequently, Few, following a plan used by Harvard, named Boyd as the first director of libraries early in 1930. He would occupy the position for four years, a period of dramatic development in the university's library holdings but also with chronic administrative problems that ultimately led to Boyd's more or less invited resignation.

Before all of that happened, however, there were noteworthy changes in the operations of the library. Circumstances forced it to be something of a "moveable feast" over a period of three or so years. In March, 1927, Breedlove capably supervised the transfer of about 100,000 volumes from Trinity's old library—the one J. B. Duke had given at the turn of the century and which Breedlove described as the "handsomest structure" on the old Trinity campus—to the elegant new Georgian or neoclassical library that was one of the eleven new buildings that J. B. Duke had given for the East campus.[38] Then in 1930 Breedlove faced the even more daunting task of arranging for about 200,000 volumes to be moved from East to the new university library and various professional libraries on West.

In the long view, however, those physical moves were perhaps not as important as the numerous significant additions that were made to the library's holdings under the direction of Boyd. Various circumstances in Europe after World War I increased the opportunities for the acquisition of valuable material for the library, and a number of Duke faculty members, backed by the administration and Boyd, took the initiative in making important purchases. Albert M. Webb in romance languages, for example, discovered while in Paris in the summer of 1927 that the private library of a distinguished French scholar and critic, Gustave Lanson, could be purchased. Authorized by Few and Flowers to close the deal, Webb thus added around 11,000 volumes to Duke's library. Jay Hubbell asked for and got special appropriations for purchases in American and especially southern literature.

In British history, W. T. Laprade became the key agent. Going on leave to do research in England during the 1926–27 academic year, Laprade reminded Few that for graduate work in the field certain basic source materials were "as essential as laboratory equipment is for the study of science." While locating the material would be time-consuming and inter-ruptive of his own research, Laprade noted, he possessed the experience and bibliographical training for the task.[39] Laprade succeeded in acquir-ing for Duke a significant number of basic collections of source material in British history, such as Hansard's *Debates*, the *Annual Register*, *British Foreign State Papers*, and others. E. Malcolm Carroll performed a similar service for European history while in Paris in 1927–28.

In Latin American history, J. Fred Rippy proved to be as energetic in book buying for Duke as he was resourceful. From Bogota, Colombia, in the spring of 1928 he cabled Flowers that he had assembled an excellent collection that would cost $1,500. Having gained that, Rippy next discov-ered a rich collection of Latin American material in Peru and persuaded Duke to buy it for $10,000.[40] Duke's Latin American holdings thus grew from about 500 volumes to 15,000 in six years, thanks in part to Rippy, who was aided by John Tate Lanning, Alan Manchester, Robert Smith, and Earl Hamilton.

The most avid collector of all, however, proved to be W. K. Boyd. Sen-sitive to the fact that his position first as chairman of the library council and then as director of libraries gave him large responsibilities, Boyd saw to it that his own particular interest in southern Americana did not distort the pattern of library expenditures. The income from the annual student library fee, the "fee fund," was divided, after deductions for periodicals and binding, among all departments, but a large portion of the annual general appropriation to the library went to build up the resources of those departments that were offering programs leading to the Ph.D. The natural sciences were not overlooked. Holdings in biology and chemistry were meager in 1925, but the purchase in one order of 2,000 volumes of periodicals and monographs in chemistry and another 1,500 volumes in biology immediately raised those collections above the collegiate level.[41]

Periodicals and newspapers, both current and extinct, are indispens-able for a research library, and Boyd took pride in Duke's strong start in that area. In 1925 there were 554 current periodicals received in Duke's libraries; by 1929 the number had risen to 844. Purchase of sets of runs of extinct periodicals led to there being over 18,200 bound volumes of them by 1929. As for bound volumes of newspapers, there were only 1,200 in 1925 but over 5,000 four years later. They came from 144 localities in 35 states of the United States and 34 localities of 26 foreign countries. Nowhere south of Washington, D.C., Duke's library leaders boasted, was there such a cosmopolitan newspaper morgue.[42]

One of Boyd's oft-reiterated ideas was that no extensive university library in the nation had ever been built by university funds alone; help from individuals and foundations was also necessary. Accordingly, in 1928 Boyd took the lead in establishing a loosely organized group known as the Associates of Duke University Library. With Boyd as chairman and R. L. Flowers, Allan Gilbert, Paul Gross, and J. B. Breedlove as cofounders, the group pledged to keep the interests of the library in mind and to contribute, if possible, to the purchase of books in their respective fields of interest.[43]

A number of alumni and friends of Duke responded to the invitation to become an associate of the library. None was more important than William W. Flowers, a younger brother of R. L. Flowers and a graduate of Trinity in 1894. Their father was George Washington Flowers, a longtime trustee of Trinity College who sent seven of his children there. President of his class for four years and a charter member of the Trinity College Historical Society, W. W. Flowers taught school in Durham after graduating and succeeded Clinton Toms as school superintendent. He received a master's degree from Trinity in 1896, and after study at Harvard and in Germany became an instructor in German at Trinity in 1899. Problems with his eyes, however, forced him to abandon his teaching career, and he, like Toms before him, went to work for J. B. Duke's American Tobacco Company. W. W. Flowers ultimately became chairman of the board of the Liggett & Myers Tobacco Company, but he always kept an interest in Trinity College and in the scholarly world.[44]

When George Washington Flowers died in 1920, his children gave a number of his books and other volumes to begin a memorial collection in Trinity's library. From time to time after that, W. W. Flowers, without any publicity, either sent Boyd a check with instructions to buy something in the area of southern history for the library or, just as frequently, Boyd discovered some desirable item and diplomatically inquired if W. W. Flowers would have any interest in adding it to the George W. Flowers Memorial Collection. The pace of this activity accelerated in the late 1920s, and Boyd, who wrote countless letters in pursuit of material as well as travelled in his own automobile all over the southeastern states in search of historical material, was in his glory. Discovering a group of important Civil War volumes for sale in May, 1930, Boyd informed W. W. Flowers and promptly received a check for $1,000. When another, unsolicited check for $5,000 arrived a couple of months later, Boyd saluted Flowers: "Now all the saints be praised that you have confidence in the enterprise." He dubbed Flowers the "Chief and Grand Sachem of the Duke Angels."[45]

Inspired and led by W. W. Flowers, other members of the family, including his sister, Estelle Flowers Spears (who would later become the first woman to serve as a trustee of Duke), helped to regularize the Flowers

Collection by establishing an endowment fund for it. Thanks to that and the labors first of Boyd and later of Robert H. Woody and others, it became the most significant collection at Duke. In 1930–31, for example, the deepening economic depression no doubt facilitated Boyd's task, and the Flowers Collection acquired a valuable group of some 4,000 letters and 1,800 books that had belonged to a nineteenth-century poet and writer in South Carolina, Paul Hamilton Hayne; the important correspondence of a prominent Alabaman in the Civil War era, Senator Clement Clay, Jr., and his wife, Virginia Clay Clopton; thirty-six letters of Robert E. Lee and his family; nearly 1,000 official memoranda and letters of the Confederate Ordnance Department; and the list even for that one year goes on. By 1940 Duke's manuscript room housed more than 600,000 items, and the collection had become one of the major repositories for the study of American and especially southern history. Indeed, when the Duke manuscript holdings, which continued to grow in subsequent decades, were considered together with the rich Southern Historical Collection at the University of North Carolina in Chapel Hill, there were few libraries in the nation that rivalled the combined resources for southern history. While there were others who headed the manuscript department for relatively short periods, two Duke-trained historians, first Nannie Mae Tilley and then Mattie U. Russell, held the post for many years and helped make the Duke library a favorite haunt for scholars from across the nation as well as for local graduate students, ambitious seniors, and faculty members.

As mentioned earlier, the impact of the great economic depression was slow in affecting Duke, but Boyd finally had to confess in his report for 1932–33 that the previous twelve months marked "Year I of the World Depression at Duke University, and the effects on the growth of the libraries have been direct and immediate." In order to prevent a reduction in salaries and personnel, the appropriations for capital expenditures had to be greatly reduced. Consequently, the amount spent for books fell from $242,000 in 1931–32 (the peak year) to $88,000 in 1932–33. On the other hand, thanks were no doubt due to W. W. Flowers for the fact that the number of manuscripts increased over the previous year.

One result of Duke's having one of the fastest growing libraries in the nation was that space began quite early to be a problem. The main library building on West, located precisely where J. B. Duke had wanted it to go on the principal quadrangle, turned out to be more architecturally pleasing than it was functional. With the circulation desk, card catalogs, and reference room located on the second floor of the building— and there were no elevators for public use—the library had clearly not been designed according to the standards of modern library construction. Moreover, the order department, headed first by Eric Morrell, and part of the cataloging department, long headed by Eva E. Malone, were housed in dark basement quarters that were far removed from the needed reference tools. Aside from those serious inconveniences, the problem of space for books began to loom early. Boyd may have been exaggerating somewhat when he announced in 1933 that the three-year-old University Library was "approaching the saturation point." When books that were already in the receiving room were placed in the stacks, he explained, there would be no more stack space available. Likewise, he reported that shelf space in the manuscript room would be exhausted within six months.[47] A. C. Lee, the engineer who supervised all construction at the university, agreed with Boyd about the critical need for lamps in the reading rooms of the libraries on both campuses and for museum cases for both libraries. On the matter of shelf space in the main library, however, Lee found that, with approximately 210,000 volumes already shelved, there was yet room for 150,000 additional volumes.[48] Yet Boyd was only a few years premature in sounding the alarm, for by late 1941, when the library collections stood at over 632,000 volumes and ranked fifteenth in the nation, books had to be boxed for storage, often in dank basement rooms. Wartime conditions made new construction impossible, and relief, in the form of an addition to the library, did not come until 1949.

A Trinity alumnus who became a prominent leader among the Duke faculty, Newman I. White, stated that as a student in W. K. Boyd's classes he never saw any special poetic or prophetic quality in Boyd. Later, however, White avowed that when he dealt with Boyd as director of libraries he became "aware of an almost fanatical quality of poet and prophet."[49] Such zeal for the task of library building makes Boyd important in Duke's history, but it came at a price.

Like many faculty members at all times, Boyd had scant patience with administrators and particularly with their rules and regulations. (In thinking of the relationship between faculty members and administrators, one is tempted to meditate upon cats and dogs.) If money had been unlimited—and it was not, even before the drastic belt-tightening that began in 1932—there would have been no problem. Few and Flowers, closely watched by two powerful businessmen in New York, George G. Allen and William R. Perkins, were determined to operate the business aspect of the university as efficiently and rationally as they could. One important step in that direction was to insist from 1927 onward that all Duke purchase orders had to be cleared through and sent from the office of the assistant treasurer, C. B. Markham. If a department had sufficient funds in its budget to cover the order, it went out promptly; otherwise, delays could and often did occur.

This system Boyd abhorred and regarded as a time-consuming, unnecessary impediment, especially in cases where the timing of rush orders from catalogs of out-of-print books was crucial. From the first, Boyd bucked the system and probably encouraged, or at least allowed, the head of the order department as well as individual professors who stumbled onto good buys for the library to do the same. By 1932, the year of the library's peak expenditure for books—and it was clearly a case of budget overrun—the problem had become serious enough for the executive committee of the trustees to name a special investigative committee. In a long memorandum to the committee, Boyd detailed his complaints about alleged obstructions in Markham's office. Among other grievances, he noted that in one instance the library had sent book orders to the assistant treasurer's office in the spring but the orders had not gone out until July. To remedy the problem, Boyd proposed that the library should order books directly, send duplicates of the orders to Markham's office, and have a monthly audit between the library and the assistant treasurer's office.

Markham, in an equally detailed rejoinder, insisted that book orders were sent out from his office on the day they were received—if they came in before 3:00 P.M. As for Boyd's example of the book orders sent over in the spring but not sent out to dealers until July, Markham pointed out that Boyd failed to mention that the library's orders in the spring were held up because the library's budgeted appropriation had been used up. When the new fiscal year began on July 1, the orders were returned to the library and orders written for those that were reauthorized.

The university's outside auditor, in an accounting firm in Richmond, Virginia, offered his opinion that Boyd's proposed plan for library orders was "exactly opposed to the procedure we have continuously advocated." Boyd, the auditor charged, wanted in effect to "divorce the fiscal activities of the Library from the Treasurer's office," but the "Treasurer must be Treasurer in fact as well as in name, . . . and there must be supervision of the expenditures of all departments at all times."[50]

Few and Flowers faced a prickly problem, for not only had Boyd labored heroically for the library while still chairing the history department and carrying a substantial teaching load, but he stood high both at Duke and in the scholarly world of historians and bibliophiles. When the university gave Boyd a much-needed leave of absence in 1933–34, Few seized the opportunity to name Harvie Branscomb, an active and influential member of the library council, as acting director of libraries and then, after Boyd's resignation upon his return to Duke, as director. Branscomb and others, including Paul Gross, helped Few mollify Boyd and steer him toward continuing his directorship of the expanded and regularized Flowers Collection.[51]

As director of libraries Branscomb managed to continue the library's growth without running afoul of the university's accounting procedures. Equally or more important, perhaps, was the effort he made to encourage and facilitate the use of the library by undergraduates. Branscomb argued that the rapid growth of university libraries had focused the attention of librarians largely on the technical processes of acquisition, cataloging, and the like; problems created by large numbers of undergraduates were often solved by highly centralized, mechanized forms of library service, and too many libraries, by separating students from books, had made access to them difficult. While some of the better endowed universities, such as Harvard and Yale, tackled the problem by incorporating small libraries into residential colleges or houses, Princeton had plans for a large open-stack library with desks or carrels for students on each stack level.

At Duke, the Woman's College Library, with its open stacks and warmly furnished Booklovers' Room, was an enviable model. Crowded conditions and inadequate space in the University Library, however, prevented it from imitating the East campus library. Pending the acquisition of additional space for the main library, Branscomb compromised by having the fairly extensive collection of books in the undergraduate reserve room moved to open shelves. In addition, seniors who wished the privilege of possessing stack permits were invited to apply for them. "All of these developments," Branscomb admitted, "involve additional labor and some additional expense." Too, a few more books might be stolen or lost. He stuck by the belief, nevertheless, that "a book on a shelf is a dead loss unless it is used, and that the most efficient library is the one that is used most." [52]

When the Association of American Colleges, with a grant from the Carnegie Foundation, invited Branscomb to undertake a study of the nation's college and university libraries, he took a leave from his post at Duke in 1937–38, visited numerous libraries in different parts of the country, and subsequently published *Teaching with Books: A Study of College Libraries* (1940). Since Branscomb was a professor of New Testament studies rather than a professionally trained librarian, some reviewers in library journals raised critical eyebrows. Breedlove, however, graciously commented that he thought the book "enlarged the librarians' conception of their practical objectives" and presented the salutary viewpoint of an experienced teacher who also knew books and libraries. [53]

Early in his directorship Branscomb no doubt alarmed Breedlove and many members of the staff by the suggestion that the library might abandon the Dewey decimal classification of books and adopt the system used by the Library of Congress. After Branscomb investigated the experience of two other large libraries that had made such a shift, however, he decided it would be an unwise move for Duke.

Branscomb was more successful in another undertaking. When Boyd went on leave, the loose organization he had formed of Associates of the Duke Library ceased to function. Picking up on the idea, Branscomb led in the organization of the Friends of the Duke University Library, which held its first meeting in November, 1935. Douglas Southall Freeman, noted journalist and prizewinning biographer of Robert E. Lee, was the featured speaker at the dinner of the organization. With over 227 members at the first meeting and approximately 200 more added during the following four months, the Friends obviously got off to a strong start.

The first issue of *Library Notes*, a bulletin for the Friends, soon appeared and proclaimed that the library was "the heart of the university." It represented "the permanent acquisition of the best thought of the world's scholars, scientists, poets, philosophers, and teachers." Not only did good teaching and all research work depend on the library, the statement continued, but it existed to serve both Duke and the entire southeastern region. "To assist in the development of such a library," the announcement concluded, "is not a task but a privilege which all friends of the University and the South are invited to enjoy."[54]

Appropriately enough, in view of Duke's history, the same issue of *Library Notes* carried an announcement that an endowed book fund in memory of Mary Elizabeth Duke Lyon, Washington Duke's only daughter, had been established by her daughter, Mrs. J. Ed Stagg. Income from the fund was to be used to purchase books in the field of child psychology.[55]

When Branscomb relinquished his job as director of libraries in October, 1940 (the same month in which President Few died), the position was dropped and full responsibility given to the university librarian, in conjunction with the library council. Breedlove, after forty-one years of service, had retired to become librarian emeritus, with certain duties, in the fall of 1939. His successor was John J. Lund, a Ph.D. in philology from the University of Chicago with library training at the University of California. Lund, who had joined the staff a year before his appointment as university librarian, did not remain long in the post, however, for he went on leave early in 1943 and resigned later that year. Breedlove faithfully returned as acting librarian and held the post until an important new appointment, that of Benjamin E. Powell, was made in 1946.

A graduate of Duke in 1926, Powell taught school for a year and returned to Duke to take a job in the library. After a year off to obtain a B.S. in library science at Columbia, he came back in 1930 to head the circulation and reference divisions of Duke's library. Urging salary increases for several people in the library around 1932, Boyd particularly noted that Powell, who was as courteous and diplomatic as he was intelligent, should get a raise, since he handled his job with rare ability. "We want to hold on to him for the future," Boyd explained, "and he should be encouraged."[56] Unfortunately, Boyd's push for salary increases coincided with the depression's impact on Duke's budget. Raise or no raise, Powell remained at Duke until 1937, when he resigned to become librarian at the University of Missouri. That experience plus the Ph.D. he obtained in

1946 at the University of Chicago made him all the more attractive as the top candidate for the position of university librarian at Duke. He accepted the post, with tenured membership on the faculty, in 1946.

The space shortage in the main library, which had begun to become discernible in the early 1930s, had grown indeed serious by the time Powell assumed his post. In fact, even before the United States entered World War II, the library staff was forced to begin boxing books for storage. Since that situation only worsened during and immediately after the war, Powell and the library council won recognition by the Flowers administration in 1946 that additional space for the library had a top priority on a long list of postwar plans.

In light of the dysfunctional design of the original library building as well as of the severe shortage of space, Powell, his staff, and many members of the library council favored turning the strategically situated "old" building to other purposes and erecting a new, carefully designed library building, one with adequate space as well as with the temperature and humidity controls that were increasingly recognized as essential for the preservation of books. One longtime staff member pointed out that careful studies had shown that the average college library doubled its holdings every sixteen years. The Duke library, however, doubled in the five years after 1924; and by 1946, that is, in sixteen years, it had increased over eightfold.[57]

Despite the arguments in favor of an entirely new building, such was not in the cards. Aside from the fact that there was no money for what would be, because of postwar inflation, a most expensive undertaking, departure from the original plan for Duke's principal Gothic quadrangles was not a viable option in the eyes of most trustees and administrators. Powell and his staff gracefully accepted the decision in favor of an addition but won agreement that eventually a subsequent, second addition to the library would be made, one that would more nearly satisfy the standards and requirements of modern library planners. (More than twenty years would pass before that second, quite extensive addition would be opened, and it would handsomely rectify the errors of the original plan.)

Mrs. Mary Duke Biddle, an alumna of Trinity and only daughter of Benjamin and Sarah P. Duke, gave the much-needed addition to the library that was begun in 1947 and opened in 1949. Increasing the maximum stack capacity from about 350,000 volumes to over 900,000, the addition brought the total number of seats in the library, including the 250 or so carrels, to 900. The awkwardness of having reference and circulation on the second floor remained, and there was still insufficient space for staff needs; but the stacks, manuscript room, and especially the handsome rare book room were all air conditioned and were among the first areas at Duke to enjoy the cool amenity that gradually came to be considered a necessity.[58]

The library that Ben Powell headed after World War II continued strongly in the tradition set by Boyd, Branscomb, and Breedlove. Containing nearly 961,000 volumes by mid-1949, the library was about to pass the one-million milestone. More important, perhaps, was the continuing high quality of many of the acquisitions. A major acquisition in 1948, for example, one that Allan Gilbert in English played a key role in making, was the private library of Professor Guido Mazzoni of Florence, Italy. Containing about 90,000 titles in Italian literature—23,000 volumes and about 67,000 pamphlets—the collection was particularly strong in the Renaissance period and the nineteenth century.

Although the university did not pay salaries to library staff members that were commensurate with book expenditures, as Boyd had early complained, some of the most dedicated professionals at Duke were key members of Powell's staff. Gertrude Merritt, an alumna who began to work in the library soon after graduating in 1931, helped in acquisitions and in 1942 organized the technical processing department. Powell would later say of her: "No university library becomes a great research library without the assistance of staff members [like Merritt] who spend their lives studying the library's holdings, its book needs for university programs and faculty research, and where to find those needed books." He added, probably truthfully, that Merritt's favorite bedtime reading was the catalogs of antiquarian book dealers from around the world.[59]

While Merritt's role brought her into a close working relationship with library-minded faculty members, her zeal and conscientiousness were matched by others on the staff, such as John P. Waggoner, who became head of the circulation department in 1948. Mary Plowden in the order department, Jane Sturgeon in descriptive cataloging, and Mary Wescott in subject cataloging were other key members of the staff in the same period; and Thomas Simkins served as curator of rare books. By 1949, the end of the era of presidents Few and Flowers, the library had indeed become one of the strongest pillars of academic and intellectual activity at Duke.

A press could hardly be described as so central to the purposes of a research university as a library. Since the establishment of the Johns Hopkins model of the 1870s, however, most of the better research universities accepted the obligation of disseminating knowledge through a university press. John Spencer Bassett, as mentioned earlier, had pushed Trinity into publishing ventures as early as the 1890s, and in 1922 an important historical study was the first volume to bear the imprint "Trinity College Press."[60] There was no question, therefore, that a press was to be included in the plans for Duke University. Indeed, Few assured John Spencer Bassett that those in charge at Duke intended to push the new university press to the limit of their ability.[61]

Unfortunately, despite good and ambitious intentions, the press got off to a somewhat shaky start. This was partly owing to the fact that Duke's resources proved to be limited. While an efficiently and imaginatively run university press can pay a large part of its own costs, that would certainly not be the case with a start-up operation. Perhaps a more basic explanation for the troubles of the press, however, were the mistakes made in the organization of the press and the selection of key personnel to run it.

The press fell under the purview of the secretary-treasurer of the university, Robert Flowers. Reporting early in 1926 to a former Trinity faculty member and close friend of the institution, Flowers insisted that he and the other leaders at Duke well understood that, despite some charges to the contrary, handsome buildings would not make a great institution. Flowers explained that in the last conversation he had held with J. B. Duke before his death, the philanthropist had declared that while he hoped to provide a physical plant adequate for the university's needs, he well knew that it would take "great men" to make the institution. "He wanted us to get the biggest men we could find," Flowers added. While Flowers went on to note that Duke would have to proceed slowly and selectively, he had felt that "one of the best things we could do, and do immediately, was to develop our press, and I do hope we can do something really worth while." [62] Deeds soon matched words, and Flowers joined Frank C. Brown from English and Boyd and Laprade from history to constitute the initial board of managers for the new press in January, 1926. Even earlier Flowers had made unsuccessful overtures to individuals at several well-established university presses. Failing there, Flowers and his colleagues turned to compromises and makeshift arrangements that proved unfortunate and probably hampered the development of the press.

In the fall of 1925 Flowers, clearly temporizing as he sought to find a qualified person, named Ernest A. Seeman of Durham as the part-time manager of the fledgling press for one year. A year later Seeman was made full-time, and the nine-year relationship of Seeman and Duke that ensued would prove to be an unhappy one for both parties. Flowers made the appointment for two reasons beyond the obvious need for someone to help organize and run the press. First, Ernest Seeman, almost thirty-eight when he took the job, was the oldest son of Henry Seeman, the founder and owner of the Seeman Printery in Durham. Close, mutually advantageous ties between it and Trinity College went back to the late nineteenth century and continued after the university was organized. The second reason was that, along with a surprising number of other subjects, Ernest Seeman knew printing. That he did not know publishing, not to mention the tricky art of dealing with learned academic types, is something that Seeman apparently never recognized or conceded and that Flowers only gradually realized. [63]

A bright, adventuresome person, Ernest Seeman was largely self-educated, for he never completed high school or set foot in a college. Yet he read widely and prodigiously while he learned to operate the printery's linotype machine. An ardent lover of nature, he explored many of North Carolina's rivers, hiked around the English countryside, and aspired at one point to become an ornithologist. He soon shifted his attention to music, however, and became a clarinetist and composer. That too proved a passing phase, and Seeman tried his hand at a wide variety of jobs, always falling back on the family's thriving printing business when one after another of his various ventures met dead ends. Service as a sailor in the United States Navy during World War I, followed by marriage in 1919, no doubt inspired him to try settling down. Serving as president of the family printing business while still seeing himself as a writer or at least as something more creative than a businessman and printer, he proved unable to get along with his two brothers and sold his share of the business to them in 1923. After his effort to start his own printing business failed and he suffered what he termed a "nervous breakdown," Seeman was no doubt grateful when Flowers offered him even a part-time job in 1925.[64]

Installed in a small office in the East Duke building on the East campus, where the headquarters of the press would be kept for many years, Seeman took to his new job in many ways. Considering himself an intellectual and a liberal in politics, he could be engaging company, and he found a number of friends among the faculty, including prominent newcomers such as William McDougall in psychology, A. S. Pearse in biology, J. Fred Rippy in history, and Justin Miller, who was named in 1930 as the dean to reorganize Duke's law school.[65]

More importantly, the press began to publish a limited quantity of books, most of them solid and appropriately scholarly, and an even more impressive number of learned journals. To the *South Atlantic Quarterly*, inherited from Trinity, were soon added several journals that brought early recognition to Duke and its young press in various scholarly fields. Among the first were the *Hispanic-American Historical Review*, *Ecological Monographs*, and *American Literature*. Other journals published by the press were *Character and Personality*, the *Duke Mathematical Review*, and the *Journal of Parapsychology*. Under a special arrangement with the Southern Association of Colleges and Secondary Schools, the press also published the *Southern Association Quarterly*. While the costs of publishing J. B. Rhine's *Journal of Parapsychology* and the *Southern Association Quarterly* were covered by special appropriations, the press went into the red on most of the journals, with the important exception of *American Literature* and the *Duke Mathematical Journal*.[66] The main point is, however, that Duke, through its press, began early to try to do its share in the process of disseminating scholarly articles and monographs. Only in that way, in a process that was admittedly less than perfect, could the marketplace of scholarly ideas function and various disciplines undergo the changes necessitated by new discoveries and new understandings. If, as many commentators have noted, American research universities were among the world's strongest by the mid- and late twentieth century, the extensive network of university presses and their publications played a significant role in making them so.

The journals published by Duke's press were mostly edited by members of Duke's faculty. Seeman, because of his keen interest in psychology and vocational guidance and his friendly relations with McDougall, served as an associate editor of *Character and Personality*; its editor resided in London, which was another reason for the arrangement. Faculty members of the press's editorial board—particularly Boyd, Laprade, Rippy in history, and Baum in English—took on the large chore of editing the books that the press published.

James A. Thomas, longtime friend of Trinity-Duke and of the Duke family, was the author of one of the early books published by the university press (as distinct from Trinity's press), *A Pioneer Tobacco Merchant in the Orient*, which was published late in 1928. Boyd's editorial labors on the project took much time and were far beyond perfunctory.[67]

The arrangement whereby faculty members performed editorial chores for the press led to trouble, however, for Ernest Seeman had limited patience with what he regarded as professorial "pedantry." Seeking to learn more about the working of some of the older university presses, Seeman visited several of them early in 1928. "Our youthful press has no cause to be ashamed of itself," he reported to Flowers. "It is already publishing in a year nearly one-third as many books as Harvard, doing it more economically, and in the light of manuscripts offered, it has apparently made good selections." The leading book dealers in New York, Seeman added, had congratulated Duke's press on "the excellent editorial and mechanical get-up of our books."[68]

After studying the operations at the University of North Carolina's burgeoning press, Seeman stressed in his report to Flowers that the "manager of the press had complete editorial supervision." While the manager remained responsible to the board of governors, Seeman explained, he was "entirely free from pestiferous pedants in his authority to edit and print the books as he sees fit." Seeman, therefore, urged a reorganization of the editorial aspect of the work at Duke; he wanted the abolition of the faculty editors and the hiring of a part-time editorial assistant under his own direction.[69]

Despite his repeated pleas, Seeman did not get the authority at the press that he wanted, though Paull Baum and others also recognized that improvements needed to be made in the organization of the press.[70] The long-simmering feud between Seeman and W. K. Boyd need not be traced in its tedious detail. While even Seeman observed that they carried on "like two cats in a bag," he failed to realize that Boyd, with his long tenure at and distinguished service to Trinity-Duke, was a rather different, less vulnerable breed of cat.[71]

Flowers no doubt felt great relief in 1929 when he could gain at least some distance from the problems at the press. This resulted from the appointment of Henry R. Dwire as director of public relations, alumni affairs, and the press. An alumnus of Trinity, Dwire was a well-to-do newspaperman from Winston-Salem whose mother, Mary Hanes Dwire, belonged to a prominent family long closely connected with Trinity-Duke. One of the outstanding civic leaders of his city and state, Dwire brought many talents to his multiple jobs at Duke. He no doubt helped to act as a buffer between Flowers and the incessant wranglings about the press, but Dwire kept his office on the West campus and exercised his directorship strictly from a distance.

Serving Few as an ever-dependable troubleshooter, Dwire had so many responsibilities that he clearly could not have given much time to the press. He and Flowers yielded in 1930 to Seeman's wishes at least to the extent of naming J. Fred Rippy as editor, which probably played a part in the strained relations that developed between Rippy on the one hand and Boyd and Laprade on the other. Dwire, reporting on the editorial change, also noted that by 1931, forty-six books had been published by the university press (and three books earlier by the Trinity press). Those books plus the seven journals represented one tangible contribution that Duke Press made in its first six years to the world of scholarship.

Problems relating to Seeman continued, however, and as Duke's budgetary situation worsened in 1932, Flowers fretted about the costs associated with the press. Coupled with his concern about what he regarded as too few book sales and the expense to Duke of most of the journals was his chagrin that Seeman "frequently gets things mixed up."[72] When the even tighter budgetary squeeze came in 1933, Flowers seized the occasion to give Seeman a year's notice about the termination of his job at Duke.[73] Seeman responded both by trying, in vain, to hold on to his Duke position and also by secretly engaging in various activities that had as their primary purpose the embarrassment of President Few and his administration. The academic year 1933–34, as is described in other chapters, was a troubled one at Duke in various ways, and Seeman played a key offstage role.[74] Many years later, as an aged man, he reminisced about his role at Duke in the early 1930s and among other things noted that he and some of his allies "were aiming to make" Justin Miller the president of Duke, for he (in contrast to Few) "would have made a real president."[75]

With Seeman's departure, friction surrounding the press abated. Dwire continued to serve as director until his death in 1944, whereupon W. T. Laprade, who had long served on the board of editors, was named acting director. In 1945 Laprade arranged for Ashbel G. Brice, a former graduate student at Duke and Columbia and an instructor in Duke's English department, to be named as an assistant editor. He soon became editor and associate director, and in 1951 Brice assumed the directorship, a position he would hold for thirty years. By 1949 the press had published 175 volumes (162 of which were still in print) and, thanks also to its sizeable number of important journals, had assumed a respectable, if not leading, place in the world of university publishing.

Just as the press had been planned as part of the reorganization and expansion that began in 1925, so too was the chapel a central feature of J. B. Duke's design for Duke's West campus. Constructed last among the original Gothic buildings at a cost of around $2,200,000, it was first used during commencement exercises in 1932. While the unusually dramatic structure had been carefully located and painstakingly constructed, the exact uses to which it would be put were not foreseen or known. Nor was it likely that anyone, including Few himself, understood what a vital role the chapel would gradually begin to play in the life of the Duke community.

Always sensitive to town-gown relations and the complexities of Methodist politics, Few, like many other faculty and staff members, belonged to and conscientiously served Duke Memorial Methodist Church, which the Duke family had helped begin in the 1880s and had always supported generously. Other Methodists associated with the university, often with Few's encouragement, belonged to the older Trinity Methodist Church, and Few wanted to do nothing at the university that would weaken or antagonize the congregations of those two churches. Trinity-Duke students had long been encouraged to attend church services in town and, those who were Methodists, to participate in the activities of the young people's Epworth League. Given that long-standing pattern, Few was understandably worried about using Duke's splendid new chapel in ways that might hurt Durham's churches.

There was another complication, too, that arose from the fact that Duke, while maintaining close and friendly relations with the Methodist church, was a nondenominational university without religious tests for faculty or students. Accordingly, any service in the chapel must necessarily be nondenominational. From the first, Few insisted that the chapel was no ordinary Protestant church, and the services that began there in the latter half of 1932 reflected that understanding. There were no robes, no processionals, no collection, no communion service, no hymnals, no any-number-of-things that would be familiar and assumed later on in the chapel. Pressures for change in the direction of a more conventional and more formal service began early, however, and Few graciously yielded to them.

Even as construction of the chapel was just getting underway, Few sought to find the special kind of preacher that he and others thought would be required to serve in it. "We have a truly noble Gothic chapel in process of construction," he wrote to Harvard's theological dean, "and we ought now to have a man to take general charge of this and university interests that should center in the chapel." Recalling a once-famous Episcopal preacher in late nineteenth-century Boston, Few avowed that Duke urgently needed "a young Phillips Brooks."[76] Elbert Russell, the dean of the School of Religion, and eighteen faculty members also urged that a university chaplain or preacher be named without waiting for the completion of the chapel.[77]

Unfortunately, Few and his colleagues did not find another Phillips Brooks, and two professors in the School of Religion, Elbert Russell and Frank S. Hickman, began serving as preachers to the university late in 1932. While they, always in consultation with Few, also invited a regular stream of visiting preachers, the university's fiscal squeeze around 1932–34 probably forced it to abandon the search for a full-time preacher in the chapel.

Despite the makeshift preaching arrangements and the bare-bones liturgy, the Sunday morning chapel services proved popular with many students and faculty, as well as visitors, from the beginning. Late in 1932, Few reported that on Sunday mornings attendance was running from 1400 to 1800 persons; the morning prayer services at 11:40 on Tuesdays, Wednesdays, and Fridays attracted from 300 to 600. A New York preacher who visited Duke a few years later advised Few that he noticed "surprise in quite a few eyes . . . when I told of the 1500 in *voluntary* chapel."[78]

Aside from the architectural splendor of the chapel, another reason for the quick popularity of the services was that, from the first, the music excelled. The Aeolian organ was a splendid one, and, perhaps equally or more important, a tradition of first-rate choral music began almost immediately. For the first service at commencement in June, 1932, Few requested J. Foster Barnes, director of the men's choir, to assemble a large choir of men and women. (Prior to that the university only had separate choirs for men and women, the latter directed by Mrs. J. F. [Myrtle] Barnes.) Since most students had already left or were leaving the campus for the summer, Barnes had to invite many townspeople to help out, but the resulting choir of 150 or so voices nicely filled the bill.[79]

In the fall of 1932 the mixed choir of students, with only a few townspeople, began to perform under Barnes's direction, and participating in the chapel choir became almost immediately an important part of being at Duke for those students involved. An energetic conductor, Barnes, according to one of the early choristers, "brought joy to the singing." Another recalled that Barnes became so animated during a rehearsal of Handel's

Messiah, the annual presentation of which began in December, 1933, that "his suspenders broke and his britches fell down."[80] Fortunately, such episodes happened only in rehearsals, and the chapel choir became a great drawing card from the beginning.

Another musical attraction in the chapel was the carillon, which George G. Allen and William R. Perkins had given to the university. In June, 1932, to inaugurate the carillon, Few sought and obtained the services of Anton Brees, then a well-known carillonneur at Bok's Singing Tower in Florida. For many summers afterwards, Brees's concerts became a popular attraction that brought numerous visitors to the campus. Thus the chapel, in addition to the stark but popular religious services held there, became a center for musical activity and cultural enrichment. That aspect of the chapel's life would increase gradually over the years, complementing the contributions that the Duke Artists Series began making in January, 1931, with a concert by the world-famous pianist Ignace Paderewski.

That Few and his advisors were willing to make changes in the chapel is indicated by the fact that in 1935 they requested Trumbauer to design an altar and altar frontals for the chapel. "As I understand it, the Duke Chapel will never be a church and will therefore have no ritualistic services," Few explained to the architect. "It is a Gothic cathedral and I have always thought [it] should have in it what essentially belongs to such a structure from the artistic or aesthetic rather than the functional standpoint." He and Hickman wanted, he added, a "simple but dignified" cross with flanking candleholders that could stand on a large altar or communion table. That would, Few thought, "satisfy every aesthetic demand without confusing anybody as to the nature of our services."[81] Thus the chapel gradually acquired more of the traditional furnishings of a large Protestant ecclesiastical structure.

In an era when relatively few Americans had travelled to Britain and the continent to see the original Gothic cathedrals, the Duke Chapel probably had a remarkable impact on many who came either to worship in it or merely to gaze upon it. Certainly one Methodist preacher from a small town in North Carolina was affected by it, for, after thanking Few for the generosity and hospitality that Duke had shown to those attending the annual Pastors' School, he noted that it was "fine to sit at last in a Methodist church [*sic*] which compels worship." He also remarked that he had been impressed by Duke's students, sufficiently so to conclude that "the jazz age had passed and that a better day is upon us."[82]

For Few himself, the manner in which the services in the chapel caught on proved highly satisfying. "Nothing since the founding of the University," Few confessed to Russell, "has pleased me more than the way the Sunday services have succeeded in the first year of the Chapel's use." It was, he later added, "the most gratifying experience in all the attempts that we have made to serve the religious needs of students that I have known in all my years at Trinity and Duke."[83]

There were problems from an early stage, however. Alongside the principle of separation of church and state that had been incorporated in the United States Constitution was the closely related tradition that voluntary participation in the life of a church involved responsibility and commitment—including monetary support in accordance with means—on the part of each member. Sensitive to that historic fact, Hickman worried about the church connections of those who worshipped in the chapel. He feared that Duke was "encouraging a loose habit among our people, namely, that of regarding the service of worship as a privilege offered by the University with no obligation on the part of the worshiper." His suggestion, which was eventually acted upon when the large and vigorous YMCA on campus also took it up, was that interested students and faculty members should be organized along denominational lines; a working federation of the denominational groups—what would become first the Student Religious Council and later the Duke University Religious Council—would relate them to each other, and unity of all the Protestant groups, at least, would come in the Sunday morning worship services. Hickman also recognized a need for pastoral consultation in the chapel offices.[84]

When the religious council was organized in 1937 along the lines that Hickman had suggested, the students who were active in it and the YMCA soon sought a way "to draw students closer to the church life on the campus as represented by the Chapel services." The method that they hit upon, and for which they obtained the support of Few and other interested faculty members and administrators late in 1937, was to organize an interdenominational church that would be affiliated with the chapel. Students and others who wished to join it would thus have the opportunity to give financial and moral support to the work of the chapel. Moreover, the authors of the plan argued, interested students would thus come to feel that they "had a real church home rather than just a chapel for religious services."[85]

The Student Religious Council also urged the employment of a full-time university pastor, and with Elbert Russell approaching retirement, Hickman was named as the first dean of the chapel in 1938. Early in 1938 these student leaders asked for and obtained an experimental collection of offerings as a part of the worship service. (There had earlier been offering boxes near the entrance to the chapel.) When the money contributed in the first offering totalled nearly $150, which went to a Duke alumnus who was a missionary in Japan, those responsible regarded the experiment as successful; once-a-month offerings were later followed by weekly ones, with the money collected going to support various social services in an underprivileged community in Durham. After the Student Religious Council succeeded in sponsoring the first open communion service in the chapel at a Sunday morning service late in 1937, the practice of holding such services three or four times a year began.

Thus the chapel services, despite Few's original idea, gradually moved closer to those in mainline Protestant churches. Thanking his old friend and ally, Clinton Toms, for the annual contribution to Duke Memorial Church in 1935, Few noted, no doubt with relief, that the downtown church had "about recovered from the shock it received when we were obliged to begin morning services in our chapel."[86]

Few did not live to see the adoption in the chapel of what might be called the full High Methodist or Low Episcopal liturgy. There would never be incense or a few other elements that might have been regarded as "papist" by Few and Russell, with their Quaker leanings. But after World War II, the chapel services grew steadily more formal, as many thought appropriate for a Gothic cathedral anyhow. A staunch supporter of the chapel suggested in 1947 that if the robed choir and ministers entered the sanctuary from the door at the right of the pulpit and sang a processional hymn, that would add dignity and effectiveness. Moreover, the ushers, and especially those who took up the offering, should wear robes.[87] All of these practices, as well as other liturgical changes, soon followed.

None of them, however, was as important as the individuals who played key roles in the life of the chapel. After Russell's retirement, the university needed to appoint another preacher, especially since Hickman too was aging and held other responsibilities in the divinity school. Harvie Branscomb, who became dean of that school in 1944, took the lead in searching for someone outstanding who could serve as professor of homiletics (preaching) in the school and also as one of the preachers to the university. Talented at seeking out the best, Branscomb wished to appoint one of the nation's most outstanding preachers, George Buttrick of New York. Since he was, however, a Presbyterian, Branscomb, possibly at the suggestion of President Flowers, sought advice from a prominent alumnus who was a Methodist bishop. Branscomb asked the bishop if he thought "the Methodists would feel that we were betraying our own genius" by inviting Buttrick. The bishop, who may have been a bowler, replied that he thought such an appointment would be "a ten strike" and that Duke should by all means pursue the matter.[88]

Although Branscomb ultimately failed in his attempt to bring Buttrick to Duke, the university managed in the following year, 1945, to score a "ten strike" anyhow: it brought James T. Cleland to serve as professor of preaching in the Divinity School and as one of the preachers to the university. A Scotsman whose tenacious brogue only added to the attractiveness of his wit and eloquence, Cleland had degrees from Glasgow University and Union Theological Seminary and came to Duke from Amherst College, where he had been since 1931. He would ultimately become a much-admired preacher in Duke Chapel for many years. Moreover, dressed appropriately as "Sandy McClaus," with his wife, Alice Cleland, as "Mrs. McClaus," the Clelands would later become the central feature of the pre-Christmas party in Brown House on East campus, only one example of the wholehearted manner in which they participated in Duke's life.

Unfortunately, Cleland and Hickman, both preachers to the university, did not relate well, and in 1948, at Hickman's suggestion, his position as dean of the chapel was abolished. He argued that, aside from the personal problems, the deanship was one in name only anyhow. Cleland, to whom President Flowers had apparently made some sort of promise about the deanship, protested its abolition, but after Hickman's retirement in 1953, the deanship was revived and in 1955 Cleland ultimately obtained the title that he wanted.[89]

The large crowds that continued to fill Duke Chapel in the postwar years knew nothing of the internal politics, which was just as well. James B. Duke, had he lived long enough, would have had every right to take great satisfaction from the fact that the tall Gothic chapel he had specifically wanted built on "the high ground" had become much more than an architectural landmark: it was a vibrant, well-loved institution in itself, one that, for many people, imparted a special flavor to a bustling research university.

While the chapel became one of the special aspects of Duke, the university serendipitously acquired another equally special feature, the Sarah P. Duke Gardens. Neither James B. Duke nor Few had included any plans for a garden in the blueprint for the university. Such would have been appropriate, for gardening was about the only hobby that J. B. Duke enjoyed. Like his father and Ben Duke, he loved flowers, shrubbery, and trees. Though he ceased to work in the soil himself when the family moved from the homestead farm into Durham in 1874, he maintained a lifelong interest in horticulture and landscaping, as was exemplified by the large sums of money he spent reshaping and planting the grounds of his country estate near Somerville, New Jersey, and having elaborate greenhouses constructed there.

Perhaps J. B. Duke believed that by having Olmsted Brothers, one of the nation's preeminent landscape design firms, plan Duke's two campuses he was making a sufficient contribution to the aesthetic aspect of the university. Moreover, he particularly liked large sprays and jets of water, and his original idea for West campus was to have large fountains cascade down terraces into the ravine between the traffic circle and the main quadrangle in front of the chapel. This in turn inspired him to envision a lake that would occupy a large portion of the ravine.[90]

When the money available to the Duke Endowment's building committee proved to be too limited to allow for the fountains, among various other things that had to be cut, the plans for the lake were also scrapped. This left an extensive tract of wooded land just across from what would later be named Flowers Drive and quite close to the center of West campus. That the medical complex, which soon (and unceasingly) began to grow like kudzu in the southern sun, never spilled across Flowers Drive to fill up the tract was a near miracle, one for which garden lovers could only be thankful.

Perhaps the miracle of Duke's eventually dedicating fifty-five close-in acres to gardens was partly explained by the fact that a prominent figure in the medical school, Dr. Frederic M. Hanes, first came up with the idea of utilizing the space, or a portion of it, for a garden and persisted in pursuing his dream until it became a reality.

A member of a prominent family in Winston-Salem, North Carolina, Hanes was an independently wealthy neurologist whom Dean Davison recruited for the faculty of the medical school. Becoming chairman of the Department of Medicine in 1933, Hanes took a keen interest in many aspects of the university and happened to possess a special love for gardening. Living first in the university-owned house later used by Alumni Affairs, Hanes subsequently swapped houses with Flowers and moved into the house on Campus Drive later occupied by Development. Thus, Hanes, in going daily from his home to the medical buildings, began in 1931 to contemplate the possibility of having the debris-filled southern area of the ravine cleared out and transformed into a garden for iris, his favorite flower.[91]

The exact nature or scope of Hanes's original idea is not known, but when news spread across the campus about the abandonment of the plan for a lake and the possibility of a garden on the site, Hugo L. Blomquist, then Duke's leading botanist, weighed in with cautionary and prophetic advice to Flowers. Blomquist explained first that, from the standpoint of those in biology, it was regrettable that there would be no lake since he thought a proper landscape needed a body of water. Blomquist went on to say, however, that he was as interested in the rumored plans for a garden as he would have been in a lake, but he would oppose a garden planted exclusively in iris. That, he thought, would look out of place in the landscape and would have the monotonous feature of a commercial plantation. He urged that, if there was to be a garden, a more or less formal one should be built, one that included a variety of shrubs and herbaceous plants and that could be arranged to blend in with the surrounding vegetation. Iris could certainly be a part of such a garden, but it should be planned carefully by an experienced landscape gardener instead of being made the object of one person's hobby.[92]

Blomquist's advice was indeed sound and may well have impressed Hanes. At any rate, he arranged for John C. Wister, a noted Philadelphia horticulturist and president of the American Iris Society, to visit Duke, study the site, and prepare a detailed report that foreshadowed a significant portion of the garden's eventual development. Wister estimated that his entire plan would cost around $100,000 but that a good start could be made for $15,000. He concluded with words that undoubtedly carried considerable weight with Few and others: "The University is dedicated to the service of the people and gives them training in many different lines of endeavor. By giving an example to the people of the great beauty they may have by the use of trees, shrubs and flowers, it will add another great service to its present field."[93]

Unfortunately, Wister's report came just as the painful effects of the economic depression were beginning to be felt at Duke. Drastic belt-tightening loomed for the 1932–33 budget, and there was a question even about the modest start-up cost that Wister had projected. Hanes nonetheless clung to his dream and explained to Flowers that he still hoped to see realized the educational as well as the aesthetic possibilities of a garden. "I hope some day it will be the means of making some real contributions to botanical science," Hanes declared.[94]

To Wister, Hanes explained that Flowers and his colleagues, like everyone else, were "sharing the current hysteria in regard to expenditures" and were "anxious to know something about the amount that would be required for the first year's work in the garden." Hanes thought that Flowers was willing to have A. C. Lee, Duke's chief of construction, do the necessary grading and laying out of walks and that the administration would come up with a reasonable sum for planting. But Wister needed to supply closer estimates as to costs.

Hanes also noted that a young man who was about to graduate in botany from the University of North Carolina, Thomas Norfleet Webb, had come to see him about a job. Webb had had some practical experience in planting, Hanes added, came with good recommendations, and was willing to work for a small starting salary. If Wister approved, Webb might serve well as the Philadelphian's "local man."[95] Young Norfleet Webb would soon begin a long association with the Duke Garden as its first superintendent.

Wister advised Flowers that the site being considered for the garden was so close to the center of the West campus and therefore so important that "unless you are willing to treat it properly and expend a proper amount upon it for construction and upkeep, . . . it would be wiser not to attempt to do anything, as no ordinary and economical treatment is going to satisfy you in this prominent position or be in keeping with the magnificent buildings of the College." Wister explained that he had not anticipated using terraces with masonry steps or balustrades, since those were expensive; but he would like to see the line of the stream that bisected the area be changed because it destroyed the picture of a "natural meadow" such as he envisioned for the site. (He may not have yet realized that the stream also frequently overflowed its banks.) He thought about $15,000 for construction and the same amount for planting would be sufficient.[96] The sum of $30,000 to start up and then an unknown annual expense for maintenance were simply not feasible in the circumstances of 1932, and all of Hanes's plans seemed to have hit a dead end.

Not one to give up, Hanes persisted and in 1934 pulled off a coup: he persuaded Sarah Pearson Angier Duke, widow of Ben Duke, to give $20,000 for "a flower garden" that would bear her name.[97] That sum would not actually cover the initial cost of what Hanes and Wister had in mind, but, with such a longtime friend of the institution as Mrs. Ben Duke interested in and committed to the garden, and with the project's approval by Allen and Perkins, Flowers and others at the university were more or less faced with a fait accompli. The university's trustees promptly endorsed the proposal.

Thus in the summer of 1934 construction began on the Sarah P. Duke Garden, though the form it took bore little or no resemblance to the gardens that would be developed later. Under the direction of Wister, with Webb as the "local man" or superintendent, more than a hundred flower beds were laid out in the southern end of the site, in what would later become the south lawn or open-sky garden. In the spring and summer of 1935 visitors trooped in to see the plantings of some 40,000 irises; 25,000 daffodils; 10,000 small bulbs; and assorted annuals. The cover of the *Alumni Register* in the spring of 1937 carried black-and-white photographs of massed plantings of tulips.[98]

No doubt that first step in developing the garden brought pleasure and satisfaction to many, especially Hanes. But there were problems and disappointments, too. Ironically, the irises so beloved by Hanes did not do well in that particular situation, and iris rot proved to be a stubbornly persistent plague. Flowers and plants, as every gardener sooner or later learns, can be, like children, contrary and mysterious; sometimes they wilt and languish despite all the tender, loving care possible. Heavy summer rains led to the small stream's overflowing its banks and washing away many of the flower beds. "Well it is still raining," Webb gloomily reported to Wister in the late summer of 1934. "Yesterday there was at least three acres of water in the garden. It was up over the top of the bridges." Those irises that had not been washed away were buried in sand, the dejected superintendent added, and it was just "a Hell'uva mess." He concluded: "What do you think about a garden in a place that is going to do like that every time there is a flood?"[99]

Despite such problems, Hanes, Wister, and Webb—all avid fanciers of iris—persisted in their efforts. To be fair, one should note that the garden contained much in addition to the iris beds, though they were prominently featured. Hanes arranged for a stone wall to be built around the southern end of the garden, on the drive, and for the main entrance to be constructed in the southwest section of the wall across from where Allen building would later stand. An entrance to the garden was also constructed near the president's house (which much later became the admissions office).

Just precisely when Hanes decided that he needed to move the garden in a different direction, to more or less start over, is not known. But Sarah P. Duke died in September, 1936. When Hanes soon afterward sought to interest her daughter, Mrs. Mary Duke Biddle, in doing something for the garden that was named for her mother, he was armed with an intriguing plan. He had asked a prominent female landscape architect, Ellen Biddle Shipman, to design a formal garden that would be quite different from the one which existed. Mary Duke Biddle, a Trinity alumna who faithfully honored her family's tradition of supporting the institution, liked Shipman's plan and agreed to pay for it as a more fitting memorial to her mother.[100]

Born into a prominent Philadelphia family in 1870, Shipman graduated from Radcliffe College but acquired her extensive knowledge about plants and horticulture largely on her own. With the major university programs in landscape architecture not open to women at that time and despite her family's opposition to her choice of a career, Shipman stuck to her guns in her determination to break into what was largely a male-dominated profession. She found encouragement from Charles A. Platt, whose book *Italian Gardens* (1894) introduced to American landscape design and architecture the concept of the house and garden designed, in the style of the Italian villa, as a whole. One of the leading designers of country houses and gardens for wealthy Americans in the early decades of the twentieth century, Platt became both mentor of and collaborator with Ellen Shipman.[101]

Teaching for many years in a school of landscape architecture and horticulture for women, Shipman made it a practice to employ women landscape architects and draftswomen in her offices in New York and Cornish, New Hampshire. Since women landscape architects obtained few public commissions in that era, Shipman did much of her best work on the estates of wealthy families in the vicinity of New York as well as in various other parts of the nation. Whether Mary Duke Biddle, who shared the Duke family's strong predilection for flowers and gardens, had ever seen one of Shipman's gardens is not known. But in selecting her to design what would become the oldest and best-known feature of the Duke Gardens, Hanes and Mary Duke Biddle made a masterful choice.

As Shipman set about her task in Durham in the summer of 1937, Few reported to Mary Duke Biddle that the landscape architect had spent a day going over her plans on the ground. While the plans were still incomplete, Few added, he thought they looked good and that a beautiful garden would soon take shape. "It will be of great interest and value to the students and to visitors," Few noted, "and a fitting memorial to your mother."[102]

President Few may have been pleased by the prospect, but Norfleet Webb certainly was not. Disappointed at the prospective downplaying of his beloved irises, he sadly reported to a friend and fellow iris fancier that "Mrs. Shipman has pushed her plans through" and a "formal garden" loomed on the horizon. "I have been sick over the thing," Webb added, "but am about to stop worrying over it as there is nothing that I can do about it." Whether the friend should send any more irises, he did not know, for with "that woman" nobody knew what was going to happen.[103] Webb no doubt gradually overcame his initial hostility to the new plan, for he remained on as superintendent until 1945 and lovingly tended his own iris beds at his home in nearby Hillsborough.

Shipman, no doubt accustomed to a lack of enthusiasm on the part of some of her male coworkers, proceeded undaunted. The twenty acres that Hanes and she chose for the new garden were just to the north of the first one. Surrounded by tall pines on all sides, the Italianate garden she envisioned would make extensive use of stone from Duke's quarry in low containing walls for a series of terraces that would descend from a large ironwork pergola or summer house (which would soon become covered with fast-growing and fragrant Chinese wisteria) at the top of the slope to a small pond at the bottom. Two small round structures made of the Duke stone would stand on the right and left of the pergola at either end of the first terrace and would serve as an office, toolhouse, and restrooms. Bisecting the terraces, a rose-colored flagstone walk would lead downward from pergola to pond and would feature on two different levels small, raised, circular pools with cherubic fountains in the middle of them. On both sides of the terraces, curved walkways would lead downwards from the first, grass-planted terrace; it would have boxwood hedges flanking the pergola and would eventually become the scene of countless weddings. On the northern and southern rims of the terraced garden, Shipman called for a planting of one of the South's greatest natural glories, the southern magnolia (*Magnolia grandiflora*), which, with its fast-growing habit and glossy, evergreen foliage—sprinkled with large, fragrant white blossoms in late spring and early summer—would quickly give the terraces the appearance of having long been in such a graciously enclosed spot.

The verticality of the surrounding pines would be echoed by planting two or three sets of upright evergreens on either side of the flagstone walk in the terraced beds, and both pines and evergreens would play against the clean horizontal lines of the stone retaining walls. The circular shape of the pergola, the two small houses, and the two pools would add further geometrical intricacy and richness to the design. Finally, the terraced beds themselves would be filled with flowers. The pattern that would eventually be followed would provide abundant flowers in all but the coldest months of the year; there would be three replacements of plantings a year—tulips and pansies in the spring, brightly colored bedding annuals in the summer, and chrysanthemums in the fall—to fill the terraced beds with color.

On the steep slope behind the pool, opposite the terraces, Shipman envisioned a rock garden, which would contrast pleasantly with the formality of the terraces. She contracted with Frederic P. Leubuscher, a leading designer of rock gardens, to undertake the task. Importing fifty tons of weathered and highly stratified limestone from northern New Jersey, Leubuscher declared that it was "the finest stone with which I have ever worked."[104] He embedded them so skillfully in the hillside that they seemed to be natural outcroppings and would eventually become the inspiration for a rich collection of dwarf conifers, whose varying shades of green and different textures would stand out dramatically against the gray stone.[105]

Closed for construction in much of 1938, the Sarah P. Duke Gardens opened formally in the spring of 1939 with a ceremony that was part of a series of events that celebrated the one hundredth birthday of Trinity-Duke. A visitor who toured the two campuses and saw the new gardens before they were formally dedicated wrote to Few that he considered the magnificent chapel, the beautiful quadrangles, the fine Woman's College, and Wallace Wade's Rose Bowl–bound football team all to be outstanding achievements. He believed, however, that none of them really set Duke apart because other colleges and universities had those things in a greater or lesser degree. "In my opinion," the visitor concluded, "the thing that will make Duke University unique and beyond compare in the coming years will be the Duke Gardens."[106]

Few, Flowers, and others at Duke came to share that viewpoint, at least in part, for the gardens quickly became popular not only with many students, faculty, and staff members but with a steady stream of visitors from near and far. Open without charge every day of the year, such a garden was a rarity in the South and not nearly as common in the rest of the country as in Britain and various other nations.

Unendowed, the gardens became an annual charge upon the university's general funds. (The cost would come to about $250,000 a year by the late 1980s.) Yet even Flowers, who admitted that he had originally believed that too much university money had to go into the project, confessed in 1944 that he had changed his mind. Thousands of soldiers encamped near Durham and elsewhere in the state poured into the gardens during the weekends. "I think now that no money spent has yielded a greater dividend," Flowers avowed. "The garden has given pleasure to thousands of people and I think it has had a splendid influence on the students."[107]

Many years later when Duke's perennial nemesis loomed again on the horizon—the attempt, with limited resources, to do well too many things—a courageous chancellor, A. Kenneth Pye, would lead in a process known as "retrenchment," which was in reality a reallocation of resources. When someone suggested that the gardens might well be targeted for cutting or elimination, Pye promptly pointed out the unwisdom, indeed the unthinkability, of such an action. Why? Because, he argued, the gardens, like the chapel, played too large a role in making Duke a special place in the minds and hearts of too many people. During lean years the gardens would take their share of belt-tightening along with other components of the university, but they would never be regarded as a mere "frill."

An important step toward integrating the gardens with the academic side of the university came in 1945. The trustees vested certain controls over the gardens in the botany department and named Paul Kramer as the first director of the gardens. (Norfleet Webb retired as superintendent in 1945 to be succeeded by Thomas Haddon.) A distinguished plant physiologist, Kramer had some interest in gardening, but more importantly, he promptly set about educating himself, through visits as well as study and correspondence, about the functions and activities of botanical gardens. As Kramer explained to the director of one of the nation's leading botanical gardens, the plan was to expand the activities of the Duke Gardens beyond "the purely ornamental function" that they had hitherto served.[108]

Articulating and implementing ideas that Hanes had more vaguely alluded to in the early 1930s, Kramer spelled out three primary purposes for the gardens. First of all was the aesthetic purpose, for the gardens were meant to provide "the maximum of beauty and pleasure to visitors." Secondly, however, the aim was to demonstrate the kinds of plants that could be grown in the southeastern region and to offer practical examples of the proper methods of planting and caring for the plants. The third purpose Kramer envisioned was in experimentation—that is, the gardens would serve as a testing ground in determining the suitability of new plants and cultural methods for gardens in the region.[109] Carrying out these policies, Kramer made sure that plants were carefully labelled so that visitors might learn if they so wished. He and Haddon, still encouraged and supported by Hanes and his wife, worked at introducing new and varied types of plants and increasingly gave the gardens an educational dimension that supplemented their primary aesthetic purpose.

Reporting to President Flowers in 1947, Kramer noted that the gardens, for the first time since before World War II, had a full crew of five or six workers. There was, he thought, a great need for one or two trained horticulturalists who could function without supervision and who could supervise the work of small groups of laborers. Parking and traffic control, especially on spring weekends, were growing problems, Kramer added, but all in all he felt for the first time since assuming the directorship that progress in improving the gardens was being made. Work on a planting of iris, which would be in honor of and contain a memorial plaque to Frederic M. Hanes, was scheduled to begin shortly.[110]

Hanes, Wister, Webb, Sarah P. Duke, Mary Duke Biddle, Ellen Shipman, Leubuscher, Haddon, Kramer—all were merely the first among many individuals who would play important roles in the evolution of the gardens over the years. Just as the gardens themselves constantly changed, so too did the people who lovingly cared for them. Still ahead, when Kramer reported so optimistically in 1947, were many developments that would vastly transform and enlarge the gardens: the spacious parking lot on the eastern side of the gardens with a handsome entrance gate on Anderson street, the smaller but no less striking entrance gate from the parking lot to the linden-tree alley leading to the circular rose garden; the colorful, hemlock-lined avenue going from the rose garden to the azalea court behind the pergola; the open-sky garden, with its crowds of frisbee throwers and sunbathers in the spring; the quiet, cool serenity of the Hugo L. Blomquist Garden of Native Plants; the lake at the northern end of the gardens, which would finally help in dealing with a long-standing problem of flood control in the drainage basin where the gardens are situated; and finally, the extensive Asiatic Arboretum in the twenty northern acres of the gardens. Truly, Frederic M. Hanes's dream would take on wonderful dimensions by the late twentieth century.[111]

To have the gardens at all is a matter of thanksgiving for many. To have them within a stone's throw of a great chapel, a vast research library, a world-class medical center, and several thousand graduate and undergraduate students and their teachers and the vast staff that supports all of them—that is a prime glory of Duke.

7

Duke Students at Work and Play in the Jazz and Big Band Era

⬿

THE TRANSITION FROM A more or less provincial liberal arts college to a regionally and nationally oriented research university brought three principal changes to Duke's undergraduates: a more challenging academic program, a more heterogeneous and cosmopolitan student body, and a more varied and sophisticated extracurricular life. Trinity College, which again became the undergraduate college exclusively for men in 1930, was always foremost in President Few's heart and in the concern of the top, all-male administrators. Yet the Woman's College under the leadership of Alice Baldwin actually outshone Trinity in certain respects during the first two or three decades of the university's life. As is discussed more fully in the next chapter, the Woman's College, for a variety of reasons, enjoyed greater selectivity in its admission of students. Moreover, Baldwin and her able staff managed to work out housing arrangements and a relationship with the women's student government that led to a healthier, more harmonious atmosphere on the East campus than existed on Trinity's West campus, especially in the early 1930s. Perhaps too the fact that seventeen- and eighteen-year-old women simply are psychologically more mature than young men of the same age accounted for certain differences between the two campuses. Despite those disparities, the undergraduate men and women shared the same faculty, the same curriculum, and, to an extent greater than Few had originally envisioned, many of the same classes, especially after the freshman year.

The curriculum that Duke inherited from Trinity, and only gradually and partially modified, was a conservative and highly restrictive one as compared to that of the late twentieth century. While Harvard and other institutions opted enthusiastically for the elective system in the late nineteenth century, Trinity never slavishly followed that trend. Greek and Latin, twin pillars of the old classical education, did lose their sway long before the mid-1920s, but Trinity-Duke's curriculum of 1924–25 remained highly restrictive. Undergraduates could obtain only the bachelor of arts degree, and they were expected to concentrate their work in one of seven groups: general, business administration, religious training, engineering, pre-medical, teaching, and pre-law. Of the 126 semester hours required for the B.A. degree, exclusive of physical education, well over half—70 hours—was taken up by work required of all students, work that long was known at Duke as the "minimum uniform requirements."[1] They consisted of English (12 semester hours—6 in composition, 6 in literature); foreign language (18 semester hours, no more than 6 of which could be in the beginning study of a language; that year-long course then had to be followed by a second course in the same language); science (16 semester hours, 8 hours of which—that is, a year-long course—had to be in any two of the three natural sciences: biology, chemistry, and physics); Bible (6 semester hours, Old Testament and New Testament); mathematics (6 semester hours); economics (which then included political science; 6 semester hours); and history (6 semester hours).

Once the students had spent all or most of their first two years clearing these numerous hurdles, they were free to concentrate on their major and minor (or related) fields, where a total of 30 hours was expected. That left 26 semester hours (or approximately 20 percent of the total required for graduation) for purely elective courses.[2]

While tinkering with the curriculum has always been the favorite indoor sport of many professors and deans, it is doubtful that most undergraduates have ever regarded the matter as earthshaking in importance. While they have no choice but to cope with the requirements as best they can in order to remain in college and, they hope, graduate, their principal interests have always been elsewhere. Certainly the students who went home from Trinity College in December, 1924, and returned to Duke University in January, 1925, had a myriad of other matters on their minds.

The *Trinity Chronicle*, the students' weekly newspaper that had been established in 1905, stubbornly kept its old name throughout the spring semester of 1925. An early concern of some students, however, was that all of their old cheers and yells about Trinity were no longer usable. Consequently, with the basketball and then the baseball season looming, there was a frantic scramble for new yells. One, which did not catch on but which possessed a certain local color, was:

Chesterfield! Bull Durham!
Strikes and Plug
Duke University
Slug! Slug! Slug! [3]

While the *Chronicle* carried a banner headline in its first issue of 1925 saying "TRINITY BECOMES A UNIVERSITY," the more immediate concern was final examinations, for Duke had (and long retained) an academic calendar that brought students back from Christmas vacation for one or two weeks of classes before the first semester's final examinations. At a mass meeting after the compulsory chapel on January 14, 1925, the Trinity men voted unanimously to forego shaves and haircuts until after finals and to form the F[ew]-B[aum]-C[ranford] Beaver Club, all three of those venerable faculty members being well bearded.

Finals behind them, the students turned to other matters. While the Taurian Players, directed on a voluntary basis by Mrs. Paul Gross, prepared to present Booth Tarkington's "Monsieur Beaucaire," the women in Southgate gathered on a Saturday evening for popcorn popping in the social room and an informal discussion on etiquette led by Alice Baldwin.[4]

Activities on campus, where absolutely no ballroom dancing was allowed, still tended to be on the tame side: meetings of the Columbia and Hesperia literary societies and of the Ministerial Club; a debate between Trinity's team and visitors from Washington and Lee; a Bible class on Sunday morning in YMCA Hall and vespers that afternoon. There was at least an on-campus soda fountain and store, located in 1925 in West Duke building and already called the "Dope Shop" for the term southerners used for the ever-popular Coca-Cola drink.

Downtown Durham was less than a mile from Duke's campus and held various attractions for students. Since prohibition reigned throughout the nation, beer halls were not among those attractions, but there were movie houses where the students flocked to see the stars of the silent film era. In addition, the "Orpheum" featured a "nice jazz orchestra" and travelling vaudeville shows, which, while not legally off-limits for Trinity's male students, were clearly regarded as in "questionable taste." The *Chronicle* reported: "Rumor has it that certain habitués of the Orpheum were required, in order to atone for their indiscretion, to reproduce before the tribunal the scenes enacted in that unholy place." [5]

The students hung out frequently at the Goody Shop on West Main Street and watched with great interest as Durham's ultramodern, sixteen-story hotel, the Washington Duke, neared completion. "There exists a feeling of kinship in the minds of the students between the University and the Hotel," the *Chronicle* explained. Aside from the name, it was "the much-loved 'Bobby' Flowers who spoke at the laying of the corner stone of the Hotel."[6]

Even before Duke began growing and changing so rapidly in the late 1920s, the *Chronicle*'s editorials struck themes that would long reappear. One perennial bemoaned the alleged loss of friendliness on campus. The custom of speaking to everyone seemed to be on the wane, the *Chronicle* declared, and the "once firmly-established custom of raising the hats to faculty members is likewise on the point of abandonment." The editor surmised that perhaps some of the newer faculty members did not know the long-standing custom and had been careless about responding.[7]

Another long-lived editorial theme had to do with the lawns. "At one time at Trinity it was a serious offense for a man even to walk across the grass," an editorial noted, "but now a casual glance across the campus on any afternoon will show just how far out-of-date" that tradition had grown.[8]

Even some students probably thought the *Chronicle* a bit on the stuffy side. While noting that some college newspapers had begun carrying crossword puzzles (perhaps the most popular single feature of the late twentieth century's *Chronicle*), the Duke editors offered two reasons for eschewing them: "Students are now in danger of flunking their work because of wasted energy on such trash, and . . . there are not enough brains on the staff to compose such a puzzle."[9]

There were no comic strips either, a popular feature in later years, but an occasional cartoon enlivened the paper. One, captioned "Irma Collegienne," depicted a young woman in a mid-thigh petticoat, hose rolled to just below the knee, pinning a college pennant to the wall. The verse underneath read: "Roses are red, violets are blue; Horses neck and so do you."[10] In an editorial on "spooning," another name for necking or petting, the *Chronicle* declared that whatever else "the age of jazz may have contributed to civilization . . . it has opened the way for the prophet of doom, furnished the columnist with material, and given pleasure to those who rejoice with youth in the glory of their morn." Were young folk really worse than their parents had been? the writer queried. He went on to add that out of a fairly representative group of women students at Duke, only 24 percent confessed to "spooning," though their precise definition of the term remained unknown. Yet the same group estimated that nearly two thirds of other girls "spooned."[11]

Growl though Dean Wannamaker and his underlings might, all sorts of changes were occurring in student life. A large advertisement for the General Electric company announced a new attraction available on the increasingly popular radio: "the world's first radio dramatic company" with sound effects that almost turned "sound into sight." A survey in the spring of 1926 found approximately a dozen radios in the Duke community with "several of the students, as well as a professor or so," reportedly "infected with that time-consuming disease which can hardly be got rid of if it once gains a slight headway." Yet who could deny, the *Chronicle* argued, that it was more profitable to hear the "monotonous voice of President Coolidge" than to "'hang out' around the Dope Shop or the Owl [a popular pharmacy just off campus]." Moreover, the jazz broadcast from Pittsburgh did not grate on one's nerves "like the shrill, nasal sounds" from the "girls who generally compose the Orpheum chorus, and who have seen younger and better days."[12]

From the Orpheum to the annual celebration of May Day on the lawn in front of the East Duke building was something of a jump. But beginning in 1921, when there had finally been a significant number of women students at Trinity, elaborate May Day pageants featuring a May Queen and her attendants became a popular feature that continued down to World War II. Although feminists of a later era might gnash their teeth at the thought, female "beauties" reigned on May Day, and the art editors of the *Chanticleer*, the yearbook, selected "eight pulchritudinous co-eds to grace the pages of the [yearbook's] beauty section."[13]

In addition to the dances and music that were part of the May Day pageant, a "tea garden" opened to the public offered "strawberry shortcake, fruit salad, home made cake, Japanese lanterns, and beautiful waitresses." The wives of male faculty members cooperated with the women students and staff members to produce the refreshments. As if all that were not enough, a May Day carnival in Memorial Gymnasium featured a twenty-piece jazz orchestra made up of African-American musicians (think of the audience's frustrated foot-tapping!), bathing beauties in the pool, fortune tellers, and pantomimes.[14]

With both the removal of several old structures and the erection of eleven new, Georgian-style buildings underway in the fall of 1925, the campus became a semi-chaotic place. Yet college life went on with remarkable continuity. Football resumed as an intercollegiate sport at Trinity in 1920 after being banned for a quarter-century and in 1925 took on new life with the naming of James DeHart as director of athletics and head football coach. A four-letter man at the University of Pittsburgh, DeHart came to Duke from the position as coach at Washington and Lee and, according to the *Chronicle*, was of a "higher caliber than it was generally expected Duke University would get."[15] Since DeHart could not assume the Duke job until 1926, that autumn's team was the first under his direction.

Before that time, an otherwise-minded editorialist in the *Chronicle* loftily observed that the general public seemed to be turning away from college football in favor of the professional game and that a "rapidly increasing group of thinking students" were ready to have colleges give the game up. Duke football, he avowed, was of no advertising value to the university, for on a football basis Duke ranked as "one of the state's minor colleges." Expansion of the program would be "decidedly unwise," and it was quite unreasonable to think that Duke could ever fill a stadium holding 40,000 people.[16]

The great majority of students, and a sizeable number of faculty and staff, strongly disagreed with the blast against football. DeHart could work no miracles, however, and Duke had to settle for what the *Chronicle* called a "long list of moral victories but actual defeats." Duke would "eventually have a great football team," the newspaper prophesied, and for the time being there was "far more glory in fighting heavier odds and losing than in combating weaker organizations and winning."[17] At the end of the season in 1927, with Duke having won four games and lost five, the *Chronicle* gamely declared in headlines that the Duke eleven had enjoyed the "Best Season in Years" and "Except for Terrible Lapses Blue Devils [are] Paramount in This Section." One of the "terrible lapses" was the loss to the University of North Carolina, which, to the frustration and mortification of the Duke students, won all the football contests with Trinity-Duke in the 1920s.

With frequent editorials calling for greater student spirit and good sportsmanship at all athletic contests, W. Frank Craven, the head cheerleader in 1926, admitted that while the spirit at Duke could be improved, there had still been plenty of it. "For three years we have won less than a dozen major games in practically all of the major sports," Craven admitted. "Yet our attendance has been good. The interest has been as keen as ever. Each succeeding game has seen the Duke students on hand, optimistic, rooting with renewed enthusiasm."[18]

Perhaps there was some consolation for Duke's less-than-glittering athletic record in the fact that social life picked up considerably in the late 1920s. Banquets, on and off campus, were a long-standing tradition, but "informal tea dances," always held off campus and in the late afternoon, livened things up. The Tombs, a secret society made up largely of upper-class athletes, held a tea dance at Forest Hills Country Club, and in May, 1927, the seniors sponsored a "garden fete" on the lawn of one of the off-campus fraternity houses. "With an abundance of moonlight and electric Japanese lanterns," the *Chronicle* reported, the formally attired partygoers were served a buffet supper as they listened to orchestra music.[19] The ballroom at the Washington Duke Hotel became the venue for countless formal dances, with the men in black-tie attire (either dinner jacket or tails) and the women in long dresses with corsages. The *Chronicle* described one of the early such dances as "the prettiest affair of the week," which featured a "grand march led by James Truesdale, during which small silver bar pins were presented to the girls as favors."[20]

Music for many of the dances was provided by an orchestra that loomed large on the Duke social scene in the late 1920s and early 1930s, that of George E. ("Jelly") Leftwich. A native of Wilmington, North Carolina, Leftwich assumed the position of band director at Duke in 1926. In addition, he assembled and led a jazz orchestra that quickly built a large, loyal following. When the Duke glee club, quartet, mandolin club, and other musical groups put on a program at Durham High School, the *Chronicle* reported that "undoubtedly the Blue Devils jazz band" led by Leftwich was the "best received." The crowd demanded encore after encore as the orchestra played "Who," "Tiger Rag," "Stumbling," and other popular numbers of the day.[21] Author of the words and music of Duke's fight song, "The Blue and White," Leftwich, according to one who knew and played under him, was a tall, slim, handsome man, "a delightful and magnetic attraction with baton in hand on the dance floor."[22]

With jazz and dancing becoming more popular each year, the students in 1926 mounted a strong campaign for permission to have on-campus dances. "The problem of social life at Duke has, in the past years, become acute," the *Chronicle* declared in the spring of 1926. New buildings would soon become available, but there was an urgent need for better and livelier activities within some of them. " 'Drop the handkerchief' and 'Ring around the roses' have had their day. They no longer satisfy," the *Chronicle* declared.[23]

Letters to the editor poured in to support the idea of on-campus dancing, and a student referendum in the fall of 1926 revealed that 704 students favored on-campus dancing, while 6 were opposed. When some opponents argued that Duke's connection with the Methodist church ruled out on-campus dancing, one student asked if the institution had "not grown quite a bit recently, and in becoming a University does it not mean that a different attitude is taken in practically all things?"[24]

That student put his finger on a crucial matter, for, as Few had repeatedly and publicly explained, the transition from small liberal arts college to nationally oriented research university did indeed involve many far-reaching changes. But was the institution's historic and friendly relationship with the Methodist church to be among those things that had to change? Few was determined that such not be the case, and in that stand he had strong support from both trustees and many faculty members. As bizarre as the matter may seem in the late twentieth century, the matter of dancing—of the social, man-holds-woman type—brought something of a crisis in Duke's relationship with the Methodist church.

President Few disliked the term "private" when applied to Trinity-Duke because, he argued, "all true colleges of whatever origin are devoted alike to the public good."[25] Consequently, as an expression of the institution's responsibility and answerability to the larger society, Few believed that the relationship which had evolved between Trinity College and the Methodist church served a highly useful, significant purpose. Those ties, formally going back to the 1850s, were carried over without modification in the charter when Duke University was organized around Trinity late in 1924. While the trustees of Trinity-Duke were in reality a self-perpetuating body of thirty-six persons, the names of one third of its members were submitted for election, which in actual practice was confirmation, by the North Carolina Conference of the Methodist Episcopal Church, South. The church's Western North Carolina Conference "elected" another third, and the alumni of the institution gave approval to the final third. In the first year of the university's existence, an official of the Carnegie Foundation sought clarification of the relationship of Duke's trustees to the church bodies. After explaining how committees of both the trustees and the two Methodist conferences handled the matter, Few noted proudly that none of the three confirming bodies had ever failed to ratify a person whom the university's trustees had nominated.[26] Through the careful, conscientious churchmanship of John C. Kilgo, Few's predecessor as president of Trinity, of Few himself (he noted in 1938 that he had not failed to attend the annual conference meetings for thirty years), and of others on the faculty and administrative staff of the institution, the arrangement evolved into one without significant friction, and the ties between the church bodies and Trinity-Duke remained cordial and close.

Even though the two Methodist conferences supplied only quite modest sums, which went toward the support of the School of Religion, they could not be allowed to become unduly alarmed or mystified about the changes taking place at Duke, for that, in turn, could disrupt the long-harmonious arrangement about the two thirds of the trustees and the institution's historic ties with Methodism.

Perhaps the most fundamental reason Few cherished the ties with Methodism is that he and a large number, perhaps most, of those associated with him in the leadership and governance of Duke University hoped to build an institution that would be distinctive in several ways. One of them had to do with religion, broadly and nondenominationally conceived. That the university took from Trinity its motto, *Eruditio et Religio* (Education and Religion); that the tall Gothic chapel stood on the highest ground of the campus and dominated the structures around it; that the School of Religion was the first of the professional schools to be organized—all of these, plus many other bits of evidence too numerous to mention, pointed to one central fact: without religious tests prescribed in its charter or statutes for either faculty or students, Duke University, in Few's words, stood for "a conception of religion as comprehending the whole of life and of education as having to do with all the powers and capacities of our human nature." To bring the two together in the generous service of humanity was the overarching aim of Duke University, and the tie with Methodism was the historic symbol of that aim.[27]

Initially, Duke followed the long-established, Methodist-sanctioned policy that Trinity had scrupulously observed: *no* dancing on campus. Off the campus and with approved arrangements concerning location, hours, and chaperones, university officials shut their eyes about what many churchgoers still regarded as a serious social vice. The school's policy worried Edmund D. Soper, the recently named dean of Duke's School of Religion who also doubled as the vice president of the Division of Student Life. Having come to Duke from Northwestern University, he explained to Few that he regarded dancing as "one of the most difficult questions" that Duke had to deal with. Now widely going on among the students, he pointed out, it would only be driven under cover if further attempts to suppress it were made, and then it would occur in possibly dangerous conditions. "The only way I can see to do justice by the parents . . . ," Soper argued, "is to assume such control over dancing that we can assure the parents that it is being conducted under conditions as favorable as it is possible for us to make them." He urged that it was the university's duty to "face the situation and to deal with it vigorously."[28]

Talk of acting vigorously about dancing came easy. Few, however, had to consider a solemn warning that came from an influential friend of the institution who believed that there was a "quiet estrangement" occurring among a part of Duke's constituency that the university could ill afford to lose unless it meant to become a purely secular institution; as a symptom of an attitude and spirit far from the demands of righteousness, dancing was a serious matter. "Indications are that there is a spirit of worldliness at Duke," the churchman concluded, "that runs counter to the things for which the college stood for more than a half a century."[29] As if such private and occasionally published statements were not enough, the Wilmington District Conference of the Methodist church passed a resolution condemning "the modern dance as one of the very worst forms of worldly amusement" and declaring that one influential institution of the church (meaning Duke University) could not "make an evil thing good by supervising it."[30]

Responding diplomatically to such critics and patiently receiving in his office visiting delegations of irate church leaders, Few rode out the storm, and, for a while at least, it subsided. Privately he admitted that if the sentiment expressed by the Wilmington conference were representative of the general state of mind among Tar Heel Methodists, rather than reflecting what he hoped was a sporadic and local idiosyncrasy, then it would be the first clear sign that he had been mistaken in persuading J. B. Duke to underwrite a national university on North Carolina soil.[31] Personally working harder than ever in leadership roles at all levels of the Methodist church—local, district, state and general conference—Few would manage finally to have the university allow carefully supervised on-campus dances and at the same time maintain its friendly and historic ties with the church. But that would come about after the undergraduate men's college (Trinity) and the graduate and professional schools moved to the new Gothic campus in the fall of 1930.

Few, Wannamaker, Soper, and others apparently explained the serious nature of the dancing question to the student leaders, for the agitation over on-campus dancing died down as abruptly as it had developed in 1926. Some students remained adept, however, at needling the administration in quite imaginative ways. As staunch, sincere Prohibitionists, Few and others at Duke took a distinctly dim view of Alfred E. Smith, New York's notoriously "wet" and highly popular Democratic governor. Yet a *Chronicle* columnist in the fall of 1926 suggested that with Boston's Watch and Ward Society giving that city a cultural black eye alongside other northern cities where "Babbitt and Women's Christian Temperance Unions flourished," it was a good time for the South to "offer some concrete testimony that it is coming out of the fog which settled after the Civil War." The quickest way to do that and attract wide public notice, the columnist urged, would be for Duke students to form an Al Smith-for-President club. That would demonstrate to the world that Duke students did not "condemn a man because he is a Catholic, or a Lutheran, or a Holy-Roller, or even a Ku-Kluxer" and that they did not care "whether a man's personal inclinations lean towards corn whiskey or pink tea." To form such a club, the essayist concluded, would "place Duke on a plane with other liberal educational institutions of the world."[32]

No such club was formed, but during the presidential campaign of 1928, Governor Smith's train halted in front of the Duke campus—about where President Theodore Roosevelt had spoken many years earlier—and Duke students made up a significant part of the crowd that gathered to greet, in the *Chronicle's* words, "the most maligned man in America." President Few saw the matter differently, and when North Carolina joined several other southern states in voting for Herbert Hoover, Few seized the occasion of a speech on Armistice Day to rejoice publicly that the Democrats' hold on the "Solid South" had been broken. Even in his closing prayer, the *Chronicle* reported, he thanked the Lord that the American people had placed "their moral courage above political expediency and party regularity."[33]

Serious political matters seldom intruded on campus life or found mention in the *Chronicle*. Both "Coolidge prosperity," which was by no means shared by North Carolina's and the South's agrarian majority, and the Jazz Age were reaching their apogee by the late 1920s, and campus life reflected some of the color. "If brevity is the soul of wit," a *Chronicle* columnist noted, "the skirt designer has about reached the end of his little joke."[34]

With the opening of the new Georgian buildings in 1927, there were many more facilities for social activity on campus. During the construction process, which seemed interminable to some students, classes had been disturbed by noise, and one student even wrote a "Campus Psalm" (with apologies to King David): "Surely pits and ditches will torment the students all the days of their lives; and mud will predominate on the campus of Duke forever."[35] But a blessed end to most construction on the old campus came in 1927, and, aside from the new dormitories occupied by undergraduate men, the new Union building, library, and auditorium added various amenities. With spacious parlors in the dormitories, the university named Mrs. Clarence (Mary Norcott) Pemberton as official hostess. Residing in an apartment in one of the dormitories, "Mrs. Pem" set about gaining the cooperation of the students in making dormitory social life "more spontaneous and liberal."[36]

To capitalize on opportunities offered by the Union building, which was (and is) as elegant and handsome inside as outside, Few, with Soper's concurrence, named J. Foster Barnes as director of student social and religious life in the summer of 1927. Among his diverse tasks, Barnes, who with his wife Myrtle Barnes lived for a while in a dormitory apartment, set about organizing the men's glee club while Mrs. Barnes directed the women's singing group. In a memorandum to Few, Barnes explained how he hoped to use the Union as a student center for receptions, "sings" in the front lobby, and a meeting place for various organizations, all with an overarching purpose of creating among the students an atmosphere that made for high ethical and moral standards.[37] Barnes, familiarly known to several generations of Duke students as "Bishop" Barnes, would become a well-known and much-admired figure on campus.

His proposed "sings," however, took a slightly different turn when the custom began of after-dinner jazz concerts in the large lobby of the Union. The *Chronicle* reported that a sizeable crowd of students and others gathered each evening to hear a dozen or so Blue Devil instrumentalists play "Three Blind Mice," "Tiger Rag," "Clarinet Marmalade," and other such tunes. "Stately gentlemen, tittering co-eds, dignified and undignified professors, jazz loving students, all sorts of folks all tap leather on marble every evening," the *Chronicle* reported.[38]

Not only did such nightly jazz concerts liven up the scene, but moving pictures began in the new auditorium early in 1928. The president of the YMCA, Ray Carpenter, promised not only that the admission fee would be modest, but that any profits would be turned over to the student governments. Moreover, pictures would be shown for entertainment, just as in the downtown theaters, and "no attempt will be made to educate or convert the students through the silver screen." A local musician organized an orchestra to accompany the silent films, and Quadrangle Pictures quickly became a popular feature of campus life on Wednesday and Saturday nights.[39] Since "talking" pictures were just coming in as Quadrangle Pictures began operation, the management added the most up-to-date equipment for their showing in 1929.

Although Duke's enrollment increased annually in the late 1920s, the campus probably retained much of the atmosphere of the old college. A larger number of students as well as faculty knew and saw each other more regularly than would be the case after 1930. An old tradition of a baseball game between male faculty members and senior men remained very much alive, with Few acting as umpire and Wannamaker, "as usual," at second base. "All students who intend to pass the spring semester's work," the *Chronicle* advised, "need to be on hand . . . to pull for the faculty."[40] An alumnus from that time much later estimated that Few knew from 25 to 40 percent of the male undergraduates and when passing would slightly raise his black felt hat and, giving a small bow of the head, greet the student by name. The alumnus remembered that Few "carried a cane in his right hand as he walked, but always upside down, and the curved handle twisted back and forth like the pendulum of a clock as it slapped against the side of his leg." One reason for the cane was that Few used it "to mark balls and strikes in the dirt to his left or right" as he umpired a practice game of Duke's usually strong baseball team. Coach Jack Coombs, addressing Few as "Prexy," would recruit him for the duty, and since Few "took his umpiring chore seriously and was very good at it," the players "loved having him there."[41] After both Few and the men moved to West campus in the fall of 1930, he would have less time for things like baseball games and would personally know a smaller number of the students.

While President Few saw only the bright side of the move to the new Tudor Gothic campus, some students perceived a few flies in the ointment. Emphasizing the students' "complete cooperation" in the large task of moving, Few told them in an assembly that the move had been made with less confusion than when the new buildings on the old campus were occupied several years earlier. Moreover, he expressed pleasure in the fact that Duke already had a more cosmopolitan student body than some of the Ivy League schools, for he thought it "a good thing for men to go to other sections of the country for education." In closing, Few "congratulated the students on the improved morale this year [1930] as exemplified in the success of the football team."[42]

On a not-quite-so-upbeat note, a *Chronicle* editorial bemoaned the fact that only the road leading to the chapel had been paved. Since students had been requested not to park in the main quadrangle, those with cars had to use other campus roads, which bore "a rather striking resemblance to a cornfield in general contour."[43] While other roads were, in fact, soon paved, complaints about unpaved parking lots would long continue, for automobiles and parking had begun their long reign as the number one extracurricular problem.

When students had to register their cars for the first time in the fall of 1930, 195 undergraduate students reported owning "everything which rolls—from Jello to Jericho." While Fords were by far the most popular cars, there were a few Whippets, Hupmobiles, and Franklins, as well as single representations of the Oakland, Willys-Knight, Hispani-Suiza, and Graham-Paige. Another breakdown showed eleven coaches, twenty-six touring cars, forty-five sedans, sixty-three coupes, and fifty roadsters.[44]

Dean Wannamaker had scant tolerance for automobile-owning students and frequently so informed them and their parents. One male undergraduate had the extreme misfortune of having an automobile accident in the vicinity of Wannamaker's home and received the following communication from the dean:

> I want to suggest that you put more time on your studies and less on joy riding in U-Drive-It Fords at midnight. Looking from my window night before last at the time you participated in a picturesque wreck, I was glad to note that you were not hurt badly but by no means pleased with some of the inexcusable language audible at some distance from the Ford in which you were riding. . . . I wish to have a talk with you before you leave.[45]

Talks with Wannamaker could be quite bracing for students, but the powerful dean fought a losing battle against automobiles. He did succeed, however, in having permission to bring them on campus denied to freshmen beginning in the fall of 1932.

Students actually had a lot more to worry about in the early 1930s than unpaved roads and parking difficulties, for the move to West coincided with what might well be termed a new academic era at Duke. More than any other single person, Walter K. Greene, a professor of English who became dean of undergraduate instruction, was responsible for leading the faculty to make a whole series of far-reaching and long-lasting changes. They helped to make Duke a more rigorous and challenging experience for its students.

A graduate of Methodist-affiliated Wofford College in South Carolina—as were Kilgo, Few, and Wannamaker—Greene received a master's degree from Vanderbilt in 1905 and then held various teaching and administrative positions before obtaining a Ph.D. in English at Harvard in 1921. The dean of Wesleyan College in Georgia when Few brought him to Duke in 1928, Greene was a prominent lay leader in Methodist affairs and also shared Few's deep belief in the central importance of effective, vital undergraduate teaching. At the time of his appointment, Few stressed not only Greene's "good training" but his "strong ethical basis of character." Few added: "We expect much of men like Dr. Greene in our big business of teaching, which we understand aims not only at intellectual development but also at the shaping of the whole personality."[46] Greene certainly lived up to Few's expectations and for more than a decade was a pivotal figure in the raising of academic standards as well as in various efforts to improve the teaching of undergraduates and especially of freshmen. Furthermore, although certain of the academic changes with which Greene was closely connected brought profound anxiety and even distress to more than a few students (especially in Trinity College), he quickly became much admired as a teacher, and in a *Chronicle* poll in 1932 the students picked him as the most popular professor.[47]

Even after the university was organized, Duke clung to the numerical system of grading that had long obtained in Trinity College. In 1930, Duke switched to the system of letter grades that was already in use in many of the better universities and colleges. At the same time, a quality-point system, new to Duke but widely used in other institutions, brought a new rigor to the requirements for graduation and for continuing from one semester to the next. Although the system could become incredibly complicated in certain cases, it was basically quite simple: a grade of A was worth three quality points; B, two, C, one; D, none; and for a grade of F, the draconian penalty of the loss of one quality point for each semester hour of the course (i.e., an F in a four-hour science course meant the loss of four quality points).

To receive the bachelor of arts degree a student had to have 126 semester hours of credit and at least 126 quality points, that is, a C average. For the bachelor of science degree, which Duke introduced for engineers in 1928 and for students majoring in science or mathematics in 1932, the requirement was 138 semester hours and 138 quality points. To rank as a sophomore, a student had to have credit for 24 semester hours and 24 quality points; in practice this meant that for many years Duke would have a sizeable group of "advanced freshmen," that is, students who should have been sophomores but who lacked the quality points to gain the class ranking. For junior ranking, a student had to have 56 and 56; and for senior ranking, 90 and 90. There were additional requirements about continuing from one semester to the next, but the essential meaning of the whole quality-point system was that academically weak or careless students were not to be allowed to "just hang around" at Duke indefinitely, much less to graduate.

While the loss of quality points for the grade of F was an obvious handicap to the marginal student, the quality-point system acquired additional potency through its entanglement with the class-attendance system. Regulations enacted by the faculty in 1930 specified that if a student incurred more than two unexcused absences or more than a total of seven absences (excused and unexcused) in a 3-semester-hour course or more than a total of nine absences in a 4-semester-hour course, that student would lose 1 quality point for the first absence in excess of the number allowed; for the second absence, 2 q.p.'s; and for each absence thereafter, 3 q.p.'s. Since absences before and after holidays were counted as double cuts, the faculty made it crystal clear that class attendance had to be taken seriously.[48]

At the same time that Duke introduced all of these new requirements, Greene worked with key members of the faculty to launch a program of honors courses. These were to provide greater opportunities for exceptionally able students to do independent and intensive work. More than a dozen departments organized honors courses, and the president appointed a chairman to head a university council on honors that supervised the whole effort.

Grades for the fall semester of 1930 revealed that a significant number of Duke students were in for painful readjustment—or for transfer or giving up on college altogether. The enrollment of men in Trinity College for 1930–31 totalled 1,359: 185 seniors, 272 juniors, 411 sophomores, and 491 freshmen. In the Woman's College the enrollment was 481: 85 seniors, 88 juniors, 110 sophomores, and 198 freshmen. Since some seniors were still on the old numerical system of grading, the figures following include fall, 1930, grades for freshmen, sophomores, and juniors only.[49]

Grades	Men (%)	Women (%)
A	7.16	10.57
B	22.16	28.6
C	33.53	35.58
D	19.8	15.8
F	12.13	6.0

Students reacted variously to the new academic dispensation at Duke. In an era when students tended to accept faculty-ordained regulations much more passively than would be the case in the late twentieth century, most students probably regarded the new system as rather like the weather: something they could not do much about even if they wished. In the late spring of 1931, a columnist in the *Chronicle* recounted the story of a senior at another university who learned well into the spring semester that he had gained enough hours and quality points to have graduated at the end of the previous semester. "This quality point business must have funny effects upon college people," the columnist continued, "but we guess the burden of staying in school just to amass quality points enough for graduation does become monotonous after the first seven or eight years and causes one to lose track of things."[50]

In the fall of 1931 the *Chronicle* warned would-be athletes that "the road to the varsity squads" was not entirely a matter of athletic ability. While the previous year's freshman teams had made an enviable record athletically, according to the reporter, their scholastic record should serve as a "grim reminder": basketball reportedly lost two men by graduation, but four left school because of low grades; baseball, hardest hit of all, had one player graduate but fifteen "flunk out"; and in football five graduated but eleven were "dropped from the rolls." The conclusion: "Being an athlete at Duke is no insurance against failure; it seems to be more of a disadvantage than anything else."[51]

Early in 1932, as the full meaning of the new system began to hit home and the nation's economy grew increasingly shaky, another columnist noted that forty seniors had already been disqualified from graduation and more would be after the first semester ended. The quality-point system was "the most merciless rule that has ever been invoked" at Duke, the columnist declared, and the current "era of depression" was the worst possible time to enforce it, when many students could not afford the extra semesters needed to earn the necessary points. Later, during the presidential campaign of 1932, a brief editorial laconically noted: "If either Mr. Roosevelt or Mr. Hoover should or would devise some alternative to the quality point system, he should or would receive the votes of many of our student body, if they could or would vote."[52]

A curriculum reform in the fall of 1932 rounded out the major academic changes for which Greene pushed. The most important change was the sharp reduction in the minimum uniform requirements: from 12 to 6 hours in English; from 18 hours in foreign language to 12 or 18, depending on the tested result of high school language study (and beginning in 1937 a student could test out of 12 hours of the requirement); from 16 to 8 hours in science; and from 12 hours in the social sciences (economics, history, and political science) to 6 hours. The religion requirement of 6 hours remained the same, and 6 hours of physical education (four semesters, each carrying 1 ½ hours of credit) became a requirement for graduation.

While the students no doubt welcomed the sharp reduction in the general requirements, the curriculum of 1932 largely took away with one hand what it gave with the other. That is, required work in the field of the major and minor was increased from 30 hours to 42 (18 to 24 in a major department in one of the three divisions—humanities, social science and history, and science, mathematics, and psychology—and 18 to 24 in at least two other departments in the same division). Furthermore, a new category of restricted electives was introduced, and a student had to take 18 hours in the two divisions not chosen for concentration, with a minimum of 6 hours each in any two departments of those divisions. The upshot of all this was that the students actually had fewer hours of free electives after 1932. An additional curricular change introduced in 1932 was the lowering of the total number of hours required for both the bachelor of arts and bachelor of science degrees to 122, and for the first time seniors were prohibited from taking for graduation credit any course open primarily to freshmen, while juniors could not take for graduation credit more than one course open primarily to freshmen.[53]

The curriculum changes of 1932 clearly kept Duke's undergraduates, like those at most other colleges at the time, still under a fairly rigid system. The new quality-point system had also introduced some stress and strain, but neither it nor the darkening economic clouds lessened the many pleasures of college life. Fraternities entertained their pledges and dates at bridge-and-supper parties in private homes in Durham, and some faculty members entertained their classes with dancing and bridge in their homes.[54] There was clearly more social interaction between students and faculty than would be true later in the century, and the gulf between faculty-style and student-style entertainment had not yet widened.

The biggest diversion of all, however, continued to be dancing—and from the fall of 1930 onward much of it took place *on* campus. Since the new Union building on West campus had on its second floor a good-sized ballroom, complete with a large fireplace, it was the logical venue for dances that involved no more than 300 people. Without any formal announcement of a change in policy, Few, Wannamaker, and others responsible had decided that the time had come to take advantage of the new facilities and yield to the long-standing request of the students. A small announcement on an inside page of the *Chronicle* informed students that any group which wished to use the Union ballroom for dances should first clear the date with Henry Dwire and Mrs. Pemberton, the university hostess, and then secure permission from Dean Wannamaker. No subscription dances would be allowed. Shortly thereafter, the YMCA opened the "fall dancing season" with music provided by Jelly Leftwich and his University Club orchestra.[55] Aside from the fact that there were now to be more dances of all types than ever, that they could be held on campus made them more accessible to the nonfraternity and nonsorority majority than had previously been the case. Nevertheless, when a Trinity alumnus and Methodist clergyman read in the newspaper about an on-campus dance in 1932, he fired off a blast to Few about feeling the "greatest mortification" in forty-three years of ministry and also indignation that "such an abomination should ever have been tolerated in my *alma mater*."[56]

Few's long, patient response to the protester was typical of many of his letters and public statements on the subject. Pointing out that only a relatively small proportion of Duke's students were now Methodists, Few went on to declare that "everybody understood when we agreed to undertake to build Duke University and make Trinity College part of it [that] the University must be for all the people without regard to faiths or social classifications of any kind." After mentioning the relative isolation of the new campus and its adaptable facilities, Few concluded with a personal and no doubt winning plea:

> I beg you to believe that I have spent most of my life so far in the effort to get funds for and to build a great university resting upon moral and religious sanctions. I have been anxious that Duke University with all its vast ramifications should never offend the moral sensibilities or religious convictions of any good man. Perhaps this may be an impossibility. The university touches life at so many points and has implications so far reaching that we must expect differences of opinion, and all of us who want to do the right thing about it must be prepared for a certain amount of give and take.[57]

Such eloquence and tact, combined with changing views among the public at large, helped Few to surmount the potential crisis in Duke's relationship with Methodism. Not only did the Duke students happily dance away on campus during the depression years and after, but they did it to the music of such outstanding student orchestras as those led by Jelly Leftwich, Johnny Long, and, later, Les Brown. Although Few perhaps exaggerated the harmony theme, he had justification for the pride he took in announcing that the preliminary adjustments necessary to change the organization and aims of an already well-established college to those of a university had been "completed without the slightest friction and with the full cooperation of our entire constituency." It meant, Few suggested, that Duke had "a constituency strong enough, intelligent enough, catholic enough to sustain a great institution of higher education."[58]

The students never had to worry, of course, about how Few handled the university's relations with the church. They proceeded to hold a variety of dances in the West campus Union, with all sorts of organizations sponsoring them. When the junior class held a dance there on a Saturday evening, the *Chronicle* reported that it was "more of a success than many thought it would be," and the freshmen proceeded to give a dance there in honor of the undefeated freshman football team.[59]

The venue for all of the large on-campus dances throughout the 1930s was Memorial Gymnasium on East campus. The first organization to demonstrate that a successful, big, formal dance could be held there was the social standards committee of the Women's Student Government Association (WSGA). Decorating the gym in red, white, and blue streamers in honor of George Washington's birthday, the women hired Leftwich's orchestra for the first of a long series of "Coed Balls" and allowed each girl to invite three men to the dance, which, as the *Chronicle* somewhat acidly noted, was "very advantageous for the girl." A large number of dateless "stags," however, was essential for a lot of "breaking-in" whereby during any number that was not announced as a "no-break" any man could tap on the shoulder or elbow of the male dancer and ask for permission to dance with the woman. For the most popular women, a veritable line of men waiting a turn was not unusual, and any thoughtful man who wished to see that his date got a "rush" could easily arrange the matter by a few whispered words to his male friends or fraternity brothers. To be stuck with a poor dancer or an inept conversationalist was the bane of both men and women, so having many stags was almost as important as a good orchestra for a successful dance.

In the case of the first Coed Ball, three no-breaks, which were often danced to the slower and more romantic tunes, were announced in advance: "Carolina Rose," "I Love You Truly," and "Drifting and Dreaming." Some sixteen women students dressed in Martha Washington costumes served punch and other refreshments during intermission.[60]

Before the first big formal dance on campus, the *Chronicle* reported that about "fifty-seven boys who didn't get bids (and some who did) are gnashing teeth and swearing they won't go near the East campus again." After the affair, an editorial stressed that the ball was "concrete evidence to the effect that large-scale dances have a social function in college life which it is neither desirable to dispense with, nor feasible to replace." Not only was Memorial gym nearly ideal for such affairs, but the dance was "full proof that Duke students can hold dances without drinking or misbehavior, and—what was perhaps more surprising to some parties— that they can hold *good* dances without the appearance of either of the above factors."[61]

What the *Chronicle* failed to explain, although there would be some complaints about the matter in later years, was that the decorous behavior did not just happen because Duke had model students. Alice Baldwin and her staff saw to it that not only were there numerous and high-powered chaperones at the dance, but also that a carefully controlled policy of entering and leaving the dance was followed: once inside, no one was allowed to leave and then return to the dance. In other words, there could be none of the "slipping out to the car for a quick one" that at other places and other times saw many a nominally "dry" dance become amazingly "wet" before the evening ended. If that strict policy at Duke lessened the pleasure of on-campus dances for any significant number of students, the *Chronicle* offers no evidence to that effect.

The move of the men to West brought many innovations besides on-campus dancing. The mile-and-a-half road between the two campuses, later officially named Campus Drive, became the focal point of strained relations between students and Durham police as the latter attempted to enforce a speed limit of fifteen miles per hour on the curving road.

When a local judge ruled that the city police had no jurisdiction on the university-owned road and ordered charges dismissed against six Duke students who had been arrested for speeding, the police changed their strategy and began arresting those who were charged with speeding at several different intersections on the road. The battle would be an ongoing one, as would the student demand for better bus service between the two campuses. "The small bus that the university furnishes—for a price [five cents]—can hold only fifty under conditions of the most expert crowding," one woman student noted.[62]

Attendance at chapel services became entirely voluntary after 1930, but weekly assemblies and class meetings, at which attendance was required, became much a part of life. In response to continuing protests from the students, the administration in 1934 agreed to have only one assembly per month for upperclassmen and three class meetings per month; freshmen continued to have weekly class meetings on Saturday mornings.[63]

Not until December, 1930 did the *Chronicle* take cognizance of the deepening economic depression. "By this time, even the proverbially cheerful and carefree college student has become aware," the paper noted, "that the country and the world in general is in the throes of what can no longer be smiled at as a temporary economic slump."[64] Not until early 1932, however, did the *Chronicle* report that some students were talking about having to leave school because of the depression, and by then there were waiting lists for virtually all of the part-time jobs available in the dining halls and elsewhere on campus.

Duke's tuition had gone up in 1928, after the new buildings on East had been made available, from $30 to $50 per semester. Then in 1930, when the West campus was opened, the tuition rose to $100 per semester, where it remained until after World War II. While $200 per year was a sizeable sum during the depression, Duke's tuition was considerably below that of the Ivy League schools and was not, in fact, much greater than that of the University of North Carolina and other state-supported institutions. As the Duke family had long subsidized Trinity College and thus allowed tuition to be kept low, so the Duke Endowment made possible the university's modest charge. While there were some wealthy students at Duke, the great majority of the students apparently had to count pennies closely in the 1930s.

While few students exhibited any deep concern about large social and political questions, there was a small minority of students at Duke who sympathized, however vaguely, with the idea of social change. In September, 1929, a dozen or so of them organized the Liberal Club and proceeded initially to invite various professors to speak on current topics. The first outside speaker came in December, 1929, from the left-wing League for Industrial Democracy in New York; with an eye toward the highly publicized textile strikes in Gastonia, North Carolina, he urged support for labor unions and their goals. In the spring of 1930 the Liberal Club invited a professor from the North Carolina College for Negroes in Durham (later North Carolina Central University) to speak on "American Negro Literature," and another speaker was the executive secretary of the New York-based League for Independent Political Action. He spoke on what the *Chronicle*'s reporter called the "rather provocative subject" of the need for a new alignment in American politics. The club also maintained a collection of about thirty or so books available for lending to interested students.[65]

When the Liberal Club helped bring Norman Thomas to speak on the campus in December, 1930, that event, unbeknownst to the students, plunged President Few into the serious crisis with George G. Allen and William R. Perkins discussed in an earlier chapter. After the field secretary of the League for Industrial Democracy spoke at Duke in March, 1931, on "The Economic Roots of Race Prejudice," the *Chronicle* reporter suggested that the choice of topic was "somewhat unfortunate" since the speaker admitted that it was not his specialty, and the talk was rather general. Yet because of the speaker's "youthfulness and his sincerity," the audience was at least made to think.[66] The Liberal Club continued to meet for a couple of years, faltered, was temporarily revived in the spring of 1934, and then disappeared, whether from the campus or merely from the pages of the *Chronicle* is not known.

On the matter of race relations, the Liberal Club was one of the few organizations on campus that dared to deal critically with the subject. In 1928, the annual conference of an organization called the Student Volunteer Union met on the Duke campus with 155 delegates from thirty colleges and universities in the two Carolinas. Writing about the meeting, the woman editor of the *Chronicle* commented, "An unusual and, shall we say, hopeful sight on a southern college campus was the presence of thirty negroes meeting with white students. . . ." A Negro college president gave one of the "outstanding addresses" at the conference, and the whole affair, the *Chronicle* writer believed, was "indicative of a changing attitude toward negroes. . . ."[67]

A month or so later, Dr. James E. Shepard, president of the North Carolina College for Negroes, spoke at the vesper service on campus under the auspices of the YMCA and the YWCA. Still following the conservative, Booker T. Washington–type approach to racial change, Shepard declared, according to the *Chronicle*, that the "Negro in the Southland is not asking for social equality, but he is asking for his just and equitable rights in the courts and in public carriers—for a chance to fit himself for the best association within his own race." Emphasizing the African-American person's demand for justice, Shepard concluded: "The Negro is patient. He is not bitter. I am pleading only that he have a chance in the race of life."[68]

Through the YWCA, ten or so Duke women continued in 1929 to cultivate exchange programs with the African Americans' college in Durham, but such activities were rare. Since de facto segregation still reigned in much of the nation outside of the South, neither most students nor most faculty members coming to Duke from other regions seemed to be shocked by the legally mandated Jim Crow system they encountered in Durham and at Duke. While more frequent attacks on the system began with the coming of World War II, one bold student columnist in 1938 dared to suggest that the German Nazis were not the only group that persecuted minorities. "Even today the 'Jim Crow' laws and Negro segregation can be traced, in part at least, to racial prejudice," the student submitted, and white Americans should remember that they were not innocent.[69]

While segregation did not bother the vast majority of the students in the 1930s, what the Trinity College men perceived as arbitrary and high-handed behavior by the administration, and particularly Dean Wanna-maker, did indeed bother them, and long-building complaints finally erupted into a vigorous, open protest in the winter of 1934. In some ways the administration did occasionally seem to go out of the way to antago-nize students. The academic calendar, for example, was fixed by a standing committee; it was not solely Wannamaker's doing. Yet he was the top dean and obviously had an important role in such matters as the calendar. With the installation of the quality-point system and the related atten-dance regulations (with double cuts before and after holidays), the days on which holidays began and ended became more important than ever, and "the powers that be" at Duke—Wannamaker, in student eyes—had a knack for making things difficult. For the Christmas holiday in 1930, for example, the dean's office announced that classes would end on Monday, December 22, at 1:00 P.M. and resume on Saturday, January 3, at 8:40 A.M., thus "killing" two weekends and making the break eleven days rather than two weeks. After editorials and letters in the *Chronicle* attacking the arrangement and protests in the various class meetings, Wannamaker an-nounced that classes would end on Friday, December 19, rather than on Monday the 22nd, but that they would resume on Saturday, January 3, as originally announced, "because the administration objects to the stu-dents traveling on Sunday."[70] There would be more such hassles about the calendar in the future.

Early in 1931, in an editorial entitled "Page Mussolini," the *Chronicle* criticized the lack of regular, publicized communication between the stu-dents and the administration. Both the abolition of required attendance in chapel and the allowing of on-campus dancing were at least partly in response to student demand, the *Chronicle* argued, yet the administrators made no effort to take the student body into their confidence. Even if the administration deemed it "inexpedient to allow the average student a voice in the affairs of the institution," the newspaper concluded, perhaps the dean and his staff might at least "recognize the psychological advantage of letting him think he has."[71]

Semi-covert digs at Wannamaker appeared in the newspaper from time to time. A columnist wrote of a "dean of a little college in the land of Nowhere," a "little monarch [who] delighted in interpreting the speeches of all intellectual visitors who addressed the student body." The dean so loved his students, the journalist continued, that he did not want to be separated from them (and therefore chaperoned many dances), and "if any of his fold got into trouble he was always kind enough to write the boy's parents about it."[72]

Wannamaker, like other deans and administrators across the nation at that time, acted *in loco parentis*: "While the relationship of the college to the student is legally and in fact quite similar to that of parent and student," Wannamaker once explained, "it must be understood that this relationship must be interpreted largely as that of parent to the more or less mature and at times even adult children, though the latter phase may seem contradictory." Wannamaker added that colleges had an obligation to give students considerable freedom, for in the acquiring of the ability to use freedom rightly lay one of the greatest sources of sound education.[73]

Since most students at that time, and certainly the overwhelming majority of parents, also subscribed to or at least acknowledged the policy described by Wannamaker, the Trinity students' growing quarrel with the dean was not about the philosophy of *in loco parentis* itself but rather about the tone and manner in which Wannamaker implemented it. Although the conscientious and highly intelligent dean certainly never intended it to be so, the students believed that he held an authoritarian and condescending attitude toward them.

The matter was also complicated by the fact that there were problems connected with the dormitory life of the undergraduate men. As mentioned earlier, J. B. Duke left generous sums of money for the rebuilding of the old campus and the building from scratch of the Gothic campus. Nevertheless, the large, ambitious plans proved more costly than was foreseen, and various cuts had to be made in most of the new buildings (except the chapel) on the West campus. The men's dormitories, therefore, were partly lacking in some of the amenities—such as large commons rooms—that might have made them more civilized and enjoyable.

President Few entertained the idea that the residential quadrangles on West, which were truly handsome on the outside but rather ordinary inside, would evolve into residential colleges or houses, much as Yale and Harvard were developing around the time that Duke's West campus was built and first occupied. Few conceded that separate dining facilities for the various residential units, as in the Ivy League schools, had been too costly for Duke, and only centralized dining halls proved feasible. Still, he clearly hoped that the men's residential patterns could be tied in with the university's larger educational and moral purposes.

Unfortunately, that did not happen. True, a few brave young faculty members, such as James Truesdale and one or two others, did agree to live in the dormitories and serve as housemasters. But their number was small, and the lump was too large to be thus leavened. Fraternities, barred from building or occupying off-campus houses after 1930, occupied sections of the dormitories; and freshmen, obviously the most untamed element, were housed in their own dormitories, where late-adolescent behavior and wild rumors could thrive without the possibly sobering influence of more mature students.

A dean at Cornell in the 1930s may have overstated—slightly—when he reportedly declared that the American college dormitory for men was, in general, "an abomination before the Lord." He insisted that there was "usually not a single refining influence within its walls" and "not a single redeeming feature about it, except as a place to hang a hat."[74] Duke's undergraduate men, like those elsewhere, would no doubt have quickly retorted that, despite the noise and unruly behavior, dormitory rooms were the venues for the beloved and often interminable "bull sessions." The *Chronicle* in 1931 offered a glimpse into that cherished institution on West campus: "Most bull-sessions have some or all of the following topics for conversation—the current football season . . . , fraternity rushing season, professors, 'crip' courses, the colossal summer, boasting on the old home state and home town, what I think of religion, voicing pros and cons on prohibition, swapping perfectly good jokes, and the other three-fourths of the conversation invariably reverts to the subject of the female race—which the boys know so much about." The columnist added that two Duke psychology majors with stop watches conducted an experiment: they got into bull sessions with twenty-five new men and began with a subject not involving women. The question was how long it would take to get to that subject. The average time turned out to be six minutes.[75]

Regardless of the vaunted camaraderie, there were numerous problems with the men's dormitories. Wannamaker alleged that he found it best to rely largely on student control of the dormitories. But he added: "Of course, our dormitories are inspected every day by good women in charge of the maids who clean the dormitory rooms up." Furthermore, he noted that he had "one man in charge of all the buildings [William E. Whitford], and, through his assistance, another sort of inspection is made."[76]

The students increasingly resented precisely the system that Wannamaker candidly described, for they saw it as an invasion of privacy, a spy network for the dean.

Tension between students and administration mounted on West campus during the 1932–33 school year. With the academic average of the fraternity men well below the average for all men and with freshmen pledges to fraternities showing the sharpest academic decline of all, even many fraternity leaders agreed that some reforms were in order. The administration wanted, and ultimately got, deferred rushing, that is, rushing at the start of the second semester rather than when classes began each fall. The men's Pan-Hellenic Council (later changed to the Inter-fraternity Council) agreed to the deferred rushing, though it posed temporary but real financial problems; but the fraternities fought hard against the administration's additional proposal that only students with a C average (fifteen quality points) on fifteen or more hours of work were to be eligible for rush. The fraternities wanted a less stringent standard, such as eligibility for rush on the basis of nine quality points on at least twelve hours of work. Since that was sufficient for a student to remain in school and for athletic eligibility, the fraternities argued that it would be unfair to hold them to a higher standard. Again, however, the administration got the higher standard that it wanted.

With tension mounting about the fraternity regulations, the quality-point system, and various other student concerns, Justin Miller, the handsome and energetic dean of Duke's reorganized law school, played an interesting role behind the scene.[77] In 1932–33 Miller hit on the idea of an informal student-faculty committee that he hoped could focus on student problems and concerns while also fostering better relations between students and faculty. When Alice Baldwin agreed to meet with this group at Miller's invitation, she was disturbed by the fact that one of the undergraduate men present "quite bitterly" attacked Wannamaker. Subsequently, Baldwin pointed out to Miller that if Wannamaker and his policies were to be the subject of discussion, she thought he should be present. If not, she declared that "she would not be a member of any group acting in such an unfair way." Although Baldwin then withdrew from the group, Miller continued to participate.[78] Just how much help and guidance Miller and his fellow faculty members were able to give to the students involved is not known, but clearly the students had some resourceful allies among at least a segment of the faculty.

"Two Seniors" bade a bitter farewell to Duke in May, 1933, with a letter to the *Chronicle*. The winner of the Wily Gray oratorical contest would no doubt spout off at commencement, they asserted, about "the four happiest years of our lives" and "equally silly twaddle in the same vein." The two seniors insisted, however, that a substantial proportion of their class had experienced a "nightmare in which we see well-built buildings . . . , a reasonably competent faculty, and a dissatisfied and disgruntled student body that is rapidly nearing the explosive point against one of the most narrow-minded administrations that can be imagined in a period characterized by liberalism rather than Victorianism." After listing a few of the "more serious grievances"—such as the refusal of the university-managed store in the Union to let students examine its balance sheet, the ban on Sunday tennis, and restrictions on student government—the seniors called for "relations of the student body to the administration on an equality basis rather than the dictatorial manner now employed."[79]

A swan-song piece by the able and outspoken editor of the *Chronicle*, James L. Stewart, probably raised even more high-powered hackles, for it got closer to the heart of the matter. He began by noting that students really could get assistance from faculty members if the students wanted it. So if "intellectual attainment" was the principal purpose in college, Stewart proposed, then perhaps "the administration of a college in its relation to students is not so important after all." He suggested that at Duke "entirely too much emphasis is placed on the functioning of this administration," which "controls far too many things." Administrators seemed to have "gone out of their way to invent duties for themselves," Stewart charged, "forcing all students to deal with them at every turn." He cited the alleged domination of class meetings by various deans who preached "innocuous sermons" to squirming students, the attendance regulations which forced students to negotiate endlessly with deans, and "the handing down of decisions made by the student council through the dean's office," a "flagrant example of the administration's forcing itself where it does not belong." Stewart's farewell indictment should have served as a cautionary warning to Wannamaker—and even to Few—but there is no evidence that it did.

The fall of 1933 brought an unusual mixture of pleasant and unpleasant developments for the students. The first big-name band, the Chicago-based "Kassels in the Air," led by Art Kassels, had come in the spring of that year to play for a men's Pan-Hellenic set of three dances, and the interest in dancing was as great as ever in the autumn. Student orchestras led by Johnny Long and Les Brown were at the peak of their popularity on campus, and Duke's football team, led by Coach Wallace Wade, seemed headed for the Rose Bowl—until Georgia Tech burst that bubble.

On the down side, however, the depression had belatedly hit the Duke Endowment and, therefore, Duke University. Luckier by far than most colleges and universities were in the early 1930s, Duke still had to make an across-the-board cut in salaries for faculty and staff for 1933–34.[80] Most faculty members recognized the necessity for the move, as well as Duke's comparative luck at a time when many other schools were forced to lay off personnel as well as make more drastic pay cuts. There were, however, some unhappy faculty and staff members, apparently rather few, who were willing at least tacitly to join the students in attacking the administration. While the students focused on Wannamaker as their chief target, Justin Miller and his friend, Ernest Seeman, the disgruntled director of the Duke Press who had been given a year's termination notice, were more eager to discredit and embarrass President Few.

A further tightening of the attendance regulations came in the fall of 1933 when the total number of allowable absences per class, excused and unexcused, was reduced from seven to five. Just as the fraternities were facing stricter academic requirements for their pledges, so too did student owners of automobiles learn during the summer that only students in the three upper classes who made satisfactory academic records during the previous semester would be allowed to register their cars on campus. Attacks on "the administration" and complaints about all of the ever-increasing rules and regulations mounted throughout the fall semester.

As has been mentioned earlier, the explosion came in February, 1934 about a relatively trivial matter, but a lot of pressure had long been building. The men's Pan-Hellenic Council ruled that one of the fraternities had violated rushing regulations and should be penalized by having its rushing period delayed for a month. Wannamaker, however, seized on the technical constitutional point that he had not been present at the council's meeting, declared the ruling void, and called for another meeting. A group of students, incensed by what they saw as the dean's high-handed behavior, gathered in one of the fraternity sections and issued a call for a mass protest meeting in the men's gymnasium the next evening. They also dispatched telegrams to W. R. Perkins and another official of the Duke Endowment declaring that "the conditions on Duke campus . . . are such that you should come at once to see for yourself that student opinion means nothing to the present administration." The students added that they were being "treated like children not men" and that "real universities do not treat student opinion with contempt."[81]

The *Durham Morning Herald* proceeded to muddy the waters at Duke by printing an erroneous headline over the story of the initial protest meeting: "DUKE STUDENTS STAGE RIOT AGAINST UNIVERSITY HEADS." There was no riot, but the story was merely the first in the *Herald* of a series of anonymously written reports on developments at Duke, reports that ingeniously mixed facts and rumors and quoted a variety of unnamed sources. Newspapers across North Carolina picked up the stories, and even *Time* magazine, in its issue of February 19, 1934, carried an account of the "Revolt at Duke" written in the style then typical of the magazine.[82]

By the time the mass meeting in the gymnasium occurred, however, President Few had stepped in. Acting through members of the faculty and the administration, he managed to steer the protest into a more orderly channel by arranging for an open assembly of the undergraduate men, faculty, and administrators in Page Auditorium. The president of the men's student government association presided at the assembly and presented the students' grievances about the administration's treatment of student organizations, the food and prices in the dining hall, the alleged spy system in the dormitories, and other matters. The assembly in Page did not deal with a surprise resolution that had been introduced and overwhelmingly endorsed at the meeting in the gymnasium: that "criticism of the administration by faculty members publicly is not only an indication of lack of loyalty on the part of such men, but is also a demoralizing influence on our student body." While the Trinity students clearly had their own quite real grievances, many of them also seem to have realized that various individuals at Duke had their own agendas, some of them not really of the students' design, in the complicated situation on campus.

A committee of nine students and three prominent faculty members, one of them Wallace Wade, proceeded to investigate the grievances and to recommend whatever remedial steps might be needed. Before the semester ended, the committee made its report, and the majority opinion, which was not shared by some dissenters, seemed to be that it had done a thorough and fair job.[83] Not only were there various changes in the fall that met many of the student demands, but Dean Wannamaker thereafter proceeded more cautiously in his dealings with student affairs. Increasingly, in fact, he allowed one of his assistant deans, Herbert J. Herring, to handle student affairs. As dean of the university and vice president for educational affairs, Wannamaker actually had under his purview both faculty and student matters that would later be divided among a sizeable group of top administrators: one or two vice presidents, a provost, and numerous deans. Although the university was admittedly smaller in Wannamaker's time, he probably had too much responsibility even then. He was reluctant to recognize that fact, but in 1935 he finally agreed to Herring's being named as dean of students in Trinity College. A graduate of Trinity in 1922, Herring taught high school English before returning to Trinity as an assistant dean and instructor in speech in 1924, and he later received a master's degree from Columbia.

At the same time in 1935 that Herring assumed his new post, Alan K. Manchester, an able historian and highly efficient administrator, became dean of freshmen in Trinity. He brought to the post a combination of firmness and fairness that earned him the respect of countless students in Trinity College.

Although probably only a minority of undergraduate men had actively participated in the student protest movement in early 1934, student morale on West apparently improved from that autumn onward, and the atmosphere, at least concerning "the administration," lightened. The *Chronicle*, edited by John L. Moorhead, became a semiweekly, and with Johnny Long and his Duke Collegians and Les Brown and his Blue Devils alternating between campuses to play after-dinner concerts in the two Unions, who could help but enjoy campus life? There was even a new student orchestra, the Duke Ambassadors, that made its debut in the fall of 1934, and early in 1935 a fourth student orchestra, the Grand Dukes, appeared. It played for an open-house dance sponsored by the YMCA that boosted of having 61 couples and 174 stags in attendance.[84]

The jazz era had evolved into the swing era by 1935, and the heyday of the famed big bands had arrived. The *Chronicle* in the mid-1930s never went as far as a later generation of music-loving students would when they gave a whole section of the paper over to stories about and pictures of rock-and-roll musicians; but at least a new column about swing and the big bands, "Rhythmania," began in the autumn of 1935. The "hep" columnist suggested that while Jelly Leftwich and Johnny Long had developed good bands at Duke, Les Brown clearly had the "top-notch group," in which every "lead man" had improved 100 percent. Earlier a *Chronicle* jazz critic noted that Brown and his Blue Devils emulated the "cacophonic or 'hoe' technique used by Benny Goodman's band." That style of playing was also known as "Dixieland," the critic explained, and went back to the early days of jazz when it was played almost entirely extemporaneously. In the 1930s, however, "no matter how disorganized a hot band may sound, the score for each player is incorporated into the orchestration." Joe "Sonny" Burke's Duke Ambassadors, the critic continued, took Hal Kemp's orchestral style as the model and imitated his "characteristic melodic and sweet rhythms, catering more to those who prefer smooth music."[85]

One student declared that despite all the complaints and disagreements that Duke men and women had about a variety of things, they were "all agreeing on one thing—swing music." It was one subject that could be discussed without harsh words. "Everyone is swinging," the aficionado proclaimed. "We're not paying attention to the cornys who give us the blues, we're getting some pep in our systems and swinging out with Goodman, Dorsey, Venuti, Novo, and the rest. When hot gents are allowed to go their own way, the result is pay dirt. Pay dirt yields swing and as long as you're swinging you're bound to be sitting on a cloud."[86]

The swing-loving and dance-loving Duke students had a problem about bringing the more expensive big-name bands to campus. Fire and insurance regulations limited the crowd in Memorial Gymnasium to 750. The university administration insisted that a ceiling of five dollars be maintained for any dance or series of dances, and the president of the men's Pan-Hellenic Council, remembering that the depression continued unabated, considered that a "perfectly fair and wise move."[87] Nevertheless, the resourceful students managed, before the 1930s ended, to bring virtually all of the best-known bands of the day to the campus. The anonymous "Bull Durham," whose column, entitled "Duke's Mixture," was a popular feature for several years, noted in the fall of 1935 that Frank Dailey and his Meadowbrook orchestra sounded fine at a Pan-Hellenic dance, regardless of whether one danced the southerners' beloved "shag" or the "suave eastern locked heads style."[88] Jimmy Lunceford, Tommy Dorsey, Paul Whiteman, and Glenn Miller were among the name bands that played on campus before World War II brought a temporary halt to the elaborate big-dance weekends.

Not all students were enamored of every phase of the dancing mania. Concerning the "Big Apple," a dance fad around 1937, a jaundiced critic described it as a "logical offspring of the square dance, Susie-Q, 'peckin',' blackbottom, Charleston, sugarfoot, shag, truckin', and 'posin'.'" He considered it a "terpsichorean terror" that had succeeded "with diabolical precision" in "incorporating the worst features of them all into a wild orgy of vicarious sex-expression not far removed from savagery." It should be, he asserted, banned from all Duke dances.[89] Another student promptly retorted that while Duke students might treat "such subjects as Chapel reform, rotten politics, Union food and service, and education with complete indifference," they certainly would not allow "a protégé of H. L. Mencken to trod upon our favorite dance with such brutal wrath."[90]

A more philosophical columnist set out to explain why dancing was by far the most enjoyable and popular pastime on campus, and he produced a classic analysis. First, he noted, it brought members of opposite sexes into "socially sanctioned proximity," and the pleasure from that was "primitive, instinctive, and natural." Secondly, dancing "ministers to the ego of one sex, in allowing it to undress with decent indecency, and in letting it be chased rhythmically—with no chance of its being caught, at least not in the Woman's College gym." Thirdly, dancing appealed to the ego of the male by allowing him to "don the garb of the leisure class (we mean tails)" and giving him the chance to "chase the other sex rhythmically—with the added stimulation of a few drops of potent aphrodisiac cunningly placed upon the lobes of the female ear." No doubt about it, he concluded, the dance was interesting—and it could be exciting too, "but, then what are chaperone lines for?"[91]

While dancing clearly occupied a prime spot in the extracurricular life of the 1930s, there were numerous other activities too. In the publications field, the *Chronicle* was obviously the most visible. Varying somewhat from one year to the next, depending on the key personnel involved, it frequently won recognition in judgings sponsored by the Associated College Press: in 1934 it was judged the best weekly college newspaper and in 1937 was one of five semiweeklies to win the All-American honor rating.

An editorial that year noted, however, that the *Chronicle* had great difficulty in obtaining news from administrative and academic offices and that Duke's professors were reluctant to give interviews, no doubt because they understandably feared being misquoted. There was also a perennial complaint about the lack of a department of journalism at Duke.[92]

Feuds between the *Chronicle* and the *Archive*, the literary magazine that had been established in 1887, were endemic. While serious reviews of the *Archive*'s issues appeared in the *Chronicle* from time to time, more typical was the newspaper's report in late 1937 that a survey of 178 students suggested that a recent issue of the *Archive* had been read by less than half of the student body and that four out of seven students favored discontinuing the magazine. The newspaper's outspoken editor, George T. Frampton, declared that it had been "many a year since a note of joy" had appeared anywhere in the *Archive*. "For the last four years, at least," he continued, "it has groaned under its own intellectual weight, bearing sometimes silently, sometimes vocally, but always with intense misery, the incurable mental inferiority of the Duke student body." Frampton conceded that the students' lack of cultural appreciation had contributed to the unpopularity of the literary magazine but thought that "this essence of sour grapes" had also played a role. He suggested that a "little brightness, a little vigor, a little pleasantness" might help.[93]

While the *Chanticleer*, the Duke yearbook, also won awards—in 1941 it could boast that it had received All-American honors in seven out of the preceding eight years—it was less controversial than both the *Archive* and a new humor magazine that was launched in the spring of 1936, the *Duke 'n' Duchess*, which would have a highly checkered career over several decades.

The glee clubs, debating teams, and the Duke Players all had their loyal followings among various segments of the student body, and in the spring of 1941 the students established a lively new musical and dramatic organization. The Hoof and Horn club took its inspiration from similar groups at Princeton and Pennsylvania. Around 1936 Sonny Burke wrote music and lyrics for a show entitled "The Devil Grins," but lack of a script or "book" prevented the show from being produced. In 1941, however, students managed to put all the necessary ingredients together to produce "Say When."[94] Although in later years, Hoof and Horn would abandon the use of student-written material and present popular Broadway musicals, a long-lasting tradition at Duke had begun.

A curious feature about Duke undergraduates in the 1930s, particularly on West campus, was their persistent worry and concern about Duke's alleged lack of traditions. The move to the new Gothic buildings in 1930 plunked the men down on a raw, new campus and separated them from the physical remnants of the old Trinity College on the East campus.

Moreover, the students, like much of the faculty and public for that matter, were struck by Duke's "newness" as a university and failed to understand that when it came to research universities, none in the United States was impressively venerable. Teased and tormented by students at the Ivy League schools or at the nearby institution at Chapel Hill, who proudly boasted that their "university" went back to the 1790s, the Duke students remained in total ignorance about the fact that their archrival had been, in fact, essentially a small, struggling liberal arts college that only began to become a real university a few years before Duke University was organized.

At any rate, Duke's undergraduates self-consciously agonized about their lack of traditions. In 1933 an editorialist noted that one of the most common criticisms of Duke was that it was "almost entirely devoid of traditions." Hollywood in the 1920s and on into the 1930s produced a large number of movies that presented a highly romantic, exaggerated view of college life. Yet Duke freshmen were said to search in vain for the "atmosphere" of "moss-covered walls and the ivied halls" that they had imagined and never to become reconciled to their absence.[95]

The seniors in 1935, clearly in search of a tradition, sponsored the creation of a "senior walk" on a lovely wooded knoll behind the chapel. Efforts to restrict use of the paths to seniors soon failed, however, and the short-lived "tradition" bit the dust. The requirement that male freshmen wear small caps known as "dinks" during the first semester (or at least until a Duke victory in the annual football game with Carolina) did take hold from 1926 onward. A sometimes rowdy sophomore organization, Beta Omega Sigma, or BOS, had as one of its primary purposes the enforcement of rules about the wearing of "dinks" and occasionally even compelled "refractory freshmen" to wear yellow caps rather than the customary blue and white "dink."[96]

Initiation rites for the rising sophomores elected to BOS constituted one tradition that, fortunately, did not forever persist. On a Friday morning in early May, 1933, fifty-three males of the class of 1936 were forced to carry buckets and brooms, wear elaborate facial makeup, and don outfits consisting of gingham dresses, bloomers, straw hats, "alarm clocks and baby nipples that dangled by strings from the neck, and loud socks." The only masculine items allowed were shoes and garters. There was reported to be much guffawing and tittering in all the classes attended by the initiates.[97]

In the more serious search for viable traditions, the Trinity seniors in 1935 tried senior blazers, but that proved to be on the expensive side. Then the class of 1936 opted for white "slouch hats" with their class numerals in blue figures. Finally, the humor—not to say absurdity—of the matter began to emerge, and a *Chronicle* columnist poked fun at the tradition-cravers. "If we must have traditions," he suggested, "let them 'tradish' into us and around us all by themselves . . . let them come naturally with a minimum of huff and puff on our part."[98] Kendrick Few, president of the organization composed of those men who had excelled academically in their freshman year, sounded much like his father, President Few, when he suggested that the significance of tradition should transcend the sentimental and the material. It should, young Few asserted, "embody a passionate zeal for scholastic achievement, a driving desire for excellence in athletics, and a will for cooperative participation in all phases of campus activity."[99]

Just as such seriousness of purpose and idealism were not alien to many students in the 1930s, so was entirely voluntary religious activity a significant component of campus life for a large number of students. The "Y's" were major organizations and quite active on both campuses. A Newman club for the Catholic students at Duke was organized in the fall of 1934, and for the Jewish students an Hillel group in the fall of 1937. The great majority of the students were Protestants, though, and various organizations and practices reflected that fact. For a number of years after 1930, the Sunday school class on West campus taught by Dean Herring was a well-attended and routinely reported event. As accompaniment for the hymns, a violinist and cornet player supported the pianist in the fall of 1930, young W. M. Upchurch sang solos, and during the following spring semester a five-piece orchestra became a feature of the popular classes.

An institution that Duke inherited from Trinity and that remained vigorous throughout the 1930s was Religious Emphasis Week. A campus adaptation of the old Protestant tradition of annual, week-long revival services or "protracted meetings," Religious Emphasis Week usually involved bringing an outstanding preacher to the campus for several days and having him preach nightly sermons in the chapel as well as speak in the Woman's College auditorium during the mornings and meet with various groups for informal discussions and prayer.

Dr. Henry Hitt Crane, whom the *Chronicle* described as the "famous 'actor-preacher'" from Scranton, Pennsylvania, proved to be the students' favorite choice for Religious Emphasis Week throughout much of the 1930s. In 1936 Crane attracted such a large audience, composed predominantly of students, that those who could not be accommodated in the chapel had to listen to loudspeakers installed in nearby Page Auditorium.[100] When Crane returned to Duke in 1939 for his sixth series of services, the *Chronicle* hailed him as "the man who has done more than any one else to make Religious Emphasis Week a Duke tradition." Crane reciprocated the kindness by declaring that of the 118 colleges and universities which he had visited, Duke was his favorite, and he planned to send his son there. He praised the religious attitude of the campus, saying that it was "the healthiest and most natural" that he had seen; and he thought that the unrestrained way in which individuals could voice their opinions on any question approached a true realization of the religious ideal.[101]

Those students who cared about religion were obviously so impressed by Crane that they regretted all the more what they regarded as a missed opportunity in the chapel. President Few, as mentioned in the previous chapter, took great satisfaction from his perception of the students' appreciation of and involvement in the chapel services on Sunday mornings. By the late 1930s, however, certain concerned students went public with their dissatisfaction about the preaching in the chapel.

The YMCA, headed by Frederick N. Cleaveland, spearheaded a campaign to invigorate religious life at Duke and particularly in the Chapel. Cleveland and the men's "Y" also received assistance and guidance from Merrimon Cunninggim, whom Few had named as director of religious activity among the undergraduate men in 1936. Joining forces with the YWCA, Cleaveland's group polled 1200 undergraduates concerning certain religious matters and got 800 responses. The study revealed that the majority of students did not attend chapel services. Of those who did attend, 78 percent of the men and 83 percent of the women said they most enjoyed the music. Only 37 percent of those who attended said they found the services helpful to them. Then on seven consecutive Sundays, "Y" checkers found that the highest number of students attending the Chapel was 807, including a choir of 140; and the lowest number was 297, also including the choir.[102]

The concerned students believed that the most essential need was the appointment of a full-time university pastor or dean of the chapel. The editor of the *Chronicle*, George Frampton, joined in the campaign. "There are not three more desperate needs of the university than those which the chapel *could* satisfy," he declared: "a need for a center of invisible spirit and activity, now lacking; a need for at least one, great purposeful tradition here; and a need for a guide to the formulation of helpful philosophies of life, giving correlation to a now uncorrelated curriculum and order to the now disordered experiences of Duke's social, fraternal, and extracurricular life." Students did not go to the chapel, Frampton continued, because they "are not being supplied what they demand in the way of college religion in their own college chapel." He believed that the overflow audiences that Crane attracted proved that he fed their hunger for "vital, living religion," and that the "Y" organizations had to do what they could to change the chapel program so that "the supply will be adjusted to the demand."[103]

Few named Frank Hickman, already one of the preachers to the university, as the first dean of the Chapel in 1938, but that failed to mollify the students. A *Chronicle* editorial subsequently called for a break from "intellectual theorizing" in the chapel sermons and a switch to "the kind of preaching that made the religion of our ancestors so powerful." [104]

While the students failed to transform the sermons preached in the chapel, they did achieve a significant success in pushing for the organization of a nondenominational church connected with the chapel. This, they hoped, would "make the students feel that they have a real church home rather than just a Chapel for religious services." The Student Religious Council asked for and got a "union communion service," the first such service in the Chapel. [105] That the idea of the nondenominational church was a good one is suggested by the fact that early in 1941 a total of 500 new members joined the group. [106]

Fred Cleaveland, who played such a key role in campus religious life in the late 1930s, may be taken as a good example of an important aspect of college life in that era: the BMOC. The cult of the Big Men On Campus— and the Big Women On Campus, too—would continue for a while after World War II but, like much else in the educational world, would vanish in the late 1960s. In Cleaveland's case, a satirical columnist in the *Chronicle* described him as having a face "like the rising sun, radiant with good humor, good deeds and good living." Responsibility, the columnist added, hung around Cleaveland's neck "like a tight necktie, knotted but neat." [107]

The pinnacle of success to which all BMOC's on West aspired was the highly secret organization known as the Red Friars. On the Woman's College campus the comparable organization was White Duchy. Established in Old Trinity in 1913, the Red Friars inspired and helped the women students to launch White Duchy in 1925. With a limit of seven seniors in each organization, competition for the coveted honor was no doubt intense, even if carefully kept undercover and discreet. The mystique of the two organizations was heightened by the impressive tapping ceremonies: in 1936, for example, the *Chronicle* solemnly announced that there would be a special undergraduate assembly in Page Auditorium at which the graduating Red Friars, garbed in special robes, would tap the seven rising seniors who were "regarded as being representative of the best ideals of Duke University as well as endowed with the greatest capacities for leadership." To become a Red Friar, the *Chronicle* declared, was to attain "the highest honor" which Duke offered, and "Tapping Day" was "one of the most important days of the year on this campus." Few, Flowers, Wannamaker, Herring and others among the administration and faculty were among the honorary members of the Red Friars; and Baldwin, Mary Grace Wilson, Ellen Huckabee and others were members of White Duchy. This resulted in the most prominent students on both campuses having a special sort of contact with the university's leaders, and that, in turn, meant that the organizations sometimes served as important channels of communication. Alice Baldwin once explained that she found White Duchy to be a helpful organization and that its members worked quietly through the larger student organizations to which they belonged and could often help create favorable opinion for some desirable reform or change.[108] The same thing was true of Red Friars, and, despite the invidious nature of such highly selective and secret organizations, it was no accident that some of the members were among the students who clearly grew to understand and sympathize with certain of the larger purposes of Duke University.

Trinity College had been proud to gain its chapter of Phi Beta Kappa in 1920, and students continued to prize membership in it as well as in several of the lesser societies based primarily on academic achievement. But the leadership honoraries also got a lot of attention on campus. A *Chronicle* editorial in 1936 explained why students respected both the honorary organizations and the students who gained membership in them: the aim of the modern college student, the newspaper declared, was "to develop himself into a well-rounded, vibrant personality, and the success of a student's striving in this direction is to a tangible extent measured by his membership in college organizations whose purpose it is to recognize such merit."[109]

Amidst all the various activities that occupied the students' time in the 1930s, many students still had to cope with the harsh economic realities of the never-ending economic depression. One reason that the members of the student orchestras played so vigorously in the after-dinner concerts on both campuses was that they earned their meals in that way. In early 1935, there were 341 Duke students who received an average of $15 per month from their part-time jobs under the Federal Emergency Relief Administration. Later that same year 370 students were paid thirty-five cents an hour for part-time jobs under the auspices of the National Youth Administration, with the schools of forestry and law employing the largest number of students.

In the spring of 1938, when the already ailing economy took an even sharper nosedive, of 152 senior men in a class assembly who hoped for a job, slightly more than 40 percent had no prospect of one at all. Of the remaining 60 percent, only 10 percent had any real assurance of a position. Perhaps it was that type of situation which helped inspire the administration to open an appointments or job placement office. Initially, the work was largely on an ad hoc basis, with Charlotte Corbin, who was Henry Dwire's secretary, handling the administrative aspect, while Dwire himself tended to business or commercial placement and A. M. Proctor, a professor of education, handled teacher placement. In 1938 a full-time person assumed responsibility for the appointment office, of which W. M. Upchurch became director late in 1940. When he left Duke during World War II, he turned the office over to Fannie Y. Mitchell, and she soon became and long remained an invaluable, widely admired link between Duke students and the corporate world.

Simply scraping up enough money to get through college, however, was the first concern of many students in the 1930s. The dining halls on both campuses employed many student workers, for there were no cafeteria-style lines; rather, waiters and waitresses served the students. On East, where there were well-observed rules about appropriate dress in the dining halls, the women students maintained at least a certain amount of decorum, and monthly dinners by candlelight were the occasions for inviting faculty members or other guests. On West, the dining situation was more problematical. Much noise, horseplay, occasional tossing of rolls, and such seem to have been the rule. When the West campus dining halls experimented by serving a turkey dinner by candlelight just before the Christmas vacation in 1935, the *Chronicle* commented that the "changed atmosphere" was a great improvement and suggested that a "monthly 'Peaceful Dinner Night' would be a step in the right direction."[110]

When someone wrote in the *Chronicle* about the alleged "slovenliness" of the student waiters in the men's dining halls, one of them retorted tellingly: "Lugging heavy trays back and forth from a kitchen whose heat would wilt a Foreign Legionnaire, . . . trying to keep abreast of the querulous pleas for 'seconds,' realizing that a broken dish will cost the breaker more money than the whole meal is worth . . . all this is not especially conducive to constant thinking about sartorial perfection." The aggrieved student-waiter added that he was paid twenty-eight cents an hour and that such a wage for some students meant the difference between remaining in college or going home. "In the face of all this," he concluded, "a tie [!] gone awry or a few soup spots on a jacket seem mighty trifling." He just did not intend to lose sleep thinking about it.[111]

Poor though a significant number of students may have been, much of the most popular entertainment on campus was either free or relatively inexpensive. In the 1930s a regular feature in many movie houses was participatory singing; a bouncing ball over lyrics flashed on the screen helped audiences to get into the act and sing all sorts of old and new favorites. After group singing proved to be a popular activity in Duke's booming summer school, Mary Grace Wilson and others in the Woman's College came up with the idea of a community sing on the East campus. With a real Carolina moon above and a musical "Carolina Moon" below, the *Chronicle* reported in the early autumn of 1936, several hundred people enjoyed Duke's first community sing on a Sunday evening on the lawn in front of the East Duke building. With words of the songs projected on a screen that was placed on the veranda of the building, the crowd seemed to favor, aside from Duke songs, "I'm an Old Cowhand," "Did I Remember," "Auld Lang Syne," and "Drifting and Dreaming." A couple of hymns were also included.[112]

Moving into the Woman's College (later Baldwin) Auditorium when cooler weather came, the Sunday evening sings immediately became, and for a number of years remained, quite popular with a wide range of students. They provided music "of the students, by the students, and for the students," the *Chronicle* explained, and included a great variety of small-group and solo numbers along with the audience-singing. It "has proved itself the most popular informal gathering the Duke campus has ever known," the newspaper declared.[113] Even as war clouds gathered over the nation in 1941, the *Chronicle* reported that more than 1500 people poured into the auditorium for a sing. In the previous year over 500 people, mostly students, had been on stage to take part, and the crowds had "never been noted for their conservatism or politeness." Good acts were received enthusiastically, but the weaker ones met loud boos and hisses.[114]

Movies shown on campus by Quadrangle Pictures remained a popular bargain. A reporter analyzed box-office receipts in 1933 and found that John and Lionel Barrymore were among the most popular stars with Duke cinema-goers. Mickey Mouse and Betty Boop led the field among the animated cartoons. "Duke students demand of their shows well written stories, good direction, and capable acting," the reporter explained. Merely sexy pictures would not draw crowds "if their only quality is that they're 'hot.'" No certain type of picture was a sure success at Quadrangle, but "those possessing clever drawing-room conversation appear to be the best received." Greta Garbo's dance in *Mata Hari*, the reporter noted, had been "the most talked of single shot" to show at Duke during the preceding year and a half, but Garbo did not enjoy a following on campus comparable to her national reputation.[115]

Perhaps because the Duke students, like other American moviegoers, saw so many films in the 1930s that featured elegant nightclub settings, they helped Durham get its own supper club. The "Palais d'Or," located on the second floor of the Masonic building at Main and Roxboro streets opened late in 1934. With music by Doug Motley and the Duke Ambassadors and broadcasting at regular intervals on the local radio station, WDNC, the club had a cover charge of $1.50 and boasted that it was "especially planned for the enjoyment of the Duke crowd by Duke student management." An important feature also was that Duke's women students, normally barred from going to "roadhouses" and popular "juke joints," were allowed to attend. The club lasted for several years, and in late 1937 featured the orchestra of Frank Gerard and his D-Men plus a floor show put on largely by Duke students.[116]

Ranking right alongside swing music and dancing among the students' top extracurricular priorities in the 1930s was Duke athletics, and particularly football, for it was the era of the legendary Coach Wallace Wade. Duke's competitiveness in football rose markedly under the leadership of Coach James DeHart after 1925. The new football stadium, the first structure to be actually used on West campus, opened with a game against the University of Pittsburgh in the fall of 1929. During the halftime of that game, the Duke band marched down the field "resplendent in shining new uniforms," and suddenly out of the band's ranks "flashed something blue, and amid the ovations of frenzied rooters, Duke University's own Blue Devil" appeared for the first time as the team's mascot.[117]

Despite Duke's loss to Pittsburgh, President Few and others were pleased that visiting sportswriters praised the new stadium, which was set amidst a pine and hardwood forest in a natural depression, as one of the finest in the nation, with excellent sight lines from all parts of the horseshoe-shaped structure. A journalist from Atlanta thought that the planners and builders of the new campus had "captured the spirit of the university and designed it into the loveliest campus in America." Hailing DeHart as a man of character as well as a fine coach, the same writer reported that DeHart was not counting greatly on a sudden flash in his football team but was building it slowly, and largely from local talent. "I've thirty-eight boys in uniform," DeHart had said, "and thirty-two of them are North Carolina boys."[118]

One of those "North Carolina boys" who played for DeHart was a person who would later return to Duke as a widely admired football coach, William D. Murray. In the fall of 1928 the *Chronicle* hailed handsome young Bill Murray as a "plunging sophomore full back" who had written his name in Duke's hall of fame by leading the Blue Devils to a 38-to-0 win over Wake Forest.[119] Although Duke then went on to beat North Carolina State for the first time, the jinx held and the University of North Carolina again triumphed over Duke, 14 to 7. In Murray's senior year, when he served also as president of the men's student government, Carolina again bested Duke, but a UNC alumnus and faculty member paid tribute to the spirit and good sportsmanship of the Duke students: "To have your hopes of victory shattered and still be able to carry your team from the field, to put on your splendid band serenade for the visitors, and to comport yourselves as if you, and not we, had gained the larger score—these things stamp you as foes worthy [of] any man's steel." In the natural course of events, the Carolina alumnus continued, the time would come when Duke would win the game, but "you have already won something much more important, and that is the unstinted admiration of your so-called foes."[120]

President Few and others no doubt appreciated the tribute to the Duke students' good sportsmanship, but Few, not to mention students and alumni, wanted that "natural course of events" to hurry along. Even after the defeat by Pittsburgh in 1929, Few had declared confidentially that "our football situation needs further development" and that it would come along soon.[121] Few, in other words, was beginning a quiet search that would lead to Wallace Wade.

Since the role of intercollegiate football in an academic context was much discussed even in the 1920s and 1930s, as would be the case later in the century with both football and basketball, Few's ideas on the subject are worthy of examination. In one of his last presidential reports, he devoted considerable attention to the matter and began by suggesting that he occupied "a somewhat unique relation to the question of inter-collegiate football." By that he meant that he had known Trinity College intimately during the years between 1895 and 1920 when football was banned. Throughout that period, Few noted, "there was a strong and constantly growing dissatisfaction on the part of students and younger alumni" and "very great" unhappiness about the ban toward the end of the period. Looking back, Few believed that Trinity's progress had been, on the whole, "hindered rather than helped by the long continued prohibition against football." He believed that he and his associates had had to spend too much time defending their position and "perhaps in explaining how we were better than other people."

"The morale is better now [1939] than it was then," Few argued, and instead of a sense of repression and resentment there was "a widespread feeling of co-operation with the students and alumni, and with our supporting public." And it was, as everyone knew, "easier to teach and to guide students where there is a spirit of co-operation and a sense of satisfaction."[122]

Few presented other arguments in support of Duke's athletic program. One important one was that the handling of admissions, scholarships, and self-help (in the form of part-time jobs) at Duke was kept in the hands of committees of faculty members and administrators and that these committees dealt with all students, including athletes. Furthermore, "all funds used for these purposes are administered by the college itself," so that it was "in control" and could change procedures whenever it felt they needed changing. "I am aware that differences of opinion may be possible," Few conceded, "but my own opinion is that athletics at Duke are on a sound and wholesome basis and not injurious to the University, that they contribute greatly to the physical well-being and pleasure of the students, and that the whole athletic program, both intercollegiate and intramural, is conducted in full cooperation with the University's educational purposes."[123]

Few did not point out, but might well have, that there were strong centrifugal forces operating in a complex research university. That is, not only did departmental lines tend to divide both faculty and students as the arts and sciences component grew larger, but the various professional schools tended to become separate spheres unto themselves. Not every member of the university community cared about intercollegiate athletics, of course. But at least some of the persons connected with each of the various parts of the university did care, often passionately, and the interest in the school's teams served as a common denominator or unifying force unlike anything else. Few would have undoubtedly preferred for religious values and beliefs to have been the great unifier, but he was sufficiently clear-eyed and realistic to understand that such was impossible in a pluralistic university that mirrored the larger society.

One important reason why Few could feel so positively about the athletic situation at Duke was the presence of Wallace Wade and the type of person he was. There were not many connected with the university whom Few rated higher than Wade. When Few and his top associates began to think about "further development" of the football situation at Duke, a development that they wanted more quickly than DeHart seemed to contemplate, Wannamaker played a key role.

Keeping a strong faculty-administrative rein on athletics, as Few explained, was important at Duke, and no less a figure than Wannamaker himself chaired the faculty committee on athletics. In that capacity he represented Duke at meetings of the Southern Conference, of which Duke was a member. There he met and was favorably impressed by Wade, who was then a highly successful coach at the University of Alabama, where he took teams to the Rose Bowl in two successive years. Obviously upon Few's request, Wannamaker wrote Wade confidentially early in 1930 and began by stating that he had "formed a high opinion of you both as man and as leader of youth in sports." Wannamaker explained that Duke had an "earnest desire to build the very best possible physical plant and to provide for the coaching of our teams the best leaders we can secure." Duke was determined "to integrate the sports of youth with the whole program of the university." Since Wade had "a broad and sane and experienced opinion on all that pertains to this part of college education," Wannamaker asked for his confidential advice about the best man Duke might be able to secure as football coach and athletic director. There was to be no publicity about the matter, for Duke did not wish to be deluged with applications and suggestions.[124]

Wade replied promptly and began by noting that he believed Duke had "a future probably second to none in the country." Though he doubted that Wannamaker could, at that date, find the kind of person he wanted who would be able to take charge for the 1930 season, Wade named several possibilities. Then came what Wannamaker had no doubt hoped for:

"If you decide to wait until the season of 1931," Wade declared, "I should be glad to talk with you about the position for myself." He would be in Atlanta in early March for the conference basketball tournament and could easily confer there with Duke representatives.[125]

Within a very short time, Duke landed Wade. His commitments at Alabama would not allow him to leave until early 1931, but he arranged for two of his assistants, Ellis Hagler and Herschel Caldwell, to precede him and begin working at Duke under DeHart in the fall of 1930. Concerning them, Wade requested Wannamaker to "guide them in their work with a personal interest," for they were "inexperienced boys who are anxious to do what is right" and would appreciate any advice or assistance that Wannamaker might give them. Meantime, Wade hoped that everything possible was being done to bring to Duke a "good lot of freshman material."[126]

While Wannamaker was happy to guide Wade's young assistants in their new duties, he also urged Wade to give careful consideration to keeping a young man, Edmund (Eddie) Cameron, who had joined Duke's athletic staff in 1926 as freshman football and basketball coach. Becoming head basketball coach in 1929, Cameron led the team in amassing a record of 226 victories and 99 losses down to 1942, winning three Southern Conference championships along the way. He was popular with the students, Wannamaker noted, his teams had been quite successful, and "his boys have almost without exception expressed great satisfaction with his handling of the men individually and as groups."[127] Fortunately for Duke, Wade agreed with the assessment of young Cameron, and the two coaches began a long, rewarding collaboration after Wade's arrival.

While the matter of the salary Duke offered to get Wade was the subject of much speculation and gossip, it was a carefully guarded secret, as were all salaries at Duke, for that matter. It was $12,500, a handsome figure indeed for that day and considerably more than twice what most full professors in arts and sciences made, but less than the $15,000 paid to the deans of the law and medical schools. Arguing that men of Wade's ilk were rare and in great demand, Few never doubted the wisdom of hiring Wade. In fact, Few quickly ranked Wade among Duke's top accessions. "The more I see of him," Few informed a close associate, "the more I am pleased with his personality and his program involving bodily development and character." Warming to an old theme, Few confessed that he had always placed moral and physical development above the abstract intellectual training of young men. He had believed that if he and his colleagues could make sure of a good character and a disciplined, fortified body for a boy, then the lad would take advantage of his opportunities and go as far in life as native endowment would permit. "His intellectual immaturities, his lack of knowledge, and his vagaries of opinion will be cured as he develops," Few argued, "provided his education has put into him an unquenchable yearning to know what is true and do what is right."[128]

Few's creed was an old-fashioned one that was fast crumbling around him under the uncertainties and moral relativism of the twentieth century. Yet Wallace Wade also shared many of Few's ideas—and proved to be a formidable winner besides. Long before his teams began to rack up the victories, however, Wade endeared himself both to Few and to many students by invigorating and expanding intramural athletics and physical education at Duke.

In Wade's first appearance before a Trinity College assembly, the *Chronicle* reported that he expressed his pleasure in being at Duke, praised the physical plant, and urged the students not to "mistake the side-issues for the real purpose," which was "mental, moral and physical development." He and his associates, he explained, hoped to carry on the athletic program in such a way as to assist in that development and to have the work in physical education integrated with the curriculum. "There can be no over-emphasis of wholesome and healthful sports in college," Wade concluded. "Where the mistaken stress lies is in the value which many people not connected with the game place on winning."[129] In a speech a few months later to college public relations officials, Wade suggested that winning football teams led to neither increased enrollments nor increased endowments. "My observations lead to the conclusion," he argued, "that colleges can best increase their endowments and enrollments by raising their academic standards, improving their equipment, and bringing to the faculty the best type of teachers."[130]

That Wade did more than just say the right words was shown by his immediate attention to Duke's intramural program. Having earlier complained about the old program's inadequacies, the *Chronicle*, only a few months after Wade's arrival, praised his expedition in organizing a basketball tournament for the undergraduate men's classes, fraternities, and dormitories, and for scheduling a comparable track meet. By early 1932 the *Chronicle* reported that of 1,436 regularly enrolled undergraduate men, 1,300 had taken part in at least one sports activity. There were 688 men in required physical education courses, 646 in intramural athletics, and 480 in intercollegiate sports and coaching classes. Basketball was the most popular of the intramural sports as measured by participation, but boxing attracted much attention on campus, with between 400 and 700 spectators on each night of the intramural tournament. Among the physical education courses, tennis was the most popular, but swimming was a close second. Four students were in a corrective gymnastics class.[131]

Wade did not, of course, achieve so much in such a short period by himself. While he was athletic director as well as head football coach, he inherited some first-rate coaches in other sports as well as added some new men to the staff. In terms of seniority, Wilbur "Cap" Card headed the list. An alumnus of Trinity, he had become director of Trinity College's gymnasium in 1902 and subsequently coached basketball, track, and baseball. While his own athletic fame derived from his prowess as a baseball player for Trinity, he later concentrated on gymnastics; when his teams began giving exhibitions at halftime during basketball games in the 1930s, interest in the sport increased on the campus.[132]

John W. (Jack) Coombs began to put Duke on the map of college baseball before Wade arrived. A graduate of Colby College in 1906, he immediately joined the Philadelphia Athletics and became a famous big-league pitcher before turning to college coaching in the 1920s. He came to Duke in 1929 and immediately attracted and kept an intensely loyal following among students, faculty, and alumni. Both students and the public followed college baseball more closely in the early decades of the century than would later be the case, and Coombs succeeded in getting on the West campus what the *Chronicle* called "one of the finest baseball plants in the South."[133] Winning numerous state and conference titles and with a significant number of his players going on to play in the major leagues, Coombs, like Wade, embodied and emphasized values that transcended his particular sport. After he had given a talk as Duke's representative to a school in Philadelphia, the principal wrote Few that Coombs had made a "most significant and forceful address on the theme of devotion to study and the worth of the educational processes." He had held his young audience enthralled by his "cogent and felicitous" remarks.[134]

In swimming, Walter S. (Jack) Persons was another important member of the athletic staff. Becoming the swim coach immediately after graduating from Duke in 1930, Persons, despite not having any scholarships to lure top swimmers, compiled an impressive record: in forty-five years as swim coach, his teams would have twenty-three winning seasons, take the state championship four times, and win the Southern Conference championship in 1934. Persons also served as the lacrosse coach for a long period after 1938.

Duke's track team, under the direction of Carl Voyles, won its share of conference titles in the 1930s, as was true also of the golf and tennis teams. Voyles, whom Wade brought to Duke in 1931, also served as end coach and chief scout for football. Students began playing intramural soccer in the early years of the decade, and in 1934 they organized an independent team, at their own expense, to play in intercollegiate competition. Winning three of the four games played, the soccer enthusiasts got 700 students to petition for soccer to be made an official sport, which was done in the fall of 1935.

Football reigned unchallenged as the premier sport, however, and it did not take Wade long to make Duke one of the nation's top powers in college football. Perhaps the fact that Duke fought Carolina to a scoreless tie in the last game of the 1930 season was an augury of things to come. The game, played in a torrential rain in Chapel Hill, was "more like a major naval engagement than an orthodox football game," the *Chronicle* declared. Not only did DeHart thus end his association with Duke on a happy note, but "Bill Murray closed his college career with a performance that left little doubt concerning the best player on the field." The breaking of what the *Chronicle* called a thirty-six-year-old jinx inspired the Duke band to play "The Old Gray Mare (She Ain't What She Used To Be)"— and then "It Ain't Gonna Rain No More."[135]

Tying Carolina was one thing but beating them was another. That joy for the Duke folk came in December, 1932, and the *Chronicle* soberly announced after the game, "We are much more convinced that we have a good school than we were a week ago."[136] In the 1933 season, as mentioned earlier, Wade's team won such a string of victories that there was much talk about a bid to the Rose Bowl, until Georgia Tech put a stop to all that. In 1935 unbeaten Carolina's team rode high and seemed surely headed for the Rose Bowl. Duke, however, pulled a stunning upset and dashed those dreams with a 25-to-0 victory over their neighboring rival.[137]

Two great football stars of the early and mid-1930s and Duke's first All-Americans were Fred Crawford and Clarence "Ace" Parker. Glenn E. (Ted) Mann, who became director of athletic publicity upon his graduation in 1930 and long remained in the position, described Crawford as "a hell-for-leather, hard-hitting, hard-charging, fast-running juggernaut" who "covered punts like a run-away express" and "charged through the line like a lion going in for the kill."[138] About Parker, Few stated that he was an outstanding undergraduate "not solely because of his athletic prowess and achievement but also because with it all he has been modest and self-effacing." Few believed that "gentleness combined with strength are the two elements which properly blended make a man such as a man ought to be," and Parker, Few asserted, possessed those two qualities.[139]

While Few focused on Parker's character, one of the country's prominent sportswriters pulled all the stops, in true sportswriter style, and avowed that Parker's running was like "a minnow going through the rushes, a fox eluding the hounds, a falcon diving on its prey, . . . an express train whipping through a whistle stop at midnight." Parker, the sportswriter continued, was said to use blockers only because people expected them and he was "willing to humor the crowd."[140]

The *Chronicle* and other commentators predicted much leaner days for Duke after Parker's graduation, but such was not to be the case. Perhaps the apogee of Wade's career at Duke came in the fall of 1938 when his team, the fabled Iron Dukes, went through the entire regular season undefeated, untied, and—almost miraculously—unscored upon.[141] With All-Americans Dan Hill and Eric Tipton as co-captains, the Iron Dukes ended the regular season in a game with a powerful and highly rated team from the University of Pittsburgh. Playing in Durham before a huge crowd of almost 50,000 people who shivered in falling snow, both teams remained scoreless through three quarters. Then in the final quarter of the game, Duke's Willard "Bolo" Perdue blocked a Pittsburgh punt and recovered in the Pitt end zone for a Duke score. When Tony Ruffa successfully kicked for the extra point, Duke led 7-0, which became the final score after the Iron Dukes successfully repulsed the Pittsburgh team's final efforts to score.[142]

An invitation for Duke to play the University of Southern California in the Rose Bowl on January 2, 1939, came soon after the victory over Pittsburgh. "WESTWARD HO!" a huge headline declared in the *Chronicle*, and a normally tough administration softened sufficiently to extend the Christmas holiday slightly and to suspend the double-cut penalty for class absences on the days immediately following the break.[143]

Many academic leaders, including Few, had long expressed doubts about the wisdom and propriety of post-season football games, whether in a bowl or otherwise. Not only did they distract both players and the general student body from their primary academic tasks, but they seemed another manifestation of football mania, of the athletic tail's wagging the academic dog. Yet when Duke, already basking in the celebration of its centennial year as an educational institution, received the invitation to play the University of Southern California in the Rose Bowl, Few and Wannamaker probably did not long hesitate in saying yes. "I wish that we might have avoided the Rose Bowl engagement," Few barefacedly avowed to Frank Graham, "but statewide interest in the game rapidly developed and it was made to appear to us that we could not decline without seeming offense, and even effrontery, to the great majority of the people in the State who take interest in such things."[144]

Despite the fact that USC beat Duke by scoring on a pass thrown in the last minute of the game, the large crowd of students and townfolk who met the train bringing the Iron Dukes back to Durham hailed them as heroes. The *Chronicle* reported that an estimated 10,000 people assembled around the railway station and along Main Street. When the players, wearing large western-style sombreros, stepped from their Pullman cars, they were escorted to a fleet of large limousines that the city had obtained and then chauffeured down Main and to the campus behind two motorcycle patrolmen. Some Durham residents declared that it was the biggest turnout the city had witnessed since the armistice ending World War I was signed in 1918. "It was a great display for a great team," the *Chronicle* concluded," and, anyway, we're still untied."[145]

While the crowd that greeted the returning Iron Dukes may have been especially large, such celebratory blending of town and gown was not unusual in that era. The annual homecoming games, when alumni and friends of the institution made a special effort to return to the campus, featured parades and campus displays that grew more lavish each year. In 1936, for example, the fraternities tried to outdo the widely noticed displays of the previous year when the fronts of the residential buildings had been decorated with everything from a wrecked airplane and a dilapidated Ford Model T car to giant cartoons featuring Mae West and President Roosevelt. Before the game on Saturday afternoon a parade featuring eight or so marching bands from the area proceeded from the intersection of Main and Roxboro streets downtown to the East campus. A motorcycle escort of state troopers headed the parade, and the grand marshal led an escort of forty horseback riders followed by fifty or so elaborately decorated floats. Duke Homecoming clearly brought a spectacle to Durham as much as to the campus.[146]

With "Gorgeous" George McAfee, who was out with an injury for part of the 1938 season, playing at his collegiate best in 1939, the Duke team established another impressive record. Perhaps the 13–3 win over a highly ranked UNC team (their only loss of the season) was the sweetest for the Blue Devils, but a one-point loss to Pittsburgh marred their otherwise sterling record.

Again in 1941, Wade's team, with Bob Barnett as captain, went undefeated in the regular season. The second highest-scoring team in the nation with 327 points, the Blue Devils received their second invitation to play in the Rose Bowl, this time against Oregon State University. The Japanese attack on Pearl Harbor, however, led to the banning of large public gatherings on the West Coast. Consequently, Duke invited the responsible officials in California to hold the game in Durham, the only time the Rose Bowl would ever be played outside of Pasadena. With temporary seating installed to increase the stadium's capacity from 35,000 to 56,000, the vast crowd sat in a cold, drizzling rain to watch Oregon State defeat Duke by a score of 20–16.

With Wallace Wade soon volunteering for military service and taking a leave of absence from Duke, Eddie Cameron became head football coach and managed to continue the winning tradition of his predecessor. But that was in the quite different circumstances of a university deeply involved in an all-out national war effort.

Campus reaction to world events in the 1930s largely reflected that of American society in general. That is, Duke students displayed no great interest in world affairs; they retreated into isolationist and semipacifistic positions as aggressive nations began to prey upon their weaker neighbors in both Europe and the Far East; and then they debated and disagreed about how the United States should respond to foreign dangers and alarms in the late 1930s.

In a talk to a Woman's College assembly in the spring of 1934, a member of the history department warned that both the Far East and Europe were moving toward war. "We can all look forward to bigger and better wars," he prophesied.[147] It was a rarely seen notion in the *Chronicle* and probably went largely unnoticed. In late 1936, as the Spanish civil war raged, a student columnist who frequently wrote about international affairs thought that the involvement of Fascist Italy and Nazi Germany on one side of that war and of Communist Russia on the other meant that "another international war" might be approaching. But a professor of German returned from Europe about a year later and reported that Germany seemed "headed toward economic stability and prosperity" with the people still regarding Hitler as a "great leader." Contrary to popular opinion in the United States, the professor noted, "Germans neither expect nor desire war" and, while fearful of possible Russian activities, were on friendly terms with the other European nations.[148]

In the early 1930s not many students showed interest in occasional antiwar or peace rallies. In 1932, for example, a woman student complained that only about fifteen women had shown up for an Armistice Day peace meeting on West campus and about a dozen of those were reportedly students actively engaged in some form of religious work.[149] In April, 1935, the Young Students' League, a self-styled pacifist organization headquartered in New York, called for a nationwide student "walkout" and "mass demonstrations against rising war clouds." The league's field representative expressed surprise that no Duke students planned to participate in the "walkout." Leaders of the local YMCA argued, however, that "little of lasting value can be accomplished by such ostentatious ballyhoo." A *Chronicle* editorial added that "there are few Duke men who would willingly go to war unless the United States were invaded, but there are fewer still who care to cheer a speaker who exclaims, 'War must be abolished.'"[150]

When a group of students at Princeton hit on the idea of launching a satirical, antiwar organization known as the Veterans of Future Wars, that found some support at Duke. A group of students in the School of Religion organized as the "Chaplains of the Veterans of Future Wars" and pledged to preach to the lay members so that they could realize that they were "engaged in doing 'God's work' while murdering the enemy." Soon after the divinity students spoke up, an estimated 125 Trinity students met in the Union Ballroom to organize a post of the VFW. Declaring that they wanted their bonus immediately, the professedly antiwar students argued that a bonus would do them no good after they had been shot.[151]

While the Veterans of Future Wars was an organization that was at least partly whimsical and prankish, the American Student Union was a serious, leftist organization that called for, among other things, the end of military training on college campuses, disarmament, and academic freedom. The *Chronicle*, while upholding free speech for "left-wingers," insisted that most Duke students would not be swayed by propaganda spread by allegedly Marxist sympathizers.[152]

When an antiwar coordinating committee representing a dozen or so different student organizations sponsored a conference in the spring of 1937, the featured speaker was Gerald P. Nye, a United States senator and "noted peace leader." He would soon become well known across the nation as one of the most extreme isolationists. Countering arguments presented by Nye and others like him, Joseph J. Spengler, a distinguished Duke economist, bluntly told a *Chronicle* reporter that "under the Nazi regime the German people will be compelled to spend half their time training for war and the other half actually engaging in war." Meanwhile, the outspoken economist continued, the Nazis would "destroy every civilized value for which men have fought—religious liberty, freedom of speech, economic liberty, and all the others." Believing that the dictators would force the world into a war, he opposed making concessions to them and thought Europe's hope for a more lasting peace lay in the distant future— perhaps fifty years—when freedom of trade would be a principal factor in making it possible.[153]

Spengler, like others who shared his prescient view of events as Germany made ready to move against Czechoslovakia, was way ahead of majority opinion on campus as well as in the nation. A student columnist, conceding that most Americans sympathized with the hapless people of Czechoslovakia, attributed that not to facts or events but to propaganda. "May it be that what is now sympathy for the oppressed will never change to hostility for the oppressor," he concluded, "and may it be that we can keep our saddle shoes and porkpies [slouch hats] and remain in college for a lifetime of peace."[154] With the Iron Dukes about to roll to glory and famous national orchestras as well as good local ones making dancing so pleasurable, one can perhaps understand the student columnists' world view even while recognizing its limitation.

When the European nations actually went to war in the fall of 1939, the *Chronicle*, like almost every other newspaper in the nation, declared that the United States could best serve its own and the world's interests by staying out of the war. Reflecting an interpretation of how the United States got into World War I, an interpretation that was then standard among academics and intellectuals, the *Chronicle*'s editors and columnists warned of "mechanized German propaganda" and "humanized British propaganda" that would soon inundate America. In the case of World War I, a *Chronicle* editorial declared, the United States had made two great mistakes: she let herself "become the prey of a propaganda of ideal-ism," and in a "rush to profit by supplying Europe with the commodities of war, she ran up the most gigantic total of bad debts in the history of the world." As the United States Congress began the angry debate about President Roosevelt's call for a modification of the nation's isolationist neutrality laws, the Duke students mostly wanted to make sure that the nation would not repeat the alleged mistakes of 1917.[155]

Dean Wannamaker, when asked about the European war's impact upon the students' selection of courses and fields of concentration, replied, "The present hostilities in Europe have not had, and I hardly expect them to have, any noticeable effect upon the intellectual interests of the student body here." He thought the situation in early 1940 was quite different from the World War I era, for the students were "much more realistic than they used to be, and they harbor a distinct disillusionment about the possibilities of bringing about a better world by engaging in another Homeric trek."[156]

As Britain stood virtually alone against Hitler's Fortress Europa in the fall of 1940, sharply differing views appeared on campus as in the deeply divided nation. Thoroughly Anglophilic, like so many Americans and especially white southerners, President Few addressed an assembly of the Woman's College and declared: "Our inheritance of English civilization, of English institutions, of English ideals, and of participation in English life should have supreme significance for us." The *Chronicle*, however, opposed a proposal to send planes to Britain because it would allegedly violate the United States' neutrality and be a long stride toward war.[157]

When Few spoke to an assembly of Trinity upperclassmen in early October, 1940, neither he nor his audience had any notion that he would die less than two weeks later. A *Chronicle* reporter, however, captured a certain drama and even poignancy about the occasion. "Speaking in a slow, moving voice," Few held his young audience "in rapt attention," the reporter noted. As the president rose to speak, he comforted latecomers who were straggling in by saying, "Go ahead and find your places, boys. That's what I'm going to talk to you about, anyhow." Few then proceeded to suggest that the United States was "being pushed into a war" for which the nation was not prepared. Not only was the country unprepared mili-tarily, but Few also thought that Americans in 1940 lacked "the old spirit of adventure and daring, and devotion to high ideals and willingness to sacrifice in behalf of causes which we have deeply at heart."

Few urged the students to use the opportunities offered by the new academic year up to their fullest possibilities. Then with his eyes moving slowly over the audience, he concluded: "This generation is to be tested as by fire. I earnestly hope that everyone of you tested by fire may prove to be of true gold." As Few returned to his seat, Wannamaker dismissed the group, and 1200 undergraduate men "filed out of the auditorium—in silence."[158]

Not long after Few's speech, a poll of a cross-section of Duke's male students conducted by the Polity Club found that 66 percent were opposed to bearing arms in a foreign war; that was down from the 76 percent of three years earlier. While the freshmen voted 60 percent in favor of fighting abroad if necessary to defend democracy, upperclassmen and especially graduate students were strongly opposed. While 80 percent were against any appeasement of Germany and Italy and 55 percent opposed direct financial aid to Britain, 75 percent claimed to favor all aid to Britain short of entering the war. As a subsequent *Chronicle* editorial suggested, Duke students (like most Americans at the time) were apparently confused or not thinking very carefully or deeply.[159]

As Congress and the nation debated the lend-lease program called for by President Roosevelt, various professors supplied the *Chronicle* with essays supporting the measure and pointing out the dangers of a Europe totally controlled by the Axis powers. An editorial, however, lucidly highlighted one of the basic reasons for the confusion among the students and their generation. Entitled "What Are We to Believe?" it noted that after World War I the scholars and teachers had emphasized "how unreasonable and unprofitable was this business of killing our fellow men." Books and lectures overflowed with "gore and disillusionment, decrying the manipulations of propagandists and the needless slaughter of war." Then, in a total reversal, "before our very eyes," the same sages had changed tunes and "tell us that war has become glorious and necessary and manly again." In view of such inconsistency, the *Chronicle* editorialist concluded that students had best reserve the right to do their own thinking and draw their own conclusions.[160]

With the military draft in operation and national preparedness a top priority by the fall of 1940, campus life reflected some of the tension and heightening anxiety of the outside or "real" world. The dances on campus became increasingly informal, such as the YMCA's "Get Acquainted Saddle Shoe Stomp" following one of the first home football games. A "Cotton Pickers' Ball" proved to be such a popular theme for a large, informal dance that it was repeated and later followed by a "Flue-Cured Frolic." Activities in support of British War Relief and other such war-related agencies flourished on both campuses, and as soldiers from nearby United States Army camps poured into Durham on weekends, many of them began to visit the gardens and the chapel. The YMCA and other organizations cooperated to extend hospitality to the visiting soldiers by giving them guided tours of the campus and taking them to dinner in the Union.

Only a few days after the campus went wild upon receiving the news that Duke had been invited to play again in the Rose Bowl, much more sobering news came from Pearl Harbor. The *Chronicle* reported that students seemed stunned by the radio bulletins that Sunday afternoon of December 7, 1941, and that (incorrect) rumors about the cancellation of all draft deferments buzzed around the campus. Dean Herring addressed a special assembly in the chapel, and a black-bordered editorial entitled "It's Our Turn" struck a solemn note: "If we are going to live the present more intensely because the future is uncertain, let that intensity be directed toward genuine things. Frustrated indifference and sensual escapism make a poor philosophy with which to face a bayonet. We can do nothing better than to utilize our remaining days in this ivory tower in finding a faith to live by."[161]

Actually, the entry of the United States into World War II made a larger psychological difference, at least at first, than anything else. Campus life and routines went on largely as before for the rest of the academic year. Total enrollment in June, 1940, was 3,685, which represented a 75 percent increase over the 2,106 students ten years earlier. Nearly three quarters of the 1940 student body was made up of undergraduates, with men outnumbering women about two to one. By early 1942 the impact of the draft began to show, and there was a drop of 167 in the enrollment of Trinity and the College of Engineering. But overall, and to the surprise of many, total enrollment held up rather well. Differences would become more noticeable after September, 1942, and especially in mid-1943, when the West campus became, in one sense, virtually a branch of the United States Navy.

The decade of the 1930s had been a colorful and crowded one at Duke. Hit with a rigorous quality-point and attendance system at the beginning of the era, the students had been forced to step up their academic performance even as they, or at least the men, adjusted to an entirely new campus. Friction with administrators whom the Trinity students perceived as high-handed exploded in the student protest movement of early 1934. Gaining certain limited changes, the undergraduate men seemed to enjoy a better morale and atmosphere from the mid-1930s on—and Wallace Wade's football teams and their shining records certainly did not lessen the pleasure of being at Duke.

There was always considerable rowdiness and foolishness in the men's dormitories, of course, and occasionally off campus too. Patriotic Durham citizens were reported to be aghast on an early spring day in 1935 when a Duke freshman stood on the steps of the post office "exhorting workers to unite against the exploitation of the corrupt capitalists." Another freshman was handing out bathroom tissue to patrons of a downtown theater, while a third "barely escaped arrest while parading through the business district without his trousers." All, it turned out, were fraternity initiates.[162]

Upon the relatively rare occasion of a heavy snowfall, monstrous snow-ball fights which shattered many window panes were de rigueur on West, and even without snow all hell could break loose for mysterious reasons on occasion. In May, 1934, as final examinations approached, someone in a freshman dormitory tossed a milk bottle from a window. Others, several hundred others, soon followed, and then a bonfire of milk crates lit up the quadrangle as cheers and Duke songs filled the air. In October, 1937, for reasons that remained hidden, students in Crowell Quadrangle began to yell out of their windows, "Thirty-two!" It threatened to surpass the old standby of the freshman quadrangle, "Who won the war?" The din of the "thirty-two" cries went on, with other numbers occasionally thrown in, until someone yelled "Bingo," and the "Crowell Crowers got to sleep."[163]

In some years, the *Chronicle* showed great imagination and revealed the high good humor of undergraduates. A columnist hit on the idea, for example, of asking a group of students this intriguing question: if you entered your room and found a member of the opposite sex under your bed, what would you do? A woman student replied, with the true ring of East campus propriety: "In a situation like that, the best thing to do is to consult the WSGA handbook. If the handbook had no rules to cover the situation, whatever I should do would be purely on the spur of the moment." A male freshman, quite uninhibited by handbooks, declared: "First, I'd take a Bromo. Then I'd run down to the rooming office and find out if she went with the room. If so, I'm glad I came to Duke."[164]

A lot of students clearly had great fun, even as they struggled for quality points. Some no doubt encountered disappointments of varying types, and clearly many more flunked out, especially in Trinity College, than would be the case later in the century. Most students probably did not then pause to think about what the years at Duke really meant, but one student did, and in a striking fashion. He wrote that he was ambling down the campus, gazing at the Gothic buildings, when out of nowhere a thought startled him:

> These buildings and all that they represented in themselves and be-yond themselves—the whacking paddles of a fraternity initiation and the learning and decorum of the classroom; the roar and color of the stadium and the painstaking accuracy of the lab; the clamorous bull-session with its cloud of tobacco smoke and the awe-inspiring hush of the Sunday chapel service; the cheerful clatter of knives and forks in the Union dining halls and the quiet of the library study rooms—these many things and more these buildings meant for me.

But all that, the student continued, was disconcerting, for what did it all mean and how could so many disparate things have any connection or unity? Then an idea hit him: "These buildings, all the manifold ideas they incorporated and represented, all the activities for which they furnished the background, all of this suddenly crystallized itself into one quality—*home*. This school, this university, this home had somehow or other got itself so tangled in my heart strings, had become so much a part of me that I knew I should never cease to belong to it, and I caught myself fervently hoping that it would never forget me."[165]

If home truly is where the heart is, then Duke, at least for some, clearly became a kind of home in the 1930s.

8

The Woman's College, 1925–1947:

Could Separate Be Truly Equal?

⌁

AMONG THE MULTITUDE OF problems involved in building this particular research university around Trinity College, President
William P. Few thought initially that the single most difficult
and baffling one of all would be the development of the coordinate
Woman's College.[1] Just why Few felt so apprehensive about that particular task is unclear, but there were two possible factors, one personal and
one inherent in the coordinate-college idea. On the personal side, Few as
a student himself had known first Wofford College, then an all-male liberal arts college in South Carolina, and in the 1890s Harvard University,
when its "Society for the Collegiate Instruction of Women" or, as it was
popularly known, "The Annex," was just in the process of becoming a
separate but coordinate institution, Radcliffe College.[2] Moreover, Few was
forty-three years old when he married in 1911 and subsequently became
the father of a family that consisted of five sons. As a teacher and administrator who dealt primarily with young men in Trinity College from
1896 onward, Few therefore had somewhat limited experience as far as
the education of young women was concerned.

As for the coordinate college idea, it was perhaps clearer for what it was
not than for what it actually was. It was not coeducation, the academic
intermingling on the college level of males and females. When Washington Duke prodded—or inspired—Trinity College by a gift of $100,000
in 1896 on the condition that it offer young women an education on an
"equal footing" with men, the college quickly agreed. Trinity had awarded
degrees, under special circumstances, to the three Giles sisters in 1878,

and after the move to Durham in 1892 some women attended the college as day students. After Washington Duke's gift, a small dormitory for women was built on campus. Yet President John C. Kilgo, taking a position that Few also embraced when he succeeded Kilgo in 1910, insisted that Trinity's ultimate aim was a coordinate college for women; that larger resources were needed before that goal could be achieved; and that Trinity College would continue to be essentially what it had been since the mid-nineteenth century: a college primarily for men.[3]

Wedded to the abstract idea of the coordinate college though Kilgo and then Few might be, there was no clear model of what the thing actually was. By the 1920s there were, in fact, only a bewildering variety of arrangements made by a number of institutions, largely in the Northeast, that wished to avoid coeducation. Some had separate faculties altogether for the women's college, while others shared the faculty but maintained separate classes through the four years. Some had their own endowments and governing bodies and gave their own degrees but were still units within larger universities.[4] If Few felt baffled and worried as he moved after December, 1924, to implement the plan that he had sold to James B. Duke concerning a coordinate college for women, it is certainly not surprising—if one avoids the ever-present temptation of twenty-twenty hindsight.

A happy, remarkably successful solution to the problem eventually emerged at Duke partly because Few had the good judgment and luck to pick a dean who played a major, formative role in building the Woman's College and shaping its position within Duke University. Moreover, Dean Alice M. Baldwin proved that she could work harmoniously, creatively, and always with integrity in what was then very largely a man's educational world. The true drama in the relationship of Baldwin and Few, however, lay not so much in the personal realm as in the intellectual. And it was in that subtle intellectual arena that the most important decisions about the Woman's College were made.

Both Few and Baldwin began with an honest commitment to the idea, however sketchily conceived at first, of a coordinate college, a separate but educationally equal college for women. Not all at once but gradually, the two administrators developed a genuine respect and even liking for each other, so that when they disagreed, as they inevitably did in such a complex and drawn-out undertaking, they did so intelligently and reasonably. From an early stage in their relationship and in the planning for and then the actual creation of the Woman's College, it became clear that Baldwin was a shade more concerned about equal educational opportunity for women than she was about their separation from males. Few, on the other hand, while absolutely honest in his support for educational equality, displayed a slightly more fervent and long-lasting concern about the academic separation of the sexes than did the dean. The largely triumphal story of the Woman's College down to Baldwin's retirement in 1947 makes it clear that she won out in the contest. The Woman's College, while residentially quite separate, was not just the educational equal of the men's college but in a number of ways somewhat embarrassingly better, and this was only partly because it was not as separate as Few had at one time envisioned. In her own distinctive way, and within the larger context overseen by Few, Alice Baldwin also became an institution-builder.

Ironically, Baldwin neither planned nor desired to become a dean. Born in Maine in 1879, she was the oldest of five children, and her father, like many of her male ancestors on both sides of the family, was a Congregational clergyman. Education received great attention in the family, and Alice Baldwin, after one year at coeducational Bates College in Maine, followed her father's advice and transferred to Cornell University, which then occupied a preeminent and relatively lonely position as a coeducational university in the East. A history major and Phi Beta Kappa graduate from Cornell, Baldwin stayed on there to receive a master's degree in history in 1902. Winning a travelling fellowship for study at the Sorbonne and the University of Berlin, Baldwin intended to obtain a Ph.D., and become a college-level teacher and scholar. That goal became temporarily unattainable, however, when poor health forced her father's early retirement, and the family's straitened circumstances led Baldwin to seek immediate employment.[5]

Going to Fargo College in North Dakota as dean of women and instructor in history, Baldwin, then only twenty-five, did not relish the job, primarily because she felt she was too young for it. Vowing to avoid such deanships in the future, she returned in 1906 to the East and an instructorship at the Baldwin School, a strong preparatory school for girls in Pennsylvania. Eventually becoming head of the history department, she remained there until 1921, when she took a leave of absence to pursue at the University of Chicago her original goal of a doctorate in history.[6]

By chance, Trinity College came into Baldwin's purview in 1923. Professor Holland Holton, head of Trinity's department of education and director of the summer session, had a brother who was also doing graduate work at Chicago. Since Trinity sought a new dean of women, Holland Holton, learning about Baldwin from his brother, inquired if she had any interest in discussing the position at Trinity. Though Baldwin replied in the negative, Holton persisted and with his third effort persuaded her to accept a job as acting dean of women in Trinity's summer session of 1923. Running low on funds, Baldwin, who had never been in the South, also decided that six weeks in North Carolina might be interesting.[7]

Fully expecting to return to Chicago to complete her dissertation, Baldwin may have been surprised that, despite the heat, she enjoyed the six weeks in Durham. After she had been there several weeks, President Few interviewed her at length and inquired if she would be interested in keeping the post she held. An earlier, unnerving experience with a dean of women who had wept during a conference inspired Few to ask a question that Baldwin never forgot: "He asked if I could take criticism and disappointment without weeping!" Although she no doubt assured him that she could—at age forty-four, after all, Baldwin was no tender novice—the proffered salary of $3,000, which was quite respectable in that era, and an assistant professorship in history failed to shake her conviction that she was not called to be a dean of women.[8]

Baldwin hoped to return to the University of Chicago, obtain her doctorate, and perhaps secure an appointment there. Her supervising professor, however, candidly advised her that there was not much future for her at Chicago. Whether just or not, he argued, "the fact is that in the University there is not much opportunity for women." He also pointed out that Trinity's history department enjoyed a good reputation in the profession and that she would probably be wise to take the job.[9]

Receiving a kind reception and similar advice from Trinity's most senior historians, William K. Boyd and William T. Laprade, Baldwin finally changed her mind and accepted the post. Since Trinity opened several weeks earlier in the fall than Chicago, she agreed to be in Durham for three weeks, return to Chicago to fulfill her obligations as a teaching assistant in the fall semester, and assume her full-time duties at Trinity in January 1924. "I came from walking the Midway in a heavy fur coat in 16° below zero weather to one of North Carolina's January hot spells," she later recalled, "so that for some weeks I felt as if I had a high fever."[10]

Climate was only one of the many differences to which Alice Baldwin had to adjust. Trinity College was on the brink of ambitious undertakings when she came as the first woman to serve as a full fledged member of the faculty; but not even Few knew precisely how and when that large development would occur. Trinity, a small liberal arts college, was a far cry from the University of Chicago. Yet resilience and adaptability were among Baldwin's attributes. When officials at Trinity had first begun to make inquiries about her, one historian who knew her wrote aptly that her background was "that of a cultured Eastern woman to which she has added enough of the breezy democracy of the Middle West to save her from any trace of intellectual snobbery." Baldwin possessed, he believed, "the rather rare combination of intellectual equipment with broad general culture and an alive and sympathetic personality."[11]

Few had made it clear to Baldwin that, at some as yet undetermined time in the future, a coordinate college for women was to be organized at Trinity. When he asked her views on that, she skillfully maneuvered around their mutual ignorance on the subject by replying that she herself "was a product of coeducation but that, if a coordinate college was to be developed, our job was to make it the best possible of its kind." [12]

Privately, Baldwin set out to educate herself about coordinate colleges, and before she was through she had become a widely recognized authority on the subject. After James B. Duke's large gifts and the formal beginning of Duke University in December, 1924, the matter ceased to be theoretical. Seeking detailed information about Radcliffe's relationship to Harvard, Baldwin confessed to a friend that she was "as ignorant of these things as a new born babe and have got to have some information on the subject." [13] Baldwin dispatched other requests for information about coordinate colleges and, inevitably, soon learned that no single exemplary model existed. The various colleges had evolved differently in response to widely different institutional circumstances. Amidst all the variety, Baldwin found only three features that the coordinate colleges possessed in common: separate living quarters, separate student organizations, and at least some separation in classroom work. [14] Consequently she, and no doubt Few also, fell back on the hope that Duke University could "take the best from the experience of others and at the same time create new methods that meet our peculiar conditions and the particular needs of young people now and in the future." [15]

Concerning many decisions that would have a far-reaching impact on the Woman's College, Alice Baldwin had no voice, which was hardly surprising in the circumstances. None other than James B. Duke himself, in consultation with Few and a small group of advisors, made the final decision in the spring of 1925 that the extensive new Tudor Gothic buildings that he would give to Duke University, rather than being crowded onto the old Trinity campus as was originally envisioned, would be built on vast acreage a mile and a half to the west of the old campus. That led to the additional plan for dedicating virtually the entire Trinity campus to the needs of the Woman's College rather than crowding it into the northwestern corner, as was first contemplated. While some of the existing Trinity buildings would be retained, some would have to go in order to make room for eleven new buildings to be constructed of red brick and white marble in the Georgian or neoclassical style. Starting in the summer of 1925, those eleven buildings were to be erected before work would begin on the Gothic campus. That meant that for an unknown period of time (five years, as it turned out), all segments of Duke University would be housed on the old Trinity or, as it later came to be known, the East campus; and the Woman's College could not become a full-fledged separate entity until September, 1930. [16]

Alice Baldwin saw James B. Duke on only one occasion before his death in October, 1925. He, together with Frank C. Brown, a professor of English and Few's chief liaison with J. B. Duke and his architects concerning the physical plant, visited Southgate dormitory, where Baldwin lived as dean of women. Given by the people of Durham and J. B. Duke's older brother, Benjamin N. Duke, Southgate was then the only dormitory for women students. Although it was relatively new, having been completed in 1921, Baldwin remembered that J. B. Duke was remarkably quick in spotting defects in the building, such as floors in bad condition and an awkward arrangement of pillars in the dining room.[17]

Well might Baldwin have regretted that she was never able again to confer with J. B. Duke. Going always for top quality in his endeavors, he may have been receptive to some of Baldwin's progressive—but expensive—ideas concerning the plant that would eventually become the home of the Woman's College. Not only did his death preclude that possibility, however, it also meant that Few, to his profound distress and embarrassment, had to cope with the ambitious plans for a complex research university that he had persuaded James B. Duke to underwrite but for which there simply were not adequate funds, as matters turned out. How much of all that Baldwin knew or understood at the time is not known. What does stand out is that she was able to exert only a minimal influence on the physical aspect of the Woman's College.

Although Few informed her that she was a member of the local building committee, she never was able to see Horace Trumbauer, the distinguished Philadelphia architect whose firm J. B. Duke had selected to design the buildings for both campuses, or the members of his staff. "Dr. Brown was all powerful," Baldwin tersely noted in her memoir. She was thinking of relatively small residential colleges or units within the larger Woman's College, as was Few for the West or men's campus for that matter, but her recommendations were not followed. She urged, for example, that separate dining halls be built for each unit of two dormitories, with kitchens in the basement for vegetables, salads, and other things and a central kitchen for breads and other foods that could be cooked more economically in bulk. Few, however, informed her that it had been decided to have a central kitchen and dining halls in a Union building across from the library.[18]

Showing Baldwin blueprints for the new Georgian buildings—two classroom buildings, a library, Union, and auditorium in addition to six new dormitories (one for faculty and staff use)—Few accepted certain of her suggestions while rejecting others. She finally persuaded him that the bathrooms should have showers (which Few thought women would not like because of their hair) and that the parlors of the dormitories should have fireplaces despite the fact that the buildings had central heating. Two things that Baldwin especially urged were first accepted and then, obviously for budgetary reasons, eliminated. Wishing to encourage younger women faculty members to live in the dormitories (something that Duke University, like certain other selective institutions, would later strive to accomplish), Baldwin wanted a suite of two rooms and a bath at each end of the front corridor on the second floor of each dormitory. They were cut from the plans. And as a result of painful knowledge gained from her experience in Southgate, she wanted but did not get a buzzer system connecting each room with the dormitory office so that a student could be summoned for visitors or messages. One small but important victory Baldwin did win: residential counselors in each dormitory loomed large in her plans for the Woman's College, and when she learned that private bathrooms for the counselors' suites had been cut from the plans, she successfully battled to have them restored.[19]

When the women came into sole, or at least primary, occupancy of the East campus (male engineering students would remain there until after World War II), Few dreamed up one physical feature that Baldwin managed to veto. He suggested that a large, decorative iron fence around the women's dormitory quadrangle, a fence which could be locked at night for added security, might be wise. Baldwin and one of her coworkers, however, fortunately persuaded him that such a fence would be both unnecessary and impractical and "would only lead to many escapades by both men and women."[20] The low stone wall that Benjamin N. Duke had given in 1915 both to define the perimeter of Trinity's campus and to decorate it would have to suffice as a "protective" barrier for the Woman's College.

As important as the physical plant was, there were actually more important decisions concerning the academic future of the Woman's College that were made in the late 1920s. Few and Baldwin then had to grapple with the task of translating the abstract idea of a coordinate college into concrete plans. Since there was never any question about or even possibility of a separate endowment or separate governing board for the Woman's College, one crucial remaining question was whether it was to have a separate faculty or to share the faculty of Trinity College, the undergraduate men's college in the new university plan. Apparently neither Few nor Baldwin had strong, clear preconceived notions on the matter, though Few's emphasis on separation may have tilted him towards the idea of two distinct undergraduate faculties. Baldwin, on the other hand, while eager to increase the number of women faculty members at Duke, was even more determined to see that women students received equal educational opportunity and that neither women faculty members nor women students were in any way subordinated to men.[21]

Always determined to have Duke University and its component parts approved by the appropriate national standardizing agencies, Few much wanted the Woman's College to be recognized by the American Association of University Women, which had been formed in 1921 when two older organizations of collegiate alumnae merged. To gain the recognition of that body, a college or university had to provide evidence of appropriate provision for women students, reasonable recognition of women on the faculty, and equal treatment for them in the matter of pay and promotion. The AAUW also required that a dean for women students be a regular member of the faculty, while the presence of women on an institution's board of trustees lent "much weight" to its application for recognition.[22]

On a more mundane level, Baldwin also initially learned from AAUW headquarters that for accreditation a women's college not only had to provide adequate health care for the students but also a well-planned program in physical education. Accordingly, with authorization from Few and Wannamaker, Baldwin secured the appointment in September, 1924, of Julia R. Grout. A graduate of Mount Holyoke who received her advanced training in physical education at Wellesley College, Grout became not only the founder and longtime head of the strong program in health and physical education in the Woman's College but an important ally and coworker of Baldwin's.[23]

As the first woman to hold a regular appointment on Trinity's faculty and the only female administrator, Baldwin obviously found herself in a lonely and sensitive situation. Like Dean Virginia Gildersleeve at Columbia University's coordinate Barnard College, Baldwin pursued a conservative strategy of planning carefully, beginning gently and slowly, sticking to the business at hand, and gradually, in Gildersleeve's words, becoming "one of a group of human beings, all trying together for the best possible solutions of the important questions before them." A colleague who long observed Baldwin at Duke and knew her well noted that she "learned quickly to urge rather than force or demand."[24]

Baldwin's cautious conservatism should not, however, be mistaken for spinelessness. Attending her first faculty meeting at Trinity in the spring of 1924, before the university was organized and the coordinate college definitely projected, Baldwin later admitted feeling hesitant. Although she recalled that she "never experienced from any of the men anything but courtesy,"[25] she well understood that mere courtesy was not the equivalent of being taken seriously or treated equally. By the following year when the initial plans were being made for the coordinate college, Baldwin suggested to Few that it might be helpful with the AAUW if a special committee or council on the instruction of women were established. It could include all the women who taught, many of whom then were instructors and therefore technically not members of the faculty, plus some of the male faculty members who taught mixed or all-female classes. Few not only accepted the suggestion but subsequently proposed that the new council be regarded as the nucleus of the faculty for the projected coordinate college and that women faculty members, therefore, could attend the council's meetings rather than the regular meetings of the Trinity College faculty. Baldwin at first agreed, but upon reflection and with important consequences for the future, she changed her mind. "I believe I made a mistake," she candidly informed Few, "and that it is very decidedly for the good of the woman's college and of the university that the women attend faculty meetings until the definite division of the various faculties has been made." The women, Baldwin argued, "should feel themselves an integral part of the whole and the men should think of them that way." Unless she heard from Few to the contrary, she would urge eligible women to attend regular faculty meetings for the time being. Few acquiesced to Baldwin's argument, and a quiet but significant step was taken toward the educational quality and equality of the Woman's College as well as the creation of one undergraduate faculty at Duke.[26]

Baldwin's own position as a faculty member was strengthened when she received her doctorate in history from Chicago in 1926, and Duke University Press published her excellent dissertation, *The New England Clergy and the American Revolution*, in 1928. Thus equipped with full scholarly credentials, Baldwin was promoted to an associate professorship in history; a decade later she became a full professor. She was made dean of the Woman's College in 1927, and at the same time Ruth Slack Smith (Mrs. Hazen Smith) became the assistant dean and social director. A native Georgian and graduate of Agnes Scott College with a master's degree in guidance and personnel work from Columbia University, Smith later became associate dean of undergraduate instruction and one of Baldwin's key helpers in building the Woman's College.[27]

Most features of Baldwin's deanship and of her administrative style emerged clearly in the late 1920s, even before the coordinate college had become a separate entity. As mentioned earlier, the collegiate philosophy of *in loco parentis* then prevailing across the nation gave administrators both the legal and the moral right to exercise control over the lives of students. Most students themselves, male as well as female, then accepted that fact, and Baldwin never questioned or challenged the concept. Yet from the beginning of her career at Trinity-Duke she attempted to deal democratically and fairly with the women students. Since her primary aim, as she expressed it, "was always the development of intellectual, social, and ethical responsibility and maturity" among the students, she chose to do what she could to strengthen and work through the women's student government association.[28]

By 1927 Duke's women students claimed that their student government association, headed by senior Ellen Huckabee, who later filled a key administrative post in the Woman's College, was probably the most vital factor in their collegiate life. With power to make regulations and decisions and responsible methods for carrying them out, the Women's Student Government Association, or WSGA, as it was known, had won a large degree of jurisdiction over the affairs of women students. Baldwin and her staff met frequently with the student council and worked diligently and apparently successfully at keeping lines of communication open.[29]

Manners and morals of the young were changing in the 1920s, to the inevitable dismay of many in the older generations, and Baldwin's handling of two then controversial social issues—dancing and cigarette smoking—well illustrate her approach. Trinity College not only prohibited dancing on campus but women students, victims of a different standard from that applied to male students, were not even supposed to attend dances off campus. By arranging to spend the night or weekend with girls who lived in Durham, however, some residents of Southgate did attend dances at the sparkling new Washington Duke hotel in downtown Durham. The hypocrisy of the situation bothered Baldwin, and no doubt some of the women students also. She therefore conferred with Few and won his permission for Duke women to go directly from Southgate to the dances provided that she served as chaperone and that a proper curfew was observed. Setting that at 1:00 A.M., Baldwin thought it "awkward and graceless" when the bandleader announced loudly, "One o'clock. Time for the Shack [Southgate] girls to leave." She accordingly arranged for the band to play a special song at 12:55 (perhaps "Goodnight, Sweetheart") as a signal for the necessary departure of the Duke women. The first real dance given on the Woman's College campus came in the spring of 1931 when the WSGA staged the first of a long series of increasingly elaborate Coed balls in the gymnasium there. "To this President Few assented, came to see the decorations, but refused to attend," Baldwin later recalled.[30]

If dancing ruffled Methodist feathers, so did cigarette smoking by "bobhaired flappers." Bryn Mawr had raised many eyebrows in the world of the women's colleges by establishing special smoking rooms in 1925. The matter came to a head only five years later at Duke when in the fall of 1930 the newly opened Woman's College saw women freshmen vastly outnumber the older returning students, and many of the newcomers openly rebelled against the no-smoking regulation. When the student council, headed by Gertrude Merritt, who would later become an important figure in the building of the Duke library's holdings, appealed in desperation to Baldwin, she suggested that WSGA should hold a public debate. "That habitual smoking slows the heart, weakens the lungs, and stunts growth, Miss Wilkerson had proved beyond a doubt," the *Chronicle* reported, "when Miss Hill rising to the full dignity of her six feet declared that she had been smoking for three years and behold her growth!" When the foe of cigarettes declared that "even your best friend won't tell you when you have halitosis from smoking," the smokers' champion did not even try to refute the point.[31]

Without strong personal feelings about smoking, though always sensitive to Duke's southern setting, Baldwin, after studying how other women's colleges had handled the matter, helped work out a widely accepted compromise: Duke's women students could smoke in their own rooms, in private homes, and, shortly afterwards, in the dormitory parlors. They were not, however, to offend prevailing community taste by smoking elsewhere on campus or in public in Durham.[32]

Larger matters than smoking and dancing loomed toward the end of the 1920s as construction of the men's Gothic campus neared completion, and Baldwin and her small staff planned as best they could for the women's takeover of the East campus and the formal launching of the Woman's College. Baldwin found herself occupied with a variety of matters from selecting furniture for the dormitories to the necessary enlargement of her staff. She had to work closely with Allen Tyree, the business and plant manager of the East campus and a person whom Baldwin, at least initially, found difficult. Baldwin, who had an interest in antiques and their refinishing, extensively studied dormitory furniture and ended up helping to design special desks and chairs, with the legs of all pieces made in such a way as to prevent runs in women's stockings as much as possible.[33]

More important, perhaps, was the selection of the counselors for the four dormitories that were to be initially used by the Woman's College—Pegram, Alspaugh, Bassett, and Brown, all names from Trinity's proud past.[34] From her earlier experience at the Baldwin School and later as a graduate student at Chicago, Baldwin acquired a strong belief in the important role that mature residential counselors should play in dormitory living. She wanted as counselors only college graduates and "women who could inspire respect as well as liking." Although she had difficulty from the beginning and later in convincing Few and the other top male administrators of the importance of the counselors, Baldwin stuck by her guns. Wishing to avoid the stereotype of the "housemother" or dormitory matron, Baldwin explained that she "did not want to have as counsellors widows of clergymen and other elderly women whose chief recommendation was that they liked young people." The quality of the women who were to be counselors and members of the dean's staff she regarded as crucial to the building of a high-quality residential college.[35]

Among the original house counselors were several who were destined to be long and valuably associated with the Woman's College. Two were Duke alumnae: in Alspaugh was Louise Seabolt, who also worked as Baldwin's secretary and then for many years as the college's recorder, and Mary Kestler (later Mrs. Paul H. Clyde) served in Pegram. Mary Grace Wilson taught in Durham High School and served as dean of girls before becoming the counselor in Brown House in 1930; she also served as the social director for the college and later as dean of undergraduate women until her retirement in 1970. Elizabeth Anderson (later Mrs. W. S. Persons) began as the counselor in Bassett but soon found herself working closely with Baldwin on admissions and served for many years as first the secretary of the committee on admissions and then the director of admissions for the Woman's College. Baldwin's emphasis on the role of the house counselors was to be vindicated early, for the cohesiveness and generally high morale of the various dormitories on East were to be vital factors in the success of the Woman's College.

From its opening in September, 1930, the Woman's College never had to worry about applicants. As the years passed, in fact, the problem of too many applicants became increasingly difficult and frequently embarrassing insofar as relations with alumni and the general public were concerned. First Trinity and, after 1924, Duke had long-standing experience with an excess of women applicants for the available spaces. As one of a relatively small group of academically strong institutions then open to women in the South and one of the few voluntarily supported research universities then open to women in the eastern half of the United States, Trinity-Duke began in the 1920s to be more truly selective among its female applicants than it could be among its male applicants. The fact that four out of ten inductees into Phi Beta Kappa in 1925 were women, though men outnumbered women in the student body three to one, and five out of seven Phi Beta Kappas in 1930 were women suggests that the women students were setting academic standards for undergraduates at Duke even before the Woman's College was formally opened.[36]

All was not rosy, however, during the academic year 1930–31. With some 300 new women students, mostly freshmen, greatly outnumbering the 137 returning students, there were obviously a lack of continuity in the student body and a painfully larger than usual number of inexperienced, no doubt confused new college students. Moreover, the fact that most of the first-year women were concentrated in two dormitories no doubt added to the problem. While the hullabaloo concerning cigarette smoking was eventually quieted, the officers of WSGA as well as Baldwin and her colleagues were understandably overworked and harassed during that first year.[37]

The year's experiences proved instructive, however. Baldwin and her coworkers decided that they would never again have all-freshman dormitories. Rather, roughly equal numbers of members of the different classes would be included in each of the houses, thus allowing upperclass students to play a large role in helping the freshmen to adjust and acclimatize. Another important feature of the residential life of the Woman's College also gradually emerged: sorority members would also be scattered among the houses rather than live in separate sections allotted especially to them, as was the pattern for the fraternities on the West campus. Few had, in fact, suggested that if Baldwin thought it desirable, the occasion of the opening of the Woman's College might be utilized to do away with the three existing sororities. After reflection, Baldwin decided in favor of continuing them and gave two main reasons for doing so. First, there was no plan to abolish fraternities, and Baldwin felt "most anxious not to have any discrimination against the women in the new college." The second reason was that Few and all those who joined with him in establishing Duke University were intensely concerned "to keep alumni closely connected with the University and to assure them that the traditions of Trinity College and friendliness characteristic of it would not be lost." Baldwin decided that sororities would be one additional means of sustaining interest among some of the alumnae and bringing them back to the campus. She and her associates, therefore, decided not only to keep the three existing sororities but to encourage the organization of others as the need arose and the students showed interest in doing so. The dean and her staff would, for their part, do what they could to emphasize the good aspects of sororities and, insofar as possible, eliminate or play down the less positive features. Succeeding years would prove Baldwin wise in her policy, for while the Duke women who joined sororities proved loyal to them, the sisterhoods never diminished or eroded the vibrant cohesiveness of the house organizations.[38]

As important as the residential and social aspects of the Woman's College were, the heart of the enterprise was academic, that is, in the classrooms, laboratories, and library. And it was in academics that the most important problems arose concerning the policy of a separate but equal education for undergraduate women at Duke. Although Few at one point had conceded that coeducation was "the logic of the future," he clung to the belief that "the prejudice of most men and many women through all the Eastern states" made its practice impolitic if not impossible at Trinity and then at Duke. Thus separate but equal academic opportunity became the logical alternative.[39] In the early conferences between Few and Baldwin, he reiterated his preference for separate classes for men and women. He hoped to make it possible, in fact, for a woman to receive a Duke degree for work done entirely on the East campus.[40] Such thinking, however, quickly gave way to harsh budgetary realities in the late 1920s. The resulting financial stringency, though largely hidden from the public, much affected the final plans for the academic side of the Woman's College.[41]

The scheme that Few and Baldwin worked out in the late 1920s envisioned separate classes for women in their first year; sophomores would also be taught separately insofar as possible; and where junior and senior women could gain access to advanced courses only on the West campus or, in the case of advanced courses taught on East, those classes would be integrated. Baldwin quickly discovered, even in the Southgate era of the late 1920s, that the economic argument against the duplication of faculty and facilities was a potent weapon in the struggle for equal educational opportunity for women. After September, 1930, when the two undergraduate colleges were separated by a mile and a half, there were inevitable difficulties in maintaining the policy of separate but equal. The Council for the Education of Women did not become the nucleus of a separate faculty, as Few had once envisioned, but it did serve as a useful watchdog or guardian for women's equality in the academic area. When, for example, certain deans on West moved to exclude women from sophomore courses taught on that campus, the council urged Few either to open the courses to women or to provide them also on East. Because Few too had made an honest commitment to equal educational opportunity for women and because there was not enough money to duplicate the smaller courses by offering them on East, women won the right to take the courses on West, and the sophomore courses with small enrollments were soon routinely integrated. By 1934 there were 70 courses on East in which only women were enrolled and 220 courses with mixed enrollment on both campuses.[42]

Aside from the insensitivity of some, not all, of the male administrators and faculty members on West, the distance between the two campuses posed logistical problems in scheduling classes. Instead of the ten-minute interval between classes that was common on most campuses, Duke found it necessary to have twenty minutes so that students could go via buses from one campus to the other if necessary. When a number of male faculty members on West, probably those who were lucky enough to have offices close by their laboratories or classrooms, complained of the loss of time caused by the twenty-minute interval, the committee on the schedule, over the strong protests of Baldwin, voted to recommend a change to a ten-minute interval. "In all of my dealings with the Administration and faculty," Baldwin later explained, "I had tried to so act as to make sure that I would not be regarded as an obstructionist but [as] cooperative and reasonable, so that, when I did definitely oppose some measure, they would trust my judgment." The strategy paid off in this instance, as no doubt in many others, for when Baldwin argued in the general faculty meeting that the change proposed by the schedule committee would be an unfair handicap to the women students, the faculty voted to reject the recommended change and retain the twenty-minute interval.[43]

While some male faculty members were either hostile or, more likely, indifferent to the women students, many of them became staunch supporters of the Woman's College and Baldwin's allies in her struggles to protect and advance its interests. While some of these male allies had their home bases on the West campus, perhaps the most outspoken of them had their offices on the old Trinity campus. Because office space was in short supply at Duke, and would remain so for many years, when the West campus was occupied in September, 1930, many members of several of the largest departments, such as history and English, remained on East. The education department remained there, as did several members of the philosophy and psychology departments. When a geology department was established in 1936, it was housed on East because there was no space for it on West. Appreciating the quiet serenity of the spacious, tree-filled East campus as well as believing in the moral obligation of Duke University to give the best education that it could to women as well as men, a significant number of men became prominent champions of the Woman's College. Among them were such leading veterans of the Trinity College era as W. K. Boyd and W. T. Laprade in history and Holland Holton in education; they were later joined by men such as J. B. Rhine in psychology (later parapsychology); C. Richard Sanders, Jay Hubbell, and Lewis Patton in English; W. H. Cartwright in education; Taylor Cole in political science; and W. B. Hamilton, Ernest W. Nelson, and Paul H. Clyde in history.[44] The fact that so many leading members of the faculty kept their offices on East helped Baldwin in her effort to make sure that the women's campus did not become merely a group of dormitories or, at the most, a junior college–type campus without an intellectual atmosphere and where only freshman and sophomore work was offered.

Another unforeseen development helped to enrich the academic and cultural life of the Woman's College—and therefore, of course, ultimately of Duke University also—and that was the beginning there of work in art and music. For all of the genuine strength and quality that Trinity College had developed in a number of areas prior to the organization of the university, it had, as mentioned earlier, sadly neglected the fine arts. Trinity was not alone in that respect, for American colleges in general were slow in moving art, music, and drama from the extracurricular into the regular course of study.[45] By the 1920s, however, the situation was changing, especially in the more progressive or experimental institutions, and Duke needed to begin to fill gaps inherited from Trinity.

President Few, while without the financial resources to give priority to the arts, acknowledged their importance to the university. Thanking a wealthy New Yorker and former associate of J. B. Duke's for the gift to the university of two fine paintings, Few declared that he and his associates were "especially grateful for such gifts because we are anxious to build up a first rate collection of paintings." They would have great educational value and be "particularly useful in places like this where high-minded boys and girls spend the formative years of their life."[46] A few years later Few confessed that the art department at Duke was in its "mere beginnings," and while it was one of the things he was "most anxious" to see developed, the nation's economic depression and its impact on Duke worked against doing so.[47]

Alice Baldwin turned out to be one of Few's most valuable allies in the effort to have Duke strengthen both art and music. Not only did she as a trained pianist herself have a personal and relatively sophisticated interest in music, but she also quickly became aware after first arriving in Durham in 1923 that neither Durham nor Trinity College then had much to offer in the area of the arts. Moreover, after the university was organized and the plans for the Woman's College began to take shape, Baldwin seized on the opportunity offered by the arts as another way in which to enrich the East campus and to avoid the junior-college model by having advanced work in those fields offered there. She by no means wanted to foster the mistaken idea that the arts were in any way peculiarly feminine, but she did want to further the cause of the arts at Duke and to strengthen the Woman's College.[48]

Chairing a music committee in 1925–26 and helping to reorganize the women's music club, Baldwin took pride in the first public appearance of the women's glee club in 1927. She spoke to various groups on and off campus about Renaissance art and conferred with Few about the urgent need of developing course work in the arts. Few, Flowers, and other male administrators were all too familiar with music and art as long taught in finishing schools for girls, both in the South and in other parts of the country, so part of Baldwin's task lay in educating them about the fact that there were more serious and academically respectable ways in which to teach both history and theory in the arts. While Few ruled out any attempt to establish schools of art and music at Duke, by the early 1930s he was firmly committed to the gradual building up of strong academic departments in those areas.[49]

Baldwin played a key role in the appointment of the faculty members, both the women and the men, who pioneered in art and music at Duke. As mentioned earlier, one of the first of these, Louise Hall, came to help launch the art department in the fall of 1931. By 1934, when Elizabeth Gilmore, a graduate of the University of Wisconsin with a doctorate from the University of Munich, joined Hall in the fledgling department, eleven courses in art were listed in the catalog.[50]

W. K. Boyd, longtime chairman of the history department and director of the university's libraries from 1930 until 1934, joined Baldwin in fostering art at Duke. Keenly aware that there were then no first-class art galleries south of the Potomac river and that no southern college or university had, in Boyd's opinion, a "high-grade curriculum and equipment" in the arts, he helped make the handsome Georgian library on the East campus the first focal point and display case for art at Duke.[51] Boyd negotiated with Mrs. Margaret L. Barber of Missouri for the extended loan to Duke University of her large, miscellaneous collection of art and antiques. He then worked with Lillian B. Griggs, head of the Woman's

College library, and others to transform early in 1931 the library's splendid foyer and several of its rooms, including a spacious "lower gallery" that later became a reserve reading room, into an art museum. Even before the exhibition was opened to the public, Boyd took the lead in organizing a Duke University Art Association, which sponsored a large number of exhibitions in the Woman's College Library after the initial fanfare about the Barber collection.[52]

With so much artistic endeavor already centered in the library, it is understandable that early in 1936 President Few requested the university's architect, Horace Trumbauer, to prepare preliminary plans and cost estimates for an addition to the Woman's College library building that could meet the needs of the small art department as well as provide for its expansion in the future.[53] Before anything was done along that line, however, Few's plans were drastically altered and his hopes raised late in 1936 by negotiations that began with William Hayes Ackland about his offer to Duke University of an art museum and endowment for it. The executive committee of the trustees subsequently rejected the Ackland bequest in 1941, after Few's death, and no art museum would be established at Duke for another generation.[54]

Just as Alice Baldwin and the Woman's College were closely involved in all the developments concerning art at Duke from the late 1920s on, such was also the case in the field of music. Baldwin welcomed the appointment in 1927 of J. Foster Barnes as director of religious and social activities; while he took over the men's glee club, his wife, Myrtle Preyer Barnes, directed the women's choral group. Likewise, Baldwin was young enough at heart to appreciate the rousing popular music—mostly jazz—provided by George "Jelly" Leftwich and his student orchestra, but she noted that he and the Duke band "aroused some ridicule from music lovers when he gave what was called a symphony concert, because he jazzed up classical music."[55] Accordingly, when a formally trained musician and alumnus, Robert Fearing, became director of the band and orchestra in 1935, Baldwin applauded the move. Prior to that, Edward H. Broadhead had joined the staff in 1933 to teach courses in the history of music. Baldwin and Broadhead then found Henry A. Bruinsma in 1938 to teach courses in theory. In 1939, as earlier, Baldwin stressed to Few and Wannamaker that Duke needed to strengthen its music department. With their approval, she took the lead in finding a young violinist trained at the Eastman School of Music, Julia Wilkinson (later Mrs. Earl Mueller), who joined the fledgling department that fall.[56]

Though both the art and music programs were slowly growing, they remained quite small and both suffered from leadership problems. When enrollment in art courses reached a point where an additional appointment seemed essential, Baldwin and Louise Hall conferred and decided that the appointment of a male scholar in the field would be wise. They hoped thus to counter any notion that the study or teaching of art was for women only.[57] Consequently, the administration authorized the appointment of Alexander D. McDonald as an assistant professor in art in 1936. But just as McDonald lacked the doctoral degree and proved not to have the administrative talents needed in a departmental chairman, Broadhead in music did not seem able to pull together his small group and also lacked a doctorate. Since Baldwin, more than any other administrator, had been actively involved in recruiting the faculty members involved and spent many hours trying to help them work out various problems, Wannamaker and Few named her acting chair of the music department in 1940. That was merely a temporary move designed to buy time, however, for Baldwin came up with an ingenious solution to the problem of the small, problem-filled departments of art and music.

Having heard of Cornell's apparently successful experiment in combining aesthetics, art, and music in one department, Baldwin suggested to Wannamaker and Few that such an arrangement might solve several problems for Duke. Katherine Everett Gilbert was, upon joining Duke's Department of Philosophy in 1930, the most outstanding scholar among the women on the faculty and the first woman to hold the rank of full professor. A graduate of Brown University, she received her doctorate in philosophy from Cornell in 1912 and specialized in aesthetics, in which she published well-received books and articles. Married in 1913 to Allen H. Gilbert, who became a professor of English in Trinity College and then Duke University, Katherine Gilbert bore two sons. Later she became a research fellow in philosophy at Cornell and then at the University of North Carolina in the late 1920s before she joined the Duke faculty.[58]

For a year or more, Katherine Gilbert, with Baldwin's encouragement and with the approval of Few and Wannamaker, investigated the multipurpose department at Cornell and in the summer of 1942 had interviews with scholars at several northeastern universities, including Cornell, and with the directors of the National Gallery in Washington and the Museum of Fine Arts in Boston. She also conferred with several of the Duke faculty members directly involved. In midsummer 1942 Wannamaker and Few gave the green light for the launching of the new department that fall.[59]

Though handicapped by lack of adequate space and with resources scattered widely on both campuses, the department that Katherine Gilbert headed from 1942 until her death in 1952 proved a viable solution, even if a transitory one, to a difficult problem that had plagued Baldwin as well as quite a few others. Gilbert explained that the rationale behind the department was to give "completeness to the acts of seeing and hearing" and to prove that "rational knowledge may coexist with a heightening of pleasure." Proudly interdisciplinary in her own approach, Gilbert once noted that three out of the seven members of the department, herself being one of the three, offered courses in other departments, and that cooperation with people in a wide range of fields—from engineering to physical education, from classics and religion to psychology and physics—seemed entirely logical to those in the department. While no credit was yet given for work in the applied arts, the department looked forward to changing that when space and staff became available.[60] While the entire university and the surrounding community benefitted indirectly from the growth of the work in art and music, the Woman's College obviously gained the most.

270

The
Launching
of Duke
University
⟨⊖⟩

Within less than a decade of the college's formal opening, Baldwin, together with many who assisted and worked with her, had made it amply clear that the Woman's College was neither a mere collection of dormitories nor a junior college. Rather, it possessed the intellectual attributes and cultural tone of a thriving undergraduate college within a research university. Another way in which that fact gained reinforcement was in the growth and character of the library of the Woman's College. Under the leadership of an imaginative and dedicated librarian, Lillian Baker Griggs, from 1930 until 1949, the library became a vital force on the East campus, as popular with many faculty members and their families as with the students. The first professionally trained librarian in a public library in North Carolina when she began work in Durham in 1911, Griggs crusaded successfully for library extension into the county's rural areas and took the lead in procuring the first bookmobile in the state. Then from 1923 until she accepted the position at Duke she oversaw the work of public libraries throughout the state as the director of the North Carolina Library Commission.[61]

With this rich background of experience, Griggs played a key role in making the Woman's College library a model one for undergraduates in several respects. Since the library was virtually emptied when the main collection was moved to the new West campus in the summer of 1930, the strength of the East campus library lay not in the size of its collection, which consisted of only some 4,000 volumes initially, but in several other innovations. From the beginning, and long before the main library on the West campus changed its policy of barring undergraduates from the stacks, Griggs insisted on having open stacks. Another innovation was an inviting Booklovers' Room close to the entrance, with a small but carefully chosen selection for browsing, which immediately became a well-loved feature of the library and the venue for informal talks by faculty and staff members to groups of students, poetry readings, and musical presentations. The students showed their appreciation of the room in 1936 when the sophomore group in the YMCA gave venetian blinds, draperies, chairs, and andirons to make it even more attractive and comfortable.[62]

Starting with the carefully selected four thousand volumes in 1930, the library's collection grew steadily, totalling almost eighty thousand by the time Griggs retired in 1949. While there were numerous ongoing problems about how much duplication there should be of books and periodicals available in the main library and exactly how various funds should be allocated, the acquisitions policy of the Woman's College library became generally set by the mid-1930s: the collection was to consist of books used in connection with courses taught on East, the most important books for collateral reading in courses taught on West in which significant numbers of women were enrolled, a limited number of books for general reading which were of permanent value, a limited number of important periodicals and newspapers, and a rapidly growing research collection in books related to the fine arts. In certain other areas the library also developed particular strength, such as children's literature, which became tied in with a course taught for many years in the Department of Education. Griggs, like so many other members of the university community, liked serious fiction, and holdings of that in English as well as in the romance languages and German grew to be substantial and much used and enjoyed by many.[63]

The splendidly accessible and user-friendly library became only one factor in the success of the Woman's College, but it was an important element. Perhaps the most obvious indicator of the college's success lay in the quantity and the quality of the applicants for admission. While Trinity first and then Duke had long enjoyed the privilege of selecting its women students from more well-qualified applicants than it could admit, there had never been such a flood of applications as that which increasingly descended upon the Woman's College. Learning from problems growing out of the large influx of new students in the fall of 1930, Baldwin set out to refine and strengthen the college's methods of selectivity. In the years before the famed tests of the College Entrance Examination Board had spread outside of a few select institutions in the Northeast, the secondary school record remained the most important item for the admissions committee to consider. To complement it, however, Baldwin hit on the personal interview as a valuable device both for evaluating the seriousness of the student and for informing her about the expectations and nature of the Woman's College. Beginning in 1931, Baldwin made regular visits to the larger cities on the East Coast in order to interview applicants, urged visits to and interviews on campus where possible, and began to utilize a loyal network of alumnae who met with prospective students across the country. For the first five years Baldwin reviewed all applications and, with Ruth S. Smith and at least one other person, made the decisions concerning admission. As the college grew, however, Baldwin found it necessary to turn more of the chore over to a Council on Admissions, for which Elizabeth A. Persons served as secretary before becoming director of admissions in 1945. Beginning in the mid-1930s Persons, who also served as dean of freshmen, also took over the extensive interview trips.[64]

By 1934 the Woman's College could accept slightly less than half of its applicants, and shortly after World War II, though the college had been expanded by then to enroll around 1,100 students, there were 1,623 applicants for the 250 places in the freshman class. Faced with the daunting task of choosing from among the growing numbers of applicants each year, Baldwin and then Persons began informally to urge women interested in applying to the Woman's College to take the aptitude test of the College Entrance Examination Board. By 1939 the college stopped giving entrance examinations to the relatively few students who applied from unaccredited secondary schools and required that those students take the tests of the college board. Efforts of the college to require the tests of all applicants were stymied, however, by the university's refusal to allow the Woman's College to have an admissions policy that was markedly different from that of Trinity College. Wannamaker, Few, and other top administrators argued that the undergraduate men's college was simply not ready for the requirement of college board examinations nor for the application fee for which the Woman's College pushed.[65]

One reason the Woman's College wanted an application fee was that, despite its obvious drawing power, there were still problems. One was the matter of able students who made multiple applications and withdrew late from the Woman's College upon receiving acceptance from another institution. The room deposit, nonrefundable after July 15, was raised from $5 to $25 in 1936, yet two years later 85 percent of the withdrawals came after August 1. As Elizabeth Persons noted, some students were clearly applying to Duke as a second choice, and to check the loss of the stronger applicants the Woman's College began to develop an early admission program.[66]

Despite continuing problems, the overall picture concerning admissions in the Woman's College was indeed bright. "Because of its unique place among the higher institutions of North Carolina and the Southeast," as Persons explained, "it did not have to meet the competition of other colleges in the area to the same extent as did Trinity."[67] She might well have added that the college's attractiveness extended well beyond the Southeast, for from an early stage Baldwin found it necessary to fix geographical quotas for the students admitted.

In employing geographical quotas she was being faithful to the larger purposes that both Few and James B. Duke, as well as the trustees, envisioned when the university was established late in 1924. It, like Trinity earlier, was meant to be of the highest, most generous service possible to the people of its state and region. Yet Duke University was also, in the words from J. B. Duke's indenture creating the Duke Endowment, charged with a mission to attain and maintain "a place of real leadership in the educational world." In other words, the university had a dual purpose: it was intended to be both a southern and a national or even international institution, to serve both the people in its own state and section and those in more distant regions who wished to enroll. Needing to avoid regional parochialism on the one hand and cosmopolitan indifference to Duke's home base and setting on the other, President Few, as well as those who worked with him in launching the university, faced a sometimes tricky task.

In the case of the Woman's College, especially when it became clear how many students from other regions wished to attend it, the matter quickly ceased to be theoretical. From the beginning Baldwin wanted students to come from a wide geographical area, both because she thought that increased the possibility of selecting able students and because she believed that the students themselves benefitted and learned from a regionally diverse student body. On the other hand, she quickly took root in Durham and North Carolina after being transplanted permanently in 1924 and was remarkably sensitive to various local conditions as well as to Duke University's dual purpose. When the administrative group discussed the matter of a tuition hike late in 1929, Baldwin argued for making any increase as gradual as possible. Most of the women students then came from the South and particularly from North Carolina, and Baldwin suggested that since the Woman's College needed as many old or returning students as possible when it opened in the following September, it would be "unfortunate to increase too rapidly the proportion of northern and western girls." Against the background of an agricultural depression that had hit the South beginning in 1921, Baldwin noted: "Times are hard in North Carolina and already some girls who are doing the finest work and are leaders in activities, etc., have had to take up dining room work and are doubting their ability to return next year."[68]

Balancing these divergent but not necessarily incompatible objectives, the Woman's College, with the approval of the university's admission committees, gradually worked out geographical quotas that, while never rigidly adhered to, allocated 65 to 70 percent of its admissions to the South, including about one third to North Carolina. The Middle Atlantic region, that is, from Washington, D.C., north to and including New York state, received from 14 to 16 percent of the places; the New England states, 5 percent; the Middle West or central region from 14 to 16 percent; the Far West, 1 to 2 percent; and foreign countries, 1 to 2 percent.[69] The Woman's College in Baldwin's time, that is, down through World War II, proved almost too popular along the Atlantic seaboard, particularly in the border South and the Middle Atlantic states where the geographical quotas were perhaps most restrictive. Yet to have admitted too many students from those areas would obviously have meant the downplaying or even neglect of Duke's historic and fiduciary obligation to North Carolina and the South.

From the national perspective, the Woman's College during its first fifteen or so years was conspicuously lacking in students from the Southwest, including Texas, and the Far West. A study made by Persons revealed remarkably few applications from those regions. That would change in the years after World War II, but during the formative period of the Woman's College its national dimension had distinct western weaknesses.[70] Despite that fact, President Few was not slow in acknowledging the remarkable success of the Woman's College in attracting able students both from within and outside of the South. In 1936, in fact, he informed an old friend that he had come to believe that Duke's thriving summer school, its medical school, and the Woman's College were the university's most direct "roads to a strong south-wide and even nation-wide student constituency."[71]

For all of his appreciation of what Baldwin and her staff—plus the Duke faculty—had achieved, Few was clearly reluctant to give up his earlier notions about the separateness of the Woman's College. A few months before acknowledging its southwide and even national drawing power, Few insisted that Duke was not a coeducational institution. Ignoring the huge fact of the shared or common faculty and the large number of integrated classes, Few argued that Duke's undergraduate women had "a college all their own, as much so as if they were located fifty miles away." Theoretically, Few continued, "a young woman could graduate with the A.B. degree and do all her work on the Woman's College campus." Few's conscience may have tweaked him slightly about that somewhat excessively theoretical statement, for he hastened to add in the next sentence that most women "prefer, and perhaps will always prefer, in the junior and senior years, to take some courses on the University [West] campus."[72]

President Few may have worried that Duke's coordinate college was not quite separate enough in the academic area, but no such matters seemed to have bothered the women students themselves. Because the college was a new unit even though partly rooted in an older institution, because the East campus was or seemed to be in some ways neglected by the chief administrators on West, or perhaps because of the excellent leadership provided by Baldwin and her staff—whatever the precise reason or mix of reasons, most of the students of the Woman's College apparently identified wholeheartedly with it. This was demonstrated in a variety of ways, but one of the clearest was the manner in which the women students worked and scrambled to provide various improvements and amenities for their campus. Lacking a recreational center other than the gymnasium, which had originally been built for men, the students, aided by Baldwin and Allen Tyree, managed to prevent the demolition of one of the oldest buildings on the campus, the wooden Angier Duke Gymnasium given by Ben Duke in 1899 and then later allowed to fall into shabby disrepair. Renovated and rechristened "The Ark," the building became a much-used social center for the East campus, the scene of countless late afternoon tea dances and informal evening dances. Refurbishing the interior of the Ark and providing it with furniture and equipment became a major project for various student organizations such as the social standards committee of the student government, the YWCA, and others. The student orchestra that played after dinner each evening in the East campus Union furnished the music for a monthly dance in the Ark, and sororities and other organizations also held formal dances there.[73]

The women were eager for the East campus to equal the manicured splendor of West, for it was an era when strict rules, ones that were enforced, allowed grass to grow where it was planted and shrubbery to survive. Members of the Woman's College class of 1932 assessed themselves to pay for landscaping in front of the library, and flower beds incorporating plants given by an alumna were created in front of the East Duke and West Duke buildings. A woman faculty member, Ruth Addoms of the botany department, led in the refurbishing of the elaborate fountain in front of East Duke that Anne Roney, Washington Duke's sister-in-law, had given to Trinity early in the century, and Ruth S. Smith established a handsome garden in the small courtyard between the Union and Faculty Apartments (later known as Wilson House). "We are anxious," a woman student candidly explained, "to make our campus as beautiful as the men's campus."[74]

Women students were involved in much more than beautification of the campus. One of the chief arguments in favor of the separate women's colleges was, in fact, that they provided women with leadership and service opportunities that were too often denied to them in coeducational situations. While the women students of Trinity College had established their own student government even before Baldwin arrived, and also before the male students established theirs, Baldwin helped in many ways to strengthen and invigorate WSGA. In the publications area, however, there was only one student newspaper, one literary magazine, and one annual, and the women students traditionally were limited to secondary roles in their production as well as on the publications council that oversaw them. Discontent among the women students about the situation led them in the fall of 1930 to tax themselves (at the rate of a half dollar per student) in order to launch their own literary magazine, *Distaff*. Despite discouraging advice about the move from administrators on West, the women stuck by their guns, published the first issue in the spring of 1931, and successfully continued the magazine for the next two years. When the men responsible for the older literary magazine, the *Archive*, agreed to make sure that women received a fairer share of the top jobs as well as better representation on the publications council, the women ceased publishing *Distaff*. Baldwin advised Few that the whole episode together with other projects run by the women had given them "a new initiative and sense of unity and power."[75]

Two other initiatives taken by the students suggest how they viewed Alice Baldwin. As the traditional gift to the college from the seniors, the class of 1935 started a fund to have a portrait of Baldwin painted by a reputable artist, one approved by both the art department and the class president. The portrait was given to Duke University and hung in the Woman's College Union as part of the May Day festivities in 1936.[76] Another gift honoring the dean addressed one of the critical needs of the college, for while a significant number of students held part-time jobs on the campus, especially in the dining halls and library, there were all too few scholarships for needy students. The class of 1943, accordingly and with assistance from other groups, began the Alice M. Baldwin Scholarship Fund to assist each year a senior woman whose academic record was outstanding and who needed the help.[77]

Urged always by Baldwin to attend to their studies as well as to community service, many of the students apparently did both. Through the YWCA, Duke's hospital and legal aid clinic, and various community agencies, a significant number of students donated their time and talents to worthy causes.[78] As for their studies, the fact soon became clear that the large degree of selectivity enjoyed by the Woman's College meant a generally able and hardworking group of students. While there were many excellent students among the male undergraduates, Trinity College in the 1930s and 1940s simply did not enjoy the same degree of selectivity as did the Woman's College, and that meant that Trinity had a larger proportion of weaker students. As a much larger college with a less well organized system of residential housing, Trinity also had certain morale problems, such as those that emerged during the student protest movement of February, 1934, that the Woman's College managed to escape.[79]

Baldwin, wise enough to know that comparisons can be odious and troublemaking, discouraged any public discussion of disparities between the two campuses. Moreover, she and her associates fully realized that the Woman's College possessed certain advantages about admissions that Trinity College did not yet have.[80] Nevertheless, a professor of English privately informed Baldwin that in one of his upper-level, integrated courses, 25 percent of the men had failed, while only 2 percent of the women had done so. Moreover, in a large sophomore course where he used identical quizzes for separate sections of men and women, 22.8 percent of the men had failed and only 6 percent of the women. He explained that he sent the information not only to cheer the dean but with the hope that something might be done towards the "eventual raising of entrance standards on the West Campus (and I don't feel inclined to broach the question myself by sending these figures to the West Campus office)." Thanking the professor and confessing that she rarely had hard evidence as to how the men and women students compared, Baldwin concluded: "It is rather a delicate matter, and there are a good many elements which make it difficult to handle as we should like to."[81]

For all the studying and good works that the women students of the 1930s and 1940s did, they—or certainly most of them—also managed to have a good time, albeit in a stylized and structured way that a later generation of students might well regard as bizarre. The traditional May Day celebration, to name one now-extinct event, disappeared without a trace during and after World War II, yet for many years it was a highlight event on the East campus. In 1933, for example, a senior from Durham, Dorothy Newsome (later Mrs. Robert Rankin), wore the May Queen's crown amidst a court of ten elaborately attired attendants. "Thousands" of spectators, including many alumnae back for the annual homecoming, crowded the lawn in front of the East Duke building as a special student orchestra performed, and "dancers representing cobblers, peasants, shepherdesses, milkmaids, morris dancers, and maypole dancers took part in the program."[82] What the public may not have known is that to help produce the popular pageant, Julia Grout and her associates in physical education contributed countless hours of extra time, calculated by Grout in one year to be 111 volunteer hours for one instructor and 60 for another, and that was on top of 19 hours per week of regular class instruction plus about 3 hours of out-of-class work each week with special clubs such as the swimmers' Nereidian club and the modern dance group.[83]

No one kept track of the hours that the students contributed to many of their own special social occasions. "More scheming, planning, work and secrecy go into the making of a Co-Ed Ball at Duke," the *Alumni Register* reported, "than into any other social event of the school year." Keeping the scheme of decoration a secret, the social standards committee in 1939 managed to turn the women's gymnasium into "a fairyland of loveliness that has meant days of work and planning and considerable expense." At a time when Europe's four-month-old war was still only a distant affair to most Americans, the theme was "Winter Wonderland," and the entire ceiling of the gym was covered with dark blue material sprinkled with stars and hung with icicles and snowballs. In the ceiling's center there revolved "the most spectacular feature of the decoration—a great ball of mirrors on which spotlights played and reflected into the crowd below." With gilded evergreens set in banks of artificial snow about the dance floor, the orchestra was seated in a "stand with a fretwork of icicles."

During the intermission, the names of twenty-one women students, selected by student balloting as the East campus "beauties," were announced. Their photographs would be sent to John Powers, head of a famous modeling agency in New York, who would then select the "ten official beauty queens of the university." Their photographs would appear in a special section of the 1940 yearbook, *The Chanticleer*.[84]

Carefully chaperoned by members of the faculty and staff, such elaborate affairs were the staple of collegiate social life. To ensure that they remained decorous, Alice Baldwin, like her male counterparts on West, took no chances. When on-campus dances were first allowed in the early 1930s, she explained privately that the conditions were carefully monitored, "the most important being the matter of invitations, allowing no one to leave the building during intermission and having the building well guarded on the outside in order to care for any trouble." She added that if the ban on leaving the building during intermission did not eliminate the problem of drinking, "any person who was objectionable would be put off the floor." Duke, she explained, was "trying to keep most of our social life on the campus and under the right kind of control, putting much of the responsibility on the students themselves but sharing with them the supervision and planning."[85]

The myriad social regulations of the Woman's College made sense in an era when most of the women students, and even more so their parents, shared the assumptions on which the regulations were based: the students were there not only to be studious but also to be "ladies," and certain rules concerning proper dress, curfews, sign-out books, and countless other matters were essential for both the sake of propriety and their safety and welfare. When women students, in the changed social climate after World War II, began gradually to rebel against a system which so sharply differentiated them from men students, the whole social structure over which Baldwin presided would begin to change. But in the 1930s and 1940s, outright challenges to the system from the women students were indeed faint and few.

In response to student pressure and evolving customs in society at large, changes did come, as in the matter of women students' use of cigarettes. But in various important areas, change came slowly and in carefully limited ways. For example, when the student council in the early 1930s requested a change in the ban on women students' riding in automobiles, Baldwin and her staff, in consultation with the students, worked out a system whereby a girl who wished to ride in an automobile outside of the city limits had to have special permission in each case from her house counselor or from the dean of residence, Mary Grace Wilson. Any girl who wished to ride within the city limits had to have on file with the house counselor a letter from her parents or guardian giving approval. "It is understood by each student," Baldwin added in what may have been wishful yet noble thinking, "that the permission means riding only and that parking or stopping at any place not on the approved list is not permitted." Freshmen and sophomores, who were restricted in the number of dates they could have weekly, could have only limited permission to ride in automobiles.[86]

Much student concern focused on automobiles, for while the Trinity men were allowed cars after the freshman year, the women were not. Baldwin urged a woman student leader in 1935 not to agitate the question, for in "permitting certain seniors to have cars after the spring vacation, we have gone as far as we intend to go, for the present at any rate. . . . Our reasons are many and seem to us so good that we cannot change our decision."[87]

Differences in viewpoint between Baldwin and the staff on the one hand and the students on the other remained few and quite marginal. As the students themselves lacked any defined feminist ideology on which to base their case, such was also the case with Baldwin. While she strove valiantly, and with considerable success, to guarantee equal educational opportunity for women, she had no agenda, hidden or otherwise, for reshaping society and particularly women's role therein. From the beginning of her career at Trinity-Duke, however, she encouraged the women students to broaden their horizon of expectations and consider professional or business careers as well as marriage. Watching Baldwin complete her doctoral dissertation, publish a book, and gain promotion in academic rank in the late 1920s, the women students in Southgate cheered and admired her. "Alice Baldwin's standards, academic and social," one historian observed after interviewing many of those students, "tended to become those of many of the Southgate women."[88] Though Baldwin obviously could not have as much direct impact on the larger student body of the 1930s and 1940s, she continued to be widely respected and admired even if she was not a role model for those students, still the large majority in that era, who planned to give top priority to marriage and family.

Baldwin, for all her encouragement of careers for women, never denigrated the role of homemaker and mother. In fact, in response to student interest, she initiated a voluntary, no-credit class on marriage and the family for senior women. Meeting with the students on Sunday afternoons in her home, which was behind Carr building and was the former residence of Robert L. Flowers, Baldwin explained that she was "not attempting to teach them, but I am studying with them and shall try to find others who know more than I to help in certain aspects of our study."[89] Thoroughgoing feminists of a later era might label as ambivalent Baldwin's support for the socially responsible homemaker as well as for the career woman. As an historian of Baldwin and the Woman's College has pointed out, however, "her philosophy approached what feminists of later generations would call counseling for choice."[90]

The same dean who studied marriage and the family with seniors helped to make the occasion of Duke University's celebration of its centennial in the academic year 1938–39 a particularly memorable and feminist event for the Woman's College. The worldwide depression of the 1930s as well as the rising tide of totalitarianism in Europe had led to what some feminist leaders regarded as a "women's recession."[91] Baldwin and her colleagues in the Woman's College, however, chose to make their contribution to the centennial in the spring of 1939 with a three-day symposium on "Women in Contemporary Life." With Katherine Gilbert chairing the committee, they set out to illustrate the accomplishments of women in the professions and the arts as well as to provide a forum for the discussion of issues that particularly concerned women. Gilbert explained in one of her letters of invitation that the Duke women wished "to emphasize women's active achievements, demonstrate it in the flesh, and particularly emphasize what women can do at this moment for the cause of peace and freedom." On the other hand, they also wanted "to consider the passive side of the situation: the present tendency to withdraw women from leading intellectual positions and to replace them by men." What had caused that development and how might it be countered?[92] In another letter Gilbert urged an invited speaker to talk about the reasons why more women were not school principals and on school boards and, in general, in more policy-determining positions. To what extent, she pondered, were women themselves "responsible for their hand-maidenly situation, etc."[93]

The careful planning of Gilbert and her committee paid off, for all of the evidence suggests that the symposium was an impressive success in every respect. With the North Carolina branch of the Association of American University Women, the North Carolina alumnae organizations of the stronger women's colleges in the nation, and various other such groups meeting concurrently in support of the symposium, many alumnae of the Woman's College also returned for the occasion. One of them, an educator herself, declared that it was "almost unbelievable that every woman who spoke was a good speaker." Declaring it "the most comprehensive array of ability I ever found on one program," she vowed that she felt "like conquering the world because of my week-end experiences [at the Woman's College]."[94]

Some of the distinguished women who won such accolades for their speeches at the Woman's College were Mary Emma Wooley, the president emerita of Mount Holyoke College, and Meta Glass, the president of Sweetbriar College. Other leading educators on the program were Marjorie Hope Nicholson of Smith College and Marion Edwards Park of

Bryn Mawr College. An ordained clergywoman and distinguished scholar, Georgia Elma Harkness, not only spoke about opportunities for leadership roles for women in the church but preached in the Duke Chapel for the regular Sunday morning service, thus becoming the first woman to fill that role. Florence Ellinwood Allen, the first woman judge of the United States Sixth District Circuit Court of Appeals, and Mary Anderson, director of the Women's Bureau of the United States Department of Labor, represented the legal and governmental realms. Two of the symposium's sessions were devoted to women in the arts. One of them focused on the work of Käthe Kollwitz, the acclaimed German etcher and painter, and an exhibit of her works in the Woman's College library complemented the session. A lecture-demonstration by Hanya Holm, an outstanding American dancer, was the other artistic presentation. There were other women leaders on the program which the president of the alumnae association, who was herself an able historian, hailed as "one of the most perfect experiences I have ever known."[95]

The threat of war that only hovered in the spring of 1939 during the symposium became a grim reality in Europe that September. The Woman's College, however, like most of the nation, was slow in reflecting any impact from what a great majority of Americans initially hoped would not be in any sense their war. College life went on largely as usual with a great deal of studying and academic activity interspersed with dances, ballgames, and the countless other diversions of the era's collegians. Yet the university's commencement speaker in June, 1940—the month France fell—warned that Nazi Germany posed a dangerous threat to American liberties.[96] While many Americans increasingly believed that to be true, a large number in the heterogeneous isolationist camp did not. That battle largely ended when the Japanese attacked Pearl Harbor on December 7, 1941, but even then the Woman's College felt the impact of the war in a much less direct way than did the West campus. There the draft, finally extending even to eighteen-year-old males, became an omnipresent reality. With some of the professional schools such as law and forestry decimated, Trinity College was transformed in 1943 into a vast assembly of student-sailors by the United States Navy's collegiate training or V-12 program. With other military units on campus and the academic calendar totally revamped to accommodate year-round operation, Trinity College became more different from the Woman's College than it had ever before been. One small sign of the times amused Alice Baldwin: she reported to a friend away in military service that it was the Navy "boys who have to get in on time now, and you would laugh to see them run, sometimes leaving the girls high and dry before they get to the dormitory."[97]

The Woman's College, while remaining close to the traditional academic calendar, did eliminate the spring break and provided for a three-year or accelerated program for those students who wished it. With a bustling Red Cross room in the East Duke building, which was heavily used by students, faculty, and staff, the students also volunteered many hours at the Army's Camp Butner near Durham and at Fort Bragg in Fayetteville, North Carolina. Professor Ruth Addoms led in the work on campus for British War Relief, and more than 600 women students received training in extracurricular courses such as first aid, home nursing, and other such war-related activities. The first women students were admitted into engineering, and the number of women majoring in the sciences increased.[98]

With the number and quality of the applicants for admission to the Woman's College increasing throughout the war years, Baldwin and her associates had every reason to take great pride in the college. Yet in one related area Baldwin may well have felt frustrated: she had not done too well in persuading the predominantly male administrators and departmental chairmen at Duke to increase the number of women on the faculty, particularly women in the upper ranks of the academic hierarchy. True, starting in the late 1920s there were, besides Baldwin and then Julia Grout, a number of women who might be regarded as pioneers at Duke: Julia Dale and Ruth Stokes in mathematics, Mary Hendren Vance and Marie White in English, Bessie W. Spence in religion, Ruth Slack Smith in education, Dorothy Mackay [Quynn] in history, and several others, some of whom did not remain long at Duke. The appointment of Katherine E. Gilbert in philosophy in 1930 was important, and in the next several years Frances C. Brown in chemistry, Louise Hall and Elizabeth Sunderland in art, Ruth M. Addoms in botany, Hertha Sponer in physics, Lois Raymond and Marie Thérèsa Dow in French, and a few other women were added to the faculty.[99] The total number of women on the faculty, however, was small both in 1930 and in 1947 when Baldwin retired. Out of 130 full-time members of the faculty in arts and sciences in 1930–31, 8 (slightly more than 6 percent) were women. A decade later, out of 220, only 19 (8.6 percent) were women.[100]

Baldwin had argued from the 1920s on that "there should be on the faculty a fair number of women whose scholarship and teaching ability should win and hold the respect of both students and faculty and who are interested in working with the women students in various ways, who are given positions of high rank, by no means always as instructors, and who will serve as examples of what women can achieve in the academic world."[101] Baldwin, however, did not have the power to select and hire faculty members. Departments, and especially their chairmen and senior members in the early period, did that in consultation with Wannamaker and Few. Baldwin's role in faculty hiring was, therefore, marginal, but some chairmen either consulted her or sought her help when appointing women faculty members.

Baldwin, while privately deploring the attitude of some of the male chairmen and faculty members, was also intelligent and fair enough to recognize that the matter of appointments in a research university was not simple. She well knew, in fact, that most research universities then had few women on their faculties, and in the case of many, none at all. When certain departments at Duke set out, because of the Woman's College, specifically to hire a woman, even Baldwin admitted that there could be unanticipated problems. Such was the case, for example, when Duke's Department of Mathematics lost its only woman member through death. As explained in an earlier chapter, Baldwin pushed for the appointment of another woman mathematician; and though Few and Wannamaker supported her position, the male members of the department resisted when no well-qualified woman candidate for the job could be found. A male got the job, but Baldwin admitted privately that she had been surprised at "how few [women] there are in the country who are making a name for themselves" in the field of mathematics.[103] Women with advanced training in physics were then also relatively rare in the United States, but when the possibility arose for Duke to employ an outstanding German woman physicist, Hertha D.E. Sponer, Few and the male physicists then on the faculty seized the opportunity, as mentioned earlier.

For those few women who were on the faculty or staff, the dean of the Woman's College proved a constant and valuable champion. In addition to trying persistently to educate Few, Wannamaker, and Flowers about the valuable but underpaid work of the residential counselors in the Woman's College, Baldwin argued in behalf of Katherine Gilbert and other women faculty members. Salary raises in the 1930s were few and far between for most faculty members, but Baldwin suggested to Wannamaker in 1939 that since Katherine Gilbert, like Hertha Sponer, had a national and even international reputation as a scholar and was the coauthor of an important new book being published by Macmillan, she well deserved a raise.[104] After not getting a satisfactory response to her suggestions in 1939, Baldwin a year later returned to the matter in a letter to President Few. "It is difficult in some cases," she declared, "for the women on the faculty to get the encouragement they should have." While some departmental chairmen were fair and impartial, she continued, others seemed to encourage men more than women. "I hope the Executive Committee will always keep in mind that the women are few in number," Baldwin added, "and are called upon to give much of their time to committee work and to various student and community activities, and that they do this generously." Baldwin's letter may have been a factor in influencing that year's decisions concerning promotions and salary increases, for at a time when Flowers had requested Wannamaker to hold the line on the budget as much as possible, four of the twelve persons promoted were women and several women were in the small, select group that received the maximum raises given for 1940–41.[105]

Baldwin apparently never complained to the administration about her own relatively modest salary, which reached $5,500. She had to borrow money from a bank to furnish her on-campus residence when she moved into it in 1932 and which the university did supply rent-free. Baldwin received no allowance for entertainment; but that never discouraged her from frequently inviting to her home and back garden a large number of students, staff, and alumnae and other visitors. In her later years as dean, she recalled, she was allowed to secure free cookies from the Union when she entertained some 300 entering women and the freshman advisors each September.[106]

With the strenuous years of World War II behind her, Baldwin, in October 1945, a few months before her sixty-seventh birthday, informed President Flowers that after twenty-three years at Duke she believed the time had come for her to retire and hand over the reins to a younger dean. She and her associates, she explained, had "tried to develop a Woman's College worthy to take its place beside the other colleges and schools of the University and to stand among the best of the coordinate colleges in the country." Thanking Flowers for his own as well as the trustees' "unfailing support" of the Woman's College, Baldwin went on to express certain ideas about how her successor should be chosen and what qualifications she should have. With ideas that were more progressive than those held by the men then in charge at Duke, Baldwin suggested that the trustees, in choosing the new dean, should be assisted or advised by a small committee that included at least two alumnae and at least one woman faculty member. Heading the list of qualifications that Baldwin wished to see in the next dean were scholarly training and experience sufficient to merit the rank of professor in some department as well as "to win and hold the respect of faculty and students for intellectual ability and attainments." Experience in working with both men and women came next on the list, followed by some eight other qualities. Baldwin conceded that her advice might seem like a counsel of perfection and graciously added that she realized that she had lacked some of the specified qualities, but she wanted "an abler and better woman than I to succeed me."[107]

What Baldwin could not mention to Flowers was that many of her friends on the faculty were increasingly concerned about the fact that Flowers, who was seventy years old when he succeeded Few in 1940, gave no indication of retiring, despite his frail health. Wannamaker, second in command, was seventy-two in 1945. Duke University, like all other colleges and universities, faced mountainous problems and challenges as the postwar era began, and vigorous leadership was never more urgently needed. "I wanted to retire myself before people began to feel and to say that it was time for me also to retire," Baldwin later confessed.[108]

Baldwin's request and suggestions fell on stony ground. Wannamaker advised Flowers against an advisory search committee because that would set an unwanted precedent, and, further, the trustees "will look to the President for recommendations of university officers."[109] Flowers himself kept putting Baldwin on hold by saying, every time she brought up the matter of her wish to retire, "I have hoped you would change your mind."[110]

Frustrated by Flowers's refusal to act, Baldwin repeated her recommendation about an advisory search committee in May, 1946. "I believe that the new Dean will have more whole-hearted support from staff, faculty, and alumnae," she argued, "if some opportunity has been given for such recommendation." Failing again to persuade Flowers about the advisability of the more broad-based and democratic procedure, Baldwin finally asked if he wished her to try to come up with some possible candidates for the deanship. When he approved of that approach, Baldwin began the search on her own and interviewed several women in Washington, D.C. One of them was Roberta Florence Brinkley, the fifty-three-year-old chairwoman of the English department at Goucher College and a well-established scholar in the field of seventeenth-century English literature. A native of Georgia and a Phi Beta Kappa graduate of Agnes Scott College in 1914, Brinkley taught for several years in the public schools of Georgia and Tennessee before going to Yale for her doctorate, which she received in 1925. Unfortunately from the standpoint of the Duke deanship, Brinkley took off for research in Britain during the academic year 1946–47.[111]

Baldwin thought a "younger woman" candidate who finally was invited to Duke for a visit made a generally favorable impression, but Flowers did not wish to pursue the matter. After months passed with nothing being done, Baldwin, "in despair," as she recalled, informed Wannamaker that she intended to retire in June, 1947, regardless. That finally started the ball rolling. Flowers was interested in Brinkley, who herself was interested in the Duke deanship, and he dispatched Baldwin to Baltimore to make careful inquiries on the Goucher campus. When Baldwin returned with positive reports concerning Brinkley as a scholar, administrator, and person, that, along with a number of strong letters of recommendation from respected sources, inspired Flowers to act. He and his advisors also liked the fact that Brinkley was a Methodist. He invited Baldwin to attend a meeting with him and five or more top male administrators. When they pressed Baldwin as to whether she would recommend Brinkley for the job, the dean bristled a bit: "I said I would recommend nobody—it was not my business to recommend my successor." She did, however, report that on the basis of both the two hours or so she had earlier spent with Brinkley and the interviews she had had at Goucher, she considered the Georgian to be well-bred, scholarly, pleasant, and possessed of a nice sense of humor. That apparently was enough for Flowers and his advisors, for he promptly cabled Brinkley, whom neither he nor any of the other men had ever seen, and inquired about her possible interest in the deanship. After more cables and letters, Brinkley, who had never seen the Woman's College, happily accepted the offer. "After this severe winter in England," she confessed to Flowers, "the offer of a heated house was wonderful psychology!" [112]

In September, 1947, Alice Baldwin yielded the leadership of the Woman's College to Florence Brinkley. If President Few had been alive he would certainly have been the first to extend the heartiest congratulations to Baldwin and to applaud the honorary degrees that the Woman's College of the University of North Carolina in Greensboro gave her in 1946 and that Duke conferred on her in 1949. She had played an indispensable role in solving a problem that Few had much feared, that of establishing a coordinate college for women. She had also helped prove that in the case of the Woman's College separate could indeed be equal, certainly not as separate academically as Few had initially envisioned but distinctly separate in residential aspects. And perhaps Baldwin might have privately agreed that it was even a bit more than equal in the academic area. Brinkley, in September 1947, took over a truly flourishing college within Duke University. Yet gradually some of the autonomy of the college and the interrelated system that Baldwin had developed—the admissions process, the mature but intellectually lively house counselors, and the social regulations worked out jointly by staff and students—would begin to erode in the years ahead. And when many of the women students themselves began profoundly to question the justification of separate but equal, as would happen in the 1960s, the fate of the Woman's College would be sealed. It would cease to exist in 1972.

9

One Recumbent Too Many: Duke University
and the Ackland Museum of Art

⊸

H L. MENCKEN, the Baltimore pundit of the Jazz Age, drew blood in his famous essay, "The Sahara of the Bozart."[1] Depicting the southern region of the United States in the early twentieth century as one vast desert as far as serious art, music, and literature were concerned, Mencken hurt sensitive southerners all the more because of the large element of painful truth in his indictment. One citizen of Durham, North Carolina, for example, pushed in 1929 for an art gallery on the campus of Duke University because, he argued, there was not a city south of Washington, D.C., "that has a first class painting, a piece of sculpture or other worthy piece of art."[2] William K. Boyd, the prominent Duke historian and director of its libraries, came at the matter from the academic side by pointing out that no southern educational institution then had a "high-grade curriculum and equipment" in the area of the fine arts.[3]

Certainly Duke's President Few felt keenly the institution's lack of adequate attention to art and music as academic disciplines. Few was hampered first, however, by a lack of funds to undertake all that he and others believed the university ought to undertake. Then, when the Great Depression struck in the early 1930s, Duke's expansion into new areas became even more difficult and, for a while, impossible. When the opportunity did arise around 1940 for Duke to acquire an endowed teaching museum of art—possibly with a small starting core collection of paintings, sculpture, and other *objets d'art*—it was blocked primarily by one powerful trustee of the university, William R. Perkins. He believed, passionately and combatively, that an unacceptable stipulation accompanied the proffered gift: that the donor should be interred in the museum in a marble sarcophagus on which rested a recumbent statue of himself. With recumbent statues of Washington Duke and two of his sons, Benjamin N. and James B. Duke, already prominently in place on sarcophagi in the Memorial Chapel within Duke's vast Gothic chapel, Perkins regarded another such statue on the campus as out of the question—simply one recumbent too many. Through a complex set of circumstances and accidents, Perkins won his battle and, to boot, managed to camouflage what he had done. Several years before that happened, however, Duke appeared to be on the verge of receiving a generous gift from William Hayes Ackland.

Born into a wealthy family of plantation and slave owners near Nashville, Tennessee, in 1855, Ackland ultimately inherited about $100,000 from an older half-sister who died only a few months after he was born. While his parents lost most of their wealth before they died, Ackland, through careful investments and conservation of income, accumulated an estate of about $1,350,000 at the time of his death in 1940. Educated at the University of Nashville and the law school of Vanderbilt University, he never had to work but developed a keen interest in art and literature, travelled extensively in Europe, and published a novel as well as several volumes of poetry. Marrying at age forty in 1896, Ackland was divorced by his wife less than a year later, and the couple had no children.[4]

Like other southerners, Ackland was perhaps stung by Mencken's jibes at the cultural desert in the South. At any rate, in 1936 Ackland drew up a will leaving the bulk of his estate in trust. Without consulting any of the educational institutions involved, he directed that his trustees should erect a memorial art gallery, containing his mausoleum, at Duke University, or the University of North Carolina in Chapel Hill, or Rollins College in Winter Park, Florida. When the trustees read the will, they urged Ackland, who was already eighty-one and in frail health, to make more definite plans for the building and to designate the institution where he wished the memorial gallery to be established. Ackland followed this advice and in December, 1936, sent a brief, handwritten letter to each of the three institutions stating his purpose and asking about the conditions under which such a gift might be received.[5]

Ackland never explained just why he picked Duke and the University of North Carolina as possible recipients of his gift. Rollins College was located near his winter home in Ormond, Florida, and, furthermore, he admired Hamilton Holt, the president of Rollins. Yet as Ackland subsequently informed Few and others, he worried about Holt's health and "definitely decided that Rollins College did not possess the financial stability to assure permanency of administration."[6] As for the University of North Carolina, Ackland received two letters in response to his initial overture but had no interview with President Frank P. Graham or other officials there. Ackland later advised Few that he had visited the campus in Chapel Hill but "was disappointed, and did not like public[-]supported universities anyhow."[7]

Ackland's letter to Duke University came at a most opportune time. Earlier in 1936 Few, intent upon trying to strengthen Duke's program in art, had asked the university's architect: "Do you think it would be feasible to add to the Woman's College Library building [of neoclassical design on the East campus] sufficiently to take care of the needs of the Art Department and provisions for its expansion?" The architect had promptly responded with the preliminary plan for such an addition as requested.[8]

Ackland's overture in December, 1936, however, gave Few hope for a happier solution to the art problem. He promptly informed Ackland that Duke would indeed be interested in the possible gift and added that he could "not think of any conditions that the University would wish to suggest." Sending pictures of Duke's buildings to give an idea of the campus architecture, Few invited Ackland to come for a visit or, if that should not be convenient, offered to go himself to confer in Ormond, Florida. Thanking Few for the cordial letter, Ackland explained that he planned to travel northward in the spring and would like to visit Duke then.[9] After the exchange of several more letters, Ackland visited Duke as the personal guest of President and Mrs. Few early in May 1937.

The two elderly southern gentlemen—Few almost seventy and Ackland eighty-one—hit it off from the first. "I should be happy," Ackland declared, "to think of having left behind [at Duke] as pleasant an impression as I carried away with me." Few responded in kind and urged Ackland to plan on spending "at least a week or so" at Duke on the way to Florida in the autumn. "Some active contacts with a young and strong institution like this would no doubt be stimulating to you," Few advised. "It is, indeed a sort of fountain of eternal youth, I find. And those who drink of it either are or at least live like the young."[10]

Even before receiving Few's letter, Ackland informed Few that, having ruled out both the University of North Carolina and Rollins, he was "so favourably impressed" during his recent visit to Durham that he had "decided on Duke." Now the question facing him, he explained, was whether to create a permanent fund or to distribute his estate; he would appreciate suggestions from Few or from the university's trustees once the matter was presented to them. Ackland noted that he should not like to see his "several hundred thousand dollars of securities" sold at a sacrifice. Moreover, the person whom he intended naming as executor of his will urged that the income be allowed to accumulate for a number of years until it amounted to a sum adequate for the erection of the museum building, with the annual income from any remainder being used to make future purchases for the collection.[11]

Few, no doubt mindful of Ackland's advanced age and delicate health, remembered the old saying about a bird in the hand. Moreover, Few genuinely liked Ackland and wished to help him realize his dream in his lifetime. Expressing Duke University's profound gratitude for Ackland's decision, Few declared that he hoped Ackland and Duke could cooperate to find a way "to make some temporary financial provision for going ahead with the building without too much delay, so that your idea . . . might be properly followed out." Tied up with several commencement exercises besides Duke's, Few informed Ackland that Robert L. Flowers, Few's longtime associate in administration, would call on him in Washington in late May, 1937.[12] Ackland gave Flowers a copy of his will, and within a few weeks William R. Perkins, the New York lawyer who served as vice chairman of the Duke Endowment and as a member of the executive committee of Duke University's board of trustees, analyzed the document in a letter to Few. Perkins always worked closely with George G. Allen, the chairman of the Endowment, who also sat on the university's executive committee. Given the fact that the Endowment contributed approximately half of the annual income necessary to run the university, Few carefully consulted both men concerning all large matters of university business.[13]

As for the will, Perkins noted that it placed the bulk of Ackland's property in the hands of trustees who were to establish and maintain the memorial on one of the three campuses specified. If Duke were selected, Perkins continued, it would therefore have on its campus a building controlled by persons not connected with the university; although Ackland's trustees would no doubt endeavor to make the dual arrangement work, "an element inheres which . . . would seriously threaten its value to the University." Perkins suggested, therefore, that Ackland revoke the old will and by appropriate legal instrument go ahead and donate to Duke the securities he wished to dedicate to the memorial. He should do so, however, on the condition that Duke, out of its own funds, would proceed at once to erect the building and pay Ackland during his life either the income from the securities or an agreed-upon annuity. In that way he could both see "the fruition of his charity" as well as save various expenses connected with administering the estate.[14] While the will contained the stipulation concerning the mausoleum and recumbent statue, it should be noted that Perkins then raised no objection to that aspect of Ackland's plans.

Following up on Perkins's advice, Few visited Ackland in Williamstown, Massachusetts, in September, 1937, and explained the preferred solution from Duke's viewpoint. Ackland, without making binding commitments as to what approach he would follow, obviously encouraged Few, for the latter no sooner had returned from New England than he requested the university's architect to prepare preliminary sketches of the proposed art museum. "We are at the beginning of that undertaking [in the art area]," Few explained to the architect, "and haven't much in the way of a collection." He thought it wisest to undertake a building costing from $200,000 to $300,000, so designed that additions could be made when needed. While the exact location had not been determined, Ackland wanted it on the West campus, and George G. Allen thought it might well be situated "on the edge of the pine forest southeast of the flower garden." Few also mentioned that he would submit the architect's sketches to the small staff of the art department, whose members Few had earlier consulted about their needs and wishes. Within a few weeks the architect submitted the preliminary sketches for a small, teaching art museum. He explained that it was to be a one-story building consisting of galleries surrounding a cloistered garden with a fountain in the middle. Top light was provided for most of the galleries, which were of various sizes, but side light could also be had where certain exhibitions might require it. A basement would provide work rooms and a lecture room, and additions could be made easily both on the sides and in the rear. The estimated cost was between $250,000 and $300,000.[15]

Ackland soon asked that the sketches be sent to him together with the cost estimates. His financial advisor urged that the memorial should not cost more than $250,000. Ackland added that he was interested in the annuity plan suggested by Perkins; but he might choose to draw up a codicil to his will stating that if no provision for the memorial should be made in his lifetime, then his executors were to turn over to Duke an amount to cover the estimated cost as soon as they were satisfied that the building would be erected in accordance with any plans that Ackland had approved.[16]

Fortunately for Duke University, Few possessed great patience. Ackland's precarious health prevented him from seeing Few in the fall of 1937. Few explained that Duke expected to be erecting several buildings in connection with the celebration in 1938–39 of the centennial of the institution's founding. If the proposed art museum could be built along with the other structures, Few noted, there would be less cost as well as better results. For example, although the university owned the quarry whence came the stone for its Gothic buildings, getting out all the stone needed at one time was the most economical procedure. "It is a policy of ours," Few declared, "to make money given to us go as far and last as long as is humanly possible." Ackland could not be budged, however, and insisted that for the time being he did "not feel equal to anything but the most urgent affairs."[17]

Although Few visited Ackland briefly in Florida in January, 1938, and the two exchanged numerous notes, not until April of that year did the two men get together again in Washington. Ackland wanted Few to meet Edson B. Olds, Jr., an investment counselor in Washington, who served as Ackland's financial advisor. He was, Ackland thought, "a young man of exceptional good judgment and business ability of which I regret to say I am very deficient." [18] After the meeting Few assured Ackland that he had enjoyed the conference with Olds, who clearly had been to Ackland "a useful adviser" as well as "a genuine friend." At an earlier stage, Few argued, Olds had well advised the creation of a trust fund; but now that Ackland had decided to build the museum at Duke he could certainly work the matter out better for all concerned. "Only one gift in the form of a trust fund has ever been made to this institution in its whole history," Few added. "And it has turned out that this has been the least satisfactory of all the gifts ever made to us." If Ackland chose not to proceed directly with the erection of the museum, then he should in his new will bequeath directly to Duke the amount he had decided upon for the building and designate that any remainder that might be left should be devoted to the purposes of the museum. [19]

To Perkins in New York, Few explained that Ackland wished him (Perkins) to draw up a tentative new will, one that substituted a direct bequest to Duke for the trust-fund arrangement. Olds had promised to send a list of securities to be put up for the building. "My feeling is that the first thing to do is to get the will in order," Few commented, "then we can understand better how to proceed with the erection of the building during Mr. Ackland's lifetime." It was all going to require more time, but Few still believed that it could be worked out satisfactorily. [20]

A small stroke kept Ackland bedridden in late April, 1938, but he continued to display the caution and apprehension of an aging person who had apparently made a lifetime practice of never spending his principal while living off its return: "I hope there may be found some way of making it possible for me to leave the fund for the care and disposal of the pictures and the building of the museum after my death without a sacrifice of stocks and bonds should there be a depression at that period." [21]

Equipped with Perkins's suggested draft of a new will, Few conferred with Ackland and Olds in Washington in late May, 1938. Soon afterward Few informed Perkins that while Ackland stuck mighty close to his financial advisor, it appeared that the will would definitely be changed in such a way, Few hoped, that Duke could accept the bequest. Hearing no more from Ackland for several months, Few dispatched an unusually candid letter in November, 1938. He first explained that he felt it his duty, in light of all the conversations and correspondence of the preceding two years, to "call your attention to some decisions that you yourself will have to make or else in the course of time circumstances will make them for you." After repeating the proposal that he had made earlier to Ackland about his putting up securities to pay for the building and receiving a lifetime annuity from Duke, Few spoke bluntly: "If, on the other hand, you leave the whole matter as it was when I was in Washington, I shall not feel hopeful of the outcome either as to an adequate memorial for you or a real service to the cause of art in the South, which you and I have alike at heart. I feel that I owe it to you to say this much to you. In any case, I am sure that neither you nor others will misunderstand my motives."[22]

Ackland referred Few's letter to both his executor-to-be, Olds, and to his lawyer. Since both men advised Ackland against relinquishing control of his securities, regretfully he felt that he "should be guided by their advice and abide by their opinion." Few could only accept that decision stoically and, as he informed Ackland, "hope that after all things will turn out most to your liking and so as best to secure the memorial that you have had in mind and that has seemed to me to be quite worthwhile."[23]

While Few kept in touch with the aged art-lover and invited him to visit Duke as he travelled to or from Florida, not until the spring of 1939 did Few learn indirectly about a new will, one which he never saw until after Ackland died. The president of Rollins College, Hamilton Holt, congratulated both Few and Duke and explained that Ackland had just informed him of a new will that gave Duke his art collection and a building for it. Holt added that since the University of North Carolina had been ruled out, he had made as strong a case as he knew how to make for Rollins; but he had also advised Ackland that "he would make no mistake" if he selected Duke. "I did this," Holt graciously added, "because I share with many others great admiration in the outstanding progress of Duke and realize its appeal in a case of this kind."[24]

Except for Holt's letter, Few remained more or less in the dark about the matter until after Ackland's death on February 16, 1940. In response to a telegram with the news from Olds, Few summed up his estimation of Ackland: "He was a gentleman of the old school with the refinement that comes out of leisure and good associations. His comrades had gone on ahead of him and he always seemed to me to be a bit lonely and even wistful." With no children of his own, "like other fine-souled men he seemed eager to leave behind him some remembering of him in a tangible form." In view of the many conversations and the correspondence about building the William Hayes Ackland Museum of Art at Duke, Few offered to be of any help that he could. "You will, of course, first need to be on your guard about federal taxes," the realistic president cautioned. "We have experienced lawyers here [at Duke]. If they are needed you can feel free to call on us."[25]

Olds assured Few that Ackland had "never wavered from his desire" to have the memorial museum at Duke and had provided for it in his will. Soon after that letter, John E. Larson, an attorney in Washington who had not known Ackland, but who represented both Olds's firm and the Ackland estate, and a representative from Ackland's bank in Washington visited Duke. Few, along with the university's counsel, T. D. Bryson of the Duke Law School, conferred at length with them, and Few reported promptly to Perkins and Allen in New York that he and Bryson "both feel that we are dealing with first-rate people." They had informed Few and Bryson that the Ackland estate, exclusive of the art collection, was worth a bit more than $1,300,000; that the money would probably be available for the building around the end of 1940; and that they, as the trustees, would want Duke to erect just such a building as it desired. "My impression at the moment," Few optimistically concluded, "is that we are not going to have much trouble with the trustees." Their main concern, in fact, was not about the museum at Duke but about the possibility of a suit to break the will. Few's visitors told him that when the will had been read in Nashville, where Ackland was buried, "there was a good deal of shaking of heads" on the part of certain relatives of the deceased and that "there have been many family complications and even feuds." Since the trustees thought that, at the worst, they could settle out of court if that seemed desirable, Few clung to the belief that "on the whole, it looks . . . to be more promising" than he, Allen, and Perkins had believed when they had discussed the matter the previous week at Duke.[26]

Few's optimism must have been shaken when he shortly thereafter received a stern cautionary letter from Perkins, who made it emphatically clear that he spoke also for Allen. Not yet revealing his particular aversion to the mausoleum aspect that had always been and still remained a part of Ackland's plan, Perkins focused on the question of the control of the museum and its contents. "By the terms of the will," Perkins declared, "the Ackland trustees will forever own, maintain and operate the Ackland memorial and mausoleum." While gifts and art centers were highly to be desired, Perkins admitted, that could not be "at the cost of the principle here involved and with the establishment of a precedent that is most likely to prove embarrassing in the future." Then Perkins seemed to make an important concession and one that precisely foreshadowed the course of action that the Ackland trustees would soon promise to take.

> Of course if a court of competent jurisdiction in a manner binding upon all parties interested should construe the will to mean that the building will become really and truly the property of Duke University, as are the other buildings on the campus, that will be an entirely different thing. And the possibility of such a construction furnishes another reason why you should now frankly state our difficulties to the representatives of the Ackland estate in order that they will have full opportunity to remove them, if possible.[27]

Few, clearly worried by Perkins's stern tone, first conferred with Bryson and then assured Perkins that he and Bryson had pointed out to Larson that "there were certain things in the Will that would have to be clarified before a building could be erected on the Duke campus, and that decisions for Duke would be made by the Executive Committee of the University." Perkins, however, repeated his assertion—which turned out to be something less than the truth—that he would "be happy if a court having jurisdiction of the proper parties should enter a binding judgment declaring that the will properly construed makes the memorial, the mausoleum and the exhibits that may be in it the property in all respects of Duke University." Since Ackland's will gave the residuary estate "absolutely and forever to trustees," however, Perkins thought that Ackland seemed to be thinking "much more of a prominent memorial and mausoleum to himself than of any gift to Duke." Ackland, as Perkins viewed the matter, had done nothing to entitle him to having a location on Duke's campus to satisfy his "posthumous vanity."[28]

Clearly disturbed by the drift of the ongoing correspondence, Few took the trouble to write a long, detailed letter—six single-spaced pages—in which he recapitulated his entire relationship and negotiation with Ackland. Repeating his personal liking and admiration for the man, Few emphasized that he had "not the slightest doubt" that Ackland meant to give outright to Duke the museum and his collection. "His advisors, keeping in mind their own interests," Few suggested, "controlled him with their advice and prepared a will that seems not to have done what I believe he intended to do." Regardless, Few concluded, he could not "escape the conviction that I, at least, am under an obligation to him and his memory to do what I can to see that his wishes are carried out." Few pointed out also that the university's architect had planned a memorial room within the museum, as Ackland had requested. Not only had Ackland approved all those plans, but the mausoleum feature had been included in Ackland's own plan from the very beginning.[29]

As Few sought to placate Allen and Perkins, John E. Larson, attorney for the Ackland estate, prepared to defend the will against those who sought to break it. Few joined most of Ackland's close friends and certain of his relatives in deposing that he was unquestionably of sound mind and judgment when he made the second will. Ackland's niece, the daughter of his deceased sister, refused to join those relatives who sought to break the will. Ackland, apparently on good terms with the niece and her two children, had left his house in Florida as well as $20,000 to the niece and $10,000 to each of her two children. Trouble came, however, from the four children of his late brother, Joseph H. Acklen [sic] of Nashville, to each of whom Ackland had left only $1,000.[30]

As the legal battle over the will unfolded, in July, 1940, Few and Bryson conferred in Washington with Ackland's trustees and their attorneys. The Duke representatives explained that the university's executive committee would desire before acting either to accept or reject the gift "a construction by the courts determining the status of the proposed building and the works of art to be placed therein." Both the Ackland trustees and their counsel gave assurance that they fully understood the situation and "would cooperate with Duke University in every way to obtain such a declaratory judgment."[31]

Given that attitude on the part of Ackland's trustees and their counsel, one may conclude that if President Few had not died of a coronary thrombosis on October 16, 1940, the Ackland Museum may well have been eventually built at Duke. But Few's death, added to an already complicated situation, proved crucial. He was succeeded as president by Robert Lee Flowers, who was seventy years old and not in robust health. Yet Flowers seemed both to the trustees who elected him and to the alumni and those faculty members who applauded the choice the logical successor to Few. As one faculty member put the matter, there seemed to be universal satisfaction that "this justly deserved recognition and honor has come to you."[32] Yet there no doubt were some in the Duke community who privately wondered if the presidency of the institution should be regarded primarily as an honor to be bestowed in recognition of past service, no matter how long or meritorious. Where Few, at any rate, probably would have fought to carry out the plans that he had come to share with Ackland, Flowers never showed the slightest inclination to do so when strong opposition arose.

In August, 1941, Duke University, or Flowers acting for it, received a summons in a civil action in the federal district court in Washington. Duke—along with Olds, Ackland's bank, his niece and her two children, and Rollins College (to which Ackland had left a small bequest)—was named as a defendant in a suit brought by the four children of Joseph H. Acklen to have William H. Ackland's will declared invalid. Having given up on the earlier attempt to attack Ackland's mental competence, the plaintiffs now sued primarily on the grounds that "defendant Duke University has not consented, and cannot consent lawfully, to the erection on its campus" of a memorial building subject to the terms and conditions prescribed in Ackland's will.[33]

The summons triggered hasty, decisive, and final action by the executive committee of Duke University. In early September, 1941, the committee, obviously led in the matter by Perkins, unanimously resolved that "Duke University should decline, and it hereby does decline, all of the provisions of said [Ackland] Will with respect to said institution . . . and that prompt notice by the counsel for Duke University be given to the executors and trustees under said will."[34]

Shocked upon receiving this news from Bryson, John E. Larson in

Washington promptly telephoned Perkins in New York. Larson first declared that the trustees and lawyers for the Ackland estate felt that they had been treated badly by Duke University and that they believed that Ackland had had a right to assume, from what Few had written and stated repeatedly, that the gift would be accepted. Thus the second will had made no alternative provisions for the property left to Duke. Perkins replied first that from the beginning he and other trustees had cautioned Few that nothing he said or approved in the matter was binding upon the university until the executive committee gave its approval. Perkins next moved to the matter of the property's being controlled by Ackland's trustees, which Perkins thought seemed to show the "distrust of Mr. Ackland of the Trustees of Duke University." Larson countered that he and his associates in the matter would get a court order clearing up all those aspects of control in a manner fully satisfactory to Duke, although Duke obviously would have to cooperate in that step.

Then Perkins finally, and for the first time, let the cat out of the bag. He informed Larson that

> there was a larger and really more important phase, namely the erection of a mausoleum with a recumbent statue [of] Mr. Ackland on the campus; that while I had nothing to say against Mr. Ackland, whom I had never met, I did have a lot to say as to such a precedent for Duke University and frankness compelled me to tell him that I would oppose to the very utmost any such precedent, and felt that there never had been a time when even Dr. Few could have gotten the sanction of the Trustees for the project set up in the will of Mr. Ackland, as much as Dr. Few was admired and respected.[35]

Flowers, upon reading Perkins's account of his conversation with Larson, immediately advised Perkins, "I approve heartily of what you said."[36]

Perkins, Flowers, and others associated with Duke would obviously have been happy if the whole matter of the Ackland will could have quickly been forgotten. But such was not at all the case. Larson, Olds, and their associates were not without connections and influence in Washington. Prominent Trinity-Duke alumni in the capital began to ask embarrassing questions. Among those alumni were Daniel C. Roper, a university trustee who had served as Secretary of Commerce under President Franklin D. Roosevelt, and George Venable Allen, who was already embarked on a distinguished career in the Department of State. Allen, a native of Durham, took a particular interest in the matter and had several conferences with Edson B. Olds, Ackland's executor. Allen, after reading all the correspondence and other documents in Olds's files, pointed out that Perkins had made no objection to the mausoleum feature when he had read Ackland's original will in 1937 nor indeed at any time prior to 1941. "Mr. Ackland went to his death," Allen concluded, "in the fullest conviction that the provisions expressed in his will would be carried out by Duke University." Allen also noted that even Flowers, when Larson had visited him at Duke in the spring of 1941, had shown great enthusiasm about the proposed art museum, according to Larson's account. All the greater was the shock, therefore, when notice arrived in Washington of the executive committee's action in September, 1941. After summarizing Perkins's concerns about both the control of the museum and the mausoleum, Allen argued: "After as impartial a consideration as I have been able to give the case, it seems to me beyond any doubt that Duke University is under moral obligation to accept the bequest, out of respect for the memory of Dr. Few if for no other reason."

Allen went on to argue that he, as a loyal Duke alumnus, was anxious for the university to accept because "no single addition to the University would add more to its cultural breadth and to the cultural development of North Carolina and the South than an important art museum and collection, with classrooms and ateliers for art study." He thought it hardly necessary to point out that Ackland had "felt justified in resting his negotiations with the President of the University." As for the question of control or ownership of the museum, Allen pointed out that the lawyers for the executors were convinced that the federal court in the District of Columbia would sustain their contention, in a case scheduled within the next few weeks, that both building and contents would belong to Duke in fee simple. Since the executive committee had not waited for the outcome of those proceedings, Allen judged (correctly) that the mausoleum feature was the true obstacle. On this point Allen turned eloquent.

He first declared that no one connected with Duke University could fail to honor the Duke family for its "many and matchless benefactions to the University." But Allen felt certain that none of that family would hesitate to welcome the "relatively small but important memorial which Mr. Ackland desired to contribute to the University which they made great." James B. Duke, Allen continued, had inherited from his father "an aspiration for Duke University as broad as the seven seas" but had also undoubtedly realized that the university he saw building during his lifetime could not become complete in a few years, or even in many years. "He wanted it to acquire the many attributes of a great institution of art and learning and culture which are acquired only in time." In short, the Dukes themselves, Allen insisted, would certainly have regarded Ackland's esteem for Duke University as "the compliment which it was intended to be." Allen closed his ten-page, single-spaced letter with a cautionary word: "The people of North Carolina and the South would regret exceedingly to know that the Trustees of Duke University had deprived them of the opportunity of adding a notable contribution to the cultural development of the State."[37]

Despite the cogency and eloquence of Allen's statement, President Flowers remained unmoved. He merely commented that "my friend George Allen is not familiar with a good many points connected with the whole matter." Flowers, who usually wrote quite brief letters anyway, explained that when he next saw Roper, and presumably Allen also, he would be glad to supply all the details and thus demonstrate that the executive committee had indeed acted wisely.[38]

Flowers, Perkins, and their fellow members of the executive committee had more to worry about than prominent alumni in Washington. As news and gossip about Duke and the Ackland will spread across North Carolina, John F. Bruton, the chairman of Duke's board of trustees, nervously informed Flowers that certain trustees believed that the full board should have a voice in the matter. While Bruton wanted Perkins to make a full and detailed statement about the Ackland will at the upcoming meeting of the board, perhaps he could also make a "delicate reference" to the matter of the executive committee's having had to act on its own in the matter.[39]

Perkins, as it turned out, proved unable to attend the meeting of the full board in late January, 1942. He sent a long letter, however, which recapitulated his version of the Ackland affair and which notably deemphasized his objection to the mausoleum feature while concentrating on the question of ownership and control.[40] If Perkins had been in attendance, he no doubt would have vigorously opposed and probably have blocked a resolution which the trustees present passed without objection: that Duke University (i.e., Flowers) should issue a public statement explaining its position in the Ackland affair.[41]

Many of Duke's trustees, clearly either half-informed or virtually ignorant of the complicated details in the matter, were embarrassed by the stories and rumors that newspapers across the state had begun to carry. The matter had become public knowledge mainly because John E. Larson and his associates, themselves left in an embarrassing and frustrating quandary by the action of Duke's executive committee, had remembered Ackland's first will, which listed the University of North Carolina as one of three possible sites for the museum. Communicating first with a former governor of North Carolina, O. Max Gardner, Larson and the Ackland trustees were soon conferring with Frank P. Graham, the president of the University of North Carolina, and other officials in Chapel Hill. It turned out that what the executive committee of Duke University had turned down in September, 1941, the comparable committee for the University of North Carolina voted to accept—if they could get it—in January, 1942.[42] The *Winston-Salem Journal* reported that former Governor Cameron Morrison had joined with Gardner and others in supporting the University of North Carolina's bid for the museum. "When Duke University, which likes money, wouldn't have it, that's a queer thing," Morrison reportedly commented. "And being a Scotchman and a dirt farmer, I want to know why."[43]

Morrison, for all his curiosity, probably never learned why. One prominent Duke trustee and member of the executive committee assured Flowers, who all along preferred silence about the matter, that "far more good than harm will come out of a tactful statement."[44] But Perkins emphatically disagreed. "Who is it that calls this action [of Duke's executive committee] in question so that thereby a public explanation is required of us?" Perkins demanded of chairman Bruton. A statement, Perkins insisted, would only fan the flames of public controversy and "produce greater trouble than any that now exists." Furthermore, Perkins vowed that if the precedent of such a public statement were set "it will make it extremely difficult for me to properly act for Duke University in the future, not knowing when this precedent may bring future trouble of the same kind on my head." George G. Allen assured Flowers that Perkins was "eternally right in his advice that it would be far better to make no public statement whatever." Bruton remonstrated that many trustees were troubled and that the "attitude of 'the public be-dammed'" was a dangerous one. There were even rumors abroad, Bruton noted, that the reason Duke declined the gift was the provision in the will for a recumbent statue of Ackland. "So far as I am concerned that is a reason sufficient for me to vote against accepting the bequest," Bruton confessed, "but that alone would be provocative of ridicule."[45] Bruton argued in vain, for Flowers assured Allen that he did not intend to issue a statement because he believed it "would be a very great mistake." Instead, Flowers proposed to talk over the matter in a face-to-face conference with Bruton.[46]

Thus neither the public nor most of Duke's trustees, for that matter, ever learned exactly why Duke declined the Ackland bequest. Something like nine years of complex, tortuous litigation were required before Larson and the Ackland trustees finally gained the green light from the federal courts to locate the museum at Chapel Hill. John E. Larson had good reason, therefore, to feel satisfied and happy on September 20, 1958, as he addressed the audience assembled there for the dedication of the William Hayes Ackland Art Museum of the University of North Carolina. He announced that several years after Ackland's death, when the trustees had paid all the taxes and other obligations of the estate, the executors had turned over approximately $955,000 to the trustees. That amount represented roughly the cost of the building being dedicated, including its equipment. There remained about $285,000 in the accumulated income fund which was immediately available for the purchase of art objects. Finally, Larson noted, the permanent endowment fund then had a value of about $1,450,000 and earned an annual income of about $65,000. Larson tactfully commented in passing that Duke had originally declined the bequest primarily for "sentimental reasons."[47] He might well have said that the statue over the sarcophagus in the new building at Chapel Hill had been for Duke University simply one recumbent too many.

One
Recumbent
Too Many

10

Theological Education
at Duke University, 1925–1950

⌀

O F ALL THE PROFESSIONAL schools that were built around Trinity College in the gradual creation of a complex research university, none was more important to President Few than what was originally called the School of Religion. This was so not simply because Few himself was a deeply religious man. Nor was it merely because James B. Duke, in his indenture making provision for the new university, had paid particular homage to religion: "I recognize that education, when conducted along sane and practical, as opposed to dogmatic and theoretical lines, is, next to religion, the greatest civilizing influence," he had declared. And J. B. Duke had gone on to urge that the courses at the new university should be arranged "with special reference to the training of preachers, teachers, lawyers and physicians."[1]

If neither Few's nor J. B. Duke's personal beliefs were the basic explanation for the priority that Few gave to the School of Religion, one might well ask, what was? The answer lay in the type of university that Few first envisioned and then persuaded his coworkers and allies, including J. B. Duke, to support. Obtaining his doctorate in English at Harvard in the 1890s, Few had watched Harvard's president, Charles W. Eliot, during a portion of the four decades that Eliot led in what Few termed the transformation of "a provincial New England college into a true American university," and Few became throughout the remainder of his life a close student of higher education in America.[2] Keenly sensitive to the inherent tension between the teaching and research functions of major universities such as Harvard, and quite properly fearing that undergraduate education could easily be given short shrift in the rush toward graduate and professional training, Few meant for Duke University to be different in several ways. One would be its emphasis on both teaching and undergraduate education, matters that some research universities notoriously downplayed.

Few also had early arrived at the belief that a serious rift had developed between many of the leading universities and religion. Not only were state-supported institutions inhibited in their approach to religion by the constitutional wall separating church and state, but many of the private or voluntarily supported universities had so distanced themselves from their church-related beginnings that few vestiges of the original ties and common purposes survived. Having fought for and gained freedom in religion, too many educational institutions took that victory to mean, according to Few, freedom from religion. A trustee of Duke who also served as the president of the Association of American Colleges, John W. Chandler, asserted late in 1988 that "in too many contemporary universities the conversational range is artificially and unrealistically narrow in that it excludes or is embarrassed by questions of values and faith."[3] Few began commenting on the same development even before he became the president of Trinity, and the avoidance of just such narrowness or embarrassment became one of his prime goals, first for Trinity and then for Duke.

"Material progress, enlightened government, and popular education are not enough to insure our well-being," Few asserted in 1909. "If in our eagerness to progress in these directions we neglect the cause of religion, we shall be like the foolish man who cut off his right hand in order that the left hand might be strengthened." In order to have a stable, vigorous civilization, Americans would always need "to cultivate a virile and aggressive religious faith" and to make "education and religion mutually helpful and both contributory to human progress."[4]

Recognizing that Trinity's location in the South posed real problems as well as offered great opportunities, Few envisioned the institution as having the "further duty of mediation between the religious conservatism of this region and the great intellectual ferment of the age."[5] The South's religious conservatism, which Few spotlighted long before World War I, had, by the time Duke University was established in the mid-1920s, developed a powerful fundamentalist wing, and the "duty of mediation" that Few had described had become more urgent than ever.

For President Few, as for a significant portion of those who worked closest with him in leading Trinity College and then in organizing and launching Duke University, the motto of the college and then of the university—*Eruditio et Religio,* Knowledge and Religion—was no mere shibboleth. Likewise, the commanding presence of the great, towering chapel that J. B. Duke wanted on the high ground in the center of the Tudor Gothic buildings that he provided for Duke University's new West campus was no simple architectural or aesthetic device. Rather it was a dramatic symbol of priorities shared by the philanthropist and the institution's leaders.

Related to these basic reasons for the prominence of the School of Religion in the plans of Few and J. B. Duke was the institution's historic ties with the Methodist church. Those ties had begun informally with the establishment of a modest, one-room school in Randolph County in 1838; they became formalized in the late 1850s when the North Carolina Conference of the Methodist Episcopal Church, South, adopted the school officially, and it changed its name to Trinity College.[6] The Methodist tie was not only crucial in the very survival of the college in the poverty-stricken decades of the late nineteenth century, but it was also the primary reason why Washington Duke and his family had become the institution's chief benefactors from about 1890 onwards.

No one worked harder or more successfully in maintaining those ties with Methodism than William P. Few. Yet a close and friendly bond had to go along with a certain distance too. By the time he became president of Trinity, the college had achieved what Few, as well as many other leading American educators, considered essential for a stable and secure college or university: a permanent and self-perpetuating board of trustees. Having learned from history as well as his personal experience in Trinity College's famed Bassett affair of 1903, Few balanced a genuine belief in democracy with a realistic awareness that, in one of his favorite phrases, periodic "gusts of unwisdom" were a characteristic and dangerous feature of democratic societies. "In the long run of years there can be no security for a college," Few avowed in 1908, "which in its actual control is too close to the untrained mass of people, whether this mass is represented by a state government subject to popular will or represented by a church organization that reflects too immediately the changing moods of the multitude." In words that echoed famous phrases of Abraham Lincoln, Few declared that to "believe in the future of America at all, or for that matter to contemplate human life with any degree of patience, one must believe that the people wish to do right and in the long run and in the main will do right; but this does not mean that they have the expert knowledge to manage a college any more than it means they are competent to argue a point of law before the Supreme Court of the United States, or to treat an acute case of pneumonia."[7]

Translated into practical terms, the formal or legal relationship that Trinity College had with Methodism came down to an arrangement concerning two thirds of the trustees, an arrangement that was continued without modification when the university was organized. As mentioned earlier, while the trustees of Trinity-Duke were in reality a self-perpetuating body of thirty-six persons, the names of one third of these were submitted for election, which in actual practice was confirmation, by the North Carolina Conference of the Methodist Episcopal Church, South. The newer Western North Carolina Conference of the same church "elected" another third, and the alumni of the institution gave approval to the final third. In explaining the arrangement to an official of the Carnegie Foundation soon after the university was organized, Few noted proudly that none of the three confirming bodies had ever failed to ratify a person whom the university's trustees had nominated.[8] While Few was a lay Methodist (unlike his predecessor, John C. Kilgo, who became a bishop in 1910), he worked diligently all of his life on every level—local, district, conference, and general conference—of the Methodist church. He noted in 1938 that he had not missed a meeting of the annual conference for thirty years, and especially during the last two decades of his life informed observers acknowledged him as one of the most influential and dedicated laymen in the church. Such loyal service to Methodism also characterized Robert L. Flowers and numerous others associated with Few in Duke's top administrative echelon.

The tie with Methodism, more historic and more meaningful in human terms than the lofty grandeur of the chapel, anchored Duke University in the community and symbolized its overarching aim. Without religious tests prescribed in its charter or statutes for either faculty or students, Duke University, in Few's words, stood for "a conception of religion as comprehending the whole of life and of education as having to do with all the powers and capacities of our human nature." To bring the two together in the "generous service of humanity" was the great purpose and aim of the university.[9]

Such were the considerations that helped give, in Few's mind, a special emphasis to the School of Religion at Duke. There especially Few understandably expected to find strong allies in the struggle to maintain the desired relationship between education and religion, and while the school would be carefully ecumenical, it would be the most directly meaningful and practical link with Methodism. Trinity had received only relatively small amounts of money directly from the two Methodist conferences in the state, and those sums had gone towards the support of instruction in Bible. That pattern would continue, with money from the church, in small amounts at first and gradually growing larger, going to the School of Religion.

In organizing what was meant to be a major, national university around what had been essentially a North Carolina Methodist college, Few well knew that there would be difficulties aplenty. For one thing, the composition of both the student body and the faculty would gradually change, with both becoming significantly larger and more religiously and geographically diverse than had been the case with Trinity. Speaking candidly of the new challenges facing Duke University, Few posed this question in 1925: "Is our constituency wise enough and good enough to produce a soil and atmosphere that will sustain a great university and one worthy of Mr. Duke's wonderful gift? Our people and their leaders must make answer in the great and eventful years that are just ahead of us."[10] The School of Religion would play a central role in helping Few a few years later to give a positive answer to the question he had posed.

A movement to strengthen religious instruction at Trinity had begun, in fact, several years before the university was organized. Eager to expand Trinity's religious work so that through academic or extension programs it might "reach directly to every nook and corner of the State," Few requested the two Methodist conferences in 1922 to underwrite two more faculty appointments in the Department of Religion. The conferences agreed to do so, and Few began speaking of Trinity's hopes for a School of Religion, one offering not only Bible studies but also church history, public speaking, and missionary training. That ambitious plan, however, like Few's abortive attempt to launch a medical school in conjunction with the University of North Carolina, never materialized.[11] The munificence of J. B. Duke finally allowed a number of Few's and Trinity's ambitious plans to start becoming realities after December, 1924.

Selection of the deans for Duke's new professional schools proved to be one of President Few's most important and challenging tasks. In terms of long tenure in the deanship, Few would not have the good fortune with the School of Religion that he had with the medical school. Yet in both cases he started the process by seeking advice from distinguished leaders in the respective fields. In the case of the School of Religion, Few invited the dean of Yale's divinity school, Charles Foster Kent, for a conference in Durham. Among other matters on which Kent offered advice, he suggested a man he considered of "unique promise and ability" and one who could prove to be, Kent believed, "one of the corner stones in the large work" being planned at Duke.[12] Although Few tried to pursue the suggestion, Professor Millar Burrows, Kent's nominee and a rising luminary in biblical scholarship, proved unavailable to come to Duke.

Few also turned to the executive secretary of the Association of American Colleges, Robert L. Kelly, for suggestions, since his work gave him a wide knowledge of academic life, and in addition he was a recognized authority on theological education in America. "We need men of size and men wise and good enough to make the best use of first rate opportunities, in the Law School, School of Religion, and in almost any subject," Few explained, "provided the man is really first class and might be available for us here."[13]

The initial suggestion of the person who was destined to become the first dean of the School of Religion apparently did not come from Kelly, however, but from James Cannon III, a future dean of the school himself. A graduate of Trinity in 1914, Cannon, after obtaining a master's degree at Princeton University and being ordained as a Methodist minister, had joined the Trinity faculty in 1919 as an assistant professor in biblical literature and missions. During the academic year of 1924–25, he was on leave while securing an advanced degree at the Princeton Theological Seminary. Edmund D. Soper, Cannon's nominee, was a professor of the history of religion in Northwestern University. A graduate of Dickinson College and Drew Theological Seminary, Soper was well known in his field as the author of two prominent books in comparative religion. Few, having learned that Soper was a good teacher as well as a thorough scholar, gained additional interest when Cannon, who had heard Soper in the pulpit, reported that his preaching was "constructive and stimulating, though not oratorical."[14] The fact that Soper was a Methodist, albeit of the northern variety, no doubt heightened his appeal, for Few and others at Trinity-Duke had long been outspoken, prominent supporters of the movement to reunify the Methodist church and end the sectional schism that had occurred before the Civil War. Another young faculty member in religion at Duke and also a Trinity alumnus, Hersey E. Spence, had urged Few to seek "a big man whose standing is unquestionable and of international reputation to head the school." Few clearly needed no such urging, for that was his oft-expressed view all along; but he probably did not agree with what Spence termed a further "sad observation" after a survey of the field in the South: "We shall have to turn to northern trained and northern born men for our new professors, especially for the head[s] of our departments," and as for the deanship especially, the sort of "first class man, trained in a university, that has a modern outlook" did not appear "to be in the Southern Methodist church."[15]

Knowing the academic side of Southern Methodism extremely well, Few apparently did not fully share Spence's gloomy assessment about regional possibilities. At any rate, while the question of the deanship remained unsettled, Few displayed his canny ability in spotting certain kinds of talent by recruiting for the School of Religion a remarkable young southerner, Bennett Harvie Branscomb. A graduate of Birmingham-Southern College with both a bachelor's and master's degree from Oxford University, Branscomb was a promising New Testament scholar. Destined also to be a future dean of the Duke school as well as a highly successful and significant chancellor of Vanderbilt University, Branscomb in 1925 was, of course, only at the beginning of his outstanding career. Few had tried in vain to bring him to Trinity two years earlier, and with the success in 1925 Few boasted to a prominent Methodist layman who had assisted in the matter, W. R. Odell, that Duke had obtained "the best available man in the South for our department of religious training."[16] Branscomb himself seemed equally pleased, for he wrote Few that with Duke's "magnificent opportunity" and "the need throughout the South of the work that Duke can do," he felt "very distinctly to have found a vocation worthy of a lifetime."[17]

No doubt cheered by that success, Few pushed to land Soper. With growing national publicity about Tennessee's law banning the teaching of Darwinian evolution in the state's schools and a furore that would lead to the famed Scopes trial in July, 1925, Soper understandably worried about whether the affair "would affect the possibility of securing men from the north, even in North Carolina." He thought Tennessee had done "a very dangerous thing."[18]

Whatever fears Soper had about the repercussions from the fundamentalists' crusade must have been allayed when he visited Duke at Few's invitation in May, 1925. Having gotten additional information on Soper even before the visit, Few soon after it reported to Cannon that Soper had "made a fine impression on practically everybody" and it was clear "that we want him."[19] Soper, however, liked his position at Northwestern. Moreover, he worried about the multiple responsibilities that Few, at least initially, envisioned for the dean of the School of Religion: he would not only have the large chore of being the organizing and foundation-laying dean, but he would also be expected to serve as vice president in the Division of Student Life as well as being the university preacher. Soper protested that the combination of the three tasks might be possible during the first year or two, but the load would become crushing after "things got under way."[20]

No doubt recognizing the reasonableness of Soper's views, Few relented about one of the three tasks, that of being the university preacher, and declared that he would largely follow Soper's advice when a decision had to be made about that. And as for salary, Soper's career would certainly be put on "an even sounder financial basis" if he came to Duke.[21]

With Northwestern struggling to hold on to Soper, Few made a strong appeal. He argued that Soper would have a better opportunity at Duke "to promote religion through education in the coming twenty-five years" than at anywhere else in the world. "Where is there another institution," Few asked, "that has at once the resources, the purpose to give the Christian program a central place in education, that has a wide open field and the human material, and all this in a liberal atmosphere of Christian freedom and truth and in a section of the country that is growing rapidly, that is full of hope, and that has its face steadily toward the future?" Soper would have a place of leadership in a formative period, and if more mundane considerations needed to be weighed, Duke would provide a house as well as a salary ($8,000) higher than Northwestern was paying. Since Duke aimed at cross-fertilization, Few argued, Soper could certainly keep his membership in the New York Methodist Conference.[22]

Soper accepted. Few, no doubt happy and relieved to have named the first of the deans for Duke's professional schools, expressed his delight at the prospect of having Soper "so intimately associated with me in that part of the work here which I have most at heart." The two of them, Few noted, would have to give a good part of the coming year to thinking through their problems. Meantime, Duke also needed a dean for its law school, and if Soper would confer with the law dean at Northwestern and then transmit suggestions, that would be appreciated.[23]

Even before Soper's acceptance, Few advised Branscomb, who wished information to pass on to possibly interested students, that Duke would certainly offer the master's degree in religious education in the 1925–26 academic year, as had been done in the previous year. Candidates for the bachelor of divinity degree should be encouraged to enroll, for Few felt sure that such a degree would be established within the next two years. He expected the School of Religion to be fairly well set up by September, 1925, and fully so by September of the following year.[24]

That Few and others at Duke rejoiced over Soper's acceptance of the deanship should occasion no surprise. That the *Christian Century*, one of the nation's leading religious journals, found the appointment hopeful and significant was a more important omen. "Tennessee is not all the South," the *Christian Century* commented, and neither had "the court at Dayton [for the Scopes trial] heard all there is to be said as to the cultural and religious future of that great part of the country." The best evidence for that, the magazine continued, was Soper's appointment at Duke. In the field of comparative religion, he occupied a position which would have been "repudiated with honor by practically all church bodies of half a century ago." Yet Soper's books revealed a "catholicity of spirit sufficient to recognize the genuine religious significance of all the ethnic faiths."

The *Christian Century* went on to explain that Soper had the promise of a free hand in building what was expected to be the most influential school of religion in the South, one that would train both ministers and scholars in religion. While serving as dean, he would also be a vice president in immediate charge of all the religious interests of the university. "It is an unusual organization for a school," the journal noted, "and gives the man chosen for the position an unusual opportunity." That a person of Soper's kind had been chosen "augurs well for the future religious life of the South."[25]

With Soper coming to Duke in September, 1925, he and Few generally proved able to work together reasonably well, as far as surviving records indicate. In fact, an historical problem arises from the fact that frequent conferences between the two men eliminated the need for most written communications, and there is uncertainty as to the precise contribution each man made to the development of the School of Religion. On one basic matter concerning standards, the two men strongly agreed: the school would be strictly professional in that only college graduates would be accepted. This was not then the case with many theological schools in the nation and certainly not with most of them in the South. The significance of the standard is further heightened by consideration of the fact that a survey of Southern Methodist clergy in 1926 revealed that only 4 percent were graduates both of college and a theological seminary; 11 percent were college graduates; and over half (53 percent) had only a high school education or less. Peter Cartwright, the famed circuit-riding evangelist of the early nineteenth century, had boasted that uneducated Methodist itinerants had set America on fire religiously before educated ministers had been able to light their matches.[26] Overthrowing the vestiges of that tradition, perhaps once suited to a raw frontier society, was one of the chief purposes of Few, Soper, and Duke's School of Religion.

Soper, as part of the planning and recruiting process, traveled to confer with various leaders in theological education. A professor at Union Theological Seminary in New York, believing that there was too much individualism and compartmentalization in the work of the leading older seminaries, urged that Duke try to start its theological work as a "cooperative enterprise, each instructor being willing to be a part of a team." As for emphases, he counseled that whatever else Duke's school might do, its graduates "should know their Bible[s], know how really to use them." Both goals were, of course, more easily pronounced than accomplished, but Soper confessed to Few that his various conferences made him "feel more than ever the responsibility of getting the best men" for the school. "We must be able to win the respect of those who are watching theological education," he urged, "—and men are the most important element."[27]

Soper also had ideas about the physical facilities that were yet to be built for the school. Construction of them on Duke's new West campus would not begin until 1927. Soper began early, however, to push for certain features in the building that would eventually house the School of Religion. He pled for a sufficient number of offices for the faculty, something perhaps taken for granted in a later and more opulent era but hard to come by in earlier decades. And he particularly desired that there should be in the school's building a small chapel seating from 250 to 500 people. "We must have such a place," he maintained, "a place that is churchly, for many things connected with teaching homiletics and the conduct of worship, as well as a quiet place for the meditation and quiet meetings we must frequently hold."[28]

Few, wrestling with an unending series of problems, may have forgotten

Soper's plea for a small chapel or may have thought that the planned proximity of the School of Religion to the great university chapel that was to be built obviated the necessity of a smaller, separate chapel. At any rate, as the planning of the Tudor Gothic buildings for the West campus proceeded, Soper became seriously disturbed at one point and, after a conference with Few in the spring of 1926, wrote him a letter explaining that their views might be so far apart as to make it difficult for them to cooperate further in making the School of Religion what it ought to be.

Soper avowed that he had two prime convictions concerning the place of the school in the life of Duke: "One is that it must be an integral part of the life of the University, socially, and intellectually, as well as religiously." Also, he believed that there had to be a certain unity within the School of Religion which would make possible certain results not possible otherwise, and above all, there had to be religious contacts between the persons in the school that would give it its characteristic atmosphere. In physical terms, Soper wanted in the building a room for a social center and, more important he said, a small chapel. The energetic chairman of the English department, Professor Frank C. Brown, was Few's chief liaison with the architects designing all the new buildings and with the building committee of the Duke Endowment that was supervising and paying all the costs. Brown, according to Soper, seemed to think that an assembly room or large classroom would suffice for the school's religious gatherings, but Soper, obviously aroused, insisted that his own idea was different. "It is to have a real Chapel," he explained again, "where at times the theological students might meet as a united body and there stimulate that sense of religious unity without which we might just as well not attempt to start a School of Religion at all."[29]

Soper got the chapel. When the new building—named for James A. Gray, an important trustee of Trinity College—that would house the School of Religion, along with various other occupants, was opened in 1930 it contained the small chapel for which Soper had battled. Named for Brantley York, the Methodist preacher who in the 1830s had served as the founding principal of the modest school that evolved into Duke University, the chapel would, as Soper predicted, play an important part in the life of the school.

Soper left his imprint on things that were more important than physical facilities. In an important memorandum in June, 1926, he spelled out for Few various important policies that needed to be settled and agreed upon before the formal opening of the school could be announced. Branscomb later recalled that he had worked closely with Soper in all of the planning for the school, so the memorandum probably reflected his thinking also.[30] At any rate, on the matter of admitting only college graduates, Few and Soper agreed, though the policy would certainly mean small enrollments for an unknown period. On the matter of scholarships for students, Soper explained that in most theological seminaries students not only received free tuition but also paid no room rent; many seminaries also gave scholarships in a range from $100 to $200 per year and helped students to secure part-time work in nearby churches. Since queries were coming in, Soper noted that clear answers to questions about costs to the students had to be forthcoming.

Here, on the matter of scholarships for theological students, Few had a brainstorm. Trinity College had long given, in effect, full tuition scholarships to pre-ministerial students. Now that Duke University was preparing to move to a higher level of theological training, it was Few, according to the later testimony of the second dean of the School of Religion, who hit on an imaginative way to solve the critical problem of student scholarships.[31] Despite widespread local and national publicity to the contrary, Duke University was actually hard pressed to find the money to do well all that Few had persuaded James B. Duke it should try to do; and the School of Religion, receiving virtually no income from tuition, would be costly enough even without the added burden of scholarships for students. Yet in the indenture creating the Duke Endowment, completely apart from special provision made for the university, J. B. Duke had stipulated that a certain percentage, 4 percent to be exact, of the annual income of the Endowment—a sum that would over the years grow progressively larger— should be used to "maintain and operate" rural churches of the Methodist Episcopal Church, South, in North Carolina.[32] Having been J. B. Duke's primary agent for aid to North Carolina Methodism, aid that began a decade or more before the Duke Endowment was created, Few was more knowledgeable and experienced in the matter than any one else. When confronted with the problem of scholarships for students in the School of Religion, he soon came up with the idea of summer apprenticeships for the students in North Carolina's rural Methodist churches, work that could be a valuable learning experience for the student and for which the Duke Endowment could pay; that pay, in turn, could cover the students' basic living expenses for the academic year. It was a plan destined to play a most important role in Duke's theological training.

If Few solved that particular problem, Soper probably deserves the credit for coming up with a solution to another difficult tangle that he described in his memorandum of June, 1926. To an extent that Few apparently had not contemplated, Soper believed that a sharp and clear demarcation had to be made between the School of Religion and the undergraduate work in Bible required of all students and in elective undergraduate courses in religion. In other words, it was Soper who argued for and won the organization of a separate faculty for the School of Religion just as in law and medicine. Declaring that decisions about the policies and personnel of the teaching staff were crucial in determining "the kind of a school it is to be for decades if not for a century," Soper warned that unless care were taken "we might easily wreck our vessel in the very act of launching it."

Soper confessed that in dealing with personalities, "sensitive natures are to be found in the religious field as in all others." But human sensitivities and egos notwithstanding, there were realities about graduate-level theological education that had to be faced. Soper then noted that "the doctor's degree is not a *sine qua non* of success in doing work of the highest grade," and he conceded that exceptions might be made in special cases. (Presumably his own case was one such exception.) The fact remained that "the schools of religion in the United States which take front rank have faculties in which most of the faculty possess the [doctor of philosophy] degree." This meant, he believed, that at least two of the men already in religion at Duke, Hersey Spence and Jesse M. Ormond, should be utilized primarily in undergraduate teaching. Soper thought that James Cannon had the potential to develop into an effective graduate-level teacher in the field of missions and that Branscomb needed to be given the opportunity to complete the doctorate (which he did at Columbia University). Hiram E. Myers, a Trinity alumnus who had served as pastor of Duke Memorial Methodist Church in Durham, had been appointed to the Duke faculty in 1925 and given leave to do more graduate work at Boston University. Soper judged that while Myers would be clearly valuable in undergraduate courses, the question of his teaching in the School of Religion could best be left open.

Aside from Soper's responsibilities as vice president for student life, he had an apparently genuine interest in enriching Duke's undergraduate program in religion. He urged that, in addition to the courses in the Bible, there should be elective courses in religious education, missions, the Christian social program, and the history of religion. The School of Religion and the undergraduate department would, of course, have a close relationship and share a number of faculty members, but Soper convinced Few that formal, organizational separation of the two entities was the soundest procedure.

For the School of Religion itself, Soper's memorandum set forth a clearcut plan. Historically there were, he suggested, five basal "chairs" or departments in most theological schools: (1) systematic theology or Christian doctrine; (2) New Testament literature and interpretation; (3) Old Testament literature and interpretation; (4) church history; and (5) practical theology and homiletics. To those fields of study various others were often added, but he thought the two most important were history of religion or comparative religion (his own field) and Christian missions. Those were the seven "chairs" that Soper believed should be filled before Duke announced the opening of its school.

Religious education could be organized separately, Soper noted, but he thought it preferable to include it as an integral part of the school. Within that field, the three particular areas that he believed should be taught were the psychology of religion, methods in teaching religion, and the administration of religious education.[33]

Just how much of Soper's somewhat elaborate memorandum was a restatement of matters that he, Branscomb, and Few had agreed upon earlier and how much of it was novel to Few is not known. What is clear is that the first dean had described and given the rationale behind the essential pattern that the School of Religion would follow. Moreover, appointments to fill most of the important "chairs" that Soper had described were being made throughout 1925 and 1926.

Two important appointments, both of men destined to be future deans of the school, came in the spring of 1926. Elbert Russell, a Quaker with ancestral roots in North Carolina, received his doctoral degree at the University of Chicago after graduating from Earlham College. Teaching at Swarthmore when Soper interviewed him there, Russell had publications in the field of New Testament studies, and Soper, obviously much pleased by him, reported to Few that he believed Russell could fit splendidly into the Duke situation. After Russell's visit to the campus, he promptly accepted Few's invitation to teach in the general field of biblical interpretation.[34]

In the field of church history, Paul Neff Garber proved easy to find, for he was already a member of Duke's Department of History. A native Virginian, he graduated from Bridgewater College and then attended Crozer Theological Seminary before transferring to the University of Pennsylvania for a doctorate in American history. Born and raised in the Church of the Brethren, he had become a Methodist, one who perhaps displayed the alleged zeal of the convert, for he worked with unusual relish and productivity in the area of Methodist church history as well as in the operations of both the School of Religion and various church bodies.[35]

The appointment made in the field of Old Testament studies proved, in the long run, much more problematical than the others. Allen H. Godbey graduated from Morrisville College and then received his doctorate at the University of Chicago. Author of an impressive number of publications in a difficult, somewhat esoteric field, he was clearly an able, albeit idiosyncratic scholar, and he was named professor of Hebrew and Oriental languages in the School of Religion in the summer of 1926. Few received a number of unambiguous recommendations of Godbey, but one correspondent, after expressing satisfaction about Duke's interest in Godbey, noted, somewhat bluntly, that he was "a queer duck, but a very great scholar."[36] Elbert Russell, in his initial interview with Soper, had spoken favorably of Godbey, and for some time after the appointment Few and others seemed pleased about it. Few, in fact, wrote in 1927 to thank the person who had first called attention to Godbey and added that he was "a bright, a learned, and an admirable man and it is a satisfaction to us all to have him here." Few thought that it was a sad reflection that in an organization like the Methodist church for a quarter of a century "so loyal and competent a man could not have been made use of."[37] Unfortunately for both Godbey and the School of Religion, the situation would drastically change for the worse within a very few years.

Ironically, the appointment that seemed to be the hardest to make also proved to be of short duration at Duke. In June, 1926, Soper advised a correspondent that for every name he and Few had suggested to them for other positions, they received at least five in religious education. Commenting that "it is easier to get a man than to get rid of him if he is not desirable," Soper went on to say: "We feel that there is much superficiality in this field [religious education] and what we are looking for is a man or men who not only have the technical training but who have religion, sound common sense and philosophical background."[38] Presumably Soper finally found a person meeting such expectations, for Howard M. LeSourd was named to the School of Religion's original faculty in the field of religious education. An undergraduate at Ohio Wesleyan who had also received a master's degree at Columbia, LeSourd was a graduate of Union Theological Seminary and was brought to Duke from his teaching post at Western Theological Seminary. In 1929 he would leave Duke for a position at Boston University.[39]

Not all of Few's and Soper's recruiting efforts were successful, of course, but one or two of their failed attempts are suggestive of the caliber of person being sought. Paul B. Kern, then dean of the theological school at Southern Methodist University, planned to leave that position in order to return to the preaching ministry. Few, undoubtedly with Soper's full concurrence, sought to bring Kern to Duke and enlisted the aid of the Methodist bishop E. D. Mouzon in the endeavor. "What we do in the next few years in setting up this institution will last as long as American civilization endures," Few declared, "and everybody who can help ought, I think, to be willing." Noting that Kern felt something of that pull towards Duke, Few admitted that Kern also felt drawn toward the pastorate. Could not Bishop Mouzon help work out an arrangement whereby Kern could both teach at Duke and take the pulpit of a Durham church?[40] Despite all of Few's arguments and efforts, he failed with Kern, who later became a Methodist bishop. Another person who was also destined to become a prominent Methodist bishop, Ivan Lee Holt, declined Duke's invitation in 1927 to teach in the School of Religion.[41]

Despite these rebuffs, a core faculty was on hand for the opening of the school in the fall of 1926: Branscomb, Cannon, Garber, Godbey, LeSourd, Russell, and Soper. There were others who taught part-time in the school, and additional appointments would be made in due course; but Duke's first professional school opened its doors to eighteen full-time students, all college graduates, in September, 1926. Formal exercises marking the opening were held on November 9, 1926, the day before the meeting in Durham of the North Carolina Conference of the Methodist church. To begin the exercises, Ralph W. Sockman, a distinguished minister from New York, preached at a special morning service at Trinity Church, the oldest Methodist church in Durham, and a communion service followed. The planners of the occasion (Few and Soper) explained: "It seemed especially fitting that the spiritual note which is to characterize the life, not only of this School, but of all of Duke University, should be prominent in the first hours of the life of the new School."

Luncheon at the sparkling new Washington Duke Hotel in the center of downtown Durham followed and featured an illustrated lecture by Professor Frank C. Brown showing the plans for the future buildings of the university, including, for the first time, a slide showing the architect's drawing of the building to be occupied by the School of Religion. Visiting guests were then taken from the luncheon for a tour of the new campus and the proposed site of the building.

The formal opening of the school, held that afternoon in Duke Memorial Methodist Church, took a more academic tone. A robed procession preceded statements by Few and the chairman of Duke's trustees, Joseph G. Brown, and an address by Bishop Mouzon to which Soper responded. Again justifying the purely graduate orientation of the school, the planners declared that the day had come "when a minister must be able to interpret the age in which he lives to his congregation, and this cannot be done without far more preparation and study than have been necessary in the years that have gone by." A reception and dinner that evening at the Washington Duke Hotel, with brief remarks by visitors representing various theological schools and universities and colleges, closed the all-day affair.[42]

Having started with an appropriate flourish, the fledgling school grew steadily. By 1931 there were 133 men and ten women enrolled as candidates for the three-year bachelor of divinity degree. They came from 35 colleges and universities, with Duke heading the list with 60 students and Wofford College next with 8 students. Well over half of the students (83) still came from North Carolina, and while Methodists constituted the overwhelming majority (130), there were 13 students from other denominations and faiths, including 2 Baptists and 1 Jewish student.[43]

Starting with only five students in 1927, the summer program for ministerial students working in rural Methodist churches had grown to sixty-seven by 1931. Since it was for many years the only source of scholarship aid in the School of Religion, the program was obviously a crucial one;

J. M. Ormond, director of the school's rural life department, was in charge of the program. Mostly serving as assistants to regular pastors and directors of religious education, the theological students had few expenses while performing the summer work, since local churches furnished their room, board, and transportation. For their work, the university (which was in turn repaid by the Duke Endowment) advanced to each student $200 per semester to cover room, board, and other basic expenses during the school year.[44]

The work plunged students quickly and directly into challenging situations. In the summer of 1931 two students who were assigned to rural churches on the Goldsboro circuit in the eastern part of the state reported that they had conducted a twelve-day revival meeting with two preaching services daily and a Bible school for about fifty children every morning at 8:30. Encouraged by the "splendid crowds" at the small church, the students added that they had "visited in practically every home" and were pleased that "eighteen new members were brought into the church on profession of faith." They were proceeding next to open another revival meeting at another church on the same circuit.[45]

Reports of similar exertions were numerous, but there were also problems. Students fresh from their classrooms at Duke were not necessarily primed for functioning well in all circumstances, although in Ormond's noncredit practicum for the students in the program he tried to alert them to possible problems and pitfalls. Despite that, an experienced minister in the mountains of western North Carolina reported on his dealings with a summer assistant from Duke and declared that "when you are dealing with mountain people you are up against circumstances that are different from those to be found at any other place." The Duke student assigned to him, he declared, had argued with him since arriving, and though he had warned the student not to go "off on a tangent on the idea of Pacifism and the Racial question," the student had done exactly that in his evening sermon. When warned again, the student avowed that "unless he could preach [on] those two things that he could not preach."[46]

Few had spoken of Duke University's having a "duty of mediation" between the South's religious conservatism and the intellectual ferment of the era. No doubt Ormond, Garber, and other professors in the School of Religion had a more immediate, literal task of "mediation" between their students and older Methodists, lay as well as clerical, in the region. At any rate, the summer program, despite occasional problems, proved to be a valuable mainstay of the school's scholarship support as well as a pioneering experiment in training for work in rural churches.

As valuable as the program was, there were also troubling limitations to it. While North Carolina in that period remained one of the nation's most rural and agricultural states, cities and towns were growing rapidly too;

yet by the terms of J. B. Duke's indenture, assistance was barred to towns having more than 1,500 people. Garber, who was a zealous member of the Western North Carolina Conference and had numerous close friends among the Methodist ministers in many Piedmont cities and medium-sized towns, complained privately about the fact that Duke theological students could not be assigned there, for he believed the benefits to them would be even greater than from the rural work.[47]

The Duke Endowment scholarships were also available only to Methodists, and for a school that wished to be ecumenical in both faculty and student body, that restriction posed problems. One dean at a neighboring college advised that he could send additional, promising students to the school if aid were not limited to Methodists.[48] A few non-Methodist applicants to the school even proposed changing their denominational affiliation, but the School of Religion strongly discouraged such a step.[49] An additional limitation was that the summer program was open only to unmarried students on the grounds that the stipend paid was inadequate to support a family.[50] Theological students, like other graduate students in that depression-wracked era, were not as apt to be married as would become the case in later decades, but the restriction still affected some persons interested in becoming ministers. On the one hand, therefore, the opportunity for scholarship aid from the Duke Endowment proved to be a vital godsend to the young school. There were troubling limitations, however, and the leaders of the school would later move to ameliorate the situation.

E. D. Soper, however, hardly remained long enough as dean to have a part in solving later problems. Having played a crucial role in establishing and shaping the School of Religion, he resigned in 1928 to become the president of Ohio Wesleyan University. While the faculty of the School of Religion passed appropriate resolutions expressing appreciation for Soper's contributions and regret at his leaving, Few commented privately that Soper had been certain to go sooner or later since he was "a rolling stone" and had not, at any rate, "been altogether satisfactory on the inside."[51] Soper, in turn, had his own reservations about Duke's president, for he warned his successor as dean that one could "work *under* President Few but not *with* him."[52]

Regardless of Soper's assessment, Few may not have been altogether fair in his appraisal of Soper. While the challenge of a college presidency plus a larger salary may have been the chief attractions for Soper, the fact that Few had assigned him not one but two quite different tasks, both of them challenging and time-consuming, might have played a part in his decision to leave Duke. In addition to the deanship, Soper had, at Few's insistence, served as vice president for student life. While the double appointment aptly demonstrated Few's aspirations for the moral tone and religious dimension of Duke University, it undoubtedly posed problems for Soper. The scope of the work was broad, for, as he had sketched it out in a memorandum to Few, Soper's task was nothing less than the promotion of the highest standard of living—physical, social, moral and religious—among the Duke students. Working with a prestigious committee that included, among others, Few, Dean Wannamaker, James DeHart (the director of physical training and football coach), and J. A. Speed (the college physician), Soper oversaw an ambitious program that was intended to have an impact upon undergraduate class work and examinations, athletic activities, social affairs, student organizations, and other facets of university life. He and his coworkers were pledged to promote "an outlook on the world and its problems which shall lead to the formation of plans [by the students] for a career which shall not only be honorable but which shall make a contribution to the good of society." Moreover, through all the work of the student life division "the voluntary principle is to be scrupulously adhered to."[53]

The whole plan, so admirable in many ways, exactly reflected President Few's thinking. Yet it was highly unusual, to say the least, to ask the dean responsible for leading in the establishment of what was intended to be a high-quality professional or graduate school of religion to expend such a large portion of his time and energies in carrying out the other task, one which had a significant but not exclusive undergraduate focus. The fact that Few, after Soper's departure, did not again attempt such a doubling up of duties also suggests that even he had learned that his original plan was probably not the best one.

Soper's successor as dean of the School of Religion, Elbert Russell, certainly never faced the double challenge that had confronted Soper. Russell, in fact, escaped a large portion of the administrative burden of the school itself, for at the same time he became dean, Paul Garber was named as registrar of the school and thereby shouldered responsibility for dealing with the students concerning their academic programs and various other concerns. Energetic and personable, Garber proved to be adept in the performance of his task and clearly relieved Russell of a great deal of work and responsibility. Russell later recalled, in fact, that he had not wanted to become dean, for he had no zeal for administrative work. When he tried to persuade Few of that fact, however, and urged that Branscomb be named dean, Few countered that he did not wish at that stage to sidetrack Branscomb from his promising scholarly career. Moreover, Few, personally proud of having had a Quaker grandmother, liked to emphasize that Methodists and Quakers had united to establish the university's forerunner, Union Institute, back in 1838, and he clearly liked the idea of a Quaker's becoming dean of Duke's School of Religion. Russell reluctantly assented.[54]

Even before Russell took over the deanship from Soper, other important additions were made to the school's faculty. Soper had been saddled with two difficult jobs and had persuaded Few that it would be impossible for him to serve also as the preacher to the university. Slated eventually to fill that spot, Franklin S. Hickman joined the faculty in 1927 as professor in the psychology of religion. He would later become also the school's first professor of preaching (or homiletics). Born in Indiana in 1886, Hickman worked for the Pennsylvania Railroad for a number of years before his ordination as a Methodist preacher in 1913. He then proceeded to obtain his formal education: an undergraduate degree from DePauw University, a theological degree from Boston University, and a doctorate from Northwestern in 1923. He taught at the Chicago Training School for Home and Foreign Missions from 1920 to 1924 and at Hamline University for one year before coming to Duke. When the Duke Chapel was opened on the West campus in 1932, Hickman was named as one of the two preachers to the university (Elbert Russell was the other), and from 1938 to 1948 Hickman served as the first dean of the chapel.

Another important addition to the faculty was made in 1928. Gilbert T. Rowe, after graduating from Trinity College in 1895, taught Greek for a year at Hendrix College before being ordained as a Methodist preacher. After serving in a number of churches, mostly in North Carolina, he became editor of the *North Carolina Christian Advocate* in 1920 and in the following year the book editor of the Methodist Episcopal Church, South, and editor of the *Methodist Quarterly Review*. Clearly one of the intellectual leaders of Southern Methodism, Rowe possessed the rare combination of extensive pastoral experience, wide knowledge of the church and its headquarters office, and scholarly interests. Few and Soper, again enlisting the assistance of W. R. Odell, set out to recruit Rowe for the faculty of the School of Religion; in 1928, after considerable debate on Rowe's part as to where he could best serve in what he regarded as a most critical time for religion in the South, they succeeded in bringing him to Duke as the professor of Christian doctrine.[55] Not only would Rowe remain at Duke for many years, serving as acting dean of the school during Russell's absence on leave in 1933–34, but he proved also to be a valuable link between the school and the Methodist church. Popular as a speaker and teacher on campus as well as off, Rowe, according to one official in the Methodist church's headquarters, was "one of a small group of men who know the general situation in the [Methodist] church and who have the ability to interpret the Bible from a liberal point of view and yet with satisfaction to the Church." Another perspective on Rowe came from a former student who said, "I had rather hear him call the roll of the class than to listen to most preachers."[56]

If Rowe's appointment worked out well, that of Allen H. Godbey, who had first been suggested by a person in the Methodist headquarters office, unfortunately did not. Apparently a prickly scholar in the Old Testament field, Godbey, according to Russell's guarded comment to a colleague at another university, had a "violent quarrel" with prevailing theories of literary criticism of the Old Testament and along with possessing "very decided views" was "somewhat disposed to believe that the newest and least conventional opinion is the right one."[57] Eccentricities and difficult personalities are, of course, not rare in academic life, but in Godbey's case the matter apparently reached extreme, even bizarre proportions. Believing himself unfairly treated and thwarted in his desires about his courses and teaching, he began at some point around 1930 publicly attacking and criticizing his colleagues in the School of Religion, and especially Few and Russell. By late 1931 the situation had become so troubling and demoralizing that Few, backed by the faculty of the school as well as by a special investigatory committee of the trustees, moved to suspend Godbey from his teaching duties while keeping him on full salary. After taking his regular sabbatical leave with pay in 1932–33, Godbey lost his position at Duke. "It is a rather sad necessity that led to this," Russell noted privately, "and I think under the circumstances the University has been very lenient."[58] To a recent alumnus of the school and former student of Godbey's, Russell explained further: "We tried very hard to get along in the hope that he could stay with us until the retiring age . . . but his trouble developed so rapidly that it became intolerable. I realize that his attitude put many of his students in a rather difficult situation before it became clear that he was a mentally sick man. I want to assure you that I never let his attitude interfere with my friendship for him and efforts to help him."[59]

Branscomb, on leave in Germany for the year, informed Russell that students had reported their resentment of Godbey's classroom attacks on Russell. "I think your attitude toward him throughout your administration has done as much to win for you the affection of the student body as any other thing," Branscomb declared. "And I might also add the faculty in that statement."[60] Godbey attempted to publicize his grievances and to write quite long, elaborate, and accusatory memoranda to Few and various others. While the whole episode was painful for all parties involved and caused embarrassment to Duke and especially the School of Religion, it proved to be transitory.

No doubt partly because of the Godbey affair, the school moved with great deliberation in making its next appointment in the Old Testament field, but what turned out to be a fortunate appointment, originally in religious education, was made in 1931. Few and Soper apparently first encountered the name of Hilarie Shelton Smith in 1926 when trying to assemble the original faculty for the school.[61] Trying in vain to obtain another person for religious education, they then settled on a friend of Soper's, Howard H. LeSourd, who, as mentioned earlier, left Duke soon after Soper did. Early in 1930, J. Q. Schisler, a prominent Methodist official to whom Russell and Few had turned for advice, wrote that Shelton Smith was "perhaps the best man in sight for your purpose." A native North Carolinian and graduate of Elon College, Smith had served as an Army chaplain in World War I and then obtained his doctorate at Yale. After a stint with the International Council of Religious Education, he had taught at Union Theological Seminary in New York but reportedly had found "the chilled atmosphere in that institution so out of harmony with his own Christian viewpoint that he did not find it pleasant." Brought back to teach at Yale, Smith, according to Schisler, possessed "those qualities which will enable him to grow with your institution"—if he could be moved from Yale.[62]

Encouraged by such letters, Russell and Few brought Smith to Duke for an interview in May, 1931, and soon afterwards offered him the job. Although Yale tried to keep him and he said he had found his situation there "delightful," Smith graciously explained that Duke had impressed him as having a great future. Furthermore, the job appealed to him, he added, "as being an opportunity to render a bit of service to the section of the country that I love."[63] Later shifting the focus of his teaching and research interests from religious education to the history of American Christianity and religious thought, Smith was destined to play a leading role in the strengthening of the scholarly dimension of Duke's religious studies.

Another appointment made in 1931, while originally meant to be temporary, also turned out to have a long-lasting impact. With Branscomb away on leave, Russell, working closely with Few, sought a one-year replacement in the New Testament field. Although Few was then "chary of Chicago theology," according to Russell, the dean held out for and finally won the appointment of young Kenneth W. Clark.[64] A native New Yorker, Clark graduated from Yale before obtaining his theological degree from Colgate-Rochester Divinity School and his doctorate from the University of Chicago. Clark proved to be an able teacher and energetic scholar, and his appointment was extended for a second and then a third year when Branscomb returned only to take on half-time duty as Duke's director of libraries. When the depression's grim consequences hit Duke, belatedly but seriously, in 1933–34, Russell had the unhappy task of first talking with Clark and then notifying him formally in June, 1933, that due to the "exigencies of preserving the departmental balance" in the School of Religion, Clark's appointment would terminate at the end of the next academic year.[65]

Happy at Duke and facing an academic job market woefully shrunken by the depression, Clark appealed directly to Few. After coming as a one-year substitute for Branscomb in 1931, Clark noted, he had been asked to remain for a second and then a third year, with the suggestion (or hope?) expressed by Russell in the spring of 1933 that the third appointment was "more permanent" than in the first two years. Clark accordingly brought his furniture down from Rochester, New York, only to be told by Russell, who was no doubt pushed by Few in the matter, that the appointment would have to end in 1934. Rather than harping on that aspect, however, Clark emphasized his contributions to the school through his teaching, which Branscomb endorsed; through his scholarly work, which was in its early stages but certainly promising; and through his service to the Duke community as well as the larger community, which included a large amount of speaking to a number of Baptist and other groups.[66]

Fortunately for Duke and its School of Religion, Few relented and Kenneth Clark did not become a victim of the depression. Neither did the young ministers who graduated from the school in growing numbers in the 1930s, for they at least found employment. The South in which most of them found their first appointment, however, was indeed a poverty-stricken region, quite different from the relatively prosperous Sun Belt of the late twentieth century. Not all of Duke's new bachelors of divinity went to stricken rural churches, of course, but many of them did—and wrote back giving glimpses of their work. One young alumnus in rural Louisiana reported that he was "literally an itinerant Methodist preacher." His first appointment had been to a circuit with four churches, but after a few months he gained a promotion to a federated church of four different denominations that paid $1,800 a year. "There are also many Jews in the town and they contribute to the support of the church, and often attend the services," he stated. "The spirit of cooperation is fine, and I find no trouble in 'Being all things to all men.'"[67] Exactly how the Duke mentors felt about such supreme adaptability on the part of their students is not known, but Garber shared the letter with his colleagues and Few.

A Duke product serving in the remoter, mountainous regions of western North Carolina, "where revivals are attended but culture unknown," informed Garber that his book, *The Romance of American Methodism*, had been a great inspiration. "When I'd see such unthinkable conditions prevailing," the fledgling minister explained, "I'd think about the pioneers that had worse conditions than I, so I really enjoyed my work."[68] Another beginning minister in a small eastern North Carolina town wrote that he hoped he could fulfill Garber's expectations, but "if my work is to be judged by the amount of money the charge gives, I am afraid I will fall short of your expectations."[69] From an isolated section of Kentucky, a young alumnus, receiving around $400 a year on a four-church charge, reported that he had had no trouble getting into the conference because he was the only candidate with the bachelor of divinity degree. But there were perhaps unexpected challenges: "Dr. Garber, we are going to show the Ky. Annual Conference that a Duke student will Go Any Where. We will also show them that we are Christ-like. Yesterday I had to stop twice during my sermon and pray, because of the disturbance." Since he said he had found the local people not in the habit of attending church, the enterprising young minister was emphasizing pastoral visiting, writing for the county newspaper, and utilizing the Parent-Teacher Association. Inviting Garber to come ride the circuit with him, he promised that there were "plenty of horses, the roads are rough and get slick with mud, but not slick for horseback riding."[70]

A similar story of spartan circumstances came from Mississippi, where an alumnus reported that his four churches were far apart and located on unimproved mud roads. Since people had been generous about bringing in gifts of food, the annual salary of $585, plus a $50 supplement from the Methodist mission board, stretched fairly far. The biggest expense had been a secondhand Ford coupe costing $225. Offsetting that expense, however, haircuts in the village cost only 15 cents. Though the parsonage had neither electricity nor running water, the young minister assured Garber that he was "very happy" and enjoying life to the fullest.[71]

Not all of the letters that came back from the alumni focused on physical circumstances. One new preacher in western North Carolina assured Garber that the most important part of his work, "next to the reverential part of it, has been the desire to make you never regret that you recommended me for the place here." Then he recounted a story that must have inspired understanding smiles in the School of Religion. Confronted with his first wedding and it a double one, the alumnus became rattled in reading the names on the licenses and tried to marry an absent mother to one of the grooms until the bride intervened (gently, one hopes) to straighten out the matter. "In spite of it all, they were well married," the minister concluded, "but the strain on my nervous system was dreadful for a week afterwards."[72]

Just as Duke's beginning ministers faced unforeseen mishaps and various economic hardships, students wishing to enter the School of Religion encountered formidable obstacles as a result of the great depression. No sociological data on the early students or their family backgrounds are available, but most of them probably came from quite modest circumstances. At a somewhat later date, Harvie Branscomb made an interesting observation about the theological students that was probably quite valid for the earlier students as well. "The ministerial student group on the whole is probably superior in character and purpose and, perhaps, equal in native ability to other professional groups," he noted, "but decidedly more limited in social background and worldly experience." Thus the school faced the double responsibility, according to Branscomb, of selecting only strong candidates for the ministry and planning their training "so as to overcome as much as possible deficiencies in social experience, cultural knowledge, and above all, good judgment."[73]

Regardless of the students' socioeconomic backgrounds, there is good evidence that many of them, especially in the 1930s, had to scramble quite a bit to attend the School of Religion. One determined entrant from Oklahoma wrote that he was bound to come to Duke even if he had to hitchhike, for he had run short of money. On second thought, he believed he could cover his transportation to Durham but would not have any money when he got there.[74] Young Kenneth Goodson, a future bishop, was unable to have his transcript from Catawba College sent to Duke because he still owed money to Catawba. The college agreed, however, to send his diploma to Duke, thus allowing him to begin his theological training. "Then I have made arrangements to pay them ten dollars a month until the bill is paid . . . ," Goodson explained, and when that was accomplished they would forward the transcript. "It would certainly be a relief to me if I could find work after I get to school," he declared.[75]

Garber and, no doubt, some of his colleagues exerted themselves to find part-time jobs for the students. Since only a limited number of scholarships were available from the summer program of the Duke Endowment, many students served as assistant or part-time pastors for churches in the Durham area and further away. The students also lined up for part-time jobs in the library of the School of Religion and elsewhere on campus. Garber's prompt response to young Goodson was typical of many such letters he wrote: "I assure you that I will be glad to help you secure outside employment if I can possibly do so."[76]

Theological students had much more to cope with, however, than their financial circumstances. The school required for the bachelor of divinity degree, in addition to the three years of demanding course work, the completion and satisfactory oral defense of a full-fledged thesis. That it was a demanding requirement is shown by the report in 1936 that thirty-two former students in the school had completed all requirements for the degree except the thesis; approximately half of the thirty-two were said to be writing their theses in absentia, for which special permission was required.[77] Garber supplied further evidence about the faculty's standards for the thesis when he wrote in 1936 that two students had failed on their theses and that "a new day seems to be dawning for us in that more respect is being given in the preparation of good theses."[78]

The pendulum may have swung too far in the direction of "respect" for the thesis. By 1938 the faculty had restudied the matter and concluded that because the thesis had come to occupy a place in the curriculum out of proportion to that intended by the faculty, it "should be strictly limited in scope and bulk." Except in unusual and especially approved cases, theses were to be limited to 100 to 125 pages in length. The faculty had also considered a comprehensive examination but after long study postponed the matter indefinitely.[79] An interesting defense of the thesis, which a majority of the school's alumni endorsed in a poll, came from Elbert Russell. He favored it, he later explained, not as an exercise in original research comparable to a doctoral dissertation but as training in the investigation of a subject and the clear, logical presentation of one's findings. "Preachers are not like lawyers who have a trained opponent to force them to be accurate and informed," Russell declared. "There is a temptation for preachers to be content with slipshod thinking and care-less statements, because of lack of [research] facilities for information and keen and competent criticism."[80] Despite these defenses of the thesis, it would gradually be eliminated after World War II.

While the School of Religion clearly struggled to balance the spiritual, practical, and scholarly elements in ministerial training, the more purely scholarly dimension of the school gained an important impetus in the late 1930s. As articulated by Few and Soper from the beginning, the university's purpose was to train both ministers and advanced scholars in religion. A program for the training of the latter group proved a bit elusive and perhaps difficult to work out. The school at first tried a plan in cooperation with the Graduate School of Arts and Sciences whereby candidates for the degree of bachelor of divinity might also receive a master of arts degree without taking additional courses. That approach, which confused the ministerial or pastoral aspect of the divinity degree with the scholarly nature of the master's, proved unsatisfactory and was abandoned in 1933.[81]

Encouraged by President Few, Shelton Smith set his mind to the problem of graduate study in religion and headed a committee to devise plans. In a memorandum in 1936 Smith argued that the South needed at least one university in which students of "exceptional ability could engage in scholarly study of religion beyond that afforded in the regular B.D. curriculum of a divinity school." It would require, in addition to a strong faculty in the divinity school, library resources, "an undenominational atmosphere," and a well-established graduate school offering a wide range of courses of cognate value for students in religion. "Duke University alone in the South affords all of these advantages," Smith concluded. President Few hardly needed persuading along those lines and, with approval of the trustees, named Smith as director of graduate studies in religion, a post exactly like those in other arts and sciences departments that offered advanced degrees through the graduate school. It made for a somewhat complicated administrative structure in the area of religious studies at Duke—with a School of Religion, a distinct but related undergraduate

Department of Religion, and a separate but also related or overlapping Graduate Department of Religion. Nevertheless, the scheme worked.

Awarding the first three doctorates in religion in 1939, Duke University by 1947 had awarded a total of sixty-one masters of arts degrees (to forty-five men and sixteen women) and seventeen doctoral degrees (all men). Smith reported that the latter group was well placed, mostly in academic positions. Over three hundred students from twenty-nine different states and eight foreign countries had been enrolled in the graduate school for either a major or minor in religion.[82]

President Few, of course, took great pleasure and pride in the development and suggested to one correspondent that Duke, at that time, was the only university affiliated with American Methodism that provided for advanced studies in religion beyond the bachelor of divinity degree. "Duke is one of the important graduate religious centers," he asserted, "and it will, I predict, be better and better understood that we are now all in all as well equipped for this kind of work as any other university in the country."[83] Few insisted that this second, scholarly function of the faculty in religion was as important as the training of ministers. "No doubt we need great preachers," he argued, "but in the conflict with the paganism of our time, as in the conflict with the pagans of an older time, we must not only 'outlive and outdie' them but we must 'outthink' them."[84]

Developments in two areas were particularly important for the graduate aspect of religious study at Duke, the library and the faculty. Attention to library resources had long been a hallmark of the academic endeavor at Trinity College even before the university was organized. Early in the century, President John C. Kilgo, clearly influenced by the young Ph.D.'s on his faculty, had declared that the library was "the one department that measures the future development of the College."[85] After the organization of the university that tradition gained even greater emphasis, and many members of the faculty in the School of Religion played significant roles in building the library's resources. By 1936 Branscomb reported that as Duke's general library took its place as one of the half dozen most rapidly growing libraries in the nation, the library of the School of Religion was growing right along with it. With an estimated 35,000 volumes, it had developed special strength in the records of Methodism, thanks largely to Paul Garber's indefatigable labor in that field; there was also one of the most complete collections in America of the diocesan records of the Protestant Episcopal Church, and there were special strengths in literature for the study of the New Testament, in comparative religion, and in literature on the rural church. Highlighting some recent acquisitions of special interest, Branscomb noted a complete file of the Palestine Exploration Society; *Journals of the Royal Asiatic Society* for the Malay and Straits Settlement Branches and the Korean Branch, resources prized by

James Cannon in his field of missions; and a rare set of the *Magdeburg Centuries*, a work which he described as begun in 1559 and one of the fountainheads of much of the rewriting of the history of the Christian church in the first fifteen centuries.[86] In the Trinity-Duke tradition, the library of the School of Religion, not content with a mere regional comparison that would place it first in the South, would long continue a policy of aggressive development.

Important new appointments to the faculty, as well as library growth, helped in the graduate program. Using part-time or temporary teachers to cover some of the courses that Godbey had taught, Russell and his colleagues proceeded slowly and carefully in their search of a person in the Old Testament field. After extensive canvassing and one or two campus visits by possible candidates in 1935, Russell stated that Duke was trying to find someone who, in addition to the usual scholarly qualifications, had gained first-hand experience in Palestinian archeology. Such a person was difficult enough to find, he added, and since rather few students were attracted to Old Testament studies, and especially Hebrew, Duke hoped to find a person "who would add the weight of personal charm to the attractions of his field."[87]

One whose name cropped up early in the search, William F. Stinespring, was out of the country at the time (1934); in fact, he was obtaining exactly the type of first-hand experience in Palestinian archeology that Russell and his colleagues at Duke desired. A native of Virginia who graduated from the University of Virginia, Stinespring had, while also obtaining a master's degree there, taught Greek and biblical literature at his alma mater for several years before receiving his doctorate from Yale in 1932. A fellowship enabled him to spend four years at the American School of Oriental Research in Jerusalem before taking a job at Smith College in 1935. Described as "a coming man" by one referee, Stinespring was endorsed by one of his teachers at Yale as one who possessed a "genuine philological talent," as suggested by his having offered Hebrew, Syriac, Aramaic, North Semitic epigraphy, and Arabic in his final examinations at Yale. Characterized as a "likeable chap" who was neither suave nor mild-mannered, he was said to be "legitimately assertive, self-reliant and forthright," one who was not so much philosophic but "more interested in facts and results than in ultimate causes."[88]

Impressed by Stinespring's promise as a scholar and by his rich experience in the field, Russell, who had met and liked him while visiting in Jerusalem, had one misgiving or doubt: while there was no question about Stinespring's exceptional competence in linguistics, history, and archeology, would he have "a sympathetic interest in church work or in the religious side of Old Testament study"? The faculty of the School of Religion, Russell explained to one referee, was "quite liberal in accepting the methods and general conclusions of a modern historical and critical study," but it also taught "a positive Christian faith and experience."[89] Unable to offer evidence about Stinespring's religious belief, the referee suggested that Duke invite Stinespring to come for a year as a visiting professor and "vet" him during that time. "He is such an honest man and so incapable of hypocrisy," this referee declared, "that there would be no trouble getting a clear idea of his adaptability to your requirements."[90] Russell, acting promptly on this advice, invited Stinespring to come as a visiting professor in the fall of 1936, which invitation he quickly accepted. No doubt his letter accepting the invitation somewhat reassured Russell and his colleagues, for Stinespring, after listing the courses he taught at Smith, stated that he did not much care what he taught "so long as it has something to do with Bible— a book which thrills me as a source of personal power, and as a cultural phenomenon of the greatest significance."[91] More important in the long run than such a letter, the opportunity to "vet" the Old Testament visitor during 1936–37 furnished ample evidence that he was indeed the type of scholar and person who filled the varied needs of the School of Religion, and Stinespring would remain at Duke for the remainder of his career.

Another young scholar who came to Duke in 1937, Ray C. Petry, also proved to be a long-term asset. A graduate of Manchester College with his doctorate in early church history from the University of Chicago (1932), he taught at Macpherson College, which was affiliated with the Church of the Brethren, for four years before coming to Duke. Russell reported a few years later that Petry had promptly won the respect of students and colleagues by his "fine personal spirit, his scholarly standards and ability as a lecturer." One insight into Petry's thoroughness, Russell suggested, was provided by the fact that when a group of divinity students from Texas and Louisiana purchased a secondhand car for their travels to and from home, they christened it the "Petry" because they expected it to cover a lot of ground. In his research and writing, Petry, having completed a book-length manuscript on Saint Francis of Assisi by 1940, was at work on a book on the "Ideal of the Christian Community in the Middle Ages" and well on his way to recognition as a distinguished scholar in his field.[92]

Joining the faculty a year after Petry, Albert C. Outler taught theology at Duke from 1938 until his resignation in 1945. A native Georgian who graduated from Wofford College before receiving his divinity degree from Emory, Outler received his doctorate from Yale the same year he came to Duke. He returned to Yale from Duke and in 1951 began a long, noteworthy career at Southern Methodist University.

Additional faculty strength for the School of Religion came from other departments at Duke, for as a relatively young university, professional schools and departments were not, perhaps, as rigidly compartmentalized as was the case at many of the older institutions. Several professors in Duke's Department of Sociology—Charles A. Ellwood, Howard Jensen, and Hornell Hart—taught courses in the School of Religion. Ellwood, the first chairman of sociology at Duke, declared that his department felt "a greater interest in training students in the School of Religion to appreciate the problems of their human world than any other class of students in Duke University, for our aim is to train and adequately equip spiritual leaders for our civilization."[93] From the Department of Philosophy, Alban G. Widgery taught a course in the philosophy of religion, and Homer H. Dubs, a specialist in East Asian religion and thought, one in the history of religion and missions. Although Duke's medical school did not at first have the resources to include a Department of Psychiatry, after such an addition had become possible, the head of the department, Robert S. Lyman, offered a course that was especially adapted to the needs of divinity students. Filling another type of need, a member of the English department, A. T. West, taught a course in public speaking that was required for all candidates for the bachelor of divinity degree.[94]

Thus by building up its own faculty while also drawing on other resources in the university, the School of Religion achieved greater strength in the mid- and late 1930s. One conspicuous asset of the school was an unusually loyal and ever growing body of alumni. While no doubt less able than the graduates of other professional schools to contribute monetarily to the university, the divinity alumni showed a strong, continuing interest in and support of both the school and the university. Forming their own alumni association in 1934, the alumni finally obtained in 1936 something that they had been urging for several years: a quarterly publication from the School of Religion that would have as its primary objective, according to the faculty's statement, the continuation "with our alumni and others interested, the educational processes which are the concern of the School of Religion."[95] With James Cannon III as managing editor, the *Duke School of Religion Bulletin* immediately became a valuable addition. Various faculty members in the school presented articles dealing with their own research or with significant developments in their fields, and there were brief reviews of new books that could be recommended "as being likely to prove of special value to ministers and others particularly interested in religious questions."[96] News about the school itself and the activities of its current students also appeared in each issue.

Various publications by the theological students themselves would not be as long-lasting as the *Duke School of Religion Bulletin*, but one student-published quarterly, *Christian Horizons*, did continue from 1938 until shortly after World War II. Claiming to be the only journal published by seminary students when it began, *Christian Horizons* reflected a lively intellectual and spiritual ferment. Long before most other students, in the

North or South, began to be concerned about then prevailing racial arrangements, an editorial on "Jim Crow" in 1938 concluded: "If Christian social ideals are to be advanced substantially in the South, they will be advanced by both colored and white people working not independently of each other, but together. Southern students are placed providentially in a position whereby they, personally, may have an enormous part in bringing about interracial justice and cooperation."[97]

Data based on questionnaires submitted to the students by the staff of *Christian Horizons* afford an even more direct insight into prevailing ideas. Concerning theology, students claimed that the "crisis theology" of Karl Barth and Emil Brunner, two leading European theologians, greatly assisted them in formulating their own positions and that it grew in influence as they progressed in their studies. Approximately three fourths of the students (78 percent) favored admission of Negroes to the School of Religion, and almost all favored a more interdenominational student body. In world affairs, and the poll was apparently taken early in 1940 before the fall of France in June of that year, 35 percent of the students professed to be, like Elbert Russell, "absolute pacifists," and only 5 percent then favored United States intervention in World War II even if "it becomes evident that England and France are being defeated in the European conflict." Reflecting the lingering impact of the depression and certain aspects of the New Deal, over three fourths of the students believed that consumers' and producers' cooperatives might help in the South's economic recovery, and 68 percent agreed, with some reservations, to government ownership of major public utilities.[98] Fast-changing world events in 1940 and 1941 would no doubt help modify at least some of the ideas of Duke's divinity students, just as happened with the great majority of other Americans in that era. But the students at least appeared to be ready to challenge various aspects of the status quo.

Students and faculty may have held certain views that often differed from those that predominated in the surrounding community and region, but both groups also tried in various ways to be of service to the larger society. Aside from the part-time preaching and other types of church work that many of the students performed, various groups among them, at different times, conducted services in the Duke Hospital and in the Durham County jail. They cooperated with the Duke Legal Aid Clinic, and several students worked in a social and recreational center in a run-down section of East Durham.[99]

The faculty's outreach or public-service activities took a different form from that of the students, but they too were conspicuously active in the local and larger community. Few, and through him the deans and departmental chairmen, strongly encouraged faculty members to have as much contact with the public as possible. Given the economic circumstances of the times, honoraria were usually not involved, and even if they were offered, faculty members often declined to accept them. Aside from frequent stints at guest preaching, faculty members in the School of Religion were, perhaps understandably in light of their profession and the role of their alumni, more in demand as high school and college commencement speakers than any other group at Duke.

In addition to such individual contributions, the faculty participated in a number of more organized, service-oriented efforts. Carrying on a tradition that came from the Trinity College era, Duke University and particularly the School of Religion hosted each summer a Pastors' School for North Carolina's Methodist preachers. An official in the church's head office declared to Few in 1929 that the arrangements at Duke were better than he had seen elsewhere and that the "spirit of the North Carolina Pastors' School is as good as any in which I have served and that is due in no small measure to the school atmosphere that is created by holding the school in the buildings of the university."[100] Elbert Russell, inviting a prominent northern Quaker to lecture in the Pastors' School, made an interesting observation about the participants: "Thee would find the ministers very open minded, liberal and responsive. It is a delight to work with them. I had no idea before coming [to Duke] that any southern church had made as great progress as I have found here."[101]

The summer school that the School of Religion ran for a number of years at Lake Junaluska in the North Carolina mountains represented another type of outreach. Duke University began a summer session at Junaluska, a well-known Methodist conference center, in order to make it easier for teachers in the public schools in the mountain area to attend. When the School of Religion joined forces with the General Sunday School Board of the Methodist church to offer a six-week summer term there beginning in 1928, they targeted a different group. Both graduate courses and undergraduate courses were offered, with the former being under the jurisdiction of the School of Religion.[102]

A Pennsylvania schoolteacher looking for an inexpensive summer sojourn in other parts attended the School of Religion's session at Junaluska in 1932 and published a colorful account of her experiences. The setting, with its "blue, blue lake hidden away among clustering mountains," she considered "one of the most beautiful spots" she had ever seen. The absence of trolleys, movies, radios, shops and other diversions added to the quiet serenity of the place; and the nominal tuition of $5 per course was also appealing. With five professors and only thirty-five students, there obviously was much opportunity for interaction, and the Pennsylvanian gave an enthusiastic report about her classes. Nine of the ten ministers in one class, she observed, came from poor churches that paid little or no salaries. "To them the summer school was a time of refreshing for body and soul," she added, "and to me a glimpse of how the other half of the world lives." The shortage of money was not matched by any shortage of food, however, for she reported that the tables in the "huge barn-like" Terrace Hotel "groaned with good things and there never was any lack, [for] great dishes piled up, were emptied and filled again and again."[103]

Durham's topography and summer climate could not compete, of course, with Junaluska's, but much of the faculty's service-oriented activity took place on Duke's main campus. A good example came in the fall of 1932 when Franklin S. Hickman invited ministers of all denominations in Durham and the surrounding area to meet at Duke. Some fifty or so ministers representing nine denominations attended a luncheon given by the university and then a lecture by Hickman with discussion following. Out of this grew an informal organization that, inspired by a famous New England preacher of the nineteenth century, took as its name the Phillips Brooks Club. Led by Hickman, it would meet monthly, with an interruption forced by travel restrictions during World War II, for two decades until his retirement in 1953.[104] Both students and faculty members engaged in many other types of service-oriented activities, and they changed somewhat with changing conditions, as, for example, during World War II.

Some months before the United States entered that war in late 1941, two significant developments occurred in the School of Religion: it acquired a new name and a new dean. The name change occurred primarily because President Few began pondering the matter at some point in 1939, possibly when many leading American educators visited Duke in the spring of 1939 for the capstone event in the year-long celebration of the centennial of the institution's founding. Receiving a letter somewhat later from a distinguished leader in theological education who defended "School of Religion" as the appropriate name, Few summoned Shelton Smith to his office to discuss the matter. Smith, firmly disagreeing with the writer, argued that "School of Religion" was "too indefinite a name to indicate the specialized function of a school designed to prepare men and women for the various types of ministry in the Christian communions." Furthermore, Smith continued, since "School of Religion" in some institutions was used to embrace undergraduate and pre-professional work as well as ministerial training, it was confusing to give the same name to a school such as Duke's that was focused solely on the graduate and professional level. Smith expressed his personal regret that Duke's school did not have the "more precise and significant name" of Divinity School, as was the case at Harvard, Yale, and certain other leading universities.[105]

Smith later recalled that President Few listened thoughtfully but expressed no immediate judgment on the matter. On several occasions thereafter, however, Few publicly used the term "Divinity School" when referring to the School of Religion, and before he died in October, 1940, he told Vice President Flowers that he had decided to seek a change in the school's name. Feeling bound by Few's wishes, Flowers, soon after becoming president, arranged for the faculty in the school to be informed of Few's thinking and to be consulted about the matter. When all of the faculty members except one (who was not identified) expressed approval of the change, Flowers gained permission from the executive committee of the board to announce in May, 1941, that the School of Religion would henceforth be known as the Divinity School.[106]

Announcement of the new dean accompanied that of the new name. Elbert Russell, dean since 1928, apparently informed Few in the spring of 1939 that the time was fast approaching for his retirement. With Paul Garber being sought by various colleges to become their president, Few and Russell moved successfully to hold him at Duke by indicating that he would, in the not too distant future, be named as Russell's successor as dean. Accordingly, when Russell submitted his resignation the trustees elected Garber to the post in January, 1941, and announced the appointment publicly in May.[107]

An energetic and apparently effective administrator in the school as its registrar from 1928 on, Garber achieved particular prominence in 1938–39 in connection with the reunification of the nation's Methodist churches. A leading proponent of reunification, as were Few and others at Duke, Garber first published in pamphlet form an historical and legal study that answered in detail the claims made by one of the leading southern foes of unification, Bishop Collins Denny, Jr., of Virginia. "I have been spending more time in the Duke University Law Library than I have in the School of Religion Library," Garber reported to one ally, "endeavoring to make an examination of every legal case dealing with ecclesiastical matters."[108] With a copy of the pamphlet sent beforehand to each delegate to the General Conference of the Methodist Episcopal Church, South, which met later in 1938, Garber was pleased when the judicial council of the church voted unanimously in favor of the constitutionality of the plan of union. "A number of the members of this Council," Garber stated, "told me that my document had been of great value in forming the decision."[109]

Not one to rest on his laurels, Garber, encouraged by Few and others, next plunged energetically into the writing of a short history of the division and reunion of American Methodism. Completing the manuscript in record-breaking time (from late July to the end of December, 1938), Garber entitled his book *The Methodists Are One People* and, no doubt to the great satisfaction of the publisher, Cokesbury Press, read the galley proofs and prepared the index with sufficient expedition for the book to appear even before the great Methodist Uniting Conference in Kansas City in May, 1939. Garber's training in historical research—he had, after all, received the doctorate in history at the University of Pennsylvania—obviously stood him in good stead. A prominent northern Methodist and scholar, after reading some of Garber's writings about the nineteenth-century schism and its long-lasting effects, made an interesting observation to Garber: "It has been our adopted policy and practice to make no reference to the era of separation. For me and those I can influence, it does not exist. Maybe such a policy is not as wise as your own in bringing everything into the open." [110]

In light of Garber's prominence in Methodist reunification, it is not surprising that various acquaintances began to speculate about a bright future for him in the church. When a divinity student showed Elbert Russell a letter and press clipping from Garber in Kansas City, Russell predicted that Garber would be "one of the biggest men in the new Methodist church" and added that he had "a genius for administration, a capacity for hard work and a fine knowledge of how to handle people" that would carry him far. When the student suggested that Garber might make a good bishop, Russell reportedly replied, "I do not know whether he would have it." [111] A prominent Methodist leader and intimate friend who knew Garber perhaps as well or better than Russell seemed somehow more prescient about an episcopal future. Congratulating Garber on his decision to remain at Duke, this friend added: "I was not joking about developments a few years from now in the Southeastern Jurisdiction [of the United Methodist Church]. I think that little difficulty will be experienced in putting that over, if you want it." [112]

Regardless of what might lie ahead and as busy as Garber obviously was, he also found time to counsel and help Duke's divinity students in various ways. One of them wrote him a fairly typical comment: "I have never before known a man who held as important a position as you hold to be as friendly to the students." A recent graduate of the school likewise hailed Garber by declaring, "Sailing the seas of this old world has lost much of its difficulties since I acquired your friendship." [113]

As is sometimes the case in human affairs, one of Garber's great strengths—his love for and zeal to serve Methodism—may have been also, in one way, a problem. The Divinity School from the beginning was carefully planned to be ecumenical, in faculty, student body, and curriculum. The fact that a Quaker, Elbert Russell, had served for a long period as the second dean of the school underscored that nondenominational principle, and in 1941 six denominations were represented on the faculty. Yet Garber declared from the beginning of his deanship that one of his major purposes was to relate the school more closely to Methodism. "We really have only one task here [at Duke]," he declared to an old friend," and that is the preparing of consecrated, trained young men for our Methodist ministry." He hoped that "we can develop a spirit of unity in our faculty so that we will all have one common purpose."[114] Such a focus at least ran the risk of slighting or downplaying the ecumenical aspect of the Divinity School as well as the scholarly dimension of the graduate program in religion. Whether that actually happened is unclear, for Garber's deanship, as things turned out, proved to be relatively short and significantly influenced by developments connected with the involvement of the United States in World War II.

As dean, Garber certainly tried to make a difference, and there were a variety of changes. For one thing, there were some indications that faculty morale or perhaps *esprit de corps* had not been quite at the optimum level. "I agree with your statement," Garber wrote to James Cannon III, "that because of the lack of any definite plan many of us have fallen into controversy and antagonisms." Garber went on to say that he did not know exactly how it could be done, but he hoped "we can secure unity in our school which we have not had up to the present time." He was, he promised, certainly planning a program aiming toward that goal.[115]

How much Garber may have succeeded in what is sometimes difficult with any group, certainly one including learned and individualistic academics, is not known. There was, however, an increase in social activities that were carefully planned to include both faculty and students. A series of teas in the school's social room began in the fall of 1941, and following Garber's installation as dean, he and Mrs. Garber were the hosts for a reception in the ballroom of the Union building to which students, faculty, and friends of the Divinity School were invited.[116]

Alongside the attempt to facilitate social interchange came a new approach to the use of York Chapel in the Divinity School. While much used from the time of the building's occupancy in September, 1930, the small chapel had remained unadorned and stark. Garber led his colleagues to modify that by installing a maroon carpet and drapes and acquiring maroon robes for members of the choir and black robes for speakers. Fresh flowers on the altar added an additional touch of beauty. To avoid the conflict with classes that had apparently hindered some of the earlier services in the chapel, Monday and Wednesday mornings from 11:30 to noon were set aside for corporate worship. While distinguished visitors were to be invited to speak occasionally, the routine plan was to have a faculty member speak on Mondays, with a student presiding, and a student speak on Wednesdays, with a faculty person presiding.[117]

A prominent Episcopalian in Winston-Salem gave copies of the Book of Common Prayer to be used in York Chapel. Thanking him, Garber explained that one of his purposes as dean was to have dignified and beautiful worship services and thereby to acquaint students with the best liturgical forms. "In my estimation there is no devotional book that can compare with the Book of Common Prayer," Garber declared.[118]

Another way in which Garber moved energetically to strengthen the school was through a drive to increase the number of scholarships. Long frustrated by the fact that the Duke Endowment's grants could go only to students who served in rural Methodist churches in North Carolina, Garber worked with urban Methodist churches to gain scholarships for students who could do their summer apprenticeships in those churches. A prominent Methodist layman and Trinity alumnus in Raleigh, N. Edward Edgerton, especially assisted in the campaign, first by personally creating a scholarship fund in the Divinity School—"the first specific donation for the exclusive benefit" of the school—and then by helping to persuade his church, the Edenton Street Methodist Church in Raleigh, and other churches to donate to the fund.[119] One year after launching the drive, Garber reported that the school was already able to admit nine additional students, and he felt confident that the five-year goal would be reached.[120]

Enrollment in the Divinity School grew as thousands of ordained ministers became chaplains in the nation's burgeoning military forces, and their replacements had to come from the seminaries. Recognizing that there were some students and faculty who held to their pacifist principles even after the United States entered World War II, Garber declared that he could not agree with that position. "I feel that the future of civilization and Christianity is at stake in this conflict," he asserted.[121] Many of the school's alumni apparently shared the dean's outlook, for by November, 1942, there were sixty-two of them serving as chaplains, and more names were added later. The *Divinity School Bulletin* printed excerpts from some of their letters to Garber and thereby revealed a new and no doubt unforeseen dimension of the school's mission. "The opportunities for service to the men are without parallel," one alumnus-chaplain reported, "—helping the square pegs to find square holes, consoling the homesick, cheering the lonely, providing proper recreation for the man with time on his hands, showing more than one man how to enter the Christian fellowship, and so on. I mean it when I say the work is truly thrilling." Another enterprising alumnus stated that he used a motorcycle to pick up the mail for distribution in the hospital wards, coached the regimental boxing team, and organized church parades led by the regimental band. "As the band marches up 7th Avenue [of the camp] those going to church fall out from their barracks and . . . march to our chapel," he wrote. "My attendance has been the best of all Protestant services on the Post."[122]

On the homefront, activities in the Divinity School could hardly match those of the chaplains for color and drama. Yet the war years did bring marked growth. Enrollment climbed steadily, reaching 152 in 1945. At a time when the ministry remained closed to women, the school responded to the call of the Methodist General Conference in 1944 for more "young women . . . prepared to be teachers of religious education in our churches" by introducing that autumn a master's degree in religious education.[123] While the alumni had always been able to borrow books from the school's library, the faculty voted early in 1944 to make the library's resources available to ministers of all denominations. Special funds provided for the purchase of multiple copies of current religious books most in demand, and lists of such books were widely distributed. Less than a year after the program started, 1,429 ministers representing 27 denominations and living in all 48 states had borrowed 2,897 volumes.[124]

Another type of outreach, one clearly foreshadowed earlier, accelerated during World War II, and that was the Divinity School's interest in and sympathy for the plight of America's blacks. An alumnus of Trinity College, N. C. Newbold, had long worked quietly but effectively in his post in the North Carolina Department of Education to improve the state's educational opportunities for blacks. Early in 1940, after a conference at Duke arranged by Newbold, Elbert Russell undertook to teach a graduate-level class for black ministers at what was then North Carolina College for Negroes (later North Carolina Central University) located in Durham. The Divinity School loaned the library materials needed for the course. The following semester Russell taught another course there while Gilbert Rowe offered a special course on the undergraduate level. At the same time, Kenneth Clark taught courses at Shaw University, a black Baptist institution in Raleigh.[125] Garber, who named a faculty committee to give special consideration as to how the school might help in the training of black ministers and church workers, spoke to various black groups. After one well-received series of lectures he had given at Gammon Theological Seminary in Atlanta, then an all-black institution, Garber advised a close friend that he had had a wonderful time, for "as you often say, I was with my own people at Gammon." Garber, Russell, Rowe, Clark, Shelton Smith, and no doubt numerous others among the school's faculty and student body were clearly more sensitized about what a famous sociologist, Gunnar Myrdal, termed during World War II "the American dilemma" than were others at Duke at that time. They probably shared the viewpoint, rather rarely encountered in that era, expressed by a white professor at Gammon who wrote to tell Garber how much the black preachers, faculty members, and students had appreciated his lectures: "How much they have been deprived of through *white supremacy*! How greatly they have used the little that has fallen to them!"[126]

Heightened awareness of racial injustice suffered by blacks was not the only by-product of World War II in the Divinity School. As early as 1929, Elbert Russell had informed the Rockefeller Foundation that the "presence of a Jewish professor on our staff would be a welcome influence for comprehension and the scientific attitude."[127] Despite that stance, however, not until the war years did the school actually move to underscore further its nonsectarian nature by adding a Jewish scholar to the faculty. A donor who wished to remain anonymous at the time—Sidney J. Stern of Greensboro, North Carolina—provided money to pay the salary of a Jewish scholar to teach courses in the history and thought of Judaism, and President Flowers requested Branscomb to lead the search. After consulting leading Jewish scholars in the country as well as a representative of the donor, Branscomb reported that the consensus was that the Divinity School should name an American Jew rather than a refugee, that the individual should be competent in the area of Judaism's beginnings, and that the person should not be a Zionist. The individual who best fitted the requirements and was available, according to Branscomb, was Rabbi Judah Goldin, who had obtained his doctorate in Hebrew literature at the Jewish Theological Seminary of America under a teacher whom Branscomb described as the most distinguished Talmudic scholar in the English-speaking world. When offered the position, Goldin, who was then with the Hillel Foundation at the University of Illinois, accepted and thus became the first Jewish member of the school's faculty.[128]

A number of constructive changes thus characterized Garber's deanship, but it turned out to be a brief one. The development that his friends had predicted at the time of Methodist unification became a reality in June, 1944: at age forty-five he was elected to the bishopric by the Southeastern Jurisdictional Conference of the United Methodist Church and assigned to the southern and central European area, with his episcopal residence in Geneva, Switzerland.[129]

Fortunately for the Divinity School, an attractive and logical successor to Garber was already on the faculty, Harvie Branscomb, and he was promptly named acting and then regular dean of the school. By the age of forty-nine, Branscomb had achieved distinction not only as a New Testament scholar but in the academic world at large: director of libraries at Duke University from 1934 until 1941 and then director of a special research project for the Association of American Libraries in 1937–38, Branscomb gained national stature as an educational administrator. Sought earlier by Union Theological Seminary as well as other institutions, Branscomb had remained at Duke partly because President Few had struggled to hold him.[130] His tenure as dean would be, as matters turned out, all too brief, but he hit the ground running.

In a long memorandum to President Flowers, Branscomb began by emphasizing the Divinity School's opportunity and obligation to provide educational leadership in the field of religion in the South. The region, he suggested, was the stronghold of Protestant Christianity in the nation: with 28 percent of the country's population, the South contained 41 percent of its Protestant church membership, and out of every $1,000 of income in the South, $16.02 went for religious purposes, as compared with $10.50 for the nation as a whole. After recapitulating the various special features of the school, Branscomb turned to problems that had to be solved if the school was to render service commensurate with its opportunities.

First among the problems, he submitted, was that of staffing. Garber for a year or more had sought a professor of homiletics who could also preach in the chapel, and that appointment still needed to be made. Outler in theology had resigned, and retirements would soon leave other critical vacancies. Branscomb asserted that no request took precedence over the importance of securing the best possible faculty for the school.

Other basic problems, according to Branscomb, related to the improvement of the quality and morale of the student body. As mentioned earlier, he believed the divinity students as a whole to be superior in character and purpose and, perhaps, equal in native ability to other professional students, but he thought them "decidedly more limited in social background and worldly experience." This meant that the school had a special responsibility to "plan its training so as to overcome as much as possible deficiencies in social experience, cultural knowledge and, above all, good judgment." The school, therefore, had to resist pressure to seek larger enrollments and concentrate on the quality of its product.

Branscomb also hoped to find ways in which the school could most effectively serve ministers out in the field. This would not be a mere advertising device, he argued; it was as much a part of the obligations of the school as were frequent public clinics and symposia in a first-rate medical school.

Finally, and one is tempted to say inevitably, Branscomb pointed to space problems. In the case of the Divinity School, however, he clearly had a point. Unlike the assertive dean of Duke's law school, who had demanded and gotten exclusive use of its new building early in the 1930s even though the students in law were not numerous, the Divinity School shared the Gray building with students and faculty in the arts and sciences. Branscomb reported, in fact, that aside from the small Divinity School library and York Chapel, the school had come to have less than half of the building at its disposal; of fifteen classrooms, only four were permanently assigned to the school. Since the Divinity School had grown, it clearly had either to recover space it had given up or to seek new space. Branscomb thought, in fact, that it might be easier to interest a possible donor in a new building for the Divinity School than in a supplementary classroom building. Since housing for divinity students was also a continuing problem, Branscomb, harking back to his experience as a Rhodes scholar at Oxford and again pushing an idea that he and others had earlier advanced, suggested that thought be given to a "single divinity quadrangle," with an instructional building as its architectural center and adjacent dormitories for students.[131]

Branscomb did not get the "divinity quadrangle," but he did gain authorization for important new appointments to the faculty. Robert Earl Cushman, a future dean of the school, came in 1945 to teach systematic theology. An undergraduate at Wesleyan with his divinity and doctoral degrees from Yale, the latter in 1941, Cushman had been chairman of the Department of Religion at the University of Oregon prior to his appointment at Duke. In homiletics and as preacher to the university, James T. Cleland brought a Scottish presence that would long have a marked impact on Duke and especially on the chapel. Serving as a pastor in several small Scottish churches after receiving his divinity degree from Glasgow University in 1927, Cleland then crossed the Atlantic to obtain another degree in theology from Union Theological Seminary in New York. He returned to Glasgow University before going to Amherst College as professor of Bible in 1931 and came to Duke from that position.

Appointments less senior than those of Cushman and Cleland were also made in 1945. Franklin W. Young, who took his doctorate in biblical studies at Duke, was named as instructor in biblical literature and would shortly become dean of students in the Divinity School. A Dartmouth graduate, he had received his divinity degree from Crozer Theological Seminar. Another new instructor, John Jesse Rudin II, was named to teach public speaking. He did his undergraduate work at Willamette University and received a divinity degree from Asbury Theological Seminary and a master's in theology from Boston University. After graduate study in Northwestern's department of speech, Rudin chaired the department of speech at Northwest Missouri State Teachers College prior to joining the faculty at Duke.[132]

Another young scholar who joined the faculty to teach Christian ethics in 1946, Waldo Beach, was destined to spend the remainder of his career at Duke. A native of Connecticut who graduated from Wesleyan University, Beach took both his divinity and doctoral degrees from Yale. Then from 1942 until he moved to Duke, he served as a professor of religion and pastor at Antioch College.

In addition to playing a key role in making the new appointments that would long influence the Divinity School, Branscomb impressively addressed another need that he had mentioned in his memorandum to President Flowers: helpful service to ministers already out in the field. An estimated 1,500 ministers and laymen attended the first annual convocation held by the Divinity School in February, 1946. Among those taking leading parts on the program were Henry Sloane Coffin, president emeritus of Union Theological Seminary; Reinhold Niebuhr, a professor at the same institution and perhaps the nation's most widely known theologian of the era; Henry R. Luce, publisher of *Time* and other magazines and a trustee at Union; G. Bromley Oxnam, bishop in the United Methodist Church; and James W. Fulbright, United States senator from Arkansas and a leading layman in the Disciples of Christ church.[133]

Clearly a mover and shaker as a scholar-administrator, Branscomb, who had resisted various earlier offers from other institutions, accepted the invitation to become chancellor of Vanderbilt University in the fall of 1946. The school's most recent historian notes that Branscomb, like each of his predecessors in the job, wanted to make Vanderbilt a great university in its part of the South. He would spend sixteen years at the task, and the historian concludes that Branscomb "came closer than any predecessor to achieving the goal."[134]

Branscomb's acceptance of the larger challenge posed by the top post at Vanderbilt may well have been partly rooted in a certain disappointment he felt about developments at Duke. In his later autobiography, Branscomb explained that among the reasons he had declined the position at Union Theological Seminary were his and his family's preference for living where they were rather than in New York City and his own liking for being part of a university rather than being confined solely to a seminary. Branscomb's library work had demonstrated his administrative ability, and Branscomb recalled that his friend, President Few, had once said that he wanted Branscomb to succeed him at Duke. That did not happen, of course, for Robert L. Flowers became Few's successor. Although Branscomb clearly admired Few as one possessing a "quick, keen mind" despite giving an initial impression of "being languid and a little shy," he also disagreed with Few on certain matters and recalled telling him so. Flowers, Branscomb noted, was the "opposite in type and personality" of Few. Jovial and popular with alumni and the business community, Flowers, according to Branscomb, had one great goal for Duke: "to produce football and baseball teams that would defeat the University of North Carolina."[135]

Regardless of the reasons for Branscomb's departure, faculty members in the Divinity School were stunned by the development and expressed deep concern about the question of his successor. Petry emphasized to President Flowers that the "academic attainments of our incoming Dean" had to be quite high if he was to "foster the scholarly work of the Divinity School in close and appreciated cooperation with the [group in] Graduate Studies in Religion and the Graduate School as a whole." On that depended "the preservation and enhancement of our steadily rising stock in the field of Graduate leadership throughout the South and the nation." Cushman, whom Branscomb had just helped recruit, confessed that he was shocked by the resignation but hoped for a successor who shared Branscomb's ideals of quality and excellence in theological education.[136]

Fate was not kind to the Divinity School in the matter of Branscomb's successor. Paul A. Root, who had received both his divinity and doctoral degrees from Duke before becoming a professor of the sociology of religion at the Perkins School of Theology at Southern Methodist University, was offered and accepted the Duke deanship in March, 1947. Declaring that he considered the position "the biggest thing that the church has to offer," Root added that he was "not ambitious for anything else."[137] Before Root could even assume the post, however, he died of a heart attack in Dallas on May 13, 1947.

In addition to the faculty's undoubted dismay, the divinity students were sufficiently disturbed by the situation to convey their concern to the chairman of the faculty, Gilbert Rowe. "The students feel that another year without centralized administrative authority," they avowed, "will have grave consequences for student morale." They also feared that the "unsettled conditions" in the Divinity School would "lessen the attraction of the school for prospective students."[138]

The plight of the Divinity School was no doubt heightened by the fact that the university as a whole was undergoing something of a quiet, half-hidden crisis in leadership at the time. At age seventy-six and in increasingly frail health, Robert L. Flowers was simply not able to cope with the demands of the university presidency. Several of his associates in the administration, none with strong academic or faculty connections, attempted to cover for him but could not actually compensate for the lack of vigorous presidential leadership. Perhaps more than Few, Flowers displayed a wary nervousness about faculty involvement in university governance and high-level decision-making, and this attitude was more or less shared by his associates.[139]

Given this situation, the fact that a new dean of the Divinity School actually was named in July, 1947, was fortunate, perhaps even remarkable. Less fortunate, however, was the fact that he would serve as dean only briefly. Harold A. Bosley, at age forty, came to become dean of the Divinity School from the Mt. Vernon Place Methodist Church in Baltimore, Maryland—the first dean to have served a pastorate. A native of Nebraska and graduate of Nebraska Wesleyan College, Bosley had received both his divinity and doctoral degrees from the University of Chicago. He had taught at Iowa State Teachers College for three years before going to the Baltimore church and was the author of three books.

Methodist Bishop William Walter Peele, a Trinity alumnus and chairman of the trustee committee on the Divinity School, apparently played a key role in selecting Bosley for the deanship. Hersey Spence praised

Bosley to Peele in enthusiastic terms: "He's got everything. He is the only man in America—and perhaps the world who is a scholar (Ph.D. Chicago, '33), a successful pastor, a great preacher, a writer of significant books, a successful teacher in a theological seminary, a director in religious activities and teacher in a church college, a he man, and at the same time teachable, modest and considerate." Spence thought Bosley would put the Divinity School and even Duke itself on the map.[140]

Spence's reference to Bosley as a "he man" no doubt related to the fact that the new dean—at six feet, three inches in height and weighing 215 pounds—was a physically large man and had in fact played football as an undergraduate. Upon arriving in Durham, Bosley was asked by someone who did not know him if he was one of Coach Wallace Wade's new football recruits.[141]

Installed as dean in an impressive service in the chapel in June, 1948, Bosley was pleased by the occasion and thought it gave "opportunity for the University to say publicly that, in its estimation, religion continues to be a central concern."[142] Apart from such academic and religious ceremony, however, Bosley faced a challenging task. Postwar inflation caused all Duke salaries, including those in the Divinity School, to be increasingly inadequate, and the frequent changes in the deanship no doubt had taken a certain toll on the school's morale. Moreover, the Association of Methodist Theological Seminaries had sponsored a study of its ten members, and the report concerning Duke's Divinity School caused some consternation among the faculty. Statements concerning inadequate salaries at Duke as well as at the other schools came as no surprise, and neither did the suggestion that the Divinity School's physical facilities had become inadequate. With scholarly reputations of several key faculty members still in the process of being made, the visiting committee's comment in that area no doubt stung but was perhaps accepted as valid: "There is probably no one on the list [of faculty members] who could be called distinguished in the international field, and there are few who could be so described with regard to the national field."

Another aspect of criticism of the school drew a vigorous rebuttal from Bosley and his new colleagues. The visiting committee believed that there was "too great a tendency toward departmental specialization within the faculty both in its selection and in the thinking of the faculty itself." This related to a criticism of the curriculum as being developed from the point of view of departments of specialized study rather than the functions of the Christian minister. While the Divinity School faculty undertook a careful restudy of the curriculum and agreed that it should be supplemented by more extensive work in the "so-called practical field," the Duke faculty, speaking through Bosley, chided the visiting committee for failing to see or stress the important fact that the Divinity School was a graduate as well as a professional school, that the dual nature of the school "laid a greater emphasis upon scholarly research as one of the most effective tools of the ministry." Bosley asserted that no change in the curriculum would be made to lessen that emphasis.

Bosley concluded his article on the visiting committee's report and the school's response by noting that one appointment had already been made in the area of "practical theology": Russell L. Dicks, a graduate of the University of Oklahoma and Union Theological Seminary who had gained considerable experience in both teaching and preaching as well as hospital work, was named an associate professor of pastoral care in 1948. To replace Ormond, who had retired, A. J. Walton was named associate professor of practical theology and director of field work. A West Virginian who had extensive experience as a Methodist pastor before receiving his doctorate in divinity from Morris Harvey College in 1935, Walton served there as a dean before becoming the director of evangelism in the extension division of the Southern Methodist church (1935–39) and then superintendent of town and country work in the United Methodist Church for the five years prior to his appointment at Duke. Bosley believed that one or possibly two additional appointments in the same general area might be made soon. Meantime, additional fellowships were urgently needed for men and women who were preparing to teach religion on the college level. He hoped too that the school's student body might grow to number at least 200, or about 50 more than were then enrolled.[143]

Funds available to the school were, in fact, slowly accumulating. Even before Bosley became dean, James A. Gray of Winston-Salem, chairman of the board of R. J. Reynolds Tobacco Company, gave a $100,000 endowment to the school to support its educational services to North Carolina churches and ministers.[144] Support of the school from the General Conference of the United Methodist Church also increased, from around $2,800 per year to $15,000, and Bosley reported that Duke could anticipate a more equitable distribution of funds to the ten Methodist divinity schools.[145]

While deans inevitably must concern themselves with money matters, they do—at least, some do—occasionally publish books. Bosley's *Main Issues Confronting Christendom* appeared in 1948, soon after his arrival at Duke, and in an interesting illustration of academic freedom, one of the more junior members of the faculty, Waldo Beach, reviewed the volume in the *Duke Divinity School Bulletin*. Praising the "sermonic essays" for their "moral seriousness" and "forthright championing of what are quite evidently the unavoidable Christian ethical causes," Beach nevertheless confessed to having a "mixed reaction" to Bosley's volume and believed "the most serious questions" about the book concerned the theological premises on which the dean's Christian ethics rested. There seemed to be,

345

Theological
Education
at Duke
✢

the reviewer continued, "some hidden ambiguity" in the dean's various definitions of God, "though in the main it would be fair to say that his God could take up residence more comfortably in Chicago than in Geneva or Basel." Beach suspected, in conclusion, that "the most real 'main issues confronting Christendom' are precisely the theological questions, even more than the ethical ones, which the new continental theology is raising, and which . . . Bosley does not confront." [146]

Beach's reference to Chicago proved strangely apropos, for a year later, in January, 1950, Bosley resigned as dean—to go to that city. To be more precise, Bosley became the pastor of the First Methodist Church in Evanston, Illinois, which the *Duke Divinity School Bulletin* described as "easily the first church in American Methodism." Bosley himself explained that as he had "studied the unfolding pattern of responsibilities in the deanship" if the Divinity School was to "continue its growth toward adequacy," he had concluded that he "could be more useful in the pulpit of the church than in the deanship." [147]

The Divinity School, having had three different leaders in less than a decade—or four, if one counts Root, who did not live to assume the post—was back to square one concerning the deanship. Despite that problem, the school which Few, Soper, Russell, Garber, Branscomb and others had launched so hopefully in 1926 had made great strides in its first quarter century, but its brightest days clearly lay ahead. As the visiting committee representing the Methodist seminaries had suggested, the school's prestige, a highly vaunted matter in the academic world, still left something to be desired. Yet if "generous service to humanity" was, as President Few had said, what Duke University truly was all about, then surely the Divinity School had conspicuously done its part.

11

Building a Medical Center from Scratch

◆

MANY COMPONENTS OF Duke University had antecedents in Trinity College, since there had been, for example, a Department of Religion that foreshadowed the School of Religion, a modest law school, and even graduate work leading to the master's degree. There was no forerunner for the School of Medicine, however, and yet within a decade of its opening in the fall of 1930 it had clearly emerged as one of the strongest parts of the new university. The marked ability of a young, ambitious, and hardworking faculty plus excellent facilities and the expenditure of a considerable amount of money largely explained the phenomenon.

That Trinity College never added even a two-year, preclinical medical school was not because it had not tried to do so. First Crowell in the early 1890s, then Kilgo around 1909, and then Few in 1916 had each broached the matter only to back off because of financial uncertainties. By the 1920s, North Carolina lacked a full-fledged, four-year medical school and only had the two-year, preclinical schools at the University of North Carolina and Wake Forest College. Because of the state's real need for a larger number of properly trained physicians and because Trinity had long aspired to add a medical school, Few in 1921–22, with support from the General Education Board as well as J. B. Duke, attempted to have Trinity and the University of North Carolina join forces to build a strong medical school that would use Watts Hospital in Durham for teaching purposes. The bold plan eventually failed, for a variety of reasons, but it had important consequences for later developments at Duke.[1]

Perhaps the most important lesson that Few learned from the abortive attempt in 1921–22 to start a medical school was that such a venture was extraordinarily expensive, by far the single most costly element of a research university. This was so not only because physicians generally enjoyed high incomes relative to other professional people, but also because scientific medicine and the importance of medical research had become well established by the time of World War I. This meant that much expensive equipment was essential for both the best in patient care and for medical research. With the Johns Hopkins medical school and hospital leading the way and serving as the models for top quality in medicine, Dr. Abraham Flexner had carefully studied the nation's 155 medical schools and recommended in 1910 that all but 31 of them should be closed. The great majority of the schools, Flexner found, were shakily managed commercial ventures that produced poorly trained doctors.[2]

Tutored in the costs and standards of medical education by none other than Abraham Flexner himself, who had become associated with the General Education Board, Few approached the subject of a medical center in the new university with the utmost caution. In the original memorandum he had submitted to James B. Duke in 1921, the blueprint for the university that Duke later incorporated in his indenture establishing the Duke Endowment, Few had named all the various components before adding these words: ". . . and, when adequate funds are available, a Medical School." The qualifying phrase was important, for Few had no desire to do as certain other universities had done and build a strong medical school at the expense of other parts of the institution. Following Few's lead, J. B. Duke in the indenture named the various parts that the proposed university might "eventually include," with a medical school being one, but added the phrase "as and when funds are available."

Even after the announcement of J. B. Duke's large benefaction and the establishment of the university late in 1924, Few still believed that adequate provision had not been made for a medical school. As a result of his hammering away at that idea, both in conversations with J. B. Duke early in 1925 and in communications sent to him during the summer and early fall, nine days prior to the death of J. B. Duke on October 10, 1925, he added a codicil to his will which, among other things, provided for $4,000,000 to be expended in erecting and equipping a medical school, hospital, and nurses' dormitory at Duke University.[3]

With that final gift, especially targeted toward the physical construction of a medical center, Few and Duke University were finally committed to its incluson. The question of whether it would be a four-year school or merely provide the last two years of clinical training remained open, however, until after the Rockefeller Foundation made its crucial grant late in 1929 to support the four-year school.[4]

Just as Few had conspicuously good luck in the selection of a dean for the Woman's College, so too was he fortunate when he picked a leader to organize and start the medical center. Wilburt Cornell Davison, like Alice Baldwin, became a most successful institution-builder, for Few, while consistently supportive of Davison and the medical center, had less direct involvement in it than in any other part of the university. Few found Davison by following the advice of his friends and mentors in medical matters at the General Education Board; they arranged for Few to visit Johns Hopkins and meet selected members of the medical faculty at a dinner in March, 1926. Two men seemed to be the likeliest candidates for the deanship at Duke, Davison and Harold L. Amoss.

Amoss was forty when Few met him, six years older than Davison, and an associate professor of medicine at the Hopkins. Harvard-trained, Amoss had worked, among other places, in the Rockefeller Institute for Medical Research (later Rockefeller University) for a number of years before going to Johns Hopkins in 1922, and he had a well-established reputation in the field of infectious diseases. Davison, on the other hand, was only an assistant professor in pediatrics who also served as the assistant dean of the medical school. An undergraduate at Princeton, Davison won a Rhodes scholarship for study at Oxford in 1913 and there fell under the influence of his lifelong inspiration and hero, Sir William Osler, the world-renowned physician who had left Johns Hopkins to head Oxford's medical school. Designing much of his own course of study, but always with Osler's approval, Davison managed to take a bachelor of arts at Oxford in 1915, a bachelor of science in 1916, and also to make extended medical forays into war-torn France and Serbia. Returning to Johns Hopkins for his final year of medical school, he chose to become a pediatrician; then in 1917, after the United States entered World War I, he served until early 1919 in a United States field hospital overseas before returning to the Hopkins. As one historian has stated, Davison's "unique experience had convinced him that medical students should take an active part in planning their course of studies in accord with their personal interests, that research should be a major part of the students' curriculum, and that for learning the art of medicine there was no substitute for close personal contact with professors."[5]

At the time of Few's visit in March, 1926, Davison's superiors had him show Few around, and one of them expressed the view that "Davison would be the best man" for Duke to get, if he would take on such a job.[6] Writing many years later, Mrs. Few suggested that Abraham and Simon Flexner had pushed Harold Amoss for the position at Duke and that on paper he seemed to be well qualified. "When Dr. Few met him," his widow continued, "he [Few] was sorely disappointed and did not even mention the Deanship to him." Apart from high professional standing,

the new dean had to be a practical man, Mrs. Few added, "and an organizer extraordinary—really a superman." She thought her late husband
had possessed "an uncanny ability in evaluating men."[7]

Despite Mrs. Few's hindsight interpretation, Few did not act hastily in
naming a dean. Months passed after the meeting in Baltimore as Few ex-
amined papers published by Amoss and Davison, sought additional advice
concerning the deanship, and began the protracted negotiations with the
Rockefeller agencies about their support for the medical school. (Few was,
of course, simultaneously tackling dozens of other problems concerning
the university.) Finally, early in 1927, Few was ready to act, returned
to Baltimore, and, after conferring with the dean of the Johns Hopkins
medical school, asked him to summon Davison. "I have come for you,"
Few announced to the young assistant dean. "Are you ready?" Davison recalled that he replied, "Yes, sir." Few then named the salary ($15,000), the
amount for building and endowment, and asked whether they were satisfactory. Again, Davison said, "Yes, sir." An outspoken man who perhaps
grew more ebullient as he aged, Davison thought Few "the quietest man
I had ever met; he rarely talked, but when he did, it was worth hearing,
and always with a twinkle in his eye."[8]

From that point on, Davison, not Few, was at the center of the stage
in the establishment of the Duke medical center. The new dean soon
moved to Durham and proceeded to immerse himself in the planning of
the medical building, to seek and largely win the support of the medical
community in North Carolina, and to coordinate the plans for the medical
center with the ambitious and unprecedented aims of the Hospital Section of the Duke Endowment. In addition to support for Duke University
and other charitable agencies, J. B. Duke had specified in the indenture
creating the Duke Endowment that nearly one third of the annual income
(32 percent, to be exact) from the corpus of the trust should be used to
provide one dollar per day for every day of care given to charity patients
by nonprofit hospitals in the two Carolinas and to help in building, equipping, and maintaining not-for-profit community hospitals, for both white
and African-American people, in the two Carolinas. In other words, long
before the federal government moved after World War II to stimulate and
assist in the building of local hospitals, the Duke Endowment began in
the mid-1920s to pioneer in that field.

The architect of that plan and the first director of the Hospital Section was Dr. Watson S. Rankin. As secretary of North Carolina's board of
health, Rankin had supported and advised Few in the abortive attempt to
build a joint UNC-Trinity medical school in the early 1920s. Then when
J. B. Duke in 1923 requested his executive secretary, Alex. H. Sands, Jr., to
survey health care needs in the Carolinas, Few put Sands in touch with
Rankin, and the eventual result had a profound, long-lasting impact in

North and South Carolina. Concerned about the acute shortage of medical care in much of North Carolina, still one of the most rural states in the nation in the 1920s, Rankin borrowed ideas from a plan in Saskatchewan, Canada, whereby an outside agency assisted counties or communities to build hospitals. These in turn provided the facilities necessary for the practice of modern medicine and helped keep physicians from flocking to urban areas. The hospitals were locally controlled but were required, as a condition of outside aid, to keep records on costs, methods, and results so that comparative studies could be made and improvements suggested.[9] "There is little doubt in the minds of any of us," Rankin declared soon after J. B. Duke's death, "that in considering rural hospitals and providing for them separately Mr. Duke had in mind all the time their further relation to a large medical school and central hospital."[10]

Davison took an immediate and lifelong liking to Rankin and, more importantly, became a strong believer in the ambitious scheme for wide-ranging medical service that J. B. Duke had envisioned. A few months after being named dean, Davison addressed the members of the Medical Society of North Carolina and, among other things, assured them that the Duke medical center, in addition to providing state-of-the-art facilities for patients and medical students, would train nurses and technicians for other hospitals and perform laboratory procedures for the smaller ones. The medical library, which Davison began carefully assembling as soon as he was named dean, would be made available to physicians throughout the state, and postgraduate symposia on various medical topics would be offered regularly. "The word Service," Davison declared, "is to be carved into the cornerstone."[11]

For the medical school's curriculum, Davison had certain unconventional ideas that he set forth early. Believing that physicians were being forced to begin their productive careers at too late an age because of the lengthy training required, Davison proposed for Duke to admit students to medical school after only two years of college, which would include all of the basic science courses. (He obviously placed no great value on liberal education for physicians, and Duke, as well as other medical schools, would later move away from such a policy.) Then, borrowing the recently liberalized medical curriculum at the Hopkins, which allowed students greater choice among electives, he proposed to have four eleven-week quarters per year, the fourth falling during the summer months. Those students who wished could accelerate and complete medical school in three years instead of the usual four. Another important innovation at Duke, however, would require that each student complete two years of internship, instead of the then usual one year, before actually receiving the Duke medical diploma.[12]

As important as curricular innovations and cooperation with the Duke

Endowment were to be, they were not as crucial for the future of the medical school as the selection of the faculty and key staff members. While numerous other relatively new or reorganized medical schools—such as Vanderbilt (1925) and Rochester (1922)—turned to Johns Hopkins for deans and key faculty members, none was to be quite the "colony" or offspring of the Hopkins that Duke proved to be. Davison's first appointment, made early in 1929, was none other than Harold Amoss to be professor of medicine and head of that important clinical department. Ironically, that first appointment, widely hailed in medical circles at the time, would be the source of serious trouble a few years later.

Davison later recalled that when Few presented Amoss's name to the board for official confirmation of the appointment, a trustee asked to what church Amoss belonged. Few promptly interjected that religion had nothing to do with medical competence, which ended that particular line of discussion. Davison himself had expressed some concern to Few about the veto power which the two Methodist conferences in North Carolina presumably possessed concerning two thirds of the university's trustees. Few reportedly replied, "Don't fuss about it, [for] if they use the veto, they will lose it."[13]

Davison often described his style of leadership in the medical school as comparable to that not of a commanding officer but of an adjutant, that is, one who coordinates and assists. That approach was illustrated in the selection of the faculty, for in picking the head of surgery, the other major clinical department, Davison worked closely with Amoss, and as additional members were named each was brought into the process of selecting the remaining members of the faculty. Later the medical center, while ultimately answerable to the university's board of trustees and its executive committee, would actually be largely controlled by its own executive committee consisting of the heads of the four original clinical departments and the four preclinical ones.[14]

The person whom Davison and Amoss picked to head the surgery department, Julian Deryl Hart, was destined to play a major role not only in the medical center but also in the university. Indeed, he would later serve as president at a critical time in the institution's life. A native Georgian and graduate of Emory, Hart received his doctor of medicine degree from Johns Hopkins and remained there for eight years as a resident in surgery; he was, in fact, chief resident when invited to become professor of surgery at Duke. Hart proceeded not only to help in the selection of other faculty members but also to write long, detailed letters to Davison in which he (Hart) specified exactly how the operating rooms in the hospital were to be arranged and equipped. No physical detail seemed too small, for while Hart, like the others, was a relatively young man, he was already richly experienced in his profession—and at one of the nation's most eminent medical centers. Hart, in consultation with Davison and Amoss, took the lead in securing Edwin P. Alyea to handle urology at Duke and boasted that "we have scored a point in taking him."[15]

Just as Hart was enthusiastic about Alyea, Amoss had high hopes for a young bacteriologist whom he picked, David T. Smith. "That boy would be one of our great assets," Amoss declared to Davison; "he is doing splendid work and is chock full of ideas." Davison and the others agreed with Amoss about Smith, and he and his wife, Susan Gower Smith, would soon head for Durham. Amoss proved to be prophetic too, for he thought that one of the first problems to be researched at Duke would be pellagra. "I have some ideas about that and am in correspondence" about it, he wrote Davison. The dean, in reply, expressed his gratification that Amoss was interested in pellagra, for the depression seemed to be making it worse and "the mortality from that condition is increasing in North Carolina."[16] Long after Amoss had left Duke, both David T. Smith and Susan G. Smith were destined to play significant roles in important research on pellagra that was done at Duke.

For obstetrics and gynecology, Davison and his associates picked Bayard F. Carter, who was a Hopkins alumnus then serving as the professor in his specialty at the University of Virginia's medical school. From Vanderbilt, Francis H. Swett came to head the anatomy department, and Wiley D. Forbus, an associate in pathology at Johns Hopkins, was an early choice to chair that department. Another early choice, William A. Perlzweig, was named professor of biochemistry, and George S. Eadie chaired the physiology department.

All of the heads of departments, and even most of the others on the original staff, had connections of one sort or another with the Hopkins, and most were relatively young. The average age of the original medical faculty at Duke was, in fact, only thirty-five, and Davison liked to point out that the average age of the four physicians who had made the Hopkins the trailblazing model for American medical schools was also thirty-five when they began the school.[17]

Though the salaries Duke offered to the medical newcomers were significantly higher than those in the arts and sciences, they were probably not the main attraction. Rather, the challenge and excitement of being in from the start on a new, ambitious medical center no doubt brought most of them to Duke. Bessie Baker, the head nurse, declared, as she contemplated the move to Durham: "I too am beginning to get a thrill out of the idea of starting in on an entirely new project; there is lots of hard work ahead of us, but I feel sure we can do it."[18] Professors in the medical school started at from $5,000 to $7,500 annually, with some (such as Amoss) promised increases to $10,000 by 1934. Associate professors were paid from $3,000 to $3,500; and instructors up to $2,500.[19] As strange as it may seem, for many of the appointees in the clinical departments these starting salaries were to become their more or less permanent salaries from the university, for, as will be explained below, they developed another and highly lucrative source of income.

Even before all of the department heads were named, Davison launched a careful search for a head nurse. "The chief nurse is the most important person in any hospital," Davison later declared, "and enquiries for candidates were made throughout the country." Many people recommended Bessie Baker, a Hopkins-trained nurse and administrator, who was then serving as superintendent of nursing at a hospital in St. Paul, Minnesota. Davison had known her at the Hopkins base hospital in France in 1917 and liked, among other things about her, her sense of humor. According to Davison, she had not reported the enlisted men of the base hospital, who were seniors in the Hopkins medical school, when they had moved the latrine which she was occupying. (Shades of "M.A.S.H."!)[20] Baker accepted the job and became not only the chief nurse but the first dean of Duke's School of Nursing.[21]

Between coordinating the selection of the faculty and certain members of the technical staff, who were most important in a teaching hospital, and overseeing the actual construction of the building, Davison was obviously an extremely busy man in the late 1920s. As far as the new Tudor Gothic structure on the West campus was concerned, he and his chief associates had more input about their building than did any other division of the university. Though changes within the vast edifice housing the medical school and hospital began to be made almost as soon as it was completed, it was not dysfunctional, as was, for example, the original university library in certain ways. The university's architect, Horace Trumbauer of Philadelphia, obtained the services of the director of the Hopkins hospital as a consultant. While the exterior of the building was another example of the artistry of Julian Abele, the then anonymous African-American architect in Trumbauer's office who actually drew the plans, the interior arrangement was partly modelled after new hospitals at Vanderbilt and Rochester. One example of the role played by the physicians in the building process came in June, 1929, when Davison requested Amoss to meet him and A. C. Lee, Duke's chief engineer and head of the construction company, at Trumbauer's office in Philadelphia. Davison wanted Amoss to show the draftsmen exactly how he wished "the dust-proof room" to be constructed. Lee was then going on with them to Atlantic City for a medical meeting, and Hart and Forbus were to bring their lists of equipment and other data to give to Lee.[22]

At one point toward the end of construction, Davison noted that he was spending a week "in trying to make sure that every door is of the right size and swings in the proper direction." There were, he added, 1,447 doors in the building, and while the task was bewildering, he thought there was "nothing that is more annoying than to try to push a 3'6" wide bed through a 3' door."[23]

The matter of securing students for the new medical school had also to be dealt with. On the basis of the facilities, early appointments, and Davison's assurances that high standards were to be met, the medical school received a class A rating in 1929, even before it opened, from the Council on Medical Education of the American Medical Association.[24] Capitalizing on that fact, Davison placed small notices about the new school in college newspapers across the country and invited applications. In addition to the announcements about the medical and nursing schools, there were also notices of the projected school of dietetics (offering a one-year course leading to the certificate of graduate dietitian), of a training program in medical technology, and of the internship program in hospital administration, another innovative feature which fitted nicely into the hospital work of the Duke Endowment.

The new building was opened for public inspection on Sunday, July 20, 1930—which turned out to be a ninety-five-degree day. Perhaps people were hardier in those days before air conditioning, for thousands flocked out to tramp through the hospital. Davison long remembered that it was "the hottest day I have ever experienced" and that, in addition to losing six pounds (which he probably did not regret), he "ruined a white linen suit showing visitors through the building and repairing overloaded elevators."[25] Covering four acres of ground and with twenty acres of floor space, the hospital had a total capacity of 416 beds. Ward beds cost $3 per day, semiprivate rooms $4, and private ones from $5 to $9.[26]

There had been skepticism on the part of some observers about the wisdom of locating a large, complex teaching hospital in a relatively small city such as Durham, which had a population of only around 50,000 in 1930. The objection was that there would not be enough patients to furnish the quantity and variety of teaching material that students and researchers needed. Davison, guided by Osler's comments about small German cities that had great teaching hospitals, never doubted that the Durham location would prove satisfactory, and the results proved him correct. The age of the automobile had arrived; North Carolina had, and prided itself on having, good roads; and patients came in ever-increasing numbers, not only from within the state but from neighboring states and eventually from other regions. The average daily patient census jumped from 91 in 1930–31 to 375 in 1939–40; the total number of patients in the hospital, public dispensary, and private clinics (not counting repeat visits) increased from 6,248 in the first year to 143,180 eight years later.[27] Talk among habitués of the medical center about the need for new buildings and more space began early, and, like kudzu in the southern sun, the medical center began to spread quickly.

In October, 1930, the entering group of medical students arrived, thirty

355

Building
a Medical
Center
↭

for the first-year class and eighteen for the third year. Since seventy students for each of the four classes was the eventual target, the small number at first allowed for informal teaching methods and close interaction between professors and students even in the preclinical courses. Much of that continued in later years, and Swett in anatomy noted that best results in teaching had been through small group conferences and individual laboratory discussions, "in which considerable care is taken to avoid the appearance of quizzing." Moreover, he thought the substitution of the teacher's careful, personal judgment of each student's ability in lieu of an examination rating had been a "long step in the right direction," and the abolition of quizzes and exams in favor of "individual encouragement and stimulation has done away with much of the student fear and worry." Such methods, he noted, took much time on the part of the staff, and since research stimulated teaching, the department needed more funds for both teaching and research fellowships.[28] As Swett's statement suggests, the faculty modified its methods and moved in the direction of lessening among the students both tension and attrition. The school steadily attracted a growing number of applications from a widening area; that the rate of attrition among such a highly selective group dropped throughout the first decade was, therefore, not surprising. The first year of medical school at Duke gradually lost the traditional image, especially among undergraduates, of unadulterated terror.

Among the thirty students admitted in the first-year class in 1930 were three women. Many years later one of them recalled that the women students were treated "wonderfully well by the faculty." Some of the male students and house staff, however, acted as if they wished the women would "get lost, permanently." The hearty survivor added: "We [women] were tolerated, usually politely, then avoided if possible. But we became accustomed to the jibes and innuendoes." She wanted an internship at Duke in medicine, but the head of the department had declared, "No women and no married students will be accepted." Since she was, in fact, already married, there were two strikes against her. Another member of the faculty interceded on her behalf, however, and she not only got the internship but went on to become a well-known and widely admired physician in Durham.[29]

Having been taught hospital laboratory techniques and procedures, as well as the basic methods of taking a case history and performing a physical examination, students at Duke went directly on to the wards in their third year. Referring to bedside teaching, Osler had declared in 1905 that the greatest achievement of the Johns Hopkins hospital had been in demonstrating to the medical profession and to the public "how medical students should be instructed in their art." Never before, he continued, had medical students "lived and worked in a hospital as part of its machinery, as an essential part of the work of the wards." The amphitheater clinic and dispensary classes, he thought, had been "but bastard substitutes" for the Hopkins method.[30]

Translated later into practice at Duke, the Oslerian method meant that a third-year transfer student in June, 1931, faced a heavy work load on the surgical service. His name was J. Lamar Callaway, and he would later become a well-known dermatologist at Duke. That summer, however, he was assigned more than twenty ward patients and had duties in the afternoon in the outpatient clinic. His day began around 7:30 A.M. with essential laboratory work; then he made daily ward rounds with the surgical staff and sometimes "worked up" as many as eleven new patients per day. In the clinics all afternoon, he got to bed around 11:30 P.M.—and felt lucky to have a room in the interns' quarters of the hospital.[31]

Beginning in January, 1931, working alongside young medical students like Callaway were thirty-five student nurses. The School of Nursing offered the diploma of graduate nurse to the student who wished to pursue only the three-year program; for the student who presented at least sixty hours of college work, taken before or after the basic nursing program, the school offered the B.S. degree in nursing. During a probationary period of six months, the nursing students had courses and laboratories taught by the faculty members in the preclinical departments and by Anne Gardiner, an assistant professor of nursing education who was much involved in the academic side of the program. After the probationary period, practical training in the hospital began, with each student spending about fifty-two hours per week on the wards and only about eight hours per week in class.[32]

Davison liked to emphasize that Duke was raising the standards of nursing by selecting "pupil nurses" on the same basis as the students for Duke's Woman's College were chosen. Furthermore, he suggested that the nursing students be afforded the same recreational and educational advantages as other women students. During the first year and a half of the school's existence, the nursing students were, in fact, housed on East campus, but in June, 1932, a new dormitory for them (later known as Baker House) was completed with accommodations for 226 persons.[33]

There were problems with the School of Nursing, however. Attrition was high: one of every ten students admitted during the first seven years dropped out for personal reasons and four in ten were dropped by the school. Put another way, during the school's first decade 402 women were admitted as first-year students and only 151 graduated (63 of them with the B.S. degree).[34]

The School of Nursing was not, in fact, a "school" as the term was used elsewhere in the university but was actually a department of the hospital controlled by Davison and the other members of his executive committee. As nurses, like doctors, found that they had to master more and more complicated skills, their national organizations insisted that nursing be placed on a par with other professions and that schools of nursing in a university, like schools of medicine and law, should be under the control of the university rather than the hospital. The national organizations also wanted student nurses to spend fewer hours on the wards and more hours in the classroom. The majority of the medical center's executive committee did not agree with that position, and, under pressure from the Association of Collegiate Schools of Nursing, Duke dropped the B.S. degree program in 1941. Davison privately reported that he thought a university-related school attracted a better type of student nurse than did a purely hospital-run school but that the majority of the executive committee disagreed with his view and that the clinicians at Duke preferred the hospital school. Davison also recognized that having one person serve as both dean of the nursing school and director of nursing services posed problems, for those responsibilities sometimes clashed.[35]

At any rate, Bessie Baker resigned as dean of the School of Nursing in 1938 for reasons of health and was succeeded by Margaret I. Pinkerton. Debates continued, however, about the direction in which nursing education at Duke should go, and after World War II there would be further changes in the program. Those nursing students who successfully completed Duke's rigorous program had good reason to be proud, and many of them became important participants in the university's alumni activities. While nursing standards in Duke Hospital in general were high, as would be expected, the fact remained that the comfort and privacy of the patient could not take first priority in a teaching hospital. Patients, at least some of them, should perhaps be forgiven if they occasionally forgot that fact. Biochemist W. A. Perlzweig, who had a penchant for speaking his mind, once commented to Davison during one of the ongoing debates about nursing at Duke, "For just straight bodily comfort, I still would not want to be a patient at Mr. Duke's hospital."[36]

Just as there was a problem about nursing education, there was a totally different kind of problem that had to do with the compensation of the clinical faculty. Complicated and rather arcane, the problem was solved in a unique manner through the pioneering creation at Duke of the private diagnostic clinic (PDC). While it brought many important benefits to the medical center as a whole, and ultimately even to the university, it simultaneously gave significant monetary benefits to the members of the clinical staff who were involved and also produced certain long-lasting problems. Furthermore, the private diagnostic clinic represented a significant departure from the policy followed at Johns Hopkins.

At the Hopkins, as at Chicago, the Mayo Clinic, and various other leading medical centers, the faculty members were full-time employees of the university. Like the lawyers in reputable law schools, the physicians at those schools foreswore income from private practice in exchange for salaries that were less than private practice would probably have brought but more than most faculty members in arts and sciences received. Originally, the Duke medical school was to follow the Hopkins model in that policy, as in so many others. Addressing the Medical Society of North Carolina in April, 1927, Davison assured his listeners, who were interested in more than one meaning of the word, that the heads of the departments in the new medical school would be on a full-time basis. "They will be given adequate salaries," he continued, "and will not engage in private outside practice." The new dean noted that there were arguments for and against such an arrangement but that two advantages of it were that the department heads would be able to give their full time to patient care and to teaching students and interns (he did not mention research), and that the faculty members would be removed from competition with the members of the profession. Davison said that he hoped there would be private patients, "but all fees collected for private patients will go to the medical school and no private patient will be seen who is not referred by his or her own physician."[37] That was all clear enough, and those who heard it were no doubt pleased.

The matter really was not so clear-cut and settled, however. Deryl Hart, writing many years later, recalled that when he was first approached about heading Duke's surgery department, he asked if it was to be on the Hopkins-style full-time basis; he got the impression that it was, and since he said he wanted to have private patients too, he initially expressed his lack of interest in the Duke position. A week or so later, Hart continued, the same person informed him that the Duke job would be on a part-time basis; thereupon Hart said he would be interested, and he became the third member of the faculty when he accepted Davison's offer in March, 1929.[38]

Hart's account suggests that Davison probably had not thought much about the compensation matter after he announced the full-time policy in 1927. Probably as a result of talks with Amoss, Hart, and others, as the first actual appointments were being made in 1929, Davison began to rethink the matter. Hard pressed for funds even to support a four-year school, Few had undoubtedly emphasized to Davison that Duke could not afford to pay many large salaries. Davison, possibly with others, also talked to leading figures in Harvard's medical school and liked the part-time plan they followed. It allowed the clinical faculty members to see and be paid by private patients but since they saw them *in* the Harvard medical buildings they were described as "geographical full-time." (Laymen had good reason to be mystified.) This was the plan and the phrase that Duke adopted, though the PDC arrangement was unique.[39]

During the first months of the medical center's operation, the small faculty was no doubt too busy getting everything started to have any time for much else. At some point prior to the opening of the PDC in September, 1931, however, Deryl Hart proposed the establishment of a voluntary, cooperative, and private group practice among the clinicians. He argued that this was the best way to achieve the best diagnoses in complicated cases. There would have to be a fixed schedule of fees for all medical services and consultations, however, and the fees should be low so that primary physicians would not hesitate to call in consulting physicians. Fees would be paid directly to a business manager for the group, thus freeing the physician from the business aspect of the practice, and the business manager would divide up the income and pay the participants according to prearranged formulas. Hart later emphasized the fact that officials of the university and medical center assured the clinicians that such a program with its increased concentration of financial information *"would not be used to pry into their earnings or to limit in any way their income from private practice* as long as they fulfilled their University responsibilities."[40] Davison supported the plan on the important condition that the participants in the PDC would have first and always to meet their obligations to the university, that is, to the students and the nonprivate patients.

Hart, supported by David T. Smith, who was acting head of medicine in the absence of Amoss, presented the plan to the clinical faculty only to find that half of them were opposed to it, some because they did not wish to limit their private practice in the proposed fashion. Two days of intense lobbying for the plan by Hart, Davison, and Smith changed the situation, however, and a majority voted to support Hart's proposal. The PDC opened on September 15, 1931.[41]

Starting modestly in improvised quarters in the hospital, the PDC steadily grew more lucrative for the physicians involved as well as beneficial to the medical center in many ways. Aside from the fact that an increasing number of private patients found excellent service in the PDC, the participating physicians agreed that a portion of the total income should be set aside to support research activities and that new faculty members in the clinical departments could be attracted and guaranteed competitive salaries through the device of having the university pay only a portion of their salaries (one third in the case of medicine), the PDC paying the remainder. This meant that even during the depression the faculty grew faster than it might otherwise have done and that more university funds were made available to support the preclinical departments. By 1937 the group practice had grown sufficiently for the PDC to split into two separate units, one for surgery and one for medicine. There was a pressing need for more space for private patients. Consequently, the university and the

Duke Endowment agreed in 1939 to add a wing to the hospital (which would later link it to Baker House); the wing would provide more private and semiprivate beds as well as a floor of offices and examining rooms for the Surgical PDC and another for the Medical PDC. In lieu of an annual rental payment of $17,500 to the university for the new examining areas, the physicians proposed that, in addition to paying all expenses of operating the clinics, they would place a percentage of the clinics' gross income (4 percent initially) in a building and development fund for the medical center, which would yield a larger sum than the proposed rental fee.[42]

While the whole question of the PDC arrangement would resurface later in the university's history, there were certain problems even in the 1930s. One was obvious: the incomes of the clinical staff began quickly to grow larger than those of the preclinical faculty members, especially since the university was in no position to increase salaries during the 1930s. Davison took great pride in the cooperative teamwork and *esprit de corps* of the original staff members, who were quite conscious that they were engaged in laying the groundwork for a medical center that aspired to be among the best. Once Davison apparently forgot himself, however, and made some remark to the effect that the preclinical people used the staff dining room in the hospital only as a matter of "courtesy and sufferance." Perlzweig promptly rebuked the dean in a note and pointed out that the sharing of the dining room should be regarded as a policy, part of the general scheme of having the medical school and hospital under one roof, with all that implied for the maximum cooperation between clinical and preclinical staff. Perlzweig added that while the Duke school already had more cooperation than any other place he knew of, he would like to see more of it. But, he concluded, "we shall never have angelic perfection, and if we did it would be deadly boring."[43]

That the matter of the salary differential grated on the preclinical staff was quickly made clear, however. In the printed *Report of the President* that appeared in 1935, Swett of anatomy declared: "I feel very strongly that full-time heads of all preclinical departments should receive remuneration equivalent to the basal salary of the part-time heads of the clinical departments." While the training of both groups was approximately equal and both contributed the same to the students and the institution, Swett argued, the "preclinical men are denied the opportunity to supplement their income while the higher paid clinicians are encouraged, though perhaps indirectly, to do so."[44]

Wiley Forbus in pathology also dealt with the matter in print but from a different angle. He argued that if the medical center was not to become "a vast therapeutic institute," then its ranking and reputation had to depend on "first-class productivity in the field of investigation." That meant, he suggested, a staff organized on a significantly different basis from that which existed, with the most radical changes needed in the clinical departments. Full-time teachers of high rank should be added there, Forbus asserted, because the existing system (the PDC system) left "virtually untouched the major problem of developing the teaching and scientific side of our medical school and hospital."[45]

Forbus obviously pointed to an important dilemma. Tension between teaching and research was (and is) always present and an overriding fact of life for both professors and administrators in a research university. Yet the clinicians in the PDC had introduced a third, time-and-energy-consuming element—private practice. Another person who worried in public about the matter was a key figure in the early years of the medical center, Frederic M. Hanes, who became professor of medicine and chair of the department in 1933. An independently wealthy man, Hanes no doubt realized that his situation was somewhat special, yet that did not prevent him from speaking his mind. In the mid-1930s, Hanes publicly declared that private patients constituted "the most serious problem" that the Department of Medicine faced. "They are inevitable," he conceded, and "their proper handling can do much to make friends for the institution; and they must be well treated." Yet he believed them to be "thoroughly demoralizing" because they consumed a large and undeterminable part of the faculty's teaching time. "*Progress in scientific medicine is almost impossible* for the teacher who accepts *private patients,*" Hanes insisted. He thought some more or less "trivial work" was possible but that, with rare exceptions, "sustained and important work" could not be done by a teacher so divided in commitment. Hanes, echoing Forbus, recommended that there be two types of teachers: part-time persons such as the medical center already had for senior teachers, and "the absolutely whole-time man who has no obligations whatsoever to private patients." The needs of the growing outpatient clinics had to be met, he observed, "if the wards are to be fed, and the need of fourth-year teaching material is to be met."[46]

A few years later Hanes returned to the matter, but a strong note of resignation had crept into his remarks. He continued to argue that from the standpoint of the effective use of the clinical professors as teachers and investigators, "private patients are a nuisance," and he still urged two distinct types of staffs—one for private patients and one for teaching and research. He confessed his realization, however, that "the present part-time arrangement is the only one possible for us [at Duke]," even if there was "a grave danger of the younger men sacrificing their scientific advancement through the rather profitless [?] drudgery of too much private practice." Yet it was probably true, Hanes wearily concluded, "that all human problems are insoluble, and this is distinctly a human problem."[47]

In one sense Hanes was correct. The problems associated with the PDC would not be solved in his lifetime. Yet at a later time the medical center would indeed move in the direction of the two types of staff that he had advocated. Moreover, his notion that "all human problems are insoluble" was much too sweeping and facile. A very human problem developed concerning interpersonal relations during the early years of the medical center, and it was certainly solved, albeit in a fairly drastic manner: the heads of all the other departments asked for and got the resignation of Harold Amoss as professor and chairman of medicine.

There remains a puzzling aspect to the Amoss affair. Insofar as the surviving letters exchanged between Davison and Amoss (who addressed each other as "Dav" or "Davy" and "Amo") may be trusted as evidence, they appear to have cooperated well in 1929–30 in selecting the other major figures on the staff and in the elaborate planning for the interior arrangement and equipping of the hospital. As mentioned earlier, Amoss was the best known of the original department heads at Duke and had published more important papers than any of the others. When he accepted an appointment as a visiting professor at Peking (Beijing) Union Medical College in China during the second half of 1931, Davison and the others may have regretted his going on leave so early in the medical center's life, but Davison wrote Amoss that he envied him the trip. Responding with an account of his activities in the exotic new setting, Amoss added that the academic year at Duke would be starting soon and that he would be homesick, so "you [Davison] and company have my prayers for a good year."[48] Soon afterwards, Davison wrote that Hanes, who was serving as a visiting associate professor of medicine in the absence of Amoss, was proving to be "splendid." The clinical staff had organized the PDC, which so far was "a great success, for it apparently fills a very great need." With the economic depression as the main topic of conversation, Davison added that stockowners like Amoss and he were "not sleeping very well at night."[49]

One of the most difficult and also embarrassing problems that the medical center faced when it began was that no funds had been earmarked to pay for a professor of psychiatry, or neuropsychiatry, as it was then sometimes called. Yet a class A medical school had to provide instruction in that field, and Davison and Amoss had approached various foundations in the hope of securing help, only to fail in their efforts. In November, 1931, Davison suggested in a letter to Amoss that perhaps the best arrangement might be to invite Hanes to become an associate professor of medicine in charge of neurology and to let the matter of psychiatry go until a well-trained person could be found. Davison thought it would be ideal to find a combined neurologist and psychiatrist, but he had discovered that one speciality always seemed to predominate at the expense of the other.[50]

Amoss responded that he was delighted about the prospect of adding Hanes and agreed that temporizing about psychiatry seemed to be in order. He noted also that he was pleased about the PDC, for it would settle several questions and would "help me tremendously to get out from under the work in regard to private patients." Amoss added that he had been glad to learn that Hart was "making good" and that before long he (Amoss) would be heading home—"with great enthusiasm." [51]

Physicians, for all of their scientific training and manner, are, of course, just as touchy and capable of dissembling in their letters as are other mortals. There probably were problems about Amoss prior to the latter's trip to China, but there is certainly nothing in the correspondence between Davison and Amoss that hints at such a state of affairs. Yet in January, 1933, less than a year after Amoss returned, he signed a notarized statement submitting his resignation as professor of medicine, the same to take effect at such time as might be determined by the executive committee of the university's trustees. (The notary public, incidentally, was Judith Farrar, librarian of the medical school and niece of W. R. Perkins.)

In a confidential memorandum that Davison later submitted to Few, the dean claimed that, knowing of Amoss's difficulties in getting along with colleagues, he had originally selected Amoss "against my better judgment." But he had known Amoss since 1917, and the leaders at Johns Hopkins as well as at the Rockefeller Foundation had recommended him highly. Davison stated that after the opening of the hospital in July, 1930, friction increased between Amoss and the other departmental heads. Aside from alleged problems of temperament, the complaints about Amoss were that he expended so much of his energy caring for private patients that he neglected his departmental duties; and also that although he was appointed at a top salary of $10,000, he refused to assign any of his fees from his private practice to the Department of Medicine. When finally confronted with the unanimous request from the other heads of departments that he resign, Amoss agreed to do so and stated that he would do it without malice or ill feeling. [52]

To complicate the matter further, friends of Amoss at Johns Hopkins and in the Rockefeller organizations were much disturbed by the goings-on at Duke. After a conference in New York with both Davison and Amoss, Abraham Flexner advised Few that he (Flexner) and others in New York believed that the course followed by the medical facility at Duke was "unacademic and would inevitably do the institution infinite damage." Flexner added that nothing was nearer to his heart than the building up of strong centers of scientific education in medicine in the South, specifically at Duke and Vanderbilt, but he thought the dismissal or "practically forced resignation" of Amoss would make that "already hard task infinitely greater." In a subsequent letter, Flexner reiterated the above ideas and emphasized his view that it was of "the highest importance that nothing should happen calculated to deter medical scientists of ability from entering the services of Duke University."[53]

Although Few apparently left the matter in the hands of Davison and his colleagues, Davison agreed, under pressure from Abraham and Simon Flexner, that Amoss should be allowed to try again to establish a more harmonious and satisfactory working relationship with his colleagues at Duke. When that attempt also failed to work out, Davison recommended, and Few agreed, that Amoss's resignation, submitted in January, 1933, be dated not later than February 1, 1934, and that he be relieved of his duty as head of the Department of Medicine not later than October 1, 1933.[54]

Knowledge of the Amoss affair might have been kept largely private, or at least limited to certain medical circles, but Duke in 1932 had employed, at Amoss's suggestion, a part-time visiting psychiatrist, Ernest M. Poate, who was then living in Southern Pines, North Carolina. When Duke failed to renew Poate's contract for the following year, he released a statement to the press in which he mixed a few facts with many distortions, exaggerations, and plain untruths about the Amoss affair and Duke's medical center in general.[55] Although Davison prepared a full rebuttal of the charges for the eyes of Few and the university's executive committee, Duke chose not to enter into a public debate with Poate.

Wiley Forbus in pathology, ignoring the fact that the depression was having its worst impact on Duke during 1933–34, urged Davison to use the small flap about Poate's allegations to show Duke's trustees and administrators that "there wasn't and isn't money and opportunity enough to attract as yet a real first-rate man [in psychiatry]." Forbus argued that the medical faculty should not deny that there was "a certain 'sweat shop' element in our organization" and that it was "only by such methods that we are able to maintain our standards under the prevailing conditions." There was a great need for a real department of ophthalmology (instead of a part-time arrangement) and for a social service department in the hospital, deficiencies which Poate had publicized. "Psychiatry is a huge problem," Forbus concluded, and "we must admit our liability to criticism when we must be satisfied with a second rater . . . because we can't afford any better."[56] Perhaps Davison realized, if Forbus did not, that in late 1933 no amount of protests about inadequate resources could change bleak realities. Fortunately for the medical center, there seemed to be no large or permanent damage to it from the brief flurry about Amoss and Poate.

Perhaps the best objective proof of the essential strength of Duke's young medical school came in the mid-1930s. The Council on Medical Education and Hospitals of the American Medical Association conducted a survey of the sixty-six approved four-year medical schools in the United States and found that Duke's already ranked in the top quarter. The educational programs in anatomy, biochemistry, physiology, bacteriology, and medicine were all rated in the top decile. No ratings were lower than the fourth decile, with the exception of the poor showing of the library's holdings of foreign-language journals and of the clinical facilities for obstetrics.[57] While the medical professors obviously took certain satisfaction from the survey, they noted too that it had been helpful in pointing out weaknesses. They suggested also that though the rating was "flattering for a school which had been organized only five years," it was "not good enough." Believing that the medical center had established satisfactory standards concerning the training of medical students and the care of patients, the faculty hoped to raise the level of research being done in the medical center in an effort to strengthen it further.[58]

One matter that the AMA's council had not investigated was the number of charity patients treated by the various hospitals. Despite the clinical faculty's concern about private patients and how they were to be dealt with, the truth was that Duke Hospital from the day it first opened faced an enormous opportunity, challenge, and burden in the matter of charity work. In the late 1920s North Carolina stood near the bottom of the list of states (forty-sixth out of forty-eight) in per capita income, and the depression that began late in 1929 made an already bad situation even worse. In the first full year of the hospital's operation, 1931, two thirds of the care given was completely free.[59] While J. B. Duke intended for the agencies that his monetary gifts supported to be of the maximum service possible to the public, and especially to the poorer black and white classes, there simply was no provision for an unlimited supply of free medical care. Deficits in the hospital's operating budget had to be covered by Duke University; and as those deficits rose in the early 1930s, Few's worst fears about the possibility of the medical center's swamping the university's boat began to loom as a possibility.

Davison, even in the late 1920s, had shared with others in the medical profession a concern about the rising cost of health care, for scientific medicine bore a price tag to which the public was not accustomed. Inspired by a small-scale hospitalization insurance plan in Roanoke Rapids, North Carolina, and in consultation with Rankin, Davison had tried in vain to start a hospital insurance program in 1929. Finally, in 1933, Davison, in collaboration with George Watts Hill, a prominent Durham capitalist, and others, helped to launch the Hospital Care Association, one of the earliest nonprofit health insurance plans in the nation.[60] It would eventually become a part of the vast Blue Cross-Blue Shield system and was an important step toward helping middle-class people and certain employed groups cope with the cost of health care. It did nothing, however, for poverty-stricken people, and their large number, especially in the 1930s, was the source of the medical center's problem about charity work.

As a first step toward dealing with the charity problem in an era when neither the federal nor the state government accepted any responsibility for health care, Duke officials remembered that J. B. Duke, like his father and brother Ben, had always operated on the principle of helping individuals as well as institutions to help themselves. That is, matching gifts to charitable institutions were usually more effective than a straight handout, for the matching gift stimulated others to pitch in and help. This philosophy lay behind a new policy that Duke Hospital introduced in April, 1933. The primary designer of the policy was F. Vernon Altvater, who had been one of the first two interns in hospital administration when Davison began the program in 1930. The other intern was F. Ross Porter, and in the fall of 1932 Altvater and Porter were named as superintendent and assistant superintendent, respectively, of the hospital.

As a result of an intensive study of records concerning the admission of patients and their bill payments, Altvater found that over 90 percent of patients (outpatients as well as hospitalized patients) were not paying anything. Altvater argued, with supporting evidence, that most patients could pay at least some part of their bills, though in many cases not the full amount. With authorization from the university and medical center authorities, he accordingly placed notices in newspapers throughout North Carolina and adjoining states that after April, 1933, Duke Hospital would not give wholly free medical care. (That turned out to be untrue, of course.) It would, however, try to reconcile costs with the patient's means (as it always had), and for the indigent, Duke Hospital would pay half the costs if the patient's county welfare department or friends, church, lodge, or some other group, would pay the other half.[61]

The plan took time to become effective, but it worked. Virtually all of North Carolina's 100 counties eventually cooperated; by 1940, while 72 percent of patients paid less than cost, through having them pay what they or their supporting agencies could afford, the hospital used the same amount of money annually to treat 15,000 patients instead of giving complete charity care to 4,000 patients.[62]

The other innovation that the hospital introduced as a result of Altvater's studies, the flat-rate or all-inclusive plan of prepayment, also helped limit the hospital's deficit. The original billing policy at Duke, as in most other American hospitals at that time, was to charge patients a daily rate for room and meals plus an additional amount for whatever special services the hospital rendered, such as x-ray, laboratory tests, and such. Altvater's studies revealed that the average patient in Duke Hospital in the early 1930s remained there for 12.8 days, was billed an average rate of $5.20 per day, but actually paid on average only $1.77 per day for care. Not knowing in advance what hospital costs would be, many patients in that era of hard times received bills and began to reflect on Duke University's allegedly "deep pockets" as they requested charity care. Altvater proposed that the hospital charge a flat rate for each day of care (varying according to the type of room) and to have it include most routine extras. Not only would this device employ the insurance principle of spreading hospital costs among the patients, but it would help both the patient and the hospital. A ward patient, for example, whose diagnosis involved only moderate difficulty would pay $49.20 for fourteen days of care under the flat-rate plan, whereas under the original plan the cost would have been $67.50.[63] The hospital would benefit in that while an admitting officer might admit an indigent patient to a ward for as little as a dollar a day, the hospital would be able to collect in advance an average bill of $2.62 per day (instead of the average of $1.77 per day that it had been collecting). Even if the collection rate were only 70 percent of charges, that would allow the hospital, with the $1.00 per day for each charity patient from the Duke Endowment, to cover operating costs and thus expand its services.[64] There were various problems about presenting the flat-rate plan both to the public and to the state's medical profession, but with Watson Rankin's help, Davison and Altvater succeeded in getting it established. In the outpatient clinic the patient's ability to pay continued to be the basic consideration. The combined impact of the flat-rate plan and the cooperative approach to charity care were highly innovative, even if partial, solutions to a problem that not just Duke Hospital but the entire nation would grapple with for the remainder of the century.

James Gifford, the historian of the medical center's first decade, concludes that there were five experiments in the financing of medical care that were started at Duke in the 1930s: the outpatient clinic, which was new only to the region; the flat-rate plan; the cooperative approach to charity care; the Hospital Care Association, in which Davison and Duke Hospital were closely involved; and the private diagnostic clinic. Only the last-named made money, but the overall purpose of the innovations was to help keep the hospital as close to being solvent as possible, a goal fervently hoped for by Few and actively pursued by Davison.[65]

In addition to important innovations in the administrative area of hospitals and health care, the medical center achieved a certain distinction even before World War II from research and technological advances. As the medical professors themselves recognized, to varying degrees and depending on who was commenting, much remained to be done to give research a higher priority in fact, not just in words. Yet from the beginning, there were able, dedicated researchers who did significant work. As Amoss had expected, pellagra received considerable attention from the start, and Perlzweig, D. T. Smith, and Susan Gower Smith began early to do meritorious work in that field. Also contributing to the pellagra research were Julian M. Ruffin, who was a professor of medicine in the original faculty group, and Elsie H. Martin, the hospital dietitian. The investigation of fungal diseases, especially blastomycosis, led to important findings at Duke by D. T. Smith and Donald S. Martin, who joined the faculty in 1932 in the field of preventive medicine. In the field of gynecology, Bayard Carter and Claudius P. Jones, who came in 1936 as a technical research instructor in obstetrics-gynecology, did useful work, while Edwin C. Hamblen, who came in 1931, pioneered in gynecologic endocrinology with highly significant results. The husband-wife team of Frederick and Mary L. C. Bernheim, in pharmacology and biochemistry respectively, conducted experiments concerning the relation of drugs to bodily processes and gained nationally recognized results. That was true also of the discovery of a vaccine against equine encephalomyelitis that was developed by Joseph W. Beard, who came in the field of experimental surgery in 1937 and whose work at Duke on virus tumors was first supported by Lederle Laboratories.[66]

While Deryl Hart regarded himself primarily as a clinician rather than a researcher in surgery, he was responsible for a highly important technological advance—and it was one that had the additional merit of being immediately understandable to laymen. Despite the most elaborate procedures against germs and infections, patients at Duke, as at other hospitals, who had to have major surgery that involved large operative wounds, as in thoracic surgery for example, occasionally became mysteriously infected from an organism known as *Staphylococcus aureus* (hence "staph infection"). This could be quite serious, even fatal, and in the winter of 1933–34 six patients who underwent such surgery and who had clean wounds died. Since that was as many deaths in a few months as had occurred in comparable circumstances since the hospital opened, Hart and his staff proceeded to study exhaustively all aseptic procedures that were employed and to test the "washed" air that was used to ventilate the operating suites. Although tests showed that the air was clean when it entered, it became contaminated from the people in the operating rooms no matter how many vaccines they were given or how thick the masks they wore.

Setting out to sterilize the air, therefore, Hart discovered that rays from a therapeutic ultraviolet light killed the offending organism within sixty seconds at a distance of eight feet. With the help of the Westinghouse company, Hart secured eight, specially designed lamps, tested them with good results on animal subjects, and in January, 1936, performed the first operation on a human patient in a field of ultraviolet radiation. The results from that and subsequent operations brought Hart and Duke hospital to the attention of the whole medical profession. Not only did the patients have less postoperative pain and lower temperatures, but more importantly, the rate of infection in clean wounds dropped dramatically—from 33 to 3.8 percent—and deaths from mysterious infections during radical surgery ceased. Subsequent tests in various parts of the nation confirmed Hart's explanation of the problem and his remedy for it, and while some surgeons complained about the protective clothing and goggles that the staff had to wear under the lamps, that seemed a small price to pay for the great benefits gained.[67]

While Hart's ultraviolet lamps and the various research achievements mentioned earlier added to the prestige of the medical center in the nation's medical profession, there were other activities that probably had a larger, more direct impact in North Carolina and the southeastern region. Beginning in October, 1934, the medical center sponsored a three-day postgraduate symposium each autumn for physicians in the state and region. With outstanding specialists from across the nation featured on the programs, the symposia focused successively on subjects within each of the major divisions in medical practice—medicine, surgery, pediatrics, and obstetrics-gynecology. Almost 300 visitors attended the first of the symposia, but by 1941 there were as many as 1,000 people attending some of the sessions. Starting in 1941 the medical center cooperated with the medical schools at the University of North Carolina and Wake Forest to sponsor two-day postgraduate clinics at Durham's Lincoln Hospital for the African-American physicians of North Carolina.[68]

Pathologist Wiley Forbus performed another type of state-oriented service, one of many activities in the medical center that fitted into the hospital program of the Duke Endowment. Small hospitals were not equipped to perform the pathological tests on tissue removed during operations, as required in hospitals approved by the American College of Surgeons. Consequently, Forbus, in consultation with the Endowment's Watson Rankin, developed an outside pathological service for those hospitals in the Carolinas that were assisted by the Duke Endowment. Not only did the participating hospitals thus secure help in maintaining their standards, but the medical school gained through the additional supply of clinical material for training pathologists and the strengthening of Duke's position as the first referral center in the state.[69]

There were many other ways in which the medical center and the Duke Endowment collaborated for the improvement of health care in the Carolinas, but the medical center itself grew significantly stronger throughout the 1930s. The embittered psychiatrist, E. M. Poate, had been careless in his public indictment of the medical center in 1934, but he had also pointed to some quite real weak spots. One of them was in the social service area, for patients needed all sorts of help with various personal problems with which already overworked physicians were not equipped to deal. The Women's Auxiliary, organized by wives of university faculty members in 1931, helped from the first to add a human dimension to the hospital and played a steadily increasing role in various ways that supported both patients and staff. The members of the auxiliary, however, were part-time volunteers and not trained social workers. When the hospital opened and for several years thereafter, a single social worker faced a daunting task in coping with the ever-increasing number of patients who sought help with bill payment, transportation and housing arrangements, care during convalescence, and countless other such matters. Finally, in 1937, Davison persuaded Doris Duke Cromwell to provide anonymous support, which, combined with funds from the university, made possible the establishment of a full social service division in the hospital. The staff, which grew by 1950 to include a director plus eight caseworkers and two secretaries, not only worked with patients but assisted in the instruction of medical students and nurses. The division also cooperated with the School of Social Work at the University of North Carolina to give practical training to graduate students in the program.[70]

Psychiatry also was a weak spot, as mentioned earlier, but in the late 1930s help finally came from two main sources. Even before the medical center opened Davison tried to find support that would enable Duke to have a department of neuropsychiatry, but he had failed. The short, unhappy experience with Poate was followed by the appointment of a Hopkins-trained psychiatrist, Raymond G. Crispell, so that medical students could be taught, but there were no facilities for primary psychiatric cases. A study paid for by the Rockefeller Foundation and inspired by Davison and his colleagues pointed up North Carolina's great needs in the field of psychiatric care, but the state government took no action in response to the report. Davison therefore again sought help from the Rockefeller Foundation to develop a department of psychiatry at Duke. While this was being considered, Dr. Robert S. Carroll, the proprietor of a long-established mental hospital in Asheville, North Carolina, gave it outright to Duke University. That, plus the availability of a psychiatric ward in old space that became available when the new wing was completed in 1940, led the Rockefeller Foundation to grant $175,000 over a seven-year period for the establishment of a full department of psychiatry. Richard S. Lyman, another Johns Hopkins product, became the first chairman of the new department, the creation of which completed the original plan for the medical school and hospital.[71]

With the completion of the new wing and the resolution of the problem about psychiatry, Hanes, thinking along lines that were quite unusual in the medical center, proposed that its executive committee should go on record against further expansion on the grounds that the center was already as large as it should ever be. How seriously Hanes himself took his proposal is not known, but it probably was greeted by a stunned silence. Deryl Hart much later recalled that at first he alone spoke up in opposition. After discussion, the committee defeated the motion, largely on the grounds that the existing committee members should not try to anticipate the needs of their successors or to restrict their freedom of action.[72]

In light of the center's subsequent history, Hanes's motion has an ironic aspect. From the perspective of a later time (1971), Hart thought that because of the depression and then World War II there had been "very slow growth" of the medical center during the period from 1930 to 1945.[73] The center's growth was, in fact, slow in comparison with what happened after 1945, and especially after 1950, but in comparison with the other parts of the university during its first quarter-century, the medical center was far ahead in terms of expansion, with reference to both buildings and personnel. Not counting alterations in the original building which resulted in more space (such as the roofing over of a courtyard to enlarge the medical library), the medical center in its first decade added the nurses' residence (Baker House) and the large PDC wing. The faculty of the medical school grew from twenty-three in 1930 to sixty-six in 1940, and that did not include instructors, fellows, and such.[74] World War II put a halt to that steady expansion that later looked so "slow" to Hart, but it would indeed be only a temporary halt.

Leaders in the medical center were no more prescient about world affairs in the late 1930s than were most other Americans. When the United States Army requested in April, 1940, that Duke form a medical unit for overseas service in case of a national emergency, the medical center refused the invitation. That was before the fall of France, however, and that shattering event—plus developments in other parts of the world that frightened the great majority of Americans—caused profound changes in many minds. When the Navy subsequently dragged its feet in response to Duke's offer to form a medical unit, Davison and his colleagues turned to the Army, and it authorized the formation of a Duke unit, North Carolina General Hospital no. 65. Appropriately enough, Hanes had commanded a general hospital with the same name and number in World War I.[75]

Two members of the original staff, Elbert L. Persons and Clarence E. Gardiner, Jr., became heads, respectively, of the 65th's medical and surgical services. Julia Elizabeth White, the assistant dean of the nursing school, served as chief nurse. These three took the lead in recruiting and organizing the 65th's large staff, which was predominantly composed of Duke-related personnel. Stationed first at Fort Bragg, North Carolina, from July, 1942, until the end of July, 1943, the unit proceeded to go overseas but did so in World War II Army fashion, that is, slowly and via several stopovers. Finally, in October, 1943, the 65th sailed for England on the converted *Queen Elizabeth*.

Assigned at first to a "cantonment type hospital" that had Nissen huts for living quarters and barracks for wards, the 65th was initially located near Malvern, a small city in central England, northwest of London. The early days there were obviously not too demanding, for the historians of the unit report that "off-duty hours were spent inspecting the English countryside via bicycle, studying cathedral architecture and adapting one's individual physiology to British beer, no perspiration [?] and Brussels sprouts."[76]

Even after the hospital opened for patients in December, 1943, things remained relatively quiet, for there were no troops stationed in the immediate vicinity. Things changed, however, in March, 1944, when the 65th was ordered to take over a hospital in East Anglia near the English Channel. On the day the 65th arrived, 1,000 heavy bombers attacked Berlin during daylight hours, and twenty-three fresh casualties came in that night. Before daylight the following day, two bombers crashed on takeoff, and their injured were brought in before the previous night's work was completed. "Thus began a continuous operation of an active hospital," the historians state, "which was maintained without interruption until the day of inactivation on 29 August 1945."[77]

Meantime, on the home front the medical center responded to the war much as did the rest of the university—with sharply reduced and overworked personnel. With one third of the medical faculty away on active military duty, those remaining took on heavy overloads in teaching, without extra pay, as their contribution to the war effort. With doctors and nurses in urgent demand, the medical center adopted an accelerated teaching program to produce as many graduates as possible in as expeditious a manner as possible. The medical school increased the size of the entering class by 10 percent and admitted a new class every nine months, thereby increasing its output of physicians by 46.6 percent.[78]

The nursing school also responded to the emergency in various ways. As requested by federal agencies, it increased its class size from fifty-eight to eighty-four (and even larger) and admitted a new class every nine months. Entrance requirements were temporarily lowered to a half year of college work, including chemistry. In July, 1943, the United States Public Health Service initiated the cadet nurses corps at Duke and other schools, and this led to even larger nursing classes. To house at least some of the student nurses, a new dormitory for nurses, paid for partly by the federal government, went up on Erwin Road. Flowers noted privately that the new dormitory was not "in keeping" with Duke's other buildings (at that time), but it could not be seen from the hospital.[79]

In 1942–43 all medical students were eligible for inactive commissions without salary in the Army Medical Corps, the Naval Reserve, or the United States Public Health Service, and over 90 percent of the eligible students took that option. Davison and his colleagues thought that arrangement worked well. In 1943, however, when the Army and Navy began their college training programs, against the better judgment of

Davison and his associates, the medical school had to alter its program to conform with those of the Navy V-12(S) and the Army Specialized Training Program (ASTP). Most male medical students thereafter became, for the duration, uniformed army privates or navy seamen and, in addition to having their tuition and maintenance paid by the government, received $65 per month ($90 if married) while in medical school.[80]

Because the medical school's first class to graduate was in 1932, Duke's medical alumni were a relatively young group, and Duke had the highest percentage in the nation of medical alumni on active duty. In fact, the majority of the 722 graduates and postgraduates (former members of the house staff) who had completed at least nine months of internship were medical officers on active duty in the Army or Navy. Elizabeth Swett, the secretary of the admissions committee and a person who significantly humanized medical school for a generation of Duke students, kept in touch with most of the military alumni through frequent newsletters.[81]

In addition to the heavy teaching load, many medical faculty and staff members were involved in various war-related research projects ranging from tropical diseases to chemical warfare. Many also served on national committees or as consultants to various boards in Washington or elsewhere. Davison was on a train for a substantial portion of the war, for he travelled to countless places on medico-military business. In 1942–43 he served as vice chairman of the National Research Council's Division of Medical Sciences and spent weekdays in Washington and weekends in Durham doing the dean's work. As he later put it, he "developed 'an infinite capacity for taking trains.'" The rail beds were so rough, however, that he claimed he had to engage in "chemical warfare" to get rest: with the help of Seconal he could sleep, but the next day he had to take benzedrine and drink numerous Coca-Colas to stay awake. Davison recounted that one night on his Durham-Washington run, he got on a troop train filled with "a very hilarious group of 'G.I.s'" and only got some sleep after introducing Seconal to the soldiers around him. There was a bright side, he avowed, to all the rough train rides. Davison was plagued by a problem with excess weight, but he found an unforeseen solution: "As I slept on my tummy, the jolting of the train over the rapidly deteriorating roadbed soon massaged off twenty pounds of my weight so, in that sense, I was a war profiteer."[82]

While Davison and others on the faculty carried on their myriad wartime activities, the hospital operated under difficult conditions. With an average daily census of 450 and an occupancy rate of 80 percent, the hospital faced an acute shortage of skilled personnel of all types. Red Cross volunteer nurse's aides, 258 of them, helped save the day, and Girl Scouts scurried about serving as messengers. Although there was no publicity about it at the time, forty-five conscientious objectors, members of the

Civilian Public Service Corps, rendered valuable services on the wards and in the operating rooms. There were even twenty prisoners of war who, under military supervision, worked in the housekeeping department.

The length of the internship required of newly graduated doctors was reduced to nine months during the war, and the shortage of interns and residents especially hurt all teaching hospitals. In 1940 Duke Hospital had a house staff of 125 (48 interns and 77 residents), but by 1945 the combined figure had shrunk to 70 (35 of each).[83]

If the wartime years were strenuous ones for those who worked in and ran the medical center, the immediate postwar years brought a new type of problem that brought serious and perplexing dilemmas: inflation. It affected the whole university, of course, as it did the nation, but charitable institutions were in a special bind as expenses soared ahead of income. In the medical school, the tuition had always been more than in the colleges—$150 per quarter from 1930 until after World War II. Then, as inflation set in, the tuition went to $200 per quarter in 1946 and to $250 in 1948.[84]

As for the hospital, patient costs increased slightly before and during the early years of the war: from $4.51 per day in 1936 to $5.35 in 1940 to $5.73 in 1942. But by 1947 the figure had reached $12.36 and was steadily climbing. Attempting to meet the rising costs, the hospital kept increasing the rates charged to patients, yet income failed to keep pace with costs. In 1947, for example, when the average daily patient cost was $12.36, the average daily collection from patients was $10.12, meaning an average daily loss of $2.24 per patient. Since the university had to cover that loss, the hospital's predicament posed a serious problem for the whole institution.[85]

In the postwar years, when the American economy was vastly different from what it had been in the early 1930s, Duke Hospital—actually Duke University—continued to carry a significant load of charity work. It was not as much proportionately as during the first years of the depression, but in absolute terms around 1950 it amounted to almost $384,000. In 1947–48 the university had to subsidize the medical center to the tune of $700,284 in order to cover the difference between expenses and income.[86] Since that amount was too large a portion of the university's income from the Duke Endowment, drastic changes had to be, and were, made. But as is discussed in the last two chapters, bloody, long-continuing battles about the budget had begun between Davison and his colleagues in the medical center on the one hand and the university administrators on the other.

Despite the problems caused by inflation, the medical center strengthened itself in various ways, and there were important changes. After F. H. Swett's death in 1934, Joseph E. Markee succeeded him as head of the anatomy department. The death of F. M. Hanes in 1946 removed a major figure not only from the medical center but also from the university, which he had served in numerous important ways. In 1947 Eugene A. Stead, Jr., who was to play a major role in the subsequent development of the medical center, succeeded Hanes as head of the Department of Medicine. Frank G. Hall succeeded G. S. Eadie as head of physiology in 1949, and Philip Handler, another major figure in the center, became head of biochemistry in 1950 following the death of William A. Perlzweig.

The increasing focus on research was facilitated in the postwar years by the vastly increased role that the federal government played in science and medicine. The first unit of a building specifically designated for research purposes went up in 1944; in 1948 a second unit was added, and three more were still to come. With funds for the construction coming from a variety of different sources, the university named the building for William B. Bell, a longtime friend of the institution and particularly the medical center, a trustee of the Duke Endowment, and president of the American Cyanamid company.[87]

While medical research at Duke had a bright future indeed, that of nursing remained more problematical. The gender issue probably played a role, for the male- and doctor-dominated American Medical Association pulled in one direction—toward the bedside—while the predominantly female nursing organizations pulled in another—toward the classroom and greater professional recognition for nurses. In 1940, as mentioned earlier, Duke took the AMA's or the male doctors' preferred route and dropped the bachelor of science degree, offering only the three-year diploma program. The following year, however, after protests from nursing alumnae and others, Duke briefly reinstated the B.S. program and then again discontinued it in 1944, probably in response to the urgent wartime need for nurses regardless of degrees. The shilly-shallying continued after the war, and in 1947 the B.S. degree in nursing came back. It could be obtained under a new arrangement whereby candidates for the degree did two years of work in the Woman's College before taking their three years of nursing instruction, with Helen Nahm named as the professor in that field.

Just as the student nurses' options about credentials kept changing, so too did their residential arrangements. With an eye toward using Baker House for the house staff, Davison and his associates tried to get a new dormitory for the nurses in 1940, at an estimated cost of $750,000.[88] That attempt failed, and new construction became quite difficult from 1941 on through the war.

Despite the acquisition of the relatively small nurses' dormitory (later known as Hanes Annex) in 1943, the idea of building a new, large dormitory and classroom building for the nurses remained much alive. Before his death in 1946, Hanes revived his prewar offer and plan, but the university's trustees refused again to assume the financial responsibility. (They were already committed to an extensive building program for engineering and physics and, as discussed in chapter 14 below, were confronting the fact that faculty salaries were being drastically eroded by inflation.) Hanes then arranged with his wife, Elizabeth Peck Hanes, who was a former nurse, that she would give $1,000,000 to the university to build the new facility for the nurses. "My heart will always be in our medical school and therefore at Duke University," Elizabeth Hanes wrote Flowers, "so that it is a joy to me to do anything that contributes in any way to the advancement of the highest ideals."[89]

Not only did the medical center gain the enthusiastic support of faculty members like Hanes, but its alumni were among the most tightly knit and loyal groups in Duke's constituency. Men and women who earned their M.D. and nursing degrees at Duke were the most numerous of the medical alumni, but to an extent that outsiders probably did not understand, many interns and residents developed strong ties with the medical center. Looking back over the first decade, Hanes insisted in 1940 that the money the hospital had spent on its large house staff was "the most productive of all its expenditures." He thought the greatest advance the Department of Medicine had made was its development of a program whereby during a twenty-five-month period and by successive three-month steps, the house officers (interns and residents) were trained in every branch of internal medicine, including three months in neurology and psychiatry.[90] Hart in surgery also emphasized the importance of the postgraduate students. Noting that the number of residents in surgery had increased from five to thirty-one during the first decade, Hart stressed that the pattern of three- to six-year training periods for residents in surgery and the surgical specialities had become firmly established. "The development of such a prolonged period of surgical training for the graduate student will turn out in this part of the South highly trained surgeons," Hart declared, "and will probably have a greater influence on surgery in this section than the undergraduate [i.e., medical student] surgical instruction in the School."[91] If many members of the hospital's house staff developed strong ties with the medical center, one reason clearly was that the faculty emphasized and apparently enjoyed teaching and working alongside the younger physicians.

Surveying the medical center's achievement in its first decade, James Gifford concluded that four factors played a predominant role. First, the long-lasting poverty of the South after 1865 meant that Duke was committed to an effort "to stop the continuing migration of patients, medical students, and doctors from the region in search of competent treatment, clinical training, and more rewarding opportunities to practice." The second major influence was the standard of medical education set by Johns

Hopkins, which was built on the principles of laboratory science in the preclinical years,bedside teaching of the art of medicine in the clinical years, and close contact between teachers and students. The third factor was J. B. Duke's generosity, which guaranteed the university the finest facilities in the South at the time and which gave the medical center the opportunity of collaborating with the Duke Endowment "in the attempt to modernize medicine in the Carolinas" (and make it more accessible to people of both races). Fourth and finally, Gifford suggests that the depression (and the fact that Duke, for all its blessings, did not have all the resources it needed) forced the medical faculty to be efficient and imaginative as teacher-clinicians and the medical administrators to be innovative.[92]

Gifford quite correctly goes on to say that those four factors alone could not have produced the strong medical center if it had not been for the imaginative leadership and contagious enthusiasm of Davison. A relatively young man when named dean, he gambled on other beginners, shared power with them (at least the heads of departments), and as Gifford notes, the subsequent "participation in achievement built confidence in individuals and individual commitment to the institution."[93]

Deryl Hart also, looking back from a later period, suggested that the most important single factor in the development of the medical center had been "a contagious *esprit de corps* which has resulted in staff enthusiasm for what we have been trying to do." That spirit was carefully nurtured from the first, Hart explained, and the staff had confidence in the future of the center. He thought too that if Duke had possessed unlimited resources during the formative early years, the staff would never have developed such a sense of loyalty, pride, and unity.[94]

Clearly, as Duke ended its first quarter-century and a new president, A. Hollis Edens, reported for duty early in 1949, the medical center had developed into one of the strongest, most widely respected components of the university. The true "glory years" lay ahead, too, for a vast new Veterans Administration hospital, affiliated with Duke and just across Erwin Road from the center, was about to open in 1950. Various agencies of the federal government were beginning to make unparalleled new resources available for medical scientists. Not only was the medical faculty cohesive, as Hart stressed, but it was aggressive in pursuit of ambitious goals. As early as 1935 and long before most other components of the university had begun to think about and prepare long-range plans, each of the medical school's department heads spelled out needs and hopes for the next decade. The unforeseen war temporarily thwarted many of those plans, but the mere fact that the medical center generated them so early was significant. Again in 1940, the medical leaders seized the occasion of the center's tenth anniversary not only to summarize the decade's achievements but to emphasize an agenda for the future.[95]

Later on, Davison would look back on the years of the Few and Flowers administrations and, drawing on biblical lore, describe them as being for the medical center "like Joseph's years of plenty in Egypt." They were followed, the dean continued, by "eleven lean years" under Hollis Edens.[96] What Davison probably could not see or certainly not agree with was the notion that for all of the medical center's great strength and success, it was not the only ambitious unit in Duke University. If, in its unrelenting drive for expansion and quality, it consumed a disproportionate share of the limited resources available for the whole institution, then the dream of Few, J. B. Duke, and others for a research university of all-around excellence would be compromised. That, however, would be a battle for the 1950s.

12

The Rebuilding of Duke University's
School of Law, 1925–1947

‹❧›

THE CREATION OF a full-fledged, nationally recognized law school proved to be another difficult task that President William Preston Few faced. Although Few began almost immediately in 1925 to search for an outstanding legal scholar to serve as dean and help plan and staff the law school, the search ended up taking five frustration-filled years. Once found, the new dean of Duke's law school, Justin Miller, played the key role in getting it off to a brilliant start insofar as its faculty and program were concerned. Yet by 1934 President Few and some of his close advisors had for a variety of reasons grown disenchanted with the young, ambitious dean, and Miller resigned from his position at Duke in somewhat ambiguous circumstances early in 1935. Prior to that time, however, Few at one point felt that the long, careful search for a dean of the law school had ended up most auspiciously indeed. What initially justified that verdict and what happened subsequently to change it?

In launching an expanded law school, Duke built on a respectable foundation that had been laid in Trinity College. Although Trinity had offered an undergraduate course in law as early as 1868 and there had been intermittent attention to instruction in law after that date, not until 1904 did Trinity establish a School of Law. Underwritten by annual payments from Benjamin N. Duke and his younger brother, James B. Duke, the school was headed by Samuel Fox Mordecai, a colorful teacher and strong legal scholar. At a time when many law schools required no previous college work of its students—indeed, many persons still prepared to become lawyers by "reading" law with a practitioner rather than by attending any college or law school—Trinity joined a select group in requiring from the first that entrants in the law school had to have completed two years of college work. In its second year Trinity's law school was invited to join the new Association of American Law Schools, which then had among its thirty members only one other institution from the South, the University of Tennessee. Employing the case method that Harvard had pioneered in the late nineteenth century, Trinity's law school remained small, but it stuck by its high standards and remained indifferent to numbers.[1]

With Dean Mordecai in his mid-seventies and unwell by the time Duke University was underway, Few at first took what was for him a most uncharacteristic stance: he sought a southerner to head the expanded law school. Few, like his predecessor at Trinity, John C. Kilgo, and like others in key faculty and administrative posts at Trinity, took great pride in Trinity's maintaining a broadly national and "reconstructed" outlook. Shunning both neo-Confederate romanticism and embittered sectional defensiveness, Trinity College sought to exemplify forward-looking aspects of the New South. The fact that both Washington Duke and his sons were staunch Republicans who combined deep Tar Heel roots and attachments with national economic interests only served to strengthen and underscore Trinity's orientation. Yet when Few began the search for a dean of the law school, he privately confessed: "For this particular place I feel that the preference should be given to a man of Southern antecedents or associations, though I have never before intimated this as a requirement for men in any of the posts here. In fact more than half the men on the Trinity College staff are not from the South."[2] Few never elaborated on his regional preference concerning the legal deanship, but the fact was obvious that law possessed more state and regional peculiarities and ramifications than, for example, medicine or theology. At any rate, Few would end up with a non-southerner, but the original preference was one factor in the long delay in the naming of the dean.

Concerning the law school, Few worked closely with William R. Perkins, legal advisor to James B. Duke and chief author of the indenture establishing the Duke Endowment. It was no wonder, then, that Few early on informed Perkins, "I shall look rather especially to you for help in matters connected with the Law School."[3]

Writing to a friend of Perkins's in Yale's law school, Few requested the suggestion of a "thoroughly first-rate man" to head up the Duke school, "a man of the calibre that you would require in a dean of the Yale Law School."[4] Letters soliciting suggestions also went to Huger W. Jervey, dean of law at Columbia, and to a Harvard law professor. One of the men whose name cropped up in response to these initial inquiries actually visited Duke at Few's request in April, 1925, but Few soon advised Perkins that "I am not quite sure that he is just the man for dean."[5] Meantime, as Few took the lead in the search for a dean of the new School of Religion, as well as participating in the searches for various key appointees in the arts and sciences, Robert L. Flowers interviewed various law deans and prospective appointees in the North. Another strategically placed ally was George B. Pegram, an alumnus of Trinity who served as dean of Columbia's School of Mines, Engineering, and Chemistry. At Pegram's request, Harlan Stone, associate justice of the United States Supreme Court, wrote Few with a list of suggestions for the Duke deanship.[6]

Having successfully recruited the new dean of the School of Religion, Edmund D. Soper, at Northwestern University, Few promptly requested him to seek advice from the dean of the law school there. Officials of the Rockefeller Foundation in New York, with whom Few conferred in June, 1925, also recommended the Northwestern dean as a likely source of sound advice, and Few promptly began corresponding with him. Warned of the substantial salaries being paid in top law schools, Few calmly replied that he was quite familiar with that aspect but "still I am desirous of getting for dean here a man of just such calibre as would be required at one of these [top] places."[7]

One bit of advice to which Few quietly, but firmly, paid no heed came from a Trinity alumnus in law. His premise was that various developments at Trinity College early in the century—such as President John C. Kilgo's "independent attitude" and the trustees' defense of academic freedom and unorthodox racial views in the Bassett affair in 1903—had estranged the lawyers of North Carolina from Trinity and inspired them to criticize it as a "Northern Methodist institution." Since Duke now needed the goodwill and interest of the South's lawyers, eighty-five percent of whom the alumnus believed to be "in sympathy with the traditions of the Old South," Duke had to "legitimately cultivate their friendship." This it could do by avoiding the mistake of other institutions in naming a "big, scholarly man" as dean and choosing instead a lawyer who had practiced extensively or served as a judge, one who had ability as an executive and a "publicity man."[8]

Although Few had a knack for graciously side-stepping unsolicited advice with which he disagreed, a "big, scholarly man," preferably of southern origins, was precisely what he wanted for the Duke deanship. And in the spring of 1926 he finally believed, after several false starts and disappointments, that he had found just the person to fill the bill. Huger W. Jervey, forty-seven-year-old dean of law at Columbia, was a native of Charleston, South Carolina, and a graduate first of the University of the South (Sewanee) and then of Columbia's law school. Recommended to Few by various persons as well as by his prestigious position and geographical origins, Jervey negotiated—or perhaps dallied—with Few about the post at Duke over an unusually long period. A visit to the campus in

March, 1926, had to be cancelled because of Jervey's illness. Then, when Few subsequently tracked him down in June, 1926, at the Mayo Clinic, where Jervey was being treated for an ulcer, Jervey preferred that Few not make the trip out to Minnesota but wait until Jervey travelled to Charleston for a rest. Since his health had become problematical, Jervey felt that tackling a new job would be impossible. "Get your dean," he urged Few, "and if some day he and you feel that you would like a Southerner to teach Constitutional Law to Southerners, it may be that the urge to go back to the South would be more than I could resist, although a thousand things might happen between now and then to make it impossible." The transplanted Charlestonian asserted his belief that, though his conscience fought against his leaving Columbia, the "South is the critical point of a good deal of our national development today." Duke had a "glorious opportunity," and, frankly, "selfish feelings lead me to wish I could have shared in it."[9]

Was it a yes, a no, or a maybe? Few, unfortunately as it turned out, interpreted the letter as a maybe, and replied that Jervey was "the only man I know who is at once thoroughly familiar with our field and with the problems of a first-class modern law school." Few therefore looked forward to talking with Jervey when he returned to the East and felt like conferring.[10] That time was slow in coming, for in July and August, 1926, Few could not locate his elusive quarry. By the time Few finally reestablished contact in November, 1926, his own sense of urgency about the law school was on hold, at least temporarily.

The less important, transitory reason for Few's slowing down about the law school was that the building program for Duke's physical plant was unusually vast as well as complex. The old Trinity campus, beginning in the late summer of 1925, was being totally rebuilt. Upon the near completion of that campus, work was to begin on the even more extensive Tudor Gothic buildings on the new campus a mile or so to the west of the old one. Until that campus was ready for occupancy (in September, 1930, as it turned out), the old Trinity campus had to house Duke's undergraduates, male and female, as well as the growing number of graduate and professional students, not to mention the burgeoning faculty. In short, when the first phase of the building program fell somewhat behind schedule in 1926, Few and his associates found themselves increasingly short of space on a crowded, construction-filled campus. Few admitted to Perkins, that under the circumstances, Duke was probably fortunate not to have "a budding law school" on its hands in September 1926.[11]

A more substantial and long-range reason for Few's temporary and partly accidental decision to slow down on the law school was, as has been mentioned earlier, that money was not actually as abundant at Duke as a dazzled public, including many at Duke and in its constituency, long and erroneously believed. Concerning the law school, Few in an early and still optimistic phase, had privately boasted that funds had been allocated to make Duke's "at this time the best endowed law school in this country; and a large amount has already been set apart from the building fund for the purchase of a great law library."[12] The embarrassing truth about inadequate funding gradually became clear, but unfortunately only after James B. Duke died in October, 1925.

One possible solution to the painful dilemma was to seek additional endowment in the form of gifts. Given the tremendous even if often misleading publicity concerning J. B. Duke's very great generosity to the university, Few could hardly go public with his campaign. Behind the scenes, however, he quietly canvassed among a number of the wealthy businessmen in New York who had been associated in one enterprise or another with J. B. Duke. One who greatly assisted in this effort was Clinton Toms, the president of the Liggett & Myers Company and longtime staunch friend of both Few and Trinity-Duke. In response to Few's appeal for help, Toms advised that he liked Few's memorandum concerning the law school, and if C. C. Dula, chairman of Liggett & Myers's board of directors, showed no interest in helping with a school of business, then Toms would talk with him concerning the law school. Many months as well as many conversations and letters later, Few supplied a more fully developed statement about the law school for Toms to use with Dula. "A million now and a million in his will might do it," Few coolly suggested, "if he can't be brought to give all now."[13] Dula fell short of having Duke's law school named for himself, for Toms could only secure from him a gift of stock worth $200,000.[14]

While searching, mostly in vain, for substantial new endowments, Few temporized concerning the law school. The law students had to be taught, however, and Mordecai's death in 1927 left a void. Few took one measure to alleviate the situation by making two appointments. The first, in July, 1927, was W. Bryan Bolich, a Trinity alumnus who had gone on to take, with high honors, degrees in jurisprudence and civil law at Oxford University before entering the practice of law in Winston-Salem, North Carolina.[15] The other appointment was Thaddeus D. Bryson, a graduate in law from the University of North Carolina who had become widely respected in the state as a judge of the Superior Court. Bryson's appointment was partly a bid for recognition and support for Duke's law school from the North Carolina bar, and as such it indeed worked well. Among others who praised the appointment, Angus W. McLean, the governor of North Carolina, considered Bryson one "who understands fully the genius of our people" and the appointment "most fortunate for Duke University and the State."[16]

Still pursuing Huger Jervey, Few had consulted him before making the two new appointments. Few's efforts to confer with him in the spring of 1928 failed, but when Jervey finally visited the Duke campus in June, 1928, he was still ambivalent about the Duke post; that is, he stated that he would like a professorship in the law school but remained uncertain about serving as dean. Moreover, he was worried about an adequate law library as well as proper support from the trustees. Few continued to hope that Jervey would at least give the deanship a try without making a final commitment.[17] By late 1928, however, Few was clearly losing patience; and, though the record is not clear, either he abandoned the pursuit early in 1929 or Jervey finally rejected the offer unequivocally. At any rate, by that time Few was fortunately primed for another line of attack on the problem of the law school deanship.

An old friend of Few's from his years at Harvard's graduate school, Francis G. Caffey, had become a prominent lawyer and then a federal judge in New York. Caffey wrote Few about a chance conversation with William Draper Lewis. Formerly dean of the University of Pennsylvania's law school, Lewis had become the founder and director of the American Law Institute, a prestigious organization of academic lawyers and practitioners who were undertaking to produce authoritative restatements concerning various aspects of the law. Lewis expressed interest in advising Few about the planned expansion in law at Duke.[18] Few, pursuing other leads, and particularly Huger Jervey, at the time of Caffey's letter, did not promptly follow up on the suggestion about William Draper Lewis. There was correspondence, however, and early in 1929 Few and several of his associates conferred with Lewis in Pinehurst, North Carolina. When Few rejected Lewis's proposal that Duke's law school become primarily a research-oriented affiliate of the American Law Institute, Lewis suggested that a committee of leading figures from the law schools and the legal profession might be assembled to advise Duke about its law school. Few liked the idea and requested Lewis to engineer "the whole thing for us, of course allowing us to pay the expenses." Few recalled that an official of the Rockefellers' General Education Board had made a similar suggestion concerning Duke's proposed medical school, and the ensuing conference at Johns Hopkins University in 1927 had resulted happily in the naming of Wilburt C. Davison as the first dean of Duke's medical school.

Among the half-dozen prominent legal scholars whom Lewis recruited to write advisory statements concerning Duke's law school were the law deans at Minnesota, Pennsylvania, and Southern California, as well as prominent professors of law at Harvard, Yale, and Columbia. While emphases varied in the statements, there was among them agreement that Duke's law school should be kept small (which quite suited the traditional Trinity-Duke preference for quality rather than large numbers) and that a carefully selected faculty of legal specialists should be expected both to teach and to do scholarly research.[19] A dinner at the Mayflower Hotel in Washington, D.C., in May, 1929, brought together Few, Lewis, and various members of the advisory panel.

The immediate upshot of the procedure which Lewis had arranged was that Few considered one of the advisors, Professor Noel T. Dowling of Columbia, as a possibility for the Duke deanship. Dowling indicated, however, that he could not work a visit to Duke into his schedule in the immediate future, so Few abandoned the idea.[20] He confessed to W. R. Perkins that he was beginning to feel a sense of urgency about the law school deanship.[21]

Loyal alumnus as well as admirer of Harvard, Few turned once more to distinguished leaders there for whatever assistance they might give about his law school problem. He prefaced his request with the explanation that he and his associates at Duke had had five strenuous years since the university was launched: "In that period we have done worlds of building, have taken on eighty new men, have dealt with fundamental problems in the government and administration of the institution, and have all along continued to widen and strengthen the financial foundations here." Few added that he felt fairly well satisfied that not only had much been done but it would stand the test of time. But now, "right up against the problem of organizing the Law School," he requested three names, in order of preference, for the deanship of the law school. "The Law School here will have an extraordinary opportunity," Few concluded, "if the man who ought to head it up can be found and secured."[22]

Even as Few wrote again seeking help in Cambridge and elsewhere, he sadly confessed to his old Harvard contemporary, Judge Caffey, that he doubted that Duke's law school dean would be a Harvard man. "You and I were at Harvard about the time the University of Chicago was being set up," Few recalled. "I distinctly remember at Cambridge an indifferent or high-hat attitude towards the great new undertaking at Chicago." Only recently at the University of Chicago, Few thought Harvard's influence there was still conspicuous by its absence. "We are certain to see here in Durham the largest university development in the country since the establishment of Chicago," he continued. "Am I mistaken or am I not, in the feeling that there is about Harvard a less real understanding of our situation than in other university centers? And is this partly my fault?" Few asserted that he had always felt that as Harvard should have led in Chicago's development, so it should be a great factor in the building of Duke. "I am puzzled about all this," the obviously frustrated Harvard alumnus concluded, "and am anxious for light as well as for light on our Law School problems."[23]

Ironically, while Few continued to hope for light from the East, he was about to find the new dean for the law school in the Far West. Even before writing to Dean Roscoe Pound at Harvard and to the other eminent educators, Few had arranged for another member of Lewis's panel of advisors, Justin Miller, dean of the law school at the University of Southern California, to visit Duke around Christmas of 1929. Shortly afterwards, Few, both relieved and hopeful, practically exulted in reporting to Perkins that he believed "that for us, everything considered," Miller was "the best man I have seen and I do not except Jervey."[24]

Waiting to learn Miller's decision about the Duke offer, Few undertook to answer the questions that Miller had posed in a letter. Few explained that while Duke had inherited Trinity's "obligations to the Methodist church," everybody clearly understood that "we are in no way undertaking to build a denominational university." Both the board of trustees and the executive committee were free from outside interference, and "there are no religious tests of any kind prescribed in our charter or statutes." In short, Few believed that Duke possessed "as good form of ultimate control as any university in America."

After reassuring the weather-conscious resident of southern California about North Carolina's mild climate, which included "much open weather" even in winter, Few explained that both students and faculty came from a wide geographical area; that "a man with ability to get on anywhere can get on here"; and that Miller need not fear any trouble on account of not being a southerner. When, in a subsequent letter, Few reported that $10,000—over half of the $18,000 total for student aid that came from the Angier B. Duke Memorial Scholarship fund—would be available for fifty tuition scholarships in the law school, Miller accepted the post.[25]

A native Californian, Miller was forty-one when he arrived at Duke in July, 1930. A Stanford undergraduate, he had obtained a law degree at the University of Montana and then a doctorate in law at Stanford. Moving upwards rapidly through a series of jobs, both as a practicing lawyer and as a public official, he had taught in the law schools of the Universities of Oregon, Minnesota, and California before becoming dean of the law school at the University of Southern California in 1927. Able, ambitious, and energetic, as well as handsome, Miller was definitely a rising star in the legal world. A specialist in criminal law, he chaired the American Bar Association's Section of Criminal Law and Criminology. He had, in fact, led in revitalizing the section's work by involving it in cooperative endeavors with the American Prison Association, the American Medical Association, and various psychiatric and social-work organizations. Problems relating to the parole and probation system, to police work, and to juvenile delinquency and rehabilitation interested Miller, and he served as vice president of the National Probation Association and was actively involved in a large number of similar organizations. His membership on the fourteen-person executive committee of the National Crime Commission—he was the only law dean in the group—brought him into contact with such prominent figures as New York's Governor Franklin D. Roosevelt, who was also a member of the executive committee. After attending one of the crime commission's meetings in the spring of 1931, Miller, who kept a low profile politically while at Duke but had earlier been a progressive Republican, reported that Governor Roosevelt had made a "splendid address" and that many North Carolinians would be happy to support him for the presidency if the opportunity should arise.[26] Miller, as one admiring chief of police wrote, was clearly "not the ordinary type of academician." Being "down on the ground with both feet," he had at one point, according to the police chief, been "one of the most famous prosecuting attorneys of this country" before becoming a professor of law; then Duke had heard of him and "doubled the salary paid to him by the University of Southern California." Miller, the chief concluded, was simply "foremost in the ranks" of those seeking to reform criminal procedure in the nation.[27]

One explanation for Miller's prominence in so many national organizations related to the law and crime is that he obviously enjoyed speaking in public and apparently did it most proficiently. One of his friends at Harvard's law school wrote teasingly that he hoped Miller would have time to reply "between the interstices" of his speechmaking. "I suppose a professional orator like yourself," the friend continued, "has to make a move every three or four years like the Methodist ministers, so you can take the old sermons out of the barrel and use them over again." The friend just hoped that Miller's "stuff" would go over in "the tobacco country" as well as it had elsewhere.[28]

The Harvard friend need not have worried, for Miller plunged enthusiastically and successfully into intensive speechmaking at Duke, in Durham, and in North Carolina and other southern states as well as on the national circuit with which he was already familiar. In fact, Miller regarded being closer to that national circuit at Duke than he had been at Southern California as one of the many advantages of his new job. Invited to address the Florida Conference on Social Work in March, 1931, Miller noted that he had spoken eight times in two and a half days; a few weeks later he commented that for the past two or three weeks he had been speaking on an average of once a day.[29]

In order to participate more effectively in the work of the local and state legal organizations, Miller promptly joined the North Carolina bar, and he and his wife became members of Duke Memorial Methodist Church, Durham's second oldest church of that denomination and the church that had been organized and long supported by members of the Duke family.[30] Within less than a year of his joining Durham's Rotary Club Miller was elected to membership on the board of directors, and by 1933 he was elected to the presidency of the North Carolina Conference of Social Service.[31]

Aside from Miller's own dynamism, his early and extensive involvement in campus as well as local and state activities was facilitated by the fact that he seems to have genuinely liked becoming a Tar Heel. After several months in North Carolina, he declared to a California friend that he liked the people he found himself among. "They are just the same sort of folks as those who live out in California," Miller suggested. "They have a good deal of the Western freedom of manner and kindliness of spirit, which is so lacking in the New England states and to a greater or less extent also throughout the Middle West."[32] As for the country itself, Miller quickly became a strong booster for the state that would much later advertise itself as "Variety Vacationland." To a friend in Los Angeles, Miller reported that he was "particularly pleased with the living and working conditions" that he had found in North Carolina. "When I consider the beauty of this country and the splendid climate which prevails here," Miller added, "I can easily understand how much oversold California is in the minds of the folks who live in this part of the United States."[33] And to a friend who worked in publicity for Los Angeles, Miller wryly noted that if there were "two or three hundred good Los Angeles boosters here [in North Carolina], my impression is that the whole middle and western part of the state would be sub-divided before long into city lots and sold to [people in] the Middle West and the North."[34]

About Duke and its leaders Miller initially was equally enthusiastic. He liked the fact that Duke's law school was not intended to emphasize large enrollment of those who would become average practitioners but rather to train leaders on the bench and at the bar. "President Few is about as liberal in his attitude toward independent work upon the part of members of his faculty as any university president I have ever known," Miller declared. Few, according to Miller, frankly urged the faculty "to feel that we are engaged in a piece of pioneering work and that he wants us to have the courage to go our own way." Miller concluded: "I have the feeling that I have come into this country just on the eve of a new and substantial industrial and intellectual development which will be noticed and remarked upon by the rest of the country."[35]

The mood of awakening and pioneering that Miller noted was no doubt enhanced, at least on the Duke campus, by the fact that in September, 1930, Duke's undergraduate men, now constituting the students of Trinity College, as well as the Graduate School of Arts and Sciences and the schools of religion and law moved from the old Trinity campus into the new Tudor Gothic buildings on the spacious West campus, where the new medical school was also situated. The handsome new law school building stood on the main quadrangle adjacent to the general library. Few and his associates, confronted with the necessity of giving names to certain classroom and dormitory buildings that did not name themselves functionally (such as the library), reached into the institution's history to come up with such names as Craven, Crowell, and Kilgo for dormitory quadrangles on the Gothic campus.[36] Several alumni of Trinity's law school promptly queried Few as to why the new law school building was not to be named for Samuel Fox Mordecai. One alumnus, noting that a few " 'bullet-headed' Preachers" had criticized the irrepressible Mordecai for using strong language and even "cussing" on occasion, insisted that "when the last great Day comes and the trumpet has sounded . . . Mr. Mordecai will be so high above . . . some few preachers that I know he cannot even look down and see the tops of their heads." Another prominent legal alumnus, also urging that Mordecai be so honored, argued: "I have never known a man to be more imbued with the spirit of fairness and justice towards all men than Mr. Mordecai, and I don't believe I have ever seen the Golden Rule as nearly approached in practice by anyone as was true in his case." The alumnus admitted that Mordecai had not been much interested in the "frills and fringe that go with academic life," but he had been "at home with any assemblage of brains and was abashed in the presence of no one."[37]

After explaining to the concerned legal alumni that only certain buildings had necessarily to be named promptly, Few went on to note that since James B. Duke had paid for and given all the buildings, his representatives had not only been consulted about the names already designated but had also agreed that "we might name the Law School as a whole for some man if he should be good enough to endow it with something like six million dollars." Few added confidentially that he was "trying very hard to get a man to do just this thing."[38]

Although Few failed, despite valiant efforts, to find the separate endowment for the law school—or for any other of the professional schools— he virtually gave Justin Miller a blank check in the first year or so after he arrived at Duke. Few, along with many others, had become well aware by the summer of 1930 that the economy was badly faltering. What neither he nor anyone else knew was that the nation was gradually slipping into what would be the longest and most severe economic depression in its history. In the fiscal years from 1927 through 1930 payments to Duke University from the Duke Endowment approximated a half million dollars each year and made up roughly half of the university's total receipts. In 1930–32, before the full impact of falling stock prices and shrunken dividends had hit, the Endowment's contribution was approximately double the earlier level; but since the size of the student body had increased and tuition had been raised, the Endowment still supplied close to half of the university's total receipts. The university would not confront a fiscal crisis until

1933–34; that year payments from the Endowment shrank back to their 1927 level.[39] In other words, while Duke University fell far short of all the funds it actually needed for an ambitious and high-quality program, the institution's economic situation in 1930 was relatively strong. President Few, no doubt encouraged especially in this case by W. R. Perkins, meant to go first class with the law school. And that suited Justin Miller exactly.

After accepting the deanship, Miller began immediately to recruit new members for the law faculty. "We must be sure," he admonished Few, "that our first appointments are of the most convincing possible character as the law school world and the university world generally will judge us upon the basis of those appointments."[40] Pursuant to authorization by Few, Miller found several of his initial appointees for Duke among the faculty he had assembled at the University of Southern California. These included John S. Bradway, Douglas B. Maggs, William R. Roalfe, and Gordon E. Dean. The first three would remain many years at Duke and play significant roles in shaping the law school. An alumnus of Haverford College and the University of Pennsylvania's law school, Bradway acquired his interest in legal aid work in Philadelphia and became one of the foremost proponents of and authorities in that field. After directing a legal aid clinic at the University of Southern California at Miller's invitation, he did the same thing for a much longer period at Duke. One historian of American legal education has pointed to Bradway's work as one of the significantly innovative teaching methods of the era.[41] Maggs received a doctorate in juridical science at Harvard after completing his undergraduate work at the University of California in Berkeley. A high-spirited scholar who enjoyed intellectual combat, Maggs would be an important figure in Duke's law school and in the university generally for many years. William Roalfe, an alumnus of the University of Southern California and law librarian there, became Duke's first full-time law librarian and bore the main responsibility for the quick building of a strong legal collection. By 1932, Duke's was the largest law library in the South, but, following the old Trinity-Duke policy of not relying on regional measurements alone, Roalfe led in the continuing push for the steady strengthening of the law library. Gordon Dean, who took his law degree at Southern California in 1930, came to Duke as Miller's assistant and also did a limited amount of teaching while obtaining one of Duke's first graduate degrees in law.

Another early appointment was H. Claude Horack, professor of law at the University of Iowa. In 1927 the American Bar Association named Horack as its first full-time advisor on legal education with the purpose of raising the standards of the nation's law schools and of the states' bar examinations. Horack also served as president of the Association of American Law Schools.[42] Horack would succeed Miller as dean in 1934 and remain in that post until 1947.

Having at Few's urging accepted both Bryan Bolich and Thaddeus

Bryson from the original Duke law faculty, as well as Marshall T. Spears, Sr., a Durham attorney who taught part-time, Miller soon recruited Malcolm McDermott, former dean of law at the University of Tennessee and president of the Tennessee Bar Association, to head an innovative department of legislative research and drafting. While several of Miller's most outstanding finds were still to be recruited, he felt justifiable pride in his first group of appointments and also in the increased size and quality of the entering class in the fall of 1930. With seventy-seven students in all (after four who had registered dropped out), Miller thought he detected "a striking contrast" between the students entering in 1930 and those that preceded them. Coming from a wider area than ever, the first-year students were, according to Miller, "very superior" and "one of the best groups" he had ever seen.[43]

Still receiving generous support from Duke's administration, Miller made significant additions to the faculty during 1930–31. He did not, of course, get everyone he sought, despite the fact that the salaries proffered were quite competitive with the best among law schools. Roswell Magill, in tax law at Columbia University, declared initially that the work at Duke appealed to him because of its "pioneer character," but he ultimately declined Miller's offer.[44] Similarly, a handsome salary of $12,000 plus an invitation to join Miller in establishing at Duke an Institute of Criminal Law failed to lure Albert J. Harno, dean of the School of Law at the University of Illinois.[45] Still, if Miller could not win every time, he succeeded sufficiently to build a most impressive faculty of twelve persons by the fall of 1931.

Miller had failed to get the Illinois dean, but he succeeded in securing a bright, younger man whom he knew on the faculty there, Lon L. Fuller. With undergraduate as well as law degrees from Stanford, Fuller faced the no doubt pleasant situation of being sought by both Duke and Chicago even as Illinois attempted to hold him. Chicago offered an associate professorship at a salary of $7,500 with an obligation to teach only contracts. In a winningly frank and detailed letter, Miller explained to Fuller that he could probably teach whatever he preferred at Duke and that while the standard teaching load in the law school was six hours of classes per week (it was officially fifteen hours in arts and sciences), if Fuller wished to engage in special research, a lighter load could be arranged—provided there was "a program to cover it which will be sufficiently illuminating to the President so that he will have no question about your loafing on the job." Miller advised that there was a $25,000 annual appropriation for the law library's purchases and that he could probably get a special appropriation for some of the European legal books which Fuller might wish to add for comparative study. Since Fuller had inquired about the others on the faculty—and he already knew Miller, Maggs, Bradway, and Horack—

Miller reported that Bryson, with a high reputation among Tar Heel lawyers, was a "typical old judge type" in his standards and teaching but "very much impressed with the importance of building a law school on proper grounds and is amenable to any type of program which we work out." He was well qualified in the specialized field of North Carolina pleading. Miller described Bolich as a person of "fine ability" and McDermott as "one of the finer representatives of law teachers in the Southern states" and "a charming fellow personally." Fuller, refusing to bargain with Illinois, accepted Duke's offer of a professorship at $8,000 a year and ultimately proved to be one of Miller's prize catches.[46]

At the same time he was recruiting Fuller, Miller sought and landed another young legal scholar of great promise. David M. Cavers, an assistant professor of law at the University of West Virginia, had, after graduating from the University of Pennsylvania in 1923, served as president of the *Law Review* board at Harvard and achieved the highest three-year academic average in his class. After practicing law in New York for three years, he served as an instructor in Harvard Law School for one year before taking the job at West Virginia. Miller explained to Cavers that, in anticipation of publishing a law review in a couple of years, Duke planned to start in the fall of 1931 a course in current decisions which all second-year students would be required to take. The group would be divided into sections and do pretty much the same sort of work which only the elite group of students on the staff of the law review did in the larger schools. In light of Cavers's experience at Harvard, Miller thought he might be interested in helping in such a course. That was indeed the case, though a $1,000 increase over the $4,500 he received at West Virginia no doubt also played a part in Cavers's decision.[47] Thurman Arnold, then a professor of law at Yale, congratulated Miller on getting Cavers, whom Arnold regarded as "one of the unusual finds running about loose in the law school world today." The most essential element in building up a law school, Arnold explained, was "the ability to pick coming men," and he thought that the case of Cavers proved that Miller had an eye for them. When Arnold concluded by warning that Yale might make it hard for Duke to keep Cavers, Miller retorted that nothing gave him greater pleasure "than to have on my faculty men who are wanted badly by other schools."[48]

As many of the appointments revealed, Miller was determined to have the Duke Law School in the forefront of the movement to have legal training deal with the major economic and social problems of the time. Another important appointment that suggested such an orientation was that of Leslie Craven. A friend of Miller's for a number of years, Craven had received both his undergraduate and law degrees at Stanford, the latter in 1911. Becoming a prominent railway attorney first in Oregon and then the nation, he was named counsel for the President's Conference Commission on the Federal Valuation of the Railroads. When Miller pushed late in 1931 to have Craven appointed to teach in the fields of public utility law and taxation at a salary of $14,000, an enormous academic salary for that era, Few finally balked. Miller had carefully studied James B. Duke's indenture creating the Duke Endowment, however, and reminded Few of the philanthropist's injunction that the university should secure for its faculty such persons as would "insure its attaining and maintaining a place of real leadership in the educational world." Miller then asked if the university wished to undertake a long, slow period of development or "go forward boldly with the objective of overtaking the leading schools and placing ourselves in the same group within the next few years." If the latter course was to be the choice, then the university would certainly have to spend even more than it had already committed.[49]

Miller could, of course, forget about the nation's economic depression. Few could not. Its impact on Duke University had been delayed but was clearly beginning to loom ahead by late 1931. Still, Miller found an important ally in William R. Perkins, who supported the appointment of Craven and ascertained that while he would definitely come to Duke for $14,000 he would consider doing so for $12,000. Craven telegraphed his acceptance of the offer at the latter figure in December 1931.[50]

Miller won the battle over Craven, but Few also scored a few points along another line. Miller believed that there were advantages in bringing in well-established legal scholars as visiting professors, especially during the period when he was recruiting his own faculty. During his first year at Duke, 1930–31, Miller was proud to have the dean of Stanford's law school, Marion Kirkwood, as a visiting professor, and during 1931–32 there were prominent, and relatively expensive, visiting professors from both Stanford and Pennsylvania. As part of a compromise concerning Craven's appointment, however, Few obtained Miller's promise that for 1932–33 the visitors would be replaced by younger men at much smaller salaries.[51] In carrying out this policy, Miller added two younger men beginning in the fall of 1932: Warner Fuller, who received undergraduate training at the University of Oregon and his law degree at Yale, and Paul W. Bruton, who also took his law degree at Yale after doing undergraduate work at the University of California in Berkeley.[52]

The able faculty that Justin Miller recruited was no doubt the major explanation for the attention that the law school world paid to Duke in the early 1930s, but it was not the only one. Another factor was the school's innovative program and curriculum. In launching the legal aid clinic Miller and Bradway had the utmost support of the general administration, for such service-oriented activity appealed strongly to Few and was, in fact, very much in the Trinity-Duke tradition. On a more mundane level, however, Miller and Bradway were careful to meet early on with the members of the Durham bar and to explain how the clinic would work and that only those persons unable to pay would be accepted as clients. Thus they won important local support for the project.[53] Personal injury cases where a contingent fee might be involved were not to be accepted; nor were most divorce cases. Drawing on his experience, Bradway believed that most cases would involve the recovery of small wage claims, landlord-tenant difficulties, and protection of women and children in various respects. In addition to the assistance for indigents Bradway emphasized that the clinic was intended "to acquaint the student, by direct contact under faculty supervision, with certain of the problems of 'law in action' which may escape emphasis in the study of 'law in books.'"[54]

After the clinic had operated successfully for almost two years out of its offices in the law school building on Duke's campus, Miller received an inquiry about the feasibility of such a clinic in small cities. He explained that the experience at Duke suggested an answer in the affirmative. While Durham then had a population of only about 55,000, the clinic had extended its cases widely, Miller noted, and gone into a number of fields that were not usually considered for clinic purposes. For example, in addition to the work with indigents, the clinic staff occasionally helped prepare opinions for various judges. Then there was the matter of remedial legislation, such as in the small loan area. When the Duke clinic took up a test case on North Carolina's sterilization law, which the state's supreme court found unconstitutional, the clinic helped prepare a new law that the legislature then adopted.[55]

An unusually conscientious and dedicated professor, John Bradway long emphasized the service and public-relations aspect of the legal aid clinic. "As far as I can see Duke University, at least during our generation, needs more than anything else," he declared, "to build up in the minds of the people of North Carolina and the South a sense of confidence and pride in its achievements." Just as Duke's medical center won friends by leaning down to individuals and showing interest in their physical well-being, he argued, the legal aid clinic could gradually build confidence in the law school. Bradway, who led the law faculty in sheer number of publications (mostly articles) during the period from 1930 to 1935, maintained that while scholarly writings gradually reached their intended audience, "the base of public confidence [in Duke] should be broader than that." Active in Durham's community welfare program as well as in the State Conference of Social Work, Bradway built a collection of photographs of prominent Tar Heel judges and lawyers as well as courthouses to display in the rooms of the clinic, asserting that he and his colleagues on the faculty could not "build a new enterprise like the Duke Law School into the general consciousness of the people of North Carolina without showing an appropriate respect for their traditions and institutions."[56]

While Bradway pushed public outreach and service through the legal aid clinic, Malcolm McDermott and a small staff found a useful as well as instructionally valuable role to play through the section of legislative research and drafting. At the request of North Carolina's chief justice, McDermott's group undertook a study of constitutional provisions concerning county and municipal government with a view toward assembling information for the state's commission on constitutional revision. A handbook, "Legislation in North Carolina," published by the department must have been useful, for requests for copies came in from across the state. Legislative research and drafting were not limited to North Carolina, however. A request from Oregon's legislature, possibly inspired by Miller's connections there, led to the drafting of a bill intended to protect public funds that were deposited in banking institutions.[57]

While the legal aid clinic and the activity in legislative research and drafting obviously had valuable instructional aspects and were not commonplace among other law schools at that time, Miller's innovative plan for a course in current decisions was more directly related to the central purpose of the law school. Maggs and Cavers had primary responsibility for the two sections into which the second-year class was divided, but all faculty members were expected to contribute. Both the relative smallness of Duke's law school—seventy-one students in 1931 when the course was introduced—and the quality of its proportionately large faculty made it possible for Duke to give all of its law students the type of closely supervised research and writing experiences that were reserved in the larger law schools only for a handful of academically elite students. Duke's plan called for each student in the course to prepare during the year three or four short case notes and two longer comments, with the better papers to be published periodically.[58]

Although Miller intended from the first for the Duke Law School to have its own publication, as did virtually all of the important law schools, he wisely refused to be hasty about the matter and waited until the school had assembled its faculty and begun to attract the type of students it wanted. He had learned while dean at Southern California, he explained, that a law review, or something like it, not only could be used "in the finest sense as an honors course," but that it was "very stimulating to more intensive work, upon the part of both faculty members and students."[59] By the spring of 1933, Miller and his colleagues were ready to launch plans for the publication of not one but two journals, and therein lay another aspect of the distinctiveness that characterized Duke Law School under Miller's leadership. Moreover, the fact that the administration, that is, Few and Flowers, supported these plans despite the severe budgetary restrictions under which the university had to operate by 1933–34 is further evidence of the strong commitment that the university's leaders continued to make to the law school.

As David Cavers argued in a memorandum, every significant American law school, with the exception of Stanford at that time, published a legal periodical. Most of these publications followed, with "inconsequential variations," the pattern that Harvard had set in 1887 with its *Law Review*. That is, the journals usually appeared eight or so times a year, and specialized articles by established scholars on miscellaneous aspects of the law were followed by a special section that featured student work. Cavers, explaining and justifying a plan with which Miller and others on the law faculty were already in agreement, called for Duke to break from the stereotype and "strive to make a distinctive contribution to legal periodical literature."[60]

Duke's law faculty, therefore, proposed to publish a quarterly journal, each issue of which would carry a symposium on one of the many problems of the law "which are so interrelated with problems in the other social [science] disciplines as to render their consideration from a variety of points of view imperative to their proper understanding." The journal would thereby be "a concrete manifestation of that interrelation concerning which so much is said and so little is actually done, at least in the domain of legal scholarship." It would emphasize "law in action" as distinguished from "law in books" and would, Cavers maintained, "inevitably attract the keenest interest among the law teaching profession" and place Duke among the leaders of the movement to broaden the function of the law school. Since the quarterly would deal with "living problems," Cavers believed that there was every likelihood that it would be read by subscribers rather than filed away, as he suggested was the usual fate of a law review. While there would be no special section for student work, significant and superior essays by students could certainly be included when they were appropriate.[61]

When the time came to name the new publication, the faculty played around and let their imaginations run wild. Leslie Craven came up with five possibilities, including "Inscrutability Unscrewed" and "Intimations of Infallibility." Cavers retorted with "The New Leviathan" or, certainly better, "Toots from Tugboats." After more serious discussion of various possibilities, they settled on *Law and Contemporary Problems*. The first issue, edited by Cavers and featuring a symposium called "The Protection of the Consumer of Food and Drugs," appeared in December, 1933. As Cavers had predicted, it and subsequent issues indeed helped put the Duke Law School on the legal world's map.[62]

The first issue of the other publication, a student-edited quarterly, appeared in March, 1933, and was initially named the *Duke Bar Association*

Journal. The name was not fanciful, for, following a plan Miller had first tried at Southern California, he had led the law students in organizing themselves into the Duke Bar Association, modelled closely on the structure of the American Bar Association and various state associations. That is, the student body was divided into nine sections with a faculty advisor for each, the sections consisting of legal education and admission to the bar, legislation, law school affairs, criminal law, comparative law, legal aid, constitutional amendments, grievances and professional conduct, and publications. With appropriate and sometimes distinguished visiting speakers invited by the various sections, Miller thought "the boys" were "on their toes regarding the Bar Association work" and that other members of the faculty besides himself were becoming more and more interested in its work. The first issue of the journal contained reports of the various sections of the Duke Bar Association and reviews of current decisions by students of the highest academic standing in the second- and third-year classes.[63]

Just how the students themselves reacted to the various developments in the law school in the early 1930s can only be inferred. There probably was an atmosphere of ferment and intellectual excitement, but the economic depression was a grim, grinding reality for many, probably most, of the students. Although there were at first fifty tuition scholarships for law students and then forty when the tuition was raised in 1931 to $250, there were no fellowships or stipends that covered more than tuition. Claude Horack thought that the school's "greatest need" was help for "exceptional southern boys" who were "nearly all going on a shoestring, hoping each day that they will be able to find at least one meal the next."[64]

To provide at least temporary, emergency help for hard-pressed students, Miller used an unexpected check for a talk he had given in a Durham church to start a law school loan fund, and he wanted publicity about it to encourage others to contribute.[65] The wives of the law faculty pitched in to help by giving a benefit bridge party to aid the loan fund. Miller reported that the fund proved most useful, with loans not exceeding $20 being made to a considerable number of students. A third-year student suggested that the Duke Bar Association should create another small loan fund whereby loans of from $1 to $3 could be made for temporary emergencies.[66]

Despite the obvious poverty of so many students, the smallness of the school made for a community spirit among the students and closer student-faculty relationships than characterized larger and often more urban law schools. Even though national prohibition under the Eighteenth Amendment prevented the type of beer-drinking conviviality that would later become a part of student life, Duke's law students enjoyed respites from their books, even in the dry and poverty-stricken early 1930s.

The Ladies' Auxiliary of the law school, composed largely of the wives of the law faculty, entertained both students and faculty at teas, sometimes given in the law school building, and as part of the pre-Christmas festivities in 1932 the school sponsored an informal dance in the ballroom of the Union building on West campus.[67]

Whether the law students always enjoyed the lessened anonymity that Duke's small classes gave them may well be debated. The professors liked, or became accustomed to, the relatively intimate classes. Douglas Maggs, as a visiting professor at Yale's law school in 1936, commented about his experience there and thus threw an indirect light on the situation at Duke: "So far, I am unconvinced that the students here are better than those at Duke—to put it mildly. The usual rumors reached me that my sarcasm & shouting frightened them & made them angry—but I think they'll get over that as my classes elsewhere have. It is fun to have 65 in a class again, but I'm not sure I'd prefer it after the novelty has worn off."[68]

Lon Fuller, visiting at Harvard and teaching contracts to a large class of first-year students, reported that he had had some surprises in his teaching. "In the first place, I have found it rather easier to teach large classes than I thought it would be," he commented. "To tell the whole truth, I'm afraid I rather enjoy the experience of presiding over a public meeting." On the other hand, Fuller found his Harvard students "terribly frightened and tense." He declared that he sometimes felt "like a captain addressing a few words to his men just before they go over the top." He got the impression that "their brains are congealed with fright," and while he hoped the atmosphere would change, he had heard that it actually worsened toward examination time. "It not only tends to spoil the classroom discussion," Fuller continued, "but I am also getting tired of having every student who gets off on the wrong foot in class run down to me immediately after class to explain just why he went wrong, for fear I'll put down a little demerit mark opposite his name."[69] Duke law students may or may not have been as tense and apprehensive as those Fuller found at Harvard, though the probability is that they were not, mainly because they were not lost in a mob.

The Duke law students, when given an opportunity to make their opinions known, did complain about their work load. In response to a questionnaire about methods of study and instruction, the students hit hard at what they believed to be the excessive assignments of cases to study and brief. When Maggs, who happened to be away on leave at the time, was informed of this, he urged the dean to set himself "firmly in the way of this Bolshevistic attempt to abolish the reading and briefing of cases by students." He insisted that the "ability to tear an opinion to pieces thoroughly and rapidly, to distinguish holding from dictum (but to be able to use dictum in an argument or brief if it will help) is almost the biggest thing a student gets from law school." Naturally the students tired of doing that, Maggs conceded, but as with the piano, "practice—repeated and repeated—does give proficiency."[70]

While the students groaned and continued briefing cases, the professors found their own satisfactions. Once again, it was Douglas Maggs who shed some light on why certain lawyers prefer the classroom. During World War II he found himself, as Solicitor of the Department of Labor, presiding over a staff of about 170 lawyers. He reported that at times he enjoyed the administrative work, but at other times he did not. "In the long run, I still think teaching can't be topped," Maggs declared. "The class room nearly makes up for the exciting moments of arguing cases, etc.—and there is real satisfaction in plugging away at one's subjects—an intellectual continuity that is lacking in private practice or government service." Maggs, already contemplating postwar possibilities for the Duke Law School, declared that his experience in Washington had convinced him that "every job a lawyer has to do is unique—and that a trained mind is the thing needed most. No—one thing more—ability to write (and talk). I wonder if we could do more about ability to write?"[71] The students, grinding away at their law books and the eternal briefing, no doubt viewed the matter somewhat differently and would have surely testified that they were already required to write quite enough.

The few women law students at Duke in the 1930s had more to worry about than their work load, for they were indeed a small minority in an overwhelmingly masculine world. In the spring of 1932 a Phi Beta Kappa senior in Duke's Woman's College applied for a scholarship in the law school. Miller consulted Few and Flowers, the other two members of the administrative committee for the school, as to whether one scholarship should be earmarked for a woman student or she should merely be allowed to compete with the male applicants. Miller added that he thought it "highly desirable that some outstanding women students should be admitted to our Law School and of course we have placed no obstacles in their way." Subsequently, the administrative committee decided that, as a matter of policy, women applicants for scholarships would be treated on the same basis as men.[72] Despite this open door, there were not many women in the 1930s to whom the law beckoned. In 1939 Horack reported that out of seventeen women who had attended Duke Law School since its reorganization in 1930, nine withdrew before completing the law course.[73] He did not go on to say so, but the eight women who did receive their Duke law degrees obviously triumphed over many subtle and quite a few not so subtle obstacles.

Friendly and open to the students, male and female, and apparently enjoying quite cordial relations with his colleagues, Miller had succeeded by the fall of 1932 in building a first-rate faculty that helped attract a slowly growing but able student body. The enrollment went up about 25 percent in September, 1932, to ninety-five students, and increasingly they came from a more geographically dispersed area. In 1929–30 80 percent of Duke's law students had come from North Carolina. By 1934–35 that figure had shrunk to 29 percent, and 40 percent came from outside the South. The law library of about 12,000 volumes in 1930 had grown to 33,443 volumes by the spring of 1932 and, despite the depression, was still growing. Having the largest law library in the South but only the sixteenth largest in the nation was not a situation at Duke that called for resting.[74] Why, having been supported generously by the administration and having achieved so much in such a relatively short period, would Justin Miller wish to wage an almost open campaign against President Few and the manner in which he led Duke University?

Some faculty members at Duke in the early 1930s believed that Miller aspired to become the president of Duke University. That may or may not have been true. Some people—students and a few anonymous journalists—expressed the opinion, publicly in the case of the latter group, that he should be president and would make a first-rate successor to Few. What the truth was about Miller's own purposes and motives remains murky and may never be known. The clear fact was, however, that he played a central and somewhat mysterious role in a complex academic drama that culminated in 1934 but began several years earlier.

Miller's administrative style became clear as soon as he arrived at Duke in the summer of 1930. Energetic and ambitious, as much for the Duke Law School as for himself, he was articulate, well organized, and efficient. Letters to him received prompt, careful replies, and in them he often displayed tact and diplomacy. He had a knack for combining candor, and sometimes stern advice to young would-be law professors, with a winning graciousness.[75]

That he immediately began bombarding Few and Flowers, the other two members of the administrative committee for the law school, with all sorts of memorandums was hardly surprising, for there was much to be done for a rapidly expanding school in a new building on a new campus. Strong pleas for quick expansion of the law library from Miller and Roalfe, the law librarian, met with consistent approval from Few and Flowers. In addition to the regular annual appropriations of $25,000 for the law library, Miller requested and got a special appropriation of $5,000 for purchases in Europe. When Miller asked a friend from Stanford's law school who was then in Europe partly on a book-buying mission to purchase books for Duke also, the friend quickly agreed to help and added: "You make me gasp with envy. The nonchalant way in which you say you took up the matter [with Duke's administration] and got a special appropriation of $5,000.00 makes me feel positively poverty stricken."[76]

Getting what he wanted for the library as well as in the way of appointments to the faculty, Miller launched a battle in May, 1931, about one of academia's favorite bones of contention—space. Both faculty offices and classrooms were in short supply on Duke's two campuses in the 1930s, and this was especially true on the West campus. Since the student body of the law school was still quite small and Miller and his colleagues talked a lot about the relationships between law and such social sciences as economics and politics, Few obviously thought that there were advantages in having Duke's Department of Economics and Political Science (then still combined in one department) share some of the excess space in the law school building. Miller thought otherwise. He explained that it was "not the practice in the better law schools to use the building for any other purpose than that of the Law School itself." Any attempt to secure cooperation between professors of law and those in the other social sciences by forcing them into contact with each other, Miller argued, was doomed to failure. The "result of such forcing is to create friction and irritation which makes it impossible for the law department or for any of the other departments properly to carry on the work which they are supposed to do."[77] The chairman of the Department of Economics and Political Science, W. H. Glasson, who was also the dean of the Graduate School of Arts and Sciences, noted that his large department had approximately fifty-four classes that met in the law school building, with a total registration of about 1600 students. Moreover, twelve of the sixteen faculty members in the department had offices there (though three and sometimes four professors had to share an office).[78]

Miller won his battle for the exclusive use of the law school building. And though the law school had no summer session, and summer classes in arts and sciences boomed in that period, Miller strenuously objected to the use of the law building even for summer classes. Because the halls rang "with student foot steps, student voices, student laughter, and student noises," he found that his plans for research and writing in his office during the summer were "ruined" and there was "no hope of my accomplishing anything of importance." Going on for six single-spaced pages in this particular document, he struck one of his favorite themes in his increasingly peevish memorandums to Few and Flowers: "I have been faced constantly during this year [1930–31] with the dilemma of having to work against the traditions and methods of the small church school which have [sic] no comprehension of what is standard method or standard policy or what is necessary in order to build a great law school." Miller went on to reject the argument that good business management required the use of the law school building during the summer, for there were many "intangible considerations" which caused "all the rules of business to go by the board when they came in conflict with proper methods of university administration." Miller suggested that the university needed an arts and social science building. If Trinity College truly was, as Few often declared, "the heart and centre of Duke University," Miller concluded, then it was "obvious that the heart and centre has been the most inadequately provided for of any department in the University organization."[79]

What, if anything, President Few said in response to Miller's blast about the traditions of a "small church school" is not known. To Miller's annoyance, neither Few nor Flowers was as enamored of written communications as was the dean of the law school. Miller's scholarly output may or may not have actually suffered in the summer of 1931, but his production of a wide range of memorandums to Few and Flowers was certainly not in any way stymied. Most of them were routine, but at the end of the summer he hit again on substantive issues and somehow failed to show the same tact and diplomacy that his letters to outsiders revealed.

Looking back over his first year at Duke, Miller first made an encouraging progress report. He regarded as the most outstanding evidence of accomplishment the fact that both the American Bar Association and the Association of American Law Schools had given their stamp of approval to Duke's reorganized school. The latter organization, moreover, had just released a classification based on the size and qualifications of the faculty, salaries, and libraries, and Duke's law school was listed as one of the seventeen leading schools in the nation. From three full-time faculty members in 1929–30, the school had expanded to have seven in 1930–31 and would have eleven by September, 1931. All of them were experienced teachers and productive scholars with degrees from the strongest law schools. While Harvard, Miller concluded, then had around 1600 students and 34 full-time faculty members, Duke aimed at 300 students, which would be about the size of Yale's law school.[80]

Miller was not content with such positive reports, however. Not long after writing so encouragingly, he again launched into a long (nine single-spaced pages) attack on the administrative methods of Few and Flowers. He noted at the outset that he was typing the document himself, so that there could be no "outside" discussion of it, and that his interest in the general administration derived from his concern about the success of the whole university as well as the proper development of the law school.

First, he pointed out that the administration was poorly organized for the proper handling of details on the apparent assumption that such details were not important. Neither Few nor Flowers had competent secretarial staffs, Miller asserted, and both had themselves attempted to handle too many details. There followed a long list of alleged problems and misunderstandings that various law professors had encountered, particularly concerning their arrangements with the university about housing, and the specific charge against Flowers of not answering letters. "In all of my

dealings with you," Miller continued, "there has been a disorderly procedure which cannot fail to produce misunderstandings and trouble." Miller
noted that he sent memorandums but that Few and Flowers preferred
conversations.

In a recent conversation with Few, Miller claimed, the president had
spoken casually about the attitudes of some of the newly appointed law
professors. Miller charged that Few thus revealed "a condition of mind
peculiar to the man who has been for a long time administrator of a small
college." Forced by a limited budget to staff the college with poorly paid,
"second-rate men," the small-college president could not trust them and
had to try to control everything himself. While Miller granted that Few
had shown no lack of vision or imagination in recruiting the "great men
needed for a great university," he had not changed his administrative style
accordingly nor realized that the new faculty could simply not be treated
in the old, small-college manner.[81]

What, if anything, Few said in response to Miller's outburst is not
known. A remarkably patient man, long accustomed to the vagaries of all
sorts of academics, Few may well have said nothing. Zeal about administrative detail was not, in fact, his forte, and the fact that Miller was put
off by Few's style is perhaps understandable. Preoccupied night and day
almost every day of the year with the plans for and problems of Duke
University, Few often had an abstract or distant quality that some people
found disconcerting. He often received visitors to his office while sitting
in a favorite rocking chair, and he might gaze off into space, reaching
across the top of his head with his right arm to scratch the left side of
his head, or make a low whistling sound through his teeth as his visitor
talked.[82] One historian who knew and worked under Few for more than a
decade, the late Robert H. Woody, admitted that Few was never an orator
and was even, to a certain degree, "inept" in faculty meetings. Woody, in
interesting contrast to Miller, saw Few like this:

> If he lacked the power of a vibrant personality, he possessed a quiet
> charm which was especially effective in small gatherings, and he was
> always listened to with respect. He had a certain air of kindliness, of
> benevolence, which was as genuine as his quiet and pleasant voice.
> In short, he looked like what he was: a college president, shy, earnest,
> devoted to the causes of education and the church and anxious to do
> great good and little harm. He was a scholar; yet, all in all, he was
> a man of sound judgment, especially when viewing large matters of
> policy rather than the petty details of routine administration. He was
> a student by preference, a scholar by training, and an administrator
> only by force of circumstances. His abilities as an administrator were
> acquired rather than native.[83]

The fact that Few refused to take Miller's criticisms too seriously or personally is best shown by the fact that late in 1931, after having received several of Miller's stinging critiques, Few nevertheless reported to W. R. Perkins that an important citizen in Durham had remarked that "Dean Miller was the best of all the men brought here in the last five years." Few added that he felt "sure that we can make a success of the Law School, but it is going to require some time and meanwhile, as we all recognize, it will cost us a good deal."[84]

Few was not the only person who kept Perkins informed about the law school, for Miller frequently saw the powerful trustee of the university who, with George G. Allen, virtually ran the Duke Endowment. Miller invited Perkins to speak to the law students and visited him frequently while in New York. On at least one occasion Miller and his wife visited the Perkinses at their home in Montclair, New Jersey, and Miller, Perkins, and Willis Smith, another university trustee and prominent attorney in Raleigh, North Carolina, traveled together to inspect the law schools at Harvard and Yale. On at least one occasion, and possibly more, Miller sent Perkins a copy of one of his memorandums about the law school.[85]

If Few did not worry too much about Miller's unhappiness with the administration of Duke, one probable reason, as explained earlier, was that the harassed president agonized deeply over a period of several years about the relationship between the university and the Duke Endowment. While the university was a special, protected beneficiary of the Endowment, its trustees, under James B. Duke's indenture establishing it, had the power under certain conditions to withhold annual appropriations even to the university. This crucial matter became something more than theoretical when Allen and Perkins exploded furiously over the fact that Norman Thomas, the longtime Socialist leader and presidential candidate, spoke on Duke's campus late in 1930. Although Few tried his utmost to educate the powerful businessmen about academic freedom and the university ethos, he fought a losing battle and was forced to appease them as best he could. The Norman Thomas issue flared up again during and after the presidential election of 1932, forcing Few finally to look to changes in the structure of the university's governance, changes that he thought would protect the university and its vital tie with the Endowment.[86]

Since the public at large knew nothing of Few's problems with Allen and Perkins, one can only surmise that Miller, both as a lawyer and as a friend of Perkins, probably had a fairly clear understanding of the situation. Not only did he study and quote from the indenture, of which Perkins had been the principal author, but more than any layperson Miller would understand the full significance of the indenture's language empowering the trustees to withhold funds to Duke University if it should "be not operated in a manner calculated to achieve the results intended hereby."[87] That was the phrase that haunted Few and kept whatever worries he had about Miller and the law school in perspective.

If Miller had concerned himself only with the law school, matters might have been simpler. The popular, energetic Miller involved himself, however, with the life and problems of the undergraduates to a degree that was unusual for a dean of a professional school. As much in demand as a speaker on the campus as he was off of it, Miller, for example, addressed a dinner meeting of Trinity College freshmen on "Law as a Profession," a group of seniors on choosing their vocations, and a Sunday afternoon vesper service on "Blasphemy and Contempt of Court"—all in about a two-week period.[88] This pattern continued during much of his stay at Duke. In addition to the speaking, Miller agreed to serve on several committees that dealt with various aspects of student life. He worked with a group that helped screen student candidates for various leadership positions in Duke's Woman's College, and in 1932–33 he conceived the idea of a joint committee of students and faculty that might, as he put it, focus on student problems and the adjustment of student difficulties while also fostering friendly relationships between faculty members and students. As mentioned earlier, Alice M. Baldwin, the dean of the Woman's College, agreed to meet with this group, but at one of the early meetings she was bothered by the fact that one of the undergraduate men present "quite bitterly" attacked Dean William H. Wannamaker. After the meeting she protested to Miller that if Wannamaker and his methods were to be the subject of discussion and criticism, then she thought he should be present. If not, "she would not be a member of any group acting in such an unfair way." Baldwin therefore withdrew from the group, though Miller apparently continued to hold the meetings.[89]

Aside from knowing and working with students on various committees, Miller had an opportunity to come into contact with a wide cross-section of the Duke community through an interesting recreational group that was active in the early 1930s, the Explorers' Club. This loosely organized group of students, faculty, and staff formed in 1931 under the leadership of Ernest Seeman, director of the Duke University Press. But for reasons discussed earlier, Flowers in September, 1933, used the university's serious budgetary difficulties at that time as the opportunity to give a year's notice of contract termination to Seeman.[90] Before that happened, however, Justin Miller and Seeman had become good friends from the earliest outings of the Explorers' Club among the heavily forested hills around the rocky rivers that traversed the northern part of Durham county.

If Seeman had grievances against Duke's leadership by the fall of 1933, Miller had been cultivating—and expressing—his own complaints for a much longer period. After the expensive addition of the new faculty members and even with the large number of tuition scholarships, Miller was embarrassed in the fall of 1931 that the total enrollment in the law school of seventy-one students actually fell below the figure of seventy-seven for the previous year. "There is no use disguising the fact," he confessed, "that I am keenly disappointed in our first-year registration [of thirty-four]." He had counted on an entering class of at least a hundred students, he explained, and could only believe that the increase of the tuition from $200 to $250 had discouraged a number of graduates of Duke and other neighboring institutions from attending Duke rather than the less expensive law schools at the University of North Carolina and Wake Forest.[91]

To Miller's chagrin, Few urged and got the appointment of a committee charged with the task of trying to increase enrollment in the law school. Even more frustrating for Miller was the fact that by the spring of 1932 Duke was finally beginning to feel the pinch of the depression from the falling income of the Duke Endowment and therefore of the university's operating funds. Having been given virtually a blank check for expenditures during his first year and a half at Duke, Miller sought in vain for approval of travel money for the law librarian and noticeably chafed under restrictions that began to be applied in 1932. Few and Flowers explained that in order to avoid the salary cuts that were already in effect at most American colleges and universities, Duke planned first to cut expenses relating to travel; then expenditures for all equipment, even including books for the libraries, were to be curtailed; and finally, as a third phase of the retrenchment, faculty and staff vacancies that might occur were not to be filled. "It is hoped, by means of all these methods," Miller's memorandum of the meeting concluded, "to avoid salary cutting or the discharging of men now on permanent appointment."[92]

Stung both by one of his first monetary rebuffs and by the inclusion of a member whom he did not want on the enrollment committee, Miller fired off another of his angry communications to Few and Flowers. Regarding the low enrollment, Miller pointed out that he had asked initially for a liberal scholarship policy, one that included a stipend as well as tuition, but had only gotten the latter. Now the depression had intensified the law school's problems. The small student body was now "urged against me, particularly by Dr. Few, as an evidence that our law school is failing to develop as it should, and as an argument against putting further money into its development along the lines which were promised to me when I came here." Miller added that he had felt constantly during his nearly two years at Duke that "ideas prevailing in the minds of the members of the Administration about the development of the law school were based largely upon their experience with the sub-standard law school" that Trinity-Duke had maintained in the earlier era. Miller concluded by asserting, somewhat vaguely, that he approved of neither those methods nor attitudes, and regardless of the depression, "we cannot build a law school unless some of these difficulties are corrected."[93] The day following this pronouncement Miller sent a memorandum requesting three new staff members for the law library, an appropriation of a minimum of $50,000 for the purchase of books, and immediate consideration of the problem of providing additional space for the library staff and shelving for books.[94] Miller could no longer get everything he requested, of course, but even as salaries at Duke finally had to be cut for 1933–34, Few and Flowers approved the plans for the two legal quarterlies that Miller and his colleagues had proposed.

The atmosphere at Duke in the fall of 1933 was a strangely mixed one. The enrollment in the law school did jump to ninety-five students, but Miller's battle with the administration only intensified. Even though Duke, compared to the great majority of educational institutions, had come late to salary cuts—and still managed to avoid the layoffs that many schools were forced to make—there was grumbling on the part of some of the faculty. One highly paid law professor (not Miller) threatened to sue the university for breach of contract because of the temporary salary cut, which, as it turned out, lasted only one year. Not grievances of faculty, however, but those of undergraduate men sparked off the student protest movement of early 1934. Since it is discussed in earlier chapters, it will not be again explored here, but several of Miller's close friends played important, offstage roles.

A strange twist was given to the student protest at Duke by stories that appeared in the Durham *Sun* and in other newspapers in the state as well as, to a certain extent, in a *Time* magazine piece. This was to the effect that underlying the affair was a struggle between those who had long been identified with Trinity College, on the one hand, and newer men whose lot was cast wholly with the new Duke University—as well as with Franklin D. Roosevelt's New Deal. The prominence and popularity of Dean Justin Miller, this story continued, "coupled with his well known modernism" and youth, made "the Duke youngsters feel that their desires in this widening democracy within academic walls would have a far better chance of expression under a new deal." The Greensboro *Daily News* carried a variation of the story that described a movement at Duke "to put in a 'progressive' as president" and named Miller as the person whom "the progressives in the great university" were pushing.[95]

William Preston Few, aged sixty-six and not talking about retiring, was never given to paranoia, so when he wrote to Perkins that there were "some people here not students who are seeking for their own purposes to get control of the University," the harassed president obviously meant what he said.[96] He need not have worried too much. Not only did he and his associates deftly handle the problems that had concerned the students, but the overwhelming majority of the faculty, the trustees, and, crucially, Allen and Perkins stood solidly behind him.

Miller kept a low profile during the student protest movement and may (or may not) have been embarrassed by the newspaper stories that touted him for Duke's presidency. At the time of the unrest at Duke, a former Duke student who had worked with Miller in 1932–33 on the committee dealing with student problems wrote back to Miller saying that he hoped the committee's work was continuing. "You do hold the confidence of any students that ever had the advantage of knowing you," this admirer declared, "and a large number of the faculty of the university, unless I'm all wrong." The young Duke alumnus concluded by saying that he looked forward to the day when Miller could "do for the whole of Duke University, unfettered, what you have done for the Law School."[97] Miller replied to this admiring alumnus that since the committee had not proved too popular (he did not say in what quarters), he and the others involved had felt it wise to hold no meetings at all during the 1933–34 academic year. During the recent unrest at Duke, Miller continued, "there has been some intimation, I understand, that perhaps this group may have been in some measure responsible for the uprising." Miller concluded, however, that the former Duke student would be able to answer that question better than he could.[98]

Miller may have been only tangentially involved with Duke's student-protest movement in the spring of 1934, but it, coupled with Miller's ongoing criticisms of the Duke administration, finally led Few quietly to organize for at least the curbing if not the ousting of the popular dean. Perkins, regardless of his earlier cordial relations with Miller, did not like either *Law and Contemporary Problems* or the law school's involvement with then current socioeconomic problems. While Miller privately described himself as a Republican as late as February, 1933, he was very much in the mold of the western, progressive Republicanism of Theodore Roosevelt's era and would later easily make the transition to a New Deal Democrat. Perkins, on the other hand, represented an eastern, Old Guard Republicanism that anathematized Franklin D. Roosevelt and his program.[99] Few was not interested at all in either Miller's or Perkins's politics, but he was concerned about his leadership of Duke University and happy to have Perkins as an ally in tackling the problem of the dean of the law school. Inviting Willis Smith also to serve on a special and confidential committee, which would also include J. F. Bruton, the chairman of the trustees, Few explained that Duke had been built up rapidly and that many additions had been made to the staff. "In the nature of things some misfits have been inevitable," Few added, and the changed financial conditions in the country also made "some readjustments" necessary. Few wanted the committee to take both of those circumstances into account and "in due course propose such suggestions as they may see fit."[100]

Since Perkins went abroad for several weeks in the spring of 1934, the special committee was delayed in its work. Before it could meet, Miller, like many other academic lawyers in the New Deal era, received an invitation to spend a year in Washington, in Miller's case as a special assistant in the office of the Solicitor General of the United States. Few promptly informed Perkins that he and Flowers thought the invitation might be "a godsend for us." Whether Miller should return to Duke after the "reconstruction" of the law school was carried out would be for him to decide. "With this out of the way," Few continued, "I think our smaller difficulties can be gradually cleared up." If Perkins and George Allen agreed, then there would be no need for the former to hurry down to Duke. "We can name our own man to serve as Dean and I think cure many of the difficulties now existing in the Law School," Few concluded.[101]

Responding quickly, Perkins noted that he "had been coming more and more to the opinion that Dean Miller was tending more towards participation in public affairs than confinement to a law school." Perkins and Allen therefore welcomed the idea of Miller's being on leave in Washington for the year and hoped he might "get permanently located where things will be more congenial to the outlook he has on life." Perkins added that he assumed that Few would call on Horack, Bryson, and McDermott to help in "recasting the Law School," and he urged Few to let "such men as Cavers, and several others whose names will come to your mind, pass out as not being of the type we desire for the best interest of the students."[102]

Although Few's own private agenda for change in the law school was much more limited than that of Perkins, saying so was hardly politic, and the skillful president kept his own counsel—and secrets. When Miller shortly announced, to Few's dismay, that he had decided not to accept the offer from Washington, Few noted that he "felt called upon to speak very frankly to him about the whole Law School situation." Perkins too, in a telephone conversation with Miller, urged the acceptance of the federal post.[103]

With the whole matter still up in the air, Few met with the faculty of the law school in late May, 1934, and, as the minutes cryptically record, opened the meeting with a brief statement on matters of policy concerning the law school and the university.[104] Exactly what Few said in that meeting is not known. Normally soft-spoken and gentle, Few could be tough and hard when he felt he had to be. But the chances are that he was not really quite as steely on that particular occasion as he made himself sound in his report to Perkins:

> I opened the way for no discussion, saying that I was there merely
> to tell them, and in addition I invited any of them who cared to come
> to see me. Those who most needed to come have already come. I have
> now with the faculty as I already had with Dean Miller as complete

an understanding as seems possible between human beings. I cannot, of course, guarantee immediate results. The school will be different next year or we must have a complete overhauling of it.

Few thought Cavers might leave, which Few said had been the trend of his advice to him, but added "although he is personally agreeable and, to me, likeable." If Cavers left, Few surmised, that would probably be the end of *Law and Contemporary Problems*. Or did Perkins think it possible, either with or without Cavers, to continue to operate the journal under the supervision of an editorial committee made up of Miller, Horack, and McDermott, the committee "to decide upon the 'problems' to be discussed and their general outlines." Even with that arrangement, the cautious president warned, "we must perhaps be prepared for articles from time to time that most of us would not fully or at all approve of. But this liability inheres in the nature of such a publication, or for that matter in the nature of any journal of opinion." Explaining that he had not discussed the matter with anyone at Duke, Few requested Perkins's advice.[105]

Although Few was actually misleading Perkins a bit, since *Law and Contemporary Problems* already had the editorial board in place and functioning, Perkins rose to the bait nicely and expressed approval of Few's idea. "For my part," Perkins advised, "I prefer to see them restricted to the scope of the law and keep away from social problems, just as I hope to see the Law School restricted and those connected with its faculty." Perkins hoped that Cavers, Paul Bruton, and "those of a like type" would leave, thus reducing the cost of the law school, but then those were matters for Few's "good judgment in connection with the Committtee on the running of the Law School."[106]

Actually, as subsequent events made clear, Few had no intention of muzzling *Law and Contemporary Problems* or forcing Cavers or any other faculty member to leave. Few did want Miller to leave, however, and felt immense relief when the dean, after more shilly-shallying, finally decided in June, 1934, to accept the post in Washington and take a year's leave of absence from Duke.[107]

Few promptly named Claude Horack, not *acting* dean, but *dean* of the law school for 1934–35, a subtle difference by which Few may have been trying to give a signal to Miller. At any rate, only two members of the law faculty resigned in the aftermath of all the strange goings-on about the law school: young Gordon Dean, Miller's assistant, and Leslie Craven, the highly paid specialist in utility regulation whom Miller had brought to Duke. Craven went on record, at least privately, about his personal reaction to what had happened and explained to a friend on the faculty that he had resigned because of an important opportunity in Washington offered to him by the Federal Coordinator of Transportation. Craven added that he could have remained at Duke despite the administration's attitude toward the law school and its treatment of Miller. "But with it I have no sympathy whatever," Craven continued, "and its inconsistency with such standards as I have learned at Stanford, and even in the hard boiled business world, made me doubt whether Duke University, as the expression of the old South, is apt to stand for the changes which I have thought it was the mission of Duke University to give to the South." Craven concluded that at any rate he felt "absolutely out of sympathy with the immutable orthodoxy and its domination of both individual thought and action."[108]

With Craven's resignation, Few predicted to Perkins (correctly, as it turned out) that there would be no more attrition in the law faculty, and he thought that "under all the circumstances perhaps that will be well." He considered the school "at the present time in very bad shape" but added that "it must be pulled out of the hole and with the least possible delay."[109] To help the morale of the law school as well as fill vacancies, Few would soon authorize new appointments to the faculty. But there were lingering problems concerning Justin Miller's situation. Aside from the inevitable gossip on campus, there was speculation in the newspapers about Miller's future. "Nobody who has come to North Carolina in a great many years has brought more 'class' than Dean Miller," a reporter commented in the Greensboro *Daily News*, and people were wondering about his leave of absence from Duke. "There is an unmistakeable Miller party over there [at Duke]," the story continued, "that is to say, a big student and faculty group which has set its heart on his ascension in time to the presidency of this great university."[110] Such newspaper comment probably did not disturb Few, but when the education editor of *Time* magazine made inquiries, no doubt in response to a tip from someone at Duke, Few thought it important to head off unwelcome publicity that might be harmful to Duke. With Willis Smith as intermediary, Few drafted a letter for Miller to send to the editor of *Time*. In it Miller was to explain that he was on leave of absence from Duke, that Leslie Craven could have remained at Duke if he had wished, and that Ernest Seeman had been at Duke in a "purely business" rather than faculty position. "No teacher at Duke, or at Trinity before Duke, has ever been in any way disciplined for opinion's sake," Few's draft continued, and if anyone claimed otherwise, names and facts should be offered. Miller was to state further that some of the trustees of the Duke Endowment might well have disagreed at certain points with the university's administration but that he had "reason to believe that no one of them has ever attempted to force his opinion upon the administration of the University."[111]

Miller, closely following Few's draft, promptly wrote to the editor at *Time* and even threw in a reference to Trinity's stand for academic freedom in the Bassett affair of 1903. In closing, Miller conceded that there had been problems at Duke, problems made more difficult by the unsettled economic and political conditions in the world, but such a large undertaking as a new university necessarily involved difficulties that called for "the exercise of patience and understanding." Miller concluded by declaring that Duke had made great progress and that "all of us who are connected with the institution are well aware of the fact that we still have a large work to do."[112]

Few thus managed to head off *Time*, though as the concluding passage in Miller's letter revealed, the absent dean had by no means come to regard himself as permanently dissociated from Duke Law School. As the months passed and Miller kept silent about his plans for the future, Few again sought advice from Perkins and Allen. He advised them that Horack, who seemed to be doing a good job as dean, favored notifying Miller no later than February, 1935, that he would "not be kept here next year." What did Perkins and Allen think about the situation? Perkins promptly urged Few to give notice to Miller, for "the sooner we can properly have a complete understanding for the future in this respect the better for all parties concerned."[113]

Whether Miller was merely awaiting clarification of his status in Washington or seriously considered returning to Duke is not known. At any rate, in February, 1935, he submitted his resignation as dean. Few, in accepting it, wished him well in the public service for which he was "extraordinarily well fitted." Thanking Willis Smith for the service he had rendered to Duke in the matter, Few observed, "So far as we are concerned we are from now on Miller's good wishers and will keep with him friendly relations so far as we can."[114]

Although Miller observed certain formal proprieties, he had rather little to do with the Duke Law School after going to Washington. At the time of his resignation Horack sent a handwritten note in which he expressed his sorrow that the relationship he and Miller had established while Miller was at Southern California "could not go on as we had contemplated."[115] Subsequently, when Horack received a confidential inquiry about Miller in connection with a university presidency—and specifically as to why Miller had left Duke—Horack politely refused to discuss the subject because he found it "quite embarrassing to go into all the matters about which you have made inquiry."[116]

Horack thus maintained a discreet silence about Miller, but Ernest Seeman went public with a vengeance. In a bitter attack in the *New Republic* on Duke University and its administrators, Seeman described Duke as, among other unflattering things, "the tail on the [Duke Power] utility kite." Concerning Miller and the law school, Seeman charged that when certain trustees of the Duke Endowment howled about the first issue of *Law and Contemporary Problems* and demanded that all New Deal-ish law professors be ousted, Miller had resisted, only to be "hounded from office and eventually forced to resign."[117]

Seeman included a wide variety of other charges in his article, but those concerning Miller and *Law and Contemporary Problems* brought a swift public rebuttal from David Cavers, Lon Fuller, and Douglas Maggs. They informed the readers of the *New Republic* that Seeman's statements and interpretation were "wide of the truth." That Miller had been at odds with the Duke administration over matters "wholly unconnected with academic freedom" was common knowledge on the Duke campus, they pointed out. Moreover, Seeman had been "an active partisan of Dean Miller in the dispute." The three professors explained that Miller had, in fact, informed the law faculty that an endowment trustee had objected to certain material in the first issue of *Law and Contemporary Problems* and had urged that the periodical avoid topics related to the New Deal. President Few, however, had assured the law professors that their freedom of speech and action would not be interfered with, and the outcome of the incident, they believed, was "precisely that which would be dictated by the best university practice." In short, contrary to Seeman's assertion, they insisted that there had been no infringement on academic freedom at Duke.[118]

Miller himself kept quiet as these charges and refutations appeared. Perhaps he chose to forget about Duke and his four years there. As crucial as they had been for Duke Law School, they were, after all, only one more episode in what had been for Miller a fast-changing, upward career. With his very marked abilities and excellent connections in the legal world, Miller easily found a new outlet for his talents in Washington in serving as a special assistant to the Attorney General. That he had become a New Deal Democrat is illustrated by the fact that he testified before a congressional committee in 1937 in favor of President Roosevelt's proposal to expand the Supreme Court. Later in that year Roosevelt appointed Miller to the prestigious United States Court of Appeals in Washington. He would after World War II become president of the Association of American Broadcasters.[119] Long after Miller left Duke, however, most of the faculty whom he had recruited remained there, and Duke Law School largely retained the curriculum and program he had given it until World War II and the draft brought lean days and drastic changes for all law schools.

No mover and shaker in the Miller style, Claude Horack apparently envisioned the deanship as largely consisting of mediation and conservation. Given the innovativeness and yet general soundness of the program that Miller had launched at Duke, perhaps stability and preservation were the wisest choices for any successor dean to make. At any rate, Horack worked harmoniously both with Few and, after Few's death in October,

1940, President Robert L. Flowers; and Horack also enjoyed, as had Miller, cordial relations with his colleagues in the law school. Horack began to suggest as early as 1936 that even with the law school's modest enrollment, which remained around a hundred students until World War II, the law building was not adequate and that a new building, possibly with a dormitory attached, would be highly advantageous.[120] That particular dream, which later deans would push more urgently, would not be realized for a quarter-century or so, but Horack met with greater success in seeking the appointment of new faculty members.

The first of these, in September, 1934, was Charles L. B. Lowndes, who was appointed in the field of taxation. After receiving his undergraduate degree from Georgetown University, Lowndes graduated from law school at Harvard and then entered private practice before returning to Harvard for a doctorate in law. He would remain at Duke for many years and serve at one point as acting dean of the school.

Another appointment that Horack sought to make in 1934 was not finally made until 1936, and though Horack appointed him, J. Douglass Poteat was actually another of Miller's finds. With both undergraduate and law degrees from Furman University, Poteat had practiced law before returning to teach law at Furman in the late 1920s. Whether he sought a job at Duke or merely asked for advice from Miller is unclear, but at any rate, on Miller's urging Poteat did graduate work in law at Yale. Thurman Arnold reported early in 1933 that he and his colleagues at Yale considered Poteat one of their best men. "He contains [combines?] a very high degree of intelligence with very charming manners," Arnold noted, "which is something which you don't always get. Personally I would grab him if I had a place."[121] Miller, in fact, much wanted to grab Poteat, but Duke's hiring freeze at that time prevented the offer. After Poteat had returned to private practice in Greenville, South Carolina, Horack first tried to lure him with a visiting professorship, for which Poteat felt he could not abandon his partnership. Finally, after Arnold had again highly endorsed the South Carolinian and Horack had visited him in Greenville, Duke succeeded in hiring him in 1936. "Picking teachers is like selecting futurity winners for a horse race," Horack confessed, but he felt convinced that in Poteat "we have a good man with lots of possibilities in him for the future."[122]

The first graduate of Duke's own rebuilt law school to be named to the faculty, Paul H. Sanders, came in 1936. A Texan who graduated from Austin College before attending Duke Law School, Sanders achieved a strong record at Duke and then worked for the American Bar Association for two years before returning to Duke to teach criminal law, among other things, and to assist Cavers with *Law and Contemporary Problems*. Cavers, to whom other law schools frequently but unsuccessfully beckoned, carried an "enormous burden," according to Horack, and Sanders was a possible "understudy who may save our lives in an emergency." [123]

Sanders did help with the school's widely respected publication, and at a subsequent period, so did another new appointee. Elvin R. ("Jack") Latty, who would eventually become an important figure in the later history of the Duke Law School, joined the faculty in 1937. An ebullient New Englander, Latty had written to Justin Miller back in 1932 and expressed an interest in teaching at Duke. He explained that he was a graduate of Bowdoin who had taught romance languages for five years at the University of Vermont before taking his law degree at the University of Michigan in 1930, winning the law review prize in the process. He had gone into practice (in no less a firm than Sullivan and Cromwell in New York) with the specific objective of acquiring some legal experience before beginning to teach law as a career. [124] Since Miller had largely completed his recruitment by the time Latty wrote, nothing came of that overture. Five years later, however, Horack brought Latty from the University of Missouri to teach corporate law at Duke, where he remained until his retirement in 1973.

Just as Latty would eventually serve as dean of the school, so would Harold Shepherd. Coming to Duke as a visiting professor in 1939, Shepherd ended up remaining when an unexpected vacancy occurred in the faculty. He had received both his undergraduate and law degrees at Stanford and then taught there before being named dean of the law school first at the University of Wyoming and later at the University of Washington. Shepherd's appointment not only illustrated Duke's continuing close ties with Stanford in the field of law but, according to the dean there, meant that with both Lon Fuller and Shepherd Duke had two of the four men who had gone through Stanford's law school during the previous two decades with a straight-A record. [125]

Aside from playing a key role in making these important new appointments, Horack made his particular contribution to the school when he conceived of a novel approach to the housing problem facing law students. Since Duke then provided no dormitories for graduate or professional students, they were often forced to scrounge for themselves as best they could in Durham and sometimes in substandard old farmhouses scattered around the fringes of the West campus in the Duke Forest. Horack persuaded the administration in 1938 to erect on the northern edge of the West campus a cluster of five large log cabins—four dormitory cabins, each accommodating eight students, and a recreational cabin—where at least a portion of the law students might live if they wished. Although spartan in some respects, the cabins were equipped with electricity, indoor plumbing and central heating, which made them more comfortable than their Lincolnesque name might suggest. They attracted a great deal of national publicity, including even the newsreels of the day, and Horack reported that "the boys are enjoying them very much indeed and all are extremely enthusiastic about the cabins and the conditions of study which they promote." He confided to the chairman of the university's trustees that privately he took economic need into account when assigning the cabins but publicly he emphasized that "selection has been on the basis of seriousness in law study rather than financial needs alone." Later, in attempting to fight off intrusion into the cabins by the medical school, Horack perhaps got carried away and described them somewhat grandiloquently as "the Duke version of a Law Commons, conceived in the spirit of the old English Inns of Court."[126]

One student who undoubtedly would have been assigned to the coveted space in the law cabins had he not graduated in 1937, a year before their erection, was Richard M. Nixon. Having seen on a bulletin board at his undergraduate institution, Whittier College in California, that Duke offered a number of tuition scholarships worth $250 a year, the hardworking future president of the United States promptly applied and was soon notified by Justin Miller in the spring of 1934 that he had been awarded a scholarship. "In those depression years," Nixon later commented "that was a decisive factor."[127] At one point young Nixon served as Horack's research assistant, being paid with funds from the New Deal's National Youth Administration, and the dean came to have great respect for his abilities. Recommending him for a job, Horack wrote that Nixon was a "very high ranking student and was president of the Duke Bar Association last year." That he was "especially capable" was also indicated, Horack thought, by the fact that Nixon was awarded the Order of the Coif, the law school's top recognition for academic excellence. In another letter Horack described Nixon as "an exceptionally brilliant and reliable young man."[128] Richard Nixon missed the experience of living in Horack's cabins, but he studied law under essentially the same strong faculty that Justin Miller had so ably assembled.

On the eve of the United States' entry into World War II, however, and then especially during and right after the war, that group underwent profound change. One of Duke's major losses came in 1940 when Lon Fuller accepted a bid to join Harvard's law faculty. He had gone to Cambridge as a visitor in the fall of 1939 and vividly described some of his experiences as a teacher there in letters to Horack. Fuller admitted that, somewhat to his surprise, he found that in teaching the large classes he enjoyed "the experience of presiding over a public meeting." When Harvard asked him to remain permanently, Fuller explained to Horack that the decisive factor for him was "the chance one has here [at Harvard] to influence large groups of able students." Money, he insisted, was not the issue, for he should only expect from Harvard at least what he already made at Duke.[129]

In the years ahead Fuller would remain at Harvard and become one of the nation's most renowned and influential legal philosophers and scholars.

In the following academic year, 1940–41, David Cavers served as a visiting professor at the University of Chicago and ended up receiving a tempting offer there. Horack argued that Duke needed him more than Chicago did and that Duke's "chances for eventual success and for a real contribution where it is worth while are much greater than theirs." The Duke dean suggested that one of the "greatest difficulties" of the Duke law faculty was "an inferiority complex, not participated in but taken advantage of by the more discriminating portion of the law school world." He had seen the same thing at Chicago, he noted, in that school's earlier days. "Esprit de corps is very essential," Horack concluded, "and I think we have the potentialities here and have done pretty well under the circumstances to avoid the development of rival camps such as have grown up in many [law] schools."[130]

While Horack's arguments may have been a factor in Caver's decision to remain on the Duke faculty, the nation's entry into World War II brought strains and pressures on the law school that no amount of letter writing or eloquence could prevent. In the first place, the draft of young men that began in 1940 and was extended even more broadly in subsequent years drastically depleted the nation's law schools. Many male undergraduates remained in college, at least for a time, under various programs of the armed services, and medical schools were jammed as they operated on accelerated schedules. Professional schools such as law and business, however, were quickly faced with shrunken enrollments. From 1939's enrollment of 123 students, the top figure for the decade, the Duke Law School's enrollment fell to 36 in 1943 and 31 in 1944. In the spring of 1943 the law dean at Stanford reported that the school there had only 29 students, and he estimated that there might be 30 in the fall—maybe 15 women and 15 men who had been rejected by the draft.[131]

The situation was sufficiently drastic at Duke as well as at Wake Forest and the University of North Carolina for there to be discussion of combining the operations of the three schools for the duration of the war. While that plan encountered obstacles and never materialized, Wake Forest's much-diminished school did move to Duke in 1943 and was operated in conjunction with Duke's until after the war.[132] If a large portion of Duke's law faculty had not been on leave during the war, either in military or government service, the situation would have been even more awkward than it was. A greatly reduced faculty, however, came closer at least to fitting the needs of a shrunken student body.

More trouble came at the war's end in 1945 when students, including large numbers of veterans, began flocking back to the law schools, including Duke's. Unfortunately, many of the original faculty members did not follow suit. David Cavers, like Lon Fuller earlier, accepted an offer from Harvard in 1945, and Maggs no doubt spoke for most if not all of his colleagues when he described it as a "big blow" for Duke.[133] In addition, William R. Roalfe, the able law librarian whom Justin Miller had secured back in 1930, resigned in 1946 to go to Northwestern in the same post. Douglas Poteat and Paul Sanders both resigned at the end of the war. Some of these resignations may have been inevitable because of changed career plans that resulted from wartime experiences, but some may have been at least partially rooted in the fact that Duke's salaries for all faculty, including the law school, began to slip during the war and continued to drop in the immediate postwar years. Whereas the salaries that Justin Miller had been able to offer for a brief but crucial period in 1930 and 1931 had been competitive with the best, that was hardly the case by 1946.[134]

At any rate, the law faculty that Justin Miller had assembled finally underwent drastic changes. True, there were important continuities: Bradway, Maggs, McDermott, and Horack—all recruited by Miller—remained, and Bolich and Bryson from the late 1920s still served. Lowndes, Latty, and Shepherd continued on the faculty. But Judge Bryson, as he was always called, retired in 1947, and when Horack retired as dean in 1947, the Miller era, or perhaps the Miller-Horack era to be more exact, had ended. *Law and Contemporary Problems* and other aspects of the school that went back to the early 1930s still continued, but the challenge of a large-scale rebuilding faced those who led and served in the Duke Law School after World War II. The shadow of Justin Miller, the dynamic Californian who had played such a key role in launching Duke's expanded law school in 1930, would not loom so large from about 1945 onward.

13

The Serendipitous Acquisition

of Assets: The Duke Forest

and School of Forestry

✑

IN THE YEARS AFTER December, 1924, President Few liked to emphasize that the expansion and reorganization that took place when Trinity College became the nucleus for a complex research university were carefully planned and rooted in past developments. To a large degree, Few was correct. But the vast Duke Forest and the later School of Forestry were different, for they largely owed their existence to the unanticipated consequences of a shrewd industrialist-philanthropist's insistence on an access road and, to a lesser extent, his interest in a potential water-power site. Put another way, the forest was an unforeseen "accident" that grew out of lessons that James B. Duke had learned in his long career as a businessman.

While the acquisition of the Duke Forest was an accident in one sense, its careful development and the subsequent establishment of the School of Forestry were not. Rather, they may be seen as a first-rate example of good problem-solving, one showing how extensive tracts of abandoned or exhausted farmlands and timbered areas could best be utilized in a particular area and at a particular time. The importance of reestablishing the South's forests as a renewable resource, one that had a vitally important relationship to the economic well-being of the region, was well matched in the Duke Forest with its variety of plant habitats; portions of existing forests could be used as models for the reforestation of worn-out farm land. While the ultimate outcome was not foreseen or intended by J. B. Duke, Few and those with whom he worked in developing the forest and then the School of Forestry combined great resourcefulness and practicality with certain idealistic purposes.

As discussed earlier, J. B. Duke and Few originally set out to buy enough land around the old Trinity campus to accommodate the expanded institution. Frustrated in that endeavor by difficulty in acquiring certain parcels and by land prices that rose as word leaked out of the large plans, J. B. Duke acceded to Few's suggestion that forest and farmland a mile or so west of the Trinity campus be considered as a possible site for the Tudor Gothic stone buildings which were planned for the new university. With authorization—and money—from J. B. Duke, Robert L. Flowers put an agent to work quietly buying land in November 1924. Since much of the land was of poor quality for farming, and southern agriculture and land prices were then depressed anyhow, Flowers found no great difficulty in buying about 3,000 acres by the spring of 1925. That included a tract near Hillsborough, North Carolina, which contained the quarry from whence would come the stone for the university's projected Tudor Gothic buildings.[1]

The critical importance of having ample land was one of the basic lessons that J. B. Duke had learned over a lifetime of building large industrial enterprises. Another learned lesson, moreover, was that good access, in the form of roads or railways, was equally vital. At a conference with Flowers and others in New York in May, 1925, J. B. Duke, after having definitely decided to locate the Gothic buildings on the "new land," indicated that he wanted an access road to the new campus to be built that would run from the Greensboro-Durham highway to the Chapel Hill-Durham highway. This road would be on the west or "back" side of the new campus and would obviously make it more accessible in general, especially to the larger cities and more heavily populated Piedmont areas of what was then still a predominantly rural state. Operating with dispatch as well as secrecy, Flowers reported in semicryptic letters during the summer of 1925 on his success in buying the land for the desired road.[2]

Despite his secrecy, Flowers did show one Trinity alumnus something of what he was up to in the way of real estate operations. After surveying parts of the new land, the dazzled visitor urged Flowers to buy another thousand acres or so, "thus extending our boundaries to Chapel Hill." He could only feel great pride and satisfaction, the alumnus declared, that "we are at last going to have enough to make those fellows [at the University of North Carolina] sit up and take notice."[3]

J. B. Duke, despite a lingering illness that began in late July 1925, also took a keen interest in the land purchases and summoned Flowers to come north, equipped with maps and surveys, for a conference around September 1, 1925.[4] In addition to the land needed for the access road, Duke had heard of a possible water-power site between Durham and Chapel Hill and, after examining a plat of the land, requested Flowers to purchase the tract below "Patterson's Mill," where two creeks entered the New Hope River.[5] This tract, a particularly scenic portion of the Duke Forest now known as the Korstian Division, lay mostly in Orange County and is one of the hilliest portions of the forest. One steep hillside is covered in native rhododendrons, and huge rocks and cliffs along the stream bank look more like they belong in the mountainous region of North Carolina than in the Piedmont.

In acquiring the land for the approximately seven-mile-long access road, Flowers obviously could not purchase mere highway-wide strips of land but had to buy whole farms and tracts of timberland, or sizeable portions thereof. This meant that when the road that became North Carolina Highway 751 (and, much later, Cameron Boulevard on the northern portion and Academy Drive on the southern) was built, considerable acreage was left on either side of the road. That surplus land became the nucleus of the Duke Forest.

Flowers happily reported to George Allen early in 1926 that the substantial cost of building the access road might not have to come out of the already squeezed building fund provided by J. B. Duke, for the building committee was having to make substantial cuts in the plans for the projected Tudor Gothic buildings. John Sprunt Hill, the state highway commissioner for the district and a prominent Durham businessman, lent a sympathetic ear to Flowers's argument that, since the road would serve the public at large as well as interests other than those of Duke University, the state should pay for its construction. Hill suggested that the university (actually the Duke Endowment) pay an engineer of the state highway commission to lay out the road: then Durham County would do the grading and the state the paving when funds became available.[6]

Following this procedure, Flowers reported early in 1928 that the road was under construction. A little more than a year later, the state took over the paving of the road, with the Duke Endowment's building committee paying $10,500 to eliminate the grade crossing over the Southern Railway's tracks. The highway, curving through handsome stands of pines and hardwood trees, became even more beautiful—at least on its northern end—when in 1936–37 Few, capitalizing on North Carolina's program in highway beautification and the New Deal's Works Progress Administration, sold state highway officials on the idea of a demonstration project there. The widened shoulders of the road, along with the absence of any commercialization, abundant dogwood blossoms in the spring, and the rich colors of hardwood trees in the autumn, made that end of the highway a rare pleasure for motorists and, in a later era, joggers, cyclists, and hikers.[7]

Thanks to J. B. Duke's foresight and money, as well as to Robert L. Flowers's skill in acquiring real estate, Duke University by late 1925 wound up owning about 5,000 acres, which with additions made in later years grew to about 8,000 acres, mostly in forests and abandoned or run-down farm land. Not all of the Duke Forest was destined to be used, however, for educational purposes and recreation. A portion of it on the southern end of Highway 751 became an important element in the university's recruitment and retention of its faculty members. In the initial halcyon days of the university's establishment, before cold budgetary truths had emerged, the plan was for the Endowment's building committee to erect houses on or near campus to rent to a substantial portion of the new faculty members who would have to be added. Though requiring a large initial investment in construction, this plan, university officials believed, could eventually be made self-supporting and certainly attractive to faculty members. A small number of new recruits for the Duke faculty were, in fact, promised such housing by Few or one of the deans so authorized by him. Those promises were kept, but fortunately the number was small. Officials of the Duke Endowment sent word early in 1929 that after careful consideration they had decided that, rather than dip further into the dwindling funds of the building committee while the new Gothic campus was still under construction, it would be best for the university to use money from its own endowment fund to build the houses. Then the housing could be managed so that the university got "around 5% or something better" on its investment.[8]

Though the university's own endowment fund was distinctly on the puny side—Few stated a few years later that the university's trustees then directly controlled less than $3,000,000—the university's executive committee voted to put up to $350,000 into faculty residences. Only ten such residences were actually built, however, on the road linking the two campuses of the university (later named Campus Drive) before financial exigencies forced a suspension of the plan.[9]

Once again the excess land made available through J. B. Duke's insistence on an access road turned out to have an unforeseen use. An Endowment official in New York suggested that the university might consider making an outright sale of building lots in certain sections of the recently acquired land, particularly along the southern end of the access road.[10] University officers, together with Endowment representatives, quickly agreed on a plan whereby the university would initially spend up to $50,000 to put in streets, sidewalks, and sewer and water lines. Then the university would sell the lots at a reasonable price to cover the cost of the improvements but would ask for only a nominal down payment on the lot. The remainder of the purchase price would be subordinated to any first mortgage on the lot that might be necessary for a faculty member to secure a loan to build a house. (Put another way, the university would take a second mortgage on the lot.) Starting in 1931 with Pinecrest Street, running from the new Highway 751 to the Chapel Hill road, Duke faculty members bought spacious, wooded lots for $1,500 and began to erect the comfortable houses that relatively modest sums paid for in that depression-wracked era. The university had launched a program that, over the next half century and beyond, played a significant role in its recruitment and retention of faculty.[11]

In addition to the forest and the faculty-staff homesites, a School of Forestry gradually, and again in an unforeseen manner, grew out of the vast expanse of new land that Duke University found itself owning. In 1921 Few had listed a significant number of professional schools for the proposed university in his original memorandum to J. B. Duke, and Duke had later incorporated them in his indenture creating the Duke Endowment. A school of forestry was not, however, among those proposed.

Both idealistic and practical considerations soon combined to suggest that Duke University put its vast forest to educational use. On the idealistic side, Few, while certainly not alone among educational leaders in espousing generous service as his institution's principal reason for existing, possessed an unusually strong commitment to the idea of Duke University's being of as much help and value as possible to its state, region, and nation. When he learned from an authoritative source, as he soon did, that the establishment of a "high-grade forest[ry] school in the South is one of the greatest single contributions that can be made to her future welfare and prosperity," Few's ears naturally perked up. The acting dean of New York state's College of Forestry at Syracuse University, Nelson C. Brown, made that suggestion to Few and went on to argue that North Carolina, because of its geography and climate, was the "logical state" in which such a school should be established. Suggesting that the South's future prosperity depended significantly upon the permanence and proper management of its forest resources, Brown noted that the vast region did not then have a forestry school of the first rank. Not content with exhortation and generalities, Brown specifically urged Duke University to take a logical first step by establishing a department or division of forestry, naming a reputable director, and then expanding slowly toward the creation of a separate school.[12]

On one point, certainly, Brown was quite correct: the South then had no strong school of forestry. Truly professional instruction in forestry had begun in the United States only toward the end of the nineteenth century—in 1898, to be exact, at Cornell University and at the Biltmore Forest School near Asheville, North Carolina.[13] By the 1920s there were over two dozen additional institutions offering work in forestry, but in the South instruction in forestry was given only to undergraduates. Yale University, however, offered forestry on a graduate basis only, and its school, established in 1900, enjoyed considerable prestige, as did a small group of state- or tax-supported schools.[14]

While the idealistic promptings of Few and his associates at Duke University thus enjoyed a wide-open field, there were practical considerations too. Not only did the vast property have to be managed efficiently, but the tax-exempt status of philanthropic, not-for-profit institutions was one that always, in the 1920s as much as later, received careful watching and protecting by vigilant educational administrators. Late in 1925, Flowers sought advice from the state forester about the 5,000 or so acres that the university owned and noted that at some time in the future Duke might "be able to give a course in forestry."[15] Such tentative thinking about work in forestry quickened late in the summer of 1927 when the sheriff of neighboring Orange County, where a significant portion of Duke's forest land was located, sent notice that the university would be expected to pay taxes on its holdings in the county. The amount was not large, but the idea was enough to inspire deeper conviction on the part of the university's leaders about the educational potential of the forest.[16]

Even before the nudge from the sheriff's office, Few had obtained approval from the executive committee of the university's trustees as well as from the leaders of the Duke Endowment to pursue the matter of a graduate or professional school of forestry at Duke. Given the financial pressures in the new university, as Few began to contemplate the creation of a school of forestry, he set about trying his best to find a donor who would underwrite all or a substantial part of the costs that such a school would entail and who would, in turn, have the school bear his or her name. Charles Lathrop Pack, a wealthy leader in forestry and resource conservation, became a prime target of Few's solicitations and hopes. The hard pressed university president failed in this endeavor, however, just as he failed in similar searches on behalf of the projected or half-organized schools of medicine, law, and business.[17]

Despite the lack of a donor, Few began carefully investigating the field of forestry education and seeking to find the most suitable person to share in the building of the type of school that Duke desired. Nelson Brown at Syracuse, one of the early contacts, informed Few that he had consulted with the chief of the Forest Service at Washington and with other leaders in forestry and that all seemed "entirely unanimous in their approval of the establishment of a good strong school of forestry somewhere in the South."[18] Strong encouragement came also from E.H. Frothingham in Asheville, the director of the Appalachian Forest Experiment Station of the United States Forest Service, who perceived in Duke's plans a "powerful means for the development of the practice of forestry in the South."[19] To a colleague in the Forest Service, Frothingham confided that

Few hoped to build one of the best forestry schools in the country, one stressing research and the advanced training of foresters for work in the South. He was looking for a person who might later, though not necessarily, become dean of the school; Few wanted the person to be at Duke for a year or more, study the situation, and help plan wisely for the future. He would have a key role in planning the curriculum, selecting additional faculty members, and making other arrangements for the school. "A similar course was followed in the organization of the medical school at Duke," Frothingham noted, "apparently with good results."[20]

Just as Frothingham and others interested in southern forestry visited Duke University to advise and encourage President Few, so did Clarence F. Korstian, a senior silviculturist in the Forest Service and one of Frothingham's colleagues at the Asheville station. A graduate of the University of Nebraska who had entered the United States Forest Service in 1912, Korstian had received his doctorate in forestry from Yale in 1926 and, through a number of scholarly publications and professional activities, had established himself both as a researcher and leader in forestry. That Korstian viewed Duke's plans favorably was indicated by his report to his former mentor and dean at Yale: "Both Frothingham and I feel that the conservative management of Duke University and the decided interest shown in education of a thorough-going and not of a superficial type will ensure the substantial background of faculty and facilities needed by an outstanding forestry school." It was not so much a "question of 'just one more forestry school,'" Korstian thought, in light of "the desirability of establishing a really high grade school in the South, where forestry is developing very rapidly and where a need exists for one good school to train men under the influence of the southern environment."[21]

If Korstian liked what he had learned and seen at Duke, the feeling was reciprocal, for in July, 1930, Duke University named the forty-one-year-old Korstian as professor of silviculture and the first director of the Duke Forest. While Korstian planned to visit important university-owned forests in the Northeast during the summer of 1931, he assumed his new position with certain ideas already in mind. He informed an official of the American Forestry Association that he expected promptly to put the Duke Forest under management leading toward sustained yield. Following a detailed cruise of the timber and a study of market conditions, he would devise a preliminary plan of management. In the course work in forestry that would be developed he hoped to train a few especially well-qualified students who were candidates for advanced degrees. The forest in Massachusetts owned by Harvard University he already knew, but it would be, he noted, one model that he expected to study closely.[22] Korstian informed another well-wisher that he leaned strongly toward making the Duke Forest a demonstration or research forest and that he believed President Few would go along with the idea of subordinating even graduate work in forestry to research.[23] Korstian also emphasized what he hoped would be an immediate and practical advantage of the forest: he planned to make it a "meeting ground for timberland owners and foresters" and a place "where forestry methods can be emphasized in a thoroughly practical and economical manner."[24]

Korstian also received encouragement from a neighboring institution in North Carolina. The State College of Agriculture and Engineering (later North Carolina State University) introduced an undergraduate department of forestry in 1929. That development posed no obstacle to Duke's possible plans, however, for the chairman at State declared that he believed that "graduate work [in forestry] should be done by an endowed institution rather than one depending on public funds." The work at the two neighboring schools would, he thought, be complementary rather than competitive.[25]

Although the opening of the School of Forestry was destined to be farther in the future than either Korstian or Few realized, mainly because of the depression's impact on Duke, the gradual realization of many of Korstian's plans began soon after he arrived in Durham. The appointment of William Maughan as assistant director of the forest late in 1930 brought another Yale-trained forester to Duke, and Korstian and Maughan together promptly initiated the first inventory of the forest's approximately 5,000 acres. Situated in the lower or eastern Piedmont at an average elevation of 300 to 600 feet, the forested portions, by far the greater part of the land, consisted of second-growth shortleaf and loblolly pines as well as various varieties of hardwood trees. With relatively little outcroppings of rock or swampland, most of the land was believed to be excellent for tree growth.[26]

The first step in the reforestation of certain open tracts in the Forest came late in 1930 when 1,200 one-year-old Oriental chestnut trees, believed to be resistant to the chestnut blight, were planted near Highway 751.[27] Soon afterward, approximately 42 acres of abandoned fields were planted in timber-producing species, 37,000 trees in all, at an average cost of $5.90 per acre.[28] By mid-1932 the initial survey of the forest had been completed; it revealed that the total area, exclusive of the campus, then consisted of 4,708 acres. Of those, 1,690 acres were in pine trees; 830 acres in hardwoods and pines; 570 acres in upland hardwoods (several varieties of oak); 313 in bottomland hardwoods (gums, poplars, sycamores, and birches); and 1,305 acres were open. A total of 125.5 acres had been planted during 1931–32.[29]

While the work of inventorying and reforestation went on, various groups began to realize what a valuable asset Duke University had acquired in the forest. While later population growth and surging economic development in the Durham area would heighten the public appreciation of the forest in the decades after World War II, even in the depressed 1930s there were those who knew a green treasure when they saw one. Korstian led one group of interested Duke people on a tour of the forest near the campus early in 1931. That one of the participants was pleased and impressed is suggested by this report: "The members of the exploring party turned away from the forest, which is so old, and yet so new, whose life is young, old and middle-aged, with a feeling that perhaps they had been close to the heart of one of the greatest parts of this great institution."[30] With the forest recognized as a national sanctuary for bird life, one avid group of watchers soon reported that 125 species had been identified there.[31]

With the launching of the New Deal in 1933, the Duke Forest received valuable assistance from an unexpected source. During the seventeen months that one camp of the Civilian Conservation Corps operated in Durham county, from mid-1933 until late 1934, the young men who made up the corps completed numerous projects that enhanced the value of the forest as a demonstration area and research laboratory. They built over 15 miles of roads in the forest, constructed 5 bridges, installed 111 culverts, removed inflammable material within 50 feet of both sides of roads, improved public recreation areas, and performed other services. In all, Korstian figured that the forest received 12,000 man-hours of free labor and 836 hours of work by a government-owned tractor.[32]

Help for the forest came not only from the CCC but also from the Federal Emergency Relief Administration. It paid about 50 Duke students for 11,619 man-hours of work related to the forest. While over half of those hours were spent in office work, some of the student workers helped to establish 18 new sample plots, to plant 37 acres of abandoned fields in 7 different species of tree seedlings, and to prune 78 acres of young stands of pine trees.[33] Later another camp of the CCC and students paid by the National Youth Administration would also benefit the forest.

Korstian argued that the forest played a role in relation to academic work in forestry comparable to that of a hospital's relationship to a medical school. While he, with the approval of Few and other top administrators, organized and improved the forest, he also moved to strengthen Duke's offerings in the field of forestry. With himself in silviculture and Maughan in forest management, Korstian thought that an important, then neglected field was forest soils. Accordingly he interested an assistant instructor already at Duke, Theodore S. Coile, in the subject and helped him to arrange a program whereby he spent one semester at Duke and then one at Yale where he worked on his doctoral degree. By hard work and getting what help he could from the few experts who then understood the basic differences between forest and agricultural soils, Coile, according to Korstian's later account, was able to develop a strong program of instruction and research at Duke.[34]

Though hampered by the economic depression in developing a school of forestry, Few was not averse to proceeding cautiously anyhow. Korstian later recalled that aspect of Few's administrative style and quoted him as saying (as he no doubt scratched his head or tugged at his beard): "Well, now, whatever we do let's give it enough thought and do it so well that we will not want to re-do it." Few added that Korstian should take all the time he needed, for "whatever we start we want to last, and we don't want to go off on a tangent, half-baked."[35] Though Korstian may at times have thought Duke and Few were moving too cautiously, he apparently adjusted with equanimity to the gradual pace of development. As early as 1931 the Duke Forest was admitted to membership in the International Union of Forest Research Organizations, thus becoming the first institution in the South and the seventh in the nation to belong to that organization.[36] In 1934 a Department of Forestry was formally organized, and work leading to the M.A. and Ph.D. degrees was offered through the Graduate School of Arts and Sciences. Joining Korstian, Maughan, and Coile in teaching the advanced-level courses were two members of Duke's botany department, Frederick A. Wolf in forest pathology and Paul J. Kramer in plant physiology.[37]

With five members of the instructional staff on hand, Korstian kept moving toward the goal of a faculty of at least eight persons, which he believed necessary for full accreditation and recognition. Seeking a wood technologist, he made various inquiries and succeeded in luring Ellwood S. Harrar away from the University of Washington. For the subject of forest mensuration, Korstian and his colleagues decided that there was only one person in the country who could fill the spot, Francis X. Schumacher, and he came to Duke in 1937.[38] With the addition of Roy B. Thomson in forest economics and policy and Albert E. Wackerman in forest utilization, Korstian and Few agreed that Duke had finally become ready to open officially its School of Forestry.

The school began in September, 1938, with Korstian as dean and twenty-one students enrolled. They came from thirteen widely scattered states and four foreign countries, suggesting that from the beginning forestry at Duke had a fairly broad national and even international drawing power. Korstian, who was elected president of the Society of American Foresters late in 1937, had good reason to be proud of what he had thus far accomplished at Duke. He later recalled that he had found Duke a congenial place to work and believed that it was not large salaries that held good faculty members there but the "freedom to teach their courses unhampered by meddling from above."[39] He also liked the fact that he was given a more or less free hand in managing the forest itself. When

Flowers asked if there should be an item in the budget to cover expenses connected with the forest, Korstian replied that he would first rather see what could be done through management of the area. Flowers agreed to set up a Duke Forest fund in the treasurer's office, with any balance left at the end of the year not reverting to a general fund, as Korstian thought would be the case in a state-supported institution, but remaining intact until needed for work in the forest. "This arrangement," Korstian later remarked, "was a very important factor in making the forest self-supporting from the beginning."

The forest fund was also the means whereby, especially during and after the years of World War II, when the market for timber and other forest products boomed, Korstian was able to purchase additional pieces of land needed to round out boundaries. By the early 1950s the size of the forest had increased from not quite 5,000 acres to 7,600 acres. All in all, Korstian believed it advantageous that he and his colleagues were "not bound by many regulations similar to those imposed upon state institutions" and that the university's business officers were generally "inclined to be helpful and desire to assist us in furthering the major objectives of the University."[40]

Not everything was rosy for forestry at Duke, however. Crowded into a room on the top floor of the biology building, which was then adjacent to the Duke Medical School and Hospital, four permanent employees of the forest and the School of Forestry, plus four or five additional people at times, labored in an area that had been originally designed to house laboratory animals. Korstian insisted that forestry desperately needed more indoor space for offices, laboratories, and classrooms, and more adequate development of its library.[41] When a new graduate dormitory, Few Quadrangle, was built on the West campus in 1939, Forestry gained the temporary use of a suite of rooms there, though the laboratories remained in the biology building. More adequate arrangements had to await the construction of a new biological sciences building in the years after World War II.

On the eve of the United States' entry into that war, both the forest and the School of Forestry seemed solidly established and ready to render increasing service on a variety of fronts. While the research and economic aspects of the forest had perhaps received the most attention throughout the 1930s, the recreational side had by no means been ignored. William Maughan noted in 1939 that the United States Forest Service took as its foremost objective in managing the national forests that they be of the greatest use to the greatest number of people, and such a goal had resulted in a multiple-use program for the forests.[42] While Maughan admitted that Duke, as a voluntarily supported institution, did not necessarily have to follow a similar policy in the Duke Forest, he declared that its staff believed generally that "the development of recreational facilities for the use of the general public, within controlled limits, will go a long way toward building up a spirit of friendliness and cooperation, or good will, on the part of those in the University community and the local community in general, not only for the Forestry program, but also for the University as a whole."[43] Accordingly, the public's use of the forest—for picnics at improved sites, hiking, and horseback riding—increased rapidly through the decade.

While World War II brought no harm to the forest, the School of Forestry was hit hard by the draft, which also drastically reduced enrollment in certain other professional schools. With several of the faculty members on leave for military or government service, the School of Forestry more or less marked time during the war. Of the nineteen persons enrolled in September, 1941, only six were able to remain in school and receive the master of forestry degree, and only one person received the doctorate in forestry. Enrollments shrank even more in the following several years.[44] Sharply rising enrollments and a host of new problems and challenges for the school would come with the return of peace in 1945.

Although James B. Duke never intended that such should happen, his insistence on an access road to the handsome new campus that he gave to Duke University led to the acquisition of assets that would vastly increase in value over the years.

14

From Few to Flowers, World War II,

and the Leadership Crisis

of the Late 1940s

⌁

WITH THE ESTABLISHMENT of the School of Forestry in 1938 and the College of Engineering in 1939, President Few completed the organization of those segments of the university that were set up during his administration and lifetime. In the late 1920s he had sought to find a large donor who would foot the bill, or a substantial portion thereof, for a graduate-level school of business administration, but he had failed in that endeavor. The depression-wracked economy of the 1930s made such a search all the more unpromising, and Few apparently ceased to worry about that particular item in the plan for the university that he had first outlined and that J. B. Duke had incorporated in the indenture creating the Duke Endowment.[1]

While much of the university's support after 1924 came from the Duke Endowment, Few continued to have close and friendly relations with various members of the Duke family. Ben Duke's widow, Sarah P. Duke, divided her time between her homes in New York and Durham. Like her late husband, she personally knew many leaders and faculty members at Duke and was on the campus for numerous occasions. Her role in the beginning of the gardens has already been discussed. After her death in 1936, her daughter, Mrs. Mary Duke Biddle, gave the handsome Durham home of the B. N. Dukes, "Four Acres," to the University, and it was long used as a guest house and as the venue for many receptions and meetings of various sorts. Mrs. Biddle had earlier in the decade given the homestead of her grandfather, Washington Duke, to the university.

With J. B. Duke's widow, Nanaline Holt Inman Duke, Few maintained cordial but hardly close relations, mainly because she evinced no continuing, close interest in the university. A native-born Georgian who seemed to have transplanted happily to New York's Fifth Avenue and Newport, Rhode Island, Mrs. Duke made only rare and infrequent visits to the university. In late 1925, Few asked her if she had any suggestions or preferences about possible names for new buildings, but that overture failed.

Few possessed his own distinctive way of dealing with the members of the family. Once, when a Methodist minister asked for help in approaching B. N. Duke about support for a missionary-run school in Japan, Few replied with an uncharacteristic sharpness: "I sometimes think that everybody in the United States has written me a letter rather similar to yours in its general import," the harassed president declared. He went on to explain that it was "quite impossible" for him to accede to such requests. "The sober truth is I have never asked Mr. [B. N.] Duke or any of the Dukes for a cent for Duke University or Trinity College," he avowed. "I have always been able to work these things out in ways other than this."[2]

One way he worked out "these things" was simply to maintain friendly communication, through either face-to-face contact when possible or through letters. He saw to it, for example, that both Mrs. J. B. Duke and her daughter Doris took part in the events surrounding commencement in June, 1928, when a cornerstone was laid for the new Gothic structures on the West campus. In 1930, as Doris Duke approached her eighteenth birthday, Few wrote her a longer, more substantial letter than usual. After mentioning that the university commemorated both her father's birthday and the anniversary of the establishment of the Duke Endowment, he noted: "Your father had the vision, the desire, and the ability to set in motion great forces that will abide in power for good to mankind." Washington Duke, in a smaller way, had done the same sort of thing, Few suggested, and he thus reminded Doris Duke of her "noble heritage in ancestors like these." Few concluded the philosophical portion of the letter with a characteristic, oft-repeated idea: "As we grow in years and have a better understanding of our human life [,] most of us, I think, come to feel that only those are fortunate who can link their lives with great and undying causes."

Turning to less weighty matters, Few mentioned that he was sending her a book of photographs of the new Tudor Gothic buildings and that those at the university looked forward to having both Doris Duke and her mother for the formal dedication of the new hospital and medical school. "You may have heard that we now have a good football team—indeed one of the good ones of the country," Few boasted, and he wished she could see some of the games.[3]

Few's efforts to bring Mrs. Duke and her daughter to the campus succeeded late in 1932, and he reported to W. R. Perkins that during their day at the university they had been shown what they wished to see, had been "duly impressed," and had been subjected to no publicity whatsoever.[4] Shortly after this visit, a friend of Few's wrote him concerning the possibility of approaching Doris Duke concerning a Methodist-related cause in which Few also had a long-standing interest. Few replied that she had just turned twenty-one, had been in school in Europe for the past two or three years, and, insofar as he knew, she took no active part in her financial affairs. "I have never seen her but twice, I believe," Few added, but she made a "favorable impression" and would probably some day "become interested in philanthropy, as her people before her have been." Meantime, Few expressed his candid opinion that there was "practically no chance at all" of interesting her in the Methodist cause involved.[5]

In 1935 Doris Duke married James H. R. Cromwell, a wealthy and socially prominent businessman with certain pronounced and well-publicized ideas about various reforms that meshed nicely with Franklin D. Roosevelt's New Deal. When Mrs. Duke sent Few an announcement of the marriage, he seized the occasion to suggest that since she might be a bit lonely, at least initially, after her daughter's marriage, she should visit Duke more often. There were many interesting things always going on.[6] The invitation went unheeded.

Throughout the 1930s Doris Duke received a vast amount of unwanted publicity, especially in the tabloid press, as the so-called "richest girl in the world." Sharing her father's passion for privacy, however, she studiously avoided public attention insofar as that was possible. From time to time she began anonymously aiding individual students to attend Duke— and probably other schools as well—from the mid-1930s onward.[7]

In the spring of 1935, Few prepared for the unveiling of the statue of J. B. Duke, which stood in the central quadrangle of the West campus. Several students wrote letters to the *Chronicle* objecting primarily to the location of the statue but suggesting also that the statue of J. B. Duke, with a cigar in one hand and a cane in the other, would bring ridicule on the university. Few promptly issued a statement explaining that plans for the West campus had always shown the statue located in the quadrangle and that it was "the glory of this university" to have been "built in accordance with carefully made plans." Furthermore, Few declared, "I have a profound appreciation of what Mr. Duke has striven to do for education and for humanity; and I would do honor to his good deeds in any way however conspicuous."[8] That closed the discussion.

Few hoped to bring the Cromwells, who were on a world cruise, for the unveiling in early June. "This is a new institution and life here is fresh and invigorating," he wrote, "rather than flat, stale, and unprofitable like Hamlet's uses of the world." He thought the newly wedded couple would enjoy occasional visits to Duke.[9] Since the Cromwells were en route to Singapore, Few's letter did not reach them in time for them to return for the occasion.

Doris Duke Cromwell, traveling incognito with a young woman friend, did visit Duke briefly in the spring of 1936. Occupying the house counselor's rooms in Brown House on the East campus, she met and socialized with a number of the women students. The *Chronicle* reported that, according to those who met her, "she is a young woman with a keen sense of humor and with interests much like their own."[10]

Few, in seeking to interest Doris Duke Cromwell in the university, obviously had its long-range interests and well-being foremost in his mind. To leave the matter at that, however, would be inaccurate and unfair to Few. Not only was he a genuinely kind person, but he well understood that extremely rich young persons often have great difficulty in finding a direction or purpose for their lives. A medical doctor from Philadelphia, who knew well both James Cromwell and his parents, visited Duke, talked with Few, and subsequently wrote Few a confidential letter. Suggesting that there was more substance to Cromwell than the newspapers had conveyed, the doctor stated, "I believe, after having seen you and the University, that it might be possible to get Jim interested in that work." The doctor intended to pass on his favorable impression of the university to Cromwell. "I hope, if it is in your power to get these young people interested in that work, that you will do so," he concluded. "Jim needs the guidance and the sort of help that you can give."[11]

The Cromwells visited Duke in the fall of 1938 for one of the excellent symposia held as part of the university's year-long celebration of its centennial. Few was not just chasing money when he and Mrs. Few had them as house guests for the occasion. Shortly afterward, just before Doris D. Cromwell's twenty-sixth birthday, Few sent her his greetings. "You must know how I feel towards your father and how easy it is for something of the same feeling to pass over to you," Few explained. "I hope you will then always understand how close I am to you in sympathy and earnest desire to be of any personal service to you if such need should ever arise."[12]

The Cromwells seem to have responded to Few's overtures, for they both returned to the campus in the spring of 1939 for the final, climactic portion of the centennial celebration. Doris Duke Cromwell also gave the university her father's desk as well as oil portraits of her grandfather, Washington Duke, and her uncle, B. N. Duke. Thanking her for those gifts and for the visit to the university, Few assured her that Duke University would throughout her life look upon her "as the cherished representative of your father." Graciously responding, she replied, in part: "No one knows better than I how interested he was in the University, and I feel privileged as his daughter to enjoy for him the realization of the dreams which you and others of his trusted friends have so splendidly achieved." She added a more personal touch also: "Mrs. Few and you make Jimmy and me feel so at home when we come to Durham that it is always a great pleasure for us to visit the University."[13]

When President Roosevelt named James Cromwell as the United States ambassador to Canada, Few wrote early in 1940 congratulating both of them. He also expressed the hope that the diplomatic post might prove to be a step in the direction in which they both might wish to go.[14]

Unfortunately, Few's death later in 1940 and the subsequent divorce of the Cromwells ended the relationship between Doris Duke and the university that seemed to have begun to emerge in the late 1930s. She would in later years make rare visits to Duke, though she appreciated and liked W. C. Davison, the dean of the medical school. But the long-term relationship and interest between her and the university that Few had hoped and worked for did not develop.

With B. N. Duke's only daughter, Mrs. Mary Duke Biddle, matters were different. Not only had she grown up and gone to the public schools in Durham, but she built a home there in the 1930s; she had also been a student and graduate of Trinity College whom Few had long known well and probably taught. Moreover, she had been in the same class of 1907 with Mrs. Few (née Mary R. Thomas). Mary Duke Biddle, therefore, had a lifelong, intimate knowledge of and association with Trinity-Duke and those who led it.

Her interest in the institution probably increased all the more when her only daughter, Mary Duke Biddle II, entered Duke in 1935. The latter was a warm, gregarious person, one who possessed a combination of seriousness and altruism or social conscientiousness that derived from her mother's family and a liveliness and charm that seemed to resemble traits of her father, Anthony D. Biddle. Few and others who knew the family well privately referred to her as "Little Mary," and Few once described her as "beyond doubt an extraordinary young person."[15] She was destined to become in later years perhaps the closest, most important link between the university and the Duke family.

A lifelong lover of music and at one point a serious student of vocal music, Mrs. Biddle early realized that the university had a long way to go in the fields of music and art. Perhaps, too, because of her earlier experiences at Trinity and those of her daughter in the late 1930s, she wished to do something for the Woman's College. Few, in close consultation with George Allen and W. R. Perkins, sought to steer her in another direction. Since the university had not yet established a department of music and did not yet have the funds to do so, Few was no doubt right in shying away from any mention of a music building. As for the possibility of a student or recreational center on East, Few argued, in a letter to Mrs. Biddle, that "we must not push that side of our development too rapidly; otherwise we might seem to be catering to students who are looking for a sort of winter resort instead of a rather stiff educational institution."

As top-priority physical needs of the university, Few named a dormitory for graduate students and an addition to the badly overcrowded main library on West campus. Perkins urged Few to give the dormitory precedence over the library addition on the grounds that the university's first duty was to house students rather than books. Few, however, stuck to his guns and finally advised Mrs. Biddle, "Personally, I have the feeling that if I were in your place I would prefer the library [addition]." [16]

Mrs. Biddle did ultimately, after World War II, give the much-needed addition to the main library. In the late 1930s, however, she helped the Woman's College by having the Alumnae Room in East Duke building redecorated and equipped with valuable furniture and art objects in the Louis XV style. She also gave noteworthy oil paintings to the Woman's College library. All of Mrs. Biddle's various gifts to the university in the late 1930s, including her parents' Durham house, became a part of the fund-raising program that Few launched in conjunction with the celebration during the academic year 1938–39 of the institution's one hundredth birthday.

Trinity-Duke had long depended heavily on the generosity and steadfast support of the Duke family, but as part of the centennial celebration in 1938–39 Few hoped to broaden the base, albeit in a quiet, low-key manner. The depression, which pushed down even further an already economically ailing South, was hardly an ideal time for fund-raising. Moreover, a completely false but nonetheless widely held image of Duke as "the richest endowed university in the nation" was another formidable handicap to fund-raising. Other endowed universities had already begun systematic, well-publicized drives for fund-raising among alumni and friends, even securing professional advice and help in some cases. A historian of research universities points out that the "soliciting of gifts became a permanent function of twentieth-century private research universities." It was not, the historian suggests, "a reaction to institutional penury but rather a consequence of ambition," and once set in motion, the process fed upon it itself.[17] Duke simply lagged behind in the matter.

Nonetheless, Few seized the occasion of the centennial to attempt to do several things for Duke. The story of the transition from Union Institute, housed in a one-room schoolhouse in Randolph County, North Carolina, to the Georgian serenity of East campus and the Tudor Gothic splendor of West was an American saga that Few quite properly wanted to highlight—and if some much-needed new money could be raised in the process, that would be icing on the cake. The centennial celebration would be one of Few's last important activities as president.

Ever mindful of the history of the institution to which he had devoted his adult life, Few broached the matter of the centennial to George Allen late in 1935. After stating his own liking for the idea, Few explained that Duke could "send out some literature setting forth our needs and opportunities and this will give our friends a chance to think about our problems in a more or less impersonal way." He assured Allen, who was apparently wary about the idea of the university's "begging" or even appealing to the public for help, that the centennial material and events would not involve in any sense "a direct appeal of the University to anyone, but it will stimulate thinking and might bring valuable results even though we do not reach all our goals." [18]

Gaining the approval of Allen and of the other trustees early in 1936, Few requested the university's architect, Horace Trumbauer, to have his staff prepare preliminary plans for an addition to the Woman's College library that might be used by the art department and for a possible building on East for the use of the engineering departments; Few noted that he already had the architect's sketches for a new dormitory group on West and for an addition to the main library.

Turning to another important quarter, the national philanthropic foundations then most interested in higher education, Few informed the Carnegie Foundation and the General Education Board of Duke's plans. "You are no doubt 'fed up' on such things," Few admitted to the head of the Carnegie Foundation, "but after all, this is a bit unique, in that we are trying to build up a great endowed university in the Southeast where one has never been." [19]

Committees in the various schools and departments went to work both to consider long-range needs that might become part of the goals of the centennial campaign and to plan a series of symposia, concerts, and other events that would be scattered throughout the academic year of 1938–39. Early in 1937 Alfred S. Brower, a Trinity alumnus who had worked in state government in Raleigh and as comptroller of North Carolina State College, arrived on campus to become the executive secretary for the centennial campaign. He would remain at Duke long after the centennial had passed and play a prominent role in the business side of the university's administration.[20]

As part of his planning for the centennial, Few, with the help of W. K. Boyd and other key members of the history department, inspired Nora Chaffin, an alumna and graduate student in history, to undertake a history of Trinity College. She promptly began her meticulous investigation into documentary sources and interviewed various veteran members of the faculty and staff. Her scholarly and useful book, which carried the story from the beginnings of Union Institute in 1838 down to Trinity's move to Durham in 1892, would not be published until 1950, but Few derived satisfaction from his knowledge that the project was underway. He supplied written answers to some of Chaffin's queries, and at one point more or less wrote his own obituary as well as revealed his unbounded, perhaps even exaggerated, hope for the long-term role and service of the university. Probably "the most significant thing I have been able to do," Few advised Chaffin, "was devising a plan for the building of Duke University, incorporating [in it] Trinity College and 'selling' the plan to Mr. Duke." Few added that he had "a growing feeling that the founding of Duke University will, in the judgments of time, stand as the most important event in the history of the Southern states since the death of Thomas Jefferson."[21]

Few, no matter how much he was interested in the university's history or how exalted his vision of its future might be, had many immediate tasks to perform. One was to find a principal speaker for the great academic convocation in April, 1939, that was to be the climax of the centennial. More than a year and a half in advance of the occasion, he extended the invitation to James B. Conant, president of Harvard. Having gone to Cambridge to confer about the matter in person, Few had missed seeing Conant, so he wrote explaining about the centennial, the overall theme of which was to be "The Southern States in American Education." He wanted Conant to speak on "The Place of the University in American Education." Few noted that President Lowell of Harvard had spoken at Few's inauguration as president of Trinity in 1910; that Duke's president (Few), its dean of the university (Wannamaker), its dean of undergraduate instruction (Greene), and the dean of the law school (Horack) were Harvard alumni; and that in the whole university there were forty-four Harvard alumni, twice as many as from Chicago, which had the next largest group. "We have done an educational task here that I dare to believe will bulk large in the judgments of time," Few declared, and because of that belief, "I am particularly anxious to have the President of Harvard come for our occasion in 1939."[22] Conant, pleading other commitments, declined. The president of Princeton, Harold W. Dodds, ultimately became the featured speaker of the occasion.

To serve as general chairman of the committee for the centennial fund, Few picked a prominent and well-to-do alumnus in Winston-Salem, P. Huber Hanes. Proceeding quietly and with a minimum of publicity, Hanes and his committee ultimately reported that over 1,200 alumni and friends had contributed almost $5,000,000 in money and gifts.[23]

The weather smiled on Duke for the convocation in late April, 1939, and the spring sun bathed the large crowd seated in the main quadrangle. Few, who believed in the importance of a certain amount of academic ceremony, personally urged his fellow presidents in the region to attend the event, and some 400 delegates were in the academic procession. Doris Duke Cromwell was the only woman in the front row of distinguished guests. One visitor for the occasion appreciated the clear sky and the play of sunlight on the chapel tower and the encircling pine forest. He said that the one scene that remained indelibly stamped on his mind, however, was President Few "standing with cap in hand, facing the quadrangle of beautiful Gothic buildings . . . , and gracefully introducing the Czechoslovakian [President Benes]."[24]

The centennial convocation climaxed a year of happy developments for the university. While the admission to the Association of American Universities was clearly the most significant academic news, the alumni and the general public no doubt paid more attention to the Iron Dukes and their spectacular record on the gridiron. While only indirectly connected with the university, Few and others at Duke took great satisfaction from the reunification in May, 1939, of the Methodist church, which had divided along sectional lines before the Civil War. The centennial convocation, therefore, took place at an auspicious moment in Duke's history.

A wise historian who had been at Trinity-Duke since 1909, W. T. Laprade, took a long-range view of both the centennial celebration and Few's purposes in having it. By 1938–39 the small contingent of faculty members who had taught at Trinity before the organization of the university was vastly outnumbered by "newcomers," that is, those who had joined the faculty of Duke University. Certain of those newcomers, like a small number of their counterparts in the late twentieth century, no doubt believed that the institution's opportunity to make real advances coincided with their arrival upon the campus. Most of the faculty recruits, however, were not so egotistical, merely ignorant of Duke's history. Laprade suggested that as much as the new funds raised during the centennial celebration were needed, "perhaps a greater gain was the progress in making the majority of members of the staff more familiar than they had previously been with things achieved before they came upon the scene." Moreover, the "very coming forward of alumni and friends to offer substantial support was inescapable evidence of work previously done."[25]

Another person whom the centennial inspired to think about Duke's future no less than its past was an able editor of the *Chronicle*, Roosevelt Der Tatevasian. Like other students before him, as well as after, he was perhaps mistaken in thinking that the "destiny of the university during the next 100 years and more lies more with the student generation than with any other group." (Another student just flatly asserted in the *Chronicle* that "the students *are* the University.") But the editor was more on the mark, at least morally and historically, when he cautioned that in Duke's "endeavors to attain lofty heights," it should never forget that charity begins at home. The university had a primary obligation, he thought, to the less privileged people of the South and should continue to seek better health care for them and to provide more and better teachers for the public schools in the area. "Duke must never permit its desire to become a national, or an international, institution to obscure its first duty," he warned. With an increasingly cosmopolitan student body (and, he might have added, faculty), an earlier provincialism had been overcome. But "great spiritual vigor" was still to be achieved during the next hundred years by carefully chosen students and faculty. He believed that Duke needed to pursue selective admission of students more vigorously than it had thus far and with more emphasis on able, deserving students for whom Duke was the first choice rather than an alternate.[26]

The editor's reference to admissions was significant, for Duke, or rather its undergraduate college for men (Trinity), faced a problem in that area. On the one hand, James B. Duke had urged that great care should be "exercised in admitting as students only those whose previous record shows a character, determination, and application evincing a wholesome and real ambition for life." Following that sensible, if somewhat vague, guideline, all segments of the university practiced a policy of selective admissions from the first. But, as mentioned in earlier chapters, the Woman's College attracted a proportionately higher number of applicants for a smaller number of places than did Trinity (and later the College of Engineering) and thus had a more truly selective policy. There were many quite able male undergraduates, fully as strong academically as the best of the women students; but there were also more academically marginal students in Trinity College.

Leading colleges and universities in the North began to use the standardized examinations of the College Entrance Examination Board even before World War I. Duke continued to shy away from that policy, however, because it was committed to serving students from the South and particularly North Carolina. Not only were the college board examinations still rarely given in the region, but it had only a few strong private secondary schools, and its public schools generally lagged behind those in other parts of the nation. Given that dilemma, which would not be resolved until after World War II, the undergraduate colleges, especially Trinity, simply muddled along as best they could.

A principal in a suburban Philadelphia school of good standing urged Wannamaker in 1934 to try to arrange for a Duke alumnus to attend the school's "college night." The reputation of Duke there, the principal explained, was that the requirements were "so easy that if a person cannot go to some other college, he is relatively sure of being accepted at Duke." No doubt affronted, Wannamaker took his time before replying that the principal had a mistaken impression about Duke's admission standards and that in the previous year fewer than 600 men had been admitted from a pool of approximately 1,400 male applicants. Furthermore, Wannamaker noted that grading at Duke was sufficiently strict so that the freshman average in the fall semester was about a C and in the second semester was between a C and a B.[27]

While the Woman's College handled its own admissions, Flowers, as secretary of the university, originally handled Trinity's admissions. He had, however, passed on the responsibility to an assistant, Charles E. Jordan, in 1925. A Trinity alumnus who had also taken a law degree under Dean Mordecai, Jordan would later play a significant role in the university's administration. A member of a prominent North Carolina Methodist family, he took a keen interest in Duke's athletic teams, especially in football, and had many connections in the state that were helpful to the university.

A sensitive and controversial aspect of college admissions across the nation in the 1930s had to do with Jewish students. Unlike many of the Eastern colleges and universities, Duke adopted no formal or set quotas for Jewish students. This was certainly not because of any greater moral sensitivity on Duke's part, for traces of the anti-Semitism that was so rampant in much of the Western world in that period could be discerned also at Duke. But there were relatively few Jewish people in North Carolina and the South in general, the area from which Duke wished, indeed felt obligated, to draw a substantial portion of its students. The geographical quotas that Alice Baldwin and her staff gradually made explicit for the Woman's College were not designed to discriminate against Jewish women. Yet in practical operation those quotas obviously limited the number of Jewish women from the North and favored those from the South. There is no evidence that Jordan had any formal or explicit geographical quotas for admission to Trinity College, but in an informal manner, young men from North Carolina and its neighboring states were distinctly favored, even if certain trustees of the institution found that hard to believe.

In reply to a confidential query in 1937, Few noted that 3 percent of the undergraduate men (44 of 1432) were Jewish and 2.3 percent of the undergraduate women (16 of 695). Of 170 students in the medical school, 28 (16 percent) were Jewish. He had no figures for the other professional schools but estimated that the percentage was approximately the same as for the undergraduate colleges.[28]

The aspect of admissions that most concerned both Few and the trustees was not the percentage of Jewish students but the gradual decline in the proportion of undergraduates from North Carolina. A trustee committee on the undergraduate colleges reported in 1934 that in the seven years since 1927, North Carolina undergraduate enrollment had declined from 79.1 percent in 1927–28 to 28.8 percent in 1933–34. The decline had been greater in Trinity College than in the Woman's College. Some trustees attributed the drop to the fact that tuition had been gradually increased from $60 per year in 1927 to $200 per year in 1931. Though the tuition was not raised after that until after World War II, the North Carolina proportion of undergraduates continued to drop. The committee concluded that tuition rates were not too high and that there was an obviously pressing need for endowed scholarships for needy and worthy North Carolina students. Unfortunately, such scholarships would be slow in coming and were certainly not possible for the university to fund during the depression.

Sometimes the trustees tended to forget that both J. B. Duke and Few had agreed on Duke's aiming toward becoming a national university. That did not, of course, preclude a serious and significant commitment to serve North Carolina and its region, but finding a balance was an ongoing, constant challenge. The decline in North Carolina attendance was inevitable, perhaps even desirable, from the standpoint of Duke's becoming a national institution. Yet the change came hard for many alumni and trustees.

The fact that the trustees normally served for life, something else that would not change until after World War II, meant that most of them had known and loved "Old Trinity." Perhaps that made them somewhat less than keenly enthusiastic about at least some developments that went along with the expansion and transformation of the institution. Under the circumstances, the remarkable thing is that the great majority of the trustees, like most alumni of the old college, rather gracefully adapted to the large new challenges that came after December, 1924.

While the full board of thirty-six trustees met only three times a year, the executive committee of the board met monthly and was the group that dealt regularly with important ongoing matters. It consisted of five trustees plus the president of the university and the chairman of the board as *ex officio* members. When Joseph G. Brown, a Raleigh banker and chairman of the board since 1917, died in 1927, he was succeeded by John F. Bruton, a banker and lawyer from Wilson, North Carolina, and a trustee since 1900.

In the late 1920s all of the trustees except three were Methodists, and those three, according to Few, had Methodist antecedents.[29] Nine of the trustees were Methodist ministers. A faculty member from Harvard who visited Duke in 1927 was duly impressed by the great "educational possibilities" that lay ahead but cautioned Few that the board of trustees seemed "thoroughly localized."[30] While that was largely true, there was also a group of trustees, most of whom served on the executive committee at one time or the other, who lived in New York and who held important positions in the corporate world. Among them, aside from B. N. and J. B. Duke in the early years, were Clinton W. Toms, William W. Flowers, George G. Allen, and William R. Perkins. Moreover, among the resident

North Carolinians on the board were such prominent and well-to-do businessmen as W. R. Odell of Concord, P. H. Hanes, Jr., of Winston-Salem, J. H. Separk of Gastonia, and M. E. Newsom of Durham. Daniel C. Roper, who became President Franklin D. Roosevelt's secretary of commerce, served conscientiously as a trustee. In 1927 Few persuaded William N. Reynolds of Winston-Salem, who had attended Trinity in the 1880s and who was the brother of Richard J. Reynolds, to become a trustee. It was "a great move for us," Few boasted to Bruton, and W. N. Reynolds subsequently became a member of the executive committee.[31] So while the trustees may have been somewhat "localized," as the Harvard professor observed, there was nonetheless an interesting mixture of North Carolina and New York businessmen with Methodist preachers and laymen.

Few enjoyed a good working relationship with the trustees, but he was personally closest to and most dependent on Clinton Toms. Because of Toms's health and pressures on him as president of the Liggett & Myers company, he had temporarily escaped from long duty on Trinity-Duke's board and executive committee in the mid-1920s. After J. B. Duke's death in late 1925, Few wanted Toms to fill the vacated seat on the board. He assured Toms that the two of them "will not any more have to make the 'die-in-the-last-ditches' sort of efforts that we used so often to have to make." Yet it was increasingly plain, Few continued, "that if we are to build up, as Mr. J. B. Duke expected us to build up, a university that will rank with the best, then we must all the time keep massed our full strength and exhaust our full resources." Few noted that he was currently "straining every nerve" to get $6,000,000 from the Rockefeller Foundation for the medical school and a smaller amount from the Carnegie Foundation for a dental school. (The latter idea Duke soon dropped.) He thought the chances for success were good if those "shrewd almoners" could be convinced that Duke had not yet reached its utmost goal but that the institution's old friends, as well as its new ones, were "still effective for new achievements and ever-enlarging usefulness."[32]

Despite such appeals, Toms insisted that his shaky health stood in the way of his returning to the board and executive committee. "Unfortunately maybe, I cannot be a dummy on any kind of board," Toms declared. When Few persisted, arguing that "circumstances might sometimes make you [Toms] indispensable," Toms reluctantly agreed, even though his health might prevent his attendance at all meetings. "There isn't anything in the world that I would not do for you and for Duke University," he declared.[33]

Not only was Toms thoroughly conversant with the institution and its various problems, but just as he had served as a unique link or intermediary between Few and the Duke brothers, he also later came to serve the same function with George Allen and W. R. Perkins. Both men were relative newcomers to Duke and, in fact, to higher education. As a highly successful and likable, albeit quiet, business leader, Toms could speak their language more easily than could Few, and the latter frequently called on the former to "educate our friends" about various matters that were crucial to Duke. When Toms, two years younger than Few, died at age sixty-seven in 1936, Few wrote Clinton Toms, Jr., that "for forty years in every critical time in my life and in the life of the institution, he was the man that saved the day."[34]

After returning to Duke duty, Toms had suggested to Few that the trustees were not being given enough information about the exact status of the university. He realized that the trustees could not actually run the institution but, nevertheless, believed that they should be as conversant as practicable with all important matters pertaining to it.[35] This nudge may have been one of the reasons that Few led the trustees in 1930 to organize themselves into six committees to investigate and report on the colleges and the graduate school, the libraries, the medical school and hospital, the law school, the School of Religion, and the business administration of the university. Few advised and pressed the chairman of each of the committees, arguing that it would be good for the university if the trustees could become more familiar with its operations.

The committees probably helped, though Few and other administrative officers often ended up writing many of the reports. Problems remained, however. When the Faculty Club proposed a reception for the trustees of the university and the Duke Endowment in 1934, Chairman Bruton confessed, "Sometimes I feel that the trustees do not know each other as well as they might, and it goes without saying that we are all more or less strangers to a large majority of the members of the faculty." Whether the trustees ever came to know each other better is not known, but the faculty's and the trustees' mutual ignorance, and perhaps slight suspicion, of each other would long continue to be a problem.

When asked by an educational leader to describe briefly the role of the trustees, Few gave a rather perfunctory, standard answer: "The first service of a Trustee, I think, is fully to understand his institution, to know it from the center, and think from thence." He added that he thought that such was the situation with "practically all" of Duke's trustees and that "a good many of them are of immense value to the financial causes of the University."[36]

Few never forgot a lesson he had learned early when a firestorm of controversy swirled around Trinity College in the Bassett affair of 1903: a board of trustees could be a highly useful buffer and bulwark for a besieged institution. Though the economic depression of the 1930s never brought a major, threatening crisis to Duke, Few feared in the early stages that it might. Late in 1931, as hard times truly hit home across the nation,

Few urged Allen and Perkins to make every effort to attend the forthcoming meeting of the board. He explained that he hoped all of the trustees, in fact, would make a point of attending throughout the year, for "out of hard times like the present come restlessness and often gusts of unwisdom."[37]

Toward the end of his life, Few made a more candid assessment of his view of the trustees' normal function than he had earlier given to the educational leader. "The Trustees can't do a great deal to help administrative officers," Few advised an old friend. "They ought to understand them and back them." There were some trustees, he continued, who were useful in raising money, but "most of them, I have found through long experience, do not look upon that as part of their function." He concluded with a confession and slight tone of resignation: "On the whole, there is a great deal of art in the handling of these Boards everywhere. We have to learn to use them when we can and not to be unduly critical of them even when we can't."[38]

In dealing with the trustees of the university, Few faced a special problem, what might even be termed a handicap, that was unique to Duke: the university depended quite largely in its early years on the financial support provided by the Duke Endowment. As mentioned earlier, that foundation's separate board of trustees had, under certain circumstances, the power to withhold annual support from the university; it also controlled substantial discretionary funds that did not fall under the legally mandated formula for the distribution of funds.[39] To make doubly sure that the most powerful and influential trustees of the Duke Endowment, George G. Allen and William R. Perkins, would stand by Duke University became Few's principal preoccupation, one might almost say obsession, from the late 1920s until the mid-1930s, when Few felt that a change in the university's by-laws had finally nailed down a solution to the problem.

This emphasis and concentration on the trustees of the Duke Endowment obviously meant a downplaying of the role of the university's trustees. As Few in 1929 prepared for the Rockefeller Foundation his privately printed pamphlet about the relationship of the university and the Duke Endowment, Clinton Toms worried that "some sensitive Trustee might think that he had not the authority which he thought he had."[40] Few reminded Toms that the pamphlet was not for public distribution. Few did not say, although such was obviously the case, that he had more critical problems to deal with than the possible sensitivity of the university's trustees.

Later, after the private but serious controversy between Few and the Allen-and-Perkins team over Norman Thomas, Few moved to lessen the danger to the university in the only way he could conceive, which was to give the Duke Endowment a statutory and powerful voice on the executive committee of the university's board of trustees. After the trustee chairman, John F. Bruton, adamantly held out against incorporating the arrangement in the university's charter, which came from the North Carolina legislature, he and Few compromised by the implementation of Few's plan through a new university by-law. Bruton was actually not enthusiastic about the by-law requiring that three trustee members of the seven-person executive committee had also to be trustees of the Duke Endowment. He feared that the plan might be "full of mischief" and that already some of the trustees felt that they were "regarded as mere figureheads."[41]

Few's prestige, record of achievement, and leadership skills were sufficient for him ultimately to gain the board's unanimous consent to the power-sharing by-law. The plan worked for the remaining five years of his administration and, under different circumstances and for different reasons, during President Flowers's administration in the 1940s. The power-sharing plan, however, was a most delicate and tricky one, and future presidents of Duke might not be as skillful in making it work as Few was.

Not only did Few manage to maintain an effective, harmonious relationship with the trustees, but during the last years of his life he achieved a gratifying rapport with the undergraduates, especially those in Trinity College. Always deeply interested in them, Few was probably too preoccupied with various worrisome problems from the late 1920s until somewhere around the mid-1930s to have the time to show his concern. He seems to have relaxed a bit after the mid-1930s, and perhaps he was less frequently forced to leave campus for trips to New York and elsewhere. At any rate, he made himself available to students and gained the warm admiration of some of them. In 1937, as the fall term began and new freshmen scrambled frantically around the campus, a reporter for the *Chronicle* went for a rare interview with Few and found him full of reminiscences about his own days as a freshman at Wofford fifty-three years earlier. He had been sixteen, he said, and suffered some homesickness, especially after his older brother had to leave college because of illness. The South had only "recently emerged from the gloom of Reconstruction," Few recalled, and students were more serious-minded than they were in the 1930s. He had played some rugby but particularly liked baseball, and he had helped organize a college newspaper. Between reading and walking, Few advised the young journalist, "a college man [in the 1880s] was expected to have enough initiative to educate himself."[42]

A few days later, the *Chronicle* reported that Few had been in "rare form" in his address at the traditional school-opening ceremony in Page Auditorium. Few was reported to have once said that he "disdained to learn the art of public speaking because he did not want to 'scratch the people's back.'" The reporter noted, however, that the small crowd attending the exercise "received a delightfully unexpected back-scratching, especially where the Roosevelt administration itches them."[43]

Few, whom some who knew him described later as a less-than-enthralling speaker, must have risen to uncharacteristic heights on occasion in his later years. Concerning his speech at the opening of the centennial celebration in the fall of 1938, the *Chronicle*'s reporter declared that only rarely did a speaker appear on a ceremonial occasion who "pours forth the beliefs, aspiration and his visions in such a way as to inspire every last one of his listeners." But such, the reporter alleged, was the case with Few in that address.[44]

Early in 1939 Few recounted to a student reporter how he had been ill with influenza in March, 1921, when a message came that J. B. Duke was at B. N. Duke's Durham home and wished to confer with him. Few said he not only got out of bed to go for the conference but subsequently accompanied J. B. Duke to Raleigh for legistlative hearings concerning utility rates. After being up for several days, Few continued, he became seriously ill with double pneumonia for several weeks. It was during his convalescence that he had had time to think through some things, he explained, such as "how to connect Trinity College with the University." The youthful reporter may not have grasped the full import of what Few was recounting, but he ended his story with this observation: "Just an incident in the noble life of a man who has given himself to a great cause."[45]

A couple of months later a *Chronicle* reporter described Few as "the easiest man to interview on campus" and gained another nostalgic gem of a story from the president. It seems that on a warm September day in 1896 a Trinity senior came upon a tall young stranger in Epworth dormitory, put his arm across the young man's shoulders, and proceeded to give him a short pep talk on "the duties of freshmen towards their betters." The next day the senior was big-eyed when he found the "freshman" lecturing to him, for young Few had just been named as a visiting professor of English at Trinity.[46]

As the new dormitory neared completion in the spring of 1939, filling in the last space on the south side of the main quadrangle, student letters and *Chronicle* editorials suggested that it should be named for Few.[47] When the trustees soon did just that, a *Chronicle* editorial declared that honoring Few was not a difficult task, for "he honors himself by his quiet manner and the unassuming way in which he directs our school." Noting that "nothing about the man is brusque," the editorial hailed Few as a "real leader in this current world-collection of tyrant dictators." Few's leadership was said to consist of "the easy-working methods of persuasion, thoughtful consideration of problems, and tactful reconciliation of opposing factors [factions?] that invariably arise in a college community." Few Quadrangle, the *Chronicle* concluded, would be a lasting memorial, "one that will stand on our campus even as the man now stands—quietly, powerfully, and beautiful."[48]

Few, whom one student described as the "best-loved man on campus," would have been less than human if such tributes from undergraduates did not warm his heart in his last years. He never grew publicly sentimental, however, but quietly went on about his life's work. In January, 1940, when the new Indoor Stadium, made possible largely by income from football, was formally opened with a Duke-Princeton basketball game, Few spoke briefly. Having what was described as one of the three largest suspension roofs in the country at that time, the stadium was said to be the largest indoor one in the South. In his remarks Few somewhat laconically noted the rising interest in basketball and speculated that it might someday pay its own way as Duke football already did. In fact, the budget-conscious president informed the crowd (which probably was not keenly interested in that aspect) that as far as he could see, the Duke Forest and the Division of Athletics and Physical Education were the only units of the university that could ever be financially self-sustaining.[49] Little could he know what a future lay ahead for Duke basketball and where athletic revenues would derive in the late twentieth century.

After a prominent northern trustee of the Duke Endowment visited a group of the leading preparatory schools in the Mid-Atlantic and New England states, he wrote Few suggesting that the university should arrange to bring a group of headmasters to the campus, at Duke's expense, and cultivate better relations with such schools. Few replied, somewhat apologetically, that he had been absent from his office with a cold and trying to work on a history of the organization of the university (a project he never finished). He promised to give attention to the suggestion about the headmasters and then added: "So far, what of time and effort I have had left over from the task of building and organizing the University I have felt I ought to give largely to the Southern states." When Duke came on the scene, Few explained, "the South did not have a climate of mind well adapted to sustain a great endowed university." He had felt a primary obligation, he stated, to attend as best he could to that, but now he would turn to those headmasters.[50]

Officials at Duke arranged such a gathering of headmasters for the fall of 1940, and on October 7, Few was dictating what his secretary noted was the "Last thing dictated by Dr. Few." Appropriately enough, the memorandum had to do with the teaching of freshmen, for Few was to lead a discussion in which Duke faculty members and the headmasters would focus on such questions as how teaching in the first year of college courses could be better adapted to the needs of students from strong preparatory schools.[51]

Feeling unwell, Few dropped his work and went home from the office; a day or so later he was admitted to Duke Hospital. There his serious heart problems were diagnosed and treated, but he died of a coronary thrombosis on October 16, 1940. He would have been seventy-three on December 29.

Since Few had become ill suddenly and died only a little more than a week later, his death came as a great and sad shock to many. At Trinity-Duke for forty-four years and president of the institution for thirty, he had come to seem something of a fixed landmark. The recipient of nine honorary degrees, Few never received one from Harvard. Once, when a politically prominent alumnus asked Few why Duke had not made him a trustee or given him more recognition, Few responded that it often happened that those things could not be worked out in wholly satisfactory ways. It was one of the limitations of democratic institutions, he explained, that many people had a voice in decisions. "For example, I have sometimes wondered why, in the light of what I have been able to do for education in the South, my alma mater, Harvard University, seems to be wholly ignorant of it," Few declared. "But this is of no serious concern to me, and I have never mentioned it before and probably never will again."[52]

Nevertheless, Few was elaborately memorialized by many individuals and groups. His fellow presidents in the Southern University Conference, meeting soon after Few's death, emphasized certain personal traits:

> President Few was a man of sound judgment and moderation, who could maintain an unruffled temper in the midst of excitement; he was gentle, unassuming and modest in manner, winning the love and esteem of his fellows; he was quietly genial in social relations, respected by all men; he had without pretense or any ostentation a deep spiritual insight and an appreciation of values. Tolerant of dissenting opinion, he was firm in his loyalty to the principles and ideal of excellence in education.[53]

A faculty committee at Duke, chaired by Malcolm McDermott of the law school, emphasized Few's role in the transformation of a small college into a respected research university. "While the University is dedicated to the memory of the family whose munificence made it possible," the committee declared, "in another sense must it stand as a monument to that man whose true greatness was instrumental in its being brought forth at this place."[54]

The *Chronicle*'s extra edition reporting Few's death noted in an editorial that students had appreciated his courteousness, his informal strolls around the campus, and his readiness to stop for a brief chat with anyone who had the time. "His utter lack of affectation was, as another has put it, 'Lincolnesque,'" the *Chronicle* declared.[55] A student columnist shortly afterward confessed that it was difficult for "the obscure undergraduate to rationalize his emotions concerning this bereavement of ours." Standing apart from the general grief and yet still a part of it, the undergraduates, the columnist wrote, were filled with a feeling of "vague helplessness, anxious for some medium of sincere expression." They could sense, he said, the end of an era, the demarcation of the transition from Trinity to Duke.[56]

To a friend on the faculty, Mrs. Few confessed her sense of loss and shock but added, in a short but wholly understandable phrase, that she felt "no sense of incompleteness in his life," for he "literally gave his life to Duke University."[57] Indeed, Few himself had often said that those who could spend their lives working hard for something in which they deeply believed were the most fortunate people of all. He was describing himself, of course, and in that sense he was indeed a profoundly happy, fulfilled man.

At a service soon after the first anniversary of Few's death, the president of the undergraduate men's student government, Lawrence E. Blanchard, Jr., noted that those students who had known Few appreciated his quiet friendliness and his tolerance of undergraduate foibles and idiosyncrasies. Others, Blanchard continued, attributed greatness to Few because he "effected the transition of a small college into a university with dignity and restraint" and because he fought "blind prejudice and haughty cynicism to make Duke University respected." The students, however, according to Blanchard, believed that Few's greatness lay in more than his accomplishments. "He was preeminent for what he was. His achievements were but the natural consequence of his character." Admiring that character, the students, Blanchard concluded, looked up to Few as a "symbol of humility, dignity, intellectual honesty and love of mankind." He was, in short, "a symbol that will never die."[58]

To place Few and his achievement in a larger and slightly different context, W. T. Laprade, an historian who knew and understood well whereof he spoke, suggested quite properly that Duke University was not entirely Few's handiwork. Laprade emphasized that Few had "an unusual sense of history and a keen and oft-repeated appreciation of the fact that a well-established institution does more to give permanence and significance to the careers of individuals associated with it than even the most influential of these individuals contributes to the shaping of the institution." Laprade then noted that had Craven, Crowell, and Kilgo "not done well their tasks and won the substance of the things for which they fought, there would have been no opportunity for Dr. Few."

After touching on various of Few's strategies in first strengthening Trinity College and then leading in the organization of the university, Laprade concluded by noting that it "happens to a man seldom to compass in a generation all that he plans." Few had aspired to administer well a small college but found himself "suddenly charged with the leading part in founding a university." Only time could fully test the mettle of his achievement, for like Craven, Crowell and Kilgo, Few had helped to lay foundations for other men and women to build upon.[59]

In the words of the show-business world, Few's act was a hard one to follow. That Robert L. Flowers, the vice president for business and secretary-treasurer of the university, should have promptly been named acting president by the trustees' executive committee was entirely appropriate and widely applauded in all quarters. At Trinity-Duke since 1891, Flowers not only had five years' seniority on Few but was probably a more widely admired and even loved man, especially by older alumni and the public at large. A handsome, always immaculately dressed man, Flowers had an affable, courtly, but gentle manner that made him more immediately accessible than Few. His devotion to Duke as well as to Methodism and its causes matched that of Few. He well deserved the honor and recognition that the acting presidency was meant to confer on him.

When the trustees subsequently elected him to the presidency of the university on January 29, 1941, however, they made a profound mistake that would ultimately be seriously detrimental to the institution and no favor to Flowers himself. The fact that Flowers was seventy years old when he became the president was not, by itself, so important, for there are persons who remain alert and vigorous well beyond that age. Flowers was not vigorous, however, and had long been hampered by some health problems; because of bronchial trouble, he had fled to Florida during late winter in numerous years. Moreover, he was not a scholar and, to his credit, never pretended to be. The "Dr." by which he was always known derived from an honorary degree. That, in itself, was also not a fatal flaw, but Flowers, for all his amiability, was probably not completely at ease in the company of serious scholars and perhaps did not truly grasp certain fundamental truths about research universities, their diverse functions, and their faculties.

Harvie Branscomb, an outstanding professor in and then dean of Duke's School of Religion, was possibly unfair when he much later recalled that Flowers was the "opposite in type and personality" of Few. Flowers, according to Branscomb, had as Duke's most important goal the production of "football and baseball teams that would defeat the University of North Carolina."[60] Branscomb also mentioned that Few, who knew Branscomb well and much admired him, had once said something about hoping that Branscomb might become Duke's president. If Few said something like that, as he may well have done, he failed to place Branscomb in any conspicuous administrative post before his (Few's) death in 1940. Branscomb became one of a number of outstanding faculty members who left Duke in the 1940s, and in his case he left to become a highly creative and successful chancellor (president) of Vanderbilt University.

Regardless of the validity or invalidity of Branscomb's evaluation of

Flowers, the 1940s would see Duke largely stand still after the impressive accomplishments of the university's first fifteen years. That was more or less inevitable, of course, during the nation's active involvement in World War II, regardless of who was president. All of the nation's large universities were, in one way or another, deeply involved in the war effort, and institutional advancement took a necessarily low priority. The years immediately after the war, however, brought major challenges, difficulties, and opportunities for universities, and Duke's top administrators at that critical juncture were simply not up to the task. Indeed, there would be a leadership crisis of major proportions. In late 1940, however, all of that lay hidden in the future.

After having named Flowers as acting president on October 18, 1940, the executive committee of the trustees proceeded to act as the de facto search committee for the new president. While Bruton served as chairman, Allen and Perkins probably had the most influence on the committee, on which M. E. Newsom, W. N. Reynolds, and J. H. Separk also served.

The committee made no attempt to ascertain the opinion of faculty members about the presidency. A. S. Pearse, the outspoken zoologist, wrote Bruton soon after Few died and, after mentioning several possible successors, bluntly asked, "What would you think of a joint committee of trustees, alumni, and faculty to consider [the choice of] the next president and make recommendations?" Pearse, who had grown antagonistic toward Few, added that in his thirteen years at Duke, after having taught at several other universities, he had regretfully observed that "the faculty here had less and less chance to express its opinions and help in shaping university policies." He believed that if faculty members were given the chance to express themselves more about such matters they would be more loyal to the institution and serve it better. "Duke University is the worst institution in this respect that I know," Pearse concluded. Bruton replied courteously but in a totally noncommittal manner.[61]

In the weeks prior to the naming of Flowers as the regular president, various newspaper stories carried "leaks" predicting such an outcome. Willis Smith, a prominent lawyer in Raleigh and longtime trustee, was probably typical of the great majority of the trustees in suggesting that Flowers should be elected promptly and "without any limitations." Flowers was more familiar with Duke's affairs than anyone could possibly be in a long time, Smith argued, and, too, the action would be heartily applauded throughout North Carolina.[62] The trustees unanimously took just that action; congratulatory messages to Flowers poured in, the state's newspapers hailed the move, and if there were any faculty members who believed that a mistake had been made, as there undoubtedly were, they kept their opinions to themselves.

Harvie Branscomb in early 1941 sang an entirely different tune about

Flowers's election than he struck several decades later in his autobiography. "A miracle has happened," Branscomb declared in a note to Flowers. He went on to say that in his sixteen years on the Duke faculty, it was the first time he had seen the faculty as united as it was about "the wisdom of the trustees" in electing Flowers to the presidency.[63] If the faculty was not as joyfully united as Branscomb stated, there is no question that the older alumni were genuinely pleased. One of them wrote Flowers that he had been pleasantly surprised upon hearing the news, for he had feared that "they would give it [the presidency] to a jitterbug type of man since everything is so streamlined now-a-days."[64] Another veteran alumnus compared the transition from Few to Flowers with the naming of Few as Trinity's president in 1910. He recalled that when chairman Southgate announced Few's election, he did so in this fashion: "Trinity has had a hard struggle. The road has been rough and the hills steep. Harness became worn, and at times the team badly fagged. I am happy to say today we are over the hill and into an improved Highway. Horses fat and fresh. Harness new and the buckles shining. Nothing to do but say to Jack [Kilgo] give Bill [Few] the lines. He will drive from now on."[65]

That Flowers would only nominally hold the lines and drive quite differently from Few was shown clearly and early in the matter of William H. Ackland's bequest of an endowed art museum to Duke University. It is discussed fully in chapter 9, but the manner in which Flowers in 1941 completely accepted W. R. Perkins's interpretation of the case and happily agreed to Duke's rejection of the bequest should be noted. Furthermore, Flowers, again following Perkins's lead, more or less ignored the university trustees' resolution calling for a statement to the public explaining Duke's action. The result was that the public, not to mention most of the trustees and the faculty, remained largely uninformed about the Ackland bequest and why it ultimately went to the University of North Carolina rather than to the donor's first choice.

There were, of course, larger, more global matters to worry about in 1941 than complicated bequests. Although the United States was not in the war when Flowers became president, it loomed larger and larger even on campus as the draft began to take its toll among male students, and some faculty and staff members began to take indefinite leaves of absence to serve the federal government or in the armed services during the emergency.

In May, 1941, Duke learned that the Department of the Navy had selected it for one of the coveted new units of the Naval Reserve Officers Training Corps. Beginning that September, therefore, there was a military presence on campus for the first time since World War I. As mentioned earlier, however, college life went on pretty much as usual in the fall of

1941. The Duke football team was again headed for the Rose Bowl, albeit in a venue that had to be changed after Pearl Harbor.

The nation's actual entry into the war accelerated changes on campus that had long been underway. Wannamaker and Brower represented Duke at a meeting in Baltimore that had been called by federal officials. There the colleges and universities agreed to implement an accelerated, three-year degree program; to give limited academic credit for certain types of military training; and to place more emphasis on physical education.[66] Many male students in the junior and senior classes began signing up for the Navy's V-7 program, which allowed them to remain in college before attending midshipmen's school and gaining commissions as ensigns. With a full year of mathematics required for that as well as other military programs, Duke's introductory classes in mathematics were soon swamped.

"Holiday Trips Home Turn Out [to be] Real Odysseys," a *Chronicle* headline read in early 1942. The wartime travel crunch had begun with a vengeance, and badly crowded trains and buses became a routine part of students' lives, especially as strict gasoline rationing forced drastic limitations on the use of automobiles. With fraternities and sororities sharply curtailing social expenses, Dean Greene announced in a special assembly that students with C averages or better would be allowed to take six courses; that spring vacation would be dropped and the examination period shortened; and that commencement would be held earlier and limited to one day. Freshmen would be admitted in June and September.

Duke's first air-raid drill came in early February, 1942, and for ten minutes classroom bells and steam whistles sounded as students and staff scrambled to get to preassigned locations. The new Wartime Social Activities Board, with student representatives from both campuses, staged a "patriotic dance" and refunded half of the admission price in the form of a twenty-five-cent United States saving stamp.

The *Chronicle*, undaunted by it all, issued two "nasty Valentines": first to Japan for "having precipitated an unpleasantness which has rationed our sugar, untreaded our tires, aroused our draft boards to vigorous activity and generally messed up our plans for the future." The Duke faculty got one also for "bending over backwards to avoid 'war hysteria' [and] for trying so hard not to lower their academic standards because of pity for war-bewildered students that they ended up by cutting a bloody swath through the undergraduate ranks during the recent exam period."[67]

Women students, pointing to the scarcity of silk, pled for an end of the requirement that they wear stockings (and hats) when in downtown Durham, at least during the daylight hours. The students' own social standards committee at first rejected the proposal, but wartime shortages soon brought greater freedom in matters of dress to the women. Even Dean Baldwin had to concede that leg makeup for young women had a place in the wartime scheme of things.

Sugar and meat shortages hit home even on campus. One of the first blows that hurt Duke students came when the Dope Shops on both campuses ran out of Coca-Cola syrup and could obtain no more until new ration coupons could be used. A *Chronicle* editorial saw a bright side to all the rationing, however. "The dating premium that always went along with the possession of an automobile seems about to be abolished," an apparently car-less journalist gloated. With both gasoline and tires strictly rationed, the dater without an automobile now found himself on a level with the formerly privileged. In this war, the editorial concluded, the United States was "striving for democracy—in dating, as in everything else."[68]

With the traditional May Day pageant on East falling victim to the war's exigencies, student governments on both campuses planned an extensive program for War Day on May 15, 1942. It was to honor the new NROTC unit, those students who had recently entered military service, and members of the various military reserves. "The day will likewise serve to express and to renew the devotion of the University to the cause for which we are fighting," the students announced. The day would begin with buglers sounding reveille, followed by drum rolls and flourishes, in the central quadrangles on both campuses. Classes were to be dismissed at 11:00 A.M. for a special service in the chapel. In the afternoon a Southern Conference track meet and a baseball game with the University of North Carolina would take place before a formal review of the NROTC unit at 4:30. For that there would be patriotic carillon music as well as military music furnished by two bands. A lawn supper for the Duke community (at thirty-five cents a person) followed by a "Buck Private Dance" in the Woman's College gymnasium would conclude the day's events.[69]

When the draft began to reach down to eighteen-year-old males, Duke, like many other educational institutions, faced an uncertain future as the 1942–43 academic year began. An increased enrollment in the Woman's College helped Duke partially to offset the loss of male students. Flowers, with obvious relief, reported in late September, 1942, that the total enrollment appeared to be down only about 4 percent rather than the 10 to 15 percent that had been feared. (In 1940–41 the enrollment was 3,716 and it dropped only to 3,493 for the fall semester of 1941.) Hospitalized with bronchial problems in the late winter of 1942 and again that fall, Flowers could not help but worry about the uncertain enrollment picture and its possible impact on the university's budget.

The Army's request to house on the Duke campus a Finance School for officers and officer-candidates came as welcome news in the summer of 1942. By adding cots and double-decker beds to the rooms in Crowell Quadrangle on West, Duke became the host to over 500 men enrolled in the school, and the number was subsequently increased substantially. Awakened at 5:30 for physical training between 6:00 and 6:30, the soldiers marched to meals in the Union and to classes in the law building and in the president's house. (President and Mrs. Flowers had remained in the university-owned house which they had occupied since the early 1930s.) With classes from 7:30 A.M. to 4:30 P.M. and then two hours of afternoon drill and more exercise, the finance officers and officer-candidates also attended classes after dinner until 9:00 P.M. Civilian students probably were awed by such rigor, which was a far cry from the carefree, leisurely campus scene of the 1930s.

With the handwriting on the wall so inescapably clear, the male undergraduates began to encounter a variety of new experiences. Eddie Cameron, the acting athletic director, converted the freshman football field into what the *Chronicle* called "a breath-taking and muscle-loosening four hundred yard commando course." Built of peeled logs, iron pipes, and stout boards, the course featured fences of varying heights, walls to scale, ditches to leap, a low-ceilinged frame to induce stooped running, a forty-five degree embankment, and other labor-requiring (and pain-causing) devices. While regular classes involving the course were included in the physical education required of freshmen and sophomores, the commando course was optional for juniors and seniors.[70]

Not to be outdone by landlubbers, Jack Persons, the swimming coach, launched a new program to train men to face emergencies that they might encounter in the armed services. This involved swimming forty minutes in deep water; swimming in water made choppy by an ingenious home-made "wave machine"; and swimming thirty or forty feet under water as well as at least 800 yards on the surface. He also taught students how to swim silently by using a slow breast stroke, how to use overturned boats and wreckage to stay afloat, and how to swim in heavy clothing.[71]

To launch the campus-wide campaign for the Student War Chest, Dean Manchester spoke to the solicitors for the twelve relief agencies included in the campaign, and drives for the collection of scrap metal, rubber goods, and other essentials kept volunteers busy on both campuses. Assisted by officers from the Army Finance School and the NROTC unit, a group of undergraduate men organized on a voluntary basis the Student Reserve Training Corps. Those participating were expected to attend two hours of drill and three hours of lectures each week, with a demerit system to ensure regular participation. Unfortunately, even in the atmosphere of wartime urgency, such a voluntary program did not work, and the Student Reserve Training Corps disappeared almost as quickly as it had materialized.

The times were not easy for the many students who were still civilians. Stung by a faculty member's charge that students were too concerned with the trivialities of college life as usual when so much of the world was in flames, a *Chronicle* editorialist conceded that student-government politics, football games, and dances were indeed trivial as compared with the battle of the Pacific, the siege of Leningrad, and the question of the second front in Europe. The editorial went on to note, however, that "the university has fallen far short of dedicating itself to an all-out war program" and that, with the exception of quartering the Finance School, "life here at the university goes on very much the same as before." Numerous exchange papers showed that "trivialities" still prevailed on campuses throughout the nation, the *Chronicle* argued, and to change the situation would require the combined efforts of all concerned.[72]

A subsequent editorial addressed the "peculiar position" of the college man in the war-focused nation. He was almost certain to enter active military service within the space of three months to a year unless classified as 4-F, that is, physically unfit. Yet in the eyes of almost everyone, the college student was still a "draft dodger" and one who was "contributing absolutely nothing to the war effort." In polite circles, the editorial continued, he was called "cagey" in exploiting opportunities to stay out of the draft. Many men in college would rather be in the armed services, the writer argued, but partly because of the desire for as much college preparation as possible—for there would be a postwar world—and partly because of family pressure, they remained in college for as long as the armed services allowed.[73]

The spiritual and mental anguish of those students who were intelligent and sensitive enough to be aware of their dilemma was quite real. Stories about Duke alumni killed in combat had begun to appear in the *Chronicle*, and a memorial service for ten of them was held in the chapel on December 8, 1942. Perhaps that is why the *Chronicle* and various student leaders on West lashed out at the father figure closest at hand, the university and "the administration." Duke was clinging to the status quo and not responding imaginatively to the challenge of total war, the *Chronicle* charged. The old course requirements should be immediately scrapped and, among other changes, a "rigorous four-year program of physical training" should be required of all students. "The bitter truth should be told," the *Chronicle* declared. "Duke University is failing the first great test of its existence; it is standing still at a time when it should be moving ahead; it is missing an opportunity for educational leadership that may never come again."[74] The men's student senate, in obvious agreement with the newspaper's sentiments, passed a resolution in favor of a four-year, compulsory physical education program by a vote of thirty-three to one. The faculty and administration, however, resisted the demand for such sweeping, immediate changes on the grounds, which normally students would have been the first to recognize, that to admit students with one set of requirements and regulations and then to change them abruptly and drastically would be a breach of contract. There were also massive problems about staffing that the students had not considered.

Duke's total enrollment in the fall of 1942 was 3,401, only 157 less than in the previous year. Big increases in engineering, nursing, and the Woman's College helped compensate for the 10 percent drop in the enrollment of Trinity College. But just as the draft began to make alarming inroads into the male student body—90 freshmen called up in January, 1943, and two groups of 100 each in the following month—the United States Navy came to the rescue.

Late in 1942, the other shoe had dropped—both for students caught in agonizing uncertainty and for many of the nation's colleges and universities. The United States Army and Navy announced that they would contract with a large number of colleges and universities to furnish instruction in curricula prescribed by the armed forces to men selected by the services. All reservists were to be called to active duty, but their education would continue, for varying lengths of time, while they were on active duty and in uniform. In the naval program, for example, men were to be allowed to remain in college for a certain number of semesters depending on how many semesters they had completed as of July 1, 1943. For example, a student who had completed two semesters as of that date would be allowed four additional, accelerated semesters before being sent to midshipmen's school.

Flowers reported to George Allen in early February, 1943, that naval officers had been on campus inspecting the facilities. His preliminary information was that the Navy wanted Duke to take about 1,600 reservists— about 300 engineers, 300 pre-medical, and 1,000 additional students. The Navy would pay room rent, board and tuition. "They do not expect to run the place," Flowers noted. "They simply wish to contract with us for certain facilities and for instruction." The West campus would be crowded, Flowers added, for the Navy wished three or four men put in double rooms and two in single rooms.[75]

To the relief of many at Duke, both faculty and students, the Navy soon made it clear that while students in the V-12 college training program would have to maintain the Navy's standard of discipline, military activities were to be kept to a minimum and to be subordinated to academic training. The V-12 students would be free to join whatever student organizations they wished and to participate in extracurricular activities as long as nothing interfered with the performance of assigned duties.

During a forty-five-minute blackout of Durham and Duke in March, 1942, observers in the chapel tower heard many raucous noises in the freshman quadrangle. Cries of "Who won the Civil War?" and "Ah'm from the Sunny South" reverberated across campus. But the days of such civilian rowdiness on West were numbered, for the fleet sailed in, en masse, on July 1, 1943.

With more than 1,600 naval trainees scrambling around the campus in their white sailor suits, a substantial portion of them formerly civilian students at Duke, Duke had one of the largest V-12 programs in the nation. While West campus shifted to an accelerated "Navy calendar," the Woman's College remained on the traditional schedule, with the fall semester beginning in mid-September. Given the inevitable turnover in the naval contingent, relations between the two campuses were probably not as close as they had been earlier. Yet when the women held open houses for the freshmen, approximately 500 Navy, Marine, and civilian men swarmed over to East. The men's student government sponsored a Fall Prom with music provided by the Duke Ambassadors, and the women were in formal dresses and many men in uniform.

Making an early evaluation of the attempt at college-and-military co-operation at Duke, the *Chronicle* judged it a success, certainly superior to the similar Army Specialized Training Program because of the Navy's more liberal approach. There were problems, however. The *Chronicle*, still put out largely by civilian men and women, noted that Duke had a hard time meeting the recreational needs of such a large number of naval trainees, especially when there were no Navy bands to play for dances or funds from the United Service Organization to help pay for them. "Dances don't just happen, yearbooks, magazines, and [news] papers don't publish themselves, and the Y.M.C.A. and similar organizations aren't run by steam," a columnist in the *Chronicle* observed.[76] Such complaining gradually sub-sided as the V-12 students began to play on Eddie Cameron's generally successful football teams and to take part in other activities. But with 395 new V-12 students (along with 100 civilian freshmen) entering as a new semester began on West around November 1, 1942, and approximately 400 having received "shipping orders" at the end of the previous semester, the rapid pace of change and turnover was all too obvious.

If students, both military and civilian, faced some new stresses and strains on the wartime campus, the same was true for the faculty. Teaching around the clock throughout the year represented a sharp departure from the normal academic routine, and the shortage of teachers and graduate assistants in many fields only added to the problem. In the natural sciences and mathematics there were fewer female graduate students than in the humanities and social sciences, and male graduate students virtually disappeared during the war. Consequently, teaching and laboratory assistants were in short supply, and teaching loads for regular faculty members frequently ranged from fifteen to twenty hours a week. "Continuous teaching the year round is not good for mind or matter," Wannamaker noted. "All of us will welcome the return to 'fore de War.'" [77]

While the faculty stretched itself as part of the war effort, an important group of faculty leaders also came to believe that the faculty should become better organized in order to gain at least a voice in university governance. While the Duke faculty, like Trinity's earlier, had long had virtually complete control of purely academic, curricular matters, it had no say at all concerning important policy decisions that very much affected the faculty but that historically, at least in the United States, had belonged to top administrators and boards of trustees. At some of the nation's stronger colleges and universities, faculty members were beginning to push for a modification in the old, traditional pattern of institutional decision-making, and Duke was no exception.

In the absence of anything resembling a true faculty senate or council, the local chapter of the American Association of University Professors functioned at Duke as the meeting place and forum for those faculty members who were not satisfied with the status quo in the university's governance. While some among the faculty and administrative staff privately referred to the leading spirits of the AAUP chapter as "radicals," they actually were not radical in any meaningful sense of the word. They simply wanted more democracy in university government.

Early in 1943, Newman I. White, a distinguished and veteran member of the English department, reported to President Flowers that the committee which he (no doubt reluctantly) had authorized to draw up a plan for a faculty senate had met several times and hoped soon to have a report. A preliminary report soon followed, and White requested that Flowers and his advisors consider it and make suggestions while various senior members of the faculty were being asked to do the same thing. [78]

It was as if the report had been dropped in a bottomless black hole, for months passed with no response from Flowers. How President Few would have responded to such a request from the faculty can only be conjectured, for none such was ever made to him. He had admired and respected Newman White, however, as well as Harvie Branscomb and other faculty members involved, and Few may well have realized that gradual, orderly change in university governance was a sensible alternative to standing pat and stoutly affirming the status quo.

Flowers, however, instinctively shied off from any such proposal as a faculty senate. Moreover, there was no one in his administrative group who might have advised him to do otherwise. Wannamaker, who turned seventy in 1943, had been an administrative officer for thirty or so years and a powerful dean for almost as long; he had no sympathy with the idea of a faculty senate. Walter Greene, a professor of English, had been an important academic voice in the administration as dean of undergraduate instruction, but he resigned in 1942 to become the president of Wofford College. Herbert Herring was then made dean of Trinity College, although his career had been largely administrative and he was only nominally a member of the faculty. Flowers's closest advisors were Charles Jordan and Alfred Brower, neither of whom had ever held a faculty appointment. After Flowers was named president, Jordan had succeeded him as secretary of the university, and Charles B. Markham, long the assistant treasurer, assumed Flowers's old job as treasurer of the university. Then when Henry Dwire died in 1944, Jordan was named to succeed him as vice president for public relations, and Charles A. Dukes took over Dwire's job as director of alumni affairs. Brower, who had come to Duke as executive secretary for the centennial, served as an administrative assistant after that and was named business manager and comptroller in 1946. In short, there were numerous persons of ability and dedication in the administration, but none of them had close or meaningful connections with the faculty.

The *Chronicle*, in a rare foray into such matters, editorialized in 1942 about "Our Ostracized Faculty" and suggested that it was unfortunate for Duke that its able faculty held "a position of such trivial importance in the life of the university outside the classroom." University policies were "completely dominated by a small, tight group of deans and executives known to the students as 'the administration,'" the *Chronicle* charged. The newspaper conceded that for the most part those in the administration were capable, sincere, and genuinely interested in Duke and its students, but that was no justification for the exclusion of the faculty from a voice in general policy-making. Duke was, the editorial concluded, leaving "untapped a tremendous reservoir of energy and talent," and by bringing the faculty out of its "academic isolation" the university's leaders could give it an "invaluable impetus along its road to greatness."[79]

Clearly, the faculty had potential allies among at least some of the students, but Flowers and his advisors obviously paid little attention to the *Chronicle*'s opinion in the matter. When ten months had passed without Newman White's having received a response to the report about a faculty senate that he had submitted, he wrote to Flowers asking about the matter. This elicited the explanation from the president that he had consulted several persons connected with Duke and "almost invariably the opinion was expressed that while everything was in somewhat of a chaotic [wartime] state it would be best to wait until the absent members of the faculty return." Also, Flowers added, because of travel restrictions and gasoline rationing, to get a full meeting of the board of trustees was proving quite difficult.[80]

Flowers obviously hoped that the matter of the faculty senate would fade and be forgotten, but such was not the case. Soon after the war, when the distinct minority of the faculty who had been on leave had returned (or, in some cases, resigned), the AAUP chapter took the lead in calling for a special meeting of the faculty. At that meeting in May, 1946, the faculty, by a large majority, endorsed a plan for a university senate and requested Flowers to transmit it to the trustees. In doing so, Flowers explained first that he did "not request that you reject the idea totally" and that the proposal seemed generally "harmless." The plan might have "some advantages in that the [proposed] body is small enough not to be un-wieldy." Opponents of the plan had made several valid criticisms, Flowers noted, and with correction of certain defects and a different name, "I could get the consent of my mind to recommend its approval at your hands." He suggested that the trustees should appoint a committee to study the matter.[81]

The proposal for the faculty senate soon got lost, at least temporarily, in the slow-motion shell game that committees sometimes play, but the called faculty meeting in May, 1946, produced another resolution that had a more immediate impact. "Within the next few years," the faculty boldly but truthfully resolved, "it will probably be necessary to choose several senior administrative officials for Duke University." The selection of proper persons for those important jobs, the resolution continued, was "delicate, tedious, and difficult," and with respect to those officers who would deal with academic matters the faculty "has a special interest and is, we believe, specially qualified to advise the trustees on certain aspects of the problem." The faculty, therefore, requested the trustees to autho-rize the faculty to select, by secret ballot, a faculty committee of not less than three nor more than five members to assist and advise the trustees in any search to fill the positions of the president, vice president in the educational division, and dean of the university.

In transmitting this resolution to the trustees, Flowers and his advisors added their own interpretation and reaction. "I do not know what you think of this," Flowers began. "My concern is not personal in that a good many of my trusted friends think it is a thinly veiled or disguised thrust at me and at one of my colleagues [Wannamaker]." Flowers went on to say that he was bothered by the fact that the resolution had been circulated in mimeographed form to all members of the faculty; that it would "give rise to speculation and various interpretations"; and that it "could only result in misunderstanding of and hurt to the Institution." He was not, in short, against the resolution per se but objected to the timing and method. The trustees had enough "sense of the eternal fitness of things," he declared, to know that when academic officers were to be chosen "it is right and proper that faculty advice and counsel should not only be received but that it should in fact be sought." In conclusion, Flowers recommended that the trustees not reject "this resolution in its entirety." Rather, they should seek an appointed (not elected) faculty committee. This was his explanation: "Events which have already transpired lead me to the belief that the proposed committee to be selected by secret ballot might well be a preconceived group which conceivably in its own mind might have already reached its conclusions and prepared its report." The trustees, therefore, should authorize a faculty committee, "to be appointed by whomsoever you might designate," to meet with a committee of the trustees to consider the whole matter and report back to the full board.[82]

In saying that all agreed that faculty opinion should always be sought when academic officers were to be named, Flowers was less than candid. As mentioned in the chapter on the Woman's College, Alice Baldwin informed Flowers in October, 1945, that as she approached her sixty-seventh birthday she thought the time had come for her to retire. She urged that a small committee that included at least two alumnae and at least one woman faculty member should be named to assist and advise the trustees in selecting her successor. In response to this suggestion, Wannamaker advised Flowers that he doubted the wisdom of naming such a committee of alumnae and faculty members, for it would probably be regarded as a precedent. "Certainly we should not wish to appear as if we were recommending to the Board such a practice in the naming of University officers," the veteran dean observed. "The Board, after all, will look to the President for recommendations of University officers."[83] When Baldwin finally succeeded, more than a year later, in prodding Flowers to act in the matter of finding her successor, the president ignored her suggestion about the committee of alumnae and faculty to assist in the matter and proceeded with the help of his own administrative advisors to select Roberta Brinkley as Baldwin's successor and to recommend her to the board of trustees.

All of these somewhat arcane goings on—small tempests in an academic teapot—were hidden from the public, of course, and the students as well as many faculty members probably knew little about them. They had to do, however, with how decisions were made and power shared, or not shared, in one of the nation's important institutions, a research university. Regardless of what might be transpiring among the leaders and top officials, routines usually continue in a university, with classes meeting, examinations being given and graded, and the myriad variety of extracurricular activities proceeding apace. All of those things were much affected by the war, certainly, yet to a surprising degree the Navy's partial takeover from mid-1943 until the contract ended in February, 1946, did little to alter the university and its operations in any fundamental way.

Veterans began to appear on campus even before the war ended in

Europe in May, 1945. The biggest wave of them, however, came in 1946, when Trinity College enrolled 2,527 undergraduate men in the fall. First priority went to former Duke students who had left to enter the armed forces, second priority to other veterans, and the lowest priority to recent high school graduates. The Woman's College had 1,000 students, and total enrollment was 5,121, an all-time high. Although admissions had to be kept within the limits of instructional and service facilities, the dormitories on both campuses were jammed, and temporary housing for married veterans became a new, postwar problem. The great majority of upperclassmen were veterans, and 60 percent of the 430 new freshmen in Trinity College were former servicemen.

The veterans generally proved to be serious, hardworking students. The idea of student evaluation of teachers, an idea that had earlier been discussed in the *Chronicle*, resurfaced after the war, and several professors wrote letters to the editor endorsing the proposal. One unidentified faculty member applauded the idea because he thought that not enough was made of good teaching at Duke. "One of the fine things about most of the veterans is that they really want to learn," this teacher noted. "They manage to get across to the instructor the idea that he mustn't let them down." Then the writer made another excellent point in a succinct manner: "Teaching is a fine art, but it is a cooperative art—a communal art. The teacher should inspire his pupils. Yes. But we don't often think of the corollary: the pupils should inspire the teachers, or, if they fall short of inspiration, they should at least have read the lessons and blown their noses."[84]

A subsequent attempt to poll a cross-section of the student body about teaching proved to be disappointing when 500 questionnaires were mailed out and only 125 were returned. Of the students responding, a bit more than half of them thought that their teachers presented material clearly. While 60 percent of the faculty members got credit for teaching interesting courses and 85 percent for having a thorough knowledge of the subject, students found that in only 38 percent of their courses were they "required to do any thinking."[85]

Faculty members at Duke in the immediate postwar years, however, had more serious things to worry about than student evaluation of teaching. Faculty salaries, still generally kept at the prewar level, were increasingly inadequate because of wartime and postwar inflation. The situation was by no means unique to Duke, but that fact was slender consolation to those who were hard-pressed to pay current bills. Some faculty members followed a course that they seldom chose in that era and wrote directly to either Flowers or Wannamaker. For example, Jay B. Hubbell, a nationally respected member of the English department and pioneer leader in the field of American literature, wrote Flowers that the increased cost of living compelled him to request a raise. His salary, he explained, was $5,200; he had been at Duke nineteen years and, despite outstanding service and the many achievements which he outlined, had not received a raise in fourteen or fifteen years. He added that he had not looked for another job because he liked Duke and had no intention of leaving.[86] Hubbell's was not an isolated case, and while the great majority of Duke's veteran faculty members felt as Hubbell did about the institution, certain outstanding faculty members did leave for better opportunities elsewhere in the immediate postwar years.

Not only were those on the faculty suffering, but Duke's attempts to recruit new faculty, especially above the beginning level, frequently failed because of the low salaries offered. A person at Oberlin whom Duke wished to hire as an associate professor in romance languages instead accepted an offer from Syracuse University. "I was unable to accept a post at Duke," he explained, "because the cost of living has risen so high that $4,500 is now worth less than $2,700 pre-war dollars." He would have liked being at Duke, he added, but simply could not "bring up a family and continue my education and writing at that figure."[87]

In 1946 Duke furnished certain data on faculty salaries and tuition charges to a distinguished economist at Harvard who, after getting similar data from eighty-seven other colleges and universities, produced a report titled "What Has Happened to Professors' Salaries since 1940." After noting that the average employee in the United States in 1946 would receive about 60 percent more pay than in 1940, he had found that in only three institutions (out of eighty-eight) had minimum salaries for full professors risen as much as 60 percent; in two thirds of the schools the increase in the minimum was 25 percent or less. Furthermore, the change in the minimum salary overstated the increase for full professors because some institutions raised the minimum but not the maximum or gave less than proportionate increases to professors who received more than the minimum. Another distorting factor was that northern and eastern schools were overrepresented in the sample, which meant that southern and western institutions (which were generally those with the lowest salaries) were underrepresented.

In late 1946, the Harvard economist maintained, the cost of living was approximately 50 percent higher than in 1940. Yet in only twelve of the eighty-eight schools had the minimum salary scales for full professors advanced by as much as 40 percent. Income after taxes per family had risen almost 80 percent since 1940, considerably more than the rise in the cost of living. Yet twenty colleges and universities (including Duke) did not raise tuition between 1940 and 1946. Of the seventy schools that did raise tuition, only seven raised it by as much as 40 percent, which was still less than the increase in the cost of living.

The conclusion that the economist drew from these data was not one to cheer the hearts of Duke's standpatters, though the AAUP members had good reason to applaud: "The unsatisfactory record of colleges and universities in meeting the salary problems of professors during recent years indicates the need of basic reform in the handling of college and university finances." In matters of educational policy, he noted, satisfactory arrangements usually existed for communication between administrators and faculty. But conditions were different in the area of finances. "Faculties are not informed or consulted," he declared, "and they are confronted with unilateral decisions on matters of vital concern to them." In all "progressive and well-administered organizations" one had come to expect "two-way communication and carefully organized consultation," but that rarely existed in the handling of college and university budgets.

The remedy the economist proposed was that a special faculty committee should be empowered to review and make suggestions concerning each year's preliminary or tentative budget. The committee should certainly not concern itself with details or with allocations as between departments. It could, however, help prevent an excessive proportion of institutional resources from being put into building programs before the prewar purchasing power of faculty salaries had been restored. "Faculties have been overly patient in watching their salaries lag behind both the cost of living and the rising level of compensation in industry and government," he concluded.[88]

The Harvard economist had an easier task than the Duke faculty. He only had to diagnose the problem and prescribe a possible remedy, but the Duke faculty had to persuade a reluctant president and board of trustees that the faculty had a right both to organize itself into a senate or council and to have a voice in the making of important institutional decisions. Both Flowers and Bruton, the chairman of the board of trustees, were, to put the case mildly, cautious in their approach to change. Their views about race relations illustrated that fact.

World War II brought an increasing militancy to many African Americans and growing conviction on the part of white liberals that American blacks had too long suffered from great injustices. The southern states' legally mandated system of racial segregation and the disfranchisement in those states of most black voters were the nation's most conspicuous monuments to white racism. Protests about those matters were not nearly as frequently heard in the 1930s as they came to be in the 1940s. At Duke some of the students in the School of Religion and certain of their professors were far ahead of others on campus in the racial views they expressed in the late 1930s.

During the war years, however, dissent from the dominant white southern orthodoxy became more common on campus. In the spring of 1941 the

Harvard glee club sang in Duke Chapel, and an African-American member of the group was allegedly not allowed to participate. Upon learning that, a columnist in the *Chronicle* asked, should not a "vauntedly Christian institution be setting a different example?" The incident, he suggested, moved the matter "from the abstract to shameful reality . . . shameful because our motto so brazenly flaunts itself now as obvious camouflage—'Eruditio et religio!'—we have struck our colors, once more, to convention and prejudice!"[89]

Late in 1943 a newspaper in Richmond, Virginia, suggested that an end to the "Jim Crow system" on urban buses might lessen racial tensions, which were increasing across the nation. A *Chronicle* editorial endorsed the idea as "a welcome innovation in a section where a great many blindly deny the existence of such a problem."[90] The following year another student journalist called on Duke to take an active part in tackling the nation's racial problems. He thought that Duke's combination of southern location and cosmopolitan student body and faculty gave it a unique opportunity. "A race problem does exist in America today," he argued, "and the sooner the anti-Semitic and anti-Negro sentiment is wiped out the quicker can America help in building a peaceful and harmonious world."[91]

After the war such ideas became even more common. In a *Chronicle* editor's farewell statement in the spring of 1945, he blasted Duke's "militant conservatism" as shown, he alleged, in refusing to allow a well-known speaker to appear at Duke because he planned to focus on the race issue. Likewise, he charged, an all-black Broadway show had been kept out of Page Auditorium because "it might stir up race tension." When, he asked, would Duke "cease being afraid to come to grips with reality?"[92]

Not by any means did all, or perhaps even most, Duke students look askance at segregation. When a student wrote a letter in 1946 protesting Duke's observance of the state's and the South's prevailing racial practices, the *Chronicle* carried an editorial that incorporated many of the standard conservative arguments of the era: "If it were not for Southern racial segregation laws, a Negro might date your sister, might be your neighbor, or might be your judge in the courts." The writer conceded that blacks should have equal opportunities in jobs, the courts, and in their "own sphere generally." That did not mean, however, that "we [whites] have to share our churches, schools, and places of recreation with the colored people."[93]

President Flowers agreed with the defenders of the racial status quo. He had long been chairman of the board of the North Carolina College for Negroes (later North Carolina Central University), and he had a strong record of interracial activity and paternalistic concern. That did not mean, however, that he had any misgivings about the basic racial arrangements of the South. President Few also had been essentially conservative in racial matters, but the 1930s had not produced the questioning of and challenges to segregation that came in the 1940s.

In 1944 a young Duke alumnus, who had been prominent on campus and who was then serving overseas, wrote a joint letter to Flowers and Bruton. The alumnus had heard that the United States Office of Education had requested that colleges and universities in the South open their doors to blacks. He thought that presented Duke with "an opportunity to demonstrate her unmistakable intention to play a leading part in the life of the South and the nation." If Duke promptly issued a statement opening its doors to all students without regard to race, creed, or color, he argued, the university could "play a unique and dramatic role of leadership in helping to resolve a problem which is otherwise pregnant with hatred and violence for the future."[94]

Flowers, in forwarding the letter to Bruton, enclosed this comment: "Personally, I don't think it needs any answer, but if I should be called on to answer it I am afraid my letter would be a little bit too hot for the mail to carry." Bruton replied that he was glad that he and Flowers agreed about the letter. Bruton added that he was inclined to believe that the writer of the letter was "not all there, and it is idle to pay any attention to the communication."[95]

The grim truth was that Duke faced a profound crisis in leadership after the war ended. Bruton, who died in March, 1946, in his eighty-fourth year, had served the university long and faithfully. He had not needed to play a dynamic role during Few's lifetime, however, and the war and its various impacts on the university had considerably lessened the demands on the trustees during the first half of the 1940s.

The leadership crisis of the late 1940s revolved primarily around Flowers and, to a lesser extent, Wannamaker. There was a very real sadness about the crisis, too, for both men had served the university faithfully and well over a long period, more than a half-century in the case of Flowers and over forty years for Wannamaker. Flowers was more widely admired and loved by the older alumni than anyone else connected with Duke, and Wannamaker, if not loved, was deeply respected by many. The labors of both men for Duke were acknowledged and appreciated. Yet, in the absence of any by-law or regulation requiring administrators to retire at a certain age (which was then sixty-nine for faculty), both men somehow missed their cues for a graceful exit and remained on stage too long. Such a by-law would soon be added for administrators, but, in one sense, it was the old story of a barn door too late locked.

The election of a forceful, dynamic chairman of the board of trustees in 1946 helped Duke gradually to work its way out of a sad, serious situation. Willis Smith was an alumnus of old Trinity and had studied law under Dean Mordecai. Having become a prominent attorney in Raleigh, he was serving as president of the American Bar Association when he was elected chairman of Duke's board of trustees. Though he had long been a trustee, with special interest in the law school, his prestige as a national leader in the legal profession would be important in his service to Duke in the late 1940s, for he was not a person to be easily intimidated or overawed.

Although Smith well knew that in becoming chairman of the board he was accepting a difficult role, he may not have realized either the dimensions or the urgency of the problem. A recent alumnus, who had been an outstanding leader while a student and who had revisited and kept in touch with the campus, promptly informed Smith that he was "now in a position to do more than anyone else to save Duke." The alumnus believed that Few's death had "left Duke leaderless and without vision and purpose" and that the presidency "should be more than a reward for long service." The alumnus had visited the campus early in 1946, soon after his discharge from the Navy, and claimed that he found the esprit de corps of both faculty and students "terrible." He perhaps exaggerated but reported that the "atmosphere of paralysis and the spirit of despair at all levels on the campus is alarming."

The main cause of the problem, he thought, was the "state of affairs" in the administration. When Walter Greene left in 1942, instead of replacing him, "they closed in the ranks, with a result that Dean Wannamaker has had more to do than he could do." Moreover, "old age has complicated his situation so that he should be retired." Alan Manchester, the alumnus noted, was the only dean who was a scholar, and while he was officially only the dean of freshmen, he had been "the guiding spirit as far as students are concerned for many years." Upperclassmen reportedly visited his office "in a ratio of about six to one freshman." The alumnus claimed that he had spoken with Duke alumni around the world during his four years in the Navy and had found many who were "deeply concerned about the state of affairs at the University." They recognized that the faculty was underpaid, that "many have gone, and more are leaving," and that "without good professors, there is no university." Aside from changes in the administration, he urged that Duke should consider adding schools in public administration, music, and possibly international relations. The sciences as well as engineering needed strengthening, he asserted.[96]

In replying to the letter from the concerned alumnus, Smith, with lawyerlike caution, stated that he realized "quite readily the correctness" of some of the alumnus's observations. While Smith explained that he did not wish to be quoted, he believed it might be necessary to "consider very carefully the ideas" that had been suggested. "In fact, several of the Board Members," Smith added, "have already expressed themselves along very similar lines."[97]

Smith displayed both his energy and his style of operation even before he had officially accepted the chairmanship. The need to appoint a new dean of the law school prompted him to write directly to the president of Harvard to ask to what extent he consulted the faculty in law when naming a new dean at Harvard. The Harvard president replied that there were no statutes about the procedure and that traditions varied from school to school. A new dean of Harvard's law school had recently been named, however, and in that case the corporation (which was somewhat comparable to the executive committee of the trustees at Duke) had decided that the president should informally canvass the faculty of the law school. He had done that in three ways: by talking personally with six or so of the twenty-member faculty; by meeting with the faculty as a group and asking them to think over the matter but hold no formal meeting; and by requesting each of them to write him a confidential letter giving suggestions as to whom should be selected as dean. On the basis of his consultations and those letters, which the president said he had shown to no one else, he reported the views of the faculty to the corporation, which was empowered to make the appointment subject to the confirmation of the board of overseers (trustees).

The Harvard president added that it was his experience that formal meetings and balloting were undesirable in such matters. If there was a clear-cut consensus among the faculty about a new dean, the governing board would do well to follow it, he thought. But if there were sharp divergencies (as there often were), then it was best for those who held the ultimate responsibility to make a decision as best they could.[98] Smith promptly saw to it that the procedure used at Harvard was followed at Duke in the search for a law school dean. In subsequent years it became standard practice not only in the naming of deans of the professional schools but also, as departmental chairmanships ceased to be long-term or indefinite in duration, in the naming of departmental chairs.

Smith also found himself quickly involved in a variety of problems and probably to a greater extent than was customary for the chairman of the board. Duke embarked on a fairly extensive building program as soon as the wartime restrictions on new construction were lifted and materials again became available for civilian use. Engineering had been left behind on East campus when most of the departments in the arts and sciences as well as the professional schools moved to West in 1930. Engineering, therefore, had first priority for new space, and construction of a red-brick engineering building of colonial or neoclassical design began in late 1946. It was located northwest of the chapel on what would later be named Science Drive and became the first of several large, serviceable but architecturally unimaginative buildings to be located there.

As welcome as the new building was to the faculty in engineering, some in the Duke community were unhappy by the abandonment of the Tudor Gothic style and the native stone. Alumni in southern California sent word that they were "quite disturbed" by the architecture of both the new engineering building and the proposed new physics building, for the alumni were concerned about maintaining the "physical beauty for which, among other qualities, Duke is renowned." Assigned the task of explaining, Charles Jordan mentioned first that the committee charged with the responsibility of planning the new structure had visited several of the nation's top engineering schools and found that they were built for utility and that "brick structures were by all odds the prevailing type of engineering building." Many walls in such buildings were not plastered, and there were often exposed steel girders overhead in spaces where heavy machinery was housed. Jordan then mentioned that the cost of building such structures in stone would be more than twice as much, and the university only had a limited amount of money for the building, money that came from "a reserve that was built up in those years when the University did not require all of its portion of the endowment earnings for maintenance and operation purposes." (The building cost around $735,000.) Jordan closed by reminding the California alumni that they and all friends of Duke had to reckon with the fact that income from the university's equity in the Duke Endowment was no longer adequate for the maintenance and operation of the university. Thus there was a new, annual Loyalty Fund through which alumni and friends could help the institution in a direct, vital way.[99]

Both Flowers and Willis Smith, as well as certain other trustees, conferred with Walter Nielsen, chairman of the physics department, about the extensive and expensive needs of that department. Its development had been hampered for a while in the 1930s, as explained earlier, and while several important new appointments were made in physics before the war, there was widespread agreement that both a new building, plus various items of expensive equipment and new appointments were important for the department after the war. The Duke Endowment quickly complied with Flowers' request for a special allocation of $900,000 for the new physics building and certain items of equipment to go in it.[100]

In the arts and sciences, Mrs. Mary Duke Biddle's gift of a much-needed addition to the main library was an important development, one that was especially crucial for the university's academic well-being. In the medical area, there was a new medical research building (later named the Bell building); outpatient, diagnostic, and private patients clinics; a hospital laundry; and a hospital service building. All in all, the late 1940s saw extensive construction at Duke. While all of the new buildings were certainly much needed, their construction at a time when faculty salaries had been allowed to slip badly in relation to the cost of living corroborated the Harvard economist's assessment of the prevailing system of governance and priorities in colleges and universities.

The trustees finally did raise Duke's tuition in 1946 from $200 to $300 a year, the first hike since 1930. The small raises that the faculty then received did help morale, but the salary scale was still on the meager side. Wannamaker reported in August, 1947, that he had just prepared the salary budget for the coming academic year and that there were increases for all ranks. The schedules were not fixed, but assistant professors received from $3,500 to $4,000; associate professors from $4,250 to $4,800; and professors from $5,000 to $7,500, with certain especially distinguished professors receiving higher salaries. In law and medicine, of course, the salaries were higher.[101]

Newman White, chairman of English, conceded that the modest, general raises had improved morale and kept down the loss of staff. He had recommended, however, virtually a 50 percent increase for the members of the English department on the grounds that "nothing less could restore the teachers to their pre-war level of living and establish them on an economic parity with most other social and economic groups." Duke had to attain substantially higher salaries in a reasonable time, White argued, if it expected to "lead more than a hand-to-mouth, year-to-year existence as a university."[102]

Another influential faculty member, Paul Gross, who succeeded Calvin Hoover as dean of the graduate school in 1946, had interesting views not only about faculty salaries but also about the interrelated matters of tuition, admissions, and Duke's future as a research university. Some months before World War II ended, Hoover requested various faculty leaders at Duke to comment on the maintenance of scholarly standards in the graduate school. Gross responded by suggesting that Duke had many able scholars and investigators. (He did not say, but certainly could have, that virtually all of them taught undergraduates as well as graduate students.) He continued, however, by noting that the university needed more such able scholars and that "they need more time for their work and better support for their research and scholarly activities than has been available in the past." To hold the scholar-teachers it already had and to attract more in the postwar years, Gross argued, would require a better salary scale than Duke then had. Gross suggested that "we have been entirely too prone to compare our Graduate School standing, salary levels and other pertinent matters with those of neighboring Southern institutions." That comparison was usually favorable for Duke, he noted, but when the comparison was with the leading graduate schools of the East and West,

Duke did not look so good. Gross also mentioned that Duke's stipends for graduate students were too low in comparison with those of the best schools.[103]

A bit later, in 1947, when Willis Smith requested Gross to offer his views on the specific matter of scholarship aid, the veteran faculty member explained that he could do that best by making a broad analysis of the entire situation concerning students and tuition. Smith and the board faced a difficult problem, for the tuition hike in 1946 had not produced a sufficient increase in revenue to go very far in raising faculty salaries. Another increase was being debated, and while the American public in later years would grow more accustomed, if not reconciled, to persistent inflation, that was not the case in 1947. Many Duke trustees recoiled strongly from the idea of a second increase in tuition.

Gross, arguing from a premise that Few would have strongly endorsed, began by asserting that Duke hoped to attain a position of high standing as a national institution yet remain firmly rooted in and integrated with the state and region where it was located. A critical matter, therefore, was the maintenance of a certain regional balance in the composition of the student body. Higher education in the South, Gross maintained, was then dominated in quantity but not quality by a large number of state-supported institutions which offered "a somewhat mediocre education at very low costs to their students." (He conceded that the University of North Carolina was an exception to that statement with reference to quality and saw that as a special problem for Duke.) In contrast, higher education in the Northeast was then dominated by first-class, endowed institutions which faced little competition from state-supported schools. As a consequence of that pattern, Duke's position was difficult if it had to depend increasingly on tuition for a substantial portion of its income. If Duke based the scope of its activities mainly on income from sources other than tuition, Gross argued, that implied a limitation of activities as well as of student body and faculty size. Alternatively, and more difficult of attainment, there would have to be a substantial increase in revenues from sources other than tuition.

Gross suggested that the best regional distribution of the student body might be roughly half from the South, 40 percent from the Mid-Atlantic and nearer Middle West, and the remaining 10 percent from the rest of the nation. Duke could maintain competitive drawing power for "*good students—which always must be our objective*—only if we maintain and continue to improve our educational standards." While admitting that other things (such as libraries, laboratories, etc.) affected educational standards, he insisted that by far the most important factor was the quality of the faculty with respect to both teaching and scholarly research. Since the maintenance of a strong faculty was related to an important extent to salaries, Gross declared, Duke's position was not satisfactory.

On the basis of data that he had gathered and studied, Gross informed Smith that Duke's salary range was $400 or $500 less for instructors and $1,000 to $1,500 less for professors in comparison not with the top three or four universities but with some half dozen institutions ranking immediately below them. Gross did not explicitly urge that additional raises be given to the faculty, but that point was undoubtedly clear to Smith.

Returning to the matter of admissions, Gross suggested that since Duke faced the special problem of competition with the strong University of North Carolina, it might "be futile to attempt to draw too heavily on North Carolina for a large fraction of our students" and wiser to attempt to draw from the South more generally. That policy, he concluded, meant that it was desirable as rapidly as possible to increase scholarships and loan funds, especially for students from the South.[104]

While Gross was clear enough about favoring an increase in financial aid to students, various trustees were even more emphatic in their opposition to another increase in tuition. A longtime trustee agreed that raising faculty salaries was "a most laudable undertaking." But because he did "not want it to become too difficult for a poor boy to go to Duke," he wondered if there were not "some other means of meeting the necessities of the situation?"[105] Another trustee warned that increasing the tuition would just be "adding fuel to the deliberate and malicious propaganda that has gone out through the state for a number of years that Duke is a rich man's college." He thought the executive committee should find an alternative way to cover any budgetary deficit.[106] Yet another trustee, arguing incorrectly that the nation was entering a deflationary period, was adamant in opposing any tuition increase. "I think we should be very frank with the faculty in telling them we do not have the funds with which to raise their salaries . . . ," he wrote, "and if they do not choose to stay at Duke there is nothing that Duke University can do about it."[107]

Amidst all the conflicting views and diverse pressures, one important resource and ally for Smith was Alex. H. Sands, Jr. William R. Perkins died in 1945, after having been unwell and inactive in Duke affairs for several years. Like Perkins, Sands had known and worked for both B. N. and J. B. Duke; he had become the executive secretary for both men in 1913, and J. B. Duke named him as one of the original trustees of the Duke Endowment in 1924. Like Allen and Perkins, then, Sands became involved with the university through his relationship with the Duke family. Because Sands quite early began to study and help with the university's business and budgetary procedures, he had a thorough knowledge of those areas. He therefore became an important trustee of the university as well as a member of the executive committee. Not the least of Sands's contributions was to help educate various segments of Duke's constituency about two crucial matters. The first was that Duke University would "have to stand more and more on its own feet" because the trustees of the Duke Endowment did not control an unlimited flow of income and were restricted in the portion of that income that they could give to the university. For 1945–46, Sands noted, Duke received about 35 percent of its total income from the Duke Endowment; the estimated amount for 1946–47 would be around 30 percent.[108] The second important point that Sands emphasized was that the university had more than enough to attend to without undertaking any new educational programs, no matter how worthy.[109]

In response to the many-sided dilemma, the university took several important steps. First, on the matter of the tuition hike something of a compromise was reached when the trustees voted to increase it only $50 per year rather than the $100 that had originally been considered. In July, 1947, accordingly, students and parents received notice that the next year's tuition would be $350 because Duke's situation was reflected in a national survey that found that university costs had increased 52 per cent at the same time that returns from endowment funds had decreased.[110]

Then, to address the crucial matter of trying to find new sources of income, Duke took a leaf from the notebook of Princeton and certain other endowed institutions and launched its first well-publicized, annual fundraising effort among alumni and friends. Sands helped arrange for Jordan and Brower to visit Princeton and study the outstanding fund-raising program there. Subsequently, Sands chaired a committee of trustees and administrators that helped plan Duke's first annual fund drive, and in April, 1947, a newly created Duke University National Council replaced the older Alumni Council as the organization behind the drive. Charles A. Dukes, the director of alumni affairs, explained that the new national council had two primary purposes: to launch a program of general education of alumni and friends about Duke's needs; and to institute in July, 1947, a program of annual giving for unrestricted support, which might be supplemented, as occasion arose, by special campaigns for specific purposes. Dukes noted that as of May, 1947, the university had almost 26,000 living alumni and over 3,500 who were deceased.[111]

Strange as it might seem in retrospect, many alumni were surprised that Duke needed money. When the alumni office mailed out a brochure, "Your Share in Duke's Future," most alumni who responded did so enthusiastically. Some, however, questioned the need for the Loyalty Fund. "I just can't believe that Duke is 'poor'," was reported to be one type of reaction. "When I was in college there seemed to be plenty of money for buildings and the operations of the institution." To this the campaign leaders replied that Duke was not poor in the sense that some small endowed colleges were at the time, but that because Duke was concerned about the quality of the work it offered, it did not want just to coast along and gradually slip into mediocrity. The institution ran the risk of losing faculty to schools that were offering 25 to 50 percent more in salary. Faculty members might wish to stay at Duke out of loyalty to the institution, "but loyalty cannot long compete with their responsibilities to their families." Duke now had to compete in faculty recruitment and retention with some of the strongest universities in the country.

To the argument that necessarily modest contributions from most alumni could hardly be worth the trouble and effort involved in the Loyalty Fund, the answer given was that Princeton relied heavily upon the $200,000 it received annually from alumni; Harvard and Yale both received considerably more, and Dartmouth, which was not heavily endowed, received more than $400,000 from its alumni to help balance its budget. Duke needed an additional $250,000 per year for operating expenses, and the national council set as the goal for 1947–48 the raising of $100,000 toward that larger figure. The appeal concluded with an expression of hope that the abnormally large enrollment of the postwar years would gradually level off at around 4,000 students (which would not happen). Even to accommodate that number, new buildings were needed for administrative offices, student activities, and other purposes. "While these needs are desirable and necessary," the statement concluded, "they are subordinate to the immediate and urgent need for further increasing teachers' salaries and for meeting the rising costs of maintenance and operation." [112]

Charles Dukes and those alumni who worked with him had good reason to be proud in June, 1948, when he reported that in approximately eight months the first Loyalty Fund drive had surpassed its goal by raising almost $109,000 for unrestricted use from 5,229 contributors. Twenty-seven persons had given $1,000 or more, and 142 gave $100 or more. Nearly $18,000 of the total had been given by the alumnae, who were considerably fewer in number than the male alumni. According to the report of the American Alumni Council for 1947, there were eleven colleges and universities that had raised $100,000 or more for unrestricted use in annual giving programs, and twelve institutions that had 5,000 or more persons as contributors. Moreover, most of those institutions had had annual-giving programs in operation for a number of years. Heartened, therefore, by the first showing, Duke set as its goal for 1948–49 the sum of $150,000 from 6,500 contributors. [113]

Not content to stop with the establishment of the Loyalty Fund, Willis Smith, Sands, and others among the trustees and administrators began to consider the feasibility of a special development campaign. In his work in the American Bar Association, Smith gained a favorable impression of the contribution that professional consultants could sometimes make to nonprofit organizations. When confronted with a tangle in the university's management of its business affairs, for example, he pushed for and got the services of an outside management consultant. "There is so much of petty jealousies and politics on a college campus," Smith explained to Sands, ". . . that you probably cannot realize quite as easily as I can the situation." Too, Smith believed that better use could be made of Alfred Brower and Charles Jordan. Smith wanted the former to be made comptroller and business manager (and therefore placed over Charles Markham, who was treasurer) and thought that Jordan was a "very valuable man" with a "sense of diplomacy and even of political sagacity." Both he and Brower, however, were somewhat frustrated "by reason of the uncertainty of their duties and the more or less nebulous situations in which they have found themselves."[114] With the help of the management consultant, Smith, Sands, and their allies among the trustees succeeded in reorganizing the business sector of the university along the lines that they had wanted.

Likewise, for the preliminary groundwork for the special development campaign that Smith, Sands, and others envisioned, Duke obtained the services of a well-known consulting firm in New York. It sent a preliminary report early in 1948 and recommended that Duke shoot for a fund-raising goal of $17,250,000, of which $6,600,000 represented urgent building and operating needs.[115]

Working closely with Sands, Smith promptly mailed copies of the report to the trustees and invited them to write him at length if they wished, or to indicate on an enclosed postal card if they approved of the recommendations in the report and if they wished to give discretionary power in the matter to the executive committee. Benjamin F. Few, nephew of the late president and an alumnus, had approved the plan in his capacity as chairman of the special projects committee of the national council. Vice president and a director of Liggett & Myers, Few would also eventually serve as chairman of the development campaign. Careful planning for it continued throughout 1948, and the targeted goal was reduced to $12,000,000, with a multipurpose building (later to be known as Allen building) to house the administration together with faculty offices and classrooms as one of the prime objects. A student recreational building on West was another much-desired addition, but that would be delayed for several decades. By the time the campaign was publicly launched in the fall of 1949, Duke had a new president and, in one sense, was opening a new chapter in its history.

Having coped with the tuition problem as well as undertaken a vigorous quest for new sources of financial support, Smith and the trustees had

also to address the old matter of admissions and particularly the maintenance of adequate North Carolina representation in the student body.
A special, continuing problem in these years had to do with admissions
to the Woman's College and the medical school, for both were swamped
with many more applicants, including quite well-qualified ones, than they
could handle. Many of the trustees, including Smith, felt frustrated and
embarrassed when children of their friends and acquaintances failed to
win admission to Duke. Both during and after the war, Flowers and Jordan
wrote many letters trying to explain the situation concerning admissions
to the Woman's College, and soothing feathers ruffled over the admissions
crunch in the medical school likewise took much time and effort.

An alumnus in the nation's capital advised Smith that he thought Duke,
like certain other universities, seemed to be overemphasizing grades in
considering candidates for admission. He worried about an alleged focus
on "super-intellectuals" but admitted that it was due "perhaps partly to
our N.C. High Schools . . . that the good young manhood and woman-
hood of North Carolina are being defeated in such a competition [for
admission] and thereby deprived of the education which Mr. Duke meant
for them to have."[116]

Among the trustees themselves, concern about the admission of North
Carolinians to Duke mounted in relation to the tuition increases. Although
in 1946–47 34 percent of the students in the Woman's College and 36 percent of those in Trinity College were from North Carolina, some trustees
felt that those percentages were already too low and feared that they
would decrease. They emphasized J. B. Duke's statement in the indenture
that he was "largely confining the benefactions to those sections served
by these water power developments [the Duke Power Company]" in their
call for the "fullest preference" to be given to applicants to Duke from the
Carolinas. (These trustees tended to downplay, however, J. B. Duke's explicit request, made earlier in the indenture, that the university attain and
maintain "a place of real leadership in the educational world.") "Duke University is not enjoying the goodwill which it should command in North
Carolina," one of these trustees insisted. "There is a growing feeling that
we [at Duke] are much more interested in becoming a national university
than we are in serving the state," and there seemed to be "a very general
disposition among high school graduates in this state to feel that they are
not wanted at Duke."[117]

In their legitimate concern about Duke's serving its state and region as
well as the nation at large, some trustees tended to deemphasize too much
the school record and academic qualifications of candidates for admission.
When one trustee, for example, argued that "scholastic standing should
not be the paramount requirement," Willis Smith himself replied, "I think

you quite correctly stated the policy that I can subscribe to." [118] Neither trustee, however, specified what should be the "paramount requirement" if "scholastic standing," that is, the academic record, was not to be.

Amidst all this debate and controversy concerning admissions, one veteran trustee from Durham, M. Eugene Newsom, sounded a strong, clarifying note that echoed Few's approach to the matter. The real question, Newsom suggested, involved not only "preference" toward students from the Carolinas and the South in general but "the larger question of the 'inferiority' of grammar and high school education which is being afforded the students of this section." Newsom, recalling one of the historic missions of first Trinity and then Duke, declared that the choice confronting Duke was "whether we shall lower the standards of admission to the basis of 'preparedness' afforded in this section, and then give preference to students of this section, or whether it is going to be possible to raise the standards of 'preparedness' and then give preference." [119] Fortunately for the university, and also for the South, Newsom's approach to the knotty problem ultimately prevailed, and the trustees imposed no rigid geographical quotas that would have compromised academic standards. Instead, the university came up with a significant and creative new type of scholarship that both signified Duke's commitment to North Carolina and at the same time promised to enhance the academic quality of the undergraduate student body.

The Angier Buchanan Duke regional scholarship program, announced in 1947, was Duke's first organized, publicized effort to bring some of North Carolina's ablest students to the university. From 1925, when Ben Duke established the Angier B. Duke Memorial fund as a special kind of monument to his deceased son, it had been the principal source of financial aid offered at Duke. Most of the income from the fund, however, had been used for low-interest loans to needy students, and while Duke was proud of its record with that form of aid, there had been no scholarship program frankly designed as a recruiting device for outstanding students. Paul Gross and others on the faculty like him saw the need for such undergraduate scholarships, and Sands became an influential supporter of the idea. Charles Jordan, working closely with Sands, studied such scholarship programs at Harvard, Yale, and the University of North Carolina. The result of all the careful study and planning was a program at Duke that initially offered six Angier B. Duke scholarships, four for men and two for women. The state was divided into six regions and candidates were to be chosen primarily on the basis of their secondary-school records, college aptitude as shown by special tests, and demonstrated leadership abilities. The candidates were to be interviewed in each region by a committee consisting of local alumni and representatives from Duke, and then five finalists from each region would be brought to the campus for more interviews by committees and the selection of the winners. The awards were to be for up to $750 per year, depending on the student's need, and were to be for four years, provided that the student maintained an average in the upper quartile of the class and showed clear evidence of developing qualities of leadership.

As one early memorandum stated, the Angier B. Duke scholarships were intended neither "to produce grade-getting machines nor the leisurely scholar." Rather, they were to bring to Duke young men and women from North Carolina who gave "promise of becoming leaders in their chosen fields." The planners hoped that the scholarships would be awarded to students who possessed academic ability of a creative, imaginative sort as well as integrity and vitality and would become mature citizens with "a genuine interest in society and the ability to influence and direct the course of affairs." [120]

The Angier B. Duke scholarship program would grow larger in future years and also take different directions. But from its inception, it had a significant impact on the university. As intended, many of those students who were involved in the competition but who failed to win one of the coveted scholarships were encouraged to come to Duke nevertheless, and financial aid was made available for them to do so. It was a happy blending of service to North Carolina and Duke's commitment to academic excellence.

Thus the university in the late 1940s had launched several new programs in fund-raising and scholarships that augured well for the future. Yet, despite the valuable services of Smith, Sands, Jordan, Brower, and one or two others, there remained a serious crisis in top leadership that had somehow to be resolved before the university community could feel confident about the future.

15

The Resolution of the Leadership Crisis and

the Finding of a New President

⌒

I N TIMES OF INSTITUTIONAL crisis, a board of trustees led by an able
chairman can indeed be a boon to a university. Such proved to be
the case at Duke in the late 1940s when Willis Smith reinvigorated
the board and then, with important help from certain influential trustees,
guided the board through a series of changes that made possible a resolution of the leadership crisis. Although it was quite real, the crisis could not
be publicly discussed because of the persons involved, and while much of
the faculty was painfully aware of the problem, the public was not.

Meeting irregularly and in a largely perfunctory manner during the
war years, the trustees found things distinctly changed for the better after
Smith became chairman. "This [was] the first meeting of the Board of
Trustees that I have attended," one of the members wrote Smith, "where
anything except a very superficial discussion was ever had."[1] Well organized himself, Smith saw to it that the board's various committees attended to their assigned tasks and had reports with substance ready for
the consideration of the full board. After a meeting during commencement in 1947, a trustee complimented Smith by declaring that it had been
"the finest meeting of the Board of Trustees that has been held since I
have been on the Board the past eighteen years."[2]

Along with this reinvigoration of the board, however, came a growing
awareness that the trustees faced a serious and, to them at least, unprecedented problem. Late in 1946 one trustee wrote Smith that he was eager
to discuss certain matters at Duke but did not wish even to put them in
writing. "It is my honest opinion," this trustee added, "that we will soon,

and the sooner the better, have to make some real changes at Duke, or it will take us a long time to build back what we are losing." Smith replied that he would, of course, welcome a talk and was glad that the trustee had "already realized some of the things that several of us have felt for some time should be attended to."[3]

The addition of Alex. Sands to the board and the executive committee helped Smith. He informed another trustee and old friend that Sands was one "who understands the problems at hand and who has the determination to do something toward solving those problems." Smith's friend replied, "There is no question that something *must* be done."[4]

An alumnus in eastern North Carolina wrote Smith that he did not mean to meddle in the affairs of the trustees, but he and other Duke alumni in the area believed that the time had come for the trustees to "set about to replace the present leadership at Duke." No one had higher regard for Flowers and Wannamaker than he did, the alumnus declared, but it had been "apparent for a number of years that neither is in physical condition to carry on the work which they are obligated to do as chief officials of Duke."[5]

Another alumnus, who chose to remain anonymous, sent a letter to the *Durham Morning Herald* stating that he had "become alarmed in recent months at the almost mass exodus of many of the best known and most able professors on the Duke staff." The explanation, he had been told, was that they were offered higher salaries elsewhere and that Duke did not have the funds to hold them. Yet the university was engaged in an extensive building program on West campus despite the "present outrageously high costs of construction." What Duke needed most at that time, the alumnus concluded, was a change in the top administration, for without that the university would probably move backward rather than forward in the next crucial years. "A younger man with an academic reputation worthy of the present stature of the school," the alumnus concluded, "and a man with a reputation for action and long range planning is required if Duke is to continue in the future its past history of great and steady progress under both President Few and President Flowers." All alumni in the area were to be invited to a meeting in the Union building on West to discuss the matter. The letter never appeared in the newspaper, however, for the editor sent it to Charles Jordan with a note stating, "I saw no reason for using this anonymous letter."[6]

The genuine affection and respect that the trustees had for Flowers and Wannamaker greatly complicated the situation. When a certain important matter got mislaid or hung up in Flowers's office, as happened increasingly after the war, one of the trustees urged Smith to see the president again about the matter but to do so gently. "Likewise, we all love the Doctor [Flowers] so much," this trustee declared, "that we had rather get off the board than to hurt his feelings."[7] Another trustee, after congratulating Smith on a "fine" meeting of the board, added: "I take it that you feel as heartbroken as I do to witness the marked change in the appearance and manner of one of the best friends we ever had [Flowers]. It will fall to somebody's lot before long to give some suggestions if he does [not] voluntarily offer them himself."[8]

Unfortunately, both Flowers and Wannamaker required prodding, presumably both gentle and diplomatic, by Smith before they "volunteered" any suggestions about their retirement. Smith grasped the nettle, however, and then led a saddened but unified board to take action. The first step came in the meeting of the board in late May, 1947. Extensive groundwork among the trustees having been done prior to the meeting, the board discussed the need for a clearer and more inclusive retirement policy at the university—that is, one that included the officers of the university as well as the faculty—and empowered Smith to appoint a committee to study the matter. Some of the trustees also began to suggest that fixed, limited terms for trustees would also be in order, and that change too would eventually be made.

With the delicate matter of mandatory retirement thus out in the open and being studied, Smith conferred with Flowers about a plan whereby the latter could be relieved of his "onerous responsibilities": a new position of chancellor of the university was to be created for Flowers. His salary would be the same as he received as president, and he would continue to occupy his university-owned house. As chancellor, Flowers could "render such further services to the University as would be designated from time to time" by the executive committee or the full board and "such duties as would not be too burdensome to him." Flowers, according to Smith, promptly and graciously approved the plan. Smith's subsequent conversation with Wannamaker about his becoming vice chancellor, with the same arrangements about salary and housing as for Flowers, resulted in the longtime dean's quick acquiescence to the plan also.[9]

The solution to at least one aspect of Duke's leadership problem was a fortunate one, for the university had found a generous, humane manner in which two men who had dedicated their entire lives to the service of the institution could retreat with dignity from their high offices to largely honorary positions. The plan was not cheap, of course, but presumably such a situation would not again develop. In June, 1948, the trustees mandated that all officers and employees of the university, except the chancellor and vice chancellor, were to retire at the end of the academic year in which they became sixty-nine.[10]

The announcement of Flowers's plans to retire from the presidency as soon as a new president could be found brought him many tributes. The *Greensboro* (North Carolina) *Record*, for example, stated: "Of friendly and democratic disposition, and a man of deep human understanding, Dr. Flowers is one of the most popular figures North Carolina has produced in educational realms."[11] Typical of letters to Flowers from older alumni was the declaration that "I know of no man so loved and admired by so many as yourself." Another veteran alumnus wrote: "If the men who have graduated throughout the years were to ballot on the one person who came nearer representing their ideal, I believe the overwhelming verdict would be—Dr. Flowers."[12]

With those retirements arranged, Smith and his fellow trustees turned to the task of finding a new president. It would prove to be more difficult than they had anticipated and would include not one but two frustrating and disappointing near-misses before the new president was actually named. The whole procedure was also quite different from that which had been followed in 1940, for Smith, supported by Sands and others, meant for the faculty to play at least a consultative role in the search. When the search committee of the trustees, which was named and headed by Smith, met in early 1948, it requested that all departmental chairmen and deans of professional schools meet and select a committee of five faculty members, including at least one woman, who could consult with the trustee committee. This resulted in the selection of W. A. Brownell in education, W. G. Davison in medicine, Katherine Gilbert in aesthetics, art, and music, C. B. Hoover in economics, and N. I. White in English.

Newman White, asked to serve as chair by his colleagues, promptly informed all members of the faculty of the arrangement and requested them to transmit nominations and suggestions to him. More importantly, since too many names poured in to Smith and others from all quarters, the faculty committee asked the members of the faculty to rate the attributes of a university president, suggest minimum and maximum ages, and indicate a preference as to an internal or external appointment. The last-mentioned matter would prove to be especially important, for a strong majority of the responding faculty turned out to favor an external appointment, and certain powerful trustees leaned toward an internal one.

On the desired qualifications of the new president, the faculty gave top rating to understanding of university problems and competence as an executive. Next came qualities of personality, such as tact, decisiveness, perceptiveness, and the like. In the middle ranking of the six qualifications that the faculty committee had listed were the ability to secure financial support and to secure moral support and favorable publicity for the university. The ability to steer wisely between the right and left social and economic extremes came out in fifth place, and regional, educational, and religious background ranked lowest. The minimum age suggested was forty and the maximum fifty-five.

Of the 107 faculty members who sent in their responses in time to be tabulated (and some came in later), twenty-one wrote in the suggestion that the president should be a recognized scholar or have an established academic reputation. The faculty committee noted that it had assumed that an understanding of university problems covered the matter of scholarship and academic reputation, but clearly many faculty members sought to make the matter more explicit.

Newman White also explained that the faculty considered the matter of Wannamaker's successor as vice president for education and dean of the university to be inseparably connected with the matter of the presidency. He and his associates on the committee believed that just as 75 percent of the faculty favored an external appointment for president, 75 percent preferred an internal appointment for Wannamaker's successor.[13]

Just why the majority of the faculty preferred an external appointment for president is not certain, but it may have been that many faculty members in arts and sciences feared precisely what George Allen and Alex. Sands wanted: to see Wilburt Davison, the highly successful and popular dean of the medical school, made president. The non-medical faculty's wariness toward Davison had nothing to do with him personally but was rooted in the fear that the medical school, already one of the most outstanding components of the university, would be developed further and faster than the other parts of the institution. Such fears were not ungrounded.

One reason that Smith and others arranged to have A. S. Brower made comptroller and business manager of the university was that they hoped he could gain at least some control over the expenditures of the medical school and hospital and rein in Davison. Warmly admired by the key persons in the Duke Endowment (first Allen and Perkins, then Allen and Sands), Davison was probably not checked in any significant way by Flowers or any of the longtime administrators under him. A lengthy battle royal began in 1948, however, when Brower, backed by Smith and others, set out to put limits on the expenditures in the medical area. "I can not stress too strongly that it will be impossible for the University to continue to increase its allocation from its endowment revenue for the purpose of the Medical School and Hospital as it has in the past," Brower informed Davison, "and you may expect this action to be typical of that which will necessarily follow in future years." Brower went on to note that there had been little increase in income from endowed funds in recent years, and the rate of return on the funds had gone steadily downward. Yet the medical school had "increased its draft upon the income of the University in an almost steady progression from $296,000 in 1939–40 to $456,000 in 1947–48." The result, Brower noted, was that the medical area had come to absorb more than half of the university's entire income from the Duke Endowment.[14] The battle would be a long-continuing one, but the point here is that non-medical faculty members were well advised to be on guard about Davison.

If Willis Smith had not opposed Davison for the presidency, however, faculty opinion might have been disregarded. While Allen, Sands, and Ben Few leaned toward Davison, Smith and other university trustees strongly disagreed. After a meeting of the search committee where the division became clear, Smith avoided a formal vote because, as he explained to Allen, he agreed with Sands that the committee's nomination should be unanimous. Smith added that, while he liked Davison personally and appreciated his fine contribution to Duke, he did not believe that Davison had ever fully realized the value and importance to the university of goodwill in North Carolina. With that achieved, Smith argued, Duke's national prestige would also increase. Many trustees shared his view, Smith noted. To Sands, Smith wrote much the same thing, saying that since he lived in the region and had much contact with "interested people" he believed he had "a better idea as to the feeling of the public generally." Loyalties to Duke that developed through many years, Smith declared, had produced "the institution's spirit and traditions."[15]

Although Smith did not mention the faculty's preference for an external appointment in his letters to the New York trustees, that preference reinforced his own position. As the presidential search got underway, in fact, Smith acquired greater appreciation of the faculty. "The more I get acquainted with individuals on the faculty," he declared to Sands, "the more I become convinced that we have an able, earnest and sincerely loyal group of professors who are most anxious to collaborate and cooperate with the administration." Even Wannamaker had conceded, Smith reported, that giving the faculty a role in the search would "result in their being thoroughly satisfied with whatever the Board does."[16] That no doubt overstated the case—since faculties are "thoroughly satisfied" about remarkably few things—but Smith had undoubtedly been wise in allowing the faculty to have a role in the presidential search.

There were many nominations made, including some self-nominations, but the first candidate to be seriously considered as well as actively pursued was Ernest C. Colwell. A forty-seven-year-old native of Pennsylvania, Colwell received his undergraduate and divinity training at Emory University before getting a Ph.D. at the University of Chicago in 1930. Immediately joining the faculty of Chicago's divinity school, he became its dean in 1939 and dean of the university faculty in 1943. When Robert M. Hutchins, Chicago's president since 1929, was made chancellor there in 1945—and the job was an active one and quite different from the honorary post created for Flowers—Colwell became president. He was also an established scholar with a creditable record of publications.

After an exchange of letters, telephone calls, and telegrams, Smith,

Sands, and another member of the trustees' committee conferred with Colwell in Chicago in May, 1948. Reporting on the meeting to another member of the committee, Smith was optimistic. "We were all very much impressed with him and with his conception of university administration," Smith explained. "I do not think any of us had any real conception of university administration on the highest level as now practiced by the most able educators." Sands reported that Ben Few had also done some checking and gotten good reports, so Smith believed that the New York group was convinced that Colwell would make a "very superior President." Smith confessed his surprise that Colwell would be willing to leave Chicago, but his wife was a southerner and Colwell's connection with Emory had given him a special interest in southern education. The plan was for him to visit Duke in early June, and if all went well, Smith hoped that the full board could act a day or two after the visit.[17]

Colwell sent a handwritten letter to Smith and said that he had done little but "carry on a continuous debate with myself over the prospects at Duke." One aspect of the situation had been cleared up for him by the meeting, he explained, for he thought the "two Boards [of the university and the Duke Endowment] have done an exceptionally fine job of organizing your inter-relations so as to remove all possibility of frustrating conflict." In fact, he thought Duke had "done better than many institutions that began with fewer obstacles." Colwell noted that he had studied the various documents left with him and thought that the report by the New York consulting firm for the development campaign seemed to "miss the mark in several very important respects." But then, rather than write down all his ideas, he would discuss them during his projected visit to the campus.[18]

Just as the search committee readied for what the members hoped would be a happy denouement, a disappointing letter came from Colwell. In a gracious yet unequivocal manner, he explained that certain things had happened at the University of Chicago during the week that convinced him that he belonged there "in every sense of the term as long as the University of Chicago wants me." There had been criticism, he noted, of certain policies of his administration and a discovery of difficulties in part of Chicago's development program that he had persuaded the trustees to adopt. Events of the preceding days had helped him, Colwell continued, "to see more clearly my general relationship to the University" and there would be no point in his visiting Duke as earlier planned.[19]

The June meeting of Duke's trustees was not, therefore, the triumphant occasion that Smith and others on the search committee had hoped it would be. Rather, the university's situation was becoming more critical, for Flowers, after the death of his wife in May, 1948, seemed to decline more rapidly. Unable even to come to his office on many days, he authorized Charles Jordan or A. S. Brower to convene and act as the university's administrative committee if either deemed such a meeting necessary.[20] The ordinary routines of the university proceeded uninterruptedly, of course, and most students and probably many faculty members remained blissfully untouched by the leadership crisis. Yet the university was actually paying a high price in lost momentum and missed opportunities.

As the months passed and no external candidate became known to the public, talk of Davison as the likeliest internal one resurfaced. An alumnus in Durham, who was also a lawyer and close friend of Smith's, warned that while he considered Davison one of the best and most capable men at Duke, the medical dean "would be one of the last men to elect to the position of President." He thought Duke was already getting "a John[s] Hopkins set-up," and the "tail will soon wag the dog, if it is not already doing it." As the alumnus saw the matter, everything at Hopkins had been "submerged to the advantage of the Medical School and Hospital," and he feared that a comparable tendency at Duke would mean that the undergraduate colleges and the graduate school would be "playing 'second-fiddle' on campus." As for Sands, one of Davison's chief backers, he was a fortunate friend for Duke to have, the alumnus declared, but Sands "never went to Trinity College nor Duke University and he can't possibly have the same feeling, not by a hell of a lot, that I have." Smith responded, in confidence, that he too thought Davison's selection as president "would be horribly disadvantageous in everything connected with the University except the Medical School."[21]

While the search committee investigated various other persons whose names had been suggested, attention soon focused on a most promising possibility indeed. James R. Killian, Jr., was a forty-four-year-old South Carolinian who had attended Trinity College for two years in the early 1920s and then transferred to the Massachusetts Institute of Technology. Upon graduating, he remained there to work on and then edit the *Technology Review* for several years before taking an administrative post. In 1943 he became vice president of MIT.

After Killian conferred with Smith and one or two others in Raleigh in July, 1948, he agreed to meet with Sands, Allen, and others in New York. "I am hopeful that this latest will not prove a water haul," Sands wrote, "and that we will have our problem settled before long." The meeting in New York made Sands feel even better, and he reported to Smith that Allen, Ben Few, and others were "very impressed" by Killian. He had declared that he was "deeply interested" in the Duke presidency but would have to delay making a definite decision until he could confer in late August with the absent president of MIT, Karl T. Compton.

Apparently in response to a request from the search committee, Killian carefully drew up a "job specification" for a university president. The document is worth a close look, for it revealed that he had a deep understanding of a most complicated and often misunderstood position. The ideal university president, he argued, should first of all possess demonstrated administrative ability. He had to be able to provide leadership that would coordinate students, staff, trustees and alumni to give them a shared enthusiasm. "He must be able to work with the faculty of the university as a 'company of scholars,'" Killian suggested, "rather than seeking to manage them through a line organization." He thought this recognition of the special nature of the faculty was fundamental if the president hoped to "stimulate the maximum of creative activity."

Second, Killian mentioned that a president had to have the ability to express the aims and ideals of the university. This required skill in both speaking and writing as well as "a keen sense of public relations." His third point was related to the second, for he thought an ideal president should have the capacity to become the "symbol of the standards and ideals of a university." As a fourth specification, Killian called for courage in maintaining high standards and the recognition that education and creative scholarship were "the principal functions of a university," which every other activity should serve to strengthen.

Killian's fifth point had particular relevance for a research university, for he insisted that a president must understand the relationship between research and teaching. They were both essential, he quite correctly explained, and "when handled in partnership they can serve each to greatly strengthen the other." A president also needed a clear understanding of the relationship between the environment and scholarly activities, and that included the environment outside the classroom. Moreover, the president should be sympathetic with the view that students and staff needed "a sense of community responsibility, a sense of belonging."

As his sixth point, Killian wanted a president to have an active interest in public service, for he believed that a "willingness on the part of an institution to make a direct contribution to the welfare of the community is a vitalizing quality." In seventh place, he called for the ability to handle the financial affairs of the university and to conserve as well as enlarge its resources. His eighth requirement was that a president had to possess the strength and stamina to perform the chief executive's many tasks; he thought too that an extrovert was more likely to succeed as the top administrator than a person who was too introspective. A successful president had to have a great interest in people and an enthusiasm about trying to help them.

In addition to those general specifications, Killian suggested that the president of a privately endowed institution needed some particular qualifications. First, the president should believe in the special opportunities and responsibilities of such institutions and understand that "their independence and flexibility enables them to be pace setters in higher education." Next (and important certainly for Duke), he wanted the president to be willing to recognize and stress the regional characteristics of a university as a source of strength and individuality. "A university, wherever it is located, if it is to function properly, must share in the background, the ideals, and the special characteristics of the community in which it lives." Killian pointed to Harvard, particularly Harvard College (for undergraduates), as a fine example of an institution with strong regional roots that had taken advantage of those regional ties to strengthen itself as a national institution.

The president also had an obligation, he noted, to put the university in contact with national educational societies and agencies, thus keeping in touch with new ideas and with "the best minds in the country." This involved encouraging the faculty to "maintain the widest possible professional and scholarly contacts." Finally, Killian urged that an ideal president should be able to deal with what he regarded as one of the central problems of contemporary education: helping students to prepare to earn a living as well as to become well-rounded, morally responsible citizens. His eloquent conclusion was that the president had to be "willing to recognize that utility in education is not enough, that training for citizenship and spiritual values must have a central place in any great university."[22]

No wonder that Smith, Sands, and the small number of others who knew of the negotiations with Killian were excited about the possibility of hiring him. Sharing many of President Few's views about the nature and purpose of the university, Killian had a clearer, more sophisticated understanding of the intertwined relationship of teaching and research than Few had possessed. Yet Killian was both sensitive and imaginative about Duke's regional obligations and national aspirations. Moreover, he shared some of the idealism and spiritual vigor that had so markedly characterized Few.

Killian wrote in early August that, as he had said in the New York conference, he was "definitely interested," in fact "quite stirred and excited by the opportunity at Duke." While still awaiting Compton's return, Killian arranged for himself and his wife to make a quiet visit to Durham, where they no doubt looked over the campus but primarily held a private meeting with Smith, Sands, and a few other trustees. "The yeast is working," Killian wrote soon after the visit, and he promised a definitive statement in a matter of days.[23]

Smith, for his part, began considering what salary to offer Killian. Sands, after making what he termed discreet inquiries among some of his well-connected acquaintances in New York, reported that the president of Princeton then received $25,000 plus a house and a generous allowance for entertainment and professional travelling. The president of New York University reportedly had a larger salary. Although Killian had stated that he did not wish his salary to be out of line and that he would make his decision before he knew what the salary would be, Sands, Allen, and others in New York thought that $30,000 (and a house) would be "not at all out of line under present conditions." Smith, however, leaned towards $27,000 and a house, perhaps because Killian was then receiving at MIT $22,000 plus $2,000 for entertainment expenses.[24]

Despite all the optimistic planning, Smith, over the many months of the presidential search, had learned to be wary. He had found, he wrote to a friend, that "there are frequently commitments outstanding and obligations incurred which prevent an educator some times from doing that which he would like to do." Colwell, Smith believed, had thus become more or less pinned down by an unforeseen "upheaval" at Chicago.[25] Well might Smith have remained cautious, for an unanticipated turn of events was about to remove another presidential candidate from Duke's reach.

A telegram from Killian in mid-September, 1948, brought the unwelcome news: "After having practically decided to accept generous and challenging offer from your group [,] unexpected and compelling developments here make it wise for me to remain. Letter follows with suggestions of other possibilities." In his letter Killian stated that he and his wife "had quite fallen in love with Duke" and had even told a few of their closest friends of their intention to make the move. President Compton, however, had requested that Killian make no final decision until after meeting with MIT's executive committee, "a perfectly proper formality which I could not, in good faith to the Institute, ignore."

Killian then explained that the executive committee had made "representations" to him that he had no choice but to consider. Also a group of his academic colleagues "made representations that were so cordial and so urgent that I was taken aback." The central argument of both groups, Killian stated, was that MIT was "at a critical juncture at the present time and that a serious loss of momentum would inevitably result if the team of Compton and Killian were broken up." There were, he continued, three reasons for that being the case: firstly, MIT was in the process of a major reconsideration of its educational program; secondly, the school had embarked on a national effort to raise $20,000,000, a program which Killian said he had been especially instrumental in starting; and lastly MIT had "certain obligations in connection with the national security which demand that there be no loss in momentum."

Killian, who mentioned several other possibilities that Smith and the committee might consider, declared that he remained convinced that Duke offered "one of the best educational opportunities in the country." Furthermore, he graciously noted that he had never encountered a situation in which an offer was made with "more skill, cordiality, and patience than you have presented the Duke proposal."[26]

What Killian could not say at the time but what became known in the following few weeks was that Karl Compton had been called to Washington by President Truman to head the research and development board of the national military establishment. In early October, 1948, came the announcement that James R. Killian, Jr., was the new president of MIT.[27]

Twice foiled by fate, Smith and the others on the search committee had every reason to gnash their teeth—and say a few strong words, too. But it so happened that Ernest Colwell had written to Smith in late July, 1948, and mentioned that he had run into an associate director of the General Education Board, Arthur Hollis Edens, after a meeting in New York with Smith and others. Colwell said that he and Edens, both Emory alumni, had talked about many aspects of higher education in the South. "I was greatly impressed with the way Edens has matured," Colwell declared, "and I could not conscientiously mention any one else as my number one candidate for the Presidency of Duke." Although Edens was then working in New York, Colwell continued, he "remains a Southerner with a deep loyalty [to] and understanding of the South." He had had varied, valuable administrative experience but still had the energy of a young man. His character was above reproach and his wife charming. "I do not believe you can do as well, let alone do better, with anyone else," Colwell concluded.[28] Colwell did not say that he and Edens were old friends and had even been fraternity brothers at Emory.

Not only was Colwell's endorsement of Hollis Edens quite strong, but the major educational foundations had already become a favorite hunting ground for the presidential search committees of American colleges and universities. Thus when the Killian candidacy collapsed, Smith and his team swiftly proceeded to gather data and letters about Edens. Born in a Methodist parsonage in rural Tennessee in 1901, he attended the Cumberland Mountain School in the early 1920s and at the age of twenty-nine received a bachelor's degree from Emory. Returning to the Cumberland school for eight years as principal, Edens received a master's degree from Emory in 1938 and began to advance quickly as an administrator, first as an associate dean at Emory Junior College in Valdosta, Georgia, and then, after 1942, on the main Emory campus in Atlanta. Having taken a master's degree at Harvard in 1944, he became in the same year an associate professor of political science at Emory; after extended leaves for more graduate study at Harvard, he was named as the dean of administration at Emory in 1946. Then he advanced so quickly and moved about so much that he chose not to record the positions in *Who's Who in America* (1950–51). But he resigned from the deanship at Emory to become the vice chancellor of the University System of Georgia under his former teacher at the

Cumberland School, who was the chancellor. Hardly settled there, Edens, after much deliberation and under considerable pressure from the General Education Board, accepted the foundation job in New York.

A tall, ruggedly handsome man, Edens looked presidential and was clearly an unusually able, energetic, and ambitious person. He had exerted himself mightily to obtain an education and had to take his graduate training in interrupted bits and pieces. With his doctoral dissertation in political science at Harvard still unfinished in 1948, he had that hurdle yet to jump before he could obtain what is sometimes referred to as the scholar's "union card," the Ph.D. Regardless of degrees, his ten-year career in higher education had been largely administrative.

Smith requested the faculty advisory committee to gather whatever data it could, including letters, on Edens and several other persons whose names had been submitted. Despite the difficulty the trustees' search committee was having in finding an external candidate, the faculty committee reiterated its view that "it would be a mistake at this time to consider candidates from the faculty" and that the faculty wanted and needed stimulating leadership from "a recognized figure from outside its own group." Meantime, the faculty committee issued a memorandum to the entire faculty reporting on the series of consultations between the search committee and the faculty committee and, despite the troubling uncertainty, urging the faculty to be patient.[29] Calvin Hoover and a small group of other senior professors agreed about the urgency of the situation but wanted no lowering of standards simply to get a president in a hurry. Some of the group thought it might be well to name an acting president in the interim, for Hoover explained that he doubted "the feasibility of our carrying on for very long without anyone really acting as President."[30]

Numerous letters about Edens came to Smith and others, but the one that carried the most weight, as Smith later said, was from the president of Emory. He began by noting that Edens had moved up rapidly in the past few years and demonstrated the capacity to carry administrative responsibilities. "Whether on the basis of this experience he is ready for a job as complicated and difficult as the Duke presidency I could not be sure," the Emory president candidly declared. He had little doubt that Edens had the capacity, but he thought the attitude of the faculty would be vitally important. "I would feel better about the whole proposal," the president explained, "if he had had three or four more years in any one of the three positions he has held recently." Edens "would then have demonstrated achievement in top-level administration, would have broadened his contacts, and any eye-brow lifting about limitations as to scholarship *or* administrative experience would be completely uncalled for." The Emory president thought Edens possessed independence, maturity of judgment, and poise; he had an unusual ability to get along with all sorts of people.

Of irreproachable character, he had a marked interest in and loyalty to the Methodist church. He also possessed a "certain kind of rugged, masculine awkwardness which, in itself, seemed to have appealed greatly to the G.E.B. people." Three or four years hence, the president concluded, he was sure Edens would be ready for a university presidency, but if Edens asked him for advice he would urge Edens to wait.[31]

Perhaps it was the unusual candor of the letter that struck Smith. The great majority of recommendatory letters tend toward nothing but glowing praise, but here was a letter that, while attributing many impressive strengths to the candidate, frankly called attention to the clear element of risk. In New York, Sands conferred with two friends on the General Education Board and found that they considered Edens qualified for the job, "although they had hoped that he would spend at least five years with them before undertaking such an assignment." Edens had also reportedly turned down two offers, one as the president of a state university in the South. Sands added that he and Ben Few were to have lunch with Edens and that he had accidentally encountered Mrs. Edens, who "impresses me favorably on first acquaintance."[32]

On the campus, as Edens's name began to circulate as a possibility, there was indeed some of the "eye-brow lifting" that the Emory president had mentioned. One member of the faculty who claimed to know Edens well considered him "personable, tactful, and amiable" but something of "the promoter type." Edens had "no standing as a scholar and apparently is not too much concerned with academic matters." This faculty member believed that "a man of some distinction, particularly as a scholar," was to be preferred.[33] When Smith met with the faculty committee to discuss Edens, Davison and Hoover were positive about Edens while Brownell and Katherine Gilbert "seemed to be more concerned with having an outstanding scholar than anything else, although they readily admitted that to find a combination of first-grade scholar and administrator was not an easy job and that very few universities possessed such a president." Smith further noted that all of the faculty members on the committee had assured him that if Edens were named, they would do their best to assist him and promote his cause among the faculty.[34]

In response to these green lights, Smith, Sands, and their trustee colleagues now moved quickly. A called meeting of the full board was set for November 19, 1948, and Edens was to meet with the trustee committee prior to the board meeting. After that meeting, telegrams went out to all presidents of Duke alumni chapters telling them that Edens had been elected as the third president of the university. One alumnus expressed his appreciation of the telegram but added that if Edens "does not continue to have 'ants in his pants,' (he having moved about so much of late) it looks as if the election is an outstanding move for the university."[35]

Congratulatory messages poured in to Smith and others, but since Edens wanted to finish his doctoral dissertation before taking up residence at the university, Smith still had many chores to perform. He told a friend that for over a year he had spent from 20 to 25 percent of his working hours—hours which certainly were not the "billable" kind that lawyers like—on Duke affairs. But the important task of naming Wannamaker's successor still remained. While Edens would necessarily make the final recommendation to the board about the vice president for education, circumstances were such that the university could not afford to wait for the new president to study the situation, which might take months, and then make his choice after he had moved to the campus.

Among faculty members who had been suggested for the presidency, the name of Paul Gross was conspicuous. Yet the majority of the faculty had preferred an external appointment. Smith turned for advice on the matter to one of his former teachers at Trinity, W. T. Laprade, and reported the conversation fully to Sands. According to Smith's account, Laprade had great respect for Wannamaker but agreed that he had "failed terribly within the last few months." He was continuing to act as dean of the university, at the board's request, but refused to make many commitments until the new president could take over. Laprade believed that the executive committee "must act immediately" if "the organization, as it should be, is held together." When Smith then asked Laprade for specific advice, in case Edens asked the trustees for the same, the veteran historian was "unqualified in his statement that of all the men on the campus, he thought Dr. Gross is the one who should be named Dean." When pressed for further recommendations, Laprade suggested that Alan Manchester was probably the "next best man" to Gross. An ideal situation, Laprade thought, would be for Manchester to serve under Gross and be more or less apprenticed to him. Smith requested that Sands or Allen or both of them talk with Edens immediately about Gross so that when Edens visited the campus briefly in December he could confer with various leaders of the faculty and promptly decide about the deanship.[36] The upshot of all this was that Edens, on the last day of 1948, requested Gross to confer with him in New York and shortly afterward revealed that he would ask the board to name Gross as vice president for education and dean of the university.

With the long months, even years, of resolving Duke's leadership crisis approaching an end, Sands thanked and congratulated Smith. "The enthusiasm with which everyone, and particularly the student body, received Dr. Edens on the occasion of Founders' Day was indeed gratifying and comforting," Sands declared, and he believed it augured well for the success of Edens's administration. When the Edens family arrived on campus, Sands predicted, "We will begin to see a revival of morale." (Edens and his wife and daughter moved to the campus in March, 1949.) Smith shared Sands's hopefulness and avowed that "we are beginning a really new era at Duke that will mean much to the Institution and to all of its supporters."[37]

There was indeed a new spirit of hopefulness on the campus, for the years immediately after World War II had been a troubling time for Duke in certain respects. The *Chronicle* hailed the trustees' selection of Edens as a happy one. "Turning outside present ranks to choose a new leader was wise," the newspaper stated, "and through using a criterion of capacity and integrity rather than one of 'name,' the board's choice was forward-looking and realistic." The *Chronicle* liked the "down to earthness" of Edens's acceptance speech and the cordiality of his standing invitation to students to visit him. "The unpleasant realization that we knew not the exact direction in which we were moving," the newspaper concluded, had been replaced by a confidence in the new president and the future.[38]

The university's problems in the late 1940s, while quite real, should not be exaggerated. True, some outstanding faculty members left for one reason or another. It was also true, however, that many promising faculty appointments, especially in the beginning ranks, were made in those years. As had been the case with so many junior appointments in the 1930s, a high proportion of those named to the faculty in the 1940s would spend their full careers at Duke and render invaluable service to the institution. Some of those in the arts and sciences who came during the 1940s, mostly after the war ended, and who spent all or a substantial portion of their careers at Duke, were, in the humanities area, Marianna D. Jenkins, Sidney D. Markman, and Earl G. Mueller in art. In English, Helen S. Bevington, Merle M. Bevington, Francis E. Bowman, Kenneth J. Reardon, Esther L. Schwerman, and Joseph C. Wetherby all were recruited in the 1940s, with only the two Bevingtons coming during the war. Music finally began to be strengthened with the appointments of Allen H. Bone, Julia W. Mueller (who had taught at Duke for two years before the war), Eugenia C. Saville, and Loren R. Withers. In religion David G. Bradley, Barney L. Jones, and James H. Phillips joined the faculty, while in romance languages the appointment of Richard L. Predmore was important for the Spanish section. In philosophy the new members were Glenn R. Negley, Robert L. Patterson, and Paul Welsh.

In the natural sciences, physics was further bolstered through the appointment of Walter Gordy, Eugene Greuling, Harold W. Lewis, and Henry W. Newson. Howard A. Strobel and Pelham Wilder, Jr., came in chemistry, and in zoology Edward C. Horn, Wanda S. Hunter, Muriel I. Sandeen, and Karl M. Wilbur were the new members.

In the social science and history area, anthropology recruited Weston La Barre, and sociology added Clarence H. Schettler and Eugenia L. R. Whitridge. In history, John S. Curtiss became the department's first

Russian specialist, and Frances D. Acomb, Joel Colton, and Irving B. Holley, Jr., were also added. In economics and business administration, Robert L. Dickens, Frank A. Hanna, Frederick C. Joerg, and Lloyd B. Saville were recruited; and Roma S. Cheek and John H. Hallowell joined the staff in political science. In education, Edward C. Bolmeier, Mabel F. Rudisill, and Wippert A. Stumpf were newcomers in the 1940s, and Luella J. Uhrhane came in health education, while Frances Holton and Carmen M. Falcone were added to the staff in physical education. Psychology added Katharine M. Banham, George Frederic Kuder, Gelolo McHugh, and Wally Reichenberg-Hackett.

Although not a faculty appointment, the arrival of Theodore M. Minah at Duke early in 1946 turned out to be highly significant, especially for students, because the Union food on West had been a source of sharp dissatisfaction for some time. As the new manager of the dining halls, Minah brought not only great expertise and experience in his field but notable diplomacy and charm. Meeting with student representatives soon after his arrival, Minah listened carefully to their suggestions and complaints, made many changes in the operation of the food services, and achieved altogether a remarkable success in a chronically sensitive area of student life. He would remain in the post for twenty-eight years and become a much-admired figure not only by students but by administrators, employees, and faculty as well.

The faculty, thwarted in its early efforts to gain a voice in university governance, would renew that campaign early in Edens's administration and gradually achieve the goal. Newman White, however, would not be present to enjoy the faculty's success. On leave in Cambridge, Massachusetts, during the fall semester of 1948, he wrote Wannamaker that he had not been able to escape a lot of departmental correspondence and sometimes wondered "whether it would be worthwhile to die." White added, "Maybe there is no post-office in Heaven, but I'll bet there's one in Hell, and I'm afraid to risk it."[39] Sadly enough, less than a month later White was stricken with a heart attack and died suddenly at age fifty-six. Saluting him, William B. Hamilton, an historian who succeeded to White's role as a leading spokesman for the faculty, declared that through White's career at Duke, first as a student and then as a faculty member, he had "added dignity and stature to each student and teacher in this university." After noting White's scholarly achievements, especially his world-acclaimed life of Percy Bysshe Shelley, Hamilton praised White's contribution to the academic and larger community, where he had possessed "the courage to espouse unpopular causes and a willingness to look authority in the eye which gave heart to many a weaker member of this university." Concerned about factory workers and "various underdogs," White had helped bring Norman Thomas to the campus when that was not an easy thing to do.

Turning to a more recent period, Hamilton continued: "At a time when many members of this university felt themselves frustrated by an atmosphere in high places of inadequacy, secretiveness and lack of trust—a failing of that academic comradeship we need here in our common enterprise—White lent his prestige and force to the protestants." Because of Newman White, Hamilton concluded, "we are each of us more learned," and "what is most important, we have more pride in ourselves and more faith in our fellows."[40]

Just as allowing the faculty to play a role in university governance, a role that was modest enough at first but one that steadily increased, ultimately strengthened Duke, so too would the fund-raising efforts that were finally begun in the late 1940s. Both the Great Depression of the 1930s and then World War II were partly responsible for Duke's somewhat tardy start on systematic, well-publicized fund-raising. The university's excessive dependence on the Duke Endowment, however, was a habit and a fact that would gradually be lessened in the decades ahead.

One inescapable source of tension and potential conflict at Duke was having a faculty that pursued excellence in both undergraduate teaching and scholarly research. While that particular source of tension was one that Duke shared with certain other research universities, that fact did not lessen its on-going and inevitable significance. As J. R. Killian, Jr., had aptly pointed out, research and teaching "when handled in partnership" could serve greatly to strengthen each other. But not all faculty members much less administrators in research universities always understood or sympathized with that insight of Killian's, and eternal vigilance on the part of the president, dean of the faculty (or provost), and departmental chairs would be required to maintain the balance. Under Few's leadership, Duke, unlike so many of its peers, had made a notable effort to avoid sacrificing its undergraduates on the high altar of research and graduate-and-professional training. The task of maintaining the priorities and policies set by Few would be a constant challenge in the years ahead.

In addition to that widespread problem among research universities, however, Duke possessed other tensions that were unique. The most obvious was the fact that one group of trustees controlled the Duke Endowment, on which the university significantly depended, and another board of trustees controlled the university. That simple but nonetheless weighty fact had turned out to be Few's greatest challenge and worry. The solution of the dilemma that he had finally worked out—having three trustees of the Duke Endowment serve as trustees also of the university and on its seven-person executive committee—had proven satisfactory during the university's first quarter-century. With each year that passed, perhaps it was true that there was a lessening of the danger of a rupture between the two boards. The matter required great tact and diplomacy on the part of all, however, and probably most of all on the part of the university's president.

Another unique problem at Duke was the university's deep commitment to and historic tradition of giving the greatest service possible to North Carolina and the South while at the same time trying to achieve a place of educational leadership as a national university. The double task was not impossible, but it was clearly difficult and highly sensitive. Just as the maintenance of the balance between teaching and research could never be solved once and for all but had to be lived with and regularly attended to, so too did Duke's regional and national commitments require virtually constant weighing and balancing. Not only the university's admissions policies but its priorities in many areas—such as faculty hiring, resource allocation, and long-range planning—were related to the manner in which regional and national obligations were handled. As Few had understood and demonstrated, the two commitments did not necessarily conflict, but great wisdom, tact, and diligence were required to keep all of the varied constituencies of the university informed and in agreement about the institution's life and undertakings.

Concerning two groups, Duke would share with the nation's other educational institutions great challenges in the 1950s and succeeding decades: African Americans and women. As for the former, nothing in Duke's charter or by-laws referred to race. In fact, however, first Trinity and then Duke had carefully observed the state's and the region's laws and customs concerning racial segregation. While de facto segregation prevailed throughout much of the nation down to and even after World War II, only the southern states had established an elaborate structure of legally mandated racial separation. With the application of that policy in higher education under attack in the federal courts from the 1930s onward, the Jim Crow system, the South's second "peculiar institution" (slavery after about 1800 having been the first), would be judicially overturned in the 1950s as the civil rights revolution gathered momentum.

In light of Trinity-Duke's history, the Duke family's conspicuous fairness toward African Americans, and the cosmopolitan nature of the university's faculty and student body, Duke stood at a crucial junction in the 1950s. One would think that Duke University might grasp the opportunity to demonstrate in a particularly difficult yet vital area "the real leadership in the educational world" that J. B. Duke had called for in his indenture. All segments of the university's constituency would face the challenge of racial justice and fairness, but perhaps the greatest responsibility would rest on the president and the board of trustees.

Concerning the role of women in higher education, Duke's future was less problematical. Nudged by Washington Duke as far back as 1896 to provide women with education on an "equal footing" with men, Trinity

College had pioneered in the South. The establishment of the Woman's College in 1930 meant not only that women became a significant component of the student body but also that there were women faculty members. The separate-but-equal arrangement would come under attack from the women themselves in the 1960s, and the Woman's College as a separate entity would finally be abolished in 1972. The fact remains, however, that Duke included women long before many of its peers in the university world.

More then, perhaps, than many research universities Duke faced an array of special challenges. Yet the opportunities afforded the institution quite matched the challenges—and as Few had once observed, "The routine at times may be dull and gray, but the vision of the future is always golden and infinitely inspiring." He added that he believed that "we have now hit the open sea and that a long journey is ahead of Duke University."[41] By 1949, over a hundred years had passed since the Methodist and Quaker farmers of Randolph County had begun their humble one-room school. Only twenty-five years had passed since the organization of a research university around Trinity College. It was a short but important phase of the institution's long journey.

Appendix 1

Original Faculty of the Schools
of Medicine, Nursing, and Health Services,
1930–1931[1]

↤

Frederick Vernon Altvater, Intern in Hospital Administration
*Edwin Pascal Alyea, S.B., M.D., Instructor in Urology
*Harold Lindsay Amoss, S.B., M.S., Dr. B.H., Sc.D., M.D., Professor of Medicine
*William Banks Anderson, A.B., M.D., Instructor in Otolaryngology
*Bessie Baker, B.S., R.N., Dean of School of Nursing and Professor of Nursing Education
*Roger Denio Baker, A.B., M.D., Instructor in Anatomy
*Frederick Bernheim, A.B., Ph.D., Assistant Professor of Physiology
*Mary Lilias Christian Bernheim, B.A., M.A., Ph.D., Instructor of Biochemistry
*Bayard Carter, A.B., B.A., M.A., M.D., Professor of Obstetrics and Gynecology
*Wilburt Cornell Davison, A.B., B.A., B.Sc., M.A., M.D., D.Sc., LL.D., Dean of School of
    Medicine and Professor of Pediatrics
*George Sharpe Eadie, B.A., M.A., M.B., Ph.D., Professor of Physiology and Pharmacology
*Watt Weems Eagle, A.B., M.D., Assistant Professor of Otolaryngology
 Judith Farrar, A.B., B.S., Medical Librarian
 Mildred Perkins Farrar, A.B., Assistant Medical Librarian
*Wiley Davis Forbus, A.B., M.D., Professor of Pathology
*Clarence Ellsworth Gardner, Jr., A.B., M.D., Resident in Surgery
 Edwin Crowell Hamblen, B.S., M.D., Associate Professor of Obstetrics and Gynecology
*Frederic Moir Hanes, A.B., A.M., M.D., Associate Professor of Medicine
*Oscar Carl Edward Hansen-Pruss, A.B., M.D., Assistant Professor of Medicine
*Deryl Hart, A.B., A.M., M.D., Professor of Surgery
*Duncan Charteris Hetherington, A.B., M.A., Ph.D., M.D., Associate Professor of Anatomy
 William Henry Hollinshead, B.A., M.S., Ph.D., Instructor in Anatomy
*Christopher Johnston, A.B., M.D., Instructor in Medicine
*Robert Randolph Jones, Jr., A.B., M.D., Assistant in Surgery
 Hyman Mackler, A.B., M.A., Ph.D., Instructor in Physiology and Pharmacology
 William deBerniere MacNider, M.D., Visiting Lecturer in Special Pharmacology
 Elsie Wilson Martin, A.B., M.S., Professor of Dietetics

Forrest Draper McCrea, M.S., Ph.D., Associate Professor of Physiology

Ernest Parrish McCutcheon, D.D.S., Instructor in Dentistry

*Mary H. Muller, R.N., Instructor in Anesthesiology

*William Alexandre Perlzweig, B.S., A.M., Ph.D., Professor of Biochemistry

Elbert Lapsley Persons, A.B., M.D., Instructor in Medicine

Francis Ross Porter, A.B., Intern in Hospital Administration

*Mary Alverta Poston, A.M., Instructor in Bacteriology

*Watson Smith Rankin, M.D., Lecturer in Public Health

Robert James Reeves, A.B., M.D., Instructor in Roentgenology

Robert Alexander Ross, B.S., M.D., Instructor in Obstetrics and Gynecology

Julian Meade Ruffin, A.B., M.D., Assistant Professor of Medicine

*Alfred Rives Shands, Jr., B.A., M.D., Instructor in Orthopaedics

*Mildred M. Sherwood, Head Nurse on Pediatric Ward

*David Tillersin Smith, A.B., M.D., Associate Professor of Medicine

*Susan Gower Smith, A.B., M.A., Instructor in Biochemistry

*Mary H. Snively, R.N., Associate In Anesthesiology

*Francis Huntington Swett, A.B., M.A., Ph.D., Professor of Anatomy

*Haywood Maurice Taylor, B.S., M.S., Ph.D., Assistant Professor of Biochemistry

Marcellus Eaton Winston, Superintendent of Duke Hospital

---

* Indicates persons with previous professional training or experience at the Johns Hopkins University.

1. From James F. Gifford, Jr., *The Evolution of a Medical Center: A History of Medicine at Duke University to 1941* (Durham, N.C.: Duke University Press, 1972), pp. 191–192.

Appendix 2

A Note on the Sources

⌒

Two important books about Trinity College, Duke University's forerunner, are discussed in the preface: Nora C. Chaffin, *Trinity College, 1839–1892: The Beginnings of Duke University* (Durham, N.C.: Duke University Press, 1950) and Earl W. Porter, *Trinity and Duke, 1892– 1924: Foundations of Duke University* (Durham, N.C.: Duke University Press, 1964). While the former book traces the survival of the institution in difficult times, the latter volume especially shows the various ways in which Trinity College strengthened itself and acquired certain features that made the transition to university status less abrupt than most outside observers realized.

Three books that are helpful in placing Duke's history in a larger framework are: Frederick Rudolph, *The American College and University: A History* (New York: Knopf, 1962); Laurence R. Veysey, *The Emergence of the American University* (Chicago: University of Chicago Press, 1965); and Roger L. Geiger, *To Advance Knowledge: The Growth of American Research Universities, 1900–1940* (New York: Oxford University Press, 1986).

The Papers and Addresses of William Preston Few, edited, with a biographical appreciation, by Robert H. Woody (Durham, N.C.: Duke University Press, 1951), is a useful volume, and the biographical sketch of almost 140 pages is perceptive. The most helpful published monograph about a major component of Duke University is James F. Gifford, Jr., *The Evolution of a Medical Center: A History of Medicine at Duke University to 1941* (Durham, N.C.: Duke University Press, 1972).

Rather than list here other, relatively few secondary sources that are cited in the footnotes, this essay will focus on the manuscript sources that are the backbone of the study, and not all of those sources but only the most important ones. They are presented in alphabetical order after a brief discussion of the papers of William Preston Few, which is by far the most important single source for the university's history in its first quarter-century. All collections, unless otherwise noted, are in the Duke University Archives, W. R. Perkins Library.

William Preston Few Papers

This voluminous collection is wonderfully rich as well as filled with many examples of Few's splendid prose style. The chronologically arranged correspondence file is both larger and more useful than the subject file, though there are some important things in the latter. In addition to these papers and the volume edited by Robert Woody, an important source for learning about Few's ideas and certain developments in the university during the 1930s is in the volumes published as *Bulletins of Duke University* and entitled *Report of the President and Reports of Other Officers*. Few's reports are of a sufficient quality to deserve to be collected, edited, and published in a single volume.

Alice M. Baldwin Papers

Except for Baldwin's unpublished manuscript, "The Woman's College, As I Remember It," this collection is disappointing. There are letters that are important from a biographical standpoint, but not many that bear significantly on the Woman's College. Baldwin's dealings with Few, Flowers, and other administrators were face-to-face, as were those among the women who worked with Baldwin to make the Woman's College so successful. The unpublished doctoral dissertation by Dianne Puthoff Brandstadter, "Developing the Coordinate College for Women at Duke University: The Career of Alice Mary Baldwin, 1924–1947" (Duke University, 1977) is both reliable and helpful.

Wilburt C. Davison Papers
(Medical Center Archives, Duke University)

This is a vast, miscellaneous collection but except for data about the naming of the original faculty of the School of Medicine and the negotiations about the interior arrangement and equipment of the first medical building, it is disappointing from the standpoint of institutional history. Historians of medicine would no doubt view the collection differently. Davison wrote a vast number of short, straight-to-the-point, and often perfunctory letters. Turning them over in the attempt to find a nugget for institutional history is a tedious chore. Davison's reminiscences, which are published in two different volumes, are colorful and lively; but, like other published records about the Medical Center, they tend to skip lightly over or, no doubt unconsciously, to camouflage controversial questions. The School of Medicine and Hospital and related "schools" have generated more hard statistical data than any other part of the university, but the tendency has always been to look at the Medical Center in isolation from the rest of the university, which was not the way the budget worked.

Robert Lee Flowers Papers

Although this collection is large, it is neither as extensive nor as important as that of Few. It is particularly useful for certain matters related to the physical plant and to those operations (such as the university press) that were under Flowers's supervision as vice president for finance. As president, Flowers received more significant letters and reports than he generated, and after World War II the record of outgoing correspondence grows progressively thinner.

Charles E. Jordan Papers

This collection is valuable for the 1940s, since during Flowers's presidency Jordan played a key role and probably drafted a number of important letters and other documents that went out over the signature of Flowers. Jordan was always keenly interested in athletics at Duke, and there is material related to that as well as to admissions, financial aid, and various other matters.

Clarence F. Korstian Papers

This collection is useful for the light it sheds on the establishment and management of the Duke Forest and the School of Forestry. Korstian's essays in the *Report of the President and Reports of Other Officers*, published annually in the 1930s, are also detailed and informative.

Records of the School of Law

The files of Justin Miller, the first dean of the reorganized law school, are silent as to whether he had any interest in becoming Few's successor, as certain of Miller's friends and admirers hoped might be the case. Miller's letters, however, shed a great deal of light on the early years of the school and the professional life of an energetic, ambitious academic lawyer and dean. The papers of Claude Horack, Miller's successor, are much less useful, since Horack seems to have regarded the job as dean as more or less that of a caretaker, one conducting a holding operation that partially failed in the 1940s.

News Service Biographical Files

Although some of the folders on individuals in this vast collection contain correspondence, this is not primarily a collection of primary source material. Rather, it affords a quick, convenient way to obtain biographical data on members of the faculty and administrative staff. Alphabetized by subject, the folders contain extensive materials about some individuals.

Records of the School of Religion (Divinity School)

The largest and richest part of these records relate to Paul N. Garber, who served as registrar for the school before becoming dean in 1941. Letters to Garber from divinity students serving summer internships and from newly ordained ministers afford an unusually rich insight into the southern Methodist church, especially in rural regions, during the hard times of the 1930s. Those letters, more than any other documents used for this volume, recall the early life of Washington Duke and suggest why he grew so deeply to love and respect the Methodist church and reared his children to share that feeling.

Records of the Board of Trustees

The official minutes of the board are kept in the office of the Secretary of the University. They are occasionally useful for pinning down dates or getting the exact wording of an important resolution or by-law. Like most official minutes, however, they conceal much more than they reveal, and the "raw," often semi-chaotic records of the trustees that are housed in Archives are more useful to the historian.

Willis Smith Papers
(Manuscripts Department)

This collection has some helpful items for the period before Smith became chairman of the board of trustees in 1946, but its main value for this study derived from the correspondence in the late 1940s. Not only are the problems that beset the university in those years illuminated, but letters showing how the search for a new president was conducted afford a rare, rich glimpse into one of academe's trickier operations.

William H. Wannamaker Papers

This large collection is divided into two parts, the correspondence file and the personnel file. The former sheds much light on a wide variety of subjects, including student behavior and discipline, but is thin on matters relating to the faculty. The personnel file, however, deals largely with faculty appointments and is indispensable. Wannamaker's conscientiousness and firm adherence to standards come through clearly in his letters, as does his sincere emphasis on the importance of good teaching. As the third member, along with Few and Flowers, of the triumvirate that led the university in its early years, the powerful dean was strong in regard to orderly procedure and probably complemented Few in that respect.

Notes

1. The Origins of the University Idea at Trinity College

1. These matters are discussed in greater detail in Earl W. Porter, *Trinity and Duke, 1892–1924: Foundations of Duke University* (Durham, N.C.: Duke University Press, 1964), pp. 6–32. Hereinafter cited as Porter, *Trinity and Duke*.

2. Porter, *Trinity and Duke*, p. 7; John F. Crowell, *Personal Recollections of Trinity College, North Carolina, 1887–1894* (Durham, N.C.: Duke University Press, 1939), pp. 10–15.

3. Laurence R Veysey, *The Emergence of the American University* (Chicago: University of Chicago Press, 1965), pp. 158–159. Hereinafter cited as Veysey, *Emergence of the American University*. Roger L. Geiger, *To Advance Knowledge: The Growth of American Research Universities, 1900–1940* (New York: Oxford University Press, 1986), pp. 7–9. Hereinafter cited as Geiger, *American Research Universities*.

4. Geiger, *American Research Universities*, pp. 2–3.

5. Ibid., pp. 18–19. Illinois, Minnesota, and Massachusetts Institute of Technology were not among the charter members of the Association of American Universities; Clark University and the Catholic University of America were.

6. Porter, *Trinity and Duke*, p. 27.

7. Wendell H. Stephenson, *Southern History in the Making: Pioneer Historians of the South* (Baton Rouge: Louisiana State University Press, 1964), p. 95. Hereinafter cited as Stephenson, *Southern History*.

8. E. C. Perrow (Trinity '03) to Harry Jackson, October 25, 1965, in Department of Alumni Affairs, Class Folders, 1903, Duke University Archives.

9. Porter, *Trinity and Duke*, p. 74.

10. Stephenson, *Southern History*, p. 99.

11. Ibid., p. 100.

12. Porter, *Trinity and Duke*, p. 91.

13. These matters are dealt with in greater detail both in Porter, *Trinity and Duke*, pp. 19–53, and Robert F. Durden, *The Dukes of Durham, 1865–1929* (Durham, N.C.: Duke University Press, 1975), pp. 82–121. Hereinafter cited as Durden, *The Dukes*.

14. Durden, *The Dukes*, pp. 108–110.

15. Porter, *Trinity and Duke*, p. 63. Although Washington Duke, who was never given to lengthy pronouncements, did not elaborate on the reasons for his interest in women's education, he may well have regarded his gift as a memorial to his only daughter, Mary Duke Lyon, who had died in 1893 at the age of thirty-nine.

16. Porter, *Trinity and Duke*, p. 86. The significance of the money that the Dukes gave to Trinity in the early years is pointed up by the fact that the state's appropriation to the University of North Carolina for 1899–1900 was $25,000, and the university's total income from all sources for that year was $48,000. Louis R. Wilson, *The University of North Carolina, 1900–1930: The Making of a Modern University* (Chapel Hill: University of North Carolina Press, 1957), pp. 31, 36.

17. William B. Hamilton, "Fifty Years of Liberalism and Learning," in William B. Hamilton, ed., *Fifty Years of The South Atlantic Quarterly* (Durham, N.C.: Duke University Press, 1952), p. 3.

18. Ibid., pp. 3–4.

19. Ibid., pp. 60–61.

20. The most balanced treatment may be found in Porter, *Trinity and Duke*, pp. 96–139. Ben Duke's role is spotlighted in Durden, *The Dukes*, pp. 117–121.

21. "Trinity College and Academic Liberty," in Hamilton, ed., *Fifty Years of the South Atlantic Quarterly*, p. 63.

22. Michael O'Brien, *Rethinking the South: Essays in Intellectual History* (Baltimore, Md.: Johns Hopkins University Press, 1988), p. 134.

23. William P. Few, "President Eliot and the South," *South Atlantic Quarterly* 8 (April, 1909): 184–191, as reprinted in Robert H. Woody, ed., *The Papers and Addresses of William Preston Few* (Durham, N.C.: Duke University Press, 1951). Hereinafter cited as Woody, ed., *Papers*. Professor Woody also wrote for this volume a useful and perceptive "Biographical Appreciation" of Few, pp. 3–141.

24. William P. Few, "The College in Southern Development," *South Atlantic Quarterly*, 10 (January, 1911) in Woody, ed., *Papers*, pp. 290–291.

25. Geiger, *American Research Universities*, p. vi.

26. William P. Few, "President Eliot and the South," in Woody, ed., *Papers*, p. 260.

27. Edwin Mims to B. N. Duke, May 5, 1897, Benjamin N. Duke Papers, Manuscripts Department, Duke University Library. Hereinafter cited as B. N. Duke Papers.

28. Porter, *Trinity and Duke*, pp. 91ff., 146. Ben and J. B. Duke made their offer of support for the coordinate college conditional on a certain level of support from the two Methodist conferences in North Carolina, but it was not forthcoming.

29. Porter, *Trinity and Duke*, pp. 143–146.

30. B. N. Duke to Mrs. W. G. McCabe, September 29, 1911, B. N. Duke Papers.

31. William R. Perkins, "An Address on the Duke Endowment: Its Origins, Nature and Purposes," delivered to the Sphex Club in Lynchburg, Va., October 11, 1929. Pamphlet in Duke University Library.

32. All of these matters, plus the family's role in textiles, are dealt with in more detail in Durden, *The Dukes*, chapters 3, 4, 7, and 9.

33. W. P. Few to J. B. Duke, March 31, 1914, William P. Few Papers, Duke University Archives. Hereinafter cited as Few Papers.

34. Durden, *The Dukes*, pp. 208–209.

35. Remarks to open the fall session of Duke University, September 16, 1931, Few Papers.

36. W. P. Few, "Southern Public Opinion," *South Atlantic Quarterly* 4 (January, 1905), reprinted in Woody, ed., *Papers*, pp. 186–199.

37. Few to J. B. Duke, December 15 (?), 1918, Few Papers.

38. Few to J. B. Duke, February 1 and February 27, 1919, Few Papers.

39. Few to Toms, June 5, 1919, Few Papers.

40. B. N. Duke to Few, September 8, 1919, Few Papers.

41. Toms to Few, September 17, 1919, Few Papers.

42. Few to J. B. Duke, January 3, 1920, and Alex. H. Sands to Few, January 6, 1920, Few Papers. Few also secured a pledge from the General Education Board of $300,000 provided the college raised an additional $700,000, with the entire $1,000,000 to be added to endowment. When a Methodist educational campaign on which Few initially pinned his hopes failed because of the depression of 1921, Trinity's share was ultimately met by the Dukes, including especially J. B. Duke's gift of $1,000,000 in 1922. The story may be followed in the Few Papers, 1920–22, or in Porter, *Trinity and Duke*, p. 211.

43. Porter, *Trinity and Duke*, pp. 181–182, 187.

44. J. S. Bassett to W. K. Boyd, September 22, 1907, as cited in Porter, *Trinity and Duke*, p. 219.

45. James F. Gifford, Jr., *The Evolution of a Medical Center: A History of Medicine at Duke University to 1941* (Durham, N.C.: Duke University Press, 1972), pp. 11–34, has a more detailed account. Hereinafter cited as Gifford, *Medical Center*.

46. Few to R. M. Johnston, January 15, 1923, Few Papers.

47. Few to Dr. J. W. Long, March 23, 1923, Few Papers, and Few's chapter "The Medical School" in his unpublished and unfinished memoir, "The Beginnings of an American University," Few Papers. The University of North Carolina would not acquire its four-year medical school until after World War II.

48. Few to H. N. Snyder, September 4, 1919, Few Papers.

49. In Few's unfinished history, Few Papers.

50. Few to J. H. Separk, May 28, 1921, and Few to Toms, July 23, 1921, Few Papers.

51. Transcript of interview with Mrs. E. C. Marshall by Frank Rounds, Charlotte, N.C., 1963, p. 51. The Duke Endowment MSS, Duke University Library. Hereinafter cited as Rounds interview.

52. Rounds interview with Bennette E. Geer, April, 1963, p. 23.

53. Arthur Link, et al., eds., *The Papers of Woodrow Wilson, XIV, 1902–1903* (Princeton, N.J.: Princeton University Press, 1972), p. 269. Contrary to an often-repeated story, J. B. Duke could not have admired the chapel at Princeton, for it was built after his death.

54. Few-Brown Scrapbook of March–April, 1924, in the Frank C. Brown Papers, Duke University Archives. Hereinafter cited as Brown Papers.

55. Few to B. N. Duke, September 9, 1924, Few Papers.

56. G. G. Allen to Few, September 18, 1924, Few Papers.

57. R. L. Flowers to Few, October 29 (two letters) and 30, 1924, Few Papers. Unfortunately, the archives of the Rockefeller Foundation contain no records pertaining to these matters.

58. Flowers to Few, November 1, 1924, Few Papers.

59. Rounds interview with Norman Cocke, pp. 106–107.

60. The indenture creating the Duke Endowment is reprinted in an appendix in Durden, *The Dukes*, pp. 268–280; a fuller discussion of the whole matter is found on pp. 228ff. of the same.

61. Few to B. N. Duke, December 13, 1924, Few Papers.

2. Building on Two Campuses

1. Banks Arendall to W. P. Few, December 10, 1924, and P. H. Hanes, Jr., to Few, December 17, 1924, Few Papers.
2. J. G. Brown to Few, December 24, 1924, Few Papers.
3. Minutes, Board of Trustees, December 29, 1924, office of the Secretary of Duke University, and Porter, *Trinity and Duke*, pp. 234–235.
4. Ibid. While none of the formal documents relating to Duke University barred African Americans, state laws at that time did.
5. H. W. Chase to Few, December 9, 1924, Few Papers.
6. J. L. Jackson to Few, November 10 and 28, 1925; Few to Jackson, November 26 and 30, 1925, Few Papers.
7. Few to J. H. Reynolds, December 29, 1924, Few Papers.
8. A bitter attack on J. B. Duke and his philanthropy by a hostile newspaperman to whom he had earlier given one of his rare interviews may be found in Ben Dixon McNeill, "Duke," *American Mercury* 17 (August, 1929): 430–438.
9. *[Duke] Chronicle*, March 13, 1973; Lawrence Wright, "A Slow Dance with Progress," *Race Relations Reporter* (March, 1973): 14.
10. Few to J. B. Duke, January 31, 1924, Few Papers.
11. Alex. Sands to Few, May 5, 1924, Few Papers.
12. Few to J. B. Duke, October, 1924, Few Papers.
13. Frank Rounds's interview with Mrs. John Williams, January and July, 1964. Mrs. Williams was the widow of J. B. Duke's nephew, Buchanan Lyon.
14. William Preston Few, "The Beginnings of an American University," unfinished manuscript, pp. 6–7.
15. A more detailed account of the acquisition of the Duke Forest is included in chapter 13 on Duke Forest and the School of Forestry.
16. R. L. Flowers to B. N. Duke, May 8, 1925, Robert L. Flowers Papers, Duke University Archives. Hereinafter cited as Flowers Papers.
17. B. M. Hall's work diary, March 29–31, 1925, in the Brown Papers.
18. Frank Rounds's interview with Dr. Watson Rankin, pp. 57–58.
19. Hall, work diary, March 31, 1925.
20. The *Duke Dialogue*, April 14, 1989, has a story on Abele.
21. F. Brown to H. Trumbauer, March 20, 1925, Brown Papers; and Flowers to G. Allen, March 21, 1925, Flowers Papers.
22. Brown to Hall, April 18, 1925, Brown Papers.
23. J. S. Bassett to Few, May 20, 1920, Few Papers.
24. J. B. Duke's involvement in the planning of East campus may be traced in the Few, Flowers, and Brown Papers. Brown served as the chief liaison between Few and his associates in Durham and Trumbauer and his staff in Philadelphia, with various matters being referred to J. B. Duke for final decision.
25. Sands to Flowers, September 9, 14, 1925; and copy of Allen to Trumbauer, September 24, 1925, Flowers Papers.
26. Nanaline Duke at "Rough Point," Newport, R.I., to Few, August 30, 1925, Few Papers.
27. After J. B. Duke's death, Dr. George R. Minot, a specialist in Boston who advised Duke's doctors in New York, studied samples of Duke's blood and advised Dr. F. M. Hanes, March 21, 1945, that he did not believe Duke died of pernicious anemia but from "one of those fundamental disorders of blood formation that have commonly been called aregeneratory anemias." Copy in the Duke Endowment Papers, Manuscripts Department, Duke University Library.

28. "Last Will and Testament of James B. Duke," J. B. Duke Papers, Manuscripts Department, Duke University Library; John W. Jenkins, *James B. Duke: Master Builder* (New York: George H. Doran, 1927), pp. 299–302.

29. Ibid.

30. Forrest Hyde to Few, August 20, 1925, and Few to Hyde, August 24, 1925, Few Papers.

31. These matters are discussed in greater detail in Durden, *The Dukes*, pp. 247–251.

32. Few to B. N. Duke, September 23 and April 27, 1926, Few Papers.

33. Veysey, *Emergence of the American University*, p. 308.

34. Few to W. Rankin, September 16, 1927, and Few to J. A. Thomas, April 4, 1928, Few Papers.

35. New York *Evening Post*, December 13, 1927; New York *Sunday News*, August 4, 1935.

36. Few to Bruce Craven, November 17, 1925, Few Papers.

37. Few to Craven, October 1, 1929, and Few to Dr. Albert Anderson, March 24, 1927, Few Papers.

38. These developments may be traced in the Flowers and Brown Papers

39. Few to E. B. Halstead, September 16, 1927, Few Papers.

40. Few to C. Toms, May 14 and 19, 1927; Toms to Few, May 24, 1927; Few to Mrs. Anthony J. D. (Mary Duke) Biddle, June 23, 1928; and Mrs. Biddle to Few, July 16, 1928, Few Papers.

41. Raleigh *News & Observer*, April 28, 1928; Few also published the plan for the institute in the *Alumni Register of Duke University* 15 (February, 1929): 50–52.

42. Duke Memorial MSS, Duke University Archives.

43. W. K. Boyd to Thomas, March 26, 1929, Duke Memorial MSS.

44. P. Gross to Thomas, June 19, 1929, Duke Memorial MSS.

45. Few to Thomas, February 26, 1929, Duke Memorial MSS.

46. Sands to Thomas, April 15, 1936, Duke Memorial MSS.

47. Few to his nephew, Benjamin Few, October 26, 1917, and Few to Mrs. J. C. Kilgo, October 9, 1922, Few Papers.

48. Roger Geiger notes in *To Advance Knowledge: The Growth of American Research Universities* (New York: Oxford University Press, 1986), p. 203, that John Grier Hibben, Woodrow Wilson's successor as president of Princeton, made a conscious attempt to educate Princeton alumni about the place of research and the graduate school in a leading university. Geiger suggests that Hibben succeeded in effectively linking the advancement of knowledge to Princeton's traditional teaching mission, and the argument became "an indispensable nexus between the donor constituency of college alumni and an erudite, research-minded faculty."

49. Few, "Government and Administration," chapter in "The Beginnings of an American University."

50. Few to W. Buttrick, February 3, 1926, and Buttrick to Few, February 6, 1926, Few MSS.

51. Few to Dr. A. Flexner, June 28, 1926, Few MSS.

52. The documents in the Few MSS supporting these statements are numerous, though not always explicit, since the GEB officials apparently explained their reasons only in oral rather than written form. One of the clearest summaries is in Few to Allen, November 6, 1929, Few MSS.

53. Few, "The Duke Endowment and Duke University," 8 pp. Privately printed, n.d. [1929], n.p. Duke University Archives.

54. Few to Perkins, March 19, 1927, and Perkins to Few, March 24, 1927. As the above letters suggest, Allen and Perkins worked together closely, and each usually spoke for the other.

55. Toms to Few, May 24, 1927, Few MSS. Whether Allen saw Flexner is not known.
56. Few to Trevor Arnett, October 10, 1929, Few MSS.
57. Arnett to Few, November 22, 1929, Few MSS.
58. Few to Toms, November 27, 1929, Few MSS.
59. Few to Perkins, January 13, 1930, Few MSS.

3. Crisis in University Governance

1. Resolution on tuition, March 3, 1928, Flowers Papers.
2. John P. Jones to W. P. Few, November 15, 1927, Flowers Papers. Letters to Few, especially concerning business matters, are frequently found in the Flowers Papers and vice versa. In 1927–28 the University of North Carolina in Chapel Hill had a tuition-matriculation charge of $111 for in-state and $136 for out-of-state students.
3. W. R. Perkins to Few, December 15, 1930, Few Papers.
4. Few to Perkins, December 19, 1930, Few Papers.
5. Perkins to Few, January 7, 1931, Few Papers.
6. Few to Perkins, January 12, 1931, Few Papers. Earlier drafts of this letter point up Few's labors on it.
7. Perkins to Few, January 15, 1931, Few Papers.
8. As late as 1939, Wannamaker informed a faculty member that all organizations at Duke were required to submit names of outside speakers whom they wished to invite to the university committee on lectures. That committee consisted of himself, Flowers, and Henry R. Dwire, the director of public relations and alumni affairs.
9. G. Allen to Few, October 10, 1932, Few Papers.
10. Few to Allen, October 15, 1932, Few Papers.
11. Allen to Few, October 18, 1932, Few Papers. Italics in original here and hereinafter.
12. Few to Allen, March 9, 1933, Few Papers.
13. Few to Clinton Toms, January 9, 1933, Few Papers. Few had three sons still living at home, and one of the family's three bedrooms he described as a small one that had been built as a servant's room.
14. Few to Allen, September 20, 1933, and Few to Alex. H. Sands, January 16, 1934, Few Papers. The amounts of the loans are not indicated.
15. Few to Perkins, January 1, 1934, Few Papers.
16. Few to Perkins, February 2, 1934, Few Papers.
17. Few to William McDougall, July 25, 1933, Few Papers.
18. Questionnaire filled out for the General Education Board, February 24, 1938, box 31, Flowers Papers.
19. R. L. Flowers to Sands, April 11, 1933, Flowers Papers; and Few to Allen, September 10, 1933, Few Papers. Flowers stated that the American Council of Education had issued a list of institutions of higher learning in the United States that had finished 1932–33 without salary cuts and without a deficit; it was a "very short list" and he was happy to see Duke's name included. Flowers to W. F. McDowell, October 23, 1933, Flowers Papers.
20. *Chronicle*, September–December 1933, Duke University Archives.
21. "The Vision of King Paucus," Few Papers; J. Miller to Perkins, November 9, 1933, with Perkins to Few, March 2, 1934, Few Papers. Most faculty members at Duke had probably never read J. B. Duke's indenture creating the Duke Endowment; Miller clearly had. Perkins replied to Miller that he never paid attention to anonymous communications. Perkins to Miller, November 14, 1933, Few Papers.
22. Mrs. Cornwall (Janet Earl) Miller to Mrs. Susan Singleton Rose, October 9, 1979,

Duke University Archives. In this letter, Mrs. Miller explains to her former classmate at Duke that Seeman suggested that she write the "spoof," which Mrs. Rose typed. For Seeman's disingenuous letter denying that he had "any part whatever in connection with the writing or circulation of the King Paucus lampoon," see E. Seeman to Flowers, February 13, 1934, Flowers Papers.

23. Biographical data in Susan S. Rose, "A Review of *American Gold* by Ernest Seeman . . . ," Duke University Archives; Seeman to Flowers, May 25, 1928, and January 17, 1929; and Seeman to W. K. Boyd, December 10, 1929, Flowers Papers.

24. Flowers to J. F. Rippy, August 24, 1932, and Seeman to H. W. Dwire, September 19, 1933, Flowers Papers.

25. Transcript of an interview with Seeman in 1971, appendix 2 of Susan S. Rose, "A Review of *American Gold* . . . ," and Exie Duncan's "Explorers' Club" photograph album, Duke University Archives.

26. *Who's Who in America* (Chicago: A. N. Marquis, 1950), vol. 26, pp. 1896–1897. Both Miller and the law school are dealt with in greater detail in chapter 12.

27. Few to Perkins, February 6, 1930, Flowers Papers.

28. Flowers to Perkins, July 25, 1931, Flowers Papers.

29. Miller to Few and Flowers, November 4, 1930, and May 5, 1931, Few Papers.

30. Miller to Few and Flowers, December 1, 1931; Perkins to Few, December 3, 1931; Miller to Few and Flowers, January 6, 1931; and Miller to Few and Flowers, April 12 and 14, 1932, Few Papers.

31. Folder on "Student Rebellion 1934," Duke University Archives; Perkins to Few, February 8, 1934, Few Papers, contains a copy of the telegram as well as Perkins's statement that he had not responded to the students and knew that Few could handle the matter adequately.

32. *Durham Morning Herald*, February 7 and 8, 1934. Ernest Seeman's probable role in the affair as well as in the writing of the stories is suggested by the story in the *Durham Morning Herald*, February 13, 1934.

33. *Durham Morning Herald*, February 9, 10, 1934.

34. *Chronicle*, February 28, March 7, and April 18, 1934.

35. Durham *Sun*, February 17, 1934.

36. Few to Perkins, February 12, 1934, Few Papers.

37. Letters between Few, Perkins, and Willis Smith concerning these matters are numerous during May and June, 1934, Few Papers.

38. Few to Perkins, June 1, 1934, and Few to Toms, July 13, 1934, Few Papers.

39. J. Bruton to Few, December 17, 1934, Few Papers.

40. Bruton to Few, January 28, February 11, and March 5, 1935, Few Papers; "Minutes of the Board of Trustees of Duke University, February 28, 1934 through May 22, 1943," March 27, 1935, office of the Secretary of Duke University. Few finally abandoned further efforts to buttress the Endowment's representation on the executive committees by further changes in the by-laws.

41. Few to Allen, October 3, 1935, Few Papers. Both the university and the Endowment at a much later time moved away from the formal, legalized linkage of boards.

42. William A. Perlzweig to the editor, *New Republic*, October 13, 1936, Few Papers.

4. The Natural Sciences, Mathematics, and Engineering

1. From the organization of the university in December, 1924, until the opening of the separate Woman's College in September, 1930, Trinity College continued to have both

male and female students; after that date, and until the separate Woman's College was abolished in 1972, there were two undergraduate colleges of arts and sciences, although both shared the same faculty and curriculum and, after the freshman year, most of the same classes.

2. Edwin B. Wilson to William McDougall, January 7, 1928, Few Papers.

3. The law school is discussed in more detail in chapter 12.

4. "Memorandum Concerning Duke University," [1927?], Few Papers.

5. Bennett Harvie Branscomb, *Purely Academic: An Autobiography* (Nashville, Tenn.: Vanderbilt University Press, 1978), p. 91. Hereinafter cited as Branscomb, *Purely Academic*.

6. This is dealt with more extensively in chapter 8.

7. W. H. Wannamaker to G. E. Hoffman, February 4, 1931, William Hanes Wannamaker Papers, Duke University Archives. Hereinafter cited as Wannamaker Papers.

8. Wannamaker to H. L. Blomquist in botany, April 4, 1932, Wannamaker Papers.

9. Blomquist to H. S. Perry at Cornell, March 7, 1932, Wannamaker Papers.

10. Wannamaker to D. H. Gilpatrick, March 13, 1945, Wannamaker Papers.

11. Wannamaker to John C. Adams, July 7 and August 3, 1935, Wannamaker Papers.

12. A. S. Pearse in Zoology to Wannamaker, February 9, 1931, Wannamaker Papers.

13. Wannamaker to Carlyle Campbell, March 5, 1947, Wannamaker Papers.

14. Wannamaker to A. S. Wilson, July 9, 1943, Wannamaker Papers.

15. William B. Hamilton, "Fifty Years of Liberalism and Learning," in W. B. Hamilton, ed., *Fifty Years of The South Atlantic Quarterly, 1902–1952* (Durham, N.C.: Duke University Press, 1952), p. 3.

16. M. A. Smith to Wannamaker, July 19, 1934, Wannamaker Papers. The other five with the twelve-hour load were the Universities of Texas and Virginia, Washington and Lee, Vanderbilt, and Agnes Scott College.

17. H. E. Myers to Wannamaker, April 3, 1944, and Wannamaker to Myers, April 6 and May 2, 1944, Wannamaker Papers.

18. In commenting on the faculty of Trinity College in 1924, before the university was organized, Branscomb noted that the college had a number of scholars of superior quality, and he named N. I. White in English, W. K. Boyd in history, and P. M. Gross in chemistry. But, he added, there was also "an adequate supply of bulbs of low wattage." Branscomb, *Purely Academic*, p. 80.

19. Wannamaker to ———, July 28, 1927, Wannamaker Papers.

20. Wannamaker to ———, November 1, 1932, Wannamaker Papers.

21. ——— to Wannamaker, February 25, 1936, Wannamaker Papers.

22. W. B. Bell to Few, December 9, 1927, and Few to Bell, December 24, 1927, Few Papers.

23. Few to J. R. McCain, November 22, 1929, Few Papers.

24. These figures are based on letters of appointment in the Few and Wannamaker Papers. That the ranges continued throughout the 1930s is shown by Wannamaker to Felix Johnson, September 2, 1941, and Wannamaker to A. R. Newsome, December 5, 1941, Wannamaker Papers. A clipping from *School and Society*, November 25, 1930, in the Few Papers announced a new salary scale for Harvard's faculty in arts and sciences: professors, $8,000 to $12,000; associate professors, $6,000 to $7,000; assistant professors, $4,000 to $5,500; and instructors, maximum of $3,000.

25. Wannamaker to P. Kramer, May 1, 1931, and Kramer to Wannamaker, May 4, 1931, Wannamaker Papers.

26. W. K. Boyd to Wannamaker, March 25, 1931, Wannamaker Papers; see also Boyd to W. Few, March 27, 1931, Few Papers.

27. Memorandum on increased salaries, 1939–40, August 2, 1939, Wannamaker Papers.

28. [P. Gross?], "The Organization and Administration of the Department of Chemistry," [1925 or 1926?], folder on "Departmental Development and Plans," box no. 1, records of the Department of Chemistry, 1924–, Duke University Archives. Hereinafter cited as Chemistry Records.

29. Memorandum of October 21, 1926, ibid.

30. There is much material in the Chemistry Records on the collaboration of the Duke chemists and Trumbauer's architectural staff, with Frank C. Brown as the busy intermediary. Because of the route of the rail line that was built up into the quadrangles during the construction of the West campus, the chemistry department could not occupy its new building until the spring of 1931, some months after the other new buildings on West were occupied.

31. Charles Bradsher to the author, October 10, 1989. No attempt will be made in the case of chemistry or any other department to name all of the faculty members; rather, names of most of those who spent a substantial part or all of their careers at Duke or who played significant roles, either at Duke or in their respective disciplines, will be included.

32. Few to T. W. Richards, March 15, 1926, Few Papers.

33. G. B. Pegram to Wannamaker, August 16, 1928, and W. Vosburgh to Wannamaker, August 17, 1928, Wannamaker Papers.

34. Gross to L. Bigelow, May 15, 1929, and C. Hauser to Gross, June 20, 1929, Chemistry Records.

35. Gross to James Kendall at the University of Edinburgh, December 9, 1931, and Gross to W. Vosburgh in Edinburgh, April 14, 1933, Chemistry Records. Gross's attempt to arrange an exchange for Saylor at the University of Aberdeen in 1934–35 fell through because of difficulties at Aberdeen.

36. Gross to Dean W. K. Greene, May 26, 1932, Chemistry Records.

37. Gross to Wannamaker, November 14, 1937, Wannamaker Papers.

38. Wannamaker to Gross, December 6, 1937, Wannamaker Papers. Leading American scientists, like their counterparts in Europe, were excited about the theoretical and experimental work then going on in the field of atomic physics.

39. Folder on "Dr. London (Paris), correspondence concerning," in box no. 3, Chemistry Records; and Vosburgh to Gross, July 26, 1938, ibid.

40. A. Pearse to F. F. Russell, February 9, 1927 in Arthur S. Pearse Papers, Correspondence, Duke University Archives. Hereinafter cited as Pearse Papers.

41. Pearse to W. G. Smilie, September 19, 1927, Pearse Papers.

42. A. S. Pearse, *Adventure: Trying to Be A Zoologist* (Durham, N.C., 1942), p. 43.

43. Pearse to ——— , October 23, 1932, Pearse Papers.

44. Blomquist to Wannamaker, July 11, 1927, and Wannamaker to Blomquist, July 15, 1927, Wannamaker Papers.

45. A. S. Pearse, "A History of Biology at Duke University," *BIOS* 20 (March, 1949): 13. Reprint in Duke University Archives; hereafter cited as Pearse, "A History."

46. Pearse, "A History," p. 16.

47. E. Seeman to Pearse, January 3, 1928, Pearse Papers.

48. W. C. Allee to Pearse, December 24, 1930, Pearse Papers. Most of the correspondence in this large collection has to do with *Ecological Monographs*, which Pearse edited, with help from Clarence Korstian in forestry, until his retirement. The journal ran a deficit of around two thousand dollars a year throughout the 1930s. In 1947, H. J. Oosting in botany persuaded the Duke University Press to take over the publication of *Ecology*, which had grown too expensive for the Brooklyn Botanic Gardens.

49. Wannamaker to K. Jeffers, February 22, 1937, Wannamaker Papers.

50. L. R. Jones to Wannamaker, August 10, 1927, Wannamaker Papers.

51. Pearse to Wannamaker, February 9, 1931, and Wannamaker to K. Blunt, February 24, 1943, Wannamaker Papers.

52. H. J. Oosting to Blomquist, January 25 and March 23, 1932, and Blomquist to Oosting, February 4 and April 1, 1932, Wannamaker Papers.

53. H. S. Perry to Blomquist, February 19 and April 5, 1932, and Wannamaker to Blomquist, April 4, 1932, Wannamaker Papers.

54. Blomquist to Wannamaker, February 19, 1937, Wannamaker Papers.

55. Pearse to Few, March 3, 1933, Few Papers.

56. Pearse, "A History," p. 11.

57. See chapter 11 on the School of Forestry.

58. Pearse, *Adventure: Trying to Be a Zoologist*, p. 44.

59. Jackson Davis of the General Education Board to Pearse, September 19, 1941; W. W. Brierley of the GEB to Flowers, November 17, 1941; Pearse to Davis, March 9, 1942; and Pearse to Flowers, May 25, 1944, Pearse Papers.

60. Pearse, *Adventure: Trying to Be a Zoologist*, p. 44.

61. Few to Pearse, October 21, 1930, Few Papers.

62. Pearse to Few, April 5, 1933, Few Papers.

63. Pearse to Few, June 20, 1938, Pearse Papers.

64. Pearse to Wannamaker, February 15, 1939, Wannamaker Papers.

65. I. E. Gray to Wannamaker, May 26, 1941, Wannamaker Papers.

66. Oosting to Wannamaker, May 29, 1942, and Wannamaker to Oosting, June 2, 1942, Wannamaker Papers. Another carryover from the Trinity College era was the custom of calling upon newcomers to the faculty, quite often on Sunday afternoon, sometimes with advance notice and sometimes without—and the latter case could be tricky. Sunday afternoon calls by many older members of the faculty continued well after World War II, and while it was regarded as quaint, if not bizarre, by less traditional newcomers, the practice represented a friendly echo of a passing era.

67. Wannamaker to Few, February 25, 1935, Wannamaker Papers.

68. C. Edwards to Few, August 17, 1926 (two letters), Few Papers.

69. Few to R. S. Kirby, August 29, 1927, Few Papers. The "or" is significant, for it suggests the dichotomy in Few's mind between two functions that would, over the long haul, be hard to separate in a research university.

70. John T. Tate to Edwards, November 25, 1927, Few Papers.

71. A. H. Compton to Few, July 16, 1929, Few Papers.

72. Few to Allen, August 2, 1929, Few Papers.

73. Few to Perkins, September 20, 1929, Few Papers.

74. Few to Bishop E. D. Mouzon, February 20, 1932, Few Papers.

75. A thick folder on Hertha Sponer in the files of the Duke University News Service Biographies, University Archives, is a convenient source of information.

76. Warren Weaver of the Rockefeller Foundation to Edwards, December 8, 1933; Edwards to Few, May 1, 1934; and Dorothy L. Mackay to Alice Baldwin, June 11, 1934, Few Papers.

77. Edwards to Sponer, March 25, 1935; Few to Sponer, April 27, 1935; Few to F. B. Hansom of the Rockefeller Foundation, March 7, 1936; and Hansom to Few, March 23, 1936, Few Papers.

78. R. A. Milliken to Few, June 24, 1936, Few Papers.

79. Few to Milliken, July 9, 1936, Few Papers.

80. Few to G. Pegram, February 13, 1935, and Pegram to Few, February 16, 1935, Few Papers.

81. Few to Pegram, January 12, 1937, for Gross's recommendation of Teller; Teller to Wannamaker, ca. March 17, 1937; Few to Teller, March 18, 1937; and Teller to Few, March 25, 1937, Few Papers.

82. Hatley to Wannamaker, April 23, 1936, Wannamaker Papers.

83. Wannamaker to Flowers, July 15, 1936, Wannamaker Papers.

84. Few to L. Nordheim, May 11, 1937, and Nordheim to Few, May 14, 1937, Few Papers.

85. E. H. McGregor to Flowers, May 12, 1944, Flowers Papers.

86. Folder on W. W. Elliott in the Duke News Bureau files.

87. R. D. Carmichael at Illinois to Few, April 20, 29, and May 13, 1927, Few Papers.

88. Pegram to Few, September 16 and 17, 1927, and R.G.D. Richardson to Few, April 11, 1929, Few Papers.

89. Richardson to Few, January 13, 1936, Few Papers.

90. See report of A. M. Baldwin, May 29, 1937, Alice Baldwin Papers, Duke University Archives. Hereinafter cited as Baldwin Papers.

91. H. H. Mitchell at Pennsylvania to J. Thomas, February 10, 1932, and G. H. Hardy at Oxford to Thomas, January 24, 1932, Wannamaker Papers.

92. Thomas to Wannamaker, March 6, 1936, Wannamaker Papers.

93. W. W. Elliott, J. H. Roberts, A. O. Hickson, E. R. C. Miles, and J. M. Thomas to Wannamaker, March 11, 1936, Wannamaker Papers.

94. G. D. Birkhoff to Elliott, February 21, 1932, Wannamaker Papers.

95. J. Gergen to Wannamaker, February 18, 1941, and Thomas to Wannamaker, March 11, 1941, Wannamaker Papers.

96. J. M. Thomas, "A Correction to the Duke University Directory, November 20, 1966," in folder on Thomas in the Duke News Bureau biographical files.

97. Rudolph, *The American College and University*, pp. 228–231, 246.

98. Earl Wolfslagel, "Big Little Man in Engineering," *Durham Sun*, September 1, 1964.

99. *Alumni Register* 17 (May, 1931): 148–150.

100. Wyatt T. Dixon, "Trinity Park School," *Durham Sun*, February 7, 1941.

101. Ralph T. Mathews, "Mechanical Engineering at Duke University—As I Knew It," manuscript of speech given to an honorary society in engineering at Duke, December 6, 1952, in the Ralph T. Mathews Papers, records of the College of Engineering, Duke University Archives. This collection also contains an interesting photograph album with Mathews's pictures of the razing of the old Branson building and the construction of the new Branson, as well as of the equipment in the mechanical engineering laboratory. Mathews left Duke in 1936 to get his master's degree at Michigan and then go into industry.

102. H. C. Bird to Few, February 3, 1936, Few Papers.

103. Few to H. Trumbauer, March 6, 1936, Few Papers.

104. Harry A. Curtis to Flowers, May 3, 1937, Few Papers.

105. W. Seeley to Wannamaker, May 21, 1934, Wannamaker Papers.

106. Few to Curtis, May 10, 1937, Few Papers.

107. Seeley to Flowers, May 12, 1937, and Flowers to Curtis, May 18, 1937, Flowers Papers.

108. Flowers to Curtis, July 6, 1937, Flowers Papers.

109. Bill Edwards, E. E. '59, "The Engineers of Southgate," *Duke Engineer* (October, 1957), p. 13.

110. "Report of the Committee on Colleges to the Trustees . . . , February 2, 1938," folder on Engineering Division in subject file, box 92, Few Papers.

111. Few to W. S. Lee, November 17, 1931, Few Papers.

112. E. W. Berry to Few, December 23, 1935, and W. J. McCaughey to Wannamaker, March 31, 1936, Few Papers.

5. The Social Sciences and the Humanities

1. W. Few to G. F. Thomas, March 1, 1927, and Few to G. W. Cram at Harvard, March 11, 1926, Few Papers.

2. Seymour H. Mauskopf and Michael R. McVaugh, *The Elusive Science: Origins of Experimental Psychical Research* (Baltimore, Md.: Johns Hopkins University Press, 1980), p. 57. Hereinafter cited as Mauskopf and McVaugh, *Elusive Science*.

3. Ibid., pp. 57–58.

4. W. McDougall to Few (ca. April 12, 1926), Few Papers.

5. Few to McDougall, April 13, 1926, Few Papers.

6. McDougall to Few, April 23, 1926, and Few to McDougall, April 27, 1926, Few Papers.

7. McDougall to Few, May 3, 1926, Few Papers.

8. Luther A. Weigle, dean of the Yale Divinity School, to E. A. Soper, dean of Duke's School of Religion, June 18, 1926, Few Papers.

9. McDougall to Few, July 4 and October 6, 1926, and Few to McDougall, July 24, 1926, Few Papers.

10. Few to McDougall, March 10, 1928, and McDougall to Few, April 9, 1928, Few Papers; Mauskopf and McVaugh, *Elusive Science*, pp. 71–80. Although Mauskopf and McVaugh have much material on McDougall in their useful study, their primary focus is on the Rhines and their lifelong work at Duke in parapsychology.

11. McDougall to Few, January 6, 1927, Few Papers.

12. McDougall to Few, January 22, 1931, Few Papers.

13. H. Lundholm to A. A. Wilkinson, May 8, 1941, in the folder on Lundholm in files of the Duke News Bureau.

14. Few to W. Stern, January 18, 1934, and Stern to Few, January 31, April 10, 1934, Few Papers.

15. The title of the quarterly was changed to *Journal of Personality* in 1945.

16. Mauskopf and McVaugh, pp. 102, 151–158.

17. Ibid., p. 135.

18. Mauskopf and McVaugh, in *Elusive Science*, pp. 136–139, give more details concerning these developments.

19. J. B. Rhine to Gardner Murphy, June 19, 1936, as quoted in ibid., p. 147.

20. Few to Rhine, August 12, 1935, and Rhine to Few, August 15, 1935, Few Papers.

21. Few to McDougall, June 1, 1934, Few Papers.

22. Few to McDougall, February 19, 1938, Few Papers.

23. Mauskopf and McVaugh, *Elusive Science*, p. 151.

24. Porter, *Trinity and Duke*, pp. 71, 74.

25. C. Ellwood to W. Glasson, December 21, 1929, Few Papers.

26. Ellwood to H. Jensen, October 21, 1930, and March 17, 1931, Few Papers.

27. Ellwood to Few, January 26, 1934, Few Papers.

28. Ellwood to Few, March 29, 1940, Few Papers.

29. George G. Wilson to Few, May 27, 1927, Few Papers.

30. R. Rankin to E. S. Corwin at Princeton, May 7, 1935, Robert S. Rankin Papers, Duke University Archives.

31. W. Y. Elliott to Wilson, April 27, 1935, and B. F. Wright, Jr., to Wilson, May 5, 1935, Robert R. Wilson Papers, Duke University Archives.

32. Cole has described his arrival and early years at Duke in *The Recollections of R. Taylor Cole* (Durham, N.C.: Duke University Press, 1983), pp. 54–69.

33. Leonard Silk in the *New York Times*, July 17, 1974.

34. Glasson to C. Hoover, July 5, 1934, C. B. Hoover Papers, University Archives; Few to Hoover, April 13, 1935, Few Papers.

35. Leonard Silk, "The Economics of Joseph J. Spengler," typed manuscript in the folder on Spengler, Biographical File, Duke University Archives.

36. Folder on Spengler, Biographical File, Duke University Archives.

37. Hoover to W. Wannamaker, August 6, 1942, Wannamaker Papers.

38. Hoover to Wannamaker, April 28, 1939, Wannamaker Papers.

39. Glasson to Few, February 22, 1937, Wannamaker Papers.

40. Nora Chaffin, in *Trinity College, 1839–1892*, elaborately documents the earlier phases, while Earl Porter, in *Trinity and Duke*, emphasizes the later aspects.

41. Durden, *The Dukes*, pp. 274, 278.

42. E. D. Soper to P. H. Vieth, May 24, 1926, School of Religion Papers, Duke University Archives.

43. Willard B. Gatewood, *Eugene Clyde Brooks: Educator and Public Servant* (Durham, N.C.: Duke University Press, 1960) p. ii; Porter, *Trinity and Duke*, pp. 148–149, 160–161.

44. H. Holton to Few, December 14, 1926, Few Papers.

45. Porter, *Trinity and Duke*, p. 216.

46. Holton to Few, August 21, 1930, Few Papers.

47. Holton to Few, December 22, 1930, Few Papers.

48. Few to C. Toms, July 10, 1936, Few Papers.

49. This is best reflected in William B. Hamilton, "Duke University and the Schools: The First Century," in W. H. Cartwright and W. B. Hamilton, eds., *The Duke University Centennial Conference in Teacher Training* (Durham, N.C.: Duke University Press, 1953), a volume in the *Historical Papers of the Trinity College Historical Society*.

50. J. S. Bassett to R. Flowers, October 26, 1925, Flowers Papers.

51. More information on Baldwin may be found in the chapter on the Woman's College.

52. W. Boyd to Flowers, January 19, 1925, Flowers Papers.

53. Boyd to Few, November 25, 1925, Few Papers.

54. Boyd to Flowers, [July 31 (?), 1925], Flowers Papers. Another important historian who joined the department in 1925, Richard H. Shryock, also left to return to his alma mater, the University of Pennsylvania, in 1938. Although he came to Duke in United States history, he later became a distinguished pioneer in medical history.

55. Boyd to Few, November 25, 1927, Few Papers.

56. W. Boyd, undated memorandum on international studies at Duke, [October 1930?], Few Papers.

57. Boyd and W. Laprade to Wannamaker, January 28, 1936, Wannamaker Papers.

58. Laprade to Wannamaker, June 25, 1946, Wannamaker Papers.

59. R. Shryock, et al., to Few, January 31, 1938, Wannamaker Papers.

60. As mentioned in an earlier footnote, no attempt is made to discuss all persons who taught in any given department; only those are discussed who spent their full careers or a large part of them at Duke or who were otherwise significant for one reason or another. Among others who taught in history at Duke in the 1930s and 1940s, but who did not remain, were Dorothy Mackay Quynn, Shelby McCloy, Joseph C. Robert, and Bayrd Still.

61. Laprade to Wannamaker, April 15, 1936, Wannamaker Papers.

62. H. Parker to Roger Marshall, January 16, 1972, in Parker folder, News Service biographical file, Duke Archives.

63. Clarence Gohdes, *Pioneers in English at Trinity and Duke* (Durham, N.C., 1988), p. 21.

This detailed and lively pamphlet is the source of part of the information that follows.

64. Few to G. Kittredge, February 27, 1925; and Few to W. A. Neilson, January 23, 1926, Few Papers.

65. Few to W. A. Neilson, May 30, 1927, Few Papers.

66. A. Gilbert to Few, April 13, 1925, and additional comments, Few Papers.

67. A. C. Jordan, Lewis Leary, and C. E. Ward, "Report of the Committee on Minimum Essentials for English 1 and 2," with letter of April 19, 1943, Wannamaker Papers.

68. Memorandum on grades in English I for fall, 1941, filed at February 29, 1942, Wannamaker Papers. That the students of the Woman's College did considerably better in English than the men in Trinity College and the School of Engineering is shown by the fact that only 1 woman (out of 276) failed English I as compared to 36 men in Trinity (out of 412) and 21 men in engineering (out of 93). At the other end of the scale, 20 women made A's as compared to 3 men in Trinity and 1 man in engineering.

69. J. Hubbell to Few, March 3, 1928, Few Papers.

70. Others in the American field who taught at Duke but who ultimately moved to other universities were Lewis N. Chase, Charles R. Anderson, and Lewis Leary.

71. These matters are discussed in chapter 7.

72. Announcement of W. K. Greene's appointment, January 3, 1928, Few Papers.

73. N. White to Few, November 4, 1937, Few Papers.

74. Few to E. T. Clarke, February 21, 1938; and Few to C. H. Barnwell, dean at University of Alabama, February 19, 1937, Few Papers.

75. Wannamaker to J. A. Walz, July 25, 1915, Wannamaker Papers.

76. Wannamaker to G. Greever, February 23, 1926, Wannamaker Papers.

77. Wannamaker to J. A. von Dohlen, May 24, 1928, Wannamaker Papers.

78. Copy, Barney Jones to J. N. Truesdale, June 24, 1974, in folder on Truesdale, Biographical File, University Archives.

79. W. P. Few, "Wm. Ivy Cranford," *Alumni Register*, 22 (September, 1936): 224.

80. Few to W. R. Perkins, June 22, 1929, Few Papers.

81. A. H. Widgery to Wannamaker, December 12, 1938, Wannamaker Papers.

82. Statement by Lewis W. Beck in folder on Widgery in Duke News Service File, University Archives. In his memoir, *A Philosopher's Pilgrimage* (London: Allen and Unwin, 1961), Widgery candidly expressed his low opinion of Duke's administrators, with the exception of Few, and declared that "the majority [of Duke's faculty] appeared to me to lack general culture" (pp. 158–159). Concerning the democratic basis of faculty meetings, where young assistant professors had a vote equal to that of the most experienced full professors, he growled: "For the incompetent to restrict the activities of the competent is a caricature of democracy" (p. 159).

83. These matters are treated more fully in the chapter on the Woman's College because Dean Alice Baldwin was also closely involved.

84. These matters are dealt with more extensively in chapter 10 on the School of Religion.

85. In his memoir, *I Remember: Recollections and Reminiscences of Alma Mater* (Durham, N.C.: Seeman Printery, 1954), Spence describes his long involvement with pageantry, Duke sports, and other aspects of campus life. Concerning his cool relations with Harvie Branscomb, a later dean of the Divinity School, Spence candidly notes: "But for some reason Dr. Branscomb did not seem to appreciate me as much as I did myself" (p. 247).

86. These matters are dealt with in more detail in chapter 10.

87. Since the dean of the Woman's College, Alice Baldwin, played a key role in the beginnings of both these departments on the East campus, the subject is treated in more detail in chapter 8.

88. Rudolph, *The American College and University*, pp. 475–476.

89. Few to H. Trumbauer, January 30, 1936, Few Papers.

90. The full story of the offer by W. H. Ackland and its ultimate rejection by Duke is told in chapter 9.

6. The Graduate School of Arts and Sciences

1. Geiger, *American Research Universities*, p. 203. Much later Duke's graduate school would drop the "Arts and Sciences" from its name because advanced degrees in various of the professional schools were offered through the graduate school.

2. W. H. Glasson to W. Few, June 1, 1925, Few Papers.

3. Glasson to Few, December 17, 1925, Few Papers.

4. W. Wannamaker to Few, January 29, 1926, Few Papers.

5. Few to Glasson, September 20, 1926, Few Papers.

6. Various professors to Few, December 22, 1926, Few Papers.

7. Copy of resolution, February 10, 1927, Few Papers; *New York Times*, February 11, 1927; and Charles W. Tillett to Few, February 11, 1927, Few Papers.

8. J. Boyd to Few, February 12, 1927, Few Papers.

9. W. D. Hooper to Few, February 12, 1927, and W. L. Poteat to Few, February 21, 1927, Few Papers.

10. W. Rose to Few, November 3, 1927, Few Papers.

11. A. Pearse to H. G. Thorkelson of the Rockefeller Foundation, September 17, 1928, Few Papers.

12. Few to C. R. Mann, December 14, 1928, Few Papers. For Few's report on the Duke program to the Association of American Colleges, see *Alumni Register* 15 (March, 1929): 85.

13. Few to G. Allen, January 3, 1930, Few Papers.

14. Few to W. Perkins, January 3, 1930, Few Papers.

15. Glasson to Few, July 19, 1930, Few Papers.

16. F. Graham to Few, July 21, 1931; Few to Graham, July 24, 1931; and Graham to Few, July 31, 1931, Few Papers.

17. Remarks of Few at inaugural dinner for Graham, November 11, 1931; and Few to Clarence Poe, editor of the *Progressive Farmer*, December 21, 1931, Few Papers.

18. Unidentified newspaper clipping, November 22, 1932, Few Papers.

19. Graham to Few, November 10, 1933, Few Papers.

20. General Education Board to Few, December 17, 1935, Few Papers.

21. Few to Perkins, March 21, 1935, Few Papers.

22. Few to Graham, November 13, 1936, Few Papers.

23. Copy of Graham to R. B. Downs, cochairman of the Committee on Intellectual Cooperation, April 28, 1937, Few Papers.

24. Report by F. M. Hanes, October 28, 1937, Few Papers.

25. Few to Allen, August 5, 1933, Few Papers.

26. Copy, Glasson to Terrell Spencer, October 26, 1936, Few Papers.

27. J. M. Thomas to Few, February 9, 1937, Few Papers.

28. Wannamaker to Few, October 10, 1937, Few Papers.

29. Few to Guy Snavely, February 21, 1938, Few Papers.

30. Few to Graham, April 22, 1938, and H. C. Horack to Few, May 4, 1938, with newspaper clipping, Few Papers.

31. C. B. Hoover to W. W. Pierson, October 25, 1938, Few Papers.

32. Few to Graham, December 22, 1938, Few Papers.

33. Few to Graham, June 16, 1939, and February 7, 1940, Few Papers.

34. Few to Chancellor O. C. Carmichael, August 12, 1939, Few Papers.

35. Porter, *Trinity and Duke*, p. 91.

36. Anne Roney was the sister of Washington Duke's second wife, Artelia Roney Duke.

37. W. K. Boyd and J. P. Breedlove, "Institutional Growth," *Duke University Library Bulletin* 1 (October, 1929): 1–2.

38. Joseph P. Breedlove, *Duke University Library, 1840–1940* (Durham, N.C.: Friends of Duke University Library, 1955), pp. 29–30. The old library was carefully dismantled and then rebuilt, as a gift, at Kittrell College, an institution for African Americans that the Dukes had long assisted. The building was later destroyed in a fire.

39. W. T. Laprade to Few, June 5, 1926, Few Papers.

40. J. F. Rippy to Few, April 29, 1928; Rippy to Flowers, December 8, 1928; and V. A. Belaunde [and Rippy] to Flowers, February 13, 1929, Flowers Papers.

41. W. K. Boyd and J. P. Breedlove, "Institutional Growth," p. 4.

42. Ibid., p. 5.

43. Memorandum on "The Associates of Duke University Library," December 31, 1928, Flowers Papers.

44. Robert H. Woody, memorial notice for W. W. Flowers, *Library Notes* 10 (May, 1941): 1.

45. W. W. Flowers to W. K. Boyd, May 1, 1930, and Boyd to Flowers, July 10, 1930, William K. Boyd Papers, Duke University Archives.

46. Breedlove, *Duke University Library, 1840–1940*, p. 38.

47. W. K. Boyd, "Memorandum Regarding Physical Defects and Needs in the General Library," March 1, 1933, Flowers Papers.

48. A. C. Lee to Flowers, April 22, 1933, Flowers Papers.

49. *Alumni Register* 18 (July 1, 1932): 188.

50. Boyd to the president and executive committee, November 8, 1932; C. B. Markham to R. L. Flowers, December 2, 1932; and G. T. Durham, CPA, in Richmond, Va., to Flowers, November 29, 1932. Papers of the Board of Trustees, Executive Committee, 1930s, folder on "Boyd, W. K. (re—Library)," Duke University Archives.

51. Few to Perkins, May 14, 1934; copy, Boyd to P. M. Gross, June 19, 1934; Few to H. Branscomb, July 11, 1934; and several letters exchanged between Few and Boyd, September, 1934, Few Papers. Boyd wanted Few to approach W. W. Flowers about support also for research and publication in southern history and letters, but Few argued that Flowers was interested in the collection of material, about both southern history and literature. Moreover, Few insisted that the "business of publication is the concern of the University and should be done, I think, through the Duke University Press, which many of us hope to see developed in due course." Few to Boyd, September 14, 1934, Few Papers.

52. H. Branscomb, "The Library and the Undergraduate," *Library Notes* 4 (March, 1939): 1–2. Branscomb's policies may have been one reason recorded use of books in Duke's libraries during 1937–38 increased almost 10 percent over the previous year, although enrollment increased only 1.8 percent.

53. Breedlove, *Duke University Library, 1840–1940*, p. 40.

54. *Library Notes: A Bulletin Issued for the Friends of Duke University Library* 1/1 (March, 1936): 1.

55. Ibid., p. 2.

56. W. Boyd, Annual Report for 1932 [December 31, 1932?], Few Papers.

57. Mary Wescott, "A New Library Building," *Library Notes* 16 (June, 1946): 21.

58. B. E. Powell to the faculty, January 23, 1947, and proceedings of the Cooperative Com-

mittee on Library Building Plans, March 18, 1947, in Papers on Libraries of Trinity and Duke, Duke University Archives.

59. B. E. Powell, "Gertrude Meritt—An Appreciation," remarks at Friends of the Library dinner, March 15, 1979, biographical file, University Archives.

60. Porter, *Trinity and Duke*, p. 220. The volume was *Political Ideas of the American Revolution* by Randolph G. Adams.

61. Few to J. S. Bassett, February 14, 1925, Few Papers.

62. R. Flowers to Randolph G. Adams, January 11, 1926, Flowers Papers.

63. The best source on Ernest Seeman is Susan Singleton Rose, "Idealist or Iconoclast: Ernest Seeman at Duke University, 1925–1934," master's thesis (Duke University, 1987); hereinafter cited as Rose, "Ernest Seeman."

64. Rose, "Ernest Seeman," pp. 6–23.

65. The relationship between Seeman and Miller is treated more extensively in chapter 12 on the law school.

66. Memoranda on circulation and cost of journals published by Duke Press, June 30, 1937, Few Papers.

67. Rose, "Ernest Seeman," pp. 30–36, has a good account of Thomas's involvement with the press.

68. E. Seeman to Flowers, February 20, 1928, Flowers Papers.

69. Seeman to Flowers, May 25, 1928, Flowers Papers.

70. P. Baum to W. D. Davison, July 9, 1928, with Davison to Flowers, July 18, 1928, Flowers Papers.

71. The quote is from Rose, "Ernest Seeman," p. 43.

72. Flowers to Rippy, August 24, 1932, Flowers Papers.

73. Seeman to H. Dwire, September 9, 1933, Flowers Papers.

74. These matters are discussed in chapter 3.

75. Rose, "Ernest Seeman," p. 76. Two years after the loss of his job at Duke, Seeman wrote an angry attack on the university and its leaders in "Duke: But Not Doris," *New Republic* 88 (September 30, 1936): 220–222.

76. Few to W. L. Sperry, December 17, 1930, Few Papers.

77. E. Russell to Few, December 10, 1930, Few Papers.

78. Few to R. E. Blackwell, November 12, 1932; T. Speers to Few, November 20, 1936, Few Papers. The New York visitor overlooked the obvious fact that not all of the 1,500 were students, but what the proportions were is not known. The chapel in the late twentieth century, when several rows of pews originally in the front of the nave had been replaced by chairs, seats about 1,470 persons in the nave and transepts, 150 in the chancel choir, 50 in the Memorial Chapel, and when needed, extra chairs may be brought in for up to about 150 persons.

79. *Chronicle*, June 19, 1988. This story quotes Walter M. Upchurch, Jr., a Duke graduate (1931) who was a member of the original choir and who in 1933 and for a number of years afterward directed the chapel choir in the summer. His papers in the University Archives contain additional information on the early choir.

80. Ibid.

81. Few to H. Trumbauer, February 25, 1935, Few Papers.

82. J. F. Phillips to Few, July 28, 1933, Few Papers.

83. Few to Russell, June 23, 1933; January 25, 1935, Few Papers.

84. F. Hickman to Few, March 9, 1933, Few Papers.

85. "Outline of the Organization and Proceedings of the Duke University Church (Interdenominational, 1937–1938)," Charles E. Jordan Papers, folder on Duke University

Church, box 5, University Archives. Hereinafter cited as Jordan Papers.

86. Few to C. Toms, December 17, 1935, Few Papers.

87. H. E. Spence to C. Jordan, December 3, 1947, Jordan Papers.

88. Branscomb to Flowers, December 21, 1944, Flowers Papers. The bishop was W. W. Peele.

89. Hickman to Flowers, March 25, 1948, Jordan Papers; Flowers to Hickman, August 16, 1948, and J. Cleland to Flowers, August 20, 1948, Flowers Papers.

90. These matters are discussed in Durden, *The Dukes*, pp. 239–240, 254.

91. Hanes's wife, Elizabeth Peck Hanes, also took a keen interest in the gardens, as in other phases of the university, and she generously supported them long after her husband's death.

92. H. Blomquist to Flowers, November 23, 1931, Flowers Papers.

93. John C. Wister, "Report to Dr. Frederic M. Hanes on Proposed Iris Garden, Duke University, Durham, N.C.," January 20, 1932, Flowers Papers. The university paid Wister's modest fee.

94. F. Hanes to Flowers, February 3, 1932.

95. Hanes to J. C. Wister, February 19, 1932, Flowers Papers.

96. Wister to Flowers, February 24, 1932, Flowers Papers.

97. Sarah P. Duke to Hanes, May 31, 1934, Flowers Papers. The letter is witnessed by W. R. Perkins. Mrs. Duke subsequently gave additional money for the project.

98. See *Alumni Register* 20 (July, 1934): 178 on the construction and *Alumni Register* 21 (February, 1935) and 23 (April, 1937) on the plantings.

99. T. N. Webb to Wister, August 27, 1934, J. C. Wister Correspondence, files in office of Duke Gardens. Larry T. Daniel, associate director of the gardens, kindly made these files available.

100. Ellen Biddle Shipman was not related, except perhaps quite distantly, to that branch of the Biddle family into which Mary Duke and her brother, Angier Buchanan Duke, had married.

101. Keith N. Morgan, "Charles A. Platt," and Leslie Rose Close, "Ellen Biddle Shipman," in William H. Tishler, ed., *American Landscape Architecture: Designers and Places* (Washington, D.C.: Preservation Press, 1989), pp. 84–89, 90–93.

102. Few to Mary D. Biddle, June 23, 1937, Few Papers.

103. Webb to Junius P. Fishburn, July 15, 1937, T. N. Webb folder, files in office of Duke Gardens.

104. F. P. Leubuscher to Webb, January 27, 1938, Webb Papers.

105. With the terraced garden and the rock garden, although they were carefully planned to complement each other, the Duke Garden became the Duke Gardens.

106. R. M. Hanes (brother of F. M. Hanes) to Few, October 31, 1938, Few Papers.

107. Flowers to W. R. Perkins, April 17, 1944, Flowers Papers.

108. P. Kramer to G. S. Avery, Brooklyn Botanical Garden, April 12, 1945, folder on correspondence and publicity to 1956, files in office of Gardens.

109. Kramer to E. I. Farrington, December 17, 1945, ibid.

110. Kramer to Flowers, June 25, 1947, Flowers Papers. The Hanes iris planting was on a walkway outside and just to the north of the terraces.

111. A brief, nicely illustrated history of the gardens, by a horticulturalist who worked in them for several years, is Marcus Embry's "Watching the Gardens Grow," *Duke: A Magazine for Alumni and Friends* 75 (July–August, 1989): 6–11.

7. Duke Students at Work and Play in the Jazz and Big Band Era

1. Students normally took five courses per semester, with those classes that met three times per week carrying three semester hours of credit and some classes, such as those in the natural sciences where laboratory work was required, carrying four.
2. In addition to the *Bulletin of Duke University for 1924–1925* and subsequent years, a convenient source for curricular information is Ann Robertson Britt, "A Chronological Study of Undergraduate Curriculum Revision at Duke University, 1856–1976," a paper done for Political Science 313 in 1976, in Small Collections, Duke University Archives.

By way of contrast, the curriculum implemented by the Duke faculty beginning in 1988 requires all undergraduate students to take only one course, the university writing course. With thirty-four one-semester courses required for graduation, students normally take four courses per semester. The old "minimum uniform requirements," which underwent various modifications before their elimination in 1969, were echoed in 1988 by the requirement that a student must take "general studies" courses in five of the following six areas of knowledge: arts and literature, civilizations, foreign languages, natural sciences, quantitative reasoning, and social sciences. In four of the five selected areas, a student must take three courses, two of which must be related and at least one of which must be at a semi-advanced level. There are other requirements concerning "small group learning experiences" (seminars, independent study, etc.) as well as the major and other matters, but the difference between the rigidity in the late 1920s and the flexibility and choice of the 1990s is obvious. Students also were required to take a larger number of courses in the earlier part of the century and did not have the option of bypassing an entire "area of knowledge" if they wished to do so.

3. *Trinity Chronicle*, March 4, 1925. All citations which follow in this chapter, unless otherwise noted, are from the *Chronicle*.
4. February 11, 1925. William Sprinkle, a star in several Taurian productions, served as president of the group.
5. February 18, 1925.
6. April 1, 1925.
7. December 10, 1924.
8. Ibid.
9. Ibid.
10. February 25, 1925.
11. April 29, 1925.
12. March 4, 1925, and April 7, 1926.
13. April 23, 1925.
14. April 29, 1925.
15. April 23, 1925.
16. Albert H. Cotton, January 13, 1926.
17. November 17, 1926.
18. March 31, 1926. Craven, after completing the requirements for the Ph.D. in colonial American history at Cornell in record time at age twenty-three, would proceed to have a distinguished academic career.
19. February 17, 1926.
20. March 16, 1929, and May 18, 1927.
21. March 31, 1926.
22. Hugo Germino in the Durham *Sun*, December 10, 1977.
23. April 21, 1926.

24. November 17 and 24, 1926.

25. W. Few to C. R. Mann, January 1, 1934; and speech by Few, n.d., in "Speeches and Writings—Miscellaneous," Few Papers.

26. Few to Clyde Furst, September 11, 1925, Few Papers.

27. Few, "How Education and Religion May Work Together," chapter in his unfinished manuscript, "The Beginnings of an American University," Few Papers.

28. E. D. Soper to Few, June 12, 1926, Few Papers.

29. M. T. Plyler to Few, February 24, 1927, Few Papers.

30. The Rev. W. A. Cade to Few, March 22, 1927, Few Papers.

31. Few to H. M. North, March 23, 1927, Few Papers.

32. October 20, 1926.

33. October 17 and November 14, 1928.

34. September 26, 1928.

35. February 2, 1927.

36. March 2, 1927.

37. [Few] to J. Foster Barnes, June 20, 1927; [secretary] to Soper, July 1, 1927; and J. F. Barnes, "What I Consider My Work to Be as Social-Religious Director," October 3, 1927, Few Papers.

38. March 5, 1930.

39. December 4, 1927; January 11 and February 8, 1928.

40. May 25, 1928.

41. William M. Werber, class of 1930, to author, February 25, 1989.

42. November 19, 1930.

43. Ibid.

44. Ibid.

45. W. Wannamaker to ————, May 28, 1926, Wannamaker Papers.

46. January 4, 1928.

47. March 20, 1929, and February 3, 1932.

48. All of these arcane matters are spelled out in the *Bulletins* for 1930–31 and thereafter and also in W. K. Greene, "Report on the Administration of the Curriculum . . . 1930–1931," box 94, subject file, Few Papers. Hereinafter cited as W. K. Greene, "Report."

49. W. K. Greene, "Report," p. 32.

50. May 13, 1931.

51. October 7, 1931.

52. January 20 and September 28, 1932.

53. Ann R. Britt, "A Chronological Study of Curriculum Revision . . . ," pp. 18–21. In 1936, the required hours in the restricted elective category were reduced from eighteen to twelve.

54. November 13, 1929; March 5 and 12, 1930.

55. October 15 and 22, 1930.

56. The Rev. R. H. Broom to Few, March 14, 1932, Few Papers.

57. Few to Broom, April 11, 1932, Few Papers.

58. Untitled statement by Few, May 30, 1930, Few Papers.

59. December 17, 1930.

60. February 18, 1931.

61. February 18 and 25, 1931.

62. October 8 and 15, 1930.

63. September 28, 1934.

64. December 17, 1930.

65. March 19 and April 30, 1930.

66. March 18, 1931.
67. February 22, 1928.
68. March 28, 1928.
69. November 18, 1938.
70. December 3, 1930.
71. February 18, 1931.
72. April 15, 1931.
73. Wannamaker to C. J. Bass, March 6, 1926, Wannamaker Papers.
74. December 12, 1936.
75. September 23, 1931.
76. Wannamaker to A. C. Zumbrunnen, February 8, 1932, Wannamaker Papers.
77. Miller's enigmatic part in Duke's affairs outside the law school is also discussed in chapters 3 and 12.
78. J. Miller to C. N. Nison, June 12, 1934, Miller Files, for the committee's purpose; Alice M. Baldwin, "The Woman's College, as I Remember It," typed MS (1959), p. 83, University Archives.
79. May 17, 1933.
80. This matter is discussed more fully in chapter 3.
81. Folder on "Student Rebellion 1934," Duke University Archives; W. Perkins to W. Few, February 8, 1934, contains a copy of the telegram as well as Perkins's statement that he had not responded and knew that Few could handle the matter satisfactorily. An older law student alleged that Walter A. Cutter, another older law student, had admitted that "he had had a hand in drafting that telegram to New York." See Henry L. Everett to Paul Garber, May 1, 1935, School of Religion Papers (D-3, box 1), University Archives. Cutter may have been something of a professional student, for after graduating from Central College in 1928, he received an M.A., then a B.D., and a Ph.D. (1933) from Duke—before entering Duke's law school. He was a friend of both Miller and Ernest Seeman and succeeded the latter as leader of the Explorers' Club in the fall of 1933.
82. The stories that appeared in the *Durham Morning Herald* may well have been written or inspired by Ernest Seeman.
83. February 28, March 7, and April 18, 1934.
84. January 11, 1935.
85. April 10, 1936; September 20 and 24, 1935.
86. March 24, 1936.
87. October 8, 1935.
88. October 11, 1935.
89. November 5, 1937.
90. November 12, 1937.
91. February 4, 1938. Robert Wilson was the columnist.
92. April 20, 1937.
93. October 19, 1937.
94. March 14 and April 11, 1941.
95. April 5, 1933.
96. November 20, 1931.
97. May 3, 1933.
98. March 2, 1937.
99. March 20, 1936.
100. February 15, 1938.
101. February 24 and March 3 (misdated February 28), 1939. The presence of a significant number of undergraduates on both of Duke's campuses who took religion seriously

and made it a part of their college experience suggests that in this respect, as in certain others, Duke's students in the 1930s do not fit neatly into the patterns that Helen L. Horowitz describes in *Campus Life: Undergraduate Cultures from the End of the Eighteenth Century to the Present* (New York: Knopf, 1987).

102. March 5, 1937.

103. October 15, 1937.

104. November 22, 1938.

105. October 26 and December 10, 1937.

106. March 7, 1941.

107. March 23, 1937. After graduating in 1937, Cleaveland served as director of student religious activities for two years and then briefly as an assistant dean of men. After World War II, he became a distinguished political scientist and eventually returned to Duke as the provost of the university.

108. A. Baldwin to Hope Vandever, December 14, 1944. Baldwin Papers.

109. November 24, 1936.

110. January 7, 1936.

111. September 29, 1936.

112. Ibid.

113. February 19, September 28, and November 9, 1937.

114. October 28, 1941.

115. April 12, 1933.

116. December 14, 1934; January 11, 1935; and September 28, 1937.

117. October 9, 1929.

118. Copy of O. B. Keeler in the *Atlanta Journal*, October 8, 1929, Few Papers.

119. November 14, 1928.

120. December 11, 1929.

121. Few to W. R. Perkins, October 18, 1929, Few Papers.

122. Few, *Bulletin of Duke University: Report of the President for 1938–1939* (March, 1940): 13–14.

123. Ibid., p. 13.

124. Wannamaker to W. Wade, February 15, 1930, Wannamaker Papers.

125. Wade to Wannamaker, February 18, 1930, Wannamaker Papers.

126. Wade to Wannamaker, August 25 and 26, 1930, Wannamaker Papers.

127. Wannamaker to Wade, August 14, 1930, Wannamaker Papers.

128. Few to Perkins, January 19, 1931, Few Papers.

129. February 11, 1931.

130. April 29, 1931.

131. March 11, 1931, and January 13, 1932.

132. March 12, 1935.

133. April 10, 1936.

134. A. O. Michener to Few, May 26, 1933, Few Papers.

135. December 10, 1930.

136. November 23, 1932.

137. In the aftermath of the 1935 season, Frank P. Graham, president of the University of North Carolina, spearheaded a movement calling for drastic reforms in college athletics. Though eventually rejected by most UNC alumni, students, and even faculty, Graham's proposals created quite a stir. At Duke, both Few and Wade, as well as many others, fought the proposals, and there is interesting correspondence about the matter in the Few Papers. See Richard Stone, "The Graham Plan of 1935: An Aborted Crusade to De-emphasize College Athletics," *North Carolina Historical Review* 64 (July, 1987): 274–293.

138. Glenn E. Mann, *A Story of Glory: Duke University Football* (Greenville, S.C.: Doorway Publishers, 1985), p. 162. Hereinafter cited as Mann, *A Story of Glory*.

139. W. Few, as quoted in the *Chronicle*, December 12, 1936.

140. Henry McLemore, as quoted in the *Chronicle*, December 1, 1936.

141. Ted Mann, in *A Story of Glory*, p. 97, says that in mid-season of 1938 he received a note from a fellow sportswriter who referred to Duke's unsurpassed defensive line as the "Seven Iron Dukes." Mann thereupon dropped the first word and began using the name that soon caught on for the team.

142. Mann, *A Story of Glory*, pp. 96–101.

143. November 29 and December 9, 1938. Despite the relaxed regulations, the athletic office reported that only about sixty Duke students made the trip to California.

144. Few to Graham, December 2, 1938, Few Papers.

145. January 10, 1939.

146. September 18 and 22, 1936.

147. April 25, 1934. Richard H. Shryock was the professor.

148. Robert G. Howard, columnist, November 24, 1936, and Professor Clement Vollmer, October 1, 1937.

149. November 16, 1932.

150. April 5 and 9, 1935.

151. April 10, 17, and 21, 1936.

152. November 13 and December 1, 1936. For an account of one of the leaders of the American Student Union at Duke, Sheldon R. Harte, '37, see Bridget Booher, "Death of an Idealist," *Duke Magazine* 77 (December, 1990–January, 1991): 14–16, 49. Harte joined the Socialist Workers Party in New York not long after graduating and was murdered by Stalinist agents while serving as a secretary-bodyguard to Leon Trotsky in Mexico in 1940.

153. March 4, 1938. E. M. Carroll, an historian of Europe at Duke, likewise asserted that Nazi Germany was "starting out where Kaiser Wilhelm left off" and thought war probable. March 22, 1938.

154. September 30, 1938.

155. October 3 and 6, 1939.

156. January 12, 1940.

157. September 27, 1940.

158. October 4, 1940. Story by Louis W. Cassels.

159. October 15 and 22, 1940.

160. February 18, 1941. Louis W. Cassels was the writer.

161. December 9, 1941.

162. March 26, 1935.

163. October 19, 1937.

164. September 26, 1941.

165. March 17, 1936. The writer was Bill Woodruff.

8. The Woman's College, 1925–1947

1. Alice M. Baldwin, "The Woman's College, as I Remember It" (1959). Typed manuscript in the Duke University Archives, p. 57. Hereinafter cited as Baldwin, "The Woman's College."

2. Rudolph, *The American College and University*, p. 320.

3. For Washington Duke's gift and his subsequent withdrawal of the conditional aspect as well as for the genesis of the coordinate college idea at Trinity, see Porter, *Trinity and Duke*, pp. 62–63, 91–92, 103, and *passim*.

4. Mabel Newcomer, *A Century of Higher Education for American Women* (New York, 1959), pp. 40–45, describes the confusing variety among coordinate colleges for women. See also Barbara M. Soloman, *The Company of Educated Women* (New Haven, Conn.: Yale University Press, 1985).

5. Biographical data are available in the Alice M. Baldwin Papers, Duke University Archives, but are more conveniently found in a solid dissertation: Dianne Puthoff Brandstadter, "Developing the Coordinate College for Women at Duke University: The Career of Alice Mary Baldwin, 1924–1947," Ph.D. dissertation, Duke University, 1977, pp. 4 ff. Hereinafter cited as Brandstadter, "Baldwin."

6. Brandstadter, "Baldwin," pp. 14–17.

7. Baldwin, "The Woman's College," pp. 2–4.

8. Ibid., pp. 4–5.

9. Andrew McLaughlin to Baldwin, July 6, 1923, Baldwin Papers.

10. Baldwin, "The Woman's College," p. 6.

11. Copy of Conyers Read to John S. Bassett, March 7, 1923, Baldwin Papers.

12. Baldwin, "The Woman's College," p. 6.

13. A. Baldwin to "My dear Betty" [Elizabeth Amen], March 4, 1925, folder on Coordinate Education, Baldwin Papers.

14. Baldwin, "The Woman's College," p. 17.

15. Baldwin to Margaret S. Morriss, dean at Brown University, April 30, 1925, folder on Coordinate Education, Baldwin Papers. Baldwin's ripened views about coordinate education are best summarized in Alice M. Baldwin, "The Woman's College of Duke University," *South Atlantic Quarterly* 55 (January, 1956): 41–48.

16. These matters concerning James B. Duke and the physical planning for Duke University are dealt with in more detail in Durden, *The Dukes*, pp. 237–242.

17. Baldwin, "The Woman's College," p. 20.

18. Ibid.

19. Wannamaker to Few, May 5, 1926, Wannamaker Papers.

20. Baldwin, "The Woman's College," p. 21.

21. The analysis is based on the Baldwin Papers and Baldwin Memoir, but the matter is also discussed carefully in Brandstadter, "Baldwin," pp. 62–63. Brandstadter fruitfully interviewed numerous women who knew Baldwin well, first as their teacher and dean and then as their coworker in the Woman's College.

22. Baldwin, "The Woman's College," pp. 14–15; Brandstadter, "Baldwin," pp. 63–72. Duke would not have a woman trustee until the 1950s.

23. J. Grout to Baldwin, April 27, 1924, personnel folder, Baldwin Papers; Baldwin, "The Woman's College," p. 13.

24. Brandstadter, "Baldwin," pp. 61–62.

25. Baldwin, "The Woman's College," p. 14.

26. Baldwin to W. P. Few, November 28, 1925, folder on Council on Education for Women, Baldwin Papers; Brandstadter, "Baldwin," pp. 66–67.

27. Baldwin, "The Woman's College," p. 22.

28. Ibid., pp. 26–27.

29. Ibid., pp. 69–70; Brandstadter, "Baldwin," p. 78.

30. Baldwin, "The Woman's College," pp. 11–12.

31. *Chronicle*, November 12, 1930.

32. Baldwin, "The Woman's College," pp. 45–46; Brandstadter, "Baldwin," pp. 81–83.

33. Baldwin, "The Woman's College," pp. 42–43.

34. Possessing a strong sense of history and eager to tie Duke University to its institutional predecessor, Few, in consultation with various others and with the approval of

the trustees, chose names only for those new buildings on East campus whose purpose did not define them. That is, the new library, auditorium, union, science, and faculty apartment buildings were not given historical names. Other buildings were named for these figures: John W. Alspaugh of Winston-Salem, North Carolina, was a long-time chairman of Trinity's board of trustees, as was also Joseph G. Brown of Raleigh, North Carolina; John Spencer Bassett was Trinity College's professor of history who founded the *South Atlantic Quarterly* in 1902 and became a key actor in the famous "Bassett affair" of 1903; William H. Pegram also represented the faculty, having taught chemistry at Trinity for forty-six years. The name of another new dormitory, one to be used initially by student nurses, honored the three Giles sisters who had been special students at Trinity College in the 1870s and received degrees from it in 1878. The general classroom building was named in honor of Julian S. Carr, important trustee and benefactor in the 1880s who also gave the land on which Trinity built its campus in Durham.

35. Baldwin, "The Woman's College," p. 42.
36. Brandstadter, "Baldwin," pp. 85–86.
37. Baldwin, "The Woman's College," pp. 44–46.
38. Ibid., p. 36.
39. Few to J. H. Reynolds, August 18, 1921, Few Papers.
40. Baldwin, "The Woman's College," p. 17.
41. Durden, *The Dukes*, pp. 252–254.
42. Brandstadter, "Baldwin," pp. 95–96.
43. Baldwin, "The Woman's College," pp. 50–51.
44. Baldwin, "The Woman's College," p. 81, names some but not all of the above plus a few others.
45. Rudolph, *The American College and University*, pp. 475–476.
46. Few to C. C. Dula, November 6, 1929, Few Papers.
47. Few to W. B. Bell, April 6, 1934, Few Papers.
48. Baldwin, "The Woman's College," pp. 29–31.
49. Ibid., pp. 60–61.
50. L. Hall to Baldwin, April 15, 1931, and Baldwin to Hall, May 26, 1931; Baldwin to E. Gilmore, May 1, 1934, Personnel File, Baldwin Papers; Baldwin, "The Woman's College," p. 61.
51. W. K. Boyd to James A. Thomas, March 26, 1929, Duke Memorial MSS, Duke University Archives.
52. These matters are dealt with in greater detail in Betty Irene Young, *The Library of the Woman's College, Duke University, 1930–1972* (Durham, N.C.: Regulator Press, 1978), pp. 43–60. Hereinafter cited as Young, *Library of the Woman's College*.
53. Few to H. Trumbauer, January 30, 1936, Few Papers.
54. This matter is dealt with in chapter 9.
55. Baldwin, "The Woman's College," pp. 30–31.
56. A.H. Larson, Eastman School of Music, to Baldwin, May 11, 1939; Baldwin to Julia Wilkinson, June 30, 1939; and memorandum of W. H. Wannamaker, July 11, 1939, Wannamaker Papers.
57. Baldwin, "The Woman's College," p. 63.
58. Memorandum on Katherine Gilbert, no date, alphabetical file, Baldwin Papers; *Durham Morning Herald*, April 29, 1952.
59. Memorandum by W. H. Wannamaker concerning the new Department of Aesthetics, Art and Music, July 13, 1941; Gilbert to Wannamaker, July 25, 1942, Wannamaker Papers. There are various other relevant documents also in this collection.

60. Memorandum by Katherine E. Gilbert on the work and purpose of the Department of Aesthetics, Art and Music, no date [early 1940s?]. Small Collections, Duke University Archives.

61. Young, *Library of the Woman's College*, pp. 10–11.

62. Ibid., pp. 15–20, 29.

63. Ibid., pp. 25–33.

64. Baldwin, "The Woman's College," pp. 46–47; Elizabeth A. Persons, "The Woman's College: Admissions, 1930–1954," pp. 3–8. Baldwin Papers. Hereinafter cited as Persons, "Admissions."

65. Baldwin, "The Woman's College," pp. 47–48; Persons, "Admissions," pp. 9–14; Brandstadter, "Baldwin," pp. 101–103.

66. Persons, "Admissions," pp. 11–12.

67. Ibid., p. 15.

68. Baldwin to Flowers, December 24, 1929, Baldwin Papers.

69. Baldwin, "The Woman's College," p. 49.

70. Persons, "Admissions," pp. 18–19.

71. Few to C. W. Toms, July 10, 1936, Few Papers.

72. Few to J.M. Higginbotham, January 13, 1936, Few Papers.

73. *Alumni Register* 19 (April, 1933): 103.

74. *Alumni Register* 19 (March 1933): 70; and *Alumni Register* 19 (August, 1933): 209.

75. Baldwin, "The Woman's College," p. 72; Brandstadter, "Baldwin," pp. 114–116.

76. Mary Wilson Meiklejohn, president of the class of 1935, to W.A. Tyree, April 16, 1935, Baldwin Papers; *Alumni Register* 21 (May, 1936): 110.

77. Baldwin, "The Woman's College," p. 73; *Alumni Register* 29 (June, 1943): 144.

78. Baldwin, "The Woman's College," pp. 73–74.

79. The student protest movement on West is dealt with in chapter 7.

80. Baldwin, "The Woman's College," p. 60.

81. C. Anderson to Baldwin, November 28, 1936, and Baldwin to Anderson, December 8, 1936, Baldwin Papers.

82. *Alumni Register* 19 (May, 1933): 123.

83. Grout to Wannamaker, March 15 and May 8, 1940, Wannamaker Papers.

84. *Alumni Register* 25 (December, 1939): 292.

85. Baldwin to Mrs. S.J. Hay, November 21, 1931, folder on Social Regulations, Baldwin Papers.

86. Baldwin to Mrs. W.H. Blank (form letter), September 28, 1933, folder on Social Regulations, Baldwin Papers.

87. Baldwin to Annie Laurie Newsom, November 27, 1935, folder on WSGA, Baldwin Papers.

88. Brandstadter, "Baldwin," p. 57.

89. Baldwin to Ernest R. Groves, November 26, 1934, Baldwin Papers.

90. Brandstadter, "Baldwin," pp. 127–128. Dara DeHaven, " 'On Educating Women'—The Co-ordinate Ideal at Trinity and Duke University," a senior honors thesis at Duke University, 1973, Duke University Archives, presents a lively critique of both Baldwin and the Woman's College for their lack of feminist ideology and for the alleged contradiction contained in the idea of separate but equal education for women. "By continually enforcing traditional patterns of behavior on educated women," DeHaven concludes on pp. 63–64, "Alice Baldwin fought against herself in the battle to widen women's horizons."

91. Brandstadter, "Baldwin," p. 131.

92. Gilbert to Marjorie Nicholson, dean of Smith College, September 26, 1938, folder on Women's Symposium, Baldwin Papers. Letters to Madame Irène Joliot-Curie in

France, Sigrid Undset in Norway, and various other Europeans reveal Gilbert's efforts to give the symposium an international character.

93. Gilbert to Mary E. Wooley, January 28, 1939, folder on Women's Symposium, Baldwin Papers.

94. Letter of Rosa Lee Walston enclosed in Walston to Gilbert, April 4, 1939, folder on Women's Symposium, Baldwin Papers.

95. Blanche Henry Clark to Baldwin, April 27, 1939, folder on Women's Symposium, Baldwin Papers.

96. William A. Neilson, president of Smith College, "Nazi Germany as a Threat to Our Liberties," *Alumni Register* 26 (June, 1940): 121–122.

97. Baldwin to Captain Tom Eaves, June 29, 1945, Baldwin Papers. The university's role in World War II is discussed in more detail in chapter 14.

98. Baldwin, "The Woman's College," p. 68; *Alumni Register* 28 (February, 1942): 36; Brandstadter, "Baldwin," pp. 130–138.

99. Baldwin, "The Woman's College," pp 15, 57.

100. Tables in a study, "Trinity Faculty Women, 1930–1985," done by Rebecca Schaller as part of her senior work in the Women's Studies Program at Duke University and used in an exhibit in Perkins Library in February, 1986; Duke University Archives. Counting women on the combined faculties of Duke in 1930, Baldwin came up with the figure of 24, as compared with 235 men. In 1947 on Duke's instructional staff, which included more than just full-time faculty, there were 57 women and 433 men.

101. Baldwin, "The Woman's College," p. 14.

102. Baldwin to J.M. Thomas, April 4, 1936, and Thomas to Baldwin, April 6, 1936, Baldwin Papers.

103. Lee Walston, May 29, 1942, Baldwin Papers. More details concerning the problem of the appointment may be found on pp 100–102 of chapter 4.

104. Baldwin to Wannamaker, July 11, 1939, Wannamaker Papers.

105. Copy of Baldwin to Few, July 4, 1940, and memorandum on the budget for 1940–41, August 1, 1940, Wannamaker Papers.

106. Baldwin, "The Woman's College," p. 78.

107. Baldwin to R.L. Flowers, October 30, 1945, Flowers Papers.

108. Baldwin, "The Woman's College," p. 88.

109. Wannamaker to Flowers, November 1, 1945, Flowers Papers.

110. Baldwin, "The Woman's College," p. 88.

111. Baldwin, "The Woman's College," pp. 88–89; Baldwin to Flowers, May 23, 1946, and "Notes Concerning Possible Candidates for Position of Dean of the Woman's College," in file on the Woman's College, Flowers Papers.

112. Baldwin, "The Woman's College," pp. 89–90; Flowers to Brinkley, March 18, 1947, and Brinkley to Flowers, May 12, 1947, folder on Women's College, Flowers Papers.

9. One Recumbent Too Many

1. Henry L. Mencken, "The Sahara of the Bozart," in *Prejudices: Second Series* (New York: Knopf, 1920).

2. W. L. Foushee to Alex. H. Sands, June 8, 1929, Duke Memorial MSS, Duke University Archives. Hereinafter cited as Duke Memorial MSS.

3. W. K. Boyd to James A. Thomas, March 26, 1929, Duke Memorial MSS.

4. The best sources for biographical information about Ackland are: a speech made by John E. Larson, an attorney in Washington, D.C., at the dedication of the William Hayes Ackland Art Museum at the University of North Carolina, Chapel Hill, September 20, 1958, a copy of which is in the folder on the Ackland Art Museum,

Small Collections, Duke University Archives; hereinafter cited as Larson speech; and Evan H. Turner, "Introduction," in Innis H. Shoemaker, ed., *The Ackland Art Museum: A Handbook* (Chapel Hill: Ackland Art Museum, 1983), pp. xi–xx. Hereinafter cited as Shoemaker, ed., *The Ackland Art Museum*. The marriage and divorce are mentioned in John E. Larson to W. P. Few, March 22, 1940, in the Few Papers. See also the *New York Times*, May 25, 1897, p. 3.

5. Larson speech; W. H. Ackland to "Dear Sir" [W. P. Few], December 5, 1936, Few Papers. Curiously enough, neither in this first letter nor in any subsequent one did Ackland explain the exact size or nature of his own art collection. Moreover, Few never mentioned that aspect in his letters, though the two may well have discussed it in one of their several conferences. Turner, in the preface to Shoemaker, ed., *The Ackland Art Museum*, p. vii, mentions that the sculpture and paintings which Ackland had inherited from his once-rich family were largely reproductions and thus "not appropriate to the realization of his ambitious plan."

6. Larson speech; Few to G. G. Allen, May 5, 1937, Few Papers.

7. Few to Allen, May 5, 1937, Few Papers.

8. Few to H. Trumbauer, January 30, 1936, and Trumbauer to Few, February 5, 1936, Few Papers.

9. Few to Ackland, December 18, 1936, and Ackland to Few, December 23, 1936, Few Papers.

10. Ackland to Few, May 3, 1937, and Few to Ackland, May 10, 1937, Few Papers.

11. Ackland to Few, May 10, 1937, Few Papers.

12. Few to Ackland, May 12 and 21, 1937, Few Papers.

13. For a fuller discussion of Duke University's relationship with the Duke Endowment and of the roles played by Allen and Perkins, see chapter 3.

14. W. R. Perkins to Few, June 16, 1937, Few Papers. A copy of Ackland's will of May 4, 1936, is in the W. H. Ackland folder in the Flowers Papers.

15. Few to Trumbauer, September 17 and 22, 1937; Trumbauer to Few, September 20 and October 9, 1937, Few Papers.

16. Ackland to Few, October 18 and 29, 1937, Few Papers.

17. Few to Ackland, November 10, 1937, and Ackland to Few, [November, 12?, 1937], Few Papers.

18. Ackland to Few, April 5, 1938, Few Papers.

19. Few to Ackland, April 19, 1938, Few Papers. Few's reference to the "least satisfactory" gift in the form of a trust fund is unclear. He could hardly have been referring to the 32 percent of the annual income from the Duke Endowment for, although it was a trust fund, that gift made possible the organization of Duke University around Trinity College in the mid-1920s and continued to play a critical role in financing Duke.

20. Few to Perkins, April 15, 1938, Few Papers.

21. Ackland to Few, May 14, 1938, Few Papers.

22. Few to Ackland, November 9, 1938, Few Papers.

23. Ackland to Few, November 16, 1938, and Few to Ackland, November 25, 1938, Few Papers.

24. H. Holt to Few, March 3, 1939, Few Papers.

25. Telegram, Edson B. Olds, Jr., to Few, February 18, 1940, and Few to Olds, February 20, 1940, Few Papers.

26. Olds to Few, February 24, 1940, and Few to Perkins, March 8, 1940, Few Papers.

27. Perkins to Few, March 13, 1940, Few Papers. Perkins also sent a copy of the letter to the chairman of Duke's board of trustees, John F. Bruton.

28. Perkins to T. D. Bryson, March 20, 1940, Few Papers.

29. Few to Allen, March 21, 1940, Few Papers. Few also noted that the architect's firm had earlier designed Harvard's Widener Library, which contained the Harry Elkins Widener Memorial Room in honor of a young man who went down with the *Titanic*.

30. Larson to Few, March 22 and April 4, 1940, Few Papers. A copy of the second will is in the Ackland folder, November 10, 1938, Few Papers. The family name was originally Acklen, but at some point after he was forty William Hayes Ackland chose what he believed to be an older, English-style spelling of the name.

31. Bryson to Perkins, July 8, 1940, Few Papers.

32. James Cannon III to R. L. Flowers, February 3, 1941, Flowers Papers. Flowers, named as acting president at the time of Few's death, was named as president by the trustees on January 19, 1941.

33. "Summons in a Civil Action. . . ," August 20, 1941, Few Papers.

34. "Resolution from Minutes of the Executive Committee of Duke University . . . ," September 6, 1941, Few Papers.

35. Perkins to Bryson, September 19, 1941, Flowers Papers. Later statements by John E. Larson confirm the gist of Perkins's letter.

36. Flowers to Perkins, September 23, 1941, Flowers Papers.

37. George V. Allen to Roper, September 23, 1941, which was enclosed with Roper to Flowers, September 25, 1941, Flowers Papers. George V. Allen was not related to George G. Allen.

38. Flowers to Roper, October 3, 1941, Flowers Papers.

39. J. Bruton to Flowers, January 19, 1941, Flowers Papers.

40. Perkins to Bruton, January 26, 1942, Flowers Papers.

41. Extract from minutes of the meeting of the board of trustees, January 28, 1942, Flowers Papers. Three different versions of the statement, which was never issued, may be found in the Flowers Papers, January 29, 1942. None mentions either the mausoleum or the recumbent statue.

42. Larson speech, September 20, 1958, Flowers Papers. The key role of former governor Gardner, who had a law office in Washington, is also emphasized in Turner, "Introduction," in Shoemaker, ed., *The Ackland Art Museum*, p. xiv.

43. *Winston-Salem Journal*, January 29, 1942. Similar stories appeared in other North Carolina daily newspapers around the same time.

44. Joseph H. Separk to Flowers, January 29, 1942, Flowers Papers.

45. Perkins to Bruton, February 4, 1942; Allen to Flowers, February 6, 1942; and Bruton to Perkins, February 9, 1942, Flowers Papers.

46. Flowers to Allen, February 13, 1941, and Flowers to Bruton, February 13, 1942, Flowers Papers.

47. Larson speech, Flowers Papers.

10. *Theological Education at Duke University*

1. James B. Duke's indenture establishing the Duke Endowment, December 11, 1925, reprinted in Durden, *The Dukes*, p. 278.

2. William P. Few, "President Eliot and the South," *South Atlantic Quarterly* 8 (April, 1909), reprinted in Woody, ed., *Papers*, pp. 259–260.

3. Speech of John W. Chandler as reprinted in the *Duke Dialogue*, March 3, 1989, p. 4.

4. William P. Few, "Constructive Educational Leadership," *South Atlantic Quarterly* 8 (October, 1909), in Woody, *Few*, p. 269.

5. Ibid.

6. These matters are fully treated in Chaffin, *Trinity College, 1839–1892*, chapters 1–4, and more briefly in Porter, *Trinity and Duke*, pp. 3–4.

7. William P. Few, "The Standardizing of Southern Colleges," *South Atlantic Quarterly* 7 (October, 1908), in Woody, *Few*, pp. 222–223.

8. Few to Clyde Furst, September 11, 1925, Few Papers. Few may have been referring only to the period since he had become president, for John C. Kilgo in 1914 stated that the conferences had occasionally refused to elect trustees. Porter, *Trinity and Duke*, p. 196.

9. Few, "How Education and Religion Can Work Together," chapter in his unfinished manuscript, "The Beginnings of An American University," Few Papers.

10. Few to D. H. Tuttle, April 25, 1925, Few Papers.

11. Porter, *Trinity and Duke*, pp. 217–218.

12. Kent to Few, February 22, 1925, and March 1, 1925, Few Papers.

13. Few to Kelly, March 7, 1925, Few Papers.

14. Cannon to Few, April 8, 1925, Few Papers.

15. Hersey E. Spence to Few, February 10, 1925, Few Papers.

16. Few to W. R. Odell, June 4, 1925, Few Papers. For the early negotiations, see Few to Odell, April 11, 1925, and Few to Branscomb, May 11, 13, 1925, Few Papers.

17. Branscomb to Few, June 4, 1925, Few Papers.

18. Edmund D. Soper to James Cannon III, March 25, 1925, Few Papers.

19. Few to Cannon, May 19, 1925, Few Papers.

20. Soper to Few, May 23, 1925, Few Papers.

21. Few to Soper, May 28, 1925.

22. Few to Soper, June 15, 1925, Few Papers.

23. Few to Soper, June 30, 1925.

24. Few to Harvie Branscomb, June 17, 1925, Few Papers.

25. *The Christian Century*, as reprinted in the *Alumni Register* 9 (October, 1925): 348–349.

26. Paul N. Garber, "The Duke University School of Religion," *Duke School of Religion Bulletin* 5 (May, 1940): 32, 40. Hereinafter cited as *Bulletin*.

27. Soper to Few, October 27, 1925, Few Papers.

28. Ibid.

29. Soper to Few, April 15, 1926, Few Papers.

30. Branscomb, *Purely Academic*, p. 81.

31. Elbert Russell, "The Debt of the School of Religion to William Preston Few," *Duke School of Religion Bulletin* 5 (November, 1940): 58.

32. J. B. Duke's indenture is discussed in Durden, *The Dukes*, p. 276.

33. E. D. Soper, "Memorandum for President Few: The Organization of the School of Religion, June 12, 1926," School of Religion Papers, Duke University Archives.

34. Soper to Few, April 23, 1926; Russell to Soper, May 11, 1926; and Few to Russell, June 15, 1926.

35. Garber to Few, May 5, 1926, Few Papers; Memorandum on the faculty [October, 1926?], School of Religion Papers, University Archives.

36. George B. Winton to Few, July 26, 1926, Few Papers.

37. Few to Fitzgerald S. Parker, March 9, 1927, Few Papers.

38. Soper to E. M. Wylie, June 16, 1926, School of Religion Papers.

39. Memorandum on faculty [October, 1926?], School of Religion Papers.

40. Few to P. B. Kern, June 16, 1926; Kern to Few, June 22, 1926; Few to E. D. Mouzon, July 19, 1926; and Few to Kern, July 19, 1926, Few Papers.

41. Holt to Few, July 10, 1927, Few Papers.

42. "The School of Religion of Duke University," October 20, 1926, Few Papers; memorandum on formal opening, November 4, 1926, School of Religion Papers.

43. *Alumni Register* 17 (April, 1931): 117.

44. *Alumni Register* 17 (June, 1931): 203; Garber to J. W. Kimbrell, October 17, 1935, School of Religion Papers.

45. J. W. Johnson and G. S. Duffie to Garber, July 13, 1931, School of Religion Papers.

46. M. B. Shives to J. M. Ormond, June 19, 1939, School of Religion Papers.

47. Garber to J. T. Mangum, May 10, 1929, School of Religion Papers.

48. M. E. Sadler, Lynchburg College, to Russell, October 17, 1933, School of Religion Papers.

49. D. X. Gass to Garber, July 17, 1934, and Garber to Gass, July 23, 1934, School of Religion Papers.

50. Garber to W. F. Johnson, September 10, 1934, School of Religion Papers.

51. For the faculty resolution, see Soper to Garber, October 15, 1928, School of Religion Papers; Few to George G. Allen, August 30, 1928, Few Papers.

52. Elbert Russell, *Elbert Russell, Quaker: An Autobiography* (Jackson, Tenn.: Friendly Press, 1956), p. 264. Russell added the comment that while he understood what Soper meant he (Russell) "managed to do both things fairly satisfactorily." Hereinafter cited as Russell, *Autobiography*.

53. [E. D. Soper], "Outline—Student Life Division," September 16, 1926, Few Papers.

54. Russell, *Autobiography*, pp. 263–264.

55. Few to Odell, April 30, 1927, and Few to T. Rowe, May 9, 1928, Few Papers; O. Lester Brown, *Gilbert T. Rowe, Churchman Extraordinary* (Greensboro, N.C.: Commission on Archives and History, Western North Carolina Conference, United Methodist Church, 1971), pp. 74–86.

56. John W. Shackford to Few, October 8, 1929, Few Papers; Brown, *Rowe*, p. 143.

57. Russell to W. F. Albright, December 10, 1930, School of Religion Papers.

58. Russell to Branscomb, February 2, 1932, School of Religion Papers.

59. Russell to W. I. Wolverton, October 19, 1932, School of Religion Papers.

60. Branscomb to Russell, [February, 1932], School of Religion Papers.

61. Soper to L. A. Weigle, May 8, 1926, School of Religion Papers.

62. J. Q. Schisler to Russell, January 2, 1930, School of Religion Papers.

63. H. S. Smith to Few, August 10, 1931, Few Papers.

64. Russell to Garber, August 15, 1931, School of Religion Papers. For background on the appointment, see Few to Russell, July 2, 6, and 29, 1931 and Russell to Few, July 4, 27, 1931, Few Papers.

65. Russell to Clark, June 21, 1933, School of Religion Papers.

66. K. W. Clark, "Statement to President Few," March 2, 1934, Few Papers.

67. R. R. Branton in Newellton, La., to Garber, April 20, 1931, School of Religion Papers.

68. Daniel C. Whitsett to Garber, July 27, 1931, School of Religion Papers.

69. J. Doyne Young to Garber, April 14, 1932, School of Religion Papers.

70. Clyde Boggs to Garber, October 26 and September 10, 1934, School of Religion Papers.

71. Martell Twitchell to Garber, January 21, 1935, School of Religion Papers.

72. James E. Scott to Garber, April 30, 1936, School of Religion Papers.

73. Harvie Branscomb, "A Memorandum Concerning the Divinity School of Duke University," [late 1944?], Flowers Papers.

74. T. S. Davis to Garber, September 14, 1934, School of Religion Papers.

75. Kenneth Goodson to Garber, September 10, 1934, School of Religion Papers.

76. Garber to Goodson, September 10, 1934, School of Religion Papers.

77. Regulations for Bachelor of Divinity thesis, July 23, 1929, School of Religion Papers; "Theses in School of Religion," *Bulletin* 1 (May, 1936): 41–42.

78. Garber to J. D. Lee, May 19, 1936, School of Religion Papers.

79. "Staff and Curriculum Developments," *Bulletin* 3 (May, 1938): 38–39.

80. Russell, *Autobiography*, p. 343.

81. H. Shelton Smith, "The Growth of Graduate Study in Religion . . . , 1926–1947," with Smith to Charles E. Jordan, January 3, 1948, Charles E. Jordan Papers, Duke University Archives. Hereinafter cited as Smith, "The Growth of Graduate Study."

82. Smith, "The Growth of Graduate Study."

83. Few to W. M. Alexander, January 4, 1940, Few Papers.

84. W. P. Few, "The Duke University School of Religion," *Bulletin* 5 (May, 1940): 30.

85. Porter, *Trinity and Duke*, p. 91.

86. Harvie Branscomb, "What's Been Happening in the Library?" *Bulletin* 1 (February, 1936): 10–12.

87. Russell to R. E. Wolfe, April 18, 1935; Russell to H. P. Van Deusen, November 18, 1935, School of Religion Papers.

88. James A. Montgomery to Branscomb, April 9, 1934, and Carl H. Kraeling to Branscomb, April 9, 1934, School of Religion Papers.

89. Russell to W. F. Albright, February 18, 1936, School of Religion Papers.

90. W. F. Albright to Russell, February 21, 1936, School of Religion Papers.

91. W. F. Stinespring to Russell, March 6, 1936, School of Religion Papers.

92. Russell to Few, June 5, 1940, Few Papers.

93. Ellwood to Garber, February 27, 1936, School of Religion Papers.

94. *Bulletin* 8 (November, 1943): 48.

95. *Bulletin* 1 (February, 1936): 1–2.

96. Ibid., p. 23.

97. *Christian Horizons* 1/3 (1939): p. 15. An incomplete file is in the Duke University Archives.

98. *Christian Horizons* 2/3 (1939–40): 8–10.

99. *Bulletin of Duke University. Report of the President . . . , 1938–1939*, p. 89.

100. J. Q. Schisler, director, Leadership and Training Department, General Sunday School Board, Methodist Episcopal Church, South, to Few, June 25, 1929, School of Religion Papers.

101. Russell to Rufus M. Jones, February 25, 1930, School of Religion Papers.

102. Memorandum from Few, with Branscomb to Few, August 15, 1927, and minutes of joint committee on Junaluska, November 8, 1927, Few Papers.

103. Alice A. Deckman, "Reminscences of a Summer Spent in the South," *The Pennsylvanian Teacher* (Fall, 1932 and Winter, 1933): 14–15, 7–9, 14–15, School of Religion Papers.

104. *Bulletin* 1 (February, 1936): 12–13; Kenneth W. Clark, "Four Decades of the Divinity School," *Duke Divinity School Review* 32 (Spring, 1967): 166.

105. H. Shelton Smith to Robert E. Cushman, November 28, 1977, in Hilarie Shelton Smith Papers, Duke University Archives.

106. Garber to Flowers, March 15, 1941, and copy of news release, May 3, 1941, School of Religion Papers.

107. Garber to Russell, April 22, 1939, and Garber to W. K. Anderson, May 12, 1941, School of Religion Papers.

108. Garber to Bishop John M. Moore, March 3, 1938, School of Religion Papers.

109. Garber to Russell, May 20, 1938, School of Religion Papers. The general conference adopted the plan of union by a vote of 434 to 26.

110. John W. Langdale, book editor of the Abingdon Press in New York, to Garber, February 18, 1939, School of Religion Papers.
111. R. Odell Brown to Garber, May 1, 1939, School of Religion Papers.
112. Elmer T. Clark, editor of *World Outlook*, to Garber, February 27, 1939, School of Religion Papers.
113. Albert Bridewell to Garber, July 1, 1939, and Kenneth Goodson to Garber, October 6, 1939, School of Religion Papers.
114. Garber to J. B. Craven, May 6, 1941, School of Religion Papers.
115. Garber to Cannon, May 8, 1941, School of Religion Papers.
116. *The Divinity School Bulletin* 6 (November, 1941): 69. This was the first issue to use the new name.
117. *Bulletin* 6 (November, 1941): 64.
118. Garber to Robert E. Lasater, September 15, 1941, School of Religion Papers.
119. *Bulletin* 4 (February, 1939): 1; P. N. Garber to H. A. Dupree, April 23, 1941, School of Religion Papers.
120. [Garber] to N. E. Edgerton, April 23, 1941, School of Religion Papers.
121. Garber to G. F. Hood, December 18, 1941, School of Religion Papers.
122. *Bulletin* 7 (November, 1942): 21; *Bulletin* 7 (January, 1943): 9–11.
123. *Bulletin* 9 (May, 1944): 20–21.
124. *Bulletin* 8 (January, 1944): 62; *Bulletin* 9 (November, 1944): 56.
125. *Bulletin* 6 (January, 1942): 82–83.
126. Garber to E. T. Clark, February 27, 1941, and F. W. Clelland to Garber, March 2, 1941, School of Religion Papers.
127. Russell to Rockefeller Foundation, March 1, 1929, School of Religion Papers.
128. Flowers to S. J. Stern, July 29, 1942, Flowers Papers; Branscomb to W. H. Wannamaker, December 16, 1942, Wannamaker Papers; and Branscomb to J. Goldin, January 5, 1943, and Goldin to Branscomb, January 8, 1943, Wannamaker Papers.
129. *Bulletin* 9 (May, 1944): p. 8.
130. Branscomb to Few, October 19, 1937, and Few to Branscomb, October 20, 1937, Few Papers.
131. H. Branscomb, "A Memorandum Concerning the Divinity School of Duke University," undated [late 1944?], Flowers Papers, subject file.
132. *Bulletin* 10 (May, 1945): 7–8.
133. *Alumni Register* 32 (February, 1946): 29.
134. Paul K. Conkin, *Gone with the Ivy: A Biography of Vanderbilt University* (Knoxville: University of Tennessee Press, 1985), p. 444.
135. Branscomb, *Purely Academic*, pp. 77–79, 99–101.
136. R. C. Petry to Flowers, August 23, 1946, and Cushman to Flowers, August 13, 1946, Flowers Collection.
137. P. A. Root to Flowers, March 5, 1947, Flowers Papers.
138. Executive Committee of Divinity School Student Body to Rowe, May 21, 1947, Flowers Papers.
139. These matters are dealt with in more detail in chapter 14.
140. Copy of H. E. Spence to Bishop W. W. Peele, June 27, 1947, in the Willis Smith Papers, Manuscript Department, Duke University Library; hereinafter cited as W. Smith Papers.
141. *Bulletin* 12 (November, 1947): 97–98.
142. H. A. Bosley to Smith, June 28, 1948, W. Smith Papers.
143. H. A. Bosley, "Duke Among the Methodist Seminaries," *Bulletin* 13 (May, 1948): 19–25.
144. Smith to J. A. Gray, June 30, 1947, W. Smith Papers.

145. Charles E. Jordan to Alex. Sands, May 10, 1948, Jordan Papers.

146. *Bulletin* 13 (January, 1949): 108–110.

147. *Bulletin* 14 (January, 1950): 117, 125.

11. Building a Medical Center from Scratch

1. The early efforts to obtain a medical school are discussed in Porter, *Trinity and Duke, passim,* and also in James E. Gifford, Jr., *The Evolution of a Medical Center: A History of Medicine at Duke University to 1941* (Durham, N.C.: Duke University Press, 1972), pp. 11–34; hereinafter cited as Gifford, *Medical Center.* This chapter will lean heavily on Gifford's scholarly and useful monograph. Although the term "medical center" did not become widely employed and official until much later, it will be used for the sake of convenience and brevity in this chapter.

2. Gifford, *Medical Center,* pp. 25–26.

3. "Last Will and Testament of James B. Duke," James B. Duke Papers.

4. This is discussed in more detail in chapter 3.

5. Gifford, *Medical Center,* p. 49.

6. Copy of William H. Welch to Lewis H. Weed, February 28, 1926, Wilburt C. Davison Papers, Medical Center Archives, Duke University. Hereinafter cited as Davison Papers.

7. Mary R. Few to W. C. Davison, March 31, 1966, Davison Papers.

8. W. C. Davison, *The Duke University Medical Center: Reminiscences . . . , 1927–1960* (n.p., n.d.; 1967?), pp. 5–7; hereinafter cited as Davison, *Reminiscences.*

9. Gifford, *Medical Center,* pp. 37–39.

10. W. S. Rankin to W. P. Few, November 14, 1925, Few Papers.

11. Gifford, *Medical Center,* pp. 52–54.

12. W. C. Davison, "An M. D. Degree Five Years After High School," *Journal of American Medical Association* 90 (June, 1928): 1812–16.

13. Davison, *Reminiscences,* p. 23.

14. The original clinical departments were medicine, surgery, pediatrics, and obstetrics-gynecology. Since both medicine and surgery contained many subspecialities, they were by far the largest departments; consequently their chairmen possessed considerable power. Subspecialities in medicine were bacteriology, neurology, psychiatry (later a separate department), dermatology and syphilology, allergy, metabolic diseases, cardiology, gastroenterology, and applied therapeutics. In surgery the subspecialities were ophthalmology, orthopedics, otolaryngology (nose and throat), urology, and dentistry. The original preclinical departments were anatomy, biochemistry, physiology-pharmacology, and pathology.

15. J. D. Hart to Davison, May 14, 1929, Davison Papers. Davison, an early member of the new Hope Valley Country Club in Durham, recruited many members of the medical faculty and staff for membership in the club as well as residence in the handsome subdivision being built around it.

16. H. L. Amoss to Davison, March 23, 1930, and Davison to Amoss, March 25, 1930, Davison Papers.

17. Jay M. Arena and John P. McGovern, eds., *Davison of Duke: His Reminiscences* (Durham, N.C.: Duke University Medical Center, 1980), p. 111; hereinafter cited as Arena and McGovern, eds., *Davison.*

18. B. Baker to Hart, October 30, 1929, in J. Deryl Hart Papers, Medical Center Archives; hereinafter cited as Hart Papers.

19. Gifford, *Medical Center,* p. 67.

20. Arena and McGovern, eds., *Davison,* p. 111.

21. Certain anomalies concerning the school of nursing are explained below. Because there were forty-six persons on the original faculty of the medical center and in order to prevent this chapter from being overcrowded with names, appendix 1 lists them and shows the large preponderance of those with connections to Johns Hopkins. For a list of all faculty members during the period from 1930 to 1950, see *The First Twenty Years: A History of the Duke University Schools of Medicine, Nursing and Health Services, and Duke Hospital, 1930 to 1950* (Durham, N.C.: Duke University, 1952), pp. 104–115. Because of the cover of this compilation of statistics, lists, photographs, etc., it is familiarly and widely known in the Medical Center as "the green book." Hereinafter cited as *The First Twenty Years.*

22. Davison to Amoss, June 8, 1929, Davison Papers.

23. Davison to Amoss, January 7, 1929, Davison Papers.

24. Arena and McGovern, eds., *Davison*, p. 113.

25. Arena and McGovern, eds., *Davison*, p. 129.

26. Gifford, *Medical Center*, p. 70.

27. Statistical table in Gifford, *Medical Center*, p. 189.

28. F. H. Swett, reporting on the Department of Anatomy, 1930–40, in "School of Medicine, 1930–1940," *Bulletin of Duke University: Report of the President and Reports of Other Officers, 1939–1940* (April, 1941): 122–124. Hereinafter cited as *Report of the President.*

29. Statement by Eleanor B. Easley, M.D., 1934, in *Aesculapian*, the yearbook of the Duke University Medical School for 1980, p. 145.

30. Reprint of a portion of Sir William Osler's farewell address at Johns Hopkins in 1905, Davison Papers.

31. Gifford, *Medical Center*, pp. 115–116.

32. Gifford, *Medical Center*, pp. 156–157.

33. W. C. Davison, "The School of Medicine," in *Report of the President, 1925–1931* (April, 1932): 81.

34. Gifford, *Medical Center*, pp. 157, 189.

35. Davison to H. J. Stauter, January 20, 1941, Davison Papers.

36. W. A. Perlzweig to Davison, May 24, 1949, Davison Papers.

37. W. C. Davison, "The Duke University School of Medicine," a paper read to the Medical Society of North Carolina, Durham, April 19, 1927; pamphlet in Medical Center Archives.

38. J. Deryl Hart, *The First Forty Years at Duke in Surgery and the P.D.C.* (Durham, N.C.: Duke University, 1971), p. 1; hereinafter cited as Hart, *First Forty Years.*

39. *The First Twenty Years*, pp. 95–96. Raymond B. Fosdick, *Adventure in Giving: The Story of the General Education Board* (New York: Harper & Row, 1962), pp. 155–173, has an interesting account of the GEB's struggle to push the full-time basis for clinical teaching.

40. Hart, *First Forty Years*, p. 9. Italics in original.

41. Gifford, *Medical Center*, p. 85. James Gifford interviewed D. T. Smith in 1969.

42. Gifford, *Medical Center*, pp. 88–89.

43. Perlzweig to Davison, May 31, 1934, Davison Papers.

44. *Report of the President* (April, 1935), pp. 129–130.

45. Ibid., pp. 137–139.

46. F. M. Hanes in *Report of the President* (April, 1935): 134. Italics in original.

47. F. M. Hanes in *Report of the President* (April, 1941): 129.

48. Davison to Amoss, August 20, 1931, and Amoss to Davison, n.d. (September, 1931?), Davison Papers.

49. Davison to Amoss, October 22, 1931, ibid.

50. Davison to Amoss, November 10, 1931, ibid.

51. Amoss to Davison, November 25 and December 15, 1931, ibid.

52. Draft of memorandum by Davison, January 27, 1933, Davison Papers. There are numerous copies and revised versions of the document.

53. A. Flexner to Few, February 1, May 9, 1933, Few Papers.

54. Davison to Few, May 16, 1933, Few Papers. Amoss tried and failed to get a position at both Minnesota and Illinois; he ultimately went into private practice in the North.

55. Raleigh *News & Observer*, November 1, 1933.

56. W. Forbus to Davison, August 8, 1933, Davison Papers.

57. Council on Medical Education and Hospitals of the A.M.A., *Survey of Medical Schools, 1934–1937* (1937), Medical Center Archives.

58. *Report of the President* (April, 1941): 105.

59. Gifford, *Medical Center*, p. 90.

60. Arena and McGovern, eds., *Davison*, p. 147.

61. *The First Twenty Years*, pp. 46, 55.

62. Ibid., p. 55. There were special, complicated circumstances concerning the hospital's large amount of charity work for people in Durham; these are described in Gifford, *Medical Center*, pp. 95–98.

63. Gifford, *Medical Center*, pp. 90–91.

64. Ibid.

65. Ibid., pp. 103–104.

66. In Arena and McGovern, eds., *Davison*, pp. 146–147, Davison highlights some of the above-mentioned research achievements; Gifford, *Medical Center*, pp. 129–154, treats them in considerable detail.

67. Hart, *First Forty Years*, pp. 118–119; Gifford, *Medical Center*, pp. 144–149.

68. *The First Twenty Years*, pp. 27–28; Gifford, *Medical Center*, pp. 170–171.

69. *Report of the President* (April, 1935): 116; Gifford, *Medical Center*, pp. 167–170.

70. *The First Twenty Years*, p. 43.

71. Ibid., p. 35; Gifford, *Medical Center*, pp. 176–178.

72. Hart, *First Forty Years*, p. 61.

73. Ibid., p. 131.

74. Gifford, *Medical Center*, appendix 7, p. 196.

75. *The First Twenty Years*, pp. 71–72; Gifford, *Medical Center*, p. 183.

76. "History of the 65th," in *The First Twenty Years*, p. 82.

77. Ibid., p. 83.

78. "The War Years," in *The First Twenty Years*, p. 67.

79. R. Flowers to W. R. Perkins, April 23, 1943, Flowers Papers.

80. "The War Years," in *The First Twenty Years*, pp. 68–71.

81. Ibid., p. 73.

82. Arena and McGovern, eds., *Davison*, p. 153.

83. *The First Twenty Years*, pp. 77–78.

84. Ibid., p. 98.

85. Ibid., p. 97.

86. Ibid., pp. 98, 152.

87. Hart, *First Forty Years*, p. 55; *The First Twenty Years*, pp. 8–9.

88. Davison and F. V. Altvater to Flowers, November 25, 1940, Flowers Papers. Since F. M. Hanes offered to give $100,000 toward the cost of the new building and $125,000 or so could come from PDC funds, Davison asked the university and the Duke Endowment to contribute the balance. See Hanes to Few and Flowers, July 17, 1940, Flowers Papers.

89. Elizabeth P. Hanes to Flowers, July 26, 1946, Flowers Papers. Information about F. M. Hanes's earlier offer is in Hart, *First Forty Years*, pp. 61–62. Mrs. Hanes received a personal annuity during her lifetime from the university as part of the arrangement. Hanes and other members of his family were indeed generous to the medical center in the years between 1930 and 1950, and Hanes left his residual estate to the medical school; as of 1967, it had a book value of over $3,373,000. Hart, *First Forty Years*, pp. 61–62.

90. F. M. Hanes on Department of Medicine, 1930–40, *Report of the President* (April, 1941): 129.

91. D. Hart on Department of Surgery, 1930–40, ibid., p. 147.

92. Gifford, *Medical Center*, p. 178.

93. Ibid., pp. 178–180. Aside from the heads of departments, the medical center was quite hierarchical, and proceedings concerning tenure were as vague as in the rest of the university, if not more so. See Davison to W. G. Morgan, December 12, 1932, Davison Papers.

94. Hart, *First Forty Years*, p. 70. To illustrate his point about loyalty, Hart mentions that he reported in 1956 that since 1930, members of the "geographic full-time" (i.e., part-time) senior staff in surgery had received thirty-one offers of academic appointment elsewhere, with all but four of the offers also carrying an appointment as chairman. The offers came from twenty-two schools in the United States and Canada, and only one of the offers had been accepted. Ibid., p. 76.

95. *Report of the President* (April, 1935 and April, 1941): 113–150, pp. 87–149.

96. Arena and McGovern, eds., *Davison*, p. 164.

12. The Rebuilding of Duke University's School of Law

1. Porter, *Trinity and Duke*, pp. 143–146. For the launching of the Association of American Law Schools in 1900 and the larger national picture of legal education in the early twentieth century, see Robert Stevens, *Law School: Legal Education in America from the 1850s to the 1980s* (Chapel Hill: University of North Carolina Press, 1983), p. 38 and *passim*.

2. W. P. Few to W. R. Vance, April 9, 1925, Few Papers.

3. Few to W. R. Perkins, April 10, 1925, Few Papers.

4. Few to Vance, April 9, 1925, Few Papers.

5. Few to Perkins, April 21, 1925, Few Papers.

6. Harlan Stone to Few, June 9, 1925, Few Papers.

7. Few to E. D. Soper, June 30, July 14, 1925, for the quote, and Few to J. H. Wigmore, July 29, 1925, Few Papers.

8. George P. Pell to B. S. Womble, November 27, 1925, enclosed in Pell to Few, November 28, 1925, Few Papers.

9. Huger W. Jervey to Few, June 15, 1926, Few Papers.

10. Few to Jervey, June 28, 1926, Few Papers.

11. Few to Perkins, August 9, 1926, Few Papers.

12. Few to W. S. Barnes, June 15, 1926, Few Papers.

13. Clinton W. Toms to Few, May 16, 1927, and Few to Toms, November 1, 1927, Few Papers.

14. Toms to Few, December 5, 1927, Few Papers. See also Few's letters about the proposed medical school to Bernard M. Baruch, May 17, 1927, and Baruch's noncommittal reply, May 20, 1927, Few Papers.

15. W. B. Bolich to Few, March 15, 1926, and July 13, 1927; also see Few to Womble,

May 28, 1927, in which Few consults Womble and other prominent Trinity-Duke alumni in Winston-Salem concerning the appointment.

16. R. L. Flowers to Few, August 3, 1927, Few to T. D. Bryson, August 30, 1927, and A. W. McLean to Few, September 2, 1927, Few Papers.

17. Few to Toms, June 23, 1928, Few Papers.

18. Francis G. Caffey to Few, November 3, 1926, Few Papers; for W. D. Lewis and the American Law Institute, see Stevens, *Law School*, p. 144 n. 21.

19. William D. Lewis, compiler, "Reports in Regard to the Establishment of the Law School at Duke University," Law Library, Duke University; memorandum, April 13, 1929, Few Papers; Glenn J. Carter, "The Rise to National Stature of the Duke University Law School, 1927–1935," seminar paper in 1978, Duke University Archives. Hereinafter cited as Carter, "Rise."

20. Few to G. G. Allen, June 18, 1929; Few to Perkins, July 11, 1929; N. T. Dowling to Few, November 8, 1929.

21. Few to Perkins, November 13, 1929.

22. Few to Dean Roscoe Pound, Harvard Law School, November 30, 1929, Few Papers. Few sent virtually the same letter to President A. Lawrence Lowell and Professor Samuel Williston, both at Harvard; to Dean Charles E. Clark at Yale Law School; and to President R. M. Hutchins, at the University of Chicago, whose inauguration Few had recently attended.

23. Few to Caffey, December 24, 1929, Few Papers.

24. Few to Perkins, January 3, 1930, Few Papers.

25. Few to J. Miller, January 23 and 29, 1930, Few Papers.

26. Miller to Louis M. Howe, March 20, 1931, Records of the Duke University Law School, Files of Dean Justin Miller, 1930–1934, Duke University Archives. Hereinafter cited as Miller Files. Biographical data concerning Miller is available in *Who Was Who in America*, vol. 5 (Chicago: Marquis Who's Who, 1973), pp. 499–500, and is scattered throughout the Miller Files.

27. August Vollmer, chief of police in Berkeley, California, to J. A. Gerk, December 13, 1930, Miller Files.

28. Thomas R. Powell to Miller, September 22, 1930, Miller Files.

29. Miller to N. Rea, March 26, 1931, and Miller to C. L. Chute, May 20, 1931, Miller Files.

30. Miller to T. C. Ridgeway, October 22, 1930, and W. A. Stansbury to Miller, July 30, 1931, Miller Files.

31. *Chronicle*, May 3, 1933.

32. Miller to L. E. Thomas, October 8, 1930, Miller Files.

33. Miller to R. H. Scott, June 2, 1931, Miller Files.

34. Miller to L. L. Hill, June 29, 1931, Miller Files.

35. Miller to W. H. Waste, October 10, 1930, Miller Files.

36. Braxton Craven, John F. Crowell, and John C. Kilgo were important earlier presidents of Trinity College.

37. R. M. Gantt to Few, October 11, 1930, and Willis Smith to Few, October 13, 1930, Few Papers.

38. Few to Gantt, October 13, 1930, Few Papers.

39. Questionnaire filled out for the General Education Board, February 24, 1938, box 31, Flowers Papers.

40. Miller to Few, February 15, 1930, Few Papers.

41. Stevens, *Law School*, pp. 162, 165 n. 14.

42. Ibid., p. 173.

43. Miller to A. B. Andrews, November 7, 1930, Miller Files.

44. Roswell Magill to Miller, November 28 and December 4, 1930, Miller Files.

45. Miller to A. J. Harno, January 20, 1931, and Harno to Miller, January 27, 1931, Miller Files.

46. Lon L. Fuller to Miller, telegram, January 7, 1931; Miller to Fuller, January 19, 1931, Miller Files.

47. Miller to D. M. Cavers, January 21 and February 24, 1931; Cavers to Miller, February 5, March 12, 1931, Miller Files.

48. Thurman Arnold to Miller, March 30, 1931, and Miller to Arnold, April 9, 1931, Miller Files.

49. Miller to Few and Flowers, December 1, 1931, Few Papers.

50. Perkins to Few, December 3, 1931; Perkins to Miller, December 1, 1931; and Miller to Few and Flowers, December 18, 1931, Few Papers.

51. Few to Perkins, December 21, 1931, Few Papers.

52. Carter, "Rise to National Stature . . . ," p. 20.

53. *Chronicle*, September 16 and 23 and October 7, 1931.

54. *Chronicle*, September 23, 1931, and John S. Bradway, memorandum on Legal Aid Clinic, February 1, 1933, Miller Files.

55. Miller to J. J. Robinson, May 2, 1933, Miller Files.

56. Bradway to H. C. Horack, August 7 and September 17, 1934, Horack Files.

57. *Chronicle*, November 11, 1931, January 18, 1933.

58. Miller to Few and Flowers, October 24, 1931, Miller Files; *Chronicle*, November 4, 1931.

59. Miller to K. N. Llewellyn, October 23, 1930, Miller Files.

60. Cavers to Miller, Memorandum on Advantages to the School of Law of the Projected Legal Periodical, n.d. [March?, 1933], folder on *Law and Contemporary Problems*, Miller Files. Hereinafter cited as Cavers Memorandum.

61. Cavers Memorandum, Miller Files. Miller sent a copy of this memorandum to Few and Flowers.

62. L. Craven to Miller and Cavers, n.d. [March, 1933]; Cavers to Miller and Craven, March 28, 1933, Miller Files.

63. Miller to Horack, March 18, 1933; *Chronicle*, April 12, 1933.

64. Horack to Kenneth Rush, December 10, 1937, Horack Files.

65. Miller to G. Dean, November 18, 1930, Miller Files; *Duke Alumni Register*, December, 1930.

66. Miller to Horack, March 18, 1933.

67. *Chronicle*, December 14, 1932.

68. D. Maggs to Horack, February 13, 1936, Horack Files.

69. Fuller to Horack, October 10, 1939, Horack Files.

70. Maggs to Horack, October 11, 1938, Horack Files.

71. Maggs to Horack, June 6, 1943, Horack Files.

72. Miller to Few and Flowers, March 24, 1932, and Minutes of Law School Administrative Committee, April 19, 1931, Few Papers.

73. Horack to C. L. Pittz, May 11, 1939, Horack Files.

74. Carter, "Rise to National Stature . . . ," pp. 22–23.

75. The Miller Files contain numerous examples of these traits; see, for example, Miller to T. A. Adams, September 24 and 26, 1930, Miller Files.

76. Miller to George Osborne (in Paris, France), November 11, 1930, and Osborne to Miller, n.d. [November, 1930], Miller Files.

77. Miller to Few and Flowers, May 5, 1931, Few Papers.

78. W. H. Glasson to Few, May 5, 1931, Few Papers.

79. Miller to Few and Flowers, June 24, 1931, Few Papers.

80. Miller to Few and Flowers, August 27, 1931, Miller Files.

81. Miller to Few and Flowers, September 9, 1931, Miller Files.

82. Interviews with various faculty members who worked with Few.

83. Woody, ed., *Papers*, p. 54. The reference to Few in faculty meetings is on p. 137.

84. Few to Perkins, December 21, 1931, Few Papers.

85. Miller to Perkins, June 22 and 29, 1931, and Miller to W. Smith, September 8, 1931, Miller Files.

86. These matters are dealt with in greater detail in chapter 3.

87. James B. Duke's indenture of December 11, 1924, is reprinted as an appendix in Durden, *The Dukes*, pp. 268–280. Quoted phrase on p. 274.

88. *Chronicle*, November 18 and 25, 1931.

89. J. Miller to C. N. Nison, June 12, 1934, Miller Files, for the committee's purpose; Alice M. Baldwin, "The Woman's College, as I Remember It," typed MS (1959), p. 83, Duke University Archives.

90. Flowers to J. F. Rippy, August 24, 1932, and E. Seeman to H. W. Dwire, September 19, 1933, Flowers Papers.

91. Miller to Few and Flowers, September 21, 1931, Few Papers. Perkins, Allen, and W. B. Bell, another trustee of the Duke Endowment, had pushed for a total fee of $300 for the law school as early as June, 1930, on the grounds that the $200 then charged made it appear that there was "something the matter" with the school. Copy of Bell to Allen, June 9, 1930, and Allen to Few, June 11, 1930, Few Papers. By early 1932 Allen agreed that because of the depression the tuition increases should be halted.

92. Miller's memorandum, April 12, 1932, Few Papers.

93. Miller to Few and Flowers, April 14, 1932, Few Papers.

94. Miller to Few and Flowers, April 15, 1932, Few Papers.

95. Durham *Sun*, February 17, 1934; Greensboro *Daily News*, February 13, 1934.

96. Few to Perkins, February 12, 1934, Few Papers.

97. Clement Doyle to Miller, February 6, 1934, Miller Files.

98. Miller to Doyle, February 20, 1934, Miller Files.

99. For Miller's description of himself as "merely a Republican" in a Democratic state, see Miller to W. A. Wiltberger, February 21, 1933.

100. Few to W. Smith, March 6, 1934, Few Papers.

101. Few to Perkins, May 14, 1934, Few Papers.

102. Perkins to Few, May 16, 1934, Few Papers.

103. Few to W. Smith, May 17, 1934, and Perkins to Few, May 18, 1934, Few Papers.

104. Minutes of Faculty Meeting of Law School, May 25, 1934, Few Papers.

105. Few to Perkins, May 28, 1934, Few Papers.

106. Perkins to Few, May 29, 1934, Few Papers.

107. President F. D. Roosevelt to Few, June 15, 1934, requesting Miller's services for a year, and Few to Roosevelt, June 18, 1934, Few Papers. As Miller's note to Willis Smith (ca. June 10, 1934, Willis Smith Papers, Manuscript Department, Duke University Library) makes clear, Duke University agreed to supplement the salary of $9,000 that Miller would receive in Washington by paying him $6,000 (plus $750 on a pension fund) so that Miller would receive the equivalent of his Duke salary.

108. Craven to A. S. Pearse, July 14, 1934, Few Papers.

109. Few to Perkins, July 6, 1934, Few Papers.

110. Greensboro *Daily News*, July 1, 1934.

111. Few to W. Smith, September 13, 1934, Few Papers.

112. Miller to Patricia McKeefe, assistant to the education editor of *Time*, September 18, 1934, with W. Smith to Few, October 3, 1934, Few Papers. In a note to Willis Smith (ca.

June 18, 1934) Miller also attacked Few as, among other things, a "jealous psychopath." Willis Smith Papers.

113. Few to Perkins, January 2, 1935, and Perkins to Few, January 4, 1935, Few Papers.

114. Few to Miller, February 15, 1935, and Few to W. Smith, February 15, 1935, Few Papers. The Durham *Sun*, February 13, 1935, printed Miller's letter of resignation.

115. Copy, Horack to Miller, February 20, 1935, Horack Files. If Miller sent a reply, it is not in the Horack Files.

116. Horack to A. J. Farrah, dean of the law school, University of Alabama, November 4, 1935, Horack Files.

117. Ernest Seeman, "Duke: But Not Doris," *New Republic*, September 20, 1936, pp. 220–222.

118. D. F. Cavers, L. L. Fuller, and D. B. Maggs, "A Communication: The Duke University Law School in Rebuttal," *New Republic*, October 21, 1936, pp. 311–312.

119. *Who Was Who in America*, vol. 5, 1969–1973 (Chicago: Marquis Who's Who, 1973), pp. 499–500. Miller died on January 17, 1973, at age eighty-four.

120. Horack to W. Smith, chairman of the trustees' committee for the law school, January 7, 1936, Horack Files.

121. Thurman Arnold to Miller, February 6, 1933, Horack Files.

122. Horack to D. Poteat, July 20, 1934, Arnold to Horack, April 20, 1936, and Horack to Maggs, May 1, 1936. Another graduate of Yale's law school whom Horack hired, Kenneth Rush, remained at Duke only one year, 1936–37.

123. Horack to Maggs, May 14, 1936, Horack Files.

124. E. R. Latty to Miller, n.d. [ca. December 1, 1932], Miller Files.

125. Marion Kirkwood to Horack, April 1, 1937, Horack Files.

126. Horack to J. F. Bruton, October 25, 1938, and Horack to W. C. Davison, May 21, 1942, Horack Files; the Durham *Herald Sun*, May 15, 1938, has pictures and a story.

127. R. M. Nixon to the author, August 20, 1987, Nixon Papers, Duke University Archives.

128. Horack to Bradway, September 4, 1936, for the research assistantship, Horack to Chisman Hanes, September 4, 1936, and Horack to John Harkrider, February 16, 1938, Horack Files.

129. Fuller to Horack, January 15, 1940, Horack Files. For Fuller's prominent place in American legal history, see Robert S. Summers, *Lon L. Fuller* (Stanford, Calif.: Stanford University Press, 1984).

130. Horack to Cavers, January 27, 1941, Horack Files.

131. Kirkwood to Horack, April 14, 1943, Horack Files.

132. On the failure of the three-school plan, see M. S. Breckenridge to Horack, March 27, 1943, and Horack to Breckenridge, April 2, 1943, Horack Files.

133. Maggs to Horack, May 14, 1945, Horack Files.

134. An example of this may be found in Horack to Paul Sanders, June 4 and October 2, 1945, Horack Files.

13. *The Serendipitous Acquisition of Assets*

1. As of April, 1928, the total cost of all of the land purchases was $1,759,715. Memorandum, Duke University, Duke Endowment Building Fund, April 11, 1928, Flowers Papers.

2. R. L. Flowers to G. G. Allen, May 26, 1925, and June 27, 1925, Flowers Papers.

3. J. M. Daniel to Flowers, July 20, 1925, Flowers Papers.

4. Flowers to Alex. H. Sands, August 28, 1925, and Flowers to Mrs. J. B. Duke, September 4, 1925, Flowers Papers.

5. Flowers to Mrs. J. B. Duke, September 4, 8, and 15, 1925, Flowers Papers.

6. Flowers to Allen, January 5 and 11, and February 3, 1926, Flowers Papers.

7. Flowers to Hill, February 3, 1928, and minutes of the Duke Endowment Building Committee, April 29, 1930, Flowers Papers; Few to State Highway Engineer, July 15, 1936, F. H. Brant to Few, July 29, 1936, and W. F. Wheeler to Few, December 31, 1936, Few Papers.

8. W. R. Perkins to Flowers, January 29, 1929, Flowers Papers.

9. Few to John F. Bruton, December 15, 1934, Few Papers, for the size of the endowment; Perkins to Flowers, January 29, 1929; memorandum of the university's executive committee, February 1, 1929; and A. C. Lee to Flowers, May 27, 1929, Flowers Papers, for the ten houses.

10. Alex. H. Sands to Flowers, April 9, 1930, Flowers Papers.

11. Minutes of Duke Endowment Building Committee, April 19, 1930, Flowers Papers; minutes of Duke University Committee on Construction of Faculty Houses, June 6, 1930, Flowers Papers; Justin Miller to Few and Flowers, August 10, 1931, Few Papers.

12. Nelson C. Brown to Few, May 5 and June 27, 1927, Few Papers.

13. Samuel T. Dana and Evert W. Johnson, *Forestry Education in America: Today and Tomorrow* (Washington, D.C.: Society of American Foresters, 1963), p. 42. The Biltmore school ceased to operate in 1913.

14. Henry S. Graves and Cedric H. Guise, *Forest Education* (New Haven, Conn.: Yale University Press, 1932), pp. 13, 22.

15. Flowers to J. S. Holmes, November 7, 1925, Flowers Papers.

16. Flowers to Perkins, August 11, 1927, and Flowers to Philip M. Payne, August 19, 1927, Flowers Papers. Few to Perkins, August 27, 1927, Few Papers.

17. Few's extensive correspondence with and about Charles L. Pack may be found in the Few Papers, 1927–1929.

18. Brown to Few, June 27, 1927, Few Papers.

19. E. H. Frothingham to Few, January 29, 1930, Few Papers.

20. Frothingham to E. H. Clapp, January 24, 1930, Clarence F. Korstian Papers, Duke University Archives. Hereinafter cited as Korstian Papers.

21. Clarence F. Korstian to H. S. Graves, January 29, 1930, Few Papers.

22. Korstian to O. M. Butler, July 18, 1930, Korstian Papers.

23. Korstian to C. R. Tillotson, July 22, 1930, Korstian Papers.

24. Korstian to G. L. Hume, July 24, 1930, Korstian Papers.

25. J. V. Hoffman to Korstian, July 23, 1930, Korstian Papers.

26. Clarence F. Korstian, "The Duke Forest," in *Bulletin of Duke University: Report of the President and Reports of Other Officers, 1925–1931* (April, 1932): 85. Hereinafter cited as *President's Report.*

27. *Durham Morning Herald*, December 8, 1930.

28. *President's Report, 1925–1931*: 87.

29. *President's Report, 1931–1932* (April, 1933): 77–88.

30. *Alumni Register* 17 (March, 1931): 77.

31. *Alumni Register* 17 (May, 1931): 152–153.

32. *President's Report, 1934–1935* (April, 1936): 125–126.

33. Ibid., pp. 127–128.

34. "Clarence F. Korstian: Forty Years of Forestry," an oral history interview by Elwood R. Maunder, February 16, 1959, Duke University Archives, p. 46. Hereinafter cited as "Korstian: Forty Years."

35. Ibid., p. 43.

36. *Alumni Register* 17 (July, 1931): 227.

37. *Bulletin of Duke University: Forestry* (February, 1935). This was apparently the first bulletin issued specifically for forestry at Duke.

38. "Korstian: Forty Years," p. 48.

39. Ibid., p. 43.

40. Ibid., pp. 44–45, 48–49.

41. *President's Report, 1937–1938* (March, 1939): 113.

42. Some of the problems and controversies related to the multiple-use policy are explored in Harold K. Steen, *The U.S. Forest Service: A History* (Seattle: University of Washington Press, 1976), pp. 278–323.

43. *President's Report, 1938–1939* (March, 1940): 116–117.

44. Unpublished Report to the President, 1941–42, in Flowers Papers.

14. From Few to Flowers

1. A School of Business Administration was finally established in 1969; it became the Fuqua School of Business in 1980.

2. W. Few to S. A. Stewart, September 28, 1926, Few Papers.

3. Few to Doris Duke, November 4, 1930, Few Papers. He received a brief but cordial, handwritten reply.

4. Few to W. R. Perkins, December 16, 1933, Few Papers.

5. Few to James Atkins, Jr., December 23, 1933, Few Papers.

6. Few to Mrs. J. B. Duke, February 25, 1935, Few Papers.

7. See Perkins to Few, March 4, 1935; Few to W. L. Baldwin, February 5, 1937, Few Papers.

8. *Chronicle*, March 8, 12, 19, and 22, 1935.

9. Few to Doris D. Cromwell, April 4, 1935, Few Papers.

10. *Chronicle*, April 24, 1936.

11. Dr. Martin E. Rehfuss to Few, January 28, 1936, Few Papers.

12. Few to Doris D. Cromwell, November 21, 1938, Few Papers.

13. Few to Doris D. Cromwell, May 15, 1939, and Doris D. Cromwell to Few, May 23, 1939, Few Papers.

14. Few to Doris D. Cromwell, January 19, 1940.

15. Few to Perkins, October 16, 1939; Mary Duke Biddle II first married Dr. Josiah C. Trent; after his death, she married Dr. James H. Semans.

16. Draft, Few to M. D. Biddle, June 22, 1937; Perkins to Few, June 30, 1937; and Few to M. D. Biddle, July 3, 1937.

17. Geiger, *American Research Universities*, p. 45.

18. Few to G. Allen, December 16, 1935, Few Papers.

19. Few to Walter A. Jessup, March 4, 1936, Few Papers. Few sent virtually the same letter to the General Education Board and one or two other foundations but was to have little to show for his efforts in that direction.

20. Technically, Brower came as executive secretary of the Duke Memorial, pet project of James A. Thomas, but in fact Brower's chief focus was on the centennial. See Few to Thomas, January 4, 1937; Brower to Few, June 17, 1937, Few Papers.

21. Few's memorandum for N. Chaffin, August 4, 1937, Few Papers.

22. Few to J. B. Conant, October 7, 1937.

23. P. H. Hanes to Few, April 22, 1939, Few Papers. Hanes broke down the total as follows: $1,561,927 for additions to the plant (not including the graduate dormitory, for which funds were in hand before the campaign began); $458,215 for scholarships and loan funds; $234,917 for research funds; $2,600,155 for endowment; and $123,029 in miscellaneous gifts. The total was $4,978,245.

24. Jerome Dowd to Few (ca. May 9, 1939), Few Papers. In late March, 1939, Few suffered a heavy personal tragedy when the youngest of his five sons, Yancey Preston Few, died.

25. W. T. Laprade, address on the life of W. P. Few, *Alumni Register* 32 (November, 1946): 280.

26. *Chronicle*, April 28, 1939.

27. G. H. Gilbert to W. Wannamaker, January 29, 1934, and Wannamaker to Gilbert, June 26, 1934, Wannamaker Papers.

28. Memorandum with Conrad Hoffman, Jr., to Few, December 4, 1933, Few Papers. The overall percentage at Duke remained at around 2.7 percent throughout the 1930s.

29. Few to J. H. Reynolds, October 29, 1927, Few Papers.

30. George F. Wilson to Few, May 27, 1927, Few Papers.

31. Few to J. Bruton, May 24, 1927, Few Papers.

32. Few to C. Toms, September 17, 1926, Few Papers.

33. Toms to Few, January 20 and February 9, 1927, and Few to Toms, February 5, 1927, Few Papers.

34. Few to C. Toms, Jr., October 19, 1936, Few Papers.

35. Toms to Few, January 2, 1928, Few Papers.

36. Few to R. L. Kelly, June 14, 1934, Few Papers.

37. Few to Allen, December 29, 1931, Few Papers.

38. Few to W. A. Lambeth, March 27, 1940, Few Papers.

39. These matters are discussed more fully in chapter 3.

40. Toms to Few, September 23, 1929, Few Papers.

41. Bruton to Few, March 5, 1935, Few Papers.

42. *Chronicle*, September 21, 1937.

43. Ibid., September 24, 1937.

44. Ibid., October 11, 1938.

45. Ibid., January 10, 1939.

46. Ibid., March 7, 1939.

47. The single vacant space on the north side of the main quadrangle would be filled by the erection of the Allen building in the early 1950s.

48. *Chronicle*, September 20, 1939. Although the editorial was not signed, Duncan C. Gray was the editor.

49. Copy of Few's remarks, January 6, 1940, Few Papers.

50. W. B. Bell to Few, August 16, 1939, and Few to Bell, September 11, 1939, Few Papers.

51. Memorandum, October 7, 1940, Few Papers.

52. Few to ———, April 23, 1938, Flowers Papers.

53. Memorial resolution adopted by Southern University Conference, October 22, 1940, Few Papers.

54. M. McDermott and others to Wannamaker, January 10, 1941, Few Papers.

55. *Chronicle*, October 16, 1940. Robert M. Lester, the editor, wrote the editorial.

56. Ibid., October 18, 1940. C. F. Sanborn was the columnist.

57. Mrs. W. P. Few to H. C. Horack (November, 1940?), records of the School of Law, Horack Files, University Archives.

58. Copy of "Tribute to Dr. Few," with W. H. Wannamaker to H. R. Dwire, November 29, 1941, Few Papers.

59. Laprade, address on life of Few, November 7, 1946, in *Alumni Register* 32 (November, 1946): 278–280.

60. Branscomb, *Purely Academic*, p. 81.

61. A. S. Pearse to Bruton, October 18, 1940, and Bruton to Pearse, October 23, 1940, records of the board of trustees for 1940, University Archives.

62. W. Smith to H. R. Dwire, January 23, 1941, records of the board of trustees for 1941, University Archives.

63. H. Branscomb to Flowers, February 2, 1941, Flowers Papers.

64. F. C. Sherrill to Flowers, January 30, 1941 (subject file, box no. 32), Flowers Papers.
65. F. M. Weaver, Sr., to Flowers, February 2, 1941 (subject file, box no. 32), Flowers Papers.
66. *Chronicle*, January 7, 1942.
67. Ibid., February 13, 1942.
68. Ibid., March 24, 1942.
69. Memorandum to faculty and staff from WSGA and MSGA, May 8 and 15, 1942, Flowers Papers.
70. *Chronicle*, September 22, 1942.
71. Ibid., October 23, 1942.
72. Ibid., October 27, 1942.
73. Ibid., October 30, 1942.
74. Ibid., November 3, 1942.
75. Flowers to Allen, February 9, 1943.
76. *Chronicle*, November 5, 1943.
77. Wannamaker to R. Fearing, June 15, 1945, Wannamaker Papers.
78. N. I. White to Flowers, January 13 and 28, 1943, Flowers Papers.
79. *Chronicle*, March 20, 1942.
80. White to Flowers, November 8, 1943, and Flowers to White, November 10, 1943. As Flowers suggested, the trustees and their executive committee met irregularly during the war. Also, Flowers neither wrote annual reports for the board (and as part of the historical record) nor asked the deans of the various schools to produce such reports. There is, therefore, a significant gap in the university's records for the 1940s.
81. Memorandum to trustees, n.d. [May, 1946], Jordan Papers, folder on board of trustees, University Archives.
82. Statement to the trustees, n.d. [May, 1946], Jordan Papers.
83. A. Baldwin to Flowers, October 30, 1945, and Wannamaker to Flowers, November 1, 1945, Flowers Papers.
84. *Chronicle*, January 17, 1947.
85. Ibid., March 14, 1947.
86. J. Hubbell to Flowers, July 24, 1946, Flowers Papers.
87. E. R. Moore to Wannamaker, March 28, 1947, Wannamaker Papers. There are other such examples in these files.
88. Sumner H. Slichter to Flowers, January 2, 1947, Flowers Papers.
89. *Chronicle*, April 4, 1941. C. F. Sanborn was the columnist.
90. Ibid., December 17, 1943.
91. Ibid., March 10, 1944.
92. Ibid., April 6, 1945. The editor was Charles B. Markham, Jr.
93. *Chronicle*, October 25, 1946. The writer was N. L. Hodgkins.
94. George T. Frampton to Bruton and Flowers, March 15, 1944, Flowers Papers.
95. Flowers to Bruton, March 22, 1944, and Bruton to Flowers, March 25, 1944, Flowers Papers.
96. Edward L. Fike to Smith, May 30, 1946, Smith Papers. Smith received a similar letter from another recent alumnus. See John Dozier to Smith, June 18, 1946, Smith Papers. Both Fike and Dozier would soon return to Duke in administrative roles.
97. Smith to E. L. Fike, June 13, 1946, Smith Papers.
98. James B. Conant to Smith, June 18, 1946, Smith Papers.
99. B. L. Elias to Dean Hall, School of Engineering, December 6, 1947, and C. Jordan to B. L. Elias, December 12, 1947, Jordan Papers. Although Horace Trumbauer himself was dead, the university still dealt with William O. Frank and Julian F. Abele in the architectural firm that kept Trumbauer's name.

100. When physics and mathematics eventually moved into the new building, the old physics building on the main quadrangle became the social science building.

101. Wannamaker to J. C. Dolley, August 6, 1947, Wannamaker Papers.

102. White to Wannamaker, March 22, 1948, Wannamaker Papers.

103. P. Gross to C. Hoover, March 19, 1945, Flowers Papers.

104. Copy of Gross to Smith, May 24, 1947, Flowers Papers. Perhaps it should be noted that the national AAUP had not yet begun collecting and publishing data on faculty salaries.

105. W. A. Stansbury to Smith, May 2, 1947, Smith Papers.

106. James A. Bell to Smith, June 2, 1947, Smith Papers.

107. R. A. Mayer to Smith, June 2, 1947, Smith Papers.

108. A. Sands's speech to the Faculty Club, *Chronicle*, February 28, 1947.

109. Sands to Smith, February 14, 1947, Smith Papers.

110. Flowers to Duke students and parents, July 14, 1947, Flowers Papers.

111. Charles A. Dukes, "Annual Report to the Duke University National Council," May 31, 1947, Flowers Papers.

112. "*More* About Your Share in Duke's Future," October, 1947, Flowers Papers.

113. Charles A. Dukes, "Annual Report to the Duke University National Council," June 5, 1948, Flowers Papers.

114. Smith to Sands, September 17, 1947, Smith Papers.

115. Byron W. Shimp, vice president of Kersting, Brown and Company, to Flowers, January 7, 1948.

116. J. G. Korner, Jr., to Smith, May 26, 1947, Smith Papers.

117. Don Elias to Smith, June 7, 1947, Smith Papers.

118. N. E. Edgerton to Elias, May 27, 1948, and Smith to Edgerton, May 29, 1948, Smith Papers.

119. M. E. Newsome to Smith, July 23, 1947, Smith Papers.

120. Memorandum from the Duke University Committee, Charles Jordan as secretary, to the trustees of the Angier B. Duke Memorial, July 20, 1946, Jordan Papers. There are other related documents in this collection.

15. *The Resolution of the Leadership Crisis*

1. Edwin L. Jones to W. Smith, February 28, 1947, Smith Papers.

2. Don S. Elias to Smith, June 7, 1947, Smith Papers.

3. Jones to Smith, November 7, 1946, and Smith to Jones, November 8, 1946, Smith Papers.

4. Smith to Elias, November 21, 1946, and Elias to Smith, November 25, 1946, Smith Papers.

5. John B. Harris to Smith, February 20, 1947, Smith Papers.

6. "A Duke Alumnus" to the editor, *Durham Morning Herald*, May 30, 1947, with a note from C. Sylvester Green to Jordan, Jordan Papers.

7. J. L. Horne to Smith, February 27, 1947, enclosing a copy of Horne to Elias, February 27, 1947, Smith Papers.

8. W. A. Stanbury to Smith, February 27, 1947, Smith Papers.

9. Smith's discreet report on his conversations with Flowers and Wannamaker is in the minutes of the executive committee of the board of trustees, October 1, 1947, office of the university secretary.

10. In later years the retirement age was made seventy for all except officers of the university, for whom it was made sixty-five.

11. January 20, 1948.

12. Henry A. Dennis to R. Flowers, January 24, 1948, and Edwin Gill to Flowers, January 26, 1948, Flowers Papers. Flowers died on August 24, 1951, a few months short of his ninety-first birthday. Wannamaker died on August 2, 1958; he would have been eighty-five on September 28.

13. The summary of the faculty ratings and other data are included in C. Jordan to Smith, February 2, 1948, Smith Papers.

14. Copy of A. Brower to W. Davison, June 8, 1948, Smith Papers.

15. Smith to G. Allen, March 26, 1948, and Smith to A. Sands, March 23, 1948, Smith Papers.

16. Smith to Sands, January 20 and 21, 1948, Smith Papers.

17. Smith to Sidney Alderman, May 22, 1948, Smith Papers.

18. E. Colwell to Smith, May 19, 1948, Smith Papers.

19. Colwell to Smith, May 27, 1948, Smith Papers. Colwell made no mention in his letter of certain personal problems of Chancellor Hutchins that had just become public knowledge (he and his wife were being divorced), but Smith believed that the "upheaval at Chicago" came just at the wrong time for Colwell to leave without appearing that "he was 'running out' on someone." Smith to J. R. Smith, August 17, 1948, Smith Papers.

20. Memorandum of Flowers, August 21, 1948, Flowers Papers.

21. Robert M. Gantt to Smith, May 31, 1948, and Smith to R. M. Gantt, June 2, 1948, Smith Papers.

22. J. R. Killian, Jr., to Smith, July 30, 1948, Smith Papers.

23. Killian to Smith, August 2, 1948, and Killian to Sands, September 13, 1948, Smith Papers.

24. Sands to Smith, September 14, 1948, and Smith to Sands, September 16, 1948, Smith Papers.

25. Smith to J. R. Smith, August 17, 1948, Smith Papers.

26. Killian to Smith, September 17, 1948 (telegram and letter), Smith Papers.

27. Killian apologized to Smith about the fact that a story about his being considered for the Duke presidency had appeared in a newspaper in Columbus, Georgia. Killian explained that a newspaper reporter had awakened his father in the middle of the night and gotten the story. Smith told him not to worry about it and added: "If my mother had been awakened in the middle of the night and asked some question about me, she would doubtless have said that I should be President instead of either Truman or Dewey." Smith to Killian, October 25, 1948, Smith Papers.

28. Colwell to Smith, July 28, 1948, Smith Papers.

29. W. A. Brownell to Smith, October 12, 1948, and undated memorandum to faculty, Smith Papers.

30. C. Hoover to Brownell, October 13, 1948, Smith Papers.

31. Copy, Goodrich C. White to J. O. Gross, October 2, 1948, Smith Papers.

32. Sands to Smith, October 5, 1948, Smith Papers.

33. Brownell to faculty advisory committee, October 20, 1948, Smith Papers.

34. Smith to Sands, October 26, 1948, Smith Papers.

35. W. W. Watson to Smith, November 22, 1948, Smith Papers.

36. Smith to Sands, December 3, 1948, Smith Papers.

37. Sands to Smith, December 14, 1948, and Smith to Sands, December 16, 1948, Smith Papers.

38. *Chronicle*, December 3, 1948.

39. N. White to W. Wannamaker, November 10, 1948, Wannamaker Papers.

40. W. B. Hamilton in the *Chronicle*, December 10, 1948.

41. Few to G. Allen, May 3 and July 3, 1930, Few Papers.

Index

❦

Bolich, W. Bryan, 384
Bolmeier, Edward C., 498
Bone, Allen H., 497
Book Lover's Room, 270
Bookhout, Cazlyn G., 83
Bosley, Harold A., 343–346
Botany, Department of. *See* Biology
Bowman, Francis E., 497
Boyd, Juliam, 160
Boyd, William Kenneth: successor to J. S. Bassett, 9; backs plan for honoring Ben Duke, 41; protests salary differential, 76–77; chairs history department, 131; and expansion in history, 133; and *American Historical Review*, 134; criticizes Harvard, 134; pushes for Far Eastern history, 135; dies in 1938, 136; as director of libraries, 170–175; spots Powell early, 177; fosters art development, 267; mentioned, 18, 19, 153, 169, 173, 180, 182, 183, 255, 266, 287
Bradley, David G., 497
Bradsher, Charles K., 82
Bradway, John S., 391, 394–395
Branscomb, Harvie: on appointments, 69 70; notes on faculty, 74; as director of libraries, 175–176; book on nation's libraries, 176; and Friends of Library, 176–177; looks for preacher, 188; appointed in school of religion, 307–308; works with dean, 311–312; praises Russell, 321; on divinity students, 324–325; search for Jewish scholar, 339; as dean of Divinity School, 339–340; assesses Few and Flowers, 342, 452; hails Flowers's election, 453–454; mentioned, 152
Branson building, 105
Breedlove, Joseph P., 169–170, 172, 177
Brees, Anton, 186
Brice, Ashbel G., 184
Brinkley, Roberta Florence, 285–286
British-American Tobacco Company, 13
British War Relief, 248
Broadhead, Edward H., 154, 268
Brooks, Eugene Clyde, 128
Brooks, Phillips, 185
Brower, Alfred S., 438, 455, 476, 478, 486, 489

Brown, Frances, 80, 282
Brown, Frank C.: and building program, 23–24; investigates local stone, 33–34; chairs English department and is comptroller, 139; mentioned, 90, 180, 256–257, 311, 316
Brown House, 533 n. 34
Brown, Joseph G., 27, 443
Brown, Les, 215, 223, 226
Brown, Nelson C., 424, 425
Brownell, William A., 129–130, 485, 495
Bruinsma, Henry A., 154, 268
Brunner, Emil, 331
Bruton, John F.: as chairman of trustees, 58, 63–64; role in Ackland matter, 299–300; dies, 469; mentioned, 409, 443, 445, 453, 464
Bruton, Paul W., 394
Bryson, Thaddeus D., 294–297, 384, 419
Burke, Joe "Sonny," 226, 228
Business Administration, School of: and donor for, 128, 432
Buttrick, Wallace, 44

Caffey, Francis G., 385
Caldwell, Herschel, 239
Callaway, J. Lamar, 357
Cameron Boulevard, 422
Cameron, Edmund, 239, 244, 457, 460
Camp Butner, 282
Cannon, James, III, 151, 307, 313, 330
Card, Wilbur "Cap," 241
Carlitz, Leonard, 100
Carnegie, Andrew, 25
Carnegie Foundation, 19, 176, 205
Carolina Geological Society, 111
Carpenter, David W., 94
Carpenter, Ray, 208
Carr Building, 533 n. 34
Carr, John W., Jr., 129
Carroll, E. Malcolm, 131–132, 171
Carroll, Robert S., 371
Carter, Bayard F., 89, 353, 369
Cartwright, Peter, 310
Cartwright, W. H., 266
Cavers, David M., 393, 396–397, 414, 418–419
Centennial: and Woman's College, 280–281; as activity of Few, 437–440

97; preference for male appointments, 96; names Nielsen as physics chair, 97; on dormitory for engineers, 106–107; moves to strengthen engineering, 107–110; and philosophy and psychology departments, 112; dislikes behaviorism, 113; supports Rhines's work, 117–118; urges Hoover to remain at Duke, 124; and disinterest in School of Education, 128; sees summer school as national magnet, 131; seeks "star" in English, 140; interest in creative writing, 144; praises Cranford, 149; involved with religion department, 151; aware of graduate school's importance, 157; on freedom in scientific teaching, 160; pushes teacher-training, 161–162; aims at membership in Association of American Universities, 162; reports on national academic organizations, 162–163; and cooperation with University of North Carolina, 163; his and Frank Graham's alleged images, 165; and nomination of Vanderbilt University, 169; on businesslike operation, 174; role in chapel's evolution, 184–189; on "private" university term, 204–205; tie with Methodist church, 205–206; keeps peace with Methodist, 214–215; handles student protest, 224–225; on intercollegiate football, 237–238; on Wallace Wade, 238–240; emphasizes students' development, 239–240; praises "Ace" Parker, 242; as Anglophile and foresees a testing time, 247–248; and Woman's College creation, 252–261; and art department, 266; sees Woman's College as nationally attractive, 274; role in establishing School of Religion, 302–316; and Quaker grandmother, 319; on cooperative medical school, 347–348; on religion and medical competence, 352; seeks law school dean, 380–387; and Harvard's disinterest in Duke, 386; criticized by law school dean, 401–408; described by Robert Woody, 404; handles student protest, 408; seeks Miller's resignation, 409–413; heads off publicity, 412; and establishing forestry school, 422–426; and Duke family members, 432–437; defends J. B. Duke

statue, 434; plans centennial celebration, 437–440; hails Clinton Toms, 444–445; relationship with trustees, 445–447; and problem of two sets of trustees, 446–447; rapport with undergraduate men, 447–449; speaks at stadium opening, 449; meets visiting headmasters, 449; death of, 449–450; on Harvard indifference, 450; memorialized, 450–451; foresees "long journey" for Duke, 501

Flexner, Dr. Abraham: advises Few, 19–20, 348; opposes Amoss resignation, 364

Flexner, Simon, 365

Flowers building, 157

Flowers, George Washington, 172

Flowers, Robert Lee: and creation of Duke Endowment, 24–25; and purchase of "new land," 31–32; on local stone, 34; cuts back on building plans, 39; hails Ben Duke's role, 40; charged with fiscal responsibility, 68; as mathematics teacher, 97–98; as engineering teacher, 103; on engineering program, 108; on businesslike operation, 174; and Duke Press, 180; gives notice to Seeman, 183; on money spent on gardens, 196; and Baldwin's successor, 284–286; and Ackland gift, 296–301; helps get "new land," 421–423; seeks advice about forest, 425; named president, 452–454; resists requests for larger role, 461–464; defends racial status quo, 468–469; stays in presidency too long, 469–470, 482–484; named chancellor and hailed upon retirement, 484–485; declines rapidly, 488–489; mentioned, 13, 172, 343, 382

Flowers, William W., 172–173, 443

Forbus, Wiley D., 353, 361–362, 365, 370

Forest Hills Country Club, 203

Forestry, School of: as component of university, 421–422; is built gradually, 424–430; has space problem, 430; is hard hit by World War II, 431

Fort Bragg, 282

Frampton, George T., 228, 231

Fraternities, 221

Freeman, Douglas Southall, 176

Friends of the Library, 176

Frothingham, E. H., 425–426

Fuller, Lon L., 392, 399, 414, 417–418

Robert F. Durden is Professor of History at Duke
University. He is the author of *James Shepherd Pike:
Republicanism and the American Negro, 1850–1882,
Reconstruction Bonds and 20th Century Politics, The
Climax of Populism: The Election of 1896, The Gray and the
Black: The Confederate Debate on Emancipation, The Dukes
of Durham, 1865–1929*, and *The Self-Inflicted Wound:
Southern Politics in the 19th Century*.

Library of Congress Cataloging-in-Publication Data
Durden, Robert Franklin.
The launching of Duke University, 1924–1949 / Robert F.
Durden.
Includes index.
ISBN 0-8223-1302-2
1. Duke University—History—20th century.   I. Title.
LD1732.D82D87   1993
378.756′563—dc20   92-27499 CIP